*The New Handbook
of Psychotherapy
and Counseling with Men*

The New Handbook of Psychotherapy and Counseling with Men

A Comprehensive Guide to Settings, Problems, and Treatment Approaches

Volume One

Gary R. Brooks
Glenn E. Good
Editors

JOSSEY-BASS
A Wiley Company
San Francisco

Printed in the United States of America.

Library of Congress Cataloging-in-Publication Data

The new handbook of psychotherapy and counseling with men :
a comprehensive guide to settings, problems, and treatment approaches /
Gary R. Brooks, Glenn E. Good, editors.—1st ed.
p. cm.
Includes bibliographical references and indexes.
ISBN 0-7879-5606-6 (v. 1 : alk. paper)—ISBN 0-7879-5604-X
(v. 2 : alk. paper)
1. Counseling. 2. Psychotherapy. 3. Men—Counseling of.
4. Masculinity. 5. Boys—Counseling of. I. Brooks, Gary R. [date]—.
II. Good, Glenn E. [date]—.
BF637.C6 N485 2000   00-010041
158′.3′081—dc21

FIRST EDITION
HC Printing   10 9 8 7 6 5 4 3 2 1

CONTENTS

VOLUME TWO

SECTION FOUR: FORMATS AND MODALITIES   525

SECTION FIVE: SPECIAL SKILLS 637

SECTION SIX: CULTURAL DIVERSITY AND VARIATIONS 735

To Gwen Stoddard,
my little sister whom I will always love.
—G.R.B.

To Laurie Mintz, Jennifer, and Allison Good,
and my parents, Robert and Jeanne Good.
—G.E.G.

ACKNOWLEDGMENTS

Sometimes ideas that seemed inspired at the outset turn out to be less creative and Promethean than originally hoped. Sometimes a product after final assemblage bears little resemblance to the one originally envisioned. At other times, however, ideas turn into finished products that emerge as even more gratifying than had ever been imagined. We believe that these volumes fall into this latter category. It is our immodest belief that the exceptional contributions of a broad range of thoughtful scholars and therapists has resulted in a handbook that adds substantially to the cause of helping counselors and therapists work more effectively with men.

First, to recognize those who made these volumes possible, we wish to acknowledge our tremendous debt to Alan Rinzler, our senior editor at Jossey-Bass Publishers. Alan's vision, involvement, and support made this set of books possible. We would also like to thank Amy Scott, the assistant editor, and Jeri Lambert, the production coordinator, for their conscientious work in helping complete this project. We also express our gratitude to the chapter contributors to this book; they have worked very hard to provide solid contributions that advance the field.

Because this set of volumes is built on the pioneering work of others, profound appreciation is offered to men's studies pioneers such as Drs. Joseph Pleck, James O'Neil, Ron Levant, Murray Scher, Mark Stevens, Gregg Eichenfeld, Michael Kimmel, Harry Brod, Robert Brannon, Tom Skovholt, and James Doyle, whose scholarly contributions provided the foundation for this project. We also express our deep appreciation to the members of the Society for the Psychological Study of Men and Masculinity (Division 51 of the American Psychological Association).

Dr. Brooks deeply values the intellectual contributions, friendship, and emotional support of his Society for the Psychological Study of Men and Masculinity colleagues—those represented in these volumes, as well as Louise Silverstein, Neil Massoth, Don-David Lusterman, Roberta Nutt, and the late Roy Scrivner. He continues to be buoyed by the love and support of his wife, Patti, and daughters Ashley and Allison. Finally, Dr. Brooks clearly realizes that he has never made a more astute move than his decision to seek partnership with Glenn Good. Glenn's breadth of knowledge and organizational skills are exceeded only by his warmth, compassion, and delightful relational style.

Dr. Good would like to acknowledge the support of his immediate family— his wife, Dr. Laurie Mintz, and their delightful daughters, Jennifer and Allison— for their patience and understanding during the completion of this project. He also expresses his gratitude to his parents, Drs. Jeanne and Robert Good, for their nurturance and encouragement, and to his sister, Ellen Wakeman, who had to tolerate him. He would also like to express his gratitude to Drs. Murray Scher, Mark Stevens, and Gregg Eichenfield, who collaborated with him on a project with similar objectives more than a decade ago. He also expresses his gratitude to his Society for the Psychological Study of Men and Masculinity colleagues, those in this set of volumes, and Drs. Neil Massoth, Louise Silverstein, and Roberta Nutt, who provide friendship and intellectual clarity. More locally, he acknowledges Drs. John Robertson, Brick Johnstone, Hank Schneider, Bernard Beitman, and Craig Anderson, who provided proper perspective along the way. He would also like to express his appreciation for his colleagues and the graduate students in the Department of Educational and Counseling Psychology at the University of Missouri–Columbia who make each work day a pleasure. Finally, it is Dr. Good's distinct pleasure to acknowledge Gary Brooks's great creativity, dedication, and everlasting upbeat energy. It is hard to imagine a guy who could get more accomplished while maintaining such delightful relational interactions along the way.

Last, yet definitely not least, we would like to express our deep appreciation for the men, women, adolescents, children, and families who have the courage to seek psychotherapeutic consultation. You have entrusted us with your secrets, hopes, concerns, and doubts. You have also challenged us to meet you where you are, challenged us to understand your experiences and their meaning to you, and allowed us to accompany you on the journey. You were willing to risk trying new ideas, experiences, and behaviors, to risk imagining better lives, relationships, and futures. Finally, you taught us how to serve you well and how to improve the services that mental health professionals might provide to others. For all of this, we are most appreciative.

November 2000

GARY R. BROOKS
Temple, Texas
GLENN E. GOOD
Columbia, Missouri

*The New Handbook
of Psychotherapy
and Counseling with Men*

PROLOGUE

Introduction

Gary R. Brooks
Glenn E. Good

Everywhere we look we see signs of deeply dissatisfied contemporary men who are fervent about change. Countless men have attended Promise Keepers rallies, the Million Man March, wilderness retreats, Fathers' Rights coalition meetings, men's therapy groups, profeminist men's activities, gay rights groups, and men's studies conventions. Although these activities are widely disparate in their underlying philosophies and politics, they reflect several common themes.

Modern men feel isolated and yearn for closer emotional connections. Many feel the need to call on men as a group to dedicate themselves to a higher standard of moral or spiritual responsibility, to counter domestic violence, substance abuse, absent fathering, and sexual exploitation. Most contemporary men are showing far greater interest in fathering than men have in the past. They are more likely to be present during childbirth, more desirous of quality time with their young children, more dissatisfied with postdivorce estrangement from children, and more deeply involved as grandparents. Many men have shown intense concern about the next generation of men and are searching for new ways to mentor young boys. Increasing numbers of men have shown willingness to forego career advancement for the sake of greater involvement with their families. Dual-career marriage, a seemingly unthinkable concept a few decades ago, is now the norm. Although men have been slow to embrace equality in domestic labor, they are nevertheless taking on more of these tasks than ever before. Finally, many men have recognized the multiple injuries of sexism,

3

racism, and gay bashing and have begun to speak out against these forms of social injustice.

MEN AT THE CROSSROADS

Contemporary men face opportunities to live lives more richly varied and broadly fulfilling than men in any previous historical era. Many men have taken advantage of these new possibilities and have begun to reshape critical aspects of their lives. But before discussing these men and these abundant possibilities, we must first take note of men whose lives are in crisis. For these men, the past few decades have been experienced as "a time of fallen heroes . . . [when] men have been brought to earth, their strengths put in perspective by their flaws" (Betcher & Pollack, 1993, p. 1). For many, the past few decades have ushered in a period that has eroded traditional male values and damaged the image of masculinity itself. In fact, over the past twenty-five years, there has been far more public attention on men's failings than on their strivings and contributions to the national interest. During this time period the "dark side of masculinity" (Brooks & Silverstein, 1995) has taken center stage.

Men as Perpetrators

No theme characterized the last decade of the twentieth century more than the constant media attention on the iniquitous acts of men. From the seemingly inexplicable shooting rampages of Columbine High School and Little Rock, Arkansas, to the hate crimes of Jasper, Texas, males have been the ones to perpetrate violence and hatred.

In the 1990s, in part because of the attention focused on the O. J. Simpson trial, domestic violence came out of the shadows and was finally recognized as a major national problem. Social scientists produced data indicating that male violence against women is far more frequent than was commonly understood. One analysis of prevalence studies indicated that between 21 and 34 percent of women in the United States are physically assaulted by an intimate adult partner (Goodman, Koss, Fitzgerald, Russo, & Keita, 1993).

Another area of increased alarm has been the recognition of the widespread perpetration of sexual harassment of women by men. Again, a public event, the Clarence Thomas hearings, seemed to galvanize public awareness of this issue. Large-scale surveys of working women have suggested that one of every two women is harassed at some point during her academic or working life (Fitzgerald, 1993).

Rape, sexual coercion, and sexual assault have also been recognized as male acts that are far more common than previously recognized (Koss, 1993). Once rape was narrowly defined and considered to be a rare behavior of a very small percentage of deviant men. Recently, however, the focus has broadened to "sexual coercion" as a relatively frequent behavior among a broad spectrum of men. Research has indicated that between one-third and one-half of men admit to some act of sexual aggression or coercion of women into unwelcome sexual activity (Kaplan, O'Neil, & Owen, 1993; Ward, Chapman, Cohn, & Williams, 1991).

Men as Psychologically Undeveloped

In the 1990s attention to male behaviors that might formerly have been dismissed as an inherent aspect of biological manhood increased. Television and films have been home to frequent comedic parodies of "macho" male behavior. More serious treatises such as the Hite Report (Hite, 1987), *Refusing to Be a Man* (Stoltenberg, 1989), *The End of Manhood* (Stoltenberg, 1993), and *Men Are Not Cost-Effective* (Stephenson, 1991) have echoed a similar message of increasing dissatisfaction with male patterns of conduct.

The sexual conduct of public figures such as Hugh Grant, Woody Allen, Mike Tyson, Gary Hart, Robert Packwood, Bill Clinton, and Rudy Giuliani has caused some to call for a serious study of normative male sexuality (Good, 1998; Levant & Brooks, 1997). Among the causes of concern are men's increasing use of pornography (Brooks, 1995; Gaylor, 1985; Kimmel, 1990) and the greater tendency for men to engage in nonrelational or casual sexual activity (Levant, 1997; Oliver & Hyde, 1993).

As more and more women have taken their place in work roles outside the home, men have been roundly criticized for failing to shoulder their proper share of work as parents and as domestic laborers. These complaints have regularly been buttressed by research indicating that although men are increasing their involvement, they still typically spend minimal time with their children (Gottfried & Gottfried, 1988; Pleck, 1997; Silverstein, 1996). Other research reflects men's laxity in taking on full responsibility as domestic labor partners (see Chapter Nineteen of this volume; Blain, 1994; Sanchez & Kane, 1996). Hochschild (1989) emphasized the extra burden falling on women because of men's resistance to change.

Men have increasingly been criticized for their failures as emotionally expressive and psychologically supportive partners. Rafts of popular self-help books have been sold to help women find ways to communicate with their withdrawn and noncommunicative male partners. Communications research has indicated that although men tend to be adept at "report talk," they are grossly deficient in "rapport talk" (Tannen, 1990, 1993). Levant (1997; see also Chapter Twenty-one of this volume) argued that alexithymia (the inability to recognize and express feelings) is normative among modern men, and Good (1998) recommended that greater emphasis be given to developing males' "emotional competence."

Men as Victims

Amidst the depressing litany of complaints against contemporary men and modern manhood, a new perspective has begun to emerge. Epitomized by Susan Faludi's *Stiffed: The Betrayal of the American Man* (1999), this perspective allows for consideration of ways that men have suffered from various cultural shifts and pressures since the 1950s. Similarly, Pollack (1998) and Gurian (1999) have provoked considerable reaction to their argument that boys, as well as girls, are harmed by a culture that poorly recognizes their needs and stresses.

Perhaps no single set of facts calls attention to men's situation as much as the repeated finding that men die earlier than do women. Men's lives are approximately seven to nine years shorter than women's (Angier, 1999; Courtenay, 1998a; Verbrugge, 1985). The death rate for American men is higher than that for women in every decade of life, and women have an overall life span expectancy that surpasses men at every age, regardless of race (Courtenay, 1998b).

Closely related to this perspective on men's mortality is a new recognition about men's violence. At a time when men's violence against women is finally receiving an appropriately high degree of attention, the realization has surfaced that men also are victims of violence. Men perpetrate the great majority of violent acts and homicides, yet they also constitute more than 85 percent of the victims of homicide (Angier, 1999; Department of Health and Human Services [DHHS], 2000). The situation for African American men is even more problematic (Franklin, 1998); some have referred to African American men as "an endangered species" (Gibbs, 1988).

Although the *Diagnostic and Statistical Manual of Mental Disorders* (American Psychiatric Association, 1994) indicates that women suffer major depression three times as often as do men, men have a suicide rate four times greater than that of women (DHHS, 2000). Men constitute between two-thirds and four-fifths of the population of those who abuse alcohol or illicit substances (see Chapter Eleven of this volume; DHHS, 2000; Diamond, 1987; Grant, Harford, Hasin, Chou, & Pickering, 1992). Men comprise more than 70 percent of the U.S. homeless population (Marin, 1991).

Lisak (1994; see also Chapter Twelve in this volume) has written extensively about the alarmingly high rates of physical abuse of young males. Based on his clinical work and reviews of the literature, he observes that childhood physical abuse of boys ranges between 10 and 20 percent. He also notes that the figures are probably gross underestimates because of the tendency of most grown men to dismiss abuse as "strict discipline."

This thesis on men's distress could go on for many more pages; it is thoroughly amplified in many chapters of these volumes. The critical point is that contemporary men, regardless of the many advantages and entitlements of a culture that generally treats men quite well, are experiencing considerable subjective pain. Men continually struggle to satisfy their fantasized male judges and harshest internalized male critics—the "male chorus" (Pittman, 1990). Men who do not live up to the rigorous standards of the manhood code are clearly experiencing anguish. But it is not just these men who are hurting. The paradox of modern masculinity is that regardless of a man's accomplishments or successes, he is in some maddening ways continually driven toward greater accomplishments— it is never enough. He is fixated on overtaking the man above him on the various hierarchical ladders of achievement and is horrified at the prospect of being overtaken by other men hell-bent on moving up on the same ladder.

The situation of men during the late twentieth century was well captured by observers of traditional men's pursuit of personal power and happiness. The pursuit of power and control denies men love and sensuality and leaves only desire and the excitement of the conquest. Men are generally distant from their children and partners, and their working lives are dominated by competition and mistrust. The higher men go on the ladder of success, the harder it is for them to trust other men and to make real friendships (McLean, 1996). The pleasures of relaxed, anonymous movement through the world, of easy conversation with others, and of trust and love as part of a community are impossible for them (French, 1991).

THEORIZING ABOUT MEN'S DISTRESS

Before considering how to ameliorate the subjective distress of contemporary men, we must first have some notion about the etiological roots of men's conduct. That is, why do men behave the way they do? This question leads to one of the most complex and perplexing areas in all of men's studies.

Essentialism

Essentialism, the idea that there are basic, inherent, or essential differences between women and men, has become an increasingly popular theory since the early 1990s. Perhaps the most visible exposition of this view has been the immensely popular work of John Gray, author of *Men Are from Mars, Women Are from Venus* (1992). For Gray, the matter is straightforward—basic *physiological* differences between women and men cannot help but create similarly basic *psychological* differences that make relationships extremely difficult.

These "essential" differences between women and men have been attributed to a range of causes. Some theorists have invoked biology, citing pronounced sex differences in hormonal makeup (Barash, 1979) or in brain structure or neurochemistry (Kimura, 1992; LeVay, 1993; Moir & Jessel, 1991). Others point to radically different evolutionary heritage and adaptive challenges faced by women and men (Archer, 1996; Buss, 1995, 2000).

These essentialist perspectives are interconnected, of course, because the evolutionary perspective is posited as a primary explanation for the essential biological differences. In terms of the age-old nature-versus-nurture debate, proponents of evolutionary psychology are outspoken in their criticism of nurture exclusivists—those they view as emphasizing social causes of behavior and ignoring evolved biological differences. "The perspective of evolutionary psychology jettisons the outmoded dualistic thinking inherent in much current discourse by getting rid of the false dichotomy between the biological and social" (Buss, 1995, p. 167).

Essentialist theorists have made important contributions to men's studies. Their work serves as a sobering reminder that practitioners must not ignore the biological aspect in the modern trend toward biopsychosocial thinking. Because of their high regard for the relative immutability of the inherent differences between women and men, essentialist theorists tend to be relatively conservative in their view of possibilities for change. Instead, they make an important plea for men and women to develop greater appreciation of each other's inherent differences and learn to create respectful communication. Gray (1990), for example, suggests that "the confusion we are experiencing today is definitely due to the lack of acceptance of our differences." For Gray the secret to relational harmony is "accepting who we are and embracing how others are different" (p. 35).

David Buss, the leading spokesperson for the evolutionary psychology perspective, offers a wide range of critical insights and thoughtful perspectives about how women and men might have come to be the way they are. Unfortunately, however, he provides a far more modest agenda about how things might be changed. Buss is appropriately critical of narrow thinking and argues forcefully for an "interactionist" perspective to social problems. He writes extensively about creating "harmony between the sexes" and has provided much food for contemplation. As yet, however, his recommendations have focused primarily on improved mutual understanding. He has provided few ideas beyond his suggestion that the key to harmony is "fulfilling each other's evolved desires" (1994, p. 221). That is, men and women need to become proficient at giving each other what they have learned to desire. Additionally, Buss noted that teaching men and women about the advantages of "cooperation" and "reciprocity" will help to "manage competitive mechanisms" that have evolved over the centuries (Buss, 2000).

The various efforts to understand the essential differences between men and women have generated enormous discussion and controversy. Despite this controversy, no serious men's studies scholar can ignore the importance of the research into sex differences in hormones and brain structure, nor the theories of differences in evolutionary adaptation. One simply must know all that one can about the building blocks and raw materials of our behavior. At the same time, this line of study is intrinsically limited, because it can only go so far in offering ideas for change. Those who hope for transcendence beyond traditional male roles need to make special efforts to understand the social construction of masculinity—the ways that the raw materials are shaped and manipulated by sociocultural pressures.

Gender Role Strain Theory

Within psychology another critical perspective has appeared—the gender role strain paradigm (Pleck, 1981, 1995). Before Pleck's work most ideas about women and men were anchored in the gender identity paradigm. According to the gender identity paradigm, there are two distinct and oppositional identities of "masculine" and "feminine," with psychological health dependent on incorporation of sufficient characteristics of the proper sex role. In this view, healthy psychological adjustment depends on achieving a secure gender identity. (Although androgyny—the incorporation of other gender characteristics—is thought to be beneficial, it is so after a comfortable sense of gender identity has been accomplished.)

The gender role strain paradigm takes a markedly different view of men's behavior. According to the gender role strain paradigm, gender roles are not only socially constructed but are also highly problematic. Among the assumptions of the gender role strain paradigm are (1) gender role norms are often inconsistent and contradictory, (2) a large proportion of gender role norms are violated frequently, (3) social condemnation and stressful psychological consequences commonly follow role violations, and (4) many characteristics and behaviors prescribed by gender role norms are psychologically dysfunctional.

Interactive Systems Model of Gender Role Strain

The interactive systems model of gender role strain (Brooks & Silverstein, 1995) has been proposed as a complex integration of cultural, psychological, and political variables affecting men's behavior. According to its developers, the interactive systems model reflects a synthesis of several theoretical approaches: the gender role strain paradigm, an ecological perspective on the origins of gender roles, the Bowen family systems theory of the effect of chronic anxiety on behavior (Bowen, 1978), and the social constructionist analysis of gender-linked power differentials within patriarchal society (Brooks & Silverstein, 1995).

The interactive systems model draws from the gender role strain paradigm in that it incorporates the idea that men's problems and challenges are best conceptualized as a product of role stress and not of problematic gender identity. That is, to be psychologically healthy men and women do not need to acquire fixed gendered identities that are inherently alien and potentially adversarial. Instead, because men's roles are socially created, they are alterable in response to changing times and social demands.

The model draws from Bowen family systems theory by adopting Bowen's (1978) belief that anxiety results when persons "give up self." In this formulation, we see that men have been resolutely socialized to limit themselves to narrow and stereotyped roles—warriors, providers, and sexual performers, but not nurturers and emotional communicators. This narrow socialization requires that men deny aspects of self, a process that generates overwhelming anxiety. The resultant anxiety perpetuates rigid definitions of acceptable male conduct and further alienation from one's full human potential.

The interactive systems model enriches the psychological perspectives of the gender role strain paradigm and Bowen theory by embracing the broader sociopolitical perspectives of feminism and the ecological perspective of the anthropologist David Gilmore (1990). Feminist theory holds that the behaviors of men and women cannot be fully understood without attention to the considerable power inequities between the groups. Miller (1986) noted that membership in a group holding power over others generates personality characteristics that are associated with the use and abuse of power. Reciprocally, membership in a disempowered group produces personality characteristics that reflect this powerlessness and dependence on the dominant group. In this analysis, women, like members of other subordinate groups, have needed to develop interpersonal empathy and emotional sensitivity. Men, on the other hand, have been free to develop entitlement and to exercise their power.

Gilmore's (1990) ecological insights add further complexity to this analysis. He studied a wide array of contemporary cultures and found that almost all societies have a "manhood cult" based on the ideas of competition, risk taking, stoic emotional reserve, and rejection of "feminine" aspects of self. But he also found that a manhood cult was not present in all societies. The presence or absence of this value system was closely tied to certain critical ecological variables. The degree to which a society adopts strict ideas of manhood is closely related to two critical ecological variables—the availability of natural resources and the degree of external threat. Within the ecological context of plentiful resources, relative ease in the production of food, and absence of external threat, role pressures are less intense. Therefore, according to Gilmore's research, rigid standards of manhood are not inevitable but depend on the ecological context.

The interactive systems model can be viewed as an effort to explain men's behavior through integration of several other perspectives. First, it incorporates the social constructionist idea that men behave in accordance with the powerful pressures of gender socialization. Further, because it identifies the role of psychological, cultural, and political variables, it offers broad potential for intervention and change.

NEW HOPE FOR MEN

Many men are in crisis. Many are resentful of the sweeping cultural changes of the last quarter of the twentieth century and seek nothing more than a return to

seemingly happier days when men were men and women [...]
place. Most men, however, recognize that the clock will not b[...]
things will never again be the same. Additionally, at some lev[...]
men sense that change may ultimately be in their own best intere[...]

Men's Movement

Beginning in the late 1960s and early 1970s, a new type of scholarship app[...]
with a curious agenda—to examine the inner workings and secrets of me[...]
lives. Admittedly, most academic scholarship had always talked about the lives
of mythical and heroic men. But this new scholarship, providing the basis for
what would become men's studies, was about the lives of ordinary men. It was
about how the average man struggled to bring meaning to his life. Several men
wrote paradigm-shifting books suggesting that men, as well as women, could
be hampered by rigid traditional gender role expectations. Brenton (1966),
Farrell (1974), Fasteau (1975), Goldberg (1976), Nichols (1975), and Pleck and
Sawyer (1980) provided impressive arguments about the hazards of traditional
masculinity in contemporary times.

This new line of men's studies scholarship heralded the appearance of a
men's movement that has gained considerable momentum and attention since
the 1970s. Similar to the women's movement that preceded it, the men's movement has been fueled by a commitment to countering sociocultural forces that
constrain people's lives. However, unlike the women's movement, the men's
movement has had no dramatically obvious mandate, no clear theoretical
underpinnings, and no central organization. In brief, there is considerable disagreement about what the men's movement actually is or has been.

For example, Shiffman (1987) observed that "the men's movement can be
described structurally as consisting of a national profeminist organization, networks of activists engaging issues of violence against women, networks of aca-
demics working on issues of masculinity, men's support groups, an annual
national conference on men and masculinity, and various local and regional
events" (p. 297). On the other hand, Williamson (1985) argued that "the North
American men's movement cannot be traced along one historical line. There
have been a number of differing directions characterized by sporadic growth
and instability" (p. 308).

Clatterbaugh (1990) described a number of men's organizations. "Non-
feminist" men joined with Fathers' Rights groups (for example Men's Equality
Now) to protest what they viewed as mistreatment of men in the court system.
Other groups of men, impressed with the work of Joseph Campbell and Robert
Bly, focused on pursuit of essential masculinity, or "the deep masculine spirit"
(Bly, 1990; Clatterbaugh, 1990). From a very different direction, the gay libera-
tion movement also provided impetus to the men's movement. Originating with
the Mattachine Society in the 1950s on the West Coast and energized by the
Stonewall Riots of 1969, the gay liberation movement not only pushed for

ut also became a leading voice against the
nic masculinity.

the philosophies and political perspectives
e subsequent Coalition of Free Men), the
inst Sexism became the group most inclu-
it philosophies. Adopting a strong profem-
d the antiviolence community, veterans of
opoetic men, men's studies scholars, and
it organization began the annual Men and
ught men together for more than twenty-

and men's issues has also reverberated in
e mental health professions. Most notably,
ation has embraced the Society for the
Psychological Study of Men and Masculinity, a group that "promotes study of
how gender shapes and constricts men's lives, and is committed to an enhancement of men's capacity to experience their full human potential" (Society for
the Psychological Study of Men and Masculinity, 2000).

The decade of the 1990s witnessed a continuation of men's search for
answers to their distress, their loneliness, and their existential or spiritual empti-
ness. Although the men of the Promise Keepers, the Million Man March, the
Fathers' Rights groups, the wilderness retreats, and the profeminist men's organizations have different faces and hold some differing philosophies, they are
united in promoting the cause of more fulfilling lives for men.

Psychotherapy for Men

Inevitably, the sweeping cultural changes have reverberated into the mental
health community. Research by Good, Dell, and Mintz (1989) found that men's
reluctance to use psychological services was closely tied to their conceptions of
masculinity. Although they were once dismissed as hopelessly resistant to any
form of help seeking, men are now finding their way, both directly and indirectly, into treatment settings. Some men recognize their distress and make independent decisions to seek therapy help. Many more, however, are urged,
coaxed, or mandated into treatment by loved ones, bosses, physicians, or legal
authorities. In the midst of sweeping cultural changes that force men to shape
new masculine roles, the resultant increase in the number of male therapy
clients poses a challenge to counselors and therapists. Are we prepared to meet
these new challenges? To what extent have we developed new therapies and
appropriate services to help men?

As is often the case, the honest answer to these questions is ambiguous—yes
and no. In some ways, the mental health community is poorly prepared to meet
the needs of many men. Many observers (Robertson & Fitzgerald, 1992; Scher,

1990; Shay & Maltas, 1998; Silverberg, 1986) have noted that men are highly unlikely to see psychotherapy as a good thing and will only seek therapy when there is no other alternative. Some (Heesacker & Prichard, 1992; Wilcox & Forrest, 1992) have argued that therapy is too reliant on "feminine" modes of intervention and that new therapies more congruent with "masculine" styles must be developed. Brooks (1998) argued that traditional men hate psychotherapy because of (1) the popular stereotypes of the male client as weak and ineffectual, (2) the conflicts between the demands of the male role and the role of the ideal therapy client, (3) traditional men's sense that there is a collusion among women and members of the therapy community against men, and (4) the failure of the therapy community to recognize men's special needs.

For some time, mental health professionals have recognized that men are reluctant to take on the client role. We have realized that men's help seeking is often tentative and complicated by conflicting motives, making it difficult for counselors to establish therapeutic alliances. But the problem is much larger: many counselors and therapists do not fully understand men's experiences. Many do not see the connection between men's problematic behaviors and their psychic pain. Many do not feel adept at engaging reluctant men in treatment. Many do not understand how to customize traditional therapy modalities to serve men better. Finally, many do not see how to integrate the progress made in a man's therapy work into systemic change that will benefit him and his loved ones.

In spite of these substantial problems, there are many positive trends. The psychotherapy community is becoming far more sensitive to cultural diversity issues (Comas-Diaz & Griffith, 1988; Sue & Sue, 1999). Within the rubric of cultural diversity, many are now recognizing that gender is a critical cultural variable and a central mediator of experience in clients' lives. Recognition came first to the many ways that gender-blind diagnoses and therapies have harmed women. Gender studies scholarship, first applied to women, soon came to be considered in terms of the experiences of both men and women. Gender scholars began to call for psychotherapies that are gender aware (Good, Gilbert, & Scher 1990), gender sensitive (Philpot et al., 1997), or gender fair (Nutt, 1991). These approaches call for therapists to consider women's and men's gender context when conducting assessments and developing intervention strategies.

We believe it is now critical that men be recognized as a special culture and that diversity training include attention to the area of men and masculinity. Further, we believe that some therapy situations should be considered as a form of cross-cultural counseling, calling for the special considerations of that sensitive situation. It is our devout belief that when men's experiences have been better understood, therapeutic bonds will be far easier to establish. Therapists will be far more empathic and compassionate toward men. Men will be far more eager to use psychotherapy. We believe ardently in the need to improve the relationship between men and the therapy community.

A landmark event in this cause was the 1987 publication of the *Handbook of Counseling and Psychotherapy for Men* (Scher, Stevens, Good, & Eichenfield, 1987). That pioneering book broke new ground, providing a single reference source that embraced many of the ideas of therapists who were working in widely diverse settings. For its time, that handbook offered the best of the information available about the diversity of therapy approaches for men.

Much has taken place in the years since the publication of that handbook. There has been an exponential increase in research and writing about men's lives and about therapy for men. Innovative new therapies have begun to appear in a wide variety of mental health disciplines. Clearly, there has been a pressing need for a new handbook that will reflect these fresh and vital new developments. We believe that these two volumes fill that void because they capture the most recent developments and offer a vital resource for counselors and therapists clamoring for new ideas.

These volumes are divided into several important sections: (1) prologue, (2) settings in which men are likely to be seen, (3) problems men are likely to present, (4) normative developmental issues men confront, (5) formats and modalities, (6) special skills for intervention, and (7) challenges of diversity among men.

In this prologue, we note that the counseling and psychotherapy communities, once inattentive to the unique aspects of men's needs, have now begun embracing the task of developing new models and processes for men. We show how scholars have begun to clarify terminology, develop more complex models of men's difficulties, and conceptualize empirical methods to validate new therapeutic approaches.

The chapters of Section One consider the counseling and therapy needs of men in terms of the physical contexts where men function. Although men may be underrepresented in therapists' offices, they are abundant in schools, colleges, medical, business and industry, sports, prison, rehabilitation, and veterans' settings. In this section, authors suggest male-friendly interventions that are sensitive to the demands and customs of their environments.

The chapters of Section Two examine some of the far-too-common problems that men experience or perpetrate—depression, substance abuse, psychic trauma, homicide, rape, sexual dysfunction, and problematic adjustment to divorce. These chapters go far beyond protesting men's offenses or bemoaning men's suffering to contextualize men's problematic behaviors. Rather than viewing dark-side behavior as the exclusive product of aberrant men, the chapters situate these problems within a framework that recognizes the social construction of masculinity. They identify how rigid male socialization processes dispose many boys to become troubled men. The chapters demonstrate how men are continually given mixed messages about violence, sexuality, alcohol, and emotional sensitivity. Finally, they incorporate the gender role strain model to show that although men are sometimes victimizers they are also victimized.

The chapters of Section Three look at the normative challenges and developmental opportunities of the male life cycle. They examine boyhood, midlife, and late-life issues. They consider the intersection of masculinity and the demands of marriage, fatherhood, career, and emotional connection with others. These chapters add a crucial perspective by broadening the focus from serious problems experienced by some men to difficulties encountered by almost all men. Even men without psychopathology are struggling to negotiate the role strain inherent in narrow definitions of proper masculine behavior. We must never lose sight of the differences between offenders and perpetrators on the one hand and those who stay within acceptable boundaries of behavior on the other hand. At the same time, however, it is also useful to recognize the commonalities among all men and to eschew excessive distancing from "sick" men.

Most men have shared (or will share) certain common experiences and challenges—the taunting and bullying of boy culture, the insidious existential dilemmas of midlife, the fears and losses of later life. Most struggle to make emotional connections with others, despite harsh pressures to maintain a rugged and stoic external facade. Most men entering or leaving marriage must unravel a myriad of conflicting messages about women, relationships, and commitment. Work and career add additional complexity to men's lives, sometimes becoming so central that all else suffers. Most men wrestle with the impossible conflict between career fixation and a broader definition of self. Finally, men confronting fatherhood face many similar challenges—to find a space in their lives for their children, to develop nurturing skills they were never taught, and to father more lovingly than they were fathered themselves.

These first sections provide many practical and applied therapeutic recommendations; the chapters of Sections Four and Five focus directly on the implications of men's studies for the practice of counseling and therapy. These chapters directly confront the formerly prevalent gender-blind models of psychotherapy training. Consistent with the welcome trend to customize therapy to the cultural values of the client, these chapters make it abundantly clear that therapists can no longer accept the notion that one size fits all. Unlike any work to date, these chapters provide explicit suggestions about how to apply existing models of psychotherapy to the special issues of men's lives. These chapters offer further ideas about how men's growth can be supplemented by activities not generally considered to fall under the therapy umbrella—psychoeducation and wilderness retreats.

The chapters of Section Five challenge assumptions about therapist neutrality. Men's pain is considered in the context of feminist politics and challenges to patriarchal power structures. Finally, therapists are acknowledged as gendered beings, in that we all bring our gender assumptions and values into our work. In the final two chapters of this section, the authors illustrate that therapists' gender awareness and self-knowledge can make a critical difference in their therapy encounters with men.

The chapters of Section Six are especially important because they challenge an assumption implicit in the preceding chapters—the myth of homogeneity in men's lives. For many years, men's studies scholars spoke of *the* masculine ideology, as if all men experienced masculinity in an identical fashion. Over the past decade, however, we have come to realize that there are many masculinity ideologies, depending on a man's ethnicity, social class, sexual orientation, and physical abilities. For example, it is absurd to speak of male dominance, privilege, power, and entitlement when considering gay men or African American men as one would speak of it when considering white, middle-class, heterosexual men. Marginalized men do not experience masculinity in the same way as do men with greater access to the historical perks of manhood.

The diversity perspective does not negate the importance of understanding the vast commonalities among all men. Rather, it simply highlights the need for therapists to simultaneously consider all critical areas of cultural influence in their clients' lives. At an extreme, it seems to call for an impossible level of accommodation from therapists. Must we develop unique therapies for every possible combination of cultural identities? For example, will my therapy be unsuccessful or unethical if I do not master *the* therapy for late-life, working-class, Hispanic males, with and without physical disabilities? Obviously, this would be an extreme stance. The point is actually far more optimistic. If therapists are familiar with the most salient values and meanings in their clients' lives, they will have many avenues of entry into their clients' worlds and will have far greater capacity for therapeutic empathy.

OUR HOPES

Our study of men and masculinity has consistently provided us with some of the most gratifying experiences of our professional lives. It has allowed us to develop many meaningful relationships and has greatly enhanced our personal lives. We are especially proud of these volumes. As excited as we have been by this dynamic field of scholarship, we have also realized that this area is one of considerable sensitivity and strongly held beliefs. It is unfortunate that this area of study has sometimes generated unnecessarily harsh acrimony and polarization. We believe that these volumes surmount the primary sources of this tension and sensitivity, because they see women's and men's interests as reciprocal, consider men as inherently well intentioned, and hold great optimism for men's capacity to accommodate the needs of a rapidly changing culture.

The gender role strain paradigm that undergirds the therapeutic interventions of these volumes recognizes that women *and* men are harmed by narrow, restrictive gender roles and unforgiving processes of gender socialization. Counselors and therapists can help women and men recognize that they are jointly invested in challenging restrictive processes and creating greater role opportunities for women and men. Rigid gender socialization into narrow roles is not in the best interests of men or women. To function successfully in a complex and changing culture, women and men must have full access to the widest range of social, emotional, and psychological skills. Counseling and psychotherapy can provide pivotal impetus and guidance for achieving those skills. Therapists and counselors can help women and men approach each other with compassion and respect and can empower them to develop their inherent capacities to be fully functioning human beings.

References

American Psychiatric Association. (1994). *Diagnostic and statistical manual of mental disorders* (4th ed.). Washington, DC: Author.

Angier, N. (1999, February 17). Why men don't last: Self-destruction as a way of life. *New York Times*, Section G, p. 8, col. 1.

Archer, J. (1996). Sex differences in social behavior: Are the social role and evolutionary explanations compatible? *American Psychologist, 51,* 909–917.

Barash, D. (1979). *The whisperings within.* New York: Penguin.

Betcher, R. W., & Pollack, W. S. (1993). *In a time of fallen heroes: The re-creation of masculinity.* New York: Atheneum.

Blain, J. (1994). Discourses of agency and domestic labor: Family discourse and gendered practice in dual-career families. *Journal of Family Issues, 15,* 515–549.

Bly, R. (1990). *Iron John: A book about men.* New York: Vintage Books.

Bowen, M. (1978). *Family therapy in clinical practice.* New York: Aronson.

Brenton, M. (1966). *The American male.* New York: Coward-McCann.

Brooks, G. R. (1995). The centerfold syndrome: How men can overcome objectification and achieve intimacy with women. San Francisco: Jossey-Bass.

Brooks, G. R. (1998). *A new psychotherapy for traditional men.* San Francisco: Jossey-Bass.

Brooks, G. R., & Silverstein, L. B. (1995). Understanding the dark side of masculinity: An integrative systems model. In R. F. Levant & W. S. Pollack (Eds.), *A new psychology of men* (pp. 280–333). New York: Basic Books.

Buss, D. M. (1994). *The evolution of desire: Strategies of human mating.* New York: Basic Books.

Buss, D. M. (1995). Psychological sex differences: Origins through sexual selection. *American Psychologist, 50,* 164–168.

Buss, D. M. (2000). The evolution of happiness. *American Psychologist, 55,* 15–23.

Clatterbaugh, K. (1990). Contemporary perspectives on masculinity: Men, women, and politics in modern society. Boulder, CO: Westview Press.

Comas-Diaz, L., & Griffith, E. H. (1988). *Clinical guidelines in cross-cultural mental health.* New York: Wiley.

Courtenay, W. H. (1998a). Better to die than cry? A longitudinal and constructionist study of masculinity and health risk behavior of young American men (Doctoral dissertation, University of California at Berkeley). *Dissertation Abstracts International, 59*(08A). (Publication No. 9902042)

Courtenay, W. H. (1998b). College men's health: An overview and call to action. *Journal of American College Health, 46,* 279–290.

Department of Health and Human Services. (2000). *Healthy people 2010. Understanding and improving health.* Washington, DC: U.S. Government Printing Office.

Diamond, J. (1987). Counseling male substance abusers. In M. Scher, M. Stevens, G. Good, & G. Eichenfield (Eds.), *Handbook of counseling and psychotherapy with men* (pp. 332–342). Newbury Park, CA: Sage.

Faludi, S. (1999). *Stiffed: The betrayal of the American man.* New York: Morrow.

Farrell, W. T. (1974). *The liberated man.* New York: Bantam Books.

Fasteau, M. F. (1975). *The male machine.* New York: Dell.

Fitzgerald, L. (1993). Sexual harassment: Violence against women in the workplace. *American Psychologist, 48,* 1070–1076.

Franklin, A. J. (1998). Treating anger in African American men. In W. S. Pollack & R. F. Levant (Eds.), *New psychotherapy for men* (pp. 239–258). New York: Wiley.

French, M. (1991). *Beyond power: On women, men, and morals.* London: Cardinal.

Gaylor, L. (1985, July/August). Pornography: A humanist issue. *Humanist,* pp. 34–40.

Gibbs, J. T. (1988). *Young, black, and male in America: An endangered species.* Dover, MA: Auburn House.

Gilmore, D. D. (1990). *Manhood in the making: Cultural concepts of masculinity.* New Haven, CT: Yale University Press.

Goldberg, H. (1976). *The hazards of being male.* New York: New American Library.

Good, G. E. (1998). Missing and underrepresented aspects of men's lives. *SPSMM Bulletin, 3*(2), 1–2.

Good, G. E., Dell, D. M., & Mintz, L. B. (1989). Male role and gender role conflict: Relations to help seeking in men. *Journal of Counseling Psychology, 36,* 295–300.

Good, G. E., Gilbert, L. A., & Scher, M. (1990). Gender aware therapy: A synthesis of feminist therapy and knowledge about gender. *Journal of Counseling and Development, 68,* 376–380.

Goodman, L. A., Koss, M. P., Fitzgerald, L. F., Russo, N. F., & Keita, G. P. (1993). Male violence against women. Current research and future directions. *American Psychologist, 48,* 1054–1058.

Gottfried, A. E., & Gottfried, A. W. (1988). *Maternal employment and children's development.* New York: Plenum Press.

Grant, B. F. Harford, T. C., Hasin, D. S., Chou, P., & Pickering, R. (1992). DSM-III-R and the proposed DSM-IV alcohol use disorders, United States, 1988: A nosological comparison. *Alcoholism: Clinical and Experimental Research, 16,* 215–221.

Gray, J. (1990). *Men, women, and relationships: Making peace with the opposite sex.* Hillsboro, OR: Beyond Words.

Gray, J. (1992). *Men are from Mars, women are from Venus.* New York: HarperCollins.

Gurian, M. (1999). A fine young man: What parents and educators can do to shape adolescent boys into exceptional men. New York: Tarcher.

Heesacker, M., & Prichard, S. (1992). In a different voice, revisited: Men, women, and emotion. *Journal of Mental Health Counseling, 14,* 274–290.

Hite, S. (1987). Women and love: A cultural revolution in progress. New York: Knopf.

Hochschild, A. (1989). *The second shift.* New York: Viking.

Kaplan, R. S., O'Neil, J. S., & Owen, S. V. (1993, August). Misogynous, normative, progressive masculinity and sexual assault: Gender role conflict, hostility toward women, and hypermasculinity. Paper presented at the annual meeting of the American Psychological Association, Toronto, Canada.

Kimmel, M. S. (Ed.). (1990). *Men confront pornography.* New York: Crown.

Kimura, D. (1992, September). Sex differences in the brain. *Scientific American,* pp. 119–125.

Koss, M. P. (1993). Rape: Scope, impact, interventions, and public policy responses. *American Psychologist, 48,* 1062–1069.

Levant, R. F. (1997). Nonrelational sexuality in men. In R. F. Levant & G. R. Brooks (Eds.), *Men and sex: New psychological perspectives* (pp. 9–27). New York: Wiley.

Levant, R. F., & Brooks, G. R. (Eds.). (1997). *Men and sex: New psychological perspectives.* New York: Wiley.

LeVay, S. (1993). *The sexual brain.* Cambridge, MA: MIT Press.

Lisak, D. (1994). The psychological consequences of childhood abuse: Content analysis of interviews with male survivors. *Journal of Traumatic Stress, 7,* 525–548.

Marin, P. (1991, July 8). Born to lose: The prejudice against men. *Nation,* pp. 46–51.

McLean, C. (1996). The politics of men's pain. In C. McLean, M. Carey, & C. White (Eds.), *Men's ways of being* (pp. 11–28). Boulder, CO: Westview Press.

Miller, J. B. (1986). *Toward a new psychology of women* (2nd ed.). Boston: Beacon Press.

Moir, A., & Jessel, D. (1991). *Brain sex: The real difference between women and men.* New York: Carol.

Nichols, J. (1975). Men's liberation: A new definition of masculinity. New York: Penguin.

Nutt, R. (1991). Ethical principles for gender-fair family therapy. *Family Psychologist, 7*(3), 32–33.

Oliver, M. B., & Hyde, J. S. (1993). Gender differences in sexuality: A meta-analysis. *Psychological Bulletin, 114,* 29–51.

Philpot, C., Brooks, G. R., Lusterman, D. D., & Nutt, R. L. (Eds.). (1997). *Bridging separate gender worlds.* Washington, DC: American Psychological Association.

Pittman, F. (1990). The masculine mystique. *Family Therapy Networker, 14*(3), 40–52.

Pleck, J. H. (1981). *The myth of masculinity.* Cambridge, MA: MIT Press.

Pleck, J. H. (1995). The gender role strain paradigm: An update. In R. F. Levant & W. S. Pollack (Eds.), *A new psychology of men* (pp. 11–32). New York: Basic Books.

Pleck, J. H. (1997). Paternal involvement: Levels, sources, and consequences. In M. E. Lamb (Ed.), *The role of the father in child development* (3rd ed., pp. 66–103). New York: Wiley.

Pleck, J. H., & Sawyer, J. (1980). *Men and masculinity.* Englewood Cliffs, NJ: Prentice Hall.

Pollack, W. S. (1998). *Real boys: Rescuing our sons from the myths of boyhood.* New York: Basic Books.

Robertson, J. M., & Fitzgerald, L. F. (1992). Overcoming the masculine mystique: Preferences for alternative forms of therapy among men who avoid counseling. *Journal of Counseling Psychology, 39,* 240–246.

Sanchez, L., & Kane, E. W. (1996). Women's and men's constructions of perceptions of housework fairness. *Journal of Family Issues, 17,* 385–387.

Scher, M. (1990). Effect of gender-role incongruities on men's experience as clients in psychotherapy. *Psychotherapy, 27,* 322–326.

Scher, M., Stevens, M., Good, G., & Eichenfield, G. (Eds.). (1987). *Handbook of counseling and psychotherapy with men.* Newbury Park, CA: Sage.

Shay, J. J., & Maltas, C. P. (1998). Reluctant men in couple therapy: Corralling the Marlboro man. In W. S. Pollack & R. F. Levant (Eds.), *New psychotherapy for men* (pp. 97–126). New York: Wiley.

Shiffman, M. (1987). The men's movement: An empirical investigation. In M. S. Kimmel (Ed.), *Changing men: New directions in research on men and masculinity* (pp. 295–314). Beverly Hills, CA: Sage.

Silverberg, R. (1986). *Psychotherapy for men: Transcending the masculine mystique.* Springfield, IL: Thomas.

Silverstein, L. B. (1996). Fathering is a feminist issue. *Psychology of Women Quarterly, 20,* 3–37.

Society for the Psychological Study of Men and Masculinity. (2000). SPSMM mission statement. *SPSMM Bulletin, 5*(3).

Stephenson, J. (1991). *Men are not cost-effective.* Napa, CA: Deimer, Smith.

Stoltenberg, J. (1989). *Refusing to be a man: Essays on sex and justice.* New York: Meridian.

Stoltenberg, J. (1993). *The end of manhood.* New York: Penguin.

Sue, D. W., & Sue, D. (1999). *Counseling the culturally different: Theory and practice* (3rd ed.). New York: Wiley.

Tannen, D. (1990). *You just don't understand: Women and men in conversation.* New York: Morrow.

Tannen, D. (1993). *Gender and conversational interaction.* New York: Oxford University Press.

Verbrugge, L. M. (1985). Gender and health: An update on hypothesis and evidence. *Journal of Health and Social Behavior, 26,* 156–182.

Ward, S. K., Chapman, K., Cohn, E., & Williams, K. (1991). Acquaintance rape and the college social scene. *Family Relations, 40,* 65–71.

Wilcox, D. W., & Forrest, L. (1992). The problems of men and counseling: Gender bias or gender truth? *Journal of Mental Health Counseling, 14,* 291–304.

Williamson, T. (1985). A history of the men's movement. In F. Baumli (Ed.), *Men freeing men: Exploding the myth of the traditional male* (pp. 308–324). Jersey City, NJ: New Atlantis Press.

CHAPTER ONE

Men's Problems
and Effective Treatments

Theory and Empirical Support

Glenn E. Good
Nancy B. Sherrod

People become therapists or counselors for a variety of reasons, including to help people and to make a reasonable living. It may seem obvious, but part of being helpful is doing things in therapy that clients find helpful. Researchers have investigated what clients find helpful (and unhelpful) in therapy, and this research offers guidance to therapists in their work. Throughout our discussion on men's problems and their treatment, we examine empirical support for treatments of problems that men experience.

The degree of importance that should be accorded to empirical support for psychological interventions is controversial. An analogy to medicine offers imperfect parallels. Over the course of history, thousands of remedies have been developed for most common human ailments. However, most contemporary U.S. consumers seek physicians who can provide effective interventions for their ailments. The relative effectiveness of medical interventions is routinely evaluated. In this vein, physicians who offer interventions that lack empirical support for their effectiveness risk malpractice claims and loss of licensure.

As we indicate in this chapter, mental health problems typically lack comparable specificity and causality to problems found in medicine. Consequently, systematic evaluation of the effectiveness of mental health interventions in treating specific psychosocial ailments is usually lacking. Nonetheless, there are excellent reasons for mental health practitioners to consider interventions that have been found to be especially effective for specific problems when they are available.

In this chapter, we discuss masculinity-related terminology, theoretical frameworks of masculinity, empirically identified problems men experience, and empirically supported treatments. Our objective is to identify findings that can guide therapists' work with men and to offer directions for expanding our understanding of men, their issues, and ways to optimally treat men's issues in the future.

THEORIES AND MODELS OF MASCULINITY

To understand men's problems and associated treatments, it is helpful to understand some of the important terminology, concepts, and theories that have developed in the study of men and masculinity. On the surface, defining concepts related to men and masculinity appears deceptively simple. Amid the growing research on men and masculinity, significant definitional and conceptual ambiguity exists. Numerous authors have attempted to clarify terms and concepts related to men and masculinity (see, for example, American Psychological Association, 1994; Deaux, 1984, 1993; Gentile, 1993; Good & Mintz, 1993; Good, Wallace, & Borst, 1994; Mintz & O'Neil, 1990; Pleck, Sonenstein, & Ku, 1993; Unger & Crawford, 1993). These authors point to the critical need to distinguish biologically determined sex-based characteristics (maleness) from societally or psychologically based conceptions of masculinity. For instance, having male genitalia is a biologically determined male characteristic, whereas being achievement oriented is a socially and psychologically constructed view of how men should be.

The area of societally or psychologically based conceptions of masculinity has been referred to by a variety of terms, including *masculine gender roles, attitudes toward the male role, conceptions of masculinity,* and *masculinity ideologies.* The term *masculinity ideologies* refers to sets of culturally defined standards of masculinity to which men are expected to adhere (Pleck, 1995). This plural term is desirable in that it reflects the notion that there are multiple standards of masculinity; various groups have different dimensions that are salient in their conception of masculinity (Brod, 1987). There are significant variations in the extent to which North American men endorse a single standard regarding masculinity ideology. For example, current observations and research indicate that there are differing conceptions of masculinity among various ethnic and racial groups (Levant, Majors, & Kelley, 1998), religious groups (Brod, 1987), age groups (Cournoyer & Mahalik, 1995), affectional or sexual preference groups (Harrison, 1995), and groups from various geographical regions (Good et al., 1995).

Another common area discussed in masculinity research is masculine role conflict and stress, which refers to the degree of distress related to men's efforts to meet the standards associated with masculinity ideologies. This concept has been called "sex role strain" (Pleck, 1981), "gender role conflict" (O'Neil, 1981), and "masculine gender role stress" (Eisler & Skidmore, 1987) by various researchers. Masculine role conflict and stress refer to such problems as restriction of emotional expression, need for success, and restriction of male friendships.

A variety of theories have sought to explain why men are the way they are. Some authors (for example, Archer, 1996; Buss, 1995) speculate that the basis for male behavior is genetic or psychoevolutionary. However, in this chapter (and book) we examine masculinity as a primarily socially constructed phenomenon (see Eagly & Wood, 1999; Silverstein, 1996). This view posits that most boys, and thus men, learn to adopt and adhere to culturally defined standards for masculine behavior (see Bergman, 1995; Kimmel & Messner, 1998; O'Neil, 1981; Pleck, 1995). Boys learn cultural messages through such routine developmental traumatic experiences as injuring oneself, experiencing pain, crying, and then receiving punitive responses to such tears. For example, when young boys are told "big boys don't cry," they are being instructed explicitly that crying is an unacceptable avenue of expression for them. This message is typically accompanied by the message that only girls cry. Hence, boys learn that there are clearly demarcated realms of gender-related behavior differentiating boys (men) from girls (women). If crying (and feeling pain) is feminine and not masculine, crying becomes a sign of weakness and vulnerability associated with femininity. Conversely, repressing emotions becomes a sign of the strength and invulnerability associated with masculinity. Therefore, to be viewed as masculine, boys typically learn to repress emotions that might be associated with vulnerability.

Boys are often called various derogatory names referring to girls or gay men if they express any sign of vulnerability and hence fail to meet cultural standards of masculinity. This process of being shamed, ridiculed, and physically assaulted is highly aversive, and most boys learn to avoid it at all costs. Some boys subsequently reinforce these beliefs and behaviors with their peers through the process of identification with their aggressors (Miller, 1998). As such, the process of indoctrination into masculine ways continues intrapersonally and interpersonally, without conscious examination of its harmful effects.

Although theories and models of masculinity ideologies have progressed, the most complete descriptions remain the "blueprint for manhood" (Brannon, 1976) and "the masculine mystique" model (O'Neil, 1981), which are based on research conducted primarily with white men of western European ancestry in the United States. According to these models, men are typically socialized toward characteristics that can be broadly categorized as independence and achievement (instrumentality, personal agency), restriction and suppression of emotions (rationality), and avoidance of characteristics associated with femininity and homosexuality (interpersonal dominance). Also mentioned in several models are the notions that men are socialized toward physical aggressiveness, toughness, and status seeking (Brannon, 1976; Thompson & Pleck, 1986).

In addition to writings and research seeking to describe masculine socialization, a related area of research has examined masculine role conflict and stress. As mentioned earlier, many men experience stresses in attempting to meet or resist societal and internalized demands to live up to the cultural standards for masculinity. For example, one of the most common findings in the masculinity research is the relation between men's level of emotional restriction and their degree of psychological distress and fear of intimacy (see, for example, Good et al., 1995). In the following sections we review issues associated with efforts to empirically assess masculinity ideologies, masculine role conflicts, and their correlates.

Measurement of Masculinity-Related Constructs

Central to an understanding of the current status of research on masculinity ideologies are issues related to the measurement of the constructs. Although a significant amount of research purports to examine aspects of masculinity, earlier studies tended to employ instruments of limited utility to the investigation of masculinity. For example, the two most widely used gender role instruments were the Bem Sex Role Inventory (BSRI) (Bem, 1974) and the twenty-four-item version of the Personality Attributes Questionnaire (PAQ) (Spence & Helmreich, 1978). Although there has been significant controversy about the relative merits of these two scales (see, for example, Spence, 1991), it is now clear that neither measures masculinity ideologies (that is, the extent to which individuals endorse numerous aspects of socialized masculine gender roles).

Both the BSRI and PAQ appear to tap the degree to which individuals (males or females) report *instrumental* ("masculinity") and *expressive* ("femininity") traits of a gender-related and socially desirable nature as being descriptive of their personalities (Spence, 1984, 1991; Spence, Losoff, & Robbins, 1991). Hence, the PAQ and BSRI "masculinity" scales should be viewed as assessing whether individuals report possessing a single personality trait that is socially desirable for males in this culture (namely, instrumentality or personal goal directedness) (Good et al., 1994). In our society, masculinity is far more complex; multiple dimensions are necessary to describe a single conception of masculinity ideology (Fischer, Tokar, Good, & Snell, 1998; Levant et al., 1992; Thompson & Pleck, 1995).

Instruments designed to more specifically assess masculinity-related constructs exist, however. Two approaches to assessing masculinity are currently in favor (Thompson & Pleck, 1995). One approach assesses dimensions of masculinity ideologies primarily derived from Brannon's (1976) "blueprint for manhood" (Brannon & Juni, 1984; Fischer et al., 1998; Thompson & Pleck, 1986) and typically includes dimensions such as status, toughness, and antifemininity.

Thompson and Pleck (1995) examined seventeen peer-reviewed scales developed since 1977 that were either attitude measures that gauge ideologies about men and masculinities or inventories for other masculinity-related constructs that reveal how males might experience their gender. They concluded that masculinity ideology appears to be distinct from gender role orientation, gender relations in general, and gender ideologies about women. They suggested that scales seeking to assess masculinity ideology should avoid using gender-comparative items, separate the concepts of gender-based personality orientation and masculinity ideology, and employ broader definitions of masculinity.

The second approach attempts to assess the degree of masculine role stresses and conflicts associated with endorsement of traditional conceptions of masculine gender roles (Eisler & Skidmore, 1987; O'Neil, Helms, Gable, David, & Wrightsman, 1986). Specifically, the Masculine Gender Role Stress (MGRS) scale (Eisler & Skidmore, 1987) is posited to assess five dimensions of masculinity-related stress, and the Gender Role Conflict Scale (GRCS) (O'Neil et al., 1986) assesses four dimensions of conflict with male gender roles. These two scales tap stress and conflict associated with culturally defined masculinity, such as restricted emotions, need for success, and restricted male friendships. In addition, researchers have conducted numerous studies of the psychometric properties of the GRCS scale; the findings strongly support the scale's factor structure (see Good et al., 1995; Moradi, Tokar, Schaub, Jome, & Serna, 2000). Not surprisingly, research using indicators of masculinity-related stress and conflict typically identifies larger relations with men's psychosocial and biomedical concerns than does research using indicators of masculinity ideologies (see Eisler, 1995; Good et al., 1995; Good, Robertson, Fitzgerald, Stevens, & Bartels, 1996; O'Neil, Good, & Holmes, 1995).

Wade's (1998) theory of reference group identity attempted to account for both conformity to and variability in standards of masculinity for individual men. This theory suggests that men's gender role self-concepts (attributes, attitudes, and behaviors) are related to their level of ego identity development (Erikson, 1968) and linked to their specific reference group (Sherif, 1962). In other words, this scale is designed to assess the extent to which a male's gender role self-concept depends on a specific male reference group. The research utility of this new model is yet to be established. In the future, it would also appear desirable to assess the degree of salience various aspects of masculinity ideology have for respondents (for example, "How important is it to you that you are perceived as successful and powerful?").

Multicultural Issues

As noted by several authors in this handbook, significant variation in conceptions of masculinity and its accompanying problems exists in different cultures and subcultures (see Chapters Thirty-five, Thirty-six, and Thirty-seven). Further, the process of acculturation (sometimes referred to as second-culture acquisition) adds further complexity to the degree to which generalizations can be made about the dominant conceptions of masculinity held by specific racial and ethnic groups. Additionally, variations in the salience of cultural identity and masculinity ideologies to individuals have been found to relate to subsequent psychological issues (Lilly, 1999). This area warrants further investigation, especially as the United States becomes increasingly multicultural.

ADVERSE AND DESIRABLE IMPLICATIONS OF SOCIALLY CONSTRUCTED ASPECTS OF MASCULINITY

A growing body of research documents both the positive and negative implications of traditional conceptions of masculinity. We discuss the negative consequences in greater detail in this chapter but first acknowledge a number of positive features associated with traditional conceptions of masculinity. Specifically, men holding more traditional conceptions of masculinity may have strengths in such areas as problem solving, logical thinking, risk taking, anger expression, and assertive behavior that may be especially beneficial in times of crisis (Levant, 1995). Examples of how these positive aspects of traditional masculinity ideologies may manifest include the ability to remain calm and problem focused in times of crisis (mental compartmentalizing) and subsuming personal needs to the greater duty of protecting and providing for one's family or country (personal sacrifice). In contemporary times, the perceived lack of need for these qualities associated with traditional conceptions of masculinity is causing distress for some men (see Faludi, 1999).

In relationships, clearly defined gender roles can provide expedient guides for division of household responsibilities and allocation of tasks. (We note, however, that all too often these responsibilities and tasks have been divided inequitably along gender lines.) Qualities embodied by more traditional masculinity ideologies can be simultaneously beneficial and injurious. This double-edged sword (noting both the pros and cons associated with some aspects of traditional masculine gender roles) is one of the reasons that men and women struggle in our society about what roles and behaviors are acceptable and appropriate for men. Although in this chapter we primarily focus on research investigating the ways in which masculinity ideologies and masculine role conflicts are deleterious for men and others in their lives, it is important to acknowledge that both men and women receive some benefits from aspects of traditional masculinity-related behaviors.

Despite the positive aspects of masculinity, researchers have identified numerous problematic links between aspects of masculinity and men's mental health. Men who report greater masculinity-related conflicts are more psychologically distressed (Good et al., 1995), have more difficulty with interpersonal intimacy (Fischer & Good, 1997), have greater biomedical concerns and poorer health behaviors (Watkins, Eisler, Carpenter, Schechtman, & Fischer, 1991), and hold more negative attitudes toward their use of mental health services (Blazina & Watkins, 1996; Good, Dell, & Mintz, 1989) than men who report few masculinity-related conflicts.

MEN'S PROBLEMS AND EFFECTIVE TREATMENTS

Research on masculinity typologies and their measurement has been progressing well; the founding of the journal *Psychology of Men and Masculinity* will likely increase the rate of progress in this area. Delineation of the link between men's conceptions of masculinity and various psychological problems has also been progressing. However, research on various treatments for men's masculinity-related problems is in its infancy. Many individuals have proposed innovative treatment programs for working with men's masculinity-related problems. At the present, researchers have evaluated the effectiveness of only a few of these interventions. What follows is an examination of research on men's problems, empirically supported interventions for those problems, and a look at promising future directions.

Identifying Problems and Accessing Mental Health Services

The first step in treating men's problems is encouraging men to recognize their problems and to access mental health services. Efforts to reconceptualize men's problems to make them more apparent have included the application of new terms, such as *alexithymia* (difficulty identifying and describing one's emotions) (Levant, 1995) and *emotional competence* (the ability to feel, experience, and communicate about the full range of human emotions) (Good, 1998). Research indicates that men have less open attitudes toward their emotions, perceive greater stigma associated with counseling, and report fewer psychological symptoms than women (Komiya, Good, & Sherrod, 2000). Hence, men's tendency to restrict emotions has been one of the most robust predictors of men's level of psychological distress to arise from research in the new psychology of men (Good et al., 1995, 1996).

Efforts to improve men's access to psychological information and use of mental health services have taken various forms. One direction has been reframing, relabeling, and repackaging how mental health services are provided. More specifically, men who hold traditional views of masculinity respond more favorably to psychological information offered via seminars and classes than that offered through counseling or therapy (Robertson & Fitzgerald, 1992). The recent growth of "coaching" may represent an extension of this approach by repackaging what is typically considered counseling and psychotherapy (see Chapter Five). Although good clinical evidence exists for the utility of this reconceptualization, it has yet to be empirically assessed.

Depression

Approximately 3 percent of U.S. men meet criteria for major depressive disorder at any particular point in time, and 13 percent of U.S. men experience major depression over the course of a lifetime (see Chapter Ten). As noted in Chapter Ten, men's depression is likely underdiagnosed because it is expressed in ways that are inconsistent with the criteria provided in the *Diagnostic and Statistical Manual of Mental Disorders* (4th edition) *(DSM-IV)*. Further, U.S. men are three times more likely than women to die of suicide (U.S. Bureau of the Census, 1997). Men fifteen to twenty-four years of age have more than five times the suicide risk, men twenty-four to forty-four years of age have four times the suicide risk, and men forty-five to sixty-four have more than three times the suicide risk of women in the same age groups (National Center for Health Statistics, 1999). Research suggests that men's depression and psychological distress are associated with conflicts and stresses related to masculinity (Cournoyer & Mahalik, 1995; Good, Gilbert, & Scher, 1990; Good et al., 1995; Good & Wood, 1995). In particular, researchers have found restrictive emotionality and conflict between work and family relations to be associated with men's levels of depression (Good et al., 1996).

Clear empirical support is available for the effectiveness of treating depression via cognitive-behavioral therapy, interpersonal therapies, and psychopharmacological interventions (Nathan & Gorman, 1998). When marital discord is a prominent part of the depressive picture, the use of marital behavior therapy has been empirically supported (O'Leary & Beach, 1990). Mahalik's pioneering suggestions about ways to address men's masculinity-related issues via interpersonal and cognitive-behavioral interventions (see Chapters Twenty-five and Twenty-six) will likely further improve the utility of these interventions for treating the masculinity-related aspects of men's depression.

When practitioners attempt to determine whether cognitive-behavioral or interpersonal therapy is the optimal initial therapeutic intervention, the "capitalization hypothesis" offers direction (Cronbach & Snow, 1977; Nathan & Gorman, 1998). The capitalization hypothesis is the notion that effective therapies seek to capitalize on clients' preexisting strengths rather than seeking to directly address clients' deficits. In terms of depression, clients with low levels of depressotypic cognitions responded preferentially better to cognitive-behavioral therapy than to other therapies (Sotsky et al., 1991). Conversely, clients with low rather than high levels of social dysfunction responded more favorably to interpersonal therapy than to other treatment interventions (Sotsky et al., 1991). In other words, the capitalization hypothesis suggests that therapists should use men's effective cognitive or interpersonal coping strategies to address their depressive concerns rather than seek to directly compensate for weaknesses. For example, a bright, rational male client might present with difficulties in interpersonal relationships and emotional insensitivity. Some therapists might approach his lack of sensitivity and emotional awareness by attempting to directly access emotions and increase sensitivity. Instead, the capitalization hypothesis suggests using the client's reasoning ability and desire to help him cognitively understand the value of emotional competence and its relation to interpersonal sensitivity before seeking to directly deepen emotional experiencing.

Anxiety and Stress

Research indicates that men's masculinity-related beliefs are related not only to their depression but also to their anxiety level (Cournoyer & Mahalik, 1995; Sharpe & Heppner, 1991). *DSM-IV* identifies six diagnoses associated with anxiety and panic. In general, people cope with anxiety and panic by avoiding the phobic stimulus or the cue associated with the phobic stimulus. Because anxiety and panic are highly aversive, men frequently use alcohol and drugs to dampen and numb themselves so that no phobic stimulus has much effect (see Chapter Eleven). As mentioned later, rates of alcohol and drug use are higher among men than among women. These higher rates of substance use and men's greater rates of violence have been hypothesized to be associated with men externalizing their feelings of anxiety and distress as opposed to internalizing them in the symptoms of anxiety and depression delineated by *DSM-IV*.

In general, treatment of anxiety and panic involves exposure to the underlying fear. Underlying fears include such concerns as abandonment, separation, rejection, death, anger, loss of control, and memory of a trauma. Anxiolytic medications may be helpful during the course of treatment. Some of the empirically supported treatments for anxiety disorders include cognitive-behavioral therapy for panic disorder and generalized anxiety disorder (Barlow, Craske, Cerny, & Klosko, 1989; Borkovec et al., 1987; Butler, Fennell, Robson, & Gelder, 1991; Clark et al., 1994) and stress inoculation training (Barlow, 1988). Some of the treatments that are probably efficacious include applied relaxation for panic disorder and generalized anxiety disorder (Barlow, Rapee, & Brown, 1992; Borkovec & Costello, 1993; Öst & Westling, 1995) and exposure therapies and stress inoculation training for posttraumatic stress disorder (Keane, 1998; Keane, Fairbank, & Caddell, 1989).

In Chapter Twelve, Lisak illustrates ways in which these empirically supported treatments may be adapted to more greatly benefit traumatized and anxious men. For example, when traumatized or anxious male clients begin to experience vulnerable emotions during an exposure intervention, they may recoil because of their internalized sense of what is appropriate for them as men. At such times, Lisak describes helping clients identify the meaning, consequences, and roots of their reflexive avoidance of emotional vulnerability.

Sexual Dysfunction

Research on male sexual dysfunction and effective treatments has been progressing. Much theoretical and clinical literature describes the link between men's masculinity-related beliefs (for example, myths) and men's levels of sexual dysfunction (see Chapter Fifteen; Zilbergeld, 1999). However, to date, little published research has examined this potential link. Research has identified five factors associated with positive outcomes of sex therapy. These predictors of favorable outcome are (1) the quality of the couple's general relationship (particularly the female partner's pretreatment assessment of the relationship), (2) the motivation of the partners (particularly the male partner) for treatment, (3) physical attraction between the partners, (4) early compliance with the treatment program, and (5) the absence of serious psychiatric disorders in both partners (Hawton, 1995; Segraves & Althof, 1998). In Chapter Fifteen, Pridal describes the empirical research supporting the effectiveness of interventions for erectile dysfunction, premature ejaculation, and male orgasmic disorder. Interestingly, studies examining whether matching the gender of the therapist with that of the client was helpful found no differences in outcome (Crowe, Gillan, & Golombok, 1981; LoPiccolo, Heiman, Hogan, & Roberts, 1985). This result is not surprising given recent findings about the importance of the therapeutic relationship to therapy outcome (Wampold, 2000).

Substance Abuse

Alcohol abuse tends to be more problematic for men than for women. In the United States, alcohol abuse and dependence are five times more prevalent in men than in women (American Psychiatric Association, 1994). Men are three times more likely than women to die from alcohol-related ailments (Doyle, 1996), and 39 percent of men have some level of psychological dependency on alcohol in their lifetime (Lemle & Mishkind, 1989).

Cultural differences in alcohol consumption have been identified. Most Asian cultures have a comparatively low prevalence of alcohol-related disorders, although men still have much higher rates than do women. This cultural difference may relate in part to the fact that approximately 50 percent of Japanese, Chinese, and Korean individuals lack the enzyme that eliminates the first breakdown product of alcohol. Hence, they are more likely to experience flushed face and palpitations when they consume alcohol. In the United States, Caucasian and African American populations have nearly identical rates of alcohol use, and Latinos have somewhat higher rates (American Psychiatric Association, 1994).

In Chapter Eleven, Isenhart reviews empirical data that suggest that aspects of traditional masculinity are associated with increased alcohol use and alcohol problems. Isenhart also discusses research on men's behavior in substance abuse treatment, efficacious treatments, and new directions for treatment.

Toughness and Violence

Statistics about men's health problems and practices suggest that adhering to the belief that men should be tough has many detrimental consequences for men. Being tough, fearless, aggressive, and restricting emotions may be considered ways in which men harm themselves. Such behaviors may also lead to detrimental consequences for others, particularly in the area of violence. Men, women, and children all suffer from the effects of male-perpetrated violence in American society. Men disproportionately perpetrate most forms of violence, including murder, sexual assault, most forms of juvenile violence, and hate crimes. Statistics suggest that men commit 95 percent of all reported violent crimes in the United States (*Sourcebook of Criminal Justice Statistics,* 1994). Men are also the most common victims of violence (Gilligan, 1996). Discussions of male victims and perpetrators of violence in the areas of homicide and rape may be found in Chapters Seven, Twelve, Thirteen, and Fourteen.

Although several areas of inquiry have examined the efficacy of treating men's violence, one area that has focused on the masculinity-related components of violence is rape prevention. We present this information as an illustration of potential research in this area.

Rape Prevention

As a result of alarming evidence of the prevalence of rape (see Koss, Gidycz, & Wisniewski, 1987), several researchers have proposed educational outreach interventions to prevent sexual assault (Berkowitz, 1994; Gilbert, Heesacker, & Gannon, 1991; Heppner, Humphrey, Hillenbrand-Gunn, & DeBord, 1995; Heppner, Neville, Smith, Kivlighan, & Gershuny, 1999; Ring & Kilmartin, 1992). Despite the widespread use of rape-prevention programs on university campuses, only a small number of studies have examined the outcomes of such interventions. Several investigators (Gilbert et al., 1991; Hamilton & Yee, 1990; Nelson & Torgler, 1990) reported significant improvement in rape-supportive attitudes after rape-prevention interventions. Although rape-supportive attitudes appear to correlate with sexual assault behavior, it remains unclear whether reported successes in changing attitudes about rape translate into reduced perpetration of sexual assault (Briere & Malamuth, 1983; Malamuth & Check, 1983; Mosher & Anderson, 1986; Muehlenhard & Linton, 1987).

There is also evidence to support the idea that even attitudinal change is temporary after such interventions (Frazier, Valtinson, & Candell, 1995; Heppner, Good, et al., 1995; Heppner, Humphrey, et al., 1995). In follow-up studies, researchers have found that although attitudes improved immediately after an intervention, they later returned to or exceeded their initial levels, sometimes called the rebound effect (Heppner, Good, et al., 1995). Thus, it appears that current rape-prevention efforts do not have an enduring impact on attitude. Rape-prevention efforts may effectively change rape-supportive attitudes for subpopulations of college men (Heppner et al., 1999). Further research may illuminate the characteristics of various subpopulations and how their attitudes do or do not change after intervention.

IMPLICATIONS AND FUTURE DIRECTIONS

Theory and clinical writing about conceptions of masculinity, associated problems, and potential treatments are expanding rapidly. However, gender-aware research investigating effective treatments for men's problems is just beginning. In this section we provide an overview of avenues and opportunities for further study.

Virtually all problems that have been associated with masculinity could be further delineated and corresponding treatments developed and assessed. Some areas in which there is particular need for investigation include the relation of emotions to men's problems and the development and assessment of interventions designed to address restriction of emotions. Research examining men's use of various psychological defenses may offer insight into the problems men develop and point toward particular therapeutic interventions (Mahalik, Cournoyer, DeFranc, Cherry, & Napolitano, 1998). Effective interventions to help men become more comfortable with interdependence, as opposed to counterdependence, could be valuable. In addition to improving remedial interventions for violence, it would also be useful to improve prevention interventions. In this vein, authors in this book offer suggestions for helping boys and adolescent males develop healthier identities. For example, Levant's discussion in Chapter Eighteen serves as a model for efforts to prevent problems from developing. Nonetheless, it is important to evaluate the effectiveness of interventions, whether they are preventive or remedial.

Therapeutic process variables in this area also need extensive investigation. As noted in Chapters Twenty-four, Twenty-seven, and Thirty-four, the quality of the working alliance between male clients and their therapists is highly associated with the outcome of therapy (Wampold, 2000). Hence, it is important to understand the connection between male clients' masculinity ideologies and their receptivity to various ways that therapists might seek to build strong working alliances. For example, male clients might have little difficulty identifying goals for treatment, some trouble with common therapeutic tasks (for example, focusing on emotions), but much trouble with bonds (letting their therapists become important to them). It would likely be of value to therapists for researchers to help clarify what therapists can do to optimize the therapeutic working alliance, especially with men for whom development of an optimal working alliance would ordinarily be difficult (see Chapter Twenty-seven).

Men, conceptions of masculinity, and associated problems and their treatments are emerging as areas of empirical research. Findings in this area that have direct applied implications are limited. Nonetheless, current research findings can assist mental health practitioners' endeavors to provide optimal services to their male clients. These initial studies indicate that an extensive array of clinically relevant questions and potentially valuable interventions await further investigation.

References

American Psychiatric Association. (1994). *Diagnostic and statistical manual of mental disorders* (4th ed.). Washington, DC: Author.

American Psychological Association. (1994). *Publication Manual* (4th ed.). Washington, DC: Author.

Archer, J. (1996). Sex differences in social behavior: Are the social role and evolutionary explanations compatible? *American Psychologist, 51,* 909–917.

Barlow, D. H. (1988). Anxiety and its disorders: The nature and treatment of anxiety and panic. New York: Guilford Press.

Barlow, D. H., Craske, M. G., Cerny, J. A., & Klosko, J. S. (1989). Behavioral treatment of panic disorder. *Behavior Therapy, 20,* 261–282.

Barlow, D. H., Rapee, R. M., & Brown, T. A. (1992). Behavioral treatment of generalized anxiety disorder. *Behavior Therapy, 23,* 551–570.

Bem, S. L. (1974). The measurement of psychological androgyny. *Journal of Consulting and Clinical Psychology, 42,* 165–174.

Bergman, S. J. (1995). Men's psychological development: A relational perspective. In R. F. Levant & W. S. Pollack (Eds.), *A new psychology of men* (pp. 68–90). New York: Basic Books.

Berkowitz, A. P. (1994). Men and rape: Theory, research, and prevention programs in higher education. San Francisco: Jossey-Bass.

Blazina, C., & Watkins, C. E. (1996). Masculine gender role conflict: Effects on college men's psychological well-being, chemical substance usage, and attitudes toward help-seeking. *Journal of Counseling Psychology, 43,* 461–465

Borkovec, T. D., & Costello, E. (1993). Efficacy of applied relaxation and cognitive-behavioral therapy in the treatment of generalized anxiety disorder. *Journal of Consulting and Clinical Psychology, 61,* 611–619.

Borkovec, T. D., Mathews, A. M., Chambers, A., Ebrahimi, S., Lytle, R., & Nelson, R. (1987). The effects of relaxation training with cognitive or nondirective therapy and the role of relaxation-induced anxiety in the treatment of generalized anxiety. *Journal of Consulting and Clinical Psychology, 55,* 883–888.

Brannon, R. (1976). The male sex role: Our culture's blueprint for manhood, what it's done for us lately. In D. David & R. Brannon (Eds.), *The forty-nine percent majority: The male sex role.* Reading, MA: Addison-Wesley.

Brannon, R., & Juni, S. (1984). A scale for measuring attitudes about masculinity. *Psychological Documents, 14,* document no. 2612.

Briere, J., & Malamuth, N. M. (1983). Self-reported likelihood of sexually aggressive behavior: Attitudinal versus sexual explanations. *Journal of Research in Personality, 17,* 315–323.

Brod, H. (Ed.). (1987). *The making of masculinities: The new men's studies.* Winchester, MA: Allen & Unwin.

Buss, D. M. (1995). Psychological sex differences: Origins through sexual selection. *American Psychologist, 50,* 164–168.

Butler, G., Fennell, M., Robson, P., & Gelder, M. (1991). Comparison of behavior therapy and cognitive behavior therapy in the treatment of generalized anxiety disorder. *Journal of Consulting and Clinical Psychology, 59,* 167–175.

Clark, D. M., Salkovskis, P. M., Hackmann, A., Middleton, H., Anastasiades, P., & Gelder, M. (1994). A comparison of cognitive therapy, applied relaxation, and imipramine in the treatment of panic disorder. *British Journal of Psychiatry, 164,* 759–769.

Cournoyer, R. J., & Mahalik, J. R. (1995). Cross-sectional study of gender role conflict examining college-aged and middle-aged men. *Journal of Counseling Psychology, 42,* 11–19.

Cronbach, L. J., & Snow, R. E. (1977). *Aptitudes and instructional methods.* New York: Irvington.

Crowe, M. J., Gillan, P., & Golombok, S. (1981). Form and content in the conjoint treatment of sexual dysfunction: A controlled study. *Behaviour Research and Therapy, 19,* 47–54.

Deaux, K. (1984). From individual differences to social categories: Analysis of a decade's research on gender. *American Psychologist, 39,* 105–116.

Deaux, K. (1993). Commentary: Sorry, wrong number—A reply to Gentile's call. *Psychological Science, 4,* 125–126.

Doyle, J. A. (1996). *The male experience* (3rd ed.). Madison, WI: Brown & Benchmark.

Eagly, A. H., & Wood, W. (1999). The origins of sex differences in human behavior: Evolved dispositions versus social roles. *American Psychologist, 54,* 408–423.

Eisler, R. M. (1995). The relationship between masculine gender role stress and men's health risk: The validation of the construct. In R. F. Levant & W. S. Pollack (Eds.), *A new psychology of men* (pp. 207–225). New York: Basic Books.

Eisler, R. M., & Skidmore, J. R. (1987). MGRS: Scale development and component factors in the appraisal of stressful situations. *Behavior Modification, 11,* 123–136.

Erikson, E. H. (1968). *Identity, youth, and crisis.* New York: Norton.

Faludi, S. (1999). *Stiffed: The betrayal of American men.* New York: Morrow.

Fischer, A. R., & Good, G. E. (1997). Masculine gender roles, recognition of emotions, and interpersonal intimacy. *Psychotherapy, 34,* 160–170.

Fischer, A. R., Tokar, D. M., & Good, G. E., & Snell, A. F. (1998). More on the structure of male role norms: Exploratory and multiple sample confirmatory analyses. *Psychology of Women Quarterly, 22,* 135–155.

Frazier, P., Valtinson, G., & Candell, S. (1995). Evaluation of a co-educational interactive rape prevention program. *Journal of Counseling and Development, 73,* 153–158.

Gentile, D. A. (1993). Just what are sex and gender, anyway? A call for a new terminological standard. *Psychological Science, 4,* 120–122.

Gilbert, B. J., Heesacker, M., & Gannon, L. J. (1991). Changing the sexual aggression–supportive attitudes of men: A psychoeducational intervention. *Journal of Counseling Psychology, 38,* 197–203.

Gilligan, J. (1996). *Violence.* New York: Putnam.

Good, G. E. (1998). Missing and underrepresented aspects of men's lives. *Society for the Psychological Study of Men and Masculinity Bulletin, 3*(2), 1–2.

Good, G. E., Dell, D. M., & Mintz, L. B. (1989). Male role and gender role conflict: Relations to help seeking in men. *Journal of Counseling Psychology, 36,* 295–300.

Good, G. E., Gilbert, L. A., & Scher, M. (1990). Gender aware therapy: A synthesis of feminist therapy and knowledge about gender. *Journal of Counseling and Development, 68,* 376–380.

Good, G. E., & Mintz, L. B. (1993). Towards healthy conceptions of masculinity: Clarifying the issues. *Journal of Mental Health Counseling, 15,* 403–413.

Good, G. E., Robertson, J. M., Fitzgerald, L. F., Stevens, M. A., & Bartels, K. M. (1996). The relation between masculine role conflict and psychological distress in male university counseling center clients. *Journal of Counseling and Development, 75,* 44–49.

Good, G. E., Robertson, J. M., O'Neil, J. M., Fitzgerald, L. F., Stevens, M., DeBord, K. A., & Bartels, K. M. (1995). Male gender role conflict: Psychometric issues and relations to psychological distress. *Journal of Counseling Psychology, 42,* 3–10.

Good, G. E., Wallace, D. L., & Borst, T. S. (1994). Masculinity research: A review and critique. *Applied and Preventive Psychology, 3,* 3–14.

Good, G. E., & Wood, P. K. (1995). Male gender role conflict, depression, and help seeking: Do college men face double jeopardy? *Journal of Counseling and Development, 74,* 70–75.

Hamilton, M., & Yee, J. (1990). Rape knowledge and propensity to rape. *Journal of Research in Personality, 24,* 111–122.

Harrison, J. (1995). Roles, identities, and sexual orientation: Homosexuality, heterosexuality, and bisexuality. In R. F. Levant & W. S. Pollack (Eds.), *A new psychology of men* (pp. 359–382). New York: Basic Books.

Hawton, K. (1995). Treatment of sexual dysfunctions by sex therapy and other approaches. *British Journal of Psychiatry, 167,* 307–314.

Heppner, M. J., Good, G. E., Hillenbrand, T. L., Hawkins, A. K., Hacquard, L. L., Nichols, R. K., DeBord, K. A., & Brock, K. J. (1995). Examining sex differences in altering attitudes about rape: A test of the Elaboration Likelihood Model. *Journal of Counseling and Development, 73,* 640–647.

Heppner, M. J., Humphrey, C. G., Hillenbrand-Gunn, T. L., & DeBord, K. A. (1995). The differential effects of rape prevention programming on attitudes, behavior, and knowledge. *Journal of Counseling Psychology, 42,* 508–518.

Heppner, M. J., Neville, H. A., Smith, K., Kivlighan, D. M., & Gershuny, B. S. (1999). Examining immediate and long-term efficacy of rape prevention programming with racially diverse college men. *Journal of Counseling Psychology, 46,* 16–26.

Keane, T. M. (1998). Psychological and behavioral treatments of post-traumatic stress disorder. In P. Nathan & J. Gorman (Eds.), *A guide to treatments that work* (pp. 398–407). New York: Oxford University Press.

Keane, T. M., Fairbank, J. A., & Caddell, J. M. (1989). Implosive (flooding) therapy reduces symptoms of PTSD in Vietnam combat veterans. *Behavior Therapy, 20,* 245–260.

Kimmel, M. S., & Messner, M. A. (1998). *Men's lives* (4th ed.). Needham Heights, MA: Allyn & Bacon.

Komiya, N., Good, G. E., & Sherrod, N. (2000). Emotional openness as a contributing factor to reluctance to seek counseling among college students. *Journal of Counseling Psychology, 47,* 138–143.

Koss, M. P., Gidycz, C. A., & Wisniewski, N. (1987). The scope of rape: Incidence and prevalence of sexual aggression and victimization in a national sample of higher education students. *Journal of Consulting & Clinical Psychology, 55,* 162–170.

Lemle, R., & Mishkind, M. E. (1989). Alcohol and masculinity. *Journal of Substance Abuse Treatment, 6,* 213–222.

Levant, R. F. (1995). Toward the reconstruction of masculinity. In R. F. Levant & W. S. Pollack (Eds.), *A new psychology of men* (pp. 229–251). New York: Basic Books.

Levant, R. F., Hirsch, L. S., Celentano, E., Cozza, T. M., Hill, S., MacEachern, M., Marty, N., & Schnedeker, J. (1992). The male role: An investigation of contemporary norms. *Journal of Mental Health Counseling, 14,* 325–337.

Levant, R. F., Majors, R. G., & Kelley, M. L. (1998). Masculinity ideology among young African American and European American women and men in different regions of the United States. *Cultural Diversity and Ethnic Minority Psychology, 4,* 227–236.

Lilly, R. L. (1999). *Gender role conflict among black/African American men: Individual differences and psychological outcomes.* Unpublished doctoral dissertation, University of Missouri, Columbia.

LoPiccolo, J., Heiman, J., Hogan, D., & Roberts, C. (1985). Effectiveness of single therapist versus cotherapy teams in sex therapy. *Journal of Consulting and Clinical Psychology, 53,*287–294.

Mahalik, J. R., Cournoyer, R., DeFranc, W., Cherry, M., & Napolitano, J. (1998). Men's gender role conflict and use of psychological defenses. *Journal of Counseling Psychology, 45,* 247–255.

Malamuth, N. M., & Check, J.V.P. (1983). Sexual arousal to rape depictions: Individual differences. *Journal of Abnormal Psychology, 92,* 55–67.

Miller, J. (1998). The enemy inside: An exploration of the defensive processes of introjecting and identifying with the aggressor. *Psychodynamic Counselling, 4*(1), 55–70.

Mintz, L. M., & O'Neil, J. M. (1990). Gender roles, sex, and the process of psychotherapy: Many questions and few answers. *Journal of Counseling and Development, 68,* 381–387.

Moradi, B., Tokar, D. M., Schaub, M., Jome, L. M., & Serna, G. S. (2000). Revisiting the structural validity of the Gender Role Conflict Scale. *Psychology of Men and Masculinity, 1,* 62–69.

Mosher, D. L., & Anderson, R. D. (1986). Macho personality, sexual aggression, and reactions to guided imagery of rape. *Journal of Research in Personality, 20,* 77–94.

Muehlenhard, C. L., & Linton, M. A. (1987). Date rape and sexual aggression in dating situations: Incidence and risk factors. *Journal of Counseling Psychology, 34,* 186–196.

Nathan, P. E., & Gorman, J. M. (1998). *A guide to treatments that work.* New York: Oxford University Press.

National Center for Health Statistics. (1999). *National vital statistics reports, 47* (19), 27. Online at: http://www.cdc.gov/nchs/fastats.htm. Accessed June 26, 2000.

Nelson, E. S., & Torgler, C. C. (1990). A comparison of strategies for changing college students' attitudes toward rape. *Journal of Humanistic Education and Development, 29,* 69–85.

O'Leary, K. D., & Beach, S.R.H. (1990). Marital therapy: A viable treatment for depression and marital discord. *American Journal of Psychiatry, 147,* 183–186.

O'Neil, J. M. (1981). Patterns of gender role conflict and strain: Sexism and fear of femininity in men's lives. *Personnel and Guidance Journal, 60,* 203–210.

O'Neil, J. M., Good, G. E., & Holmes, S. (1995). Fifteen years of theory and research on men's gender role conflict: New paradigms for empirical research. In R. F. Levant & W. S. Pollack (Eds.), *A new psychology of men* (pp. 164–206). New York: Basic Books.

O'Neil, J. M., Helms, B. J., Gable, R. K., David, L., & Wrightsman, L. S. (1986). Gender-Role Conflict Scale: College men's fear of femininity. *Sex Roles, 14,* 335–350.

Öst, L. G., & Westling, B. E. (1995). Applied relaxation versus cognitive behavior therapy in the treatment of panic disorder. *Behaviour Research and Therapy, 31,* 383–395.

Pleck, J. H. (1981). *The myth of masculinity.* Boston: MIT Press.

Pleck, J. H. (1995). The gender role strain paradigm: An update. In R. F. Levant & W. S. Pollack (Eds.), *A new psychology of men* (pp. 11–32). New York: Basic Books.

Pleck, J. H., Sonenstein, F. L., & Ku, L. C. (1993). Masculinity ideology and its corre-lates. In S. Oskamp & M. Costanzo (Eds.), *Gender issues in social psychology* (pp. 85–110). Newbury Park, CA: Sage.

Ring, T. E., & Kilmartin, C. (1992). Man to man about rape: A rape prevention pro-gram for men. *Journal of College Student Development, 33,* 82–84.

Robertson, J. M., & Fitzgerald, L. F. (1992). Overcoming the masculine mystique: Preferences for alternative forms of assistance among men who avoid counseling. *Journal of Counseling Psychology, 39,* 240–246.

Segraves, R. T., & Althof, S. (1998). Psychotherapy and pharmacotherapy of sexual dysfunctions. In P. Nathan & J. Gorman (Eds.), *A guide to treatments that work* (pp. 447–471). New York: Oxford University Press.

Sharpe, M. J., & Heppner, P. P. (1991). Gender role, gender-role conflict, and psycho-logical well-being in men. *Journal of Counseling Psychology, 38,* 323–330.

Sherif, M. (1962). The self and reference groups: Meeting ground of individual and group approaches. *Annals of the New York Academy of Sciences, 96,* 797–813.

Silverstein, L. B. (1996). Evolutionary psychology and the search for sex differences. *American Psychologist, 51,* 160–161.

Sotsky, S. M., Glass, D. R., Shea, M. T., Pilkonis, P. A., Collins, J. F., Elkin, I., Watkins, J. T., Imber, S. D., Leber, W. R., Moyer, J., & Oliveri, M. E. (1991). Patients' predic-tors of response to psychotherapy and pharmacotherapy: Findings in the NIMH Treatment of Depression Collaborative Research Program. *American Journal of Psychiatry, 148,* 997–1008.

Sourcebook of Criminal Justice Statistics, 1994. (1994). Washington, DC: U.S. Department of Justice, Bureau of Justice Statistics.

Spence, J. T. (1984). Masculinity, femininity, and gender-related traits: A conceptual analysis and critique of current research. In B. A. Maher & W. B. Maher (Eds.), *Progress in experimental research* (Vol. 3, pp. 1–97). New York: Academic Press.

Spence, J. T. (1991). Do the BSRI and PAQ measure the same or different concepts? *Psychology of Women Quarterly, 15,* 141–165.

Spence, J. T., & Helmreich, R. (1978). Masculinity and femininity: Their psychological dimensions, correlates, and antecedents. Austin: University of Texas Press.

Spence, J. T., Losoff, M., & Robbins, A. S. (1991). Sexually aggressive tactics in dating relationships: Personality and attitudinal correlates. *Journal of Social and Clinical Psychology, 10,* 289–304.

Thompson, E. H., & Pleck, J. H. (1986). The structure of male role norms. *American Behavioral Scientist, 29,* 531–543.

Thompson, E. H., & Pleck, J. H. (1995). Masculinity ideologies: A review of research and instrumentation of men and masculinities. In R. F. Levant & W. S. Pollack (Eds.), *A new psychology of men* (pp. 129–163). New York: Basic Books.

Unger, R. K., & Crawford, M. (1993). Commentary: Sex and gender—The troubled rela-tionship between terms and concepts. *Psychological Science, 4,* 122–124.

U.S. Bureau of the Census. (1997). *Statistical abstract of the United States: 1997* (117th ed.). Washington, DC: U.S. Government Printing Office.

Wade, J. C. (1998). Male reference group identity dependence: A theory of male identity. *Counseling Psychologist, 26,* 349–383.

Wampold, B. E. (2000). Outcomes of individual counseling and psychotherapy: Empirical evidence addressing two fundamental questions. In S. D. Brown & R. W. Lent (Eds.), *Handbook of counseling psychology* (4th ed., pp. 711–739). New York: Wiley.

Watkins, P. L., Eisler, R. M., Carpenter, L., Schechtman, K. B., & Fischer, E. B. (1991). Psychosocial and physiological correlates of male gender role stress among employed adults. *Behavioral Medicine, 17,* 86–90.

Zilbergeld, B. (1999). *The new male sexuality* (Rev. ed.). New York: Bantam Books.

SECTION ONE

SETTINGS

CHAPTER TWO

A Male-Friendly Therapeutic Process with School-Age Boys

Mark S. Kiselica

O utpatient psychotherapists, school counselors, school psychologists, and school social workers typically require their clients to visit their offices for formal counseling sessions, during which clients are expected to be introspective and to verbalize intimate thoughts and feelings. Although many clients are comfortable with and helped by this approach to counseling and psychotherapy, it is incompatible with the relational styles of many boys and with their conceptions about the helping process. For example, males with a traditional gender role orientation tend to prefer group activities (Andronico, 1996; Jolliff, 1994) that are competitive (Griffin-Pierson, 1990) and involve sports or the manipulation and organization of data and objects (Kiselica, 1995). Furthermore, traditional teenage boys experiencing adjustment difficulties tend to respect and trust professionals who are willing to leave their offices, participate in youth recreational activities, and help their clients to address the clients' practical concerns (Hendricks, 1988; Kiselica, 1995; Kiselica, Stroud, Stroud, & Rotzien, 1992; Sander & Rosen, 1987). Consequently, traditional young men are likely to feel ill at ease with counseling and psychotherapy as it is customarily practiced (Kiselica, 1992, 1995; Kiselica & Horne, 1999) and may be reluctant to work with practitioners who either condemn or do not understand traditional

---

This chapter is a revised version of "A Male-Friendly Therapeutic Process with Adolescent Boys," which was presented at the Annual Convention of the American Psychological Association, Boston, Massachusetts, August, 1999.

male relational styles and expectations about the helping process (Hendricks, 1988; Kiselica, 1992, 1995; Kiselica & Horne, 1999; Sander & Rosen, 1987).

To correct for this mismatch between the parameters of conventional counseling and psychotherapy and the relational styles and expectations of traditional adolescent males, practitioners must make adjustments in the process of counseling and psychotherapy with traditional young men. The purpose of this chapter is to recommend that such adjustments adhere to a male-friendly therapeutic process with traditional school-age boys. A male-friendly process is one in which the counselor employs a wide variety of strategies and activities that are likely to appeal to traditional male youth and facilitate the establishment and maintenance of rapport with this population.

I begin this chapter with a description of the traditional male relational style. I argue that there is a mismatch between the characteristics of the conventional counseling environment and the relational styles of traditional school-age boys, and I present a proposal for transforming the therapeutic process with boys through the application of a male-friendly approach to counseling and psychotherapy. Data from empirical research evaluating the efficacy of counseling with teen fathers are used as the foundation for recommending the following: questioning the rigid use of fifty-minute sessions; using informal activities, alternative time schedules, and alternative settings; employing humor, self-disclosure, and other rapport-building tactics; and helping boys through group counseling. I consider the implications of a male-friendly approach for redefining professional conceptions about boundaries in the client-therapist relationship and transforming the practice of school-based counseling. I conclude the chapter with a discussion of the myths and realities about alexithymia in boys.

As a preliminary note, I recognize that there are many theoretical approaches to working with troubled school-age boys. Many mental health professionals prefer to counsel the entire family in an attempt to change the family system in a way that facilitates the growth and emotional well-being of the identified client. Other practitioners are inclined to work with boys in individual counseling or psychotherapy, while still others artfully juggle family and individual sessions. The recommendations discussed here are offered as suggestions for establishing and maintaining rapport during individual and group therapeutic encounters between clinicians and boys who have a traditional male relational style.

WHAT IS A TRADITIONAL MALE RELATIONAL STYLE?

Boys who exhibit a traditional male relational style tend to be uncomfortable verbalizing their intimate thoughts and feelings in contexts in which there is likely to be disapproval regarding the expression of emotions by males (Fischer et al., 1993; LaFrance & Banaji, 1992; Shields, 1995). For example, many traditional males are wary of acknowledging when they are frightened or sad or of allowing themselves to cry because they believe that others will view such expressions as a sign of weakness (Levant, 1995). Traditional boys also develop friendships and experience closeness to others through instrumental activities, such as participating in sports, going fishing or swimming, hanging out in the streets, working on a project that requires manual labor, or playing on a computer (Clinchy & Zimmerman, 1985; Kiselica, 1992, 1995; Surrey, 1985). Simply put, traditional boys present themselves to the world as "doers" rather than as "feelers" (Kiselica, 1992), even though they experience and are capable of expressing very powerful emotions, such as joy, sorrow, happiness, and anger (see Heesacker et al., 1999).

TRADITIONAL BOYS IN COUNSELING AND PSYCHOTHERAPY

Traditional boys are often ill suited for counseling and psychotherapy as it is commonly practiced. More than twenty years ago, Monroe Bruch (1978) explained in a special issue of *The Counseling Psychologist* on helping men that there is a mismatch between the relational styles of traditional males and that of most helping professionals. Borrowing Holland's (1973) typology, Bruch (1978) suggested that the helping environment is best suited for individuals who would be classified as having a "social" personality type (p. 27). That is, clients who are skilled at and comfortable with the self-disclosure of thoughts and feelings and who are introspective can easily relate to counselors because counselors use the same relational style. Thus, males who have social personality types tend to respond well to counseling activities. However, many males, especially traditional males (and, I might add, many females) are not social types, and their relational styles are not congruent with the social environment of counseling. For example, men who have "conventional" and "realistic" personalities avoid less structured interpersonal and exploratory activities, such as counseling, and prefer activities involving the manipulation and organization of data and objects. Consequently, they are likely to feel ill at ease with counseling as it is customarily practiced (Bruch, 1978).

Because of this mismatch between the relational style of the client and the norms of the counseling setting, the traditional male client tends to feel uncomfortable, has difficulty responding in a manner that the counselor prefers, and is disinclined to continue in counseling. Many counselors erroneously view these behaviors as acts of resistance (Kiselica, 1992, 1995) and as evidence that the client is hypoemotional (Heesacker et al., 1999) and does not want to address his problems rather than viewing the situation as a possible problem of a lack of fit between the client and the counseling environment (Kiselica, 1992, 1995). In a conference address pertaining to this issue (Kiselica, 1992), I argued that this problem is analogous to a clothing manufacturer who has designed a one-size-fits-all glove, in which the glove actually fits a small percentage of customers. The remainder of people whose hands do not fit into the gloves either will have very numb hands on a bitter cold day because the gloves are too small to wear or their hands will feel lost inside the gloves because the gloves are too large. In this situation, is it surprising that the hands of some of the customers become stiff? That other customers dislike the gloves because they are over-sized? Would it not behoove the manufacturer to develop different gloves for different people?

Returning from this analogy back to therapeutic considerations, I contend that many boys avoid and drop out of counseling and psychotherapy because they are uneasy with the manner in which helpers typically relate to them (Kiselica, 1992, 1995). If this hypothesis is true, and there is considerable empirical support for this conjecture (see Achatz & MacAllum, 1994; Brown, 1990; Hendricks, 1988; Sander & Rosen, 1987), then it makes sense that helping professionals adapt their relational styles to the personalities of traditional boys to make the helping process more appealing and more effective with this population.

A MALE-FRIENDLY APPROACH TO COUNSELING AND PSYCHOTHERAPY

How can this adaptation be accomplished? How should the helper relate to young men with a traditional relational style? To put it in another way, how can we construct and deliver a male-friendly approach to counseling and psychotherapy with school-age boys?

In my attempt to answer these questions, I will draw extensively from the findings of a variety of studies pertaining to the provision of services to teen fathers. Historically, adolescent fathers have been greatly misunderstood, under-served, and treated in a pejorative manner by social service providers in the United States (Kiselica, 1995, 1999). Consequently, they have been unlikely to participate in teen parenting programs, even though the best available data demonstrate that the majority of teen fathers want help with the challenges of parenthood (Achatz & MacAllum, 1994; Brown, 1990; Hendricks, 1988; Sander & Rosen, 1987). Other data, which are summarized here, indicate that the use of counseling services by teen fathers increases substantially when service providers tailor teen parenting programs to the needs of adolescent fathers and employ nontraditional approaches to counseling (Achatz & MacAllum, 1994; Brown, 1990; Hendricks, 1988; Sander & Rosen, 1987). Because these data are drawn from studies that were conducted in many different rural and urban areas of the United States and with samples of white (non-Hispanic), African American, and Hispanic males, they are likely to have strong external validity for working with other boys. Collectively, these data suggest that effective helping must begin with a reexamination of the time constraints imposed on male clients and the use of formal office settings during counseling and psychotherapy.

A Reexamination of the Fifty-Minute Hour and the Use of Formal Office Settings

Traditional boys tend to develop trusting relationships with their friends over time, by hanging out, doing things together, and gradually letting others into their psychological world. Consequently, they are a bit like fish out of water when they are thrust into formal counseling situations in which they are expected to remain seated and spill their guts for an hour at a time once a week. The so-called fifty-minute hour, which has become the standard time frame for counseling and psychotherapy sessions in the United States, is an artificial and odd concept to many boys and is especially foreign to some ethnic groups, such as Native Americans. For many boys meeting a counselor or psychotherapist for the first time, fifty minutes is too long a period to sit around talking. For others who are in a crisis, a fifty-minute session—particularly fifty minutes once a week—is inadequate for managing a crisis. Some teenage boys perceive mental health practitioners who adhere rigidly to this one-hour-per-week standard as being hypocritical about wanting to be helpful (Kiselica, 1992).

The reliance on formal office settings for the work of counseling and psychotherapy is also problematic for many boys with a traditional relational style. Most practitioners who work with school-age boys do so within the confines of their offices. Yet traditional boys are accustomed to developing intimate relations in less formal settings. Boys who are good buddies with one another get to know each other inside and out through the instrumental activities they share. For example, over the course of any sporting season, boys on the same team get to know each other quite well, including significant information about each other's psyche. Although boys on the same team may not sit down and have face-to-face, heart-to-heart chats, they do share stories and bits and pieces of significant emotional material about their lives with one another while changing in the locker room, horsing around together and hanging out after practice and between games, and traveling to and from practices and games. In a similar fashion, guys who tinker with automobiles or youths who are members of gangs develop close friendships through their shared activities in garages and street hangouts, respectively. Intimate kinships develop in these varied settings. However, traditional males view formal office settings as, well, formal, and not as the kind of place where you let others see what makes you tick inside. Asking a traditional male to step into a formal office setting and open up his psyche is analogous to asking an opera singer to perform an inspired rendition of an aria in a toolshed without the support of an orchestra. The setting is just not conducive to the production of one's best performance.

Alternative Time Schedules and Settings

In light of these considerations, it is time for mental health professionals to reexamine the standard use of the fifty-minute hour and formal office settings with traditional male adolescents. Instead, as Hendricks (1988) has suggested, to the extent possible, the time for meetings with boys should be convenient for them. It is better to be more general rather than rigid and specific regarding the scheduling of appointments and to establish drop-in periods. For example, a practitioner can ask, "Can you come in the morning between the hours of nine and eleven, or is the afternoon better for you between the hours of three and six?" Because some boys, especially those from emotionally disengaged families, are not very good at following through on making and keeping appointments, Brown (1990) advised counselors to be persistent in their efforts to serve young men, even though they may feel frustrated at times. She noted that patience and persistence frequently prove successful in engaging this population in counseling. Furthermore, as I have discussed elsewhere (Kiselica, 1995, 1999), once boys gradually get to know their counselors and experience the benefits of good treatment, they tend to become more committed to counseling and psychotherapy and tolerant of higher expectations by the therapist that the client show up for expected appointments.

Having initial interactions outside the office setting can speed up the process of establishing rapport with traditional boys. The professional can conduct much of the early information gathering in a gym or outside, where the clinician and boy take turns shooting baskets or tossing a football while they talk about each other's favorite teams (Kiselica, 1995, 1999). Or the two might go for a walk, share a snack and a soda, and chat about the young man's interests as they walk side by side (Kiselica, 1995, 1999). Other strategies include conducting sessions in the client's home, at a park, or in a restaurant and talking about each other's lives while playing checkers, working together on a manual project, or fishing or hiking in the woods together.

Without question, school-based practitioners who attempt to employ these nonconventional, rapport-building strategies are likely to be discouraged by school officials who have rigid expectations about how and where counseling should occur. As a solution to this problem, in a later section of this chapter I suggest some of the system-change strategies that can help school officials to accept a transformed practice of school-based counseling with boys.

Humor and Self-Disclosure

Across the many different settings suggested earlier, the counselor should be prepared to inject a little humor and self-disclosure into the conversation. Traditional boys tend to relieve tension by telling jokes, and they typically feel comfortable with people who can loosen things up a bit with a well-timed joke or two. Although traditional boys may find it difficult to disclose very personal matters to others directly, they tend to open up to others who take the lead with self-disclosure. Therefore, it is recommended that the counselor be prepared to share an appropriate amount of personal information about himself or herself with the client. For example, when I have determined that it is safe to do so, I often show boys I counsel photos of my wife and children and tell them about where I was raised and where I live. Telling a little bit about oneself to the client engenders trust and models self-disclosure for the client. In summary, sharing light conversations that are characterized by gradual and mutual self-disclosure and are held outside of the office can pave the way for discussions regarding more substantive matters.

Other Rapport-Building Tactics

Once the practitioner senses that it is OK to broach more personal topics, heavy reliance on open-ended questions such as "How are you feeling?" tends to be ineffective. Instead, it is recommended that the counselor conduct issue-specific discussions (Barth, Claycomb, & Loomis, 1988) centered on how the counselor can help the young man with his most pressing concern (Hendricks, 1988). I emphasize the word *his* because the client may have a different agenda for the counseling session than the clinician does. For example, it is common for adolescent boys to want help with practical matters, such as finding a job, getting a car license, or settling a dispute with a girlfriend, whereas the counselor may intend to discuss the boy's academic difficulties or conflicts between the youth and his teacher or family. Although the counselor cannot ignore the latter issues, which are often the basis for counseling referrals, he or she is advised to proceed carefully and to follow the client's cues regarding his comfort level with any topic. In other words, the counselor should take it slow and follow the boy's lead. After the youth grows more comfortable and trusting, the counselor can be more direct and less tentative and switch the focus of counseling to more emotionally charged issues.

Empathy, availability, and honesty are essential to the development and maintenance of rapport (Brindis, Barth, & Loomis, 1987; Kiselica, 1996). A troubled boy needs to know that he can count on the counselor during times of crisis. Therefore, it is essential early on to assure him of one's availability for as long as it is needed and to empathize with his feelings about his problems. Furthermore, it is a good idea for the counselor to act in a way that demonstrates respect for the lad's autonomy. For example, the counselor is advised to provide his or her business card, which should list the counselor's name, work address and phone number, and the hours during which the counselor can be contacted (Hendricks, 1988).

These measures will help many boys to feel comfortable visiting a counselor in his or her office. In the following section I recommend additional tactics for making office visits a success.

Male-Friendly Strategies During Office Visits

According to Hendricks (1988), there are many things the clinician can do to put a boy at ease once he arrives at the clinician's office:

1. Ask the client for his permission to call him by his first name.
2. Encourage him to relax by offering a soft drink before beginning the session.
3. Have all calls held during the interview. Doing so contributes to his sense of importance.
4. Have magazines displayed with which a teenage boy can identify, especially sports publications.
5. Be knowledgeable about the slang he may use.
6. Be prepared to discuss events going on in the community.
7. Keep interview sessions brief—a maximum of forty-five minutes.

The manner in which one talks to a boy can greatly influence his response. During the early stages of counseling, it is advisable to not ask too many questions because boys often associate such questioning with being in trouble. Once again, the counselor should be prepared to do a lot of listening and to follow the boy's lead about what topics he is ready to discuss. This approach communicates to the youth that the counselor is there to address the youth's own pressing needs (Hendricks, 1988). "Moreover, trust, rapport, and constructive communication are likely to be established more rapidly when the youth and clinician sit side-by-side rather than opposite each other" (Hendricks, 1988, p. 719). This seating arrangement tends to reduce suspicion and self-consciousness (Hendricks, 1988). Kiselica (1999) recommended that a counselor wearing a long-sleeved shirt role up his or her shirtsleeves, thereby conveying to the youth that the counselor is ready to work for and with the youngster. It can also help to toss a miniature football around while the counselor and client talk about disturbing subjects (Kiselica, 1995).

Another critical task during the initial stages of counseling is to explore the boy's view about counseling. Through this process misconceptions about the purpose of counseling can be corrected. In addition, the counselor can prepare the client for some of the work that might lie ahead (Kiselica, 1995).

Working Efficiently: Group Counseling Services for Boys

Practitioners who work in school settings understandably might be concerned about how they can follow the recommendations offered here in light of the many demands that tax their time and energies. For example, on average there is only 1 counselor for every 513 students in U.S. elementary and secondary schools

(Barstow, Urbaniak, & Holland, 1999). I have personally supervised school counseling practicum students and interns working in school districts in which the student-to-counselor ratio is nine hundred to one. School counselors employed in these districts will have difficulty finding the time to work individually with troubled boys, especially in the manner that I have suggested here. Yet school counselors and other professional helpers who work in schools have an ethical obligation and face public pressure to address the needs of troubled boys.

These conflicting demands place some school-based helpers in a difficult if not impossible situation. It is highly unlikely that school-based practitioners who are overwhelmed with student-to-counselor ratios of five hundred to one or higher can deliver effective counseling services. Such circumstances call for systematic changes in the schools, which is an issue I address later in this chapter. Until such changes occur, however, school-based helpers must strive to find an efficient way to help troubled boys in the face of such difficult circumstances.

Counseling boys in groups may be a partial solution to this problem. Group counseling approaches are more efficient than individual approaches to counseling because they allow counselors to address the needs of many clients in the same session. In addition to this practical advantage, group counseling makes clinical sense for counseling with boys in school, agency, and private practice settings because, as Jolliff (1994) and Andronico (1996) have observed, boys and men are accustomed to working and playing together in groups. Therefore, group counseling is a powerful treatment modality with males (Andronico, 1996; Jolliff, 1994), and it works particularly well with school-age boys when it is incorporated into holistic programs that include recreational and educational activities (Kiselica, 1996; Kiselica, Rotzien, & Doms, 1994).

Over the course of the past ten years, I and several of my colleagues have designed an approach to group counseling that is designed to appeal to the relational styles of traditional boys (see Kiselica, 1995, 1996, 1999; Kiselica, Rotzien, & Doms, 1994). In brief, our approach involves incorporating informal, rapport-building strategies such as helping boys to establish rapport through participation in recreational activities integrated with group psychoeducational activities that target the particular concerns of the group. For example, we have developed after-school programs for expectant teenage fathers in which the participants introduce themselves and then play basketball for approximately half an hour. Afterward, while having a drink or a snack, the boys watch and react to educational videos that are designed to help them clarify their attitudes about fatherhood and to express their feelings about becoming a parent. Other sessions are focused on teaching the participants important life skills, such as child care and financial and time management skills. This approach to counseling taps the instrumental, group-oriented relational style of traditional boys while capitalizing on the support that is created through the formation of a therapeutic group.

Professionals can apply this model in their work with boys facing a wide range of emotional difficulties. Informal recreational activities can be merged with psychoeducational sessions targeting the stereotypic problems of boys, such as disruptiveness and aggression, as well as other problems, such as shyness, gender identity issues, and incest, problems that hundreds of thousands of boys experience but that are commonly ignored by society (see Kiselica & Horne, 1999).

A REEXAMINATION OF PROFESSIONAL CONSTRAINTS

Undoubtedly, some practitioners will be uncomfortable with the ideas that I have proposed here because they are at odds with traditional conceptions of boundaries in the client-practitioner relationship. As Arnold Lazarus (1990, 1995) has pointed out, most mental health practitioners are trained to maintain a high degree of professional distance from their clients in order to maintain their objectivity about their clients' problems. Furthermore, the ethical standards used in psychology, counseling, psychiatry, and social work discourage practitioners from developing dual relationships with clients—that is, from having a personal and a professional relationship with a client at the same time. Although these conventions of clinical practice certainly have many merits, such as preventing the exploitation of clients, Lazarus and other prominent leaders of the mental health professions, such as Nancy Boyd-Franklin (1989) and Derald Wing Sue (1997), and organizers of highly acclaimed, successful community-based service programs for adolescents, such as Michael Carrera (1992), have questioned the strict interpretations of and adherence to these conventions. For example, Lazarus (1990, 1995) has argued that rigid boundaries between client and therapist sometimes have the effect of shackling the humanity of the therapist and consequently impair the client-therapist relationship. Similarly, Boyd-Franklin (1989) and Sue (1997) have noted that the standard way of conducting psychotherapy creates such a distance between the client and the practitioner that some populations, such as impoverished, inner-city African Americans, consider counseling and psychotherapy to be a strange and foreign endeavor that should be avoided. Carrera (1992) urged that traditional service programs, which impoverished inner-city boys view as lacking heart, be replaced by holistic, highly personal educational programs.

I argue that the same types of problems permeate much of the mental health work going on with traditional boys and that it is time to transform counseling and psychotherapy with boys, a transformation that requires us to reexamine how rigidly we interpret concepts such as client-therapist boundaries and dual relationships. We have to do a better job of creating safe but humane boundaries in counseling and psychotherapy with boys. Although confused and troubled boys can be helped by someone who listens to and analyzes their problems with an objective stance, there is strong empirical evidence that they can be helped even more by practitioners who are also willing to get out of their offices, visit their clients' homes, take boys out to lunch, play with boys in school yards, drive them to job interviews, and work on projects with them (Achatz & MacAllum, 1994; Brown, 1990; Hendricks, 1988; Sander & Rosen, 1987). This is not to say that professionals should take the place or do the work of parents and other family members. On the contrary, it is preferable that the practitioner assist families to engage and help troubled boys with their intrapsychic and extrapsychic concerns. Nevertheless, whether the work is focused on mobilizing the family members to help their sons or on working with boys individually in therapy, I am convinced that the most effective practitioners are those whom boys perceive to be active, involved mentors who make a positive difference in boys' lives by addressing their practical needs and their emotional difficulties in a friendly, loving, and involved manner.

Addressing Constraints Imposed by School Systems

School counselors, school psychologists, and school social workers remain somewhat limited in their attempts to help boys by the constraints imposed by school systems. On the whole, school district policies regulating and defining the work of school-based helpers dictate and reward a conservative, outdated approach to counseling boys. School practitioners cannot help boys if they continue to be overwhelmed by inexcusably high student-to-counselor ratios and if they are forced to practice in a way that comes across as being foreign to U.S. boys. The legions of boys who are struggling with cultural values conflicts, confusion about what it means to be male, sexual identity issues, teenage fatherhood, physical and sexual abuse, aggressive tendencies, learning difficulties, anxiety, depression, hyperactivity and attention difficulties, and substance abuse warrant a radical transformation of the way we conduct counseling and psychotherapy with boys (see Horne & Kiselica, 1999; Kiselica & Horne, 1999). Schools must play an integral part in this transformation, beginning with a reexamination of the demands placed on school-based counselors and the manner in which they are required to provide their professional services.

School counselors, school psychologists, and school social workers can be crucial agents for changing school-based services for boys by participating in several initiatives. First, it is recommended that helpers employed in archaic school systems obtain and read *Developing and Managing Your School Guidance Program,* by Gysbers and Henderson (2000). This resource is necessary reading for any school-based counselor who is frustrated by high student-to-counselor ratios and by responsibilities that have nothing to do with counseling, such as performing the quasi-administrative tasks of monitoring hallways and processing student schedules. Gysbers and Henderson describe a model for how school counselors can work over time with other school personnel, parents, school board members, and students to create support for the hiring of additional school counselors and to update and expand the roles of counselors in schools. Second, school practitioners are urged to read the works of Carrera (1992), Dryfoos (1994), and Tyack (1992), all of whom describe the benefits (for example, reduced vandalism, dropout, delinquency, and teen parenthood rates) of innovative counseling and social services for youth, and to inform key power brokers in their communities about the effectiveness of these innovative approaches to counseling in schools. Lastly, school-based helpers can fortify their arguments for transforming counseling with boys by capitalizing on the growing public discontent regarding the failure of schools to address adequately the social and emotional needs of schoolchildren. Sadly, the gruesome killings and suicides at Columbine High School and similar tragedies at many other schools throughout the United States have awakened the country to the disturbing fact that "too many of our nation's sons are in trouble and troubled in a society that tends to disregard their problems or give them mixed messages about receiving help" (Kiselica & Horne, 1999, p. xvii). In response to this problem, there has been an urgent demand by the public to place more counselors in schools. As evidence of this demand, Congress is currently reviewing new legislative proposals that are designed to fund the hiring of one hundred thousand new school counselors, psychologists, and social workers (Barstow et al., 1999). Mental health professionals must continue to support this type of legislation so that we can ensure that caring and competent counseling professionals help boys to reach their fullest potential.

MYTHS AND REALITIES REGARDING ALEXITHYMIA AND BOYS

As a closing note, any mental health practitioner, whether employed in a school or a nonschool setting, should understand the subject of alexithymia and its alleged occurrence in boys. *Alexithymia* is defined as a very serious emotional disturbance characterized by a constellation of symptoms, including stiffness of posture and an expressionless face, difficulty identifying and describing feelings, a concrete and reality-based cognitive style, an impoverished imagination, and psychosomatic ailments (Krystal, 1982; Sifneos, 1973). According to Krystal (1982), alexithymia is common among people who have suffered from severe trauma and individuals with addictions who are going through drug withdrawal.

Unfortunately, recent writings about alexithymia have created the widespread impression that the disorder is gender specific and limited to males. For example, Pollack (1995, 1999) and Pollack and Chu (1997) have proposed that boys experience a normative developmental trauma of a premature, forced emotional separation from their mothers, which creates low levels of alexithymia, which in turn is the root cause of aggression, suicide, drug abuse, and other difficulties in boys. Although it is true that some boys experience alexithymia, there is no empirical support for the claim that boys are more likely than girls to suffer from alexithymia. On the contrary, the best available data indicate that there are no significant gender differences in the occurrence of alexithymia (Levant, 1999; Mallinckrodt, King, & Coble, 1998). Nevertheless, widespread misconceptions about alexithymia have contributed to stereotypes depicting boys as emotionally mummified creatures (Kiselica, 1997). These stereotypes have the potential to cause practitioners to view male clients as being more psychopathological than they actually are (Heesacker et al., 1999).

As I have argued here and elsewhere (Kiselica, 1997), a more accurate portrayal of boys is to understand that they are not emotionally constricted but that they tend to express their emotions in ways that are different from those used by most females and most counselors. Furthermore, the counseling process strategies described in this chapter are designed to help practitioners to understand the relational styles of traditional boys and how to adapt counseling to match those styles.

What, then, should counselors do with the minority of boys who display the serious condition of alexithymia? Levant (1995) has appropriately argued that males with alexithymia need training in how to access and express a wide range of emotional states, especially vulnerable and caring emotions. Clearly, boys (and girls) with alexithymia can benefit from the type of emotional self-awareness training techniques that Levant and his colleagues have developed (see Levant, 1993, 1995; Levant & Kelly, 1989). Although it is beyond the scope of this chapter to describe these techniques in detail, practitioners interested in an overview of emotional self-awareness procedures are referred to the writings of Levant on the subject (Levant, 1993, 1995; Levant & Kelly, 1989). The male-friendly therapeutic process described in this chapter can help practitioners working with boys with alexithymia to develop a sound foundation of trust on which the construction of emotional self-awareness skills can begin.

If we really intend to help school-age boys, we must understand that their ways of relating tend to be different from the preferred relational style of most mental health professionals. Consequently, we must adjust counseling and psychotherapy to fit the ways that boys approach the world so that boys will feel comfortable with counselors and the work they do. By reexamining our use of the fifty-minute hour, working with boys in informal settings, using humor and self-disclosure, employing male-friendly rapport-building strategies, counseling boys in groups, confronting professional and institutional constraints, and understanding the myths and realities pertaining to alexithymia among boys, we will succeed in helping school-age boys to lead more happy and fulfilling lives.

References

Achatz, M., & MacAllum, C. A. (1994). *Young unwed fathers: Report from the field.* Philadelphia: Public/Private Ventures.

Andronico, M. P. (1996). Introduction. In M. P. Andronico (Ed.), *Men in groups: Insights, interventions, and psychoeducational work* (pp. xvii–xviv). Washington, DC: American Psychological Association.

Barstow, S., Urbaniak, J., & Holland, H. Z. (1999, June). Washington update: "100,000 New Counselors" voted in. *Counseling Today, 1,* 10–11.

Barth, R. P., Claycomb, M., & Loomis, A. (1988). Services to adolescent fathers. *Health and Social Work, 13,* 277–287.

Boyd-Franklin, N. (1989). *Black families in therapy: A multisystems approach.* New York: Guilford Press.

Brindis, C., Barth, R. P., & Loomis, A. B. (1987). Continuous counseling: Case management with teenage parents. *Social Casework: The Journal of Contemporary Social Work, 68,* 164–172.

Brown, S. (1990). *If the shoes fit: Final report and program implementation guide of the Maine Young Fathers Project.* Portland, ME: University of Southern Maine, Human Services Development Institute.

Bruch, M. A. (1978). Holland's typology applied to client-counselor interaction: Implications for counseling with men. *Counseling Psychologist, 7,* 26–32.

Carrera, M. A. (1992). Involving adolescent males in pregnancy and STD prevention programs. *Adolescent Medicine: State of the Art Reviews, 3,* 1–13.

Clinchy, B., & Zimmerman, C. (1985). *Growing up intellectually: Issues for college women* (Work in Progress No. 19). Wellesley, MA: Wellesley College, Stone Center for Developmental Services and Studies.

Dryfoos, J. G. (1994). Full-service schools: A revolution in health and social services for children, youth, and families. San Francisco: Jossey-Bass.

Fischer, P. C., Smith, R. J., Leonard, E., Fuqua, D. R., Campbell, J. L., & Masters, M. A. (1993). Sex differences on affective dimensions: Continuing examination. *Journal of Counseling and Development, 71,* 440–443.

Griffin-Pierson, S. (1990). The competitiveness questionnaire: A measure of two components of competitiveness. *Measurement and Evaluation in Counseling and Development, 23,* 108–115.

Gysbers, N. C., & Henderson, P. (2000). *Developing and managing your school guidance program* (3rd ed.). Alexandria, VA: American Counseling Association.

Heesacker, M., Wester, S. R., Vogel, D. L., Wentzel, J. T., Mejia-Millan, C. M., & Goodholm, C. R. (1999). Gender-based emotional stereotyping. *Journal of Counseling Psychology, 46,* 483–495.

Hendricks, L. E. (1988). Outreach with teenage fathers: A preliminary report on three ethnic groups. *Adolescence, 23*(91), 711–720.

Holland, J. L. (1973). *Making vocational choices: A theory of careers.* Englewood Cliffs, NJ: Prentice Hall.

Horne, A., & Kiselica, M. S. (Eds.). (1999). *Handbook of counseling boys and adolescent males: A practitioner's guide.* Thousand Oaks, CA: Sage.

Jolliff, D. (1994). Guest editorial: Group work with men. *Journal for Specialists in Group Work, 19,* 50–51.

Kiselica, M. S. (1992, March). Alternative models of masculinity. In L. H. Glenn (Chair), *Connectedness not dependence: Gender issues and relationship excellence.* Symposium conducted at the annual convention of the American Association for Counseling and Development, Baltimore.

Kiselica, M. S. (1995). *Multicultural counseling with teenage fathers: A practical guide.* Thousand Oaks, CA: Sage.

Kiselica, M. S. (1996). Parenting skills training with teenage fathers. In M. P. Andronico (Ed.), *Men in groups: Insights, interventions, and psychoeducational work* (pp. 283–300). Washington, DC: American Psychological Association.

Kiselica, M. S. (1997). Is emotional constriction in boys and men the product of a normative or an aberrant developmental pathway? In W. S. Pollack (Chair), *Rescuing Ophelia's brothers: What about boys?* Symposium conducted at the annual convention of the American Psychological Association, Chicago.

Kiselica, M. S. (1999). Counseling teen fathers. In A. Horne & M. S. Kiselica (Eds.), *Handbook of counseling boys and adolescent males: A practitioner's guide* (pp. 179–197). Thousand Oaks, CA: Sage.

Kiselica, M. S., & Horne, A. (1999). Preface: For the sake of our nation's sons. In A. Horne & M. S. Kiselica (Eds.), *Handbook of counseling boys and adolescent males: A practitioner's guide* (pp. xv–xx). Thousand Oaks, CA: Sage.

Kiselica, M. S., Rotzien, A., & Doms, J. (1994). Preparing teenage fathers for parenthood: A group psychoeducational approach. *Journal for Specialists in Group Work, 19,* 83–94.

Kiselica, M. S., Stroud, J., Stroud, J., & Rotzien, A. (1992). Counseling the forgotten client: The teen father. *Journal of Mental Health Counseling, 14,* 338–350.

Krystal, H. (1982). Alexithymia and the effectiveness of psychoanalytic treatment. *International Journal of Psychoanalytic Psychotherapy, 9,* 353–378.

LaFrance, M., & Banaji, M. (1992). Toward a reconsideration of the gender-emotion relationship. In M. S. Clark (Ed.), *Review of personality and social psychology* (Vol. 14, pp. 178–201). Newbury Park, CA: Sage.

Lazarus, A. A. (1990). Can psychotherapists transcend the shackles of their training and superstitions? *Journal of Clinical Psychology, 46,* 351–358.

Lazarus, A. A. (1995). Boundaries in the physician-patient relationship. *JAMA, 274,* 1345–1346.

Levant, R. F. (1993, August). *Men and psychotherapy: Assessment and treatment of alexithymia in men.* Paper presented at the annual convention of the American Psychological Association, Toronto.

Levant, R. F. (1995). Toward the reconstruction of masculinity. In R. F. Levant & W. S. Pollack (Eds.), *A new psychology of men* (pp. 229–251). New York: Basic Books.

Levant, R. F. (1999, August). Boys in crisis. In R. F. Levant (Chair), *New work in the psychology of boys.* Symposium conducted at the annual convention of the American Psychological Association, Boston, MA.

Levant, R. F., & Kelly, J. (1989). *Between father and child.* New York: Viking.

Mallinckrodt, B., King, J.L., & Coble, H.M. (1998). Family dysfunction, alexithymia, and client attachment to therapist. *Journal of Counseling Psychology, 45,* 497–504.

Pollack, W. S. (1995). No man is an island: Toward a new psychoanalytic psychology of men. In R. F. Levant & W. S. Pollack (Eds.), *A new psychology of men* (pp. 33–67). New York: Basic Books.

Pollack, W. S. (1999). *Real boys: Rescuing our sons from the myths of boyhood.* New York: Henry Holt.

Pollack, W. S., & Chu, J. (1997, August). Lost boys: Finding boys' voices. In W. S. Pollack (Chair), *Rescuing Ophelia's brothers: What about boys?* Symposium conducted at the annual convention of the American Psychological Association, Chicago.

Sander, J. H., & Rosen, J. L. (1987). Teenage fathers: Working with the neglected partner in adolescent childbearing. *Family Planning Perspectives, 19,* 107–110.

Shields, S. A. (1995). The role of emotion beliefs and values in gender development. In N. Eisenberg (Ed.), *Review of personality and social psychology* (Vol. 15, pp. 212–232). Thousand Oaks, CA: Sage.

Sifneos, P. E. (1973). The prevalence of "alexithymic" characteristics in psychosomatic patients. *Psychother. Pychosom., 22,* 255–262.

Sue, D. W. (1997, November). The psyche of the nation in terms of racial and cultural relations. Address conducted for the Multicultural Lecture Series, The College of New Jersey, Ewing, NJ.

Surrey, J. L. (1985). *Self-in-relation: A theory of women's development* (Work in Progress No. 13). Wellesley, MA: Wellesley College, Stone Center for Developmental Services and Studies.

Tyack, D. (1992). Health and social services in public schools: Historical perspectives. *Future of Children, 2,* 19–31.

CHAPTER THREE

Counseling Men in Medical Settings

The Six-Point HEALTH Plan

Will H. Courtenay

Gender-based medicine and health care are receiving increased attention among health professionals (Courtenay, 2000c; Courtenay & Keeling, 2000a, 2000b; Eisler & Hersen, 2000; Lent & Bishop, 1998). In addition to having different reproductive health needs, women and men have different risks for specific diseases and disabilities (Courtenay, 1999, in press-a). They also differ in their perceptions of health. Research consistently indicates, for example, that men are less likely than women to perceive themselves as being at risk for most health problems, even for problems that men are more likely than women to experience (see Courtenay, 1998b, in press-b). Furthermore, gender-specific interventions are often necessary to achieve positive clinical outcomes. As noted elsewhere (Courtenay, 1998a), a substantial body of research has demonstrated that—based on their readiness to change health-related behaviors—women and men require different interventions and that failure to tailor interventions to these gender-specific needs significantly reduces the chance of behavioral change. Other studies have found that using such approaches as future awareness and imagining symptoms to modify risk behaviors is more effective with men than with women (DePalma, McCall, & English, 1996; Rothspan & Read, 1996).

MEN, MASCULINITY, AND HEALTH

Feminist scholars were among the first to address gender and health, noting, for example, the absence of females as subjects in health research and the use of males as the standard for health. The result, however, is that "gender and health" has now become synonymous with "women's health" (see, for example, Bayne-Smith, 1996). Although health science has frequently used males as study subjects, research typically neglects men's gender. The health risks associated with men's gender are taken for granted and have remained largely unexamined. In fact, several authors have recently argued that medical researchers, psychologists, and other health professionals have all contributed to cultural portrayals of men as healthy and women as the "sicker" gender and thus to the "invisibility" of men's poor health status (Annandale & Clark, 1996; Courtenay, 2000a; Gijsbers van Wijk, Vliet, Kolk, & Everaerd, 1991). Little is understood, for example, about why men in the United States, on average, die nearly seven years younger than women and have higher death rates than women for all fifteen leading causes of death (Courtenay, 2000d).

The explanatory power of biological factors in predicting gender differences in morbidity and mortality is comparatively small (Krantz, Grunberg, & Baum, 1985; Verbrugge, 1989). In working with men, it is therefore particularly relevant to address psychological and social factors. A growing body of research indicates, for example, that masculinity and men's beliefs about manhood are significantly associated with men's health. Men who adopt traditional beliefs about manhood and dominant norms of masculinity have greater health risks than their peers with less traditional beliefs and engage in riskier behaviors, such as smoking; alcohol and drug use; and unhealthy behaviors related to safety, diet, sleep, and sex (see Copenhaver & Eisler, 1996; Courtenay, 1998a; Eisler, 1995). Indeed, many of the attitudes and behaviors that men and boys in the United States are typically encouraged to adopt are the very same attitudes and behaviors that increase their health risks (Courtenay, 2000a, in press-b). Taken together, these findings demonstrate that men's gender—not simply male biological sex—mediates men's health and preventive practices. They also show why it is necessary for medical and mental health professionals to address the influences of men's gender when working with men.

Any contact a health professional has with a man provides an important opportunity. Men represent 65 percent of those who have not visited a physician in two to five years and 70 percent of those who have not visited a physician in more than five years (U.S. Department of Health and Human Services, 1998a). Even among persons with health problems, men are significantly more likely than women to have had no recent physician contacts, regardless of income or ethnicity (U.S. Department of Health and Human Services, 1998b).

Therefore, any encounter a health professional has with a man—particularly a young or middle-aged man—may be the only opportunity for assessment and intervention that any health professional will have with that man for a very long time. Furthermore, even one contact with a male patient can have significantly positive effects on both behavioral and clinical outcomes. A meta-analysis demonstrated that it is not the number of contacts or the amount of time spent with patients but rather how the time is spent that produces positive results (Mullen, Mains, & Velez, 1992).

Although many counseling and psychological interventions with men have been recommended in the past two decades (Courtenay, 2000b), few psychosocial techniques have been developed for health professionals who work with men in health care settings (Courtenay, 1998c; Sutkin & Good, 1987). Even more rarely are health interventions designed to address the unique needs of various populations of men, such as gay and bisexual men (Scarce, 1999) and men in prison (Courtenay & Sabo, in press). Despite the fact that on average African American men die eight years younger than European American men (U.S. Department of Health and Human Services, 1996), only recently have the specific psychosocial health needs of African American men been addressed (L. E. Davis, 1999). Given this lack of clinical guidance, it is not surprising that men receive significantly less physician time in medical encounters than women, and that men are provided with fewer and briefer explanations—both simple and technical (see Courtenay, 2000b).

PRACTICE GUIDELINE FOR THE TREATMENT OF MEN

I have developed a clinical practice guideline health professionals who work with men (Courtenay, 1996a). Its recommendations are based on an extensive review of biopsychosocial research related to men's gender and health, located through keyword searches in MEDLINE and PsycLIT. This guideline identifies behavioral and psychosocial factors that affect the onset, progression, and management of men's health problems; reviews evidence demonstrating the effectiveness of various interventions; and outlines specific recommendations for addressing these factors when working with men in clinical practice. I summarize its findings and recommendations in this chapter.

Communication between clinicians and their patients—and the health education provided through this relationship—is emphasized here. Health professionals whose responsibility it is to counsel men in medical settings are in a unique position to assist men. An extensive review of scientific evidence reveals that patients are more likely to be helped to prevent future disease by clinicians who ask, educate, and counsel them about personal health behaviors than by those who perform physical examinations or tests (U.S. Preventive Services Task

Force, 1996). Furthermore, patients' feelings and attitudes about their health are influenced both by the information they receive and by the way in which they receive it (Hall, Roter, & Katz, 1988; Horne, Vatmanidis, & Careri, 1994). These findings have led to the recent conclusions that "talking is more important than testing" (Woolf, Jonas, & Lawrence, 1996, p. xxxvii) and that offering prevention advice and communicating effectively with patients is the most important skill for clinicians to acquire in the twenty-first century (Koop, 1996).

The American Medical Association (1991a) has referred to the lack of effective clinician-patient communication as a health hazard for men. Poor communication is associated with inaccurate diagnoses, poor compliance and outcomes, and low knowledge and knowledge retention (H. Davis & Fallowfield, 1991).[1] Conversely, effective patient and clinician communication has been found to be associated with improved compliance and better patient health status as measured physiologically, behaviorally, and subjectively (Cramer, 1991; Cramer & Spilker, 1991; Hall et al., 1988; Kaplan, Greenfield, & Ware, 1989; Meichenbaum & Turk, 1987). Because the learning patterns and conversational styles of women and men in this society differ distinctively and because women and men respond to and accept information differently (Golombok & Fivush, 1994; Tannen, 1990), it is imperative that health professionals incorporate what is currently understood about these gender differences into their interventions with men if these interventions are to be effective.

This chapter consists of six sections. Each section represents one of six types of interventions discussed in the guideline. Together, the section titles form the acronym HEALTH: humanize, educate, assume the worst, locate supports, tailor plan, and highlight strengths.

HUMANIZE

The first step in working with men is to humanize. Humanizing means validating, legitimizing, or normalizing their health problems and concerns. Conveying to patients that their feelings and experiences are understandable or legitimate—and that other people would probably feel the same way—is considered essential to effective communication with patients (Grüninger, 1995). Humanizing is especially important with men. Attending to health matters has historically been socially sanctioned and encouraged among women but not among men (Courtenay, 2000a, 2000e; Oakley, 1994). Consequently, many men associate health matters with womanly matters, and men receive strict social prohibitions against doing anything that women do (Courtenay, 2000e). Because disease, disability, and behavioral responses to illness are antithetical to tradi-

---

[1]The terms *compliance* and *adherence* are used interchangeably throughout this chapter.

tional meanings of manhood (Courtenay, 2000a), men can experience shame when they have health problems. For example, one in five men report embarrassment as a reason for not discussing prostate, colon, or rectal cancers with a physician (American Medical Association, 1991b). Humanizing is especially important with patients who have chronic or permanently disabling or life-threatening conditions, which can seriously undermine men's identity as men (Charmaz, 1995).

Permission to have physical problems or health concerns and to discuss them openly has been referred to as a primary health care need of men (DeHoff & Forrest, 1984). Clinicians can help men learn that asking for help, acknowledging pain, expressing fear, crying, or needing bed rest are normal, human experiences—they are not unmanly. Other authors reviewing research on masculinity have suggested that when male patients have difficulty expressing discouragement, fear, or concern about giving up control during physical or psychological examinations, clinicians should communicate that these experiences are both normal and appropriate (Copenhaver & Eisler, 1996). Humanizing is a form of validation that some practitioners consider to be the most effective approach in beginning consultation with men (Rappaport, 1984). Humanizing may also contribute to the development of trust, which is also considered to be a critical first step in helping men (R. May, 1990). Specific factors that should be humanized include help seeking, illness and vulnerability, pain, and sexuality.

Humanizing Help Seeking

Men are significantly less likely than women to seek health care, except perhaps when their condition is serious (Courtenay, 2000a). There is evidence that this difference is seen because men have less intention to seek help from a variety of sources when they need it (see Ashton & Fuehrer, 1993; Good, Dell, & Mintz, 1989; Rule & Gandy, 1994; Sawyer & Moss, 1993). In fact, it has been suggested that men are least likely to ask for help when they are most in need of it (Rappaport, 1984). Among people who are depressed, for example, men are more likely than women not to seek mental health services, to withdraw from others, and to try to manage their depression on their own (Courtenay, 1998b, 2000a). Men learn these behaviors early in their lives. Parents and other adults not only actively discourage boys from seeking their help but often punish them when they do (Courtenay, 2000e). Seeking help can undermine men's sense of independence, which for some men is essential for self-respect (Tannen, 1990); this requirement for independence is believed to be true as well for African American men (Lee, 1990) and Latino men (Marks, Garcia, & Solis, 1990). Men can experience needing help as demeaning (Charmaz, 1995) and may subsequently develop feelings of inadequacy (Heppner & Gonzales, 1987) and shame (Brooks, 1998). Consequently, men may undergo considerable inconvenience rather than ask for help (DePaulo, 1982).

Health care visits pose a variety of threats to the roles most familiar to men (Sutkin & Good, 1987). They necessarily mean surrendering some autonomy and relinquishing some control. Lying still in bed or on a consulting table is contrary to the action-oriented and problem-solving coping styles that many men adopt. Clinicians' reconceptualization of help seeking as positive behavior can disconfirm men's anticipated response of disdain. Clinicians can offer reinforcement by saying, "I'm glad you phoned me. It's an important first step" or "Contacting me when you did was the best thing you could have done." Reframing men's help seeking as an act of strength, courage, and self-determination may decrease any embarrassment or self-doubt that they may experience in asking for help. Some clinicians consider reframing to be important when beginning work with men (J. A. Allen & Gordon, 1990). Clinicians could say, for example, "I know it can be a real challenge to ask for help, but I'm glad to see that didn't stop you." Clinicians can also assess men's intention of keeping follow-up appointments by saying, "You know, a lot of men have trouble keeping their follow-up appointments. Does that ever happen to you?" When asked nonjudgmentally, such questions help to predict future adherence and determine the need for treatment compliance techniques (Meichenbaum & Turk, 1987).

Humanizing Illness and Vulnerability

Because illness and vulnerability threaten stereotypically masculine notions of competence, vitality, and strength (Charmaz, 1995), men may experience illness and vulnerability as personal flaws or as failures to successfully demonstrate manhood (Courtenay, 2000d). Simply saying, "You know, everybody gets sick sometimes" can bring relief to men and help to establish rapport. Clinicians can also directly label the influence of gender: "Getting sick doesn't mean you're less of a man." When they are ill, men are less likely than women to restrict their activities or stay in bed for both acute and chronic conditions (Courtenay, 2000d). Some men consider staying in bed to rest or recover to be pampering, and by traditional standards men should not pamper their bodies (Courtenay, 2000e). Men may think of themselves as lazy if they miss work after an operation. Clinicians can humanize the need for convalescence and bed rest by saying to men, "Staying in bed and taking care of yourself when you're sick doesn't mean you're a bad employee or not a team player."

Humanizing Pain and Fear

It is also important for clinicians to make human the experience of pain and fear and to give men permission to acknowledge physical discomfort. Research consistently indicates that, compared with women, men report less pain for the same pathology, less severe pain, greater tolerance of pain and higher pain thresholds, and shorter duration of pain (Miaskowski, 1999; Unruh, 1996;

Unruh, Ritchie, & Merskey, 1999). Men and society in general often view admitting and displaying fear and pain as unacceptable behaviors for men (Brooks, 1998; Courtenay, 2000a; Sutkin & Good, 1987). Not surprisingly, men are less likely than women to cry (Kraemer & Hastrup, 1986; Lombardo, Cretser, Lombardo, & Mathis, 1983) and they report less fear than women do (Croake, Myers, & Singh, 1987; Liddell, Locker, & Burman, 1991). Men are often uncomfortable in situations that require the expression of tender or painful emotions, because they believe that expressing such emotions is a violation of traditionally masculine behavior (Copenhaver & Eisler, 1996). Men may need to experience literally intolerable pain before they can acknowledge to themselves or to others that they are hurting. Failing to acknowledge or display physical pain can have far-reaching implications for men's health: it can influence the decision to seek help, delay intervention, and undermine diagnosis and treatment planning.

Clinicians should label conditions known to be painful as such: "Kidney stones can be very painful. I don't want you to hesitate for a moment if you think you might need to come back to the emergency room." Clinicians could express surprise when men deny that their kidney stones are painful. It may also be necessary to humanize the need for pain medication. Sutkin and Good (1987) suggest that a "tough guy" will characteristically wait six hours before requesting or taking a pain medication that is effective for four hours. Clinicians can compensate for this behavior by saying, "There are no medals for enduring pain, so I want you to let me know if you experience even the slightest bit of discomfort." For men who are refusing medication, clinicians can say, "It's routine for people to receive pain medication for this procedure. Are you sure you don't want the doctor to write you a prescription?"

Humanizing Sexuality

It is also important to humanize sexuality. Men's sexual performance is a measure of masculinity in this society (Fracher & Kimmel, 1992). Furthermore, masculinity is measured by superhuman standards that require men to be perpetually interested in and ready for sex (Zilbergeld, 1992). These cultural stereotypes, however, are inconsistent with many men's experience. At least one out of four American men is unable to get or maintain an erection for sex (Goldberg, 1993). Erectile dysfunction is also a common side effect of prostate surgery and a variety of medications. Difficulty getting or maintaining an erection can threaten a patient's self-image as a man and undermine a fundamental aspect of his gender identity (Charmaz, 1995). Not surprisingly, at least three out of four men with sexual concerns report not discussing those concerns with their physician and report that they are deterred from doing so by embarrassment (American Medical Association, 1991b; Metz & Seifert, 1990).

Humanizing sexuality gives men permission to discuss their concerns by normalizing sexual problems or fears among men (Fracher & Kimmel, 1992;

Kaplan, 1974). Clinicians can say, "Most men have concerns about sex; it's normal. And I hope you're comfortable telling me if you do" or "I'd be surprised if you didn't worry about that; most men do." In fact, one study found that most men with sexual concerns preferred that clinicians initiate the discussion (Metz & Seifert, 1990). Many men can also use help in identifying unrealistic and less-than-human perceptions of manhood that contribute to sexual anxiety and help in learning how more human perceptions of sexuality can reduce stress and sexual dysfunction. Men with erectile dysfunction may benefit from being told that it is a common condition—that almost every man experiences occasional and transient erectile problems at some point in his life (Fracher & Kimmel, 1992; Zilbergeld, 1992). Clinicians can say, "Although the world often expects you to act like a machine, you aren't one. Your body can't really be expected to turn on and off at will. If you relax and don't expect so much out of yourself, you'll be surprised. Your anxiety will diminish and you'll feel a lot more pleasure."

Defining a Healthy Manhood

Although disease and disability are often unpleasant, they also provide men with the opportunity to redefine their lives and their manhood (Charmaz, 1995; D. F. Gordon, 1995). Indeed, many men may need to undergo this "reconstruction" of masculinity if they are to substantially improve their health (Levant & Kopecky, 1995). In a supportive manner, clinicians can challenge their patients' preconceived beliefs about what a man should be or what a man must do and discuss how these beliefs can damage them physically and psychologically (Brooks, 1998; Copenhaver & Eisler, 1996). This strategy is considered a consciousness-raising intervention (Copenhaver & Eisler, 1996), and research indicates that raising consciousness is an effective means of helping people to begin changing unhealthy behavior (Prochaska, Norcross, & DiClemente, 1994). For example, when humanizing help seeking, clinicians can say, "How do you think being a man influences your ability to ask for help?" Clinicians can then help male patients to see how their options are often limited not by their disability or illness but by their beliefs about manhood and other gender-related factors and help them explore more realistically human and healthy self-perceptions. Moderate self-disclosure by clinicians—particularly if the clinicians are men—may make male patients feel safer in exploring these issues. Self-disclosure establishes a basis of similarity and promotes trust; it has also been found to increase treatment adherence and to increase patients' sense of competence and self-efficacy (Copenhaver & Eisler, 1996; R. May, 1990; Meichenbaum & Turk, 1987). Clinicians might say, "I know what you mean, I have a hard time admitting when I'm sick too" or "I often feel like I'm just supposed to handle things on my own."

THE IMPORTANCE OF EDUCATION

The next step is to educate men about their health. As noted, health education interventions are an essential aspect of disease and injury prevention (Council on Scientific Affairs, 1990; U.S. Preventive Services Task Force, 1996; Woolf et al., 1996). According to strong evidence from recent reviews and meta-analyses, besides increasing patient and health practitioner satisfaction (Grüninger, 1995) health education improves compliance (Cramer, 1991; Cramer & Spilker, 1991; Hall et al., 1988; McCann & Blossom, 1990; Meichenbaum & Turk, 1987); reduces risk factors, disease, and death; and promotes healthy behaviors such as exercise, healthy diet, and blood pressure control (R. G. Frank, Bouman, Cain, & Watts, 1992; Grüninger, 1995; Mullen et al., 1992; U.S. Preventive Services Task Force, 1996). Similarly, psychoeducational interventions have been found to have a significantly positive effect on pain, psychological distress, and recovery and to be cost-efficient as well (Byers et al., 1995; Devine, 1992; Horne et al., 1994). Education is also essential if patients are to become active participants in their own health care (Make, 1994).

Educating Men About Their Health

There is strong evidence that men need to be educated about their health. If they are to maintain good health, it is critical that they be familiar with symptoms of life-threatening disease, know how the body should function, and know their family health histories (DeHoff & Forrest, 1984; Goldberg, 1993). Research consistently indicates, however, that men are less knowledgeable than women about health in general and about specific diseases such as heart disease, cancer, and sexually transmitted diseases (Courtenay, 2000e). Men also ask fewer questions than women do when visiting a physician (Wallen, Waitzkin, & Stoeckle, 1979; Waitzkin, 1984, 1985). Asking a question necessarily means admitting that there is something one does not know, which is often difficult for men to acknowledge (Tannen, 1990). Consequently, the American Medical Association has concluded, based on two national surveys, that men are "surprisingly uninformed" about basic health issues and that health professionals have a responsibility to educate men (American Medical Association, 1991a, 1991b).

Too often, however, health professionals fail to provide the health education that could reduce men's risks. Historically, health education generally and cancer education specifically have been directed primarily at women (Oakley, 1994; Reagan, 1997). Men also receive less information from physicians. In fact, no study has ever found that women receive less information from physicians than men do (Roter & Hall, 1997). This failure to educate men can result in a self-fulfilling prophecy and reinforce a damaging irresponsibility toward health matters among men. This need not be the case. Research indicates that health promotion and education can produce positive changes in knowledge, behavior, and health outcomes among men (Baer, 1993; Danielson, Marcy, Plunkett, Wiest, & Greenlick, 1990; Little, Stevens, Severson, & Lichtenstein, 1992); indeed, these changes are sometimes even greater than those found among women (Bjornson et al., 1995; Hornbrook et al., 1994; Oleckno & Blacconiere, 1990). Furthermore, obtaining information from conversation appeals to many men (Tannen, 1990) and can also be reassuring. Hendricks (1999) cites evidence, for example, that learning about diabetes, its associated health-related problems, its treatment, what outcomes can be expected from treatment, and when patients can expect these outcomes reduces fear and anxiety among African American men with the disorder.

Specific educational interventions vary depending on a man's current health, his presenting concern, and his future risks, as well as on the clinician's role and responsibilities. In general, clinicians can begin to educate men by saying, "I don't know about you, but most men know very little about their bodies and their health, and that lack of knowledge actually increases their health risks" or "Most of the things that have the biggest impact on your health are completely within your control." Because they have had relatively little experience with the health care system, many men need basic information such as how to ask for help, whom to contact to schedule a follow-up appointment, whom to phone with questions after discharge, and what kinds of questions to ask their health care providers. When counseling men, clinicians should word advice clearly, simply, and directly (Make, 1994; U.S. Preventive Services Task Force, 1996). Because patients see health professionals as experts, a direct statement such as "I must insist that you do your rehabilitation exercises daily" can have a strong positive effect (U.S. Preventive Services Task Force, 1996). To promote preventive care and behavioral change, it is considered essential to provide alternative behaviors (R. G. Frank et al., 1992). It is not enough simply to educate men about the importance of taking medication as prescribed. Clinicians must also suggest strategies for adhering to the prescribed regimen, such as establishing a dosing schedule and checklist and using a pillbox with daily compartments or an alarm (Cramer, 1991; Meichenbaum & Turk, 1987).

Clinicians should not be afraid to be enthusiastic in their interventions with men. Research indicates that men respond positively to active encouragement to engage in preventive health behavior (Myers et al., 1991). Because many men are less comfortable receiving information than giving it (Tannen, 1990), clinicians can communicate to male patients that the information they are being offered is provided routinely; patients may be less likely to feel that clinicians have singled them out as being ignorant (Rappaport, 1984). Clinicians can say, "We tell all of our patients . . ." or "You may already know this, but let me review it for the sake of good form." Then, clinicians can supplement what they say with written materials. Although written materials alone may not help patients to change their behavior (Grüninger, 1995), they may be more helpful to men than to women (R. May, 1990). It is essential, however, to make sure that patients can read and understand these materials (Meichenbaum & Turk, 1987).

Despite some inconsistent findings regarding the use of fear in motivating people to change unhealthy behaviors, health educators agree that some aspects of fear can be used effectively with some patients (Meichenbaum & Turk, 1987). In one study, fear of developing cancer was among the best predictors of testicular self-examination among young men (Katz, Meyers, & Walls, 1995). It is essential, however, that an intervention using fear also foster men's sense of efficacy in remedying the problem (Meichenbaum & Turk, 1987). Clinicians can offer information that induces a relatively low level of fear, provides positive reinforcement, and focuses on the immediate effects of modifying behavior, such as the reduction in high blood pressure and increased lung capacity that occur when patients stop smoking (Job, 1988): "Your diet is raising your risk of heart disease. But even the minor changes we've discussed will not only reduce this risk but also lower your cholesterol and increase your vitality."

Conveying the Importance of Screening, Self-Examination, and Early Detection

Men need to be taught how to do self-examinations. They also need to be taught the importance of screenings and early detection. Screening tests are essential for preventing disease, detecting preclinical conditions, and identifying a variety of diseases at an early stage when successful treatment is more likely (Courtenay, 2000d; U.S. Preventive Services Task Force, 1996; Woolf et al., 1996). Men, however, are less likely than women to practice self-examination or to attend health screenings (Courtenay, 2000d); African American men may be even less likely than European American men to do so (Pierce, 1999). Self-exams are particularly important for men. Because they seldom visit physicians, self-examination is the only way most men will detect a variety of diseases when they are still curable (Goldberg, 1993). Self-exams relevant to men include those for skin and testicular cancer, hypertension (for men at risk for heart disease or stroke), and sexually transmitted diseases. Health professionals can do much to encourage men to practice self-examination. Expressions of concern and personal instruction by clinicians have been associated with the intention to conduct self-exams (Brubaker & Wickersham, 1990; Neef, Scutchfield, Elder, & Bender, 1991).

Educating patients about their specific health risks is an essential aspect of disease and injury prevention (U.S. Preventive Services Task Force, 1989). It is particularly important to provide this information for men. One recent and extensive review of large studies, national data, and meta-analyses demonstrates that males of all ages are more likely than females to engage in more than thirty behaviors that increase the risk of disease, injury, and death (Courtenay, 2000d). Despite these findings, men receive less advice from physicians about changing risk factors for disease during checkups than women do (C. Friedman, Brownson, Peterson, & Wilkerson, 1994). Only 29 percent of physicians routinely provide age-appropriate instruction on performing self-exams for testicular cancer, compared with 86 percent who provide age-appropriate instruction to women on performing breast self-exams (Misener & Fuller, 1995). Clinicians must assess the need for self-examination skills among all their male patients.

To determine a man's specific risks, a health risk assessment can be useful. One such assessment has been developed specifically for men and includes items addressing both health behaviors and beliefs, including beliefs about manhood (Courtenay, 1996b). Once men's risks are identified, clinicians can provide counseling as indicated. When counseling men about modifying unhealthy behaviors, clinicians may emphasize the personal relevance of change and link it with individual men's circumstances (Meichenbaum & Turk, 1987), such as being healthy for their children. Men should also be invited to discuss what they believe they can do to reduce their health risks or modify their behaviors (J. P. May & Martin, 1993). In general, there is sufficient evidence regarding effective outcomes to strongly recommend counseling patients about avoiding tobacco, exercising regularly, limiting consumption of dietary fat, not driving while impaired by alcohol or other drugs, wearing bicycle helmets, and using condoms (U.S. Preventive Services Task Force, 1996). There is also sufficient evidence to recommend counseling patients about avoiding excess sun exposure; consuming fiber, fruits, and vegetables; using safety belts; reducing alcohol consumption in drinkers who may misuse alcohol; avoiding recreational activities while intoxicated; removing from the home or safely storing firearms in the home to prevent youth violence; and caring for their teeth (U.S. Preventive Services Task Force, 1996). Because most of these factors are significantly more common among men than among women (Courtenay, 2000d), it is particularly important to provide counseling to men.

Ensuring Comprehension

To foster compliance, it is important to make sure that patients understand what they have been told (Meichenbaum & Turk, 1987). Ensuring comprehension is especially important in the case of men, who can have difficulty admitting that they do not understand (Moore, 1990; Tannen, 1990). Simply asking patients to restate the information they have been given or to rehearse a regimen is an effective technique (Meichenbaum & Turk, 1987). If a clinician has explained to a patient how to perform a certain task—how to use a mechanical ventilatory support, for example—he or she should ask the patient to demonstrate the procedure (Kacmarek, 1994). The clinician can further clarify whether the patient has understood the information he was given—and how he will implement that knowledge—by asking, "Given what we discussed about your diet, what changes do you think are realistic for you to make to lower your blood pressure?"

Similarly, it is important for clinicians to recognize that men may have questions that they will not ask. Admitting that there is something they do not know or that they need to learn from someone else may be difficult for men (Rappaport, 1984; Tannen, 1990). Women ask more questions—and more direct questions—than men do when visiting a physician (Kaplan, Gandek, Greenfield, Rogers, & Ware, 1995; Waitzkin, 1984, 1985; Wallen et al., 1979). Consequently, clinicians should actively encourage men to ask questions, by saying, for example, "I'll try to cover everything, but your questions will be very helpful." Regardless of what exactly one says, it is essential to issue a direct invitation; merely informing patients that one is open to questions is not enough (Robinson & Whitfield, 1985). Clinicians can conclude a consultation by saying, "I've explained a lot to you. I'd be surprised if you didn't have some questions" or "You know, people often leave here without talking about the things that they're most concerned about."

ASSUMING THE WORST

One of the most common and enduring cultural stereotypes about men is that they are healthier and more resistant to disease than women are, despite a wealth of evidence to the contrary (Courtenay, 2000e). Men who attempt to conform to these cultural stereotypes increase their health risks. They may try to appear strong and healthy, believe that they are invulnerable to risk, minimize pain and deny feelings that others may perceive as signs of weakness, and report their health inaccurately (Courtenay, 2000a, in press-b).

Men's Perceived Invulnerability to Risk

Studies consistently indicate that men are less likely than women to perceive themselves as being at risk. This difference holds true for a variety of health problems (see Boehm et al., 1993; Cohn, Macfarlane, Yanez, & Imai, 1995; Cutter, Tiefenbacher, & Solecki, 1992; Flynn, Slovic, & Mertz, 1994; Savage, 1993; Weissfeld, Kirscht, & Brock, 1990), including problems associated with sun exposure (Banks, Silverman, Schwartz, & Tunnessen, 1992; Mermelstein & Riesenberg, 1992); cigarette, alcohol, and other drug use (Spigner, Hawkins, & Loren, 1993); and physically dangerous activities (Zuckerman, 1994). Men's perceived invulnerability can prevent them from practicing preventive care or changing unhealthy behavior, thus actually increasing their health risks (Janz

& Becker, 1984; Kreuter & Strecher, 1995; Mermelstein & Riesenberg, 1992; Reno, 1988; Rosenstock, 1990; Taylor, 1986; Weinstein, 1987). Perceived invulnerability has also been linked with poor compliance (H. S. Friedman & DiMatteo, 1989).

Men's Reported Health Needs

The American Medical Association contends that clinicians need to be more active than they are in inquiring about men's symptoms (American Medical Association, 1991a). This inquiry is especially important because the information men provide to clinicians does not always accurately reflect their needs. Research indicates that, except for anger, men express fewer emotions and disclose fewer fears and feelings of vulnerability than do women (Allen-Burge, Storandt, Kinscherf, & Rubin, 1994; Balswick, 1982; Belle, Burr, & Cooney, 1987; Chino & Funabiki, 1984; Grigsby & Weatherley, 1983; Hyde, 1986; Stapley & Haviland, 1989; Tannen, 1990; Williams, 1985). This stoicism is especially true of men who endorse traditional beliefs about masculinity (Copenhaver & Eisler, 1996; Saurer & Eisler, 1990; Thompson, Grisanti, & Pleck, 1985). These factors influence men's clinical consultations. Men provide less emotional and personal information than do women in reporting their health (Corney, 1990; Verbrugge, 1985). Men may deny their physical or emotional distress and conceal their illnesses or disabilities in an effort to preserve their masculinity or in the hope that their doctor will admire their stoicism or courage (Charmaz, 1995; Sutkin & Good, 1987). Men may also deny that they engage in risky behavior. One large study of safety belt use that compared self-reports with actual use found that among drivers who had been observed not wearing safety belts—more than three out of four of whom were men—one-third had reported that they always wore safety belts (Preusser, Williams, & Lund, 1991).

Assessing Men's Health Needs

Taken together, the preceding research suggests that men fail to convey the information clinicians need to provide effective medical care and that clinicians must therefore assume the worst. It is also essential to assume the worst in order to compensate for gender stereotypes, which influence the diagnostic decisions of—among others—mental health clinicians (Adler, Drake, & Teague, 1990; Fernbach, Winstead, & Derlega, 1989; Ford & Widiger, 1989; Potts, Burnam, & Wells, 1991; Waisberg & Page, 1988). One large study found that clinicians were less likely to identify the presence of depression in men than in women and that they failed to diagnose depression in nearly two-thirds of men who were depressed (Potts et al., 1991). Similarly, when patients are matched by symptoms or diagnoses, men are less likely than women to receive prescriptions for antidepressants and other psychotropic drugs (Hohmann, 1989; Taggart, McCammon, Allred, Horner, & May, 1993).

Men's desire to appear strong and healthy, to believe that they are invulnerable to risk, to conceal physical and emotional distress, and to report their behaviors inaccurately are all factors that must be considered when working with men. First, these factors make it difficult to conduct an accurate assessment. Second, as a result of these factors, men's physical and mental conditions are often serious when they finally seek help (Fabrega, Pilkonis, Mezzich, Ahn, & Shea, 1990; Gerber, Thompson, Thisted, & Chodak, 1993; Sawyer & Moss, 1993; Thomas & Kelman, 1990; Verbrugge, 1980, 1982). Assuming the worst compensates for these factors and for the tendency among clinicians to underestimate men's vulnerability.

Getting the Necessary Information

To diagnose men's condition accurately and to plan their treatment, it is essential to elicit information about their symptoms and feeling states. Asking men how they feel is not recommended, however. It has been argued that this question is difficult for men to respond to (Rubin, 1983) and that it often elicits nothing more than a shrug of the shoulders or an unreflective "Fine" (Rappaport, 1984). Instead, clinicians should inquire indirectly: "Tell me, how do you experience that?" or "What is that like for you?" These questions are uncommon and may be less likely to prompt an automatic response. Similarly, when assessing depression in men, it may be helpful to avoid the words *feel* and *depressed* and instead ask, "Do you ever get a little down?" Men may find it easier to admit that they get down than that they feel depressed.

A clinician who suspects that a man may be concealing his symptoms should question him further. If a sixty-year-old African American man who has diabetes and a family history of stroke is not reporting any symptoms, the clinician should ask him if he has experienced any sudden weakness or numbness, any loss of vision or speech, and any dizziness or headaches. Individualized feedback on specific health risks can increase men's accurate perceptions of their own susceptibility to these risks (Kreuter & Strecher, 1995). In response to perceptions of vulnerability that are inconsistent with men's actual risks, a clinician can say, "I know it's important to you to think of yourself as strong and healthy. But that attitude can lead you to take unnecessary risks with your health."

LOCATING SUPPORTS

Men are taught to value independence, autonomy, and self-sufficiency in themselves (Courtenay, 2000e; Majors & Billson, 1992; Marks et al., 1990). Consequently, compared with women, men have significantly fewer and less intimate friendships, fewer lifetime ties, and smaller and less multifaceted social networks, and they receive less support from network members (Courtenay,

2000d). Traditional beliefs about masculinity may make men even less likely to seek help from their friends, partners, and families (Burda & Vaux, 1987; Good et al., 1989; Pleck, 1981).

Exaggerated self-sufficiency and lack of social support contribute to the shortening of men's lives. There is overwhelming evidence that a lack of social support constitutes a major risk factor for mortality, especially for men. Men with the lowest levels of social support are two to three times more likely to die than those with the highest levels of support, even after controlling for health status and other possible confounding factors (Courtenay, 2000d). In contrast, high levels of social support are associated with the maintenance of positive health practices, modification of unhealthy behavior, and compliance with treatment (Courtenay, 2000d). Marriage also plays an important role in men's health; whether single, separated, widowed, or divorced, unmarried men have greater health risks than any other group (Courtenay, 2000d).

Involving Friends and Family

Assessing social support is considered essential to promoting behavioral change and preventive behavior (R. G. Frank et al., 1992). Involving friends and family as sources of support can also be essential to improving clinician-patient relationships and clinical outcomes (Delbanco, 1992). Clinicians should recognize the importance of extended family for African American men specifically and the need to involve family members collaboratively in these patients' care (Pierce, 1999). Because men have fewer social supports than do women and are less likely to use the ones they have, it is essential for clinicians to help men to identify the sources of support that are available to them. Sources of support may include significant others, friends, family members, coworkers, classmates, and groups. Clinicians can ask men, "Who are the people you are most comfortable asking to give you a hand?"

Clinicians should assess—and help patients to assess—whose involvement patients find helpful. Other people's involvement, in and of itself, is not necessarily supportive (Meichenbaum & Turk, 1987). A family member, friend, or health professional who has difficulty seeing vulnerability in men can undermine male patients' motivation to mobilize support. Once men's supports are identified, clinicians can encourage them to reach out to others. Otherwise, they may not. In a postoperative consultation, one man said, "You know, I was going into surgery and no one knew. It seemed like it would have been complaining to tell them." Clinicians can assist men in recognizing that everyone needs help sometimes and remind them that people really like to help and that their friends are probably happy to be asked.

Using Familiar Concepts

In talking with male patients about social support, clinicians should consider using concepts that are easily recognizable and familiar to many men (B.

Gordon & Pasick, 1990), such as teamwork, networking, and strategic planning. Clinicians can suggest that men set regular times to meet with friends. It may be difficult for men to contact other men to get together; they may think that doing so puts them in a one-down position (Tannen, 1990). The regular ball game, movie, or dinner out provides men with regular contact and support without having to ask for it or betray their need for it. Clinicians can provide encouragement for any attempts—however small—men make to reach out to others (B. Gordon & Pasick, 1990). Clinicians should also consider referring men to support or educational groups that are available to and appropriate for male patients and should encourage them to participate if a referral is made. It is also important not to overlook or underestimate contacts that men already have with others through activities such as work, church, or sports (B. Gordon & Pasick, 1990; Pasick, 1990).

Clinicians as Sources of Support

Health care providers are also an important source of support for men (Kaplan et al., 1989). For unmarried men in particular, professionals may be one of the few sources of support that are available. Although men may be reluctant at first to look to clinicians for support, research indicates that they will respond positively to efforts at follow-up contact. Telephone follow-up specifically has been found to improve counseling effectiveness and behavioral change (U.S. Preventive Services Task Force, 1996), reduce noncompliance, and improve appointment keeping (Meichenbaum & Turk, 1987).

CUSTOMIZING EACH PLAN

The importance of developing and implementing realistic health maintenance plans with patients has been addressed elsewhere; a well-tailored plan fosters behavioral change and improves treatment adherence (see Grueninger, Goldstein, & Duffy, 1990; Meichenbaum & Turk, 1987; Prochaska et al., 1994). Tailoring a plan is especially important with men, who are much less likely than women to persist in caring for a health problem (Courtenay, 2000d). The type of plan, the extent of the plan, and its specific components depend on each man's individual needs, as well as on the clinician's role and functions. The following discussion identifies aspects of a plan that warrant particular attention when working with men.

Planning a Healthy Future

Essentially, tailoring a plan means developing a health maintenance schedule, like the maintenance schedule for a car; this analogy may prove useful when introducing the concept to male patients. Tailoring the plan means individualizing it to the patient's needs, age, intellectual capacity, attitudes, cultural background, and circumstances; this information is considered essential both in establishing a plan and in fostering adherence (Meichenbaum & Turk, 1987). For the plan to be successful it must be realistic, it must be broken down into attainable steps, and the patient must have the skills necessary to carry it out (Meichenbaum & Turk, 1987; Prochaska et al., 1994; U.S. Preventive Services Task Force, 1996). Discussing the pros and cons of various treatment possibilities with patients and inviting their suggestions and preferences is useful not only in tailoring a plan but also in fostering compliance (Meichenbaum & Turk, 1987). For example, clinicians may suggest that men choose a day of the month to do self-examinations—a day with personal relevance that they can easily remember, such as a birth date.

Ideally, men's comprehensive health maintenance plans include periodic physicals, screenings, self-examinations, preventive behaviors, self-care techniques, and vitamin and medicine schedules. The plans should include a physical examination every few years for young men and every year for men over fifty (Goldberg, 1993). Physical examinations provide the opportunity for screenings, further assessment, referrals, and the early detection of disease. Screenings should include periodic blood pressure measurement, periodic weight measurement, blood cholesterol screening every five years, periodic sigmoidoscopy, and annual fecal occult blood testing for colorectal cancer for men over fifty; the plan should also include annual flu and pneumonia immunizations for men sixty-five and older (U.S. Preventive Services Task Force, 1996).

Fostering Adherence

It is well-known that patients do not always follow their doctors' advice. Men's beliefs about masculinity may undermine their compliance with the plan. Among men with heart disease, men with traditional beliefs have been found to be less likely to follow their physicians' orders and to make fewer healthy lifestyle changes after hospital discharge than their less traditional peers (Helgeson, 1995). Therefore, in tailoring a plan with a patient it is important to assess his intention of complying with treatment recommendations and to utilize adherence-enhancement techniques as necessary (Meichenbaum & Turk, 1987). Clinicians may ask their male patients to describe specifically how they intend to carry out their plans (U.S. Preventive Services Task Force, 1996). For example, they can assess men's intention to rest during recovery by asking, "What arrangements have you made at work to cover your absence?" The more specific patients are in describing how they intend to carry out their regimen, the more likely they are to be compliant (U.S. Preventive Services Task Force, 1996).

It is important to anticipate nonadherence. Inquiring into patients' history of compliance can be effective in fostering adherence if it is done in a nonjudgmental and nonthreatening manner (Meichenbaum & Turk, 1987; U.S.

Preventive Services Task Force, 1996). Several studies have found that clinicians who work with patients to overcome obstacles to adherence increase compliance (McCann & Blossom, 1990). Male patients can be asked, "Do you ever miss your medical appointments?" and "Do you sometimes stop taking your medicine when you start to feel better?" Clinicians can also assess patients' commitment to a proposed plan by asking directly, "Will you stick to this plan?" or "How are you going to carry out this plan?" (Grueninger et al., 1990; Hewson, 1993). Developing a written or verbal contract is also effective in fostering compliance in some patients (Meichenbaum & Turk, 1987).

HIGHLIGHTING STRENGTHS

Men's behavior and coping styles are associated with both positive and negative health outcomes. Being aggressive, competitive, and achievement oriented, for example, increases men's risk of heart disease (see Strube, 1991). But these same characteristics can be turned into a health advantage. Being competitive and achievement oriented may be exactly what makes men more successful than women at quitting smoking, even though more women than men say they want to quit (Courtenay, 2000d). Similarly, although traditional beliefs about manhood can increase men's risks, certain characteristics that are considered traditionally masculine ways of coping are highly adaptive for men (and women). These characteristics include having the ability to act independently, to be assertive, and to be decisive (Cook, 1985; Eisler, 1995; Nezu & Nezu, 1987; Sharpe & Heppner, 1991; Sharpe, Heppner, & Dixon, 1995). Reliance on traditionally masculine characteristics can help to enable men to cope with cancer (D. F. Gordon, 1995) and chronic illness (Charmaz, 1995). Interpreting testicular cancer as a battleground for proving their courage gives some men greater self-confidence (D. F. Gordon, 1995).

Highlighting patients' strengths fosters motivation and compliance (Meichenbaum & Turk, 1987). It also conveys respect for their efforts and achievements, which is an important aspect of effective patient-clinician communication (Grüninger, 1995). Commenting on men's strengths before exploring their feeling states may reduce embarrassment and allow them to express their emotions more freely (Rappaport, 1984). For example, clinicians may say, "It's great that you took control of things the way you did and got yourself in here so quickly. But even when we take decisive action, it doesn't always reduce our fears." Identifying men's strengths may also foster clinicians' sense of empathy and compassion, which some contend are essential factors in helping men to change (Brooks, 1998; Schinke, Cole, Williams, & Botvin, 1999). Highlighting men's strengths can also mean drawing on their cultural strengths. When discussing diet planning with African American men, for example, Hendricks

(1999) suggests identifying high-fiber soul foods familiar to these patients and incorporating those foods into the plan.

In the following sections I discuss how to highlight men's strengths by reinforcing specific coping strategies.

Teamwork

The most fundamental way to begin highlighting men's strengths is to encourage them to become active participants in their own health care. The relationship between health professionals and patients is increasingly viewed as a partnership in which health care is the shared work of patients and clinicians (Grüninger, 1995; Make, 1994; Meichenbaum & Turk, 1987; Woolf et al., 1996). Collaborative treatment that encourages patients' active involvement is associated with treatment adherence and improved outcomes (Deber, 1994; McCann & Blossom, 1990; Meichenbaum & Turk, 1987; O'Brien, Petrie, & Raeburn, 1992). Men may tend to perceive health care as something that is done to them, not something that they participate in. The patient-clinician relationship, however, can be the ideal type of interaction for men, provided it is approached as teamwork. Although men are taught to value independence and self-sufficiency, many men have also learned to value the camaraderie and partnership fostered among men through sports, the military, and fraternities (Heppner & Gonzales, 1987). Similarly, men's friendships often focus on working together on tasks or activities (Buhrke & Fuqua, 1987; Miller, 1983).

Asking "Where do you want to start?" (Grüninger, 1995) enlists men's involvement and reinforces their active participation. Clinicians can convey to male patients that they are an integral part of the clinical team and that the success of their treatment depends on their cooperation. Clinicians may ask, "How do you think I can best help you to follow this regimen?" or "What do you think is the best way for you to track your cholesterol levels?" Exploring patients' expectations and prior experiences, answering their questions, inviting their opinions, inquiring into their priorities and preferences, avoiding jargon, and being friendly will all help to make them feel like part of the team (Grüninger, 1995; Meichenbaum & Turk, 1987).

Denial as a Positive Coping Strategy

The negative effects of men's tendency to deny or minimize risk were cited earlier. Denial, however, can also help men to cope with illness—particularly when denial is used not to dismiss that one is ill but to minimize the severity of a problem (Helgeson, 1995). Denial is associated both with noncompliance and with positive consequences, such as resuming work and sex, better medical outcomes, and effective coping after surgery (Helgeson, 1995; Levine et al., 1987). This research suggests that clinicians need to recognize how patients are using denial. Identifying how men use denial as a positive means of coping will also convey respect (Grüninger, 1995). Clinicians can say, for example, "I admire the positive perspective you have on your recovery."

Intellectual Coping

Intellectual, logical, and rational approaches are highly valued coping mechanisms among men (Eisler, 1995; Meth, 1990). Although these coping mechanisms can create problems for men in their interpersonal relationships, they are an asset when men are learning about their health. Because men's conversational styles tend to focus on conveying and exchanging factual information (Moore, 1990; Tannen, 1990), men may be particularly responsive to health education interventions (Helgeson, 1995). Similarly, effective decision making about changing unhealthy behavior requires that individual patients assess the pros and cons of change (Grüninger, 1995; Prochaska et al., 1994). Clinicians should make positive use of men's tendency to weigh their options rationally by discussing with them the costs and benefits of change and emphasizing the intellectual aspects of health care.

Action-Oriented, Problem-Solving, and Goal-Setting Coping

Men engage in more action-oriented, problem-solving, and goal-setting coping than women do (Nezu & Nezu, 1987; Stone & Neale, 1984), including when they are coping with health problems (Fife, Kennedy, & Robinson, 1994; D. F. Gordon, 1995; Helgeson, 1995). Although an action-oriented, problem-solving coping style can hinder men's recovery from illness, it can also help them to recover and reduce their future risk (Charmaz, 1995; D. F. Gordon, 1995; Helgeson, 1995). Clinicians may help patients conceptualize their task as conquering or outsmarting an illness by saying, "I'm impressed by how determined you are to outsmart this disease. And if you keep up that approach, there's a good chance you will!" Men with traditional attitudes about masculinity may be particularly responsive to interventions that emphasize problem-solving skills (Robertson & Fitzgerald, 1992). Teaching problem-solving skills has also been found to be effective in reducing risks among young African American men (Schinke et al., 1999).

A goal-oriented approach to solving problems can be used to men's health advantage. For example, setting dates for achieving specific health goals can contribute to positive outcomes and foster adherence (Little et al., 1992; Meichenbaum & Turk, 1987). Clinicians can reconceptualize patients' goals after surgery as recovery and reframe health goals as targets to shoot for. Clinicians can also capitalize on men's interest in keeping score when monitoring cholesterol or blood pressure by saying, "What are the odds that you can bring your cholesterol down by the next time I see you?"

Healthy Sense of Control

For many men, being in control is an essential part of being a man. As noted earlier, illness can threaten men's sense of being in control. Furthermore, men are more likely than women to believe that they have very little or no control over their future health, a belief that can increase men's risk-taking behaviors (Courtenay, 1998a). To maintain healthy behaviors and modify unhealthy ones, it is essential that patients have a sense of self-efficacy and that they believe that they can respond effectively to reduce a health threat (Grüninger, 1995; Schinke et al., 1999; Taylor, 1990). Patients are also more likely to adhere to treatment when they feel that they have some control over their illnesses (O'Brien et al., 1992). College men who have a personal sense of control over cancer, for example, are significantly more likely to practice monthly testicular self-examination than those who do not (Neef et al., 1991). These findings suggest that clinicians should attempt to foster men's sense of self-efficacy by focusing on the positive aspects of control. Clinicians can suggest to men that they take "personal responsibility" for their well-being and "take charge" of their health, for example.

CONCLUSION

In this chapter I have summarized the findings and recommendations of a clinical practice guideline for working with men. I identified six general strategies, represented by the acronym HEALTH: humanize, educate, assume the worst, locate supports, tailor plan, and highlight strengths. These interventions are critical because men have serious health risks and because these risks are compounded by men's gendered health behaviors and beliefs.

It is important to note that clinicians—particularly male clinicians—need to examine their own health behavior. Like male patients, male clinicians are more likely than their female counterparts to engage in behaviors that increase their health risks (D. G. Allen & Whatley, 1986; Council on Scientific Affairs, 1990; E. Frank & Harvey, 1996; Lewis, Clancy, Leake, & Schwartz, 1991; Norman & Rosvall, 1994), and this gender difference influences their work with male patients. Physicians who themselves practice good health habits are more likely to counsel their patients about healthy behaviors, and those with poor health habits are especially unlikely to do so (Lewis et al., 1991; Wells, Lewis, Leake, & Ware, 1984). Similarly, mental health professionals who have difficulty accepting or expressing their own feelings may have difficulty assisting male patients to express their emotions (Heppner & Gonzales, 1987).

Clinicians should also be aware of their views about what it means to be a man and of how these views influence their work with men. Health professionals may subtly or even unconsciously convey contempt for male patients who do not "act like men" (Heppner & Gonzales, 1987). To assess their beliefs, clinicians should ask themselves, "How do I feel when I see a man who is not in control of his emotions?" "Am I likely just to see a man's hostility and fail to see the pain and sadness underneath?" "Do I simply assume that all male athletes are heterosexual?" "Does my manner make men feel safe?" Clinicians may need to find means of compensating for their own stereotypes and means to validate, respect, and foster the unique ways each man becomes involved in his health care.

References

Adler, D. A., Drake, R. E., & Teague, G. B. (1990). Clinicians' practices in personality assessment: Does gender influence the use of *DSM-III* axis II? *Comprehensive Psychiatry, 31,* (2), 125–133.

Allen, D. G., & Whatley, M. (1986). Nursing and men's health: Some critical considerations. *Nursing Clinics of North America, 21*(1), 3–13.

Allen, J. A., & Gordon, S. (1990). creating a framework for change. In R. L. Meth & R. S. Pasick (Eds.), *Men in therapy: The challenge of change* (pp. 131–151). New York: Guilford Press.

Allen-Burge, R., Storandt, M., Kinscherf, D. A., & Rubin, E. H. (1994). Sex differences in the sensitivity of two self-report depression scales in older depressed inpatients. *Psychology and Aging, 9*(3), 443–445.

American Medical Association. (1991a, October). *Lack of doctor-patient communication hazard in older men* [News release]. Chicago: Author.

American Medical Association. (1991b, October). *Results of 9/91 Gallup survey on older men's health perceptions and behaviors* [News release]. Chicago: Author.

Annandale, E., & Clark, J. (1996). What is gender? Feminist theory and the sociology of human reproduction. *Sociology of Health and Illness, 18*(1), 17–44.

Ashton, W. A., & Fuehrer, A. (1993). Effects of gender and gender role identification of participant and type of social support resource on support seeking. *Sex Roles, 28*(7–8), 461–476.

Baer, J. T. (1993). Improved plasma cholesterol levels in men after nutrition education program at the worksite. *Journal of the American Dietetic Association, 93*(6), 658–663.

Balswick, J. O. (1982). Male inexpressiveness: Psychological and social aspects. In K. Solomon & N. B. Levy (Eds.), *Men in transition: Theory and therapy* (pp. 131–150). New York: Plenum.

Banks, B. A., Silverman, R. A., Schwartz, R. H., & Tunnessen, W. W. (1992). Attitudes of teenagers toward sun exposure and sunscreen use. *Pediatrics, 89*(1), 40–42.

Bayne-Smith, M. (Ed.). (1996). *Race, gender, and health.* Thousand Oaks, CA: Sage.

Belle, D., Burr, R., & Cooney, J. (1987). Boys and girls as social support theorists. *Sex Roles, 17*(11–12), 657–665.

Boehm, S., Selves, E. J., Raleigh, E., Ronis, D., Butler, P. M., & Jacobs, M. (1993). College students' perception of vulnerability/susceptibility and desire for health information. *Patient Education and Counseling, 21,* 77–87.

Brooks, G. R. (1998). *A new psychotherapy for traditional men.* San Francisco: Jossey-Bass.

Brubaker, R. G., & Wickersham, D. (1990). Encouraging the practice of testicular self-examination: An application of the theory of reasoned action. *Health Psychology, 9*(2), 154–163.

Buhrke, R. A., & Fuqua, D. R. (1987). Sex differences in same and cross-sex supportive relationships. *Sex Roles, 17*(5–6), 339–352.

Burda, P. C., & Vaux, A. C. (1987). The social support process in men: Overcoming sex-role obstacles. *Human Relations, 40*(1), 31–44.

Byers, T., Mullis, R., Anderson, J., Dusenbury, L., Gorsky, R., Kimber, C., Krueger, K., Kuester, S., Mokdad, A., Perry, G., & Smith, C. A. (1995). The costs and effects of a nutritional education program following work-site cholesterol screening. *American Journal of Public Health, 85*(5) 650–655.

Bjornson, W., Rand, C., Connett, J. E., Lindgren, P., Nides, M., Pope, F., Buist, A. A., Hoppe-Ryan, C., & O'Hara, P. (1995). Gender differences in smoking cessation after 3 years in the Lung Health Study. *American Journal of Public Health, 85*(2), 223–230.

Charmaz, K. (1995). Identity dilemmas of chronically ill men. In D. Sabo & D. F. Gordon (Eds.), *Men's health and illness: Gender, power, and the body* (pp. 266–291). Thousand Oaks, CA: Sage.

Chino, A. F., & Funabiki, D. (1984). A cross-validation of sex differences in he expression of depression. *Sex Roles, 11,* 175–187.

Cohn, L. D., Macfarlane, S., Yanez, C., & Imai, W. K. (1995). Risk-perception: Differences between adolescents and adults. *Health Psychology, 14*(3), 217–222.

Cook, E. P. (1985). *Psychology androgyny.* New York: Pergamon Press.

Copenhaver, M. M., & Eisler, R. M. (1996). Masculine gender roles stress: A perspective on men's health. In P. M. Kato & T. Mann (Eds.), *Handbook of diversity issues in health psychology* (pp. 219–235).

Corney, R. H. (1990). Sex differences in general practice attendance and help seeking for minor illnesses. *Journal of Psychosomatic Research, 34*(5), 525–534.

Council on Scientific Affairs. (1990). Education for health: A role for physicians and the efficacy of health education efforts. *JAMA, 263*(13), 1816–1819.

Courtenay, W. H. (1996a). *Clinical practice guideline for the treatment of men.* Paper submitted in partial fulfillment of the doctoral degree, University of California, Berkeley.

Courtenay, W. H. (1996b). *Health Mentor: Health Risk Assessment for Men.*™ Berkeley, CA: Author. (Copies available from Men's Health Consulting, 2811 College Avenue, Suite 1, Berkeley, CA 94705-2167.)

Courtenay, W. H. (1998a). Better to die than cry? A longitudinal and constructionist study of masculinity and the health risk behavior of young American men (Doctoral dissertation, University of California at Berkeley). *Dissertation Abstracts International, 59*(08A). (Publication No. AAT 9902042)

Courtenay, W. H. (1998b). College men's health: An overview and a call to action. *Journal of American College Health, 46*(6), 279–290.

Courtenay, W. H. (1998c). Communication strategies for improving men's health: The 6-Point HEALTH Plan. *Wellness Management, 14*(1), 1, 3–4.

Courtenay, W. H. (1999). *Youth* violence? Let's call it what it is. *Journal of American College Health, 48*(3), 141–142.

Courtenay, W. H. (2000a). Constructions of masculinity and their influence on men's well-being: A theory of gender and health. *Social Science and Medicine, 50*(10), 1385–1401.

Courtenay, W. H. (2000b). Social work, counseling, and psychotherapeutic interventions with men and boys: A bibliography. *Men and Masculinities, 2*(3), 330–352.

Courtenay, W. H. (2000c). Teaming up for the new men's health movement. *Journal of Men's Studies, 8*(3), 387–392.

Courtenay, W. H. (2000d). Behavioral factors associated with disease, injury, and death among men: Evidence and implications for prevention. *Journal of Men's Studies, 9*(1), 81–142.

Courtenay, W. H. (2000e). Engendering health: A social constructionist examination of men's health beliefs and behaviors. *Psychology of Men and Masculinity, 1*(1), 4–15.

Courtenay, W. H., & Keeling, R. P. (2000a). Men, gender, and health: Toward an interdisciplinary approach. *Journal of American College Health, 48*(6), 1–4.

Courtenay, W. H. (Guest Ed.), & Keeling, R. P. (Ed.). (2000b). Men's health: A theme issue. *Journal of American College Health, 48*(6).

Courtenay, W. H., & Sabo, D. (in press). Preventative health strategies for men in prison. In D. Sabo, T. Kupers, & W. London (Eds.), *Confronting prison masculinities: The gendered politics of punishment.* Philadelphia: Temple University Press.

Cramer, J. A. (1991). Overview of methods to measure and enhance patient compliance. In J. A. Cramer & B. Spilker (Eds.), *Patient compliance in medical practice and clinical trials* (pp. 3–10). New York: Raven Press.

Cramer, J. A., & Spilker, B. (Eds.). (1991). *Patient compliance in medical practice and clinical trials.* New York: Raven Press.

Croake, J. W., Myers, K. M., & Singh, A. (1987). Demographic features of adult fears. *International Journal of Social Psychiatry, 33*(4), 285–293.

Cutter, S. L., Tiefenbacher, J., & Solecki, W. D. (1992). En-gendered fears: Femininity and technological risk perception. *Industrial Crisis Quarterly, 6*(1), 5–22.

Danielson, R., Marcy, S., Plunkett, A., Wiest, W., & Greenlick, M. R. (1990). Reproductive health counseling for young men: What does it do? *Family Planning Perspectives, 22*(3), 115–121.

Davis, H., & Fallowfield, L. (1991). Counseling and communication in health care: The current situation. In H. Davis & L. Fallowfield (Eds.), *Counseling and communication in health care* (pp. 3–22). New York: Wiley.

Davis, L. E. (Ed.). (1999). *Working with African American males: A guide to practice.* Thousand Oaks, CA: Sage.

Deber, R. B. (1994). Physicians in health management, 7: The patient-physician partnership: Changing roles and the desire for information. *Canadian Medical Association Journal, 151*(2), 171–176.

DeHoff, J. B., & Forrest, K. A. (1984). Men's health. In J. M. Swanson & K. A. Forrest (Eds.), *Men's reproductive health* (pp. 3–10). New York: Springer.

Delbanco, T. L. (1992). Enriching the doctor-patient relationship by inviting the patient's perspective. *American College of Physicians, 116*(5), 414–418.

DePalma, M. T., McCall, M., & English, G. (1996). Increasing perceptions of disease vulnerability through imagery. *Journal of American College Health, 44*(5), 227–234.

DePaulo, B. (1982). Social-psychological processes in informal help-seeking. In T. Wills (Ed.), *Basic processes in helping relationships* (pp. 255–280). New York: Academic Press.

Devine, E. C. (1992). Effects of psychoeducational care for adult surgical patients: A meta-analysis of 191 studies. *Patient Education and Counseling, 19*(2), 129–142.

Eisler, R. M. (1995). The relationship between masculine gender role stress and men's health risk: The validation of a construct. In R. F. Levant & W. S. Pollack (Eds.), *A new psychology of men* (pp. 207–225). New York: Basic Books.

Eisler, R. M., & Hersen, M. (2000). *Handbook of gender, culture, and health.* Mahwah, NJ: Erlbaum.

Fabrega, H., Pilkonis, P., Mezzich, J., Ahn, C. W., & Shea, S. (1990). Explaining diagnostic complexity in an intake setting. *Comprehensive Psychiatry, 31*(1), 5–14.

Fernbach, B. E., Winstead, B. A., & Derlega, V. J. (1989). Sex differences in diagnosis and treatment recommendations for antisocial personality and somatization disorders. *Journal of Social and Clinical Psychology, 8*(3), 238–255.

Fife, B. L., Kennedy, V. N., & Robinson, L. (1994). Gender and adjustment to cancer: Clinical implications. *Journal of Psychological Oncology, 12*(1), 1–21.

Flynn, J., Slovic, P., & Mertz, C. K. (1994). Gender, race, and perception of environmental health risks. *Risk Analysis, 14*(6), 1101–1108.

Ford, M. R., & Widiger, T. A. (1989). Sex bias in the diagnosis of histrionic and antisocial personality disorders. *Journal of Consulting and Clinical Psychology, 57*(2), 301–305.

Fracher, J., & Kimmel, M. S. (1992). Hard issues and soft spots: Counseling men about sexuality. In M. S. Kimmel & M. A. Messner (Eds.), *Men's lives* (2nd ed., pp. 428–450). New York: Macmillan.

Frank, E., & Harvey, L. K. (1996). Prevention advice rates of women and men physicians. *Archives of Family Medicine, 5*(4), 215–219.

Frank, R. G., Bouman, D. E., Cain, K., & Watts, C. (1992). Primary prevention of catastrophic injury. *American Psychologist, 47*(8), 1045–1049.

Friedman, C., Brownson, R. C., Peterson, D. E., & Wilkerson, J. C. (1994). Physician advice to reduce chronic disease risk factors. *American Journal of Preventive Medicine, 10*(6), 367–371.

Friedman, H. S., & DiMatteo, M. R. (1989). *Health psychology.* Englewood Cliffs, NJ: Prentice Hall.

Gerber, G. S., Thompson, I. M., Thisted, R., & Chodak, G. W. (1993). Disease-specific survival following routine prostate cancer screening by digital rectal examination. *JAMA, 269*(1), 61–64.

Gijsbers van Wijk, C.M.T., Vliet, K. P. van, Kolk, K. P., & Everaerd, W. T. (1991). Symptom sensitivity and sex differences in physical morbidity: A review of health surveys in the United States and the Netherlands. *Women and Health, 17*(1), 91–124.

Goldberg, K. (1993). How men can live as long as women: Seven steps to a longer and better life. Fort Worth, TX: Summit Group.

Golombok, S., & Fivush, R. (1994). *Gender development.* Cambridge, MA: Cambridge University Press.

Good, E. G., Dell, D. M., & Mintz, L. B. (1989). Male role and gender role conflict: Relations to help seeking in men. *Journal of Counseling Psychology, 36*(3), 295–300.

Gordon, B., & Pasick, R. S. (1990). Changing the nature of friendships between men. In R. L. Meth & R. S. Pasick (Eds.), *Men in therapy: The challenge of change* (pp. 261–278). New York: Guilford Press.

Gordon, D. F. (1995). Testicular cancer and masculinity. In D. Sabo & D. F. Gordon (Eds.), *Men's health and illness: Gender, power, and the body* (pp. 246–265). Thousand Oaks, CA: Sage.

Grigsby, J. B., & Weatherley, D. (1983). Gender and sex role differences in intimacy of self-disclosure. *Psychological Reports, 53*, 891–897.

Grueninger, U. J., Goldstein, M. G., & Duffy, F. D. (1990). A conceptual framework for interactive patient education in practice and clinic settings. *Journal of Human Hypertension, 4*(Suppl. 1), 21–31.

Grüninger, U. J. (1995). Patient education: An example of one-to-one communication. *Journal of Human Hypertension, 9*(1), 15–25.

Hall, J. A., Roter, D. L., & Katz, N. R. (1988). Meta-analysis of correlates of provider behavior in medical encounters. *Medical Care, 26*(7), 657–675.

Helgeson, V. S. (1995). Masculinity, men's roles, and coronary heart disease. In D. Sabo & D. F. Gordon (Eds.), *Men's health and illness: Gender, power, and the body* (pp. 1–21). Thousand Oaks, CA: Sage.

Hendricks, L. E. (1999). *Working with African American males: A guide to practice.* Thousand Oaks, CA: Sage.

Heppner, P. P., & Gonzales, D. S. (1987). Men counseling men. In M. Scheer, M. Stevens, G. Good, & G. A. Eichenfield (Eds.), *Handbook of counseling and psychotherapy with men* (pp. 30–38). Thousand Oaks, CA: Sage.

Hewson, M. G. (1993). Patient education through teaching for conceptual change. *Journal of General Internal Medicine, 8*(7), 393–398.

Hohmann, A. A. (1989). Gender bias in psychotropic drug prescribing in primary care. *Medical Care, 27*(5), 478–490.

Hornbrook, M. C., Stevens, V. J., Wingfield, D. J., Hollis, J. F., Greenlick, M. R., & Ory, M. G. (1994). Preventing falls among community-dwelling older persons: Results from a randomized trial. *Gerontologist, 34*(1), 16–23.

Horne, D. J., Vatmanidis, P., & Careri, A. (1994). Preparing patients for invasive medical and surgical procedures, 1: Adding behavioral and cognitive interventions. *Behavioral Medicine, 20*(1), 5–13.

Hyde, J. S. (1986). Gender differences in aggression. In J. S. Hyde & M. C. Linn (Eds.), *The psychology of gender* (pp. 51–66). Baltimore: Johns Hopkins University Press.

Janz, N., & Becker, M. (1984). The health belief model: A decade later. *Health Education Quarterly, 11*(1), 1–57.

Job, R. F. (1988). Effective and ineffective use of fear in health promotion campaigns. *American Journal of Public Health, 78,* 163–167.

Kacmarek, R. M. (1994). Make discussion. *Respiratory Care, 39*(5), 579–583.

Kaplan, H. S. (1974). *The new sex therapy: Active treatment of sexual dysfunctions.* New York: Brunner/Mazel.

Kaplan, S. H., Gandek, B., Greenfield, S., Rogers, W., & Ware, J. E. (1995). Patient and visit characteristics related to physicians' participatory decision-making style: Results from the Medical Outcomes Study. *Medical Care, 33*(12), 1176–1187.

Kaplan, S. H., Greenfield, S., & Ware, J. E. (1989). Assessing the effects of physician-patient interactions on the outcomes of chronic disease. *Medical Care, 27*(Suppl.), S110–S127.

Katz, R. C., Meyers, K., & Walls, J. (1995). Cancer awareness and self-examination practices in young men and women. *Journal of Behavioral Medicine, 18*(4), 377–384.

Koop, C. E. (1996). Foreword. In S. H. Woolf, S. Jonas, & R. S. Lawrence (Eds.), *Health promotion and disease prevention in clinical practice* (pp. vii–ix). Baltimore: Williams & Wilkins.

Kraemer, D. L., & Hastrup, J. L. (1986). Crying in natural settings: Global estimates, self monitored frequencies, depression, and sex differences in an undergraduate population. *Behavior Research and Therapy, 24*(3), 371–373.

Krantz, D. S., Grunberg, N. E., & Baum, A. (1985). Health psychology. *Annual Review of Psychology, 36,* 349–383.

Kreuter, M. W., & Strecher, V. J. (1995). Changing inaccurate perceptions of health risk: Results from a randomized trial. *Health Psychology, 14*(1), 56–63.

Lee, C. C. (1990). Black male development: Counseling the "native son." In D. Moore & F. Leafgren (Eds.), *Problem solving strategies and interventions for men in conflict* (pp. 125–137). Alexandria, VA: American Association for Counseling and Development.

Lent, B., & Bishop, J. E. (1998). Sense and sensitivity: Developing a gender issues perspective in medical education. *Journal of Women's Health, 7*(3), 339–342.

Levant, R. F., & Kopecky, G. (1995). Masculinity reconstructed: Changing the rules of manhood—at work, in relationships, and in family life. New York: Dutton.

Levine, J., Warrenburg, S., Kerns, R., Schwartz, G., Delaney, R., Fontana, A., Gradman, A., Smith, S., Allen, S., & Cascione, R. (1987). The role of denial in recovery from coronary heart disease. *Psychosomatic Medicine, 49*(2), 109–117.

Lewis, C. E., Clancy, C., Leake, B., & Schwartz, J. S. (1991). The counseling practices of internists. *American College of Physicians, 114*(1), 54–58.

Liddell, A., Locker, D., & Burman, D. (1991). Self-reported fears (FSS-II) of subjects aged 50 years and over. *Behavior Research and Therapy, 29*(2), 105–112.

Little, S. J., Stevens, V. J., Severson, H. H., & Lichtenstein, E. (1992). Effective smokeless tobacco intervention for dental hygiene patients. *Journal of Dental Hygiene, 66*(4), 185–190.

Lombardo, W. K., Cretser, G. A., Lombardo, B., & Mathis, S. L. (1983). Fer cryin' out loud—there is a sex difference. *Sex Roles, 9*(9), 987–995.

Majors, R., & Billson, J. M. (1992). *Cool pose: The dilemmas of black manhood in America.* New York: Simon & Schuster.

Make, B. (1994). Collaborative self-management strategies for patients with respiratory disease. *Respiratory Care, 39*(5), 566–579.

Marks, G., Garcia, M., & Solis, J. M. (1990). Health risk behaviors of Hispanics in the United States: Findings from HHANES, 1982–84. *American Journal of Public Health, 80*(Suppl.), 20–26.

May, J. P., & Martin, K. L. (1993). A role for the primary care physician in counseling young African-American men about homicide prevention. *Journal of General Internal Medicine, 8,* 380–382.

May, R. (1990). finding ourselves: Self-esteem, self-disclosure and self-acceptance. In D. Moore & F. Leafgren (Eds.), *Problem solving strategies and interventions for men in conflict* (pp. 11–21). Alexandria, VA: American Association for Counseling and Development.

McCann, D. P., & Blossom, H. J. (1990). The physician as a patient educator: From theory to practice. *Western Journal of Medicine, 153*(1), 44–49.

Meichenbaum, D., & Turk, D. C. (1987). *Facilitating treatment adherence: A practitioner's guidebook.* New York: Plenum.

Mermelstein, R. J., & Riesenberg, L. A. (1992). Changing knowledge and attitudes about skin cancer risk factors in adolescents. *Health Psychology, 11*(6), 371–376.

Meth, R. L. (1990). The road to masculinity. In R. L. Meth & R. S. Pasick (Eds.), *Men in therapy: The challenge of change* (pp. 3–34). New York: Guilford Press.

Metz, M. E., & Seifert, M. H. (1990). Men's expectations of physicians in sexual health concerns. *Journal of Sexual and Marital Therapy, 16*(2), 79–88.

Miaskowski, C. (1999). The role of sex and gender in pain perception and response to treatment. In R. J. Gatchel & D. C. Turk (Eds.), *Psychological factors in pain: Critical perspectives* (pp. 401–411). New York: Guilford Press.

Miller, S. (1983). *On men and friendship.* Boston: Houghton Mifflin.

Misener, T. R., & Fuller, S. G. (1995). Testicular versus breast and colorectal cancer screen: Early detection practices of primary care physicians. *Cancer Practice, 3*(5), 310–316.

Moore, D. (1990). Helping men become more emotionally expressive: A ten-week program. In D. Moore & F. Leafgren (Eds.), *Problem solving strategies and interventions for men in conflict* (pp. 183–200). Alexandria, VA: American Association for Counseling and Development.

Mullen, P. D., Mains, D. A., & Velez, R. (1992). A meta-analysis of controlled trials of cardiac patient education. *Patient Education and Counseling, 19*(2), 143–162.

Myers, R. E., Ross, E. A., Wolf, T. A., Balshem, A., Jepson, C., & Millner, L. (1991). Behavioral interventions to increase adherence in colorectal cancer screening. *Medical Care, 29*(10), 1039–1050.

Neef, N., Scutchfield, F. D., Elder, J., & Bender, S. J. (1991). Testicular self-examination by young men: An analysis of characteristics associated with practice. *Journal of American College Health, 39*(4), 187–190.

Nezu, A. M., & Nezu, C. M. (1987). Psychological distress, problem solving, and coping reactions: Sex role differences. *Sex Roles, 16*(3–4), 206–214.

Norman, J., & Rosvall, S. B. (1994). Help-seeking behavior among mental health practitioners. *Clinical Social Work Journal, 22*(4), 449–460.

Oakley, A. (1994). Who cares for health? Social relations, gender, and the public health. *Journal of Epidemiology and Community Health, 48*(5), 427–434.

O'Brien, M. K., Petrie, K., & Raeburn, J. (1992). Adherence to medication regimens: Updating a complex medical issue. *Medical Care Review, 49*(4), 435–454.

Oleckno, W. A., & Blacconiere, M. J. (1990). Wellness of college students and differences by gender, race, and class standing. *College Student Journal, 24*(4), 421–429.

Pasick, R. (1990). Raised to work. In R. L. Meth & R. S. Pasick (Eds.), *Men in therapy: The challenge of change* (pp. 35–53). New York: Guilford Press.

Pierce, R. (1999). Prostate cancer in African American men: Thoughts on psychosocial interventions. In L. E. Davis (Ed.), *Working with African American males: A guide to practice* (pp. 75–90). Thousand Oaks, CA: Sage.

Pleck, J. H. (1981). *The myth of masculinity.* Cambridge, MA: MIT Press.

Potts, M. K., Burnam, M. A., & Wells, K. B. (1991). Gender differences in depression detection: A comparison of clinician diagnosis and standardized assessment. *Psychological Assessment, 3*(4), 609–615.

Preusser, D. F., Williams, A. F., & Lund, A. K. (1991). Characteristics of belted and unbelted drivers. *Accident Analysis and Prevention, 23,* 475–482.

Prochaska, J., Norcross, J., & DiClemente, C. (1994). Changing for good: The revolutionary program that explains the six stages of change and teaches you how to free yourself from bad habits. New York: Morrow.

Rappaport, B. M. (1984). Family planning: Helping men ask for help. In J. M. Swanson & K. A. Forrest (Eds.), *Men's reproductive health* (pp. 245–259). New York: Springer.

Reagan, L. J. (1997). Engendering the dread disease: Women, men, and cancer. *American Journal of Public Health, 87*(11), 1779–1787.

Reno, D. R. (1988). Men's knowledge and health beliefs about testicular cancer and testicular self-exam. *Cancer Nursing, 11*(2), 112–117.

Robertson, J. M., & Fitzgerald, L. F. (1992). Overcoming the masculine mystique: Preferences for alternative forms of assistance among men who avoid counseling. *Journal of Counseling Psychology, 39*(2), 240–246.

Robinson, E. J., & Whitfield, M. J. (1985). Improving the efficiency of patients' comprehension monitoring: A way of increasing patients' participation in general practice consultations. *Social Science and Medicine, 21*(8), 915–919.

Rosenstock, I. M. (1990). The Health Belief Model: Explaining health behavior through expectancies. In K. Glanz, F. M. Lewis, & B. K. Rimer (Eds.), *Health behavior and health education: Theory, research, and practice.* San Francisco: Jossey-Bass.

Roter, D. L., & Hall, J. A. (1997). Doctors talking with patients/patients talking with doctors: Improving communication in medical visits. Westport, CT: Auburn House.

Rothspan, S., & Read, S. J. (1996). Present versus future time perspective and HIV risk among heterosexual college students. *Health Psychology, 15*(2), 131–134.

Rubin, L. B. (1983). *Intimate strangers.* New York: Harper & Row.

Rule, W. R., & Gandy, G. L. (1994). A thirteen-year comparison in patterns of attitudes toward counseling. *Adolescence, 29*(115), 575–589.

Saurer, M. K., & Eisler, R. M. (1990). The role of masculine gender role stress in expressivity and social support network factors. *Sex Roles, 23*(5–6), 261–271.

Savage, I. (1993). Demographic influences on risk perceptions. *Risk Analysis, 13,* 413–420.

Sawyer, R. G., & Moss, D. J. (1993). Sexually transmitted diseases in college men: A preliminary clinical investigation. *Journal of American College Health, 42*(3), 111–115.

Scarce, M. (1999). Smearing the queer: Medical bias in the health care of gay men. New York: Haworth Press.

Schinke, S., Cole, K., Williams, C., & Botvin, G. (1999). Reducing risk taking among African American males. In L. E. Davis (Ed.), *Working with African American males: A guide to practice* (pp. 103–112). Thousand Oaks, CA: Sage.

Sharpe, M. J., & Heppner, P. P., (1991). Gender role, gender role conflict, and psychological well-being in men. *Journal of Counseling Psychology, 38,* 323–330.

Sharpe, M. J., Heppner, P. P., & Dixon, W. A. (1995). Gender role conflict, instrumentality, expressiveness, and well-being in adult men. *Sex Roles, 33*(1–2), 1–8.

Spigner, C., Hawkins, W., & Loren, W. (1993). Gender differences in perception of risk associated with alcohol and drug use among college students. *Women and Health, 20*(1), 87–97.

Stapley, J. C., & Haviland, J. M. (1989). Beyond depression: Gender differences in normal adolescents' emotional experiences. *Sex Roles, 20*(5–6), 295–308.

Stone, A. A., & Neale, J. M. (1984). New measure of daily coping: Development and preliminary results. *Journal of Personality and Social Psychology, 46*(4), 892–906.

Strube, M. J. (Ed.). (1991). *Type A behavior.* Newbury Park, CA: Sage.

Sutkin, L., & Good, G. (1987). Therapy with men in health-care settings. In M. Scher, M. Stevens, G. Good, & G. A. Eichenfield (Eds.), *Handbook of counseling and psychotherapy with men* (pp. 372–387). Thousand Oaks, CA: Sage.

Taggart, L. P., McCammon, S. L., Allred, L. J., Horner, R. D., & May H. J. (1993). Effect of patient and physician gender on prescriptions for psychotropic drugs. *Journal of Women's Health, 2,* 353–357.

Tannen, D. (1990). You just don't understand: Women and men in conversation. New York: Ballantine.

Taylor, S. E. (1986). *Health psychology.* New York: Random House.

Taylor, S. E. (1990). Health psychology: The science and the field. *American Psychologist, 45*(1), 40–50.

Thomas, C., & Kelman, H. R. (1990). Gender and the use of health services among elderly persons. In M. G. Ory & H. R. Warner (Eds.), *Gender, health, longevity: Multidisciplinary perspectives* (pp. 25–37). New York: Springer.

Thompson, E. H., Grisanti, C., & Pleck, J. H. (1985). Attitudes toward the male role and their correlates. *Sex Roles, 13*(7–8), 413–427.

Unruh, A. M. (1996). Gender variations in clinical pain experience. *Pain, 65*(2–3), 123–167.

Unruh, A. M., Ritchie, J., & Merskey, H. (1999). Does gender affect appraisal of pain and pain coping strategies? *Clinical Journal of Pain, 15*(1), 31–40.

U.S. Department of Health and Human Services. (1996). Report of final mortality statistics, 1994. *Monthly Viral Statistics Report, 45*(3, 2 Suppl.).

U.S. Department of Health and Human Services. (1998a). *Vital and health statistics: Current estimates from the National Health Interview Survey, 1995* (DHHS Publication No. PHS 98-1527). Hyattsville, MD: Author.

U.S. Department of Health and Human Services. (1998b). *Health, United States, 1998: Socioeconomic status and health chartbook* (DHHS Publication No. PHS 98-1232-1). Hyattsville, MD: Author.

U.S. Preventive Services Task Force. (1996). *Guide to clinical preventive services* (2nd ed.). Baltimore: Williams & Wilkins.

Verbrugge, L. M. (1980). Sex differences in complaints and diagnoses. *Journal of Behavioral Medicine, 3*(4), 327–355.

Verbrugge, L. M. (1982). Sex differences in legal drug use. *Journal of Social Issues, 38*(2), 59–76.

Verbrugge, L. M. (1985). Gender and health: An update on hypotheses and evidence. *Journal of Health and Social Behavior, 26*(3), 156–182.

Verbrugge, L. M. (1989). The twain meet: Empirical explanations of sex differences in health and mortality. *Journal of Health and Social Behavior, 30*(3), 282–304

Waisberg, J., & Page, S. (1988). Gender role nonconformity and perception of mental illness. *Women and Health, 14*(1), 3–16.

Waitzkin, H. (1984). Doctor-patient communication: Clinical implications of social scientific research. *JAMA, 252*(17), 2441–2446.

Waitzkin, H. (1985). Information giving in medical care. *Journal of Health and Social Behavior, 26*(2), 81–101.

Wallen, J., Waitzkin, H., & Stoeckle, J. D. (1979). Physician stereotypes about female health and illness: A study of patients' sex and the information process during medical interviews. *Women and Health, 4*(2), 135–146.

Weinstein, N. D. (1987). Unrealistic optimism about illness susceptibility: Conclusions from a community-wide sample. *Journal of Behavioral Medicine, 10*(5), 481–500.

Weissfeld, J. L., Kirscht, J. P., & Brock, B. M. (1990). Health beliefs in a population: The Michigan Blood Pressure Survey. *Health Education Quarterly, 17*(2), 141–155.

Wells, K. B., Lewis, C. E., Leake, B., & Ware, J. E. (1984). Do physicians preach what they practice? A study of physicians' health habits and counseling practices. *JAMA, 252*(20), 2846–2848.

Williams, D. G. (1985). Gender, masculinity-femininity, and emotional intimacy in same-sex friendship. *Sex Roles, 12*(5–6), 587–600.

Woolf, S. H., Jonas, S., & Lawrence, R. S. (Eds.). (1996). *Health promotion and disease prevention in clinical practice.* Baltimore: Williams & Wilkins.

Zilbergeld, B. (1992). *The new male sexuality.* New York: Bantam Books.

Zuckerman, M. (1994). *Behavioral expressions and biosocial bases of sensation seeking.* New York: Cambridge University Press.

CHAPTER FOUR

Working with Men in Sports Settings

John M. Robertson
Fred B. Newton

G ender is not a disorder. Neither is being athletic. Therefore, male athletes are not a disordered group necessarily in need of psychological treatment. Even so, gender matters. It especially matters for counselors when they work with men in sports settings because in North American culture, masculinity and sports are virtually inseparable experiences (Messner, 1992; Sabo & Runfola, 1980). Discovering masculinity expectations in sports settings begins early with little boys hitting baseballs from the top of a tee ball support. The process continues through the life span, as older men become "master" participants in golf, running, weights, and countless other settings. Men who do not or cannot play usually watch. Men who neither play nor watch risk paying a huge price—personal shame, humiliation, poor self-esteem. Sports are a lifelong interest for many, many men. The masculinity issues that sports raise for men may vary over the life span and among cultures, but the need to address these issues continues all through life.

How does this interest begin? Why do young boys get involved in sports? The motivations of parents focus more on personal development than on external rewards and include such explanations as developing competency with new skills, building friendships, learning about the importance of group cooperation, developing good health habits, experiencing competition, and simply having fun (Gould & Petlichkoff, 1988; Weiss, 1995; Weiss & Chaumeton, 1992; Weiss & Petlichkoff, 1989). Stories in the popular sports press reinforce this message. Years later, men who played competitive sports in their youth are quoted touting the benefits they received from playing (see G. Smith, 1999).

Many of the implications of these desired benefits have a traditionally masculine overtone. To illustrate, notice the goals in a counseling program for athletes called Life Development Intervention (Danish, Petitpas, & Hale, 1995). Developed by university professors who have assisted the U.S. Olympic Committee, this model describes a set of goals for the athletes who join the program. Some of the goals include to perform under pressure, to meet challenges, to handle both success and failure, to take risks, to make a commitment and stick to it, to know how to win and how to lose, to have self-control, to push yourself to the limit, to accept responsibility for your behavior, to evaluate yourself, to make good decisions, to set and attain goals, and to be self-motivated.

Most of these ideas are direct expressions of traditional masculine socialization. Compare this list, for example, with some of the themes found in Brannon's (1976) "blueprint" for men or Pollack's (1998) "boy code": success, status, toughness, confidence, self-reliance, aggression, daring, antifemininity, and so forth. For many men, the values found in sports settings are consistent with what they have learned about the expectations of being male.

It is not surprising, therefore, that when men with sports-related issues come to counselors, they typically present questions related to athletic performance in some way (negative thoughts about their skills, coping with injuries, concerns with motivation or confidence, dealing with substance abuse, or problems with weight or eating). The typical interventions of sports psychologists are also consistent with these masculine themes: goal setting, stress reduction, imagery for performance, positive self-talk, and similar strategies (see Singer, Murphey, & Tennant, 1993). Because gender issues are so central for men in sports, a closer look at some of these themes seems appropriate. Although they are not likely to be the presenting issues by men who are active in sports, these issues are nevertheless in the background for most questions presented to the counselor.

GENDER ISSUES INVOLVED IN COUNSELING MEN IN SPORTS SETTINGS

Given the realities of masculine socialization and the values inherent in North American sports, counselors may find it helpful to review several gender-related themes as they think about their male clients who are athletic: the importance of winning and losing, the role of sports in personal identity, career pressures for athletic men, body image issues, the impact of competition, aggression and violence, and father-son relationships.

Winning and Losing

For many years, gender theorists have identified success as a major theme in masculine socialization (Brannon, 1976; O'Neil, 1981). In team sports, success and failure are central. Competitive games have winners. Winners create losers. These themes seem more significant to men than to women. That is, men appear to be more affected by success and failure than women are, keep score during games more frequently than women do, set more outcome goals for games than women do, and are more interested than women are in experiencing the success that comes from winning competitive activities (Vodde, 1997; Weinberg & Jackson, 1979; Weinberg & Ragan, 1979).

Success in sports is certainly about winning games, races, and championships, but it is much more than that. It means a boy has been chosen by a third-grade recess captain to be on his team. It means making the team in high school, earning a starting position, making a play that people cheer, getting an athletic scholarship for college, getting a tryout with a professional team, starting for your team, not feeling embarrassed on the racquetball court at age forty, or being able to play competitive basketball in a city league at age sixty-two.

The desire to succeed in sports continues at every level. Those who do succeed are rewarded handsomely. Children are praised in front of their peers, high school students get their names in the local newspaper, and professional athletes get national coverage for their "successes." It is no wonder that many boys grow up wanting to be athletes. Athletes can epitomize success.

However, failures are also publicized. Consider the double standard on a typical university campus. On the same night, a chemistry major and a student athlete are arrested in separate incidents for driving under the influence of alcohol. The community newspaper, however, writes a story and publishes the picture of only the student athlete. Only his failure to meet community standards gets publicized. In addition, athletic failures become news events that people discuss among themselves; fumbles, missed shots, errant passes, and arrests for legal offenses all become part of the community's knowledge and everyday conversation.

Jim was an all-state high school baseball player who played on championship teams beginning at the age of eight. During his junior year of high school, he was regarded as the team's best hitter and leader. Batting third in the order, he hit nearly .500 during the season. Colleges offered him athletic scholarships. He accepted one during his senior year but then went into a prolonged batting slump. He got depressed and sullen. He slept excessively, withdrew from others, and expressed doubts about himself in general. Then one day he said to his father, "If I am not good at baseball, what am I good at? This is the only goal I've really worked on. I should give the scholarship back. I don't deserve it!"

What was happening here? In truth, Jim was living the adage on his T-shirt: "Baseball is Life!" The implication was clear—to succeed in baseball was to succeed in life. Jim was not just in a batting slump. He was failing—failing to perform, failing to lead his team, failing to impress his family and friends, failing to merit his scholarship. Much was at stake for him: his self concept, his personal worth, his evaluation by others. A simple batting slump had precipitated a major developmental crisis about his ability to succeed as a man.

Jim's story is common for many boys with exceptional talent in high school and college. Other young men in this situation may act out or use substances to numb the sense of conspicuous failure. As a counselor, how do you address these issues? Do you work with the mental blocks and the performance problems to get Jim through his slump? Do you work with the stress and depression? Do you suggest medication? Is this an opportunity to help Jim look at his life in a broader perspective and to discuss additional ways of defining success and failure outside of sports? Once the batting slump ends, do you take advantage of the moment to raise career questions in light of the probabilities of actually making a living as a player?

This latter point is crucial. What makes athletic success and failure so problematic for young men is that the odds of succeeding professionally in an organized sport are extremely small. Only one of every ten thousand high school athletes plays professional sports (Simons, 1997). In basketball, one out of every fifty thousand high schoolers makes it to the National Basketball Association (Simons, 1997). Only about fifteen hundred men play in the National Football League. Very, very few "succeed" as professional players. The overwhelming majority of boys and men exit the system early. Unfortunately, many highly athletic boys see any exit as a failure.

Personal Identity

In almost every elementary classroom in the country, one or two boys are known as the fastest and the strongest boys in class. Typically, they are acknowledged as the best players on every team they join. With the reinforcement provided by peers, family, and spectators, their athleticism becomes a major part of their identity. Such a boy is not just Mario, he is Mario the jock or Mario the quarterback. When he is prevented from performing in this role (by an injury, by not making the team at the next level, or by losing a starting position), he can lose part of his core identity and suffer immensely. He may then act out in aggressive ways or perhaps withdraw and become depressed.

Kelly played basketball as far back as he could remember. He was shooting hoops as a four-year-old on his driveway, using the smaller backboard made for children. He was good. Neighbors and friends told him so as they stood around his driveway. Being an athlete became part of his identity. When he got to high school, his coaches raved. They told him that they expected big things from him by the time he was a junior. "You will be the leader on the team. We need your scoring ability." Friends and family talked about his potential as an all-state player and their expectation that he would win a state championship before he finished high school. He lived in a relatively small town of about fifty thousand in the Southeast, so the attention he received placed him at the center of the entire community.

Kelly's junior year started as promised. He was averaging more than thirty points a game, and his team was undefeated halfway through the season. Then he broke his foot. He went up for a rebound and came down awkwardly on another player's foot. Kelly's season was over. The injury was severe: three bones were broken, and metal pins were screwed into his leg and ankle. Unfortunately, his body did not respond well to the treatment. A year later, when he was a senior and supposed to be leading his team to a state championship, he just could not jump or run as well as he had before. All his numbers were down—rebounds, points, and eventually minutes. He complained about his loss of playing time. His coach finally benched him. More importantly, all the universities lost their interest. No scholarship was offered.

By the time Kelly got to college (he enrolled only because his parents insisted), he was so depressed that he could not study. He had no idea what he wanted for an academic major, because his entire life had been pointing toward basketball. When he started talking about suicide, his parents finally brought him to the campus counseling center.

Kelly's identity and ability were no longer in sync. He had always been Kelly the great basketball talent. Rebounding and slam dunking were all he had ever wanted to do. He could not imagine himself in any other setting, doing anything else. And so, for two years, he floundered. He flunked classes, drank too much, and got into legal trouble.

Kelly illustrates a difficult truth. Identity for men in sports settings is shifting, precarious. It can be changed in an instant. For Kelly, it happened with an injury. For others, it happens when parents punish them by not letting them join a junior high team, when a coach gets angry and benches them, or when they simply do not make the team at the next level.

Identity issues that involve athleticism are not restricted to young men, either. Take the case of Sam, who was forty-four at the time he sought counseling. He came because he was facing a major career change. A strongly independent man, he had taken much pride in his ability to be a rancher, until a farm crisis led him to file for bankruptcy. Because he had numerous skills, he was able to find several jobs. But he remained dissatisfied and unhappy with his life. He got depressed. He went through a divorce. He then had a health crisis. He came to therapy looking for some "career testing."

However, it quickly became clear that physical prowess was a major part of Sam's identity. He stood well over six feet and weighed a muscular three hundred pounds. His size and strength were very central to his sense of self and to the way others viewed him. His gentle and unassuming personality belied his tremendous strength. Sam disclosed that for many years, he had competed at a national level in weight-lifting competitions and had won many trophies. He had later become a legend in his county for being able to load large round hay bales weighing several hundred pounds onto trucks by himself.

For Sam, many issues needed attention. But central to his situation was his awareness that he no longer was physically able to perform feats that others admired. He had always enjoyed being able to impress people by his lifting or hoisting skills. Now that was gone. On one level, his question was how to find meaningful work. But on a deeper level, it was how to think of himself as someone no longer able to perform feats of strength in a work setting. Could any work be meaningful if it did not allow for this part of his identity to be expressed?

Another identity issue that needs to be addressed is the notion of team identity. Much of a young boy's identity can be wrapped up in a team. His identity as jock on a team actually can become more salient to him than his identity as an individual among his peers (in his team role he is better known, more publicized, more rewarded, and more penalized). As he gets older, coaches take charge of all the details of his life, including eating and drinking, career choices, social activities, sleep schedules, and so forth. This highly controlled setting again de-emphasizes individual identity. Then, suddenly, he is off the team. He has gotten too old for the age bracket, graduated, or been cut. He is on his own, having to make his own decisions as an individual. For some men, this transition to an autonomous identity can be very difficult.

Although athletes are highly envied by many, having a sports-related identity is not altogether positive for young men. Many people strongly dislike sports and athletes and criticize the publicity they receive, their supposed bullying of others, or their disproportionate income potential. One of the most tragic news events covered around the world in 1999 was the high school shooting that occurred at Columbine High School in Littleton, Colorado. Although such tragedies are complex and involve numerous variables, news reports indicated that some of the rage in the young men who shot their classmates was directed specifically toward athletes (Cannon, Streisand, & McGraw, 1999).

It works both ways. Sometimes male athletes are put on a pedestal and given much adulation by peers, family, and strangers. At other times, they are ridiculed and made targets by peers and teachers. We are aware of high school teachers in our community who say very directly to students, "I don't expect much from you; you're an athlete," and other teachers in the same school who say, "Don't worry about finishing this assignment; you have to get to practice." Either way, when a young man identifies himself as an athlete, he is saying a great deal about himself. He is describing a crucial part of his identity, his role in life.

Career

It is our experience on a university campus that most exceptional male athletes do not make a considered career choice before they come to college. Further, most resist facing that question for at least the first two years on campus. They came to college on a scholarship to play sports, not to train themselves for a career. In fact, those who do try to make career plans are often blocked by their coaches from pursuing a field that interests them. For example, on many campuses male athletes in revenue sports cannot major in teacher education because student teaching and other responsibilities would cause them to miss too much practice. For a male athlete to become a teacher, he has to stay another two years after his scholarship runs out. When young men challenge this system, the pressures to conform are intense.

Reggie was a six-foot, eleven-inch college freshman who had been recruited to a Division I-A university to play basketball (Division I-A is the highest level of university sports). Reggie was offered a full-ride scholarship. As far back as he could remember, he had been highly regarded as a player. People told him how much money he could make in the pros. Not surprisingly, Reggie was swept along by all this attention. Everyone he knew was proud of him because he had been selected to receive a university scholarship.

However, when he got to college, Reggie began to struggle with his personal realization that he did not want to play basketball. He had other dreams that were important to him. On his own, without telling anyone, he made an appointment with a counselor in the campus counseling center. Over a period of several months, he decided that he wanted to major in engineering physics. With his high American College Test (ACT) scores and his strong interests in mathematics and physics, this choice seemed reasonable. Announcing this decision, however, was terribly wrenching for Reggie. For most students, telling parents and close friends about their choice of an academic major is an important, positive event. But for Reggie, this event was momentous and frightening. As he expected, his announcement was greeted with shock and disappointment. How could he let so many people down? How could he turn down a full scholarship? How could he walk away from so much money? What was wrong with him?

But with the support of his counselor, Reggie stood up for himself and acted on his own. Losing the scholarship meant that he had to drop out of school for a year in order to establish residency. But he followed through with his plan and got his degree five years later.

Most successful athletes who start college on a scholarship expect to make a living in their sport. We have seen classes of sophomores, for example, in which student athletes are asked, "How many of you plan to make a living as an athlete?" Nearly all the men in these classes raise their hands. For most of these sophomore men, the odds do not matter. But the odds are overwhelmingly against such a career. Even in the most successful university athletic programs, only one to three football players graduate with even a slight chance of making a living in the pros (about one hundred students are connected with the football program as players every year). Many of these men come to college for only one reason—to play and go to the pros. It is an unfortunate irony; at a time when career counseling resources are virtually free and easy to obtain, the interest of most student athletes in career counseling is very low. They gamble much, these select students, on their dreams of an athletic career. And the vast majority of them lose their gamble.

Body Performance

For a long time, much attention has been paid to eating and body image issues for females (see Hutchinson, 1985; Mintz & Betz, 1988; Orbach, 1988), and such concern is certainly warranted. However, body issues can become highly problematic for men as well (Zucherman, Colby, Ware, & Lazerson, 1986). Boys with higher-than-average levels of coordination, strength, and speed are rewarded on the playing field. The more of these physical abilities they have, the better off they are.

For some athletic young men, weight becomes a dominant concern. And with good reason. Performance in many sports can be influenced by body size. Poor weight management can be critical in such sports as wrestling, cross country, gymnastics, sprints, football, and swimming. If they do not pay enough attention to body size, they will be less effective. Several sports, of course, organize the competition around very specific weight classifications (wrestling, weight lifting, boxing, rowing, horse racing, and some of the martial arts). In these sports, if athletes weigh too much, they cannot compete against opponents they have prepared to face. Other sports (figure skating, diving, gymnastics, synchronized swimming, and male cheerleading) use judges to decide winners. The criteria these judges use are related very directly to body image preferences for such things as attractiveness, aesthetics, grace, and proportion. Still other sports (swimming, skiing, bicycle racing, and track and field events) emphasize the need for low body fat percentages. The demands change according to the sport (bulk up or thin down), but the body is always of primary concern to men with athletic interests.

In an effort to reduce weight, athletes use many different strategies, including exercising excessively, drastically reducing food intake, fasting for twenty-four hours, vomiting, taking laxatives or diuretics, and using enemas (Burckes-Miller & Black, 1988). The results of these efforts can be very damaging to the body. One study of male athletes found that 1.6 percent of the sample met the criteria for anorexia nervosa, and just over 14 percent were clinically bulimic (Burckes-Miller & Black, 1988). It should be noted that men in treatment for eating disorders generally do worse than do women (Swoap & Murphy, 1995).

Weight and body size issues are critical to men not only while they are performing but also after they "retire" from active competition. Some men who have bulked up are able to slim down to their presport weight. Others may stop exercising altogether but continue previous eating patterns and gain much extra weight. Either way, men are highly aware of the function, strength, agility, and appearance of their bodies.

Weight, however, is not the only body image issue for men. Strength is just as important. Machines devoted to building strength are located in many settings for boys and men—high school gyms, college recreational centers, athletic complexes, community health and fitness centers, even home basements. It is difficult to miss the message: strength is good. In most university athletic departments, there are lists of record holders for various weight-lifting categories (for example, bench press and squat). On some campuses, men who reach a certain level of strength have their picture taken as a group and make the posters available around town.

The emphasis on strength introduces a highly controversial topic: the use of anabolic-androgenic steroids. Although they are widely banned from competitive settings, men who want to maximize their efforts to increase muscle size and strength are often tempted to use anabolic-androgenic steroids. They can be taken orally or injected into muscles. Typically, boys and men who use these substances exceed the recommended dose by ten to one hundred times (Duchaine, 1989). The theory is that these substances prolong the presence of testosterone in the blood but without any other masculinizing effects (Winters, 1990). For a summary of what is known so far about the effects of anabolic-androgenic steroids on the body, see Bahrke and Yesalis (1993).

A related area that has received much attention is the use of substances that are more "natural" than anabolic-androgenic steroids, such as creatine kinase and androstenedione. Because these substances are not universally banned, they are highly recommended by coaches and trainers at many levels of competition. The argument runs, "It's natural and they haven't found anything wrong with it, so it must be alright." Manufacturers make strong claims about these substances. A one-hundred-milligram dose of androstenedione, for example, is said to increase testosterone levels by 300 percent; the effects are supposed to last for about three hours ("New 'roid," 1998). It is likely that more information about these substances will be discovered in time. The concern about the use of various "natural" substances to enhance performance is often reported in the news (see, for example, Dickey, Helmstaedt, Nordland, & Hayden, 1999). According to these reports, runners are tempted to use sodium bicarbonate to delay muscle fatigue; beta-blockers are thought to steady the hands of archers; and other substances are often tried by swimmers, skiers, tennis players, and shot-putters. These two body image issues—weight and strength—remain important for men through the life span.

Aging Issues

It is not only the young and competitive athletes who pay attention to body size and performance. In fact, many older men start exercise activities to change body shape, to lose weight, or to build more muscle.

One of the indications for men that they are beginning to age is a drop in athletic performance. Chronic injuries and aging simply slow the body down. And for many men, this drop in athletic performance becomes an immediate and very difficult sign that midlife has arrived. Sports activities become an unwelcome reminder of the passing of time or of the loss of physical skills. It can be a difficult transition to move from daily competitive basketball in college to other sports later in life. And yet this transition can be made, with great benefits for men.

We explored this issue by interviewing several men above the age of fifty. The story of Stan illustrates the challenges of continuing to be active as the body changes. When we talked with him, Stan was sixty-two. He had been very successful in his career as a university professor.

Stan described himself as extremely involved in sports during high school. He lettered in three different sports in a very large high school of four thousand students. The athletic program in his high school was successful, and teams in various sports had won several district and state championships. Stan recalled that his high school basketball team was unusually successful (with twenty-six wins and only one loss) and that seven members of that team went on to play college ball. Half the starters on the football team went to college on scholarships. Stan himself was good enough to be offered several college scholarships, and he was given a tryout with a Major League baseball team.

After playing basketball in college, Stan found his way back into very competitive athletic venues. He played volleyball, basketball, softball, and tennis at city and regional levels. He became a very successful amateur tennis player in a region that included several states. He also played on an international basketball team during his sabbatical overseas; his team made it to the final round in a tournament of one hundred teams.

Clearly, Stan found a way to remain active over the course of his life. He described several benefits: better physical health, stress relief ("it gets my endorphins going"), and sharpened leadership skills that he used in developing teamwork in his department or in inspiring students to produce good work.

As he got older, Stan confronted the fact that his body was changing. He had to undergo lung surgery. His knees weakened from the pounding over the years. Other aches and pains developed as a result of playing sports. But he decided that in the long run, his body responded better to exercise than to inactivity.

For counselors, Stan's story offers several pointers. If men have been actively competitive early in their lives, they are not likely to want to quit when they get into their fifties and sixties. Aging gracefully in sports may require adaptations, but growing older does not mean giving up competitive sports. These can become difficult decisions for older athletic men: Do they continue playing and risk further injury or deterioration of their bodies? Do they undergo hand surgery so that they can continue playing basketball? Do they find a different sport? Or do they quit competition altogether and start walking around the block? The body image implications of these questions are significant and often quite emotional in nature.

Competition

Researchers have struggled to define competition in psychological terms. One approach has been to see competition as behavior driven by the promise of rewards (Deutsch, 1973; Johnson, Maruyama, Johnson, Nelson, & Skon, 1981). From this perspective, competition is seen as the opposite of cooperation. With competition, the rewards can be divided up in limited ways. What one person wins, another loses. With cooperation, what one person wins, another can also win. The argument is that participation in competitive activities is driven by the desire to gain significant rewards.

Another approach has suggested that competition is primarily a social process. This perspective attempts to capture the experience of competing, the actual dynamic that operates during the competition. Martens's (1976) work defined competition as a process that compares a person's performance with some standard or criterion and required that this comparison be made in the presence of someone who could evaluate the activity. Similarly, Scanlan (1988) argued that competition is a process that involves social comparisons. These interactive comparisons begin early; children compare themselves with each other in many ways. People eventually compete in sports in order to compare themselves with others. The focus is not so much on the rewards but on the enjoyment of the processes. This approach has resulted in the development of several instruments designed to measure such things as competitive anxiety (Martens, 1977), achievement orientation (Gill, 1993), and other sport-specific issues (Martens, Vealey, & Burton, 1990; Vealey, 1986).

The competitive environment in organized sports settings can be intense and passionate. Spontaneous play in young boys very quickly gives way to an emphasis on winning. The joy of play is replaced by a focus on technique, strategy, practice, and other interests that increase the odds of winning.

The sayings and exhortations of coaches reinforce this atmosphere. Some of these dictums have been quoted so often that they have become cultural folklore and no longer need to be referenced. Think of how many times men have heard the words often attributed to football coach Vince Lombardi: "Winning isn't everything; it's the only thing." Although that line was apparently first used in the 1930s by Vanderbilt and University of California at Los Angeles coach Red

Sanders (Maraniss, 1999), it has become part of the Lombardi legend of toughness, courage, and extreme competitiveness. Most men who played competitive
sports can recall decades later similar sayings written on the walls of locker
rooms or the pet phrases coaches used to inspire them to work harder. Of
course, not every male athlete values these words after leaving competitive
sports. Note, for example, Sabo's (1980) personalized rewriting of Lombardi's
line: "Winning isn't everything; it is nothing." Nevertheless, while on the team,
coaches use these attitudes and beliefs to motivate young men.

Competition can be fierce, even among friends. A basketball team may have
a dozen players on the roster, but only five men can play at a time. Similar ratios
exist for football, soccer, and other team sports. The starting positions are filled
by those who have successfully competed against their teammates. So, before
a team ever plays its first game of the season, the players have engaged in some
intense competition.

Competition can influence friendships. A man may not want to get too emotionally close to another, because they might end up competing for a place on
the team. Lifelong friendships develop, of course, but they tend to be few (Sabo,
1980). Most of the friendships are associated with the team effort itself and tend
to weaken once the men are off the team.

Competitive values are a primary motive of parents in encouraging little boys
to begin playing team sports (Gould & Petlichkoff, 1988; Weiss & Chaumeton,
1992; Weiss & Petlichkoff, 1989). And in many ways, this emphasis is not surprising. Competitive sports offer an experience consistent with many themes in
North American culture: participating in a group effort to reach a goal, understanding the importance of rules and laws, expressing emotions in ways appropriate to the setting, discovering leadership skills, and learning to deal with both
winning and losing in life.

Competition for men can be a lifelong interest. Many cities have competitive
leagues for older men. The city of Topeka, Kansas, is typical of many cities of
modest size (150,000 population). Topeka has a fifty-plus softball league of
many teams (Anderson, 1999). Some concessions are made to age. Players are
not allowed to slide on the base paths. To avoid collisions at home plate, there
are two home plates—one for the runner and one for the catcher. Topeka is just
one of many cities involved in the U.S. Specialty Sports Association, a slow-
pitch program for older players. Started in the mid-1990s, the organization sanctioned six hundred teams nationally the first year. Five years later, the number
of teams was more than twenty-five hundred. Clearly, the opportunities for older
men to remain active in highly competitive sports are increasing.

Aggression and Violence Issues

The literature on aggression and sports is extensive. Literally hundreds of
research articles on this topic have been written since 1970. In many ways, the

concern with violence in sports reflects the larger concern with violence in North American society (Eitzen & Sage, 1989; M. D. Smith, 1983). It is an unresolved issue. Consider such controversial issues as gun registration, armed guards in high schools, the growing use of metal detectors in public buildings, loitering laws designed to lessen gang aggression, video games that emphasize aggression and violence, and the use of safety locks on guns. These issues generate more disagreement than agreement in the political arena, and some of these questions have reached the U.S. Supreme Court for review.

Several theories of aggression have implications for men in sports. Parens (1987) suggested that there is a difference between destructive aggression and nondestructive aggression. When it is destructive, aggression is hostile, nasty, hurtful, rageful, bullying, torturing, and vengeful, according to Parens. But when it is nondestructive, aggression is assertive, nonhostile, and focused on goal attainment and mastery.

It is often argued that violence is the physical side of aggression. But when does aggression in a game become violence? Some have defined violence during sports contests as behavior that intends to injure or hurt another player (Siann, 1985; M. D. Smith, 1983). Some argue that this type of violence is relatively rare (Anshel, 1990). Instead, what is often regarded as violence may instead be a very assertive playing style. Most sports offer examples of assertive playing: baseball pitchers who throw inside fastballs, wide receivers in football who throw downfield blocks, centers who throw elbows while blocking out in basketball, tennis players who use a serve and volley style, or volleyball players who use "kill" shots. These behaviors are not inherently violent but are aggressive because they do not violate the rules and their purpose is not necessarily to injure an opponent. Nevertheless, the line between aggression and violence in a game is often blurred, and aggressive play has sparked many of the brawls and fights that have occurred during games. Even when such violence occurs in the context of a game, prosecution by law enforcement seems to be a rare event.

Increasingly, the violence appears to be spreading beyond the game itself. Stories involving coaches, managers, parents, and other spectators have made the national news in North America. Some of the more widely covered stories have described a brawl involving fifty parents after a football game played by eleven- to thirteen-year-olds, a parent striking his son's hockey coach in the face with two hockey sticks, the father of another young hockey player killing a coach after the game by beating his head into the ground, the father of a soccer player punching a fourteen-year-old boy on the opposing team, and a baseball coach breaking the jaw of an umpire during a game for high school players (for details of these and other incidents, see Nack & Munson, 2000). Many of these cases end up in court, and convictions are no longer rare.

Explanations of aggression are many: that it is instinctual, that it is cathartic, that it is an expression of frustration, or that it is learned (see Thirer, 1993, for an overview of these theories). More specific to the purposes of this chapter, it has been argued that aggression is part of masculine socialization in this culture. In the mid-1970s, Brannon's "blueprint" for masculine socialization included "the aura of aggression, violence, and daring" as one of the four central themes in masculine socialization (David & Brannon, 1976). He called this theme "give 'em hell" and included several illustrations of socialized male aggression from sports.

Jeremy was a highly talented high school athlete who was offered a scholarship by several major universities. He enrolled in a university and showed many glimpses of his potential during his first two years. Fans and sportswriters talked about this young man as a "hero ready to emerge." However, at the end of his sophomore year, a sportswriter assessed Jeremy's performance on the team as "a disappointment" and then proceeded to blame him for the team's losses and severely criticized him for a lackluster performance. The sportswriter's language was highly derisive and sarcastic.

Jeremy felt very hurt by the public commentary on him and acted on his feelings by verbally challenging the sportswriter and then by physically attacking him off campus. Of course, the assault only brought more headlines, court charges, and disciplinary action by the university. Psychotherapy was mandated for him to deal with his aggressive feelings. The experience was so trying for Jeremy that he considered withdrawing and possibly transferring to another college to start over.

It is our experience that writers and talk-show sportscasters make very personal judgments about sports performers when they often know very little about the individual involved or the circumstances of an incident. Student athletes are truly living in a glass house and experience a level of personal scrutiny unknown to other students. Like other students, they go through a wide range of personal experimentation during their college years. But unlike other students, their experiences may end up being discussed in the media by people who have only a partial understanding of their lives.

Jeremy objected to being required to attend counseling. For him, it was more salt in the wound. He did not see himself as the problem but as a victim. And, in many ways, he was right. Intervention had to begin with establishing a supportive relationship, which was no easy task. And then the counselor tried to help Jeremy turn the experience into something more positive. Rather than "therapize" his situation, his counselor considered two approaches. The first was to suggest enrollment in a leadership class, so that Jeremy could begin to focus on ways to positively influence his teammates. And the other was a personalized workshop on how to interview and respond to the press. One outcome was that Jeremy reframed his anger and channeled it into a personal drive to "show up" the reporter who had publicly humiliated him. The result was evident over the next year, as he became an all-conference performer.

Jeremy's story highlights several questions about aggression. What is the connection between sports activities and off-field aggression? Is aggression in sports more acceptable than aggression outside sports? To what degree should aggression be channeled into sports? These are confusing questions to many young men in North America. On the one hand, aggression in sports is widely praised. To say that someone is "an aggressive linebacker" because he hits other players especially hard during a football game is to praise him. On the other hand, aggression by athletes can be condemned. Physically attacking a sportswriter is a violation of the law, and a player who does so is subject to arrest and prosecution. Why is aggression acceptable in one setting and prosecuted in another?

Another illustration of this confusion about aggression is the taunting or trash-talking controversy. A company began manufacturing T-shirts with trash-talking slogans on them such as "Your game is as ugly as your girl" and "You like that move? so does your girl." For a while, they were marketed by JCPenney, the large department store. When objections began appearing in the media, the department store pulled the shirts from its shelves ("Trash-talking," 1999). Aggressive talk on the basketball court has become part of the game in most places, but that very same language is regarded as offensive when it leaves the gym and shows up on boys' T-shirts.

Not all counselors, of course, have played competitive sports. In working with predoctoral psychology interns, we have found that counselors who never played sports can have a difficult time understanding the experience of aggression in sports. Counselors who fail to recognize and understand the significance of aggression in a male athlete's life will miss a central feature of his experience. Men who are drawn to active participation in competitive sports are drawn in part by the aggression inherent in these sports.

If you are a counselor who believes that aggression in sports is morally wrong, then we believe you are likely to have difficulty working effectively with men heavily involved with sports. Your values are going to clash sharply with theirs. Given that most presenting issues for male athletes are directly related to their involvement in sports, aggression is not likely to be an irrelevant issue in their counseling.

Sexual Assault and Harassment

One other point deserves much more attention than the scope of this chapter will allow. Sexual harassment and assault are terribly significant issues for male athletes. Accounts indicate that compared with other men, male athletes are particularly prone to commit sexual assault. Contributing factors may be male bonding and the macho image of sports (Gill, 1993; Lenskyj, 1992; Messner,

1992). Many universities have developed counseling or prevention programs for harassment and sexual violence issues (Guernsey, 1993) and have established various procedures for dealing with these incidents when they occur. The challenge in these programs is to teach male athletes how to avoid using aggression in their personal lives. Others have recommended that counselors become active in asking campus officials for better lighting, stronger and more enforceable policies, and more secure facilities (Gill, 1993).

Coaches as Surrogate Fathers

Although father issues are important for all athletes in some way (fathers living out their own dreams from youth in their sons, attending their sons' games, rewarding or punishing performance, wanting to make "men" out of their sons, and so forth), one aspect of the father-son relationship in sports deserves particular attention. Some African American males from urban areas face unusually difficult challenges. Many of these demands have been discussed in popular magazines such as *Sports Illustrated* (Wahl & Wertheim, 1998), *U.S. News & World Report* (Simons, 1997), and *Essence* (J. Amber, 1997).

It should be noted that many African American boys grow up in middle-class families and are not confronted with many of the challenges faced by African American boys in urban settings. The differences can be significant. African American boys from urban settings grow up in a world others find very difficult to grasp. Brown and A. Amber (1997) cite U.S. Census data suggesting that 91 percent of urban African American boys do not live with their fathers. That is not to say that these boys do not know their fathers or that they have no male role models at all; it simply indicates that the biological father is not a daily presence in the home. These boys are raised primarily by their mothers, by women in Head Start programs, by female elementary school teachers, and by various male figures in the extended family or neighborhood. The shortage of male role models in their daily lives often makes their high school coach (who is usually white) one of the first adult males they have known in this capacity. When this coach then talks about the possibilities available in sports, many boys listen. Their desire to be like a sports hero is often greater than their desire to be like their own fathers. A study conducted by Northeastern University's Center for the Study of Sport in Society indicated that about two-thirds of all African American boys between the ages of thirteen and eighteen believe that they can make a living as a professional athlete (Simons, 1997). The implications of these factors for counselors are enormous.

Some counseling programs are beginning to address the larger developmental issues involved in working with athletes who fit this particular profile— African American males who have grown up in urban settings without the daily presence of a father. One example is a program developed by Franklin (1997) that begins with a set of needs that are especially important to young urban men: the need to be loved and valued as a person; the need to belong to something larger than themselves; the need to feel competent; the need for power and control over one's own life; the need to resolve the pain, shame, and anger that come from a fatherless childhood through the sensitive engagement of a father figure; the need to find some meaning and purpose in spiritual values; and the need to find their own place in a diverse culture. Franklin argues that for most rural and suburban boys—in both African American and non–African American communities—the possibilities for meeting these needs are greater. But among certain African American young men from urban settings, these needs go largely unmet. Adult men simply are not a significant, prosocial presence in their lives. As a result, their normal developmental processes in these areas are "arrested," he contends.

E. B. Franklin (personal communication, July 28, 1999) suggests that the fifty-minute counseling hour cannot address these issues in a meaningful way because of deep-seated mistrust and misunderstanding directed toward authority figures outside the African American culture. Rather, he suggests a very different approach, in which the notion of traditional counseling does not even apply. Franklin works for professional football teams, providing not only workshops but also highly individualized mentoring in which he addresses the previously mentioned needs in young African American athletes. Spontaneously, many of the men he works with begin calling him Dad. Clearly, this moves him out of the role of a traditional counselor. Instead, he becomes more like a male role model and a social advocate. His model has been developed with one National Football League team and is now being explored by other professional teams.

INTERVENTIONS FOR MEN IN SPORTS SETTINGS

Counselors who work with men in sports settings may do so in either individual or group formats. The literature suggests that both approaches can be successful. In this section we review some of what is practiced in both areas.

Individual Counseling

We have found that most male athletes do not come to individual counselors on their own. Typically, they are referred by coaches or trainers concerned about performance. Common presenting issues include the emotional consequences of a physical injury, substance abuse problems, eating disorders, performance-inhibiting anxiety, attention and learning issues, and problems with motivation.

In educational settings, the referral source is usually the coach or someone associated with the athletic department. In professional settings, these issues are often addressed by psychologists affiliated with the team. About half the teams in the National Football League, for example, now include a team psychologist in their staff directory (Pasquarelli, 1999). Amateur and professional athletes also find counselors on their own when these issues need specialized attention.

Although it is beyond the scope of this chapter to provide full details of treatment protocols for these issues by individual counselors, we can offer some brief guidelines and resources for working with men around various sports-related issues.

Counseling men with injuries. Petitpas and Danish (1995) have summarized the literature that explores the psychological consequences athletes face when injured. These men may struggle with loss issues (shock, denial, and various mood disturbances). Their identity may be threatened. They may feel dejected about the goals that will be unmet or opportunities for the future that are lost. They may feel lonely, because they are separated from team practices and games. Doubts about fully recovering from the injury can develop. Self-confidence can plummet. Petitpas and Danish (1995) offer a series of symptoms that suggest an athlete might be adjusting poorly to the injury, including denial of the importance of the injury, exaggerated storytelling about past accomplishments, expressions of guilt about letting the team down, withdrawal from his social support network, rapid mood swings, and expressions of helplessness.

Treatment options for men with athletic injuries include attention-control training (Nideffer, 1995), biofeedback for muscle control (Crews, 1992; Gould & Udry, 1994; Zaichkowsky & Fuchs, 1989), goal setting while regaining strength or dexterity (Wiese & Weiss, 1987), imagery work (Gordon, 1986; King & Cook, 1987; Suinn, 1993), progressive relaxation (Jacobson, 1928), cognitive strategies for modifying unhelpful self-talk (Wiese & Weiss, 1987), and systematic desensitization (King & Cook, 1987).

Counseling male athletes with substance abuse problems. Most athletes use alcohol. Every four years, the National Collegiate Athletic Association (NCAA) examines alcohol and substance use patterns among athletes. In the most recent study (National Collegiate Athletic Association, 1997), it found that 80 percent of those who responded to the survey had used alcohol during the previous year. Similar rates have been found for high school athletes (92 percent using alcohol) (Carr, Kennedy, & Dimick, 1990). This latter study also found higher rates of use among male athletes than male nonathletes and higher rates of intoxication. Similar rates of alcohol usage have been found in elite athletes (90 percent using in the previous year) (Carr, 1992).

Drinking patterns for male athletes differ from those of other men. One study of 140 university campuses found that among male students who were not in athletics, 43 percent had been involved with binge drinking in the previous two weeks, whereas 61 percent of the male athletes had binged—a nearly 50 percent increase. A binge was defined as five drinks in a row (Weschsler,

Davenport, Dowdall, Grossman, & Zanakos, 1996). Drinking for athletes appears to increase during the off-season. A study on one large campus found a significant increase in the percentage of male athletes who drank at least once a week during the off-season as compared to the percentage who drank during the season; the rate went from 42 percent to 60 percent during the off-season, an increase of about 50 percent (Selby, Weinstein, & Bird, 1990).

Male athletes use illicit drugs less frequently than alcohol. According to studies of university athletes, about a third have used marijuana in the previous year, and less than 20 percent have tried cocaine (National Collegiate Athletic Association, 1985, 1997). About 20 percent use smokeless tobacco, and 3 percent acknowledge the use of amphetamines.

An obvious question is why? Why do male athletes use alcohol and other substances in often abusive ways? Heyman (1986) has suggested two answers: the pressure from peers and sensation seeking. Another suggestion is the influence of advertising (Griffin, 1985). Athletes themselves report that they use for social or recreational reasons (endorsing the idea that "it makes me feel good") or because they believe that they experience higher levels of stress than do nonathletes (National Collegiate Athletic Association, 1997).

Several educational programs have been developed for athletes at risk for developing dependency on alcohol or other substances. Designed mostly for those who have problems but are still functioning, these programs are relatively short in duration. Most athletes have very full schedules, and even something as important as an alcohol or drug education intervention needs to be scheduled around team meetings, practices, and games.

Carr and Murphy (1995) have developed a three-session educational program for athletes at the U.S. Olympic Training Center in Colorado Springs. Each session lasts two and a half hours. They offer an education component (prevalence data, pharmacological effects, nutrition, and symptoms of abuse and dependency), a decision-making and coping skills component (stress management, assertiveness training, role playing, and decision-making skills), and a social skills and self-esteem component (values clarification).

Similar programs have been developed for university athletes. One widely used program was developed by Boosting Alcohol Consciousness Concerning the Health of University Students (BACCHUS), an international organization of university-based peer education programs that focuses on alcohol abuse issues, among other concerns. It has joined the NCAA in developing the Student Athletes as Peer Educators Training Program. It offers a video, a facilitator manual, and work sheets for participants (http://www.linkmag.com/bacchus/).

Counselors at some universities tailor educational programs to individuals at risk. One typical approach (Arck, 1999) is a three-session program for any athlete who has been identified as having potential alcohol or drug problems. In the first session, the athlete is given an assessment that identifies in detail the man's drinking patterns, his attitudes toward drinking, his family history with regard to substance use, and any personal problems that he might be facing. This assessment information is then used in preparing for the second session, which is organized from a series of possible modules on such topics as the effects of substance use on athletic performance (for example, reaction time, strength reduction, attention loss, and sound recognition), prevalence information, risks for aggression, or when to avoid alcohol (for example, when hungry, angry, lonely, or tired). This information is presented via videos, handouts, and personal conversation. The third session focuses on intervention strategies. Various approaches may be recommended, including anxiety control, anger management, responsible drinking practices, alcohol intake monitoring, journaling, diet and nutrition concerns, and family interaction issues. When appropriate, the athlete is referred for ongoing psychotherapy. These sessions are "confidential" in the sense that nobody in the athlete's life is told about any information discussed in the three sessions; the athlete signs a release giving permission for a letter verifying attendance to be sent to the athletic department when attendance at these three sessions is mandated.

The educational programs identified in this section are designed more as prevention and education strategies than as detailed treatment protocols. Counselors are likely to know about resources in their own areas for the treatment of alcohol and substance use.

Counseling male athletes with eating disorders. Given that athletes must push their bodies to perform at high levels, it is perhaps not surprising to learn that eating and weight issues are problematic for many male athletes. Research has demonstrated that eating problems severe enough to warrant a clinical diagnosis are more common among athletes than among nonathletes (Burckes-Miller & Black, 1988; Thornton, 1990).

Athletes have been surveyed in a search for explanations for the higher incidence of eating problems (Guthrie, 1986). Results suggest that a variety of factors are involved, including the demands of a particular sport to meet weight, strength, or aesthetic expectations; pressure from coaches to meet certain criteria during training; poor eating habits while traveling for games; fear of not being able to play because of not meeting a weight requirement stipulated by a coach; and the pressure from peers who ridicule an athlete's height, weight, or appearance. Although men do not suffer from these issues as frequently as do women, the rates are much higher than might be imagined (Burckes-Miller & Black, 1988).

The implications are clear. Counselors working with male athletes need to ask about eating patterns or concerns. These questions should be part of the counselor's standard assessment when talking with a male athlete of any age. Given the reluctance of many athletes to volunteer problems in these areas, it is well worth asking about these matters as a standard practice.

Once identified, treatment recommendations or referrals can proceed in ways familiar to counselors, ranging from individual therapy (addressing power issues, athletic pressure, assertiveness, negative self-talk, restricted emotional expressions, and possible medication), group therapy (with the added benefits that come from peer support), family therapy (when the man is still closely tied to his parents), and inpatient treatment that involves medical as well as psychological treatment for severe cases (Swoap and Murphy, 1995).

Counseling male athletes with performance-inhibiting anxiety. Anxiety in sports settings can be stimulated by many variables. Sports carry the risk of injury, which creates the possibility not only of pain and the cost of recovery but also of the loss of playing time. In addition, male athletes can get caught in intense struggles with coaches over playing time, training habits, or injury recovery behavior. Anxiety can also come from conflicts with other players on a team. These conflicts may be focused on competition for positions, ethnic conflicts, or other personality variables. Some roles in sports carry the added pressure of making decisions quickly during a contest, decisions that involve other players on the team and the outcome of the game.

Anxiety can be caused by other factors as well. The reactions of spectators can be anxiety provoking, especially when tens of thousands of people express their displeasure at a particular move by an athlete. Some sports require acceptance of high risk simply to perform them—rock climbing, bungee jumping, parachute jumping, auto and cycle racing, and contact team sports such as lacrosse, hockey, football, basketball, and baseball. Athletes who cross international boundaries may experience stress and anxiety as they face unfamiliar languages, foods, and customs.

Psychological theories about anxiety have been available in the literature for a long time (Cattell & Scheier, 1961; Spielberger, 1966). Theories that define anxiety more specifically for athletes are also readily available (Hackfort, 1986, 1990). Anxiety seems to have both cognitive components (consider the self-talk of a short-distance runner just before the race) and emotional factors (the physiological changes that come with anxiety, for example).

Counselors can assess anxiety by using both cognitive and physiological measures. Examples of accessible instruments that measure the cognitive variables include the revised Minnesota Multiphasic Personality Inventory (MMPI-2) (Butcher, Dahlstrom, Graham, Tellegen, & Kaemmer, 1989), the Manifest Anxiety Scale (Taylor, 1953), and the State-Trait Anxiety Inventory (Spielberger, Gorsuch, & Lushene, 1970). Physiological indicators of anxiety include respiratory, cardiovascular, biochemical, and electrophysiological functions (see Hackfort & Schwenkmezger, 1995), and changes in these areas can be measured by easily available biofeedback equipment.

Treatments for sports-related anxiety are often adaptations of strategies described and illustrated more generally for anxiety. Counselors have used versions of systematic desensitization (Wolpe, 1958), in which the athlete first learns to relax, then moves mentally through an anxiety hierarchy of events, and finally applies the technique in real-life situations. A modification of this approach includes cognitive restructuring. The athlete may be taught to remember his own strengths, for example, thus allowing him to become more self-reliant and self-controlled as he performs (Hackfort & Schwenkmezger, 1995).

Biofeedback training enables an athlete to become aware of the significance of his heart rate, blood pressure, respiratory frequency, muscle tension, brain waves, and other indicators of anxiety. Using visual or auditory cues provided by the equipment enables him to monitor and then regulate his physiological indicators of anxiety, typically in a laboratory setting (Crews, 1992; Gould & Udry, 1994). Some researchers are currently exploring the use of biofeedback equipment during actual athletic activities.

Another approach to anxiety management is to focus on the cognitions and images that accompany sports activities. The connection between language and motor behavior has been asserted for quite some time (Luria, 1961). For athletes, the task is to develop a mental exercise that accompanies the physical exercises for the sport. These cognitions and images then increase confidence in one's performance, thereby reducing anxiety (Mahoney & Meyers, 1989; Paivio, 1971). R. E. Smith (1989) has developed a program that combines both cognitive and somatic strategies (cognitive restructuring, self-instructional training, and relaxation skills).

Other approaches suggested for the management of athletic anxiety include meditation in various forms, especially transcendental meditation (Layman, 1978), muscle relaxation (Bernstein & Borhovec, 1973; Poppen, 1988), muscle stretching (Carlson, Collins, Nitz, Sturgis, & Rogers, 1990), and sustained vigorous exercise (Morgan, 1987).

Counseling male athletes with attention and learning problems. Athletes can experience attention problems in several ways. For example, they may find it difficult to maintain alertness in their sport. Events happen quickly in most sports, so when an athlete finds that he was not highly alert at the right moment, his performance suffers. Think of the football player not ready for the snap of the ball or the hurdler who misses the starting gun. Attention is also a problem for men who struggle to filter out unwanted or unnecessary information so that they can remain focused on their roles. Illustrations include basketball or hockey players who find themselves noticing the crowd sounds and miss their assignment in an offensive pattern. Coaches sometimes complain about attention problems when they are trying to explain complex plays on the chalkboard. Some athletes find it difficult to sustain attention long enough to adequately master the information being presented.

Abernathy's (1993) lengthy review of the literature on attention offers several practical suggestions for working with attention problems in sports. When the attentional problem is difficulty in maintaining arousal at critical times, biofeedback training may be helpful. Suppressing electroencephalogram theta waves, which are often related to low arousal states, has been shown to be help-ful in some settings (Beatty, Greenberg, Deibler, & O'Hanlon, 1974). Not every counselor has access to this equipment, however. Other strategies that may help men sustain attention include breaking larger tasks down into smaller ones or providing natural breaks from attention to prevent boredom. Examples include giving the athlete something constructive to do between plays in the action, such as something encouraging or affirming to think about, a quick relaxation exercise, or positive self-talk about his role or assignment (Magill, 1989).

When the problem is an inability to filter out unimportant stimuli, one solu-tion may be to practice the task in the midst of distracting sounds or sights. It is common knowledge among those who follow team sports that teams prac-tice to the sounds of extremely loud crowd noises before performing in an arena or stadium where the sounds may confuse some players. There is some evi-dence that athletes who practice their attention-switching skills may benefit from this approach (Allport, 1980). Another approach is to emphasize the devel-opment of dual-task performance skills. Adding secondary tasks to an athlete's primary task in practice settings may improve his attentional skills (Spelke, Hirst, & Neisser, 1976), as may breaking complex tasks down into smaller ones so that they can become automatic (Magill, 1989).

Another factor that influences attention is learning style. On our campus, we have found it helpful to assess a student athlete's learning style by using estab-lished instruments. One is the Learning Style Inventory, which evaluates how people learn and "deal with ideas and day-to-day situations" (Kolb, 1993, p. 2). A second instrument is the College Learning Effectiveness Inventory (Newton, 1997), which measures six psychosocial factors that influence a student's learn-ing effectiveness (Wilcox & Johnson, 1996). The purpose for using learning style instruments is to enable a student athlete to make adjustments in his learning activities and study planning. We have found that many athletes learn more by doing than by reading, more by experiencing than by analysis. That is, they can "listen and copy" easier than they can "read and memorize." An athlete with this learning style is more likely to succeed by studying in groups or organizing question competitions than by studying alone.

Counseling males with motivation issues. In conventional language, motiva-tion in athletics describes the desire to perform. When motivation is high, ath-letes practice longer, take more risks, gather more information, and feel more highly aroused to compete. When motivation is low, these variables are less appealing.

Psychologists have developed several detailed theories of motivation. Fifty years ago, McClelland and others (McClelland, 1961; McClelland, Atkinson, Clark, & Lowell, 1953) argued that there are two motive states in people—the motive to achieve success and the motive to avoid failure. These two constructs interact with the emotional responses of pride and shame, which then influence behavior. A decade later, social learning theory argued that the expectation of reinforcement was central in motivation and that we are driven by the need for approval from others. When the expectation of approval is high, we are more highly motivated (Crandall, 1963, 1969).

More recently, the focus has shifted to cognition. Motivation is now often thought to begin with thoughts, which then influence behavior. Researchers have examined several thought patterns theorized to motivate behavior, including thoughts about competence (Klint & Weiss, 1987), the achievement of goals (Duda, 1992), or attributions for success or failure (McAuley & Duncan, 1990).

The work of Ames (1984, 1992) implies that motivation can be improved by focusing on the motivational climate in which a person functions. Research has been conducted on children in school settings. Researchers have found that when the expectations from teachers or coaches to achieve are direct and explicit and when the rewards are significant, children develop motivation. Central to this perspective is the notion of mastery. As young people master a behavior, they likely become more motivated to perform it. For example, Ames and her colleagues found that when students focused on mastery, their motivation improved—that is, they exerted more effort, chose more challenging tasks, liked their class more, and developed the belief that their efforts contributed to success (Ames & Archer, 1990).

This work has implications for boys and men in sports. It is our experience that most coaches of boys emphasize a competitive environment more than a mastery environment. The focus is on the few who win, not the many who try. Boys who are exceptional athletes become more motivated than others to improve. Nevertheless, it is intriguing to wonder how these two approaches (competition and mastery) might be combined. Is it possible to design many smaller mastery tasks in a much larger competitive environment? Does the successful repetition of individual skills within a sport make motivation in the competitive environment higher? The research seems to support this possibility. Coaches who work with young boys might improve motivation by focusing on short-term goals and by emphasizing the mastery of new skills. As the boys learn these skills, they can be rewarded for their learning. This awareness of personal improvement appears to have a direct bearing on motivation (Evans & Roberts, 1987; Roberts, 1993).

Workshops and Classes for Student Athletes

Evidence exists that many traditional men prefer classes and workshops to individual counseling (see Robertson, 1992). This appears to be especially true for men involved in athletics. Several examples of group and class protocols for various topics exist in the literature (see, for example, Carr, 1992; National Collegiate Athletic Association, 1998). In this section, we highlight two programs not described elsewhere in the literature.

Performance enhancement. On our university campus, we offer a program called Performance Enhancement Training. The program includes thirty hours of structured activities designed to give male student athletes an in-depth exposure to various mental improvement strategies. The program is offered as a class for which students receive academic credit. Like other classes it meets in a blocked time each week. The credit and regularity provide incentives to students to follow through with commitments of time and energy. The athletes who enroll come from a variety of sports, including football, baseball, basketball, golf, tennis, and track.

We call the program Performance Enhancement Training because this phrase emphasizes a familiar and significant theme for competitive athletes—the need to improve to meet higher levels of performance. We broaden the scope of the class, however, to talk about the importance of applying these strategies to academic activities and other areas of a student athlete's life.

The format uses both process and content learning models. The process portion is organized around a thorough self-assessment program that identifies personal characteristics, strengths, and limitations. Using various checklists, this assessment addresses learning styles, leadership tendencies, stress management skills, personality style, physiological responsiveness (using biofeedback equipment), study habits and patterns, athletic abilities, communication skills, motivation, and career interests.

An important feature of the program is the requirement that students translate their assessments into something visual—pictures, graphs, or other creative expressions. The purpose is to give them an opportunity to conceptualize and integrate the findings of their personalized assessment and to present it in ways that peers can understand. Students then use these findings to develop a set of personal goals.

The next step is to develop action plans designed to help them reach their individual goals. These plans include writing measurable objectives, selecting specific activities to move them toward their objectives, developing ways of monitoring their progress, and choosing incentives that function as rewards.

The content portion of the course introduces themes that focus on performance (Gallwey, 1977; Niednagel, 1997). Topics include the use of visualization and mental rehearsal, motivational strategies, use of self-regulation for altering physiological arousal levels, time management, focus and attention skills, cooperative team behavior, the importance of nonverbal behavior, overcoming self-defeating attitudes, and many other issues. The purpose of these theme sessions is to demonstrate particular strategies that can then be applied in more depth through personalized plans. One of the major assignments for the content portion of the class is to research areas of interest in the library and then present and demonstrate the findings to fellow students.

Because the course results in a personalized plan to achieve specified outcomes, it has been fairly easy to chart how well students have done. For example, one basketball player outlined a plan to improve his rebounding capability. The plan outlined steps that he would take both in practice and in games, with a goal that defined the results he anticipated. He implemented the plan over a five-month period and demonstrated a 20 percent increase in the number of rebounds per game. This improvement placed him among the top three rebounders in a major athletic conference.

In a recent class, twenty-three scholar athletes developed plans to improve their academic performance. Indicators of their successes were significant. Over the next two years 73 percent of them remained in school (with only one leaving for academic reasons), a figure that is encouraging when compared with an overall graduation rate of 45 percent for all students. Further, the group demonstrated a combined increase in overall grade point average of 0.6 (from 2.07 to 2.63).

A further benefit of the class is that it breaks down some of the inhibitions that many students have in seeking counseling for personal or performance concerns. A large portion of these students (well over half) return in one way or another to seek advice, counsel, or referral information.

This program has been developed for university student athletes. However, it is our view that many of these concepts could be adapted easily for other groups of men. Teams of various kinds, summer camp programs that emphasize athletics, and other programs for boys and men could include many of these strategies under the performance enhancement heading.

Leadership training. Coaches often complain that they never have enough leaders on their teams. At the same time, it must be acknowledged that boys often find it difficult to learn leadership from team settings, because their parents and coaches make nearly all the decisions. For example, a group of excited ten-year-old boys organized a pregame pizza party the night before their very first game. The parents thought that the boys had a good idea and decided to formalize it. They organized a party before every game. They circulated a schedule that detailed responsibilities for hosting, food selection, and costs. What started as an idea led by the boys themselves became a program led by their parents.

An example of a university-based group format for male athletes is the Leadership Training Seminar. Developed by Newton, Rathbun, and Arck (1999), this seminar is an intensive experience offered as a credit course during two-week intercessions (between semesters) on campus. Although the seminar is open to any student wishing to register through a continuing education program, it is often recommended to students who are athletes.

The objectives of the seminar include understanding and applying knowledge in several areas: group dynamics, leadership styles, team interactions, intergroup communication, teamwork, motivation, and task accomplishment. The course emphasizes group experiential activities and an active process discussion of the activities. Assignments are completed by group cooperation.

A sample activity is the completion of the Outdoor Physical Initiatives Course. This course is an adaptation of the type of group training offered in wilderness settings (Schroeder, 1976). Students move through a series of challenges to test their personal behavior within a team context. One task is for a group of eight to ten students to climb up and over the Y in a sturdy tree about fifteen feet from the ground. After providing basic instructions on safety and outlining ground rules (such as once you are over the Y you can no longer touch or assist other teammates), the strategies and individual responsibilities are up to the team to determine within a time limit. At the end of the activity, the group discusses what happened and how each individual experienced the event. The learning in these discussions can be significant. To illustrate, one very athletic man with an army training background asserted that he knew the best way to master the climb and promptly demonstrated it by hurtling himself over the Y. Only then did he realize that by reaching the goal he had eliminated himself from being part of the team effort to get weaker members over the limb. The team had to deal with his "showing-off" behavior, by which he had given up his service to the team.

Traditional masculinity themes are especially significant for men in sports. These themes include the importance of winning and losing, the significance of competition with other men, the development of a personal identity, the relationship of sports to career, their attitudes toward their bodies, their experiences with aggression, and any relationships with their fathers. Although masculinity is not likely to be identified as the presenting problem, these issues are certainly in the background for most concerns brought to counselors. More likely to be presented are issues related to athletic performance: the impact of injuries on their emotions, their cognitions, or their futures; substance abuse problems; eating issues, including concerns about strength or weight; performance anxiety; attention and learning problems; and motivation.

We have reviewed some of the suggestions in the literature for working with these issues in both individual and group formats. We have presented this information because we believe that it is important to address these issues at face value for men who are athletic. When a man presents an athletic performance issue to a counselor, he wants specific help with that issue. Even so, his underlying ideas about masculinity are critically important. When these ideas negatively affect his health, his relationships, or his career, we believe that it is essential for the counselor to explore these gender issues openly with him.

References

Abernathy, A. (1993). Attention. In R. N. Singer, M. Murphey, & L. K. Tennant (Eds.), *Handbook of research on sport psychology* (pp. 127–171). New York: Macmillan.

Allport, D. A. (1980). Attention and performance. In G. Claxton (Ed.), *New directions in cognitive psychology* (pp. 112–153). London: Routledge & Kegan Paul.

Amber, J. (1997). The many ways of looking at a black man. *Essence, 28*(7), 87–126, 184–189.

Ames, C. (1984). Competitive, cooperative, and individualistic goal structures: A cognitive-motivational analysis. In R. Ames & C. Ames (Eds.), *Research on motivation in education: Vol. 1. Student motivation* (pp. 177–208). New York: Academic Press.

Ames, C. (1992). The relationship of achievement goals to student motivation in classroom settings. In G. C. Roberts (Ed.), *Motivation in sport and exercise* (pp. 161–176). Champaign, IL: Human Kinetics.

Ames, C., & Archer, J. (1990). *Longitudinal effects of mastery goal strategies on student learning strategies and motivation.* Unpublished manuscript, University of Illinois, Champaign, IL.

Anderson, R. (1999, July 1). Slow pitch "gray leagues" come of age. *The Topeka Capital-Journal,* p. B1.

Anshel, M. H. (1990). *Sport psychology: From theory to practice.* Scottsdale, AZ: Gorsuch Scarisbrick.

Arck, W. (1999). *Psycho-educational program for student-athletes at risk for the misuse of alcohol and other substances.* (Available from Alcohol and Other Drug Education Service, Lafene 232, Kansas State University, Manhattan, KS 66506)

Bahrke, M. S., & Yesalis, C. E. (1993). Psychological/behavioral effects of anabolic-androgenic steroids. In R. N. Singer, M. Murphey, & L. K. Tennant (Eds.), *Handbook of research on sport psychology* (pp. 877–890). New York: Macmillan.

Beatty, J., Greenberg, A., Deibler, W. P., & O'Hanlon, J. P. (1974). Operator control of occipital theta rhythm affects performance in a radar monitoring task. *Science, 183,* 871–873.

Bernstein, D. A., & Borhovec, T. D. (1973). *Progressive relaxation training.* Champaign, IL: Research Press.

Brannon, R. (1976). The male sex role: Our culture's blueprint for manhood and what it's done for us lately. In D. S. David & R. Brannon (Eds.), *The forty-nine percent majority: The male sex role.* New York: Random House.

Brown, K., & Amber, A. (1997). The *Essence* dialogue: Do our children need fathers? *Essence, 28*(7), 82.

Burckes-Miller, M. E., & Black, D. R. (1988). Male and female college athletes: Prevalence of anorexia nervosa and bulimia nervosa. *Athletic Training, 23,* 137–140.

Butcher, J. N., Dahlstrom, W. G., Graham, J. R., Tellegen, A., & Kaemmer, B. (1989). *Minnesota Multiphasic Personality Inventory (MMPI-2): Manual for administration and scoring.* Minneapolis: University of Minnesota Press.

Cannon, A., Streisand, B., & McGraw, D. (1999, May 3). Why teens kill. *U.S. News & World Report, 126,* 16–19.

Carlson, C. R., Collins, F. L., Jr., Nitz, A. J., Sturgis, E. T., & Rogers, J. L. (1990). Muscle stretching as an alternative relaxation training procedure. *Journal of Behavior Therapy and Experimental Psychiatry, 21,* 29–38.

Carr, C. M. (1993). Substance abuse education with athletes (Doctoral dissertation, University of Michigan, 1993). *Dissertation Abstracts International, 53*(7-A), 2244–2255.

Carr, C. M., Kennedy, R., Sr., & Dimick, K. M. (1990). Alcohol use and abuse among high school athletes: A comparison of alcohol use and intoxication in male and female high school athletes and non-athletes. *Journal of Alcohol and Drug Education, 36*(1), 39–45.

Carr, C. M., & Murphy, S. M. (1995). Alcohol and drugs in sport. In S. M. Murphy (Ed.), *Sport psychology interventions* (pp. 283–306). Champaign, IL: Human Kinetics.

Cattell, R. B., & Scheier, J. H. (1961). *The meaning and measurement of neuroticism and anxiety.* New York: Ronald Press.

Crandall, V. C. (1963). Achievement. In H. W. Stevenson (Ed.), *Child psychology* (pp. 416–459). Chicago: University of Chicago Press.

Crandall, V. C. (1969). Sex differences in expectancy of intellectual and academic reinforcement. In C. P. Smith (Ed.), *Achievement-related motives in children* (pp. 11–45). New York: Academic Press.

Crews, D. J. (1992). Psychological state and running economy. *Medicine and Science in Sports and Exercise, 24*(4), 475–482.

Danish, S. J., Petitpas, A., & Hale, B. D. (1995). Psychological interventions: A life development model. In S. M. Murphy (Ed.), *Sport psychology interventions* (pp. 21–38). Champaign, IL: Human Kinetics.

David, D. S., & Brannon, R. (1976). *The forth-nine percent majority: The male sex role.* New York: Random House.

Deutsch, M. (1973). The resolution of conflict: Constructive and destructive processes. New Haven, CT: Yale University Press.

Dickey, C., Helmstaedt, K., Nordland, R., & Hayden, T. (1999, February 15). The real scandal. *Newsweek,* pp. 48–54.

Duchaine, D. (1989). *Underground steroid handbook II.* Venice, CA: HLR Technical Books.

Duda, J. L. (1992). Motivation in sport settings: A goal perspective approach. In G. C. Roberts (Ed.), *Motivation in sport and exercise* (pp. 57–91). Champaign, IL: Human Kinetics.

Eitzen, D. S., & Sage, G. H. (1989). *Sociology of North American sport.* Dubuque, IA: W. C. Brown.

Evans, J., & Roberts, G. C. (1987). Physical competence and the development of children's peer relations. *Quest, 39,* 23–35.

Franklin, E. B. (1997). As the world turns: The shifting developmental issues facing today's college man, part 2 (African American men). *Campus Activities Programming, 30*(2), 60–75.

Gallwey, W. T. (1977). *Inner skiing.* New York: Random House.

Gill, D. L. (1993). Competitiveness and competitive orientation in sport. In R. Singer, M. Murphey, & L. Tennant (Eds.), *Handbook of research on sport psychology* (pp. 314–327). New York: Macmillan.

Gordon, S. (1986). Sport psychology and the injured athlete: A cognitive-behavioral approach to injury response and injury rehabilitation. *Science Periodical on Research and Technology in Sports, 3,* 1–10.

Gould, D., & Petlichkoff, L. M. (1988). Participation motivation and attrition in young athletes. In F. Smoll, R. Magill, & M. Ash (Eds.), *Children in sport* (3rd ed., pp. 161–178). Champaign, IL: Human Kinetics.

Gould, D., & Udry, E. (1994). Psychological skills for enhancing performance: Arousal regulation strategies. *Medicine and Science in Sports and Exercise, 26*(4), 478–485.

Griffin, T. M. (1985). *Paying the price.* Minneapolis, MN: Hazelden Foundation.

Guernsey, L. (1993, February 10). More campuses offer rape-prevention programs for male athletes. *Chronicle of Higher Education,* pp. A35, A37.

Guthrie, S. R. (1986). The prevalence and development of eating disorders within a selected intercollegiate athlete population (Doctoral dissertation, Ohio State University, 1985). *Dissertation Abstracts International, 46,* 3649A.

Hackfort, D. (1986). Theoretical conception and assessment of sport-related anxiety. In C. D. Spielberger & R. Diaz-Guerrero (Eds.), *Cross-cultural anxiety* (Vol. 3, pp. 79–91). Washington, DC: Hemisphere.

Hackfort, D. (1990). Self and social perception of sport-related trait anxiety. In C. D. Spielberger & R. Diaz-Guerrero (Eds.), *Cross-cultural anxiety* (Vol. 4, pp. 123–131). Washington, DC: Hemisphere.

Hackfort, D., & Schwenkmezger, P. (1995). Anxiety. In R. N. Singer, M. Murphey, & L. K. Tennant (Eds.), *Handbook of research on sport psychology* (pp. 328–364). New York: Macmillan.

Heyman, S. R. (1986, Summer). Psychological problem patterns found with athletes. *Clinical Psychologist, 39* (3), 68–71.

Hutchinson, M. (1985). *Transforming body image: Learning to love the body you have.* Freedom, CA: Crossing Press.

Jacobson, E. (1928). *Progressive relaxation.* Chicago: University of Chicago Press.

Johnson, D. W., Maruyama, G., Johnson, R., Nelson, D., & Skon, L. (1981). The effects of cooperative, competitive, and individualistic goal structures on achievement: A meta-analysis. *Psychological Bulletin, 89,* 47–62.

King, N. J., & Cook, D. L. (1987). Helping injured athletes cope and recover. *First Aider, 3,* 10–11.

Klint, K. A., & Weiss, M. R. (1987). Perceived competence and motives for participating in youth sports: A test of Harter's competence motivation theory. *Journal of Sport Psychology, 9,* 55–65.

Kolb, D. A. (1993). *Learning style inventory* (version 3). Boston: Hay/McBer.

Layman, E. (1978). McCloy: Meditation and sports performance. In W. F. Straub (Ed.), *Sport psychology: An analysis of athlete behavior* (pp. 169–176). New York: Mouvement Publications.

Lenskyj, H. (1992). Unsafe at home base: Women's experiences of sexual harassment in university sport and physical education. *Women in Sport and Physical Activity Journal, 1,* 19–33.

Luria, A. (1961). The role of speech in the regulation of normal and abnormal behaviors. New York: Liveright.

Magill, R. A. (1989). *Motor learning: concepts and applications* (3rd ed.). Dubuque, IA: W. C. Brown.

Mahoney, M. J., & Meyers, A. W. (1989). Anxiety and athletic performance: Traditional and cognitive-developmental perspectives. In D. Hackfort & C. D. Spielberger (Eds.), *Anxiety in sports* (pp. 77–94). Washington, DC: Hemisphere.

Maraniss, D. (1999). *When pride still mattered.* New York: Simon & Schuster.

Martens, R. (1976). Competition: In need of a theory. In D. M. Landers (Ed.), *Social problems in athletics* (pp. 9–17). Urbana: University of Illinois Press.

Martens, R. (1977). *Sport competition anxiety test.* Champaign, IL: Human Kinetics.

Martens, R., Vealey, R. S., & Burton, D. (1990). *Competitive anxiety in sport.* Champaign, IL: Human Kinetics.

McAuley, E., & Duncan, T. (1990). The causal attribution process in sport and physical activity. In S. Graham & V. S. Folkes (Eds.), *Attribution theory: Applications to achievement, mental health, and interpersonal conflict* (pp. 37–53). Hillsdale, NJ: Erlbaum.

McClelland, D.C. (1961). *The achieving society.* New York: Free Press.

McClelland, D.C., Atkinson, J. W., Clark, R. A., & Lowell, E. W. (1953). *The achievement motive.* New York: Appleton-Century-Crofts.

Messner, M. A. (1992). Power at play: Sports and the problem of masculinity. Boston: Beacon Press.

Mintz, L. B., & Betz, N. E. (1988). Prevalence and correlates of eating disordered behaviors among undergraduate women. *Journal of Counseling Psychology, 35,* 463–471.

Morgan, W. P. (1987). Reduction of state anxiety following acute physical activity. In W. P. Morgan & S. E. Golston (Eds.), *Exercise and mental health* (pp. 105–109). Washington, DC: Hemisphere.

Nack, W., & Munson, L. (2000, July 24). Out of control. *Sports Illustrated, 93*(4), 86–95.

National Collegiate Athletic Association, Drug Education Committee. (1985). *Drugs, the coach, and the athlete.* Overland Park, KS: Author.

National Collegiate Athletic Association. (1997). *1997 study of substance use and abuse habits of college student-athletes.* Research Ann Arbor Staff; University of Michigan.

National Collegiate Athletic Association. (1998). *NCAA CHAMPS/life skills program* [On-line]. Available: http://www.ncaa.org/news/19980601/active/3522n29.html

New 'roid is all the rage. (1998, September 8). *The Manhattan Mercury,* p. B1.

Newton, F. (1997). *The college learning effectiveness inventory.* (Available from F. N. Newton, University Counseling Services, Kansas State University, Manhattan, KS 66506)

Newton, F., Rathbun, A., & Arck, W. (1999). *Leadership training seminar syllabus.* (Available from F. N. Newton, University Counseling Services, Kansas State University, Manhattan, KS 66506)

Nideffer, R. N. (1995). Attention control training. In R. N. Singer, M. Murphey, & L. K. Tennant (Eds.), *Handbook of research on sport psychology* (pp. 542–556). New York: Macmillan.

Niednagel, J. P. (1997). *Your key to sports success.* Laguna, CA: Laguna Press.

O'Neil, J. M. (1981). Male sex role conflicts, sexism, and masculinity: Psychological implications for men, women, and the counseling psychologist. *The Counseling Psychologist, 9*(2), 61–80.

Orbach, S. (1988). Hunger strike: The anorectic's struggle as a metaphor for our age. New York: Avon.

Paivio, A. (1971). *Imagery and verbal processes.* New York: Holt, Rinehart & Winston.

Parens, H. (1987). *Aggression in our children.* Northvale, NJ: Jason Aronson.

Pasquarelli, L. (1999, July 4). Athlete's worst nightmare when sharp skills vanish. *The Manhattan Mercury,* p. B1.

Petitpas, A., & Danish, S. J. (1995). Caring for injured athletes. In S. M. Murphy (Ed.), *Sport psychology interventions* (pp. 255–281). Champaign, IL: Human Kinetics.

Pleck, J. H. (1987). *The myth of masculinity.* Cambridge, MA: MIT Press.

Pleck, J. H., Sonenstein, F. L., & Ku, L. C. (1993). Masculine ideology: Its impact on adolescent males' heterosexual relationships. *Journal of Social Issues, 40*(3), 11–29.

Pollack, W. S. (1998). *Real boys: Rescuing our sons from the myths of boyhood.* New York: Random House.

Poppen, R. (1988). *Behavioral relaxation training and assessment.* New York: Pergamon Press.

Roberts, G. (1993). Motivation in sport: Understanding and enhancing the motivation and achievement of children. In R. Singer, M. Murphey, & L. Tennant (Eds.), *Handbook of research on sport psychology* (pp. 405–420). New York: Macmillan.

Robertson, J. (1992). Overcoming the masculine mystique: Preferences for alternative forms of assistance among men who avoid counseling. *Journal of Counseling Psychology, 39*(2), 240–246.

Sabo, D. F. (1980). Best years of my life? In D. F. Sabo & R. Runola (Eds.), *Jock sports and male identity* (pp. 74–78). Englewood Cliffs, NJ: Prentice Hall.

Sabo, D. F., & Runfola, R. (1980). *Jock: Sports and male identity.* Englewood Cliffs, NJ: Prentice Hall.

Scanlan, T. K. (1988). Social evaluation and the competition process: A developmental perspective. In F. L. Smoll, R. A. Magill, & M. J. Ash (Eds.), *Children in sport* (3rd ed., pp. 135–148). Champaign, IL: Human Kinetics.

Schroeder, C. C. (1976). Adventure training for residence assistants. *Journal of College Student Development, 17*(1), 11–15.

Selby, R., Weinstein, J. M., & Bird, T. S. (1990). The health of university athletes: Attitudes, behaviors, and stressors. *Journal of American College Health, 39*(1), 11–18.

Siann, G. (1985). *Accounting for aggression.* Boston: Allen & Unwin.

Simons, J. (1997, March 24). Improbable dreams. *U.S. News & World Report,* pp. 46–57.

Singer, R. N., Murphey, M., & Tennant, L. K. (1993). *Handbook of research on sport psychology.* New York: Macmillan.

Smith, G. (1999, May 25). Moment of truth. *Sports Illustrated,* pp. 133–149.

Smith, M. D. (1983). *Violence and sport.* Toronto: Butterworths.

Smith, R. E. (1989). Athletic stress and burnout: Conceptual models and intervention strategies. In D. Hackfort & C. D. Spielberger (Eds.), *Anxiety in sports* (pp. 183–201). Washington, DC: Hemisphere.

Spelke, E., Hirst, W., & Neisser, U. (1976). Skills of divided attention. *Cognition, 4,* 215–230.

Spielberger, C. D. (1966). Theory and research on anxiety. In C. D. Spielberger (Ed.), *Anxiety and behavior* (pp. 3–20). New York: Academic Press.

Spielberger, C. D., Gorsuch, R. L., & Lushene, R. E. (1970). *Manual for the State-Trait-Anxiety Inventory (STAI).* Palo Alto, CA: Consulting Psychologists Press.

Suinn, R. (1993). Imagery. In R. N. Singer, M. Murphey, & L. K. Tennant (Eds.), *Handbook of research on sport psychology* (pp. 492–510). New York: Macmillan.

Swoap, R. A., & Murphy, S. M. (1995). Eating disorders and weight management in athletes. In S. M. Murphy (Ed.), *Sport psychology interventions* (pp. 307–329). Champaign, IL: Human Kinetics.

Taylor, J. A. (1953). A personality scale of manifest anxiety. *Journal of Abnormal and Social Psychology, 48,* 285–290.

Thirer, J. (1993). Aggression. In R. N. Singer, M. Murphey, & L. K. Tennant (Eds.), *Handbook of research on sport psychology* (pp. 365–378). New York: Macmillan.

Thornton, J. S. (1990). Feast or famine: Eating disorders in athletes. *Physician and Sportsmedicine, 18,* 116–122.

Trash-talking T-shirts taken off racks at JCPenney stores. (1999, July 6). *Kansas State Collegian Summer Edition,* p. 2.

Vealey, R. S. (1986). Conceptualization of sport confidence and competitive orientation: Preliminary investigation and instrument development. *Journal of Sport Psychology, 8,* 221–246.

Vodde, R. J. (1997). The development of a measure to evaluate scorekeeping: A process of competitive social comparisons involving preoccupation with winning and other negative male role characteristics. *Dissertation Abstracts International, 57*(9-A), 4136.

Wahl, G., & Wertheim, L. J. (1998, May 4). Paternity ward. *Sports Illustrated,* pp. 62–71.

Wechsler, H., Davenport, A. E., Dowdall, G. W., Grossman, S. J., & Zanakos, S. I. (1996). *Secondary effects of binge drinking on college campuses.* Newton, MA: Education Development Center.

Weinberg, R. S., & Jackson, A. (1979). Competition and extrinsic rewards: Effect on intrinsic motivation. *Research Quarterly, 50,* 494–502.

Weinberg, R. S., & Ragan, J. (1979). Effects of competition, success/failure, and sex on intrinsic motivation, *Research Quarterly, 50,* 503–510.

Weiss, M. R. (1995). Children in sport: An educational model. In S. M. Murphy (Ed.), *Sport psychology interventions* (pp. 39–69). Champaign, IL: Human Kinetics.

Weiss, M. R., & Chaumeton, N. (1992). Motivational orientations in sport. In T. S. Horn (Ed.), *Advances in sport psychology* (pp. 61–99). Champaign, IL: Human Kinetics.

Weiss, M. R., & Petlichkoff, L. M. (1989). Children's motivation for participation in and withdrawal from sport: Identifying the missing links. *Pediatric Exercise Science, 1,* 195–211.

Wiese, D. M., & Weiss, M. R. (1987). Psychological rehabilitation and physical injury: Implications for the sportsmedicine team. *Sport Psychologist, 1,* 318–330.

Wilcox, D. W., & Johnson, A. (1996, March 9). *A self-management problem-solving model of learning enhancement.* Paper presented at the annual convention of the American Counseling and Personnel Association, Baltimore.

Winters, S. J. (1990). Androgens: Endocrine physiology and pharmacology. In G. D. Lin & L. Erinoff (Eds.), *Anabolic steroid abuse* (pp. 113–130). (NIDA Research Monograph 102). Rockville, MD: National Institute on Drug Abuse.

Wolpe, J. (1958). *Psychotherapy by reciprocal inhibition.* Stanford, CA: Stanford University Press.

Zaichkowsky, L. D., & Fuchs, C. Z. (1989). Biofeedback-assisted self-regulation for stress management in sports. In D. Hackfort & D. D. Spielberger (Eds.), *Anxiety in sports: An international perspective.* Washington, DC: Hemisphere.

Zucherman, D. M., Colby, A., Ware, N. C., & Lazerson, J. S. (1986). The prevalence of bulimia among college students. *American Journal of Public Health, 76,* 1135–1137.

CHAPTER FIVE

Consulting with Men in Business and Industry

Hope I. Hills
Aaron Carlstrom
Margaret Evanow

James Autry, the president of the Meredith Corporation, said: "Work can provide the opportunity for spiritual and personal, as well as financial growth. If it doesn't, we're wasting far too much of our lives on it" (Autry, 1991, p. 13). Companies that recognize the truth of Autry's statement are actively working to create environments that support the growth and development of their employees and are recognized as the leaders in their industries. This leadership is measured by decreased turnover, increased job satisfaction, more effective product development, quicker response time, increased profitability, and more citations on listings of the best places to work as compared with other companies. Many use the help of consulting psychologists who employ executive coaching, team building, and other leadership development tools to support the changes that are necessary for success.

As scientist practitioners, consulting psychologists can promote changes that are based on solid theory and research and measure the efficacy of their efforts through the many records kept as normal business practice. At the same time, they can help their clients develop scientific and strategic approaches to decision making and leadership. When business clients discover the basic set of beliefs (theory) they hold about leading their organizations (and themselves) and recognize the effects of these beliefs on their company's productivity, they are often motivated to take the personal risks inherent in changing their outmoded beliefs. They can become "scientist practitioners of leadership" and thus become successful at choosing and testing the strategies needed for success in the ever-changing business environment.

Many business leaders are becoming aware of the need to recognize and change the dysfunctional aspects of old leadership paradigms built around the masculine gender role. New approaches to leadership that incorporate the positive aspects of both gender roles are being tried and tested. As leaders try these new strategies, incorporating more cooperation and attention to the needs of their followers and less autocratic decision making that consciously includes the input of those affected by the decisions, they find that the results support the new theory behind these changes.

CHANGES IN CONTEMPORARY ORGANIZATIONS

To be profitable, businesses are flattening their organizations, becoming involved in the global marketplace, creating team-oriented cultures, intensifying their customer focus, and increasing the inclusion of women and minorities in the management ranks. The byword of contemporary business environment is *change*. To be successful in this constantly changing environment, leaders must develop open, flexible, and inclusive leadership styles. Paul Wieand was one of the banking industry's youngest-ever chief executive officers (CEOs) but was fired from that post because of his rigid leadership style. The experience changed his life and career path. He is now a psychologist who works with executives. He said:

> In today's free-flowing team environment, leaders have to have a strong core
> (values that they remain true to) but they also have to be adaptive. To achieve a
> flexible-yet-resilient identity, you have to be willing to look inward. (Kruger,
> 1999, p. 124)

But looking inward is clearly not something that most men readily choose. Men still underutilize traditional counseling services and underreport their difficulties in living, even if they do seek help (Robertson & Fitzgerald, 1992). The consulting psychologist is in a perfect position to help business leaders take this inward journey, in the context of becoming better leaders, able to create more productive business environments.

This inner journey toward increasing flexibility while maintaining a strong inner core could be a description of counseling and therapy (especially for those who espouse interpersonal theory). Whatever the reason may be for enhancing flexibility, whether productive business relationships and profit or effective personal relationships and happiness, these changes are likely to affect every area of life. If a man becomes more interpersonally effective, he will probably become both a better leader and a better friend, father, and partner.

Approach to Coaching and Consulting

In this chapter we outline an approach to consulting and the individually focused activity of coaching that looks at the early experiences and resulting beliefs about self, others, and the world that are affecting the ability to productively lead in the present. The process very often results in profound changes in self-concept, relationships, and leadership style, very similar to the objectives in therapy and counseling. There are, however, some reasons to clearly distinguish between coaching (or consulting) and counseling (or therapy).

Consulting psychologists use various techniques to help organizations increase productivity and profit by focusing a trained strategic eye on the human system and then working with key leaders and teams to most effectively create the needed changes. The purpose of consulting interventions, whether individual coaching or team facilitation and development, is to increase the productivity of the organization, not to increase the mental health of an individual. The relationship that a consultant develops with a leader in an organization is much different than the more narrowly defined relationship between a therapist and a client. Although it is critical to maintain clear ethical boundaries, the business consultant may meet with an executive to report on a project that the executive assigned on one day and the next day spend time with that same executive in a coaching mode exploring the underlying experiences of childhood that make it difficult to be assertive. The course of a coaching intervention is very different from the regularly scheduled weekly sessions one expects throughout a therapy or counseling relationship. While necessarily moving through the similar stages of establishing a trusting relationship, exploring and challenging beliefs, and then helping the individual strengthen new behaviors as in therapy, these stages may be the result of a variety of both individual and group interactions with the leader. Individual coaching (which looks most similar to counseling or therapy) may take place each time the consultant visits the company, or it could happen only once or twice, with other interventions then supporting the desired change. And very critically, whereas a therapy client pays for therapy and therefore "owns" the process, in consulting and coaching the company pays, with the expectation that whatever changes are made will benefit the company. This reality makes defining confidentiality with all interested parties and maintaining those trust agreements a complex and pivotal issue that affects the viability of the consultant's practice throughout the organization. It is also important to cast the work consultants do not as therapy but as coaching, for the very reasons Robertson and Fitzgerald (1992) would predict. Most business leaders see therapy or counseling as an option only if one has mental health problems, not business or leadership concerns. Coaching, even when focused on early childhood experiences, does not carry this stigma and so arouses less of the resistance that many men would experience.

Starting at the Top

This book is focused on the treatment of varied personal and relational problems that the masculine roles engender. The men whom a business consultant works with look like they have mastered society's demands and have become successful. Some are enormously successful by the external standards of money and status. Mental health professionals typically do not focus on the upper management ranks as a place where many are in need of help. However, there are many painful examples of men who have broken under this set of rigid expectations, revealing the very real and often extreme dysfunction hidden under the successful facade. News reports of outwardly successful men "suddenly" killing family members or themselves are just the tip of the iceberg of the underlying pain. Wealth and power can be a great camouflage for tremendous pain, confusion, and loneliness. Men are caught in a double bind, because the masculine gender role also makes it unacceptable to ask for help (Robertson & Fitzgerald, 1992).

Researchers and practitioners in both psychology and business have recognized that the behaviors prescribed by this culture's masculine roles can interfere with men's inner peace, family relationships, sexual fulfillment, and physical health (Meth, 1990). Because most businesses are still run by men, this gender role is mirrored in the generally accepted models of leadership behavior, which affects the peace, relationships, enjoyment, and financial health of entire organizations. Consulting with organizations offers a tremendous opportunity to work with men who would not otherwise seek to look inward for the answers to their own life dilemmas and the organizational dilemmas that mirror those personal dilemmas. Managers and executives have generally been successful at pointing the finger elsewhere. But opportunity knocks when their position or the positions of their companies are threatened. This is often the point of "optimum pain" when the stakes are high enough to motivate action but not so high that the individual feels that failure is the only possible outcome.

Coaching executives and their teams can be an extraordinary opportunity that can improve the lives of the executives as well as those of everyone in the organization and often the customers and partners (for example, vendors and distributors) of the organization. Working with the CEO or president of a multinational corporation offers the very real possibility of supporting changes that could touch the world. When a man in this position chooses to look inward and learn to care for himself and those around him more effectively, that new approach can reshape the leadership paradigm of the entire organization (Tobias, 1995).

The necessity of remaining profitable creates the demands for measurable and strategic changes in the ways that people lead organizations and for consultants who can help leaders to make those changes. For the consulting psychologist trained to look at systems, this bottom-line imperative is not the enemy. Seen from the human systems perspective, enhancing the bottom line can be the motivation to create humane environments in which to work.

In this chapter we describe a consulting practice based on an integrated theoretical approach (interpersonal theory). The executive coaching examples focus on two men with rigid but very different leadership styles. One was dominant and critical, and the other was more modest and nurturing. To reach their personal and business goals, each of them had to face the experiences, beliefs, and values that had created the need to rigidly use their interpersonal styles at work (as well as at home). As they faced these issues, they both broke through the barriers to their personal growth, happiness, and success as well as the success of their corporation.

CONSULTATION WITH ORGANIZATIONS

Despite the fact that "women held 46% of executive, administrative, and managerial positions in 1998, up from 34% in 1983" (Farrell, 1999, p. 35), the power brokers of most modern corporations and organizations continue to be men. Male leaders who continue to avoid conventional contact with psychologists because of their attitudes toward success, power, and restricted emotionality (Robertson & Fitzgerald, 1992) are being faced with a market-driven need to loosen their rigid leadership paradigms or face individual or corporate extinction. Organizational consultation and executive coaching are powerful means of providing men with the opportunity to examine their own maladaptive patterns and change. These changes can create humane, flexible, and diverse corporations capable of responding successfully to the fast-paced marketplace.

Historically, American organizations have been patriarchal hierarchies run by white men. As such, American corporations tend to mirror both the functional and dysfunctional sides of this culture's masculine gender stereotypes. The dysfunctional side clearly reflects a rigid, defensive style. Such organizations resist change, have rigid attachments to "successful" product lines, are reluctant to introduce change into the organizational culture, and reflect an ingroup narcissism (Byrne, Diepke, Verity, Neff, Levine, & Forest, 1991; Levinson, 1994). A leading authority on corporate leadership indicates that most companies underestimate their external market threats and overestimate their internal power or abilities, a mirror of the narcissist's approach to the world (Taylor, 1999).

Facing today's global marketplace, with its increasingly complex demands, more diverse business partners, managers, and employees, and faster and more chaotic changes, is like rafting in "permanent white water" (Vaill, 1989). To stay afloat, leaders must recognize that inflexible personal and corporate beliefs and myths create a corporate "personality disorder." Recognition of this rigidity is the first step in changing to an open, flexible, and functional approach.

However, just as Robertson and Fitzgerald (1992) would predict, most executives do not recognize how their own psychological dynamics affect their organizations. If they have attended a workshop that has focused on self-awareness (a key to leadership success in the current business literature [Bridges, 1991; Covey, 1990; Farr, 1997; Lundin & Lundin, 1993; Rosen, 1996; Schutz, 1994; Senge, 1990]), they tend to cling to the personal value they experienced but, unless consistently coached to recognize it, do not readily see the parallel psychological dynamics at work in their organizations. They continue to cling to financial strategies, operational plans, and technological advances as prime targets for increasing organizational productivity and shareholders' value. But it is the focus on human dynamics, the very work that they resist, that could ensure the maximum competitive edge. Indeed, "There is a very compelling business case for this idea: Companies that manage people right will outperform companies that don't by 30% to 40%" (Webber, 1998, p. 154).

APPLICABLE MENTAL HEALTH SKILLS

Mental health workers who understand and empathize with the damage that gender role stereotypes have done to men, women, and whole organizations have the basic knowledge and skill level to work successfully in organizations. In addition, as scientist practitioners, they need to recognize the importance of working from a theoretical base that is consistently questioned, measured, and revised. With programs such as Total Quality Management (TQM), managers already see the value of following an accepted approach to the production system that is then measured to check its validity. As the consultant helps them to recognize the parallel process involved in recognizing, questioning, and measuring the effectiveness of their theory—their underlying belief system—about the human system, leaders can become scientist practitioners of leadership.

The conscious commitment to a clear ethical standard is another essential ingredient for success in this field. The questions of "Who is the client?" and "What will you share with others?" accompany consulting psychologists wherever they go in an organization (Newman, 1993; Newman & Robinson, 1991; Tobias, 1990). To remain effective, we must clearly outline our confidentiality agreements in every setting and follow up on any possible mistrust.

Training in learning, motivation, systems, and therapy provides a working knowledge and skill base to support change in organizations. A crucial ingredient for success is a sense of humility and continual solicitation of honest feedback from the businessmen and businesswomen who have poured their minds, hearts, and lives into the organizations they lead. This approach is also model-ing good leadership skills.

INTERPERSONAL THEORY

As the core of this consulting model, interpersonal theory (see Figure 5.1) has been an exceptionally valuable tool not only to help clients recognize the effects of their personal interactions and style but also to shed light on corporate strate-gies, attitudes, and direction. In this section we briefly outline the theory (the references cited are excellent sources for further understanding) and some exam-ples of its application in organizations.

The initial research into interpersonal theory took place under the auspices of the Kaiser Foundation. Timothy Leary and his colleagues, following the ideas of Harry Stack Sullivan (1953), studied the interpersonal behaviors of groups of subjects with various psychiatric diagnoses. They hypothesized that each dis-order might have a discernible interpersonal pattern that then produced reac-tions from others that reinforced the pattern. They found that the map of these behaviors took the shape of a circumplex (Guttman, 1966) called the inter-personal circle (Figure 5.1), on which similar behaviors are close to each other and differing behaviors are on the opposite side of the circumplex (Leary, 1957). What interpersonal theory offers is a concrete operational definition, a behav-ioral map, of the very predictable actions and reactions among people. Understanding the dynamics of interpersonal behavior as defined by interper-sonal theory can help anyone clarify the often mystifying reactions we experi-ence in our daily lives.

Complementarity

The primary pattern seen in most interactions among people is called comple-mentarity. There are two attributes to this pattern. The first is that one person's dominance (top half of the circle) will predictably pull, or evoke, submission from the other (bottom half of the circle). Just as powerfully, submission will evoke dominance. The second attribute is that when one person is hostile (the left half of the circle), it is most likely that the other will respond in kind. If the interaction is initially friendly (the right half of the circle), it is likely that the response will be friendly as well. When integrated, we see that behaviors from the dominant hostile quadrant of the circle will provoke submissive hos-tile behaviors, and submissive hostile behaviors will just as powerfully arouse dominant hostile reactions. Similarly, dominant friendly behavior is highly likely to pull a submissive friendly reaction, and submissive friendly behavior will attract dominant friendly reactions.

Figure 5.1. The Interpersonal Circle, a Classification of Interpersonal Behavior.

Source: Adapted from Strong and Hills, 1986.

Other patterns are variants of complementarity. *Anticomplementary* inter-actions can be seen when one of the parties realizes at some level that the com-plementary pattern is not useful. For instance, he or she may not wish to be submissive hostile and would like to get the other person to stop being domi-nant hostile. The most powerful place to come from on the circle will then be dominant friendly, which would attract the other to be friendly and submissive. A way to think about this pattern is to recognize what outcome is desired for the interaction and then move to the place on the circle that will pull the other person to the place desired. Although this approach seems manipulative, it is actually something we all do without recognizing it.

The last basic pattern is *acomplementarity.* This, of course, is every other interactional pattern. One that is very damaging but is an almost automatic response is when a submissive hostile interaction pulls a dominant friendly response, usually a nurturant one. The first person claims, from the submissive hostile quadrant, that he or she is not good enough or some other self-critical statement. The almost automatic response is, "No, you are fine" (from the nurturing octant of the dominant friendly quadrant). Unfortunately, this response just reinforces the submissive hostile person's means of getting a nurturing response; it is likely that on the private level the nurturer feels resentful and critical and eventually will respond from this quadrant. When managers recognize this pattern, they immediately realize how frequently they fall into this trap and begin to try the anticomplementary response instead.

When managers are trained to recognize these patterns, they regularly report that they are becoming much more successful as leaders. One of the most startling revelations to most of them is that to create the environment for employees to act empowered, the most effective stance for the leader is submissive friendly. It is necessary to have a new definition of power to recognize that being submissive friendly is the most effective way to empower. This definition is that true power is creating a situation so that the desired outcome is achieved. To have true power, then, leaders must develop flexibility.

Flexibility

The key to effective functioning from the perspective of interpersonal theory and research (Benjamin, 1996; Kieser, 1996; Leary, 1957; Strong et al., 1988) and the theory and research on leadership and management (Hersey & Blanchard, 1988; Kruger, 1999; Vaill, 1989) is flexibility. Paul Weiand's definition of the effective leader as having a "flexible yet resilient identity with a strong inner core" (Kruger, 1999, p. 124) is an excellent place to start.

A person who is flexible is able, in interpersonal terms, to move around the circle as the situation demands. So, rather than always needing to be dominant if he or she is a leader, the truly powerful and flexible leader could comfortably be modest or seek help from his or her followers without losing face. The result would be empowered and helpful employees, often eager to be able to take the lead from someone who is not actually giving up his or her authority.

INTERPERSONAL THEORY AND THE MASCULINE ROLE

In light of this theoretical perspective, it becomes clear why the masculine gender role sets men up for the eventual failure of many relationships in all areas of their lives. Mahalik (1999; see also Chapter Twenty-six) outlined the interpersonal behaviors seen in men who adhere rigidly to this society's expected male role (O'Neil, 1981a, 1981b, 1982). These men are dominant, emotionally distant, inflexible in their interpersonal behaviors, and unwilling to seek help from others. As expected, these attributes are also part of the accepted management style in many companies.

According to interpersonal theory, truly functional people are able to successfully use behaviors from any octant on the interpersonal circle (Strong & Hills, 1986) to get what they want or need without losing their sense of personal identity (see Figure 5.1). According to Mahalik's description, men who experience gender role conflict restrict themselves to operating their lives primarily from the critical and self-enhancing octants. These octants also define the leadership style of the majority of men who are struggling with their performance as managers and executives.

The theory predicts that those with whom these men interact will also feel restricted. They will be powerfully pulled to react primarily from the behaviors outlined in the distrustful and self-effacing octants. This submissive hostile profile is unfortunately prevalent in the subordinates of these men. The effects of this restricted profile can be recognized in most of the complaints that managers lodge about employees (for example, that they are resistant to change, are not self-starting, and only do the minimal job required to avoid getting fired). The double bind is obvious: set someone up to act in a certain way, then complain about the results.

Even if leading and perhaps nurturant are added to round out the currently practiced manager or leader profiles, leaders still have only half of all the available interpersonal strategies needed to be truly effective with all their employees. All of the dominant octants pull submissive behavior, not the dominant, empowered behavior that is needed from experienced workers.

Other leadership models, mirroring the hypotheses outlined in interpersonal theory, recommend that managers assess the needs of their employees and respond appropriately and flexibly. One such example that is used in many training programs for managers is the Situational Leadership Model (Hersey & Blanchard, 1988).

The Situational Leadership Model outlines how, as an employee becomes more task mature (for any task, from flipping hamburgers to the multifocused task of being the president), the supervisor must vary his or her leadership style from an initial telling mode that is very task oriented to an eventual delegating mode when the employee may actually have more expertise at the job than the supervisor has. Unfortunately, delegation is a skill that many managers have not developed. When they do delegate well, they will have much more committed and mature employees. This model fits neatly into a consulting practice that is based on interpersonal theory. It has been the basis of management training in many companies; the material Hersey and Blanchard have designed clearly demonstrates the importance and value of letting go of unidimensional leadership styles.

INTERPERSONAL PROCESS IN CONSULTING AND COACHING

Inflexible and restricted behavioral repertoires have very real effects on productivity and leadership effectiveness. Consultants must hone the ability to initially notice how a person pulls them and then self-confidence to disengage without withdrawing from the other. This task is actually much harder than it seems, especially when a person is new to the field of consulting. Leaders often question the seemingly "soft stuff" consultants bring into organizations. Until consultants gain experience and confidence in the concrete and measurable value of this work, they might feel that this critical reaction has merit and, caught in their own defensive maneuvers, may not recognize that this response may also be the leaders' defensive pattern signifying their real fear of change.

STAGES OF COACHING

We now discuss the three stages of coaching—social, asocial, and authentically social.

Stage 1: Social

Just noticing how one is pulled is the first step in the consulting process, which is clearly parallel to Kieser's (1988) description of therapy. Initially, it is important to notice the pattern before making any changes. During this social stage the consultant is building the trust needed for real change and may do things that create first-order change. In corporations, this stage is filled with many activities, which may include leadership training; consulting with leaders to solve various problems with employees, human resources programs, or personal issues; strategic planning and facilitation of team-building programs; succession-planning meetings; and staff meetings.

Stage 2: Asocial

Once an individual relationship with an executive is solid (the timing itself indicating the person's ability to trust and connect) the consultant would advance to the asocial stage, meaning that he or she would no longer respond to the complementary pull and instead respond from a different part of the interpersonal circle and actively pull for different behaviors. Over time, as the consultant remains "unhooked" from the old patterns, the client develops a healthy style and can move around the circle flexibly.

As leadership development in organizations becomes a planned strategy with increased productivity as its goal, some powerful change interventions are possible. The consultant can involve supervisors, peers, and subordinates in creating new "interpersonal worlds" for an individual. Through retreats and team meetings designed to share personal leadership plans that involve real change in leadership style, leaders can make agreements with various groups to change their patterns of responding. This strategy is extraordinarily powerful; it encircles the individual with new reactions and reinforces a new style. Some companies and leaders also include spouses and families in the process to complete the circle. These opportunities give the consultant tools to support the change process that are unavailable to most therapists.

Stage 3: Authentically Social

At the authentically social stage, the consulting psychologist notices that he or she is comfortable, does not feel as manipulated, and looks forward to being with the client. Reactions to one another move flexibly around the interpersonal circle. The consultant notices that many people find it easier to argue with, agree with, support, or question the leader. If the consulting psychologist were acting as a personal therapist, he or she would be close to termination. In a consulting practice, it is likely that the leader would now have much more success with his or her various relationships and support the consulting psychologist's work with other leaders and teams to further enhance the productivity of the organization.

These three stages vary in length, much as in the therapy process. If an organization is rigidly hierarchical and dominated by the masculine gender role leadership style, the length of the stages is likely to be extended. A leader with years in such an organization, especially one who is high in the organizational hierarchy, may never be willing to truly transform his or her style, given the reinforcers that are in place to support the status quo. Often the desire is there, and such a leader may be able to change the personally damaging style in retirement, perhaps even working with the consultant to facilitate the process. The following story demonstrates that consultants must be flexible and willing to build trust for perhaps years before there is a chance to support real change.

THE STORY OF VICTOR

One of my (Hills) first experiences with "Victor" was in a training meeting with the officers in his company. He sat apart, but even if he had been in the circle, his critical demeanor would have set him apart. It was early in my consulting career, and I remember very clearly thinking that I would never be able to connect with him. His disdain for leadership training was palpable, and I had to work to maintain my composure with the group. I did not know the real history of how other consultants had operated with this group until later (an important piece of information, like finding out a client's past experience with therapy). Once I did, it was clear why Victor had reacted as he had. The last consultant operated very clearly out of the dominant hostile quadrant, and Victor was just much more obvious about his distrust than the others. But the CEO was committed to leadership development, so I continued to work within the company and with the officers every month.

It was more than two years before Victor and I had the opportunity to break through his resistance and move to the second stage. During the first period, I had the chance to help many people in his organization learn effective management strategies, demonstrated by increased productivity and improved employee retention. By the time we had the chance to work together in a coaching mode, he had softened his opinion of me. This process and variety of roles demonstrate the very real differences in therapy and consulting. As a vice president, Victor was responsible for contracting with me for various assignments and then giving me feedback on the outcome. I needed to maintain my flexibility to respond to his sometimes negative feedback authentically and also be able to become his coach. Sometimes this task was very challenging. I am sure that there were times that I may have pulled his critical attacks on me as he may have sensed my insecurity and task immaturity. However, more times than not, the outcome was positive.

The CEO decided to make some changes in the organization and consulted with me about ways to pave the way for that change. We planned a multiphase process to help the officers become more of a team. Each officer met with me to explore his "lifeline" for answers to ongoing problems in his approach to leadership. This process can take from three to six hours or more, during which we use a piece of newsprint to graphically show the person's life history. Family history, test scores, and dreams for the future are all included in the basic format. Various themes that become apparent are noted at the bottom of the page. For the first time, an hour or two into our exploration, Victor found some answers that surprised him. He had long been criticized for his very dominant and critical leadership style but was able to "make things happen" so he had consistently moved up the ladder. He was in a group of three peers being considered for president, and his style stood in his way. He was at the point of optimum pain. He had been to a self-awareness workshop and valued the increased care he had for himself and his family but had not made the crucial connections to his unyielding leadership flaws.

I have found that, for most of the men I have coached, the initial place to look for the keys to their leadership behavior is in their relationship with their fathers. As we explored this relationship, it became very apparent that Victor's father's ever critical and punitive treatment had created a set of beliefs and defenses that drove him to mirror the same style while at the same time feeling insecure, distrusting, and fearful of men in authority over him. I always frame these early decisions as very valid "safety measures" a child would take to care for himself. He needed to honor that early decision and, in the present, discover other ways to deal with men in authority over him, as well as find new ways to express his own authority.

At a two-day retreat at which the officers shared their lifelines with each other, he shared his story. His tears surprised him and evoked tears from almost all of the other men. It was a pivotal moment not only for him and his colleagues but for the company as a whole. When men cry together over their pain and loss, nothing can be quite the same again. The change was not immediate. Masculine roles are strong. But others' defenses were markedly softer, much less intense, and there were many more invitations to reopen the doors after this experience.

His boss recognized the parallels between Victor's relationship with his father and Victor's relationship with him and began to change his reactions. The change in their relationship was hard won, because Victor's boss was also very critical. I call my client Victor (not his real name) because he did not stop his quest with these experiences. He used my support with him and his direct reports to do similar interventions in his organization. He also continued to challenge my leadership, helping me to grow at the same time, for which I will always be grateful.

He also became the president. As with anyone with a long-standing pattern, his "natural" first response often is critical. But he catches himself, often checking the interpersonal circle he keeps in a prominent place behind his desk to remind himself of more productive responses.

KEY PRACTICES

In this section we examine key business and consulting practices. More specifically, we discuss return on investments, ongoing consultation to executives, succession planning, team building, and leadership training.

Return on Investments

Whether we would normally use this language or not, we are all interested in a return on our investments. Indeed, "the continuous improvement of productivity is one of management's most important jobs" (Drucker, 1974, p. 111). If consultants recognize and honor this primary function of leaders and can help them fulfill it more effectively, leaders will be much more open to hearing consultants' proposals. The more clearly consultants understand that the purpose of being in business is to make a return on investments and frame the work they do in those terms, the greater the consultant's return on investments will be. Assessment is not the primary purview of this chapter, but it is important to explore the many measures that are useful for gauging the organization's baseline in order to guide initial planning and measure eventual results, the company's return on investment from the consultant's services.

Ongoing Consultation to Executives

It is critical for consultants to have ongoing approval and support from the highest possible level, preferably the CEO or president. One way to accomplish this objective is to have regularly scheduled meetings with the CEO or president to keep him or her abreast of the consultant's work, observations, and recommendations. Initially, this relationship may be simply a courtesy, but as the consultant's insights become valuable, the relationship can become one of a confidant to the executive, who often feels very alone. Notice the stages apparent in this statement from a retired CEO:

> I would characterize our relationship [between the CEO and consultant] as one that was guarded by me initially, and then grew to a warm, trusting one over a very few meetings. The trust that I developed in you was based on your clear, honest but compassionate analysis of our management situation. It was especially important to me that I had a knowledgeable, intelligent individual to exchange ideas with when there was no one else in the organization with whom I could fully discuss the bank's human problems. You were very helpful in demonstrating to our whole management team that inclusion went a long way further than maintaining individual fiefdoms. (Bill Viklund, personal communication, April 3, 1999)

Succession Planning

One of the most important responsibilities that managers and leaders have at all levels of an organization is career counseling or succession planning. Failure to select and develop leaders at every level is detrimental and costly (Bobo, 1999). Over the past ten years there has been an estimated 50 percent failure rate among corporate executives (DeVries, 1992; Sloan, 1994). If all the costs of this failure rate were calculated, it would begin to explain Webber's (1998) statement that companies that manage people right will outperform those that do not by 30 to 40 percent. Consultants, especially those with training in career assessment and planning, can play a pivotal role in helping executives to assess and plan for the leadership development of their managers and critique the clarity with which they outline the path to various kinds of success in their organizations.

Team Building

Because "teams outperform individuals acting alone or in larger organizational groupings" (Katzenbach & Smith, 1994, p. 9), many companies want to take advantage of this opportunity for greater productivity. However, the seemingly commonsense logic behind creating high-performing teams is difficult to successfully apply. The consultant must be keenly aware of both cultural and psychological issues that impact the successful productivity of teams. In those cultures, like the United States, that glorify individual effort, many revolt against the communal focus of teams. Working in teams may also create situations in which old family patterns are reenacted, confusing the seemingly clear business objective. Helping teams to recognize these issues and move beyond them is an exciting challenge.

There are many opportunities for consultants to help organizations learn to create high-performing teams. It is very important, though, to begin by helping leaders understand what it takes to make teams work in their environment. They must understand that high-performing teams depend on having clear direction and purpose (Katzenbach & Smith, 1994). If they autocratically demand that teams be the new "way" and do not invest time and money in the process, the teams will fail and become just another program of the day.

The Myers-Briggs Type Indicator is a good initial step in the team-building process. It is a step into self-disclosure and learning styles that will enable the leaders to work together effectively. It also begins to support the need to value diversity but in a mode that is not the threat that other kinds of diversity training can be for a company that has not addressed these issues. Many aids to this process are available.

Leadership Training

The consultant needs to develop and constantly fine-tune a set of models and collateral materials to use consistently with various individuals and groups. This set of models must be congruent with the consultant's own core theoretical approach and have research support. However, the models need to be in language that connects with the business world. People need to be able to remember a catchy phrase or an amusing image that reminds them of their new skills and models when they are under pressure to perform. Using the same handouts in various situations takes advantage of the learning value of repetition. The goal is to train scientist practitioners of leadership who eventually can rely on a solid theory of behavior, not an inconsistent set of skills learned at various quickie workshops.

Leadership training needs to be integrated into almost any meeting. Periodic workshops in which large groups learn about a certain topic are an excellent way to introduce and practice leadership theory and skills. Team-building sessions and retreats provide events at which the models can be used to help the team understand its dynamics as well as each other. Strategic planning retreats present the opportunity to help executives see that solid theory can be a practical tool when applied to the whole system. Whether they are planning employee succession, setting goals, or evaluating operations, a good theory will help to strengthen their assessment of the current state, clarify predictions about the future state, and improve the planning on how to get there. Meetings with problem employees and their supervisors provide powerful practice, in which using the models will improve their chances of understanding and resolving their issues. Executive coaching sessions offer the perfect opportunity for leaders to use the leadership training on themselves to create a new and self-affirming understanding of their current performance problems.

HENRY'S STORY

Victor's story outlines the basic format of the executive coaching model I (Hills) have developed over time. In 1998, after facilitating an in-depth succession-planning retreat, the officers of one firm contracted to put seven of their managers through an intensive program focused on dealing with their long-standing leadership issues. These seven individuals were seen as possible future officers. It was a critical juncture in the life of this company, and the officers wanted to see if these seven would make use of this program and change.

One of the seven had just been elevated to the human resources manager. He filled the function of a retired vice president and realized the statement it made about his leadership that he was not given the title of vice president. This, for him, was a point of optimum pain. The opportunity to participate in the intensive program of executive coaching finally brought him to do his lifeline, which he had now put off for seven years.

Most people in the company had valued "Henry" throughout his career for his caring, confidential, and growing professionalism in human resources. His former boss had been a micromanager in the extreme, so it had been difficult to truly ascertain what part of some ongoing feedback was a result of his place under this man or his own style. Now that the boss was gone, it was clear that Henry continued to appear less assertive and proactive than would be expected of someone who could be an officer in the company. He realized that he had always "hung back" from the pressure of confronting some people and had constructed his life so that he was comfortable with his back-seat role. But at this point, he was no longer comfortable and was ready to change.

His lifeline offered an answer to the long-standing feedback that has changed his self-appraisal and his leadership since that day. I noticed, as I explored his lifeline, that he did not say anything about his early childhood. I knew he came from an intact family and had lived in the community all his life. I finally asked what the blank was around his birth. His response shocked me. "Oh, I was a twin, actually a triplet, but the other two were dead. That has not had any effect on me, though." I told him that the deaths had not only affected him, but it was probably in this area of his life that we would discover the answers he sought.

We then reconstructed how his mother must have reacted to him and found that, of course, she had protected him and worried about his health much more than she had worried about the health of his siblings. We discussed how she must have felt during his first years, having lost two children, and what impact being the survivor could have on his sense of self. He saw very quickly how this situation had affected his willingness to risk and had created many beliefs about his own weaknesses. Once he had felt the impact and recognized how the many other deaths in his life had reinforced these beliefs, he was able (because he had truly worked on his self-awareness and leadership diligently for years) to make some remarkable changes rather quickly.

The next step in the process was to share his lifeline (which is on a newsprint sheet, written in a fashion that only the person could actually decipher its contents, which keeps the subject in control of what is said to others) with his boss, a person who had long questioned his ability to be an officer. He was able (in a three-way meeting with me) to share his insights and set challenging and clear agreements with his boss. He went on to share his lifeline and agreements in retreats with his peers and subordinates, as well as with his wife and children privately.

The change in Henry's energy level, demeanor, and personal expectations was dramatic. He became much more clear and forceful in his proposals about his area of responsibility. People began to comment on the change. The company merged with another similar chain, and Henry was in charge of all the processes involved in merging the human resources systems of the two. He is now the vice president of a much larger and more complex corporation.

His appraisal is that he was able, because of the lifeline and other meetings, to recognize that he had always avoided confrontation and then blamed others for the problems that resulted. He had protected others and rescued the weak (which he detested the most in others he counseled). But when he realized that he was no longer considered for the future he wanted it woke him up, and then the lifeline helped him to make changes from the position of understanding and caring for himself rather than criticism. He said he now works harder and smarter, even makes people angry at times with his challenges. He reports being "more at peace with who I am, and what I have to offer."

The men whose stories appear in this chapter came from very different early life experiences and therefore opposite public defenses. Victor was dominant and hostile, and Henry was more submissive and hostile. Both had been successful to a point. Then they had the chance to take a deep look at themselves and share their findings with other men, who also shared their findings. By sharing their insights and especially their emotions about these early experiences, as well as the results that had played out in their lives, they committed to new behaviors to replace the rigid ones that had held them back. The changes they made resulted not only in career advancement but also, and even more important to the two of them, in more authentic, warm, and satisfying relationships.

Consulting with businesses provides an amazing opportunity to affect the lives of many people by affecting the lives of a few. For those who decry the negative effects of rigid adherence to the masculine and feminine role stereotypes, the time is perfect for challenging the status quo. The chance to help leaders question their basic beliefs and theories about life and leading is exhilarating, challenging, fun, and profitable.

References

Autry, J. A. (1991). *Love and profit: The art of caring leadership.* New York: Morrow.

Benjamin, L. S. (1996). *Interpersonal diagnosis and treatment of personality disorders.* New York: Guilford Press.

Bobo, J. (1999). The care and feeding of our leaders. *National Underwriter* (National Underwriter Company, Cincinnati) 103(8), 19–20.

Bridges, W. (1991). *Managing transitions: Making the most of change.* Reading, MA: Addison-Wesley.

Byrne, J., Diepke, D. A., Verity, J., Neff, R., Levine, J. B., & Forest, S. A. (1991, June 17). IBM. *Business Week,* p. 25.

Covey, S. R. (1990). The 7 habits of highly effective people: Powerful lessons in personal change. New York: Simon & Schuster.

DeVries, D. L. (1992). Executive selection: Advances but no progress. *Issues & Observations* (Center for Creative Leadership) 12(4), 1–5.

Drucker, P. F. (1974). *Management: Tasks, responsibilities, practices.* New York: Harper Business.

Farr, J. (1997, September). Leadership vs. management: Do you know the difference? *Business Leader,* p. 9.

Farrell, C. (1999, August 9). Women in the workplace: Is parity finally in sight? *Business Week,* p. 35.

Guttman, L. (1966). Order analysis of correlation matrixes. In R. B. Cattell (Ed.), *Handbook of multivariate experimental psychology.* Chicago: Rand McNally.

Hersey, P., & Blanchard, K. H. (1988). *Management of organizational behavior: Utilizing human resources* (5th ed.). Englewood Cliffs, NJ: Prentice Hall.

Katzenbach, J. R., & Smith, D. K. (1994). *The wisdom of teams: Creating the high-performance organization.* New York: HarperBusiness.

Kiesler, D. J. (1988). *Therapeutic metacommunication.* Palo Alto, CA: Consulting Psychologists Press.

Kiesler, D. J. (1996). Contemporary interpersonal theory and research: Personality, psychopathology, and psychotherapy. New York: Wiley.

Kruger, P. (1999, June). A leader's journey. *Fast Company, 25,* 116–129.

Leary, T. (1957). Interpersonal diagnosis of personality: A functional theory and methodology for personality evaluation. New York: Ronald Press.

Levinson, H. (1994). Why the behemoths fell: Psychological roots of corporate failure. *American Psychologist, 49,* 428–436.

Lundin, W., & Lundin, K. (1993). The healing manager: How to build quality relationships and productive cultures at work. San Francisco: Berrett-Koehler.

Mahalik, J. R. (1999). Interpersonal psychotherapy with men who experience gender role conflict. *Professional Psychology: Research and Practice, 30,* 5–13.

Meth, R. L. (1990). The road to masculinity. In R. Meth & R. Pasick (Eds.), *Men in therapy: The challenge of change* (pp. 3–34). New York: Guilford Press.

Newman, J. L. (1993). Ethical issues in consultation. *Journal of Counseling and Development, 72,* 148–156.

Newman, J. L., & Robinson, S. E. (1991). In the best interests of the consultee: Ethical issues in consultation. *Consulting Psychology Bulletin, 43,* 23–29.

O'Neil, J. M. (1981a). Male sex-role conflicts, sexism, and masculinity: Psychological implications for men, women, and the counseling psychologist. *Counseling Psychologist, 9,* 61–81.

O'Neil, J. M. (1981b). Patterns of gender role conflict and strain: Sexism and fear of femininity in men's lives. *Personnel and Guidance Journal, 60,* 203–210.

O'Neil, J. M. (1982). Gender role conflict and strain in men's lives: Implications for psychiatrists, psychologists, and other human service providers. In K. Solomon & N. B. Levy (Eds.), *Men in transition: Changing male roles, theory, and therapy* (pp. 5–44). New York: Plenum.

Robertson, J. M., & Fitzgerald, L. F. (1992). Overcoming the masculine mystique: Preferences for alternative forms of assistance among men who avoid counseling. *Journal of Counseling Psychology, 39,* 240–246.

Rosen, R. H. (1996). Leading people: Transforming business from the inside out. New York: Viking.

Schutz, W. (1994). The human element: Productivity, self-esteem, and the bottom line. San Francisco: Jossey-Bass.

Senge, P. M. (1990). The fifth discipline: The art and practice of the learning organization. New York: Doubleday/Currency.

Sloan, E. B. (1994). Assessing and developing versatility: Executive survival skill for the brave new world. *Consulting Psychology Journal, 46*(1), 24–31.

Strong, S. R., & Hills, H. I. (1986). *Interpersonal Communication Rating Scale.* Richmond: Virginia Commonwealth University.

Strong, S. R., Hills, H. I., Kilmartin, C. T., DeVries, H., Lanier, K., Nelson, B. N., Strickland, D., & Meyer, C. W., III. (1988). The dynamic relations among interpersonal behaviors: A test of complementarity and anticomplementarity. *Journal of Personality and Social Psychology, 54,* 798–810.

Sullivan, H. S. (1953). *The interpersonal theory of psychiatry.* New York: Norton.

Taylor, W. C. (1999). The leader of the future. *Fast Company, 25,* 130–142.

Tobias, L. L. (1990). Psychological consulting to management: A clinician's perspective. New York: Brunner/Mazel.

Tobias, L. L. (1995). Eleven ideas that have influenced my practice of psychological consulting. *Consulting Psychology Journal: Practice and Research, 47,* 56–63.

Vaill, P. B. (1989). *Managing as a performing art.* San Francisco: Jossey-Bass.

Webber, A. M. (1998, November). Danger: Toxic company. *Fast Company, 19,* 152–161.

CHAPTER SIX

Counseling Men in College Settings

John M. Robertson

D o universities make people think? In a word, yes. More than that, most students actually change the way they think. Attitudes, values, morals, ideas, relational patterns—all are subject to change.

The evidence is abundant. Pascarella and Terenzini (1991) reviewed hundreds of studies about college life, then used an effect size strategy to estimate the change that occurs between the first and last years of college. When expressed as standard deviation units, an effect size can be converted to an estimate of the percentile point change. Using this technique, they provided strong evidence that young people change in college. For example, students show an improvement in their ability to communicate. Increases are seen in their verbal skills (+21 percentile points), their written communication skills (+19), and their oral communication skills (+22). Stronger changes are seen in their ability to think. Critical thinking improves (+34), as does their ability to use reason and evidence to address problems (+34) or to deal with conceptual complexity (+38). In short, students gain more than a knowledge base in their major fields of study. They learn thinking skills and begin to apply them to various questions they face.

Attitudes and values change as well. Students become interested in art, music, literature, and history. In general, their views broaden. They become aware of freedoms, inclusiveness, complexity, and tolerance. By the time they graduate, students are likely to have changed their relational views. They have become more autonomous (+36), less authoritarian (−81), and less ethnocentric (−45) over the course of their college years. They also are better adjusted psychologically (+40), and their views of religion and gender have become more flexible (Pascarella & Terenzini, 1991).

Although cautions may be offered about these findings (for example, group differences may hide individual differences, college may not actually cause these changes, or these shifts may represent development not change), the overall difference is unmistakable. During the years that young people are in college, they modify the way they communicate, think, value, and relate. These trends have been consistent for decades (Bowen, 1977; Corey, 1936; Jacob, 1957; Feldman & Newcomb, 1969; Pascarella & Terenzini, 1991) and do not therefore seem confined to a particular era. These findings are also consistent with what theorists have argued for quite some time (see Chickering, 1969; Perry, 1970); that is, people change (evolve, mature, develop) during their college years as they form an identity and think more carefully about the world in which they live.

It is not surprising, therefore, that many college students seek counseling. With so much change in the air, with so many new influences, ideas, and people in their lives, the challenges can become intense. Talking with someone about these issues becomes appealing to many students. Magoon's (1999) annual summary of information about university counseling centers tracks utilization patterns. Counseling centers at large universities (with more than ten thousand students) in a typical year see about nine hundred students for emotional or social problems and another two hundred students for educational or vocational questions. Many more students are seen in workshops, theme groups, outreach presentations, and guest lectures in classes. A conservative estimate is that campus counseling centers serve no less than 10 percent of the student body in any given year. Some campuses conduct exit surveys of seniors that ask about the services they have used during their educational careers. Results indicate that around 40 percent of graduating seniors at some universities report some contact with counseling staff at the counseling center while getting their degree (*Survey Results,* 1997).

HOW MEN USE COLLEGE COUNSELING CENTERS

Although college men may be reluctant to seek counseling, they do find their way to campus counseling centers. The most frequently presented questions address their relationships, their careers, their moods, and their use of alcohol and other drugs.

Rates of Psychological Services Utilization

Men do not visit counselors as frequently as do women. The ratio in North America is about one to two, with one male visit for every two or more female visits (Cheatham, Shelton, & Ray, 1987; Newton, 1999; Vessey & Howard, 1993). This pattern has not changed for many years (see Shueman & Medvene, 1981). The use rates do not mean that men have fewer problems than women; evidence indicates very similar levels of distress in men and women (Robins et al., 1984). In fact, men appear to have even higher rates of risk for some issues. Although younger boys and girls have similar rates of suicide, by the time they are in college (between the ages of twenty and twenty-four) men are actually six times more likely to commit suicide than are women (U.S. Department of Health and Human Services, 1992). This pattern continues throughout adulthood, as four of every five suicide deaths in North America are men (U.S. Department of Health and Human Services, 1992).

Another potential explanation for the differential rates of using counseling services is that referral sources might have a bias toward referring women. This explanation, however, does not appear to have much support. One study (Lott, Ness, Alcorn, & Greer, 1999) presented analogue cases (students, staff, and faculty) to potential referral sources on three college campuses and did not find that women were referred at higher rates than men. It is interesting to note, however, that this same study found that men were less likely than women to make referrals of students for counseling. Even as referral sources, men are less likely to think about counseling options than are women.

If men do not have fewer or less severe problems than women or are not referred less frequently than women, other explanations for their lower utilization rates can be considered. Several have suggested that the difference is related to male gender role socialization (see, for example, Wilcox & Forrest, 1992). Somehow, the desire to "be a man" may steer men away from counselors (Good & Wood, 1995). Several studies have found that traditional men do indeed have negative ideas about the traditional counseling process (Johnson & Brock, 1988; J. M. Robertson & Fitzgerald, 1992; Sipps & Janeczek, 1986). These negative attitudes about counseling seem to correlate with a general unwillingness to seek psychological help (Wisch, Mahalik, Hayes, & Nutt, 1995). Men also may be reluctant because they may hear on campus about some of the vast social problems that involve male oppression, male violence, or male sexual assault. Some may conclude that there is something bad or wrong with being male. Some have argued that it may seem that therapists treat masculinity as a pathology (Heesacker & Pritchard, 1992; Kelly & Hall, 1992). Traditional male behaviors have even been described as "chronic, terminal, and without redeeming value" (Long, 1987, p. 316).

Traditional counseling requires that men set aside much of their masculine socialization simply to get through the door and ask for help. Once they start talking with a counselor, they may discover other expectations that are difficult to meet. They are supposed to be verbal, expressive, and open. Counselors may want them to be emotionally aware, to acknowledge problems and uncertainty, and to think about their inner lives. Men are likely to feel less independent in such settings, less successful, and less in control. For many traditional men, these factors make counseling feel awkward and unfamiliar. Strong evidence now links these two variables—masculine socialization and a reluctance to seek psychological assistance. Good, Dell, and Mintz (1989) found that traditional attitudes about the male role, concern about expressing emotions, and a concern about expressing affection toward other men were all related to a negative attitude toward seeking counseling.

Reasons for Seeking Counseling

Many men in college begin counseling with the hope that they will be given direction and good advice. It is not uncommon for a man to start a session with, "Well, I came here to get some answers" or "I hope you've got some suggestions, because I've run out of them." Men often see their problems as situational rather than internal. They know they feel badly inside, but they tend to look for explanations in the situations around them. If a change might be made in the external world, then they will feel better inside. As a result, men are more likely than women to feel cautious about opening up and talking about their vulnerabilities and uncertainties. This perspective can change as counseling proceeds, but these expectations and feelings are often present at the outset.

In some ways, these tendencies in men are reinforced by some aspects of the academic environment. Classes teach men about the value of hypothesis testing, sequential thinking, and logical analysis. Professors and textbooks explain solutions to problems. For many classes, the focus is on external elements— cells and chemicals, numbers and treaties, blueprints and structures. Not many classes require men to consider their internal emotional states, their skills at communicating, or their personal limitations.

A taxonomy of presenting issues seen at university counseling centers (Chandler & Gallagher, 1996) suggests that most concerns cluster into only four or five categories: relationship issues, career concerns, mood difficulties, substance misuse, and, perhaps, eating disorders. It may be useful to consider briefly some of these presenting issues in college counseling centers, noting how strongly they are influenced by male gender role attitudes and expectations.

Relationship Issues. First, a primary concern for men in college is relationships. For heterosexual men, the questions are many. Because gender role expectations now vary, norms are unclear. Men must think through their own values on a wide range of gender issues. What sort of relationship does the man want? How does he want to address such issues as decision making, task allocation, and sexual behavior? What appeals to him in the women he meets?

Independence? Strong career goals? Sexual assertiveness? Given the overall changes he is likely experiencing in his life (in communication and critical-thinking skills, for example), these questions may not have immediate and compelling answers for him. He may find himself experimenting in these areas, as he "tries on" various possibilities. This concern with relationships is central for many men. At many counseling centers, it is the most common presenting issue for men. It is not unusual for male-female couples to present themselves for couples counseling. The presenting issues must be taken seriously (for example, "we argue too much" or "we don't see each another enough"), but the underlying questions about gender role behavior are always close to the surface. Questions about sexuality may occur in this context as well. Making decisions about one's sexual behavior can be fraught with uncertainty, socialized pressures, and an awareness of health risks. These factors can lead men to ask for help in sorting out questions about sexual expectations, sexual practices, and sexual dysfunctions.

For gay and bisexual men, questions about relationships are also common, though shaped by additional challenges. It is still true that gay and bisexual men are harassed on campus. They face verbal insults hurled from windows of residence halls and fraternities, physical threats, and exclusion from social groups. This treatment leads some men to hide their sexuality for fear of discrimination. The fact that they may possess numerous skills and intelligence does not eliminate the reality in which they must live—a campus or community environment that can present an unexpected challenge or threat at any moment. These factors make the development of relationships a particular challenge for gay and bisexual men on campus. How does a gay or bisexual man meet other men? Should he attend a campus group of gay, lesbian, and bisexual students? If so, others will know about his sexual orientation, and he might be reluctant to make such a public statement while still in college. More manageable for some men is the experience of a support group for gay and bisexual men, provided by either the campus counseling center or an active group in the community. In this more supportive and private setting, he might begin the process of making friends and developing closer relationships.

Another relationship issue is the ongoing process of individuation from parents. A primary developmental concern for boys is creating a sense of independence from their parents. The awareness that they are being pushed away from a nurturing parent can begin early and can be traumatizing (Pollack, 1995). This early separation is consistent with what many men are socialized to idealize as adults—autonomy. Men do not easily give up this idealization of autonomy. They believe others expect them to be independently successful. Theorists have long noted this tendency in men (David & Brannon, 1976; Pleck, 1987).

In college, men face individuation issues very directly. They begin college as teenagers, with all the financial and emotional dependence implied in that role.

They are expected to graduate as adults, fully ready to assume a productive and financially independent role in society. Along the way, men must redefine their familial and personal relationships. This can be exceedingly painful work, both for men and for their parents and siblings. Parents are not always eager to stop being parental. Drawing new boundary lines can be a formidable task for men.

Career Concerns. A second set of male presenting issues at campus counseling centers is the collection of career concerns. It is nearly axiomatic in this culture: able men must work. Although the number of male homemakers is increasing (U.S. Department of Commerce, 1992), virtually all men in college expect to work. It is often the primary reason for attending college. Men believe (and with reason) that a college degree increases their income potential. Enormous pressure is experienced when a man cannot answer the simple question, "What's your major?" It is a question asked early in nearly every conversation with a new person on campus. Much depends on this choice: his identity, his sense of himself, his economic future. Men who do not have a major field of study risk being thought of as indecisive and confused. If by some chance he should actively consider leaving college to become a full-time homemaker, he would be violating traditional definitions of masculinity. Criticism would follow (Bose, 1980, J. M. Robertson & Verschelden, 1993), and if he ends up talking with a counselor about his life he runs the risk of being given a more severe diagnostic label based only on his nontraditional choices (J. M. Robertson & Fitzgerald, 1990). The importance of career aspirations for college men can hardly be overestimated.

It is no wonder, then, that many men begin counseling by presenting career-related questions. It is familiar and socially appropriate for men to talk about occupational issues in college. They may inquire about testing to see what career might be best for them or begin by reporting difficulties sustaining an interest in a core class.

It should be noted, however, that career uncertainties often accompany personal difficulties. For example, a man may be struggling with external pressures to choose a certain career. A romantic partner or a parent may want him to consider a different career. The other person may criticize his choice ("You can't make any money with a music major" or "You'd make a great architect"). These challenges may lead to questions about his interactions with others. Is his partner correct? Will the relationship end if he remains a music major? Will his parents withdraw their financial support if he does not change his major? These questions are not hypothetical for men, because the threats can be very real. In the counseling center, a man may begin to struggle with such issues as developing his own autonomy, how he might become more assertive with his family, or how to be more expressive of his own needs in a romantic relationship.

Regional and economic factors can shape these career issues. In the Midwest, for example, male students may come from a family farming background that stretches back one hundred years or more. When the family tells him that he is next in line to take over the farm, the pressure to major in some aspect of agriculture or the animal sciences can be intense. If he wants to leave the farm and pursue a career in some other field, the issue is no longer simply a career decision. It is a personal crisis about his male role in the family and the meaning of his life. Similar illustrations of the connection between career and personal issues can be found in other regions of the country and within various religious traditions or ethnic groups. The intergenerational conflict within families over career decisions can be intense.

Mood Difficulties. A third cluster of presenting issues involves moods, especially depression. For about twenty-five years, researchers have been exploring differences in the ways men and women experience depression. Empirical studies have demonstrated that women experience crying spells and feelings of dislike, whereas men tend to withdraw from their worlds and do so without as many tears. Men also tend to somaticize their depression (Funabiki, Bologna, Pepping, & Fitzgerald, 1980; Oliver & Toner, 1990). A particularly notable difference is that many men with depression do not talk about their distress. This theme has appeared in popular literature as well. Note the success of the book by Real (1997), *I Don't Want to Talk about It: Overcoming the Legacy of Male Depression;* Real described this pattern as "male covert depression." This factor may account for much of the difference in reporting rates, with men reporting depressive symptoms only half as often as women (Amenson & Lewinsohn, 1981). Men simply do not talk about mood disorders as readily as do women.

College men do get depressed, whether they report it as readily as women do or not. One factor that has been shown to be related to the depression and psychological distress of college men is traditional masculinity (Good & Mintz, 1990; Good et al., 1995). And the stronger the beliefs in the traditional male gender role, the more likely men are to withdraw socially and to somaticize their depression (Oliver & Toner, 1990). For a long time, it has been noted that college men have difficulty expressing their emotions with words (J. G. Allen & Haccoun, 1976; Pillemer, Krensky, Kleinman, & Goldsmith, 1991). Girls cry; boys do not. Girls talk about their feelings; boys do not. Two decades ago, this tendency of males to avoid things feminine was called a "fear of femininity" (O'Neil, 1981).

In many ways, this avoidance is experienced as positive. An unemotional style in business creates a reputation of being "on top of things" or not being "ruled by his heart." Men who can gather data and make impersonal judgments based on information are praised. Nevertheless, while in college, many men find that women want them to talk more, share more, feel more. It is no longer uncommon for men to actually present this issue to counselors at the beginning of their work. "What does my girlfriend mean when she says to me, 'Tell me about your feelings?' "

One exception to the general reluctance to express emotions is college men's experience with anger. It is not unusual for college men to be required to seek counseling for anger. Typically, this request follows an incident that has gotten the man in trouble with his residence hall, fraternity, athletic department, or the law enforcement community. This issue presents particular difficulties for university counseling centers, because most staff members see themselves as supportive, not punitive. Some counselors refuse to work with mandated cases, noting that their overall goals are educational or that they do not have time to participate in the legal proceedings that might be required. Students may be referred off campus to agencies in the private sector that provide this service rather readily.

Substance Misuse. A fourth group of issues involves the misuse of alcohol and the illegal use of other drugs. Substance abuse continues to be a significant problem on college and university campuses. Exactly how big the problem is can be difficult to quantify. Surveys and other studies use different methods and designs, but they all conclude that substance use is a troublesome problem on campuses in North America. One of the largest studies about the scope of the problem collected information from more than fifty-six thousand students on seventy-eight campuses (Presley & Meilman, 1992). Results showed that about 85 percent of all college students report drinking at least once during the previous year and about 66 percent report drinking at least once during the previous thirty days. Other studies have found similar rates of drinking, ranging from about 80 percent to more than 95 percent of all college students (Meilman, Stone, Gaylor, & Turco, 1990; Wiggins & Wiggins, 1987).

The total amount of alcohol consumed by college students in a single year is staggering. Eigen (1991) has calculated that students consume 430 million gallons of alcohol a year. That is enough to fill an Olympic-sized swimming pool thirty-five hundred times. If the empty beer cans were stacked end to end, they would reach the moon and continue for another seventy thousand miles.

Not surprisingly, most of the alcohol-related problems come with heavy drinking. The percentage of heavy drinkers has remained constant at about 20 percent for many years (Engs & Hanson, 1988). A heavy drinker is usually defined as someone who has drunk an average of more than one ounce of absolute alcohol a day for the previous thirty days.

Even more striking is the level of binge drinking, defined for men as drinking five or more drinks in a row at least once in the two weeks prior to the survey.

Using this definition, the Harvard School of Public Health College Alcohol Study (Wechsler, Dowdall, Maenner, Gledhill-Hoyt, & Lee, 1998) found that nearly half of all college men (48 percent) are binge drinkers. Most college men (58 percent) drink to get drunk, and about one-third get drunk three or more times a month. Similar results have been found in others studies (Douglas, Collins, & Warren, 1997; Johnston, O'Malley, & Bachman, 1997; Presley, Meilman, Cashin, & Lyeria, 1996). A consistent finding in these studies is that college men are more likely than college women to use alcohol, although that gap appears to be narrowing. This difference remains evident even when correcting for body weight. More than twice as many male students as female students drink daily. Men also drink larger quantities when they drink, drink more frequently, are less likely to be abstainers, and have more problems related to alcohol than do women. Most of the differences appear to be found in the heavy drinker category. In one study of first-year students in Massachusetts (Wechsler & Isaac, 1992), about 20 percent of underage men drank at least ten times a month, but only 9 percent of women drank that often. One curious pattern is that college men drink more heavily than noncollege men. College students report higher levels of alcohol use than other young people on virtually all measures (Prendergast, 1994).

For a long time, it has been true that men in fraternities are more likely to drink than other men in college (Canterbury, Gressard, & Vieweg, 1991; Globetti, Stem, Marasco, & Haworth-Hoeppner, 1988; Werner & Greene, 1992). The most recent studies (for example, Wechsler et al., 1998) indicate that four of every five members of a fraternity are binge drinkers.

Binge drinking results in serious problems for men. The Harvard study (Wechsler et al., 1998) asked students to report on the consequences of their drinking. The most frequent problems were having study or sleep interrupted (61 percent), missing a class (65 percent), blackouts (56 percent), getting behind in schoolwork (48 percent), arguing with friends (47 percent), and engaging in unplanned sexual activity (45 percent). Another 29 percent reported being insulted or humiliated. Other studies have found additional consequences, many of them tragic: driving and boating accidents, falls, suicides while intoxicated, criminal behavior including assault and rape, and physical discomfort from drinking too much (Prendergast, 1994). Academically, first-year college men who drink heavily are more likely than those who do not to be on probation, earn lower grade point averages, and drop out of college during their first year (Eigen, 1991). In all, nearly four of every five students reported at least one significant negative consequence related to their drinking.

For counselors of college men, alcohol abuse raises the question of motivation for drinking. Prendergast (1994) reported that college students give several reasons for using alcohol. Some reasons are personal, such the desire to escape or forget problems or to deliberately induce a mood change. Other reasons include the desire to be more social with others or simply to get drunk. It is unfortunate, but many initiation rituals in college involve excessive drinking. These customs, norms, and traditions are difficult to break. Add to the mix the heavy promotion of alcohol to college students at athletic events by the alcohol industry, and it is easy to see why so many college men drink at such high rates.

Illegal drugs are used at various levels. Again, the self-report estimates vary, depending on age, how the questions are asked, region of the country, and so forth. Nationally, the percentage of those who have used marijuana in the past year is about 30 percent; during their college years, about 70 percent try it at least once. Other drugs (hallucinogens, amphetamines, heroin, tranquilizers, inhalants, and cocaine) are used by 6 percent or fewer students (Prendergast, 1994). Men show higher rates of usage of these drugs than do women, although the differences are generally slight (Johnston, O'Malley, & Bachman, 1993).

Knowing about a particular man's motivation for using alcohol or illegal drugs and the specific problems he is facing as a result provides an insight into his story that might point to other psychological or social issues that need to be addressed. Although alcohol itself can become a problem in college, it is also possible that the use of alcohol is experimental, and so exploring the reasons and problems associated with drinking can open up other areas of his life for discussion. Because men become old enough to use alcohol legally while they are students, their earliest experimenting occurs while they are making decisions about many values.

This list of major presenting issues for college men (relationships, careers, moods, and substance abuse) certainly is not exhaustive. Rather, it summarizes the arenas in which most of the common problems presented by college men are found and also highlights the significance of gender role issues in thinking about these concerns.

HELPING COLLEGE MEN

As noted earlier, college men seek counseling less frequently than do college women (Kirk, 1973; Nadler, Maler, & Friedman, 1984; Newton, 1999; M. F. Robertson, 1988), and the role of masculine gender role socialization appears to be a significant deterrent for many men in seeking counseling.

Making Therapy More Appealing to Men

The initial challenge for counselors of college men is to find ways to make it easier for men to seek and experience help (Dickstein, Stein, Pleck, & Myers, 1991; J. M. Robertson & Fitzgerald, 1992). Counselors must thus develop alternative approaches based on the socialization of men, with an awareness of the social and cultural influences that make traditional therapy unappealing (Kilmartin, 1994). Sher (1990) argued that counseling cannot be effective unless the gender role context in which a man seeks therapy is considered. To consider this context, several authors have suggested that new approaches be developed for men, approaches that are more congruent to masculine socialization (J. A. Allen & Gordon, 1990; Brooks, 1998; Levant, 1990; Prosser-Gelwick & Garni, 1988). In general, these approaches suggest that rather than change men to make them comfortable in therapy, it may be more effective to change the traditional therapy model itself (J. M. Robertson & Fitzgerald, 1992; Wilcox & Forrest, 1992).

There is now evidence that when attention is given to this issue, college men's unwillingness to seek help might change. When men are given a choice about the type of help they might receive, their attitudes toward help seeking change. For example, Wisch et al. (1995) found that undergraduate men with increased levels of conflict about gender roles became more open to counselors after viewing a videotape that described cognitive approaches than they did after viewing a videotape about emotional approaches. Hurst (1997) found similar results when college men were given a choice about various types of available help, including solution-focused and cognitive approaches. These results are consistent with the general notion that men are more comfortable when they can think their way to solutions and less comfortable when asked to rely on their emotions or intuition.

J. M. Robertson and L. F. Fitzgerald (1992) found that traditional college men preferred descriptions of help offered in workshops, classes, seminars, and library materials. Similar suggestions have been made by Wilcox and Forrest (1992), who recommended developing psychoeducation groups and individual therapy with a focus on problem solving, action, and cognition. Similarly, Kelly and Hall (1992) presented a model that emphasizes focusing on men's strengths, affirming that what they bring to therapy is positive, addressing the need for active interventions in their personal networks, and avoiding blaming men for not seeking help sooner.

Taken together, these notions suggest that counseling approaches to traditional college men might be more appealing when they are congruent with masculine socialization. That is, if counseling does not require men to set aside their sense of independence, their comfort with goals, tasks, and activities, or their preference of developing an understanding of a situation, then the idea of seeking help might be more appealing. When thinking about providing therapy to both women and men, it is no longer tenable to assume that "one size fits all" (Hurst, 1997). Thinking about therapy for college men from this perspective does indeed make them a "special population" that deserves attention based on social and cultural norms (Heppner, 1995).

Individual Counseling with College Men

Consistent with the previously mentioned themes, a few guidelines for one-on-one counseling of traditionally socialized men can be offered. First, it may be helpful to acknowledge the strength implied when a college man asks for help. Deciding to walk into the counseling room may have taken much time and effort. He is countering much of what he has been socialized to believe about himself just by sitting in the chair. If the counselor can acknowledge this step in some comfortable way and then frame his decision as a strength rather than as an admission of failure, then the man will experience the counseling atmosphere as positive at the outset.

Second, the counselor can experiment with language. The use of language familiar to traditionally socialized men may make the counseling room feel more familiar. Words such as *success, improvement, goals, agreements, progress, tasks, skills, homework, measurable differences,* and *baseline* are all familiar to college men. These concepts are also congruent with traditional socialization. Other words may be less familiar or appealing: *feelings, vulnerability, self-awareness, exploration, internalize, weakness,* and *expressiveness.* The use of familiar words may be helpful at the outset of therapy, when a man is feeling his way (so to speak) in a new environment.

Naturally, over time the therapist can begin to introduce new ideas and define them for male clients. Although talking about cognition and activities may be more comfortable for men, counselors need not avoid introducing ideas related to emotions, systemic relationships, or interactive processing. It helps to define these concepts clearly as they are introduced into the conversation. In the long run, widening his repertoire of skills to include emotional expressiveness, comfort with intimacy, and willingness to share power and resources is very important work for counselors. Rather than think of these issues as either/or (that is, counseling must focus on either masculine-congruent or masculine-incongruent themes), it may be more inclusive and promising to think of both/and. Counselors might begin with masculine-familiar themes and ideas and move toward a broader exploration of more nontraditional tendencies, such as expressiveness, inclusion, and intimacy.

Third, it may help to move slowly when working with emotional issues. The counselor can watch for expressions of anxiety and fear and normalize them. He or she can facilitate rather than push for the expression of affect and recognize that although men want relief from emotional pain, they find vulnerability to be extremely uncomfortable. They may be afraid that they will say too much and then be regarded as weak, unsuccessful, or foolish. They may feel a risk of being exploited, even by the warm and caring therapist. Although many men may deliberately withhold information about affect, it is often more likely that they simply do not have the language to describe their experiences. And so they can try to guess at what they "should" feel, which is often inaccurate. It can be relieving simply to acknowledge this frustration at trying to find that right word to describe an emotion. Supplying men with a list of words used to express common feelings can be helpful. When given such a list, many men actively consult it during sessions, looking for the right word to describe how they are feeling.

Another approach is to suggest to college men that emotions have a purpose, a function. They are not mere interruptions or distractions that get a man off course. Emotions can be described as tools to aid in understanding his personal strengths, his agenda for self-improvement, or his environment. This understanding may be experienced as giving him an edge in meeting various goals and objectives.

When working with men along these lines, I often provide a male-friendly definition of the word *emotion* to make sure we are speaking the same language. I explain that an emotion begins as a response to an Antecedent event (say, meeting a bear on the trail in the Sierras). As soon as the problem is identified, physiological Arousal occurs (for example, changes in heart rate, skin temperature, and pupil size). The purpose of this Arousal is to focus our attention on the event that needs to be addressed. As we survey the scene (quickly, in this case), we Appraise the situation and consider various options that might address the problem of the bear (fleeing, fighting, or freezing). When we make our choice, we then Act to solve the problem that the emotion identified for us in the first place. This whole experience can be given a name (such as fear or panic). For many men, this simple definition of an emotion in the form of a mnemonic (Antecedent, Arousal, Appraisal, Action) allows them to see emotions as significant and adaptive, not simply as "something women do." Far from leaving men feeling weak and vulnerable, emotions give them a sense of being adaptive and constructive (Plutchik, 1980; J. M. Robertson & Freeman, 1995).

It is important for counselors to be aware of their own emotions as they work with college men. Being willing to talk about their emotions at appropriate times may provide a model for men, especially when the therapist is male. It is not always easy to work with men who are beginning to experience intense emotions that have been blocked for years. Counselors who monitor their own levels of comfort in working with these issues are likely to avoid pitfalls associated with their own issues related to intimacy or power.

Fourth, counselors must take rationalizations seriously. Men can become rather skilled in offering plausible reasons and explanations for their behavior. In many college classes, men are rewarded when they think carefully, logically, analytically. And when they have finished college, they hope to be paid well for being incisive in their analysis of a problem. But to engage in exclusively cognitive discussions about problems makes therapeutic progress difficult. In some ways, responding to rationalizations requires a balancing act by counselors. On the one hand, it can be useful to avoid criticizing the tendency to look for rational explanations of a problem, given that society often sees such explanations as strengths for men. On the other hand, it is also helpful to broaden the scope of inquiry, so that men can include more affective, relational, and systemic elements in their work as clients.

Fifth, counselors can give men an opportunity to practice new patterns. College men are familiar with the ideas of homework, labs, and practice sessions. Extending this notion into the personal domain is familiar and reasonable for many college men. Conducting "little experiments" as men try a new approach to a problem gives them the impression that they are actually doing something, trying something. The variety of options for homework is virtually endless. Both counselor and client can participate in the creation of assignments outside the counseling hour. Although this approach may seem to represent a preference for cognitive-behavioral therapy, it does not need to be limited to that approach.

Groups and Workshops for College Men

Even though many counselors believe that men are seeking individual psychotherapy in greater numbers (see, for example, Betcher & Pollack, 1993; Meth & Pasick, 1990), many men are still highly resistant to the idea of one-on-one counseling. The idea is too threatening, too bewildering, or too confusing for them consider. For these treatment-resistant men, Brooks (1996) has argued that the all-male group is the best alternative. In a similar vein, Andronico (1996) suggests that "men are more familiar" with groups "than with any other type of format that is currently used for interpersonal growth and change" (p. xviii).

Brooks (1996) has noted that the group format offers several specific benefits to men. Groups provide a familiar terrain to men who have been in groups all their lives—sports, scouting, work groups, and so forth. Because the idea of talking about important issues in groups is already familiar, it is relatively easy to imagine using a group or class to gain information about personal questions as well. Groups also decrease men's social isolation. Even though men participate in other groups in their lives, the focus typically is on the sharing of activities, such as hunting, car repairs, and sports (Brehm, 1985). As a result, men can experience a social isolation and loneliness that groups can directly address. Brooks (1996) further argues that groups help men counter an overdependence on women, provide opportunities for self-disclosure, instill hope, help men discover emotional connections, and help men improve communication skills.

Numerous protocols have been developed for working with groups. McKay and Paleg (1992) and Andronico (1996) have edited volumes filled with practical ideas on running various theme and therapy groups. Andronico's book is designed specifically for male groups. Although counselors likely have their own preferences for organizing and developing groups, these resources offer many ideas. Group leaders have written about a wide variety of issues that have implications for men. Examples of group themes from just these two collections include shyness, depression, anger, assertiveness, incest offenders, addictions, male mentoring, gay issues, fathering, noncustodial fathering, parenting, sexual abuse survival, and men who batter.

Many of these groups present a workshop format, which offers a specific focus for men. These workshops or classes usually meet for a specified number of sessions and limit their focus to the announced topic. It is common for groups to consider various activities and exercises outside the group session. The purpose of the homework is to facilitate continuity during the week and to increase the rate of change. Written protocols are detailed (McKay & Paleg, 1992) and include such issues as screening and selection of group members, time and duration, structure, and goals. On college campuses, workshops are experienced somewhat like classes. They meet at the same time every week and have an informal syllabus that describes the group's purpose and focus.

Other groups focus less on given topics and more on therapy. As such, the intervention strategies are more broadly stated. For example, Jolliff and Horne (1996, pp. 65, 66) list twenty such strategies, including "teach clients the skills of authenticity and self-disclosure," "focus always on empowering the client," "normalize and encourage self-care," "model spontaneity, emotional expression, and self-disclosure," and "communicate affection, warmth, and gentleness."

The absence of women in these groups can offer several benefits. When heterosexual men do not have the opportunity to interact with women in a group, they cannot flirt. They may become more genuine and self-reflective than when they are with women. Men then tend to be more expressive, more relaxed, and more talkative. They seem to share their feelings with each other more easily. Men are socialized to talk about emotions more with women than with men. With no women present, they must turn to each other for support. The result is greater closeness with other men. They develop friendships with other men that are open, trusting, and caring. They can express feelings and thoughts in an all-male group that they would be reluctant to address in a mixed group. For example, they can talk openly about sexual questions and relationship issues. They can be expressive of anger without worrying about how a woman might interpret the rage. Techniques that have been tried in therapy groups for men include storytelling, genograms, role playing, unsent letter writing, poetry, and many more (see Jolliff & Horne, 1996).

McPhee (1996) recommends that therapy groups for men begin with a brief check-in at the beginning of the session, during which each member talks for one to two minutes about his week and what he wants from the group. He also suggests that the group end with closing statements, during which each member summarizes his experience in that particular session. Most groups emphasize confidentiality and develop policies for members missing meetings.

Men's Clinics on Campus

Some campuses are organizing clinics that coordinate medical and counseling services directed toward men (Stevens, 1998). Team members include psychologists or other counselors, physicians, physician assistants, and health educators. Together, this group forms the staff in the clinic, sometimes with health center space devoted to examination and interview rooms. These teams tend to be interested in offering proactive activities, such as presentations in fraternities, residence halls, and classrooms. They may participate in a panel at a public meeting in the student union. Presentation topics include sexually transmitted diseases, general health questions related to the genitals (for example, circumcision, contraception, urination, and testicular cancer), alcohol and recreational drug use, and sexual behavior.

Those who staff these clinics report that it is important to create a strong media awareness of their presence on campus. Men are more likely to use services that are well advertised and seem readily available (L. Moeller, personal communication, September 13, 1999; Stevens, 1998). Plans can be developed to market the clinic through posters, campus newspaper advertising, and public service announcements on the campus radio or low-power television station. The content of the advertisements not only announces the clinic's services but also focuses attention on particular health-related issues that the health team staff addresses.

Several themes have emerged in working with men in these settings (Stevens, 1998). Practitioners have discovered that many college men feel especially concerned about removing their clothing during an exam. Health team members have noted several explanations, including concerns that some men have about the appearance or responsiveness of their genitals. Homophobia appears to be an additional concern. Many men also seem uneasy about the possibility of being judged by their practitioners, especially with regard to sexual behavior. Initial questions are often tentative and asked indirectly. When they feel safe and are given permission to ask questions, most college men will talk about difficult issues. They may appear eager or even obsessive in their questioning. Perhaps this eagerness should not be surprising, because for many of these men, these conversations are the first they have had with anyone about these issues. It is not unusual to find that after men have presented their initial concern, they will then have questions about other personal matters, such as sexual identity, sexual compulsions, relationship interactions, prostitution, or other health matters. Given the psychological nature of many of these questions, the idea of working as a team is quite appealing to many physicians.

Other ideas associated with a men's clinic include the use of assessments and inventories to highlight concerns, a resource library for private reading, and a Web page that offers information of particular interest to men. Folders can be developed and distributed to men in groups on campus; the folders may include brochures on a variety of health topics such as testicular self-exams; the use of nicotine, alcohol, and other substances; rape awareness; anger management; and sexually transmitted diseases.

Using Media to Help College Men

Given the masculine socialization themes described earlier in this chapter and else-where in this book, it is not surprising that the use of media to convey informa-tion to men can be quite effective. I highlight three ideas in this section. The first is the social norms approach to drinking behavior on campus. The staff at Northern Illinois University began an experiment in 1990 that has been effective for more than a decade (Haines, 1998). Over that time, campus officials have mea-sured a reduction in binge drinking of 44 percent. Other universities have started similar projects based on the same research and have found similar reductions. The approach is based on research (Berkowitz, 1991; Perkins & Berkowitz, 1986) that found that college students generally overestimate the amount of alcohol their classmates consume. They called this impression a "false norm." Other research indicates that social norms have a powerful influence on behavior. The staff at Northern Illinois University put these two ideas together and used the media to inform students about the actual social norms on campus. At Northern Illinois, the media campaign was built around stating a simple fact over and over again: "Most Northern Illinois students drink zero to five drinks when they party." The first year after introducing this campaign, binge drinking went down 18 percent, and the trend has continued every since. The same approach has been used at several other campuses, each time with a measurable reduction in binge drinking. This approach has been much more effective than media campaigns based on fear or campaigns that emphasize the harm that can come from abusive drinking. The typical stu-dent is portrayed as a moderate drinker, not an abusive drinker. In addition to advertisements in the campus newspaper, the campaigns include a weekly col-umn, regular press releases, and other stories about normal drinking. Posters and leaflets are displayed in various locations. Although this approach may not seem like counseling in the traditional sense, counseling centers can participate in such activities with a strong expectation that the drinking behavior of men who would never come to counseling might be altered. Counselors can also refer to social norms data from the campus in talking directly with students in counseling.

A second example is the use of campus radio stations. Many campuses have radio stations that offer programming to students. Radio station personnel are often interested in the perspectives of staff members at the counseling center. In addition to providing interviews on topics of interest in the news, counselors can be creative in their use of this medium. Radio spots have been used on col-lege campuses to provide psychological information directly to students on such issues as study skills, relationship issues, diversity, and holiday concerns (Wendt & Johnston, 1987). Brief dramatizations have also been used to illustrate com-mon problem situations for students (Godin et al., 1986).

An interactive use of radio is also possible. At Kansas State University, a physi-cian and a psychologist from the counseling center have teamed up to produce a call-in talk show on the topic of sexuality. The purpose of the show is "to provide information about sexually related issues to the students" on campus (Van Haveren, Blank, & Bentley, 1999, p. 5). Each program opens with the physician and psychologist providing information about a given topic and then inviting listeners to join the conversation by calling in with their questions. Common topics include date rape, sexually transmitted diseases, how to talk with partners about sexual behavior, alcohol and sexual responsiveness, birth control issues, sexual etiquette, and relationship issues. It is interesting to note that men are quite willing to call the show and actually do so at much higher rates than they visit counselors. Callers can remain anonymous. In fact, a caller can leave a question with the producer and not go on the air at all. Even though conversation is not private (thousands are listening), the caller can remain anonymous. This approach is consistent with the finding that men with traditional values are drawn to services that offer information directly to them (J. M. Robertson & Fitzgerald, 1992).

A third idea is to make men aware of self-help resources. Simply making information available so that men can find it without having to set up an appointment to talk with a counselor makes it easier for many men to inform themselves. The full range of media can be used: print, the Internet, radio, and television. With regard to written resources, counseling centers and other campus offices may cooperate in the development of posters, space ads in the campus newspaper, or a campus-specific Web site. Counseling centers around the country have coordinated their efforts and put many of their handouts and brochures on the Web. Men can simply look up a topic and do some initial reading on their own. An address that contains many of these psychoeducational "handouts" is the Counseling Center Village (http://ub-counseling.buffalo.edu /ccv.html). The site contains self-help information on about twenty-five topics. Although these resources are not intended to be exhaustive or to take the place of psychotherapy, they provide men with introductory information. If they make an appointment, men are more likely to come with questions raised by the brochures.

The use of media by counselors may seem different from "doing therapy" with men. And yet the purpose is very similar—to provide men with assistance in addressing significant problems. Developing alternatives to the one-on-one counseling relationship clearly brings more men into contact with helping professionals and is respectful of the socialization still experienced by traditional men.

Men undergo many changes while in college. They modify many of their attitudes, values, morals, ideas, and relationship styles. They improve their ability to think critically and to communicate their ideas. They become more autonomous, less authoritarian, and more flexible about gender roles.

Given the breadth of these changes, it is not surprising that college men seek counseling. Yet they seek help only half as frequently as do women. One widely regarded explanation for this gender difference is that masculine socialization simply makes individual therapy unappealing.

When they do ask for help, men commonly present issues about relationships, career concerns, mood disorders, and substance use problems. All of these issues are heavily colored by gender role expectations and themes. Suggestions for working with these issues in one-on-one counseling include acknowledging the strength involved in asking for help, using masculine-congruent language, working slowly with emotional issues, describing emotions as functional and adaptive, taking rationalizations seriously, and providing ample opportunity for men to act on the insights they are gaining in therapy.

Structured workshops and open-ended groups provide a setting for men that is comfortable and familiar. Groups seem especially helpful to college men otherwise resistant to individual therapy. In addition, campus counselors may want to explore the development of a men's clinic with medical staff or consider a creative use of campus media to reach men.

The college years are critical in the development of a man's life story. He trains for a career. He looks for a primary relationship. He develops his own values and goals for life. Counselors who work with men during this phase of their lives are given both an enormous opportunity and an awesome responsibility.

References

Allen, J. A., & Gordon, S. (1990). Creating a framework for change. In R. L. Meth & R. S. Pasick (Eds.), *Men in therapy: The challenge of change* (pp. 131–151). New York: Guilford Press.

Allen, J. G., & Haccoun, S. M. (1976). Sex differences in emotionality: A multidimensional approach. *Human Relations, 29,* 711–722.

Amenson, C. S., & Lewinsohn, P. M. (1981). An investigation into the observed sex differences in prevalence of unipolar depression. *Journal of Abnormal Psychology, 90,* 1–13.

Andronico, M. P. (1996). *Men in groups: Insights, interventions, and psychoeducational work.* Washington, DC: American Psychological Association.

Berkowitz, A. D. (1991). Following imaginary peers: How norm misperceptions influence student substance abuse. In G. Lindsay & G. Rulf (Eds.), *Project direction* (Module No. 2). Muncie, IN: Ball State University.

Betcher, R. W., & Pollack, W. S. (1993). *In a time of fallen heroes: The re-creation of masculinity.* New York: Atheneum.

Bose, C. (1980). Social status of the homemaker. In S. F. Berk (Ed.), *Women and household labor* (pp. 69–87). Beverly Hills, CA: Sage.

Bowen, H. (1977). Investment in learning: The individual and social value of American higher education. San Francisco: Jossey-Bass.

Brehm, S. (1985). *Intimate relationships.* New York: Random House.

Brooks, G. (1996). Treatment for therapy-resistant men. In M. P. Andronico (Ed.), *Men in groups: Insights, interventions, and psychoeducational work* (pp. 7–19). Washington, DC: American Psychological Association.

Brooks, G. (1998). *A new psychotherapy for traditional men.* San Francisco: Jossey-Bass.

Canterbury, R. J., Gressard, C. F., & Vieweg, W.V.R. (1991). Alcohol abuse among college freshmen in Greek societies. *Virginia Medical Quarterly, 118*(3), 171–172.

Chandler, L. A., & Gallagher, R. P. (1996). Developing a taxonomy for problems seen at a university counseling center. *Measurement and Evaluation in Counseling and Development, 29*(1), 4–12.

Cheatham, H. E., Shelton, T. O., & Ray, W. J. (1987). Race, sex, causal attribution, and help-seeking behavior. *Journal of College Student Personnel, 28*(6), 559–568.

Chickering, A. (1969). *Education and identity.* San Francisco: Jossey-Bass.

Corey, S. (1936). Attitude differences between college classes: A summary and criticism. *Journal of Educational Psychology, 27,* 321–330.

David, D. S., & Brannon, D. (1976). *The forty-nine percent majority: The male sex role.* New York: Random House.

Dickstein, L. J., Stein, T. S., Pleck, J. H., & Myers, M. F. (1991). Men's changing social roles in the 1990s: Emerging issues in the psychiatric treatment of men. *Hospital and Community Psychiatry, 42*(7), 701–705.

Douglas, K. D., Collins, J. L., & Warren, C. (1997). Results from the 1995 National College Health Risk Behavior Survey. *Journal of American College Health, 46,* 55–66.

Eigen, L. D. (1991). Alcohol practices, policies, and potentials of American college and universities: An Office for Substance Abuse Prevention White Paper. Rockville, MD: U.S. Department of Health and Human Services, Alcohol, Drug Abuse, and Mental Health Administration.

Engs, R. C., & Hanson, D. J. (1988). University students' drinking patterns and problems: Examining the effects of raising the purchasing age. *Public Health Report, 103,* 667–673.

Feldman, K., & Newcomb, T. (1969). *The impact of college on students.* San Francisco: Jossey-Bass.

Funabiki, D., Bologna, N., Pepping, M., & Fitzgerald, K. (1980). Revisiting sex differences in the expression of depression. *Journal of Abnormal Psychology, 89,* 194–202.

Globetti, G., Stem, J. T., Marasco, F., & Haworth-Hoeppner, S. (1988). Student residence arrangements and alcohol use and abuse: A research note. *Journal of College and University Student Housing, 18*(1), 28–33.

Godin, S., Angevine, J., Asher, M., Clorez, S., Combs, B., Jacobson, S., Juskowski, R., & Miller, R. (1986). A psychoeducational prevention program for college radio stations. *Journal of College Student Personnel, 27,* 87–88.

Good, G., Dell, D., & Mintz, L. (1989). Male roles and gender-role conflict: Relationships to help-seeking in men. *Journal of Counseling Psychology, 3*, 295–300.

Good, G. E., & Mintz, L. B. (1990). Gender role conflict and depression in college men: Evidence for compounded risk. *Journal of Counseling and Development, 69*, 17–21.

Good, G. E., Robertson, J. M., O'Neil, J. M., Fitzgerald, L. F., Stevens, M., DeBord, K. A., & Bartels, K. M. (1995). Male gender role conflict: Psychometric issues and relations to psychological distress. *Journal of Counseling Psychology, 42*(1), 3–10.

Good, G. E., & Wood, P. K. (1995). Male gender role conflict, depression, and help seeking: Do men face double jeopardy? *Journal of Counseling and Development, 74*(1), 70–75.

Haines, M. P. (1998). Social norms: A wellness model for health promotion in higher education. *Newsletter of the National Wellness Association, 14*(4), 1, 8.

Heesacker, M., & Pritchard, S. (1992). In a different voice, revisited: Men, women, and emotion. *Journal of Mental Health Counseling, 14*(3), 274–290.

Heppner, P. P. (1995). On gender role conflict in men: Future directions and implications for counseling. *Journal of Counseling Psychology, 42*(1), 20–23.

Hurst, M. A. (1997). *The best fit in counseling men: Are there solutions to treating men as the problem?* Unpublished doctoral dissertation, Ball State University, Muncie, IN.

Jacob, P. (1957). Changing values in college: An exploratory study of the impact of college teaching. New York: Harper & Row.

Johnson, R., & Brock, D. (1988). Gender-specific therapy. *Journal of Psychology and Christianity, 7*(4), 50–60.

Johnston, L. D., O'Malley, P. M., & Bachman, J. G. (1997). National survey results on drug use from the Monitoring the Future Study, 1975–1992: Vol. 2. College students and young adults (NIH Publication No. 93–3598). Rockville, MD: National Institute on Drug Abuse.

Jolliff, D. L., & Horne, A. M. (1996). Group counseling for middle-class men. In M. P. Andronico (Ed.), *Men in groups: Insights, interventions, and psychoeducational work* (pp. 51–68). Washington, DC: American Psychological Association.

Kelly, K. R., & Hall, A. S. (1992). Toward a developmental model for counseling men. *Journal of Mental Health Counseling, 14*(3), 257–273.

Kilmartin, C. T. (1994). *The masculine self.* New York: Macmillan.

Kirk, B. A. (1973). Characteristics of users of counseling centers and psychiatric services on a college campus. *Journal of Counseling Psychology, 20*, 463–470.

Levant, R. (1990). Psychological services designed for men: A psychoeducational approach. *Psychotherapy, 27*(3), 309–315.

Long, D. (1987). Working with men who batter. In M. Sher, M. Stevens, G. Good, & G. A. Eichenfield (Eds.), *Handbook of counseling and psychotherapy with men* (pp. 306–320). Newbury Park, CA: Sage.

Lott, J. K., Ness, M. E., Alcorn, J. S., & Greer, R. M. (1999). The impact of gender and age on referrals to psychological counseling. *Journal of Counseling Psychology, 46*(1), 132–136.

Magoon, T. M. (1999). *College and university counseling center directors' 1998–1999 data bank: Analysis by enrollment.* (Available from Thomas M. Magoon, University of Maryland, College Park, MA 20742)

McKay, M., & Paleg, K. (1992). *Focal group psychotherapy.* Oakland, CA: New Harbinger.

McPhee, D. M. (1996). Techniques in group psychotherapy with men. In M. P. Andronico (Ed), *Men in groups: Insights, interventions, and psychoeducational work* (pp. 21–34). Washington, DC: American Psychological Association.

Meilman, P. W., Stone, J. E., Gaylor, M. S., & Turco, J. H. (1990). Alcohol use among undergraduates: Current use and 10-year trends. *Journal of Studies in Alcohol, 51,* 389–395.

Meth, R. L., & Pasick, R. S. (1990). *Men in therapy: The challenge of change.* New York: Guilford Press.

Nadler, A., Maler, S., & Friedman, A. (1984). Effects of helper's sex, subject's androgyny, and self-evaluation on males' and females' willingness to seek and receive help. *Sex Roles, 10,* 327, 339.

Newton, F. (1999). *Annual report of university counseling services.* (Available from University Counseling Services, 232 Lafene Student Health Center, Manhattan, KS 66503–3301).

Oliver, S. J., & Toner, B. B. (1990). The influence of gender role typing on the expression of depressive symptoms. *Sex Roles, 22,* 775–790.

O'Neil, J. M. (1981). Male sex role conflicts, sexism, and masculinity: Psychological implications for men, women, and the counseling psychologist. *Counseling Psychologist, 9*(2), 61–80.

Pascarella, E. T., & Terenzini, P. T. (1991). *How college affects students: Findings and insights from twenty years of research.* San Francisco: Jossey-Bass.

Perkins, H. W., & Berkowitz, A. D. (1986). Perceiving the community norms of alcohol use among students: Some research implications for alcohol education programming. *International Journal of the Addictions, 21,* 961–976.

Perry, W. (1970). Forms of intellectual and ethical development in the college years: A scheme. New York: Holt, Rinehart & Winston.

Pillemer, D. B., Krensky, L., Kleinman, S. N., & Goldsmith, L. R. (1991). Chapters in narratives: Evidence from oral histories of the first year in college. *Journal of Narrative and Life History, 1*(1), 3–14.

Pleck, J. H. (1987). *The myth of masculinity.* Cambridge, MA: MIT Press.

Plutchik, R. (1980). *Emotion: A psychoevolutionary synthesis.* New York: Harper & Row.

Pollack, W. S. (1995). Deconstructing dis-identification: Rethinking psychoanalytic concepts of male development. *Psychoanalysis and Psychotherapy, 12*(1), 30–45.

Prendergast, M. L. (1994). Substance use and abuse among college students: A review of recent literature. *College Health, 43,* 99–113.

Presley, C. A., & Meilman, P. W. (1992). *Alcohol and drugs on American college campuses: A report of college presidents.* Carbondale: Southern Illinois University, Student Health Program Wellness Center.

Presley, C. A., Meilman, P. W., Cashin, J. R., & Lyeria, R. (1996). Alcohol and drugs on American college campuses: Use, consequences, and perceptions of the campus environment: Vol. 4. 1992–1994. Carbondale: Southern Illinois University.

Prosser-Gelwick, B., & Garni, K. F. (1988). Counseling and psychotherapy with college men. *Changing roles for men on campus.* New Directions for Student Services, No. 42. San Francisco: Jossey Bass.

Real, T. (1997). I don't want to talk about it: Overcoming the legacy of male depression. New York: Scribner.

Robertson, J. M., & Fitzgerald, L. (1990). The (mis)treatment of men: Effects of client gender role and life-style on diagnosis and attribution of pathology. *Journal of Counseling Psychology, 37*(1), 3–9.

Robertson, J. M., & Fitzgerald, L. F. (1992). Overcoming the masculine mystique: Preferences for alternative forms of assistance among men who avoid counseling. *Journal of Counseling Psychology, 39*(2), 240–246.

Robertson, J. M., & Freeman, R. (1995). Men and emotions: Developing masculine-congruent views of affective expressiveness. *Journal of College Student Development, 36*(6), 606, 607.

Robertson, J. M., & Verschelden, C. (1993). Voluntary male homemakers and female providers: Reported experiences and perceived social reactions. *Journal of Men's Studies, 1*(4), 383–402.

Robertson, M. F. (1988). Differential use by male and female students of the counseling service of an Australian tertiary college: Implications for service design and counseling models. *International Journal of the Advancement of Counseling, 11,* 231–240.

Robins, L. N., Heltzer, J. E., Weissman, M. M., Orraschel, H., Gruenberg, E., Burke, J. D., & Reiger, D. A. (1984). Lifetime prevalence of specific psychiatric disorders in three sites. *Archives of General Psychiatry, 41,* 949–958.

Sher, M. (1990). Effect of gender role incongruities on men's experience as clients in psychotherapy. *Psychotherapy, 27*(3), 322–326.

Shueman, S. A., & Medvene, A. M. (1981). Student perceptions of appropriateness of presenting problems: What's happened to attitudes in 20 years? *Journal of College Student Personnel, 22,* 264–267.

Sipps, G. J., & Janeczek, R. G. (1986). Expectancies for counselors in relation to subject gender traits. *Journal of Counseling Psychology, 33*(2), 214–216.

Stevens, M. A. (1998). *Men's health team at the University of Southern California.* Symposium conducted at the meeting of the American Psychological Association, San Francisco.

Survey results summary for University Counseling Services. (1997). Unpublished manuscript, Kansas State University, Manhattan.

U.S. Department of Commerce, Bureau of the Census. (1992). *Current Populations Reports, Series P-20, No. 458, Household and family characteristics: March, 1991.* Washington, DC: U.S. Government Printing Office.

U.S. Department of Health and Human Services, National Center for Health Statistics. (1992, January 7). *Monthly Vital Statistics Report, 40* (Suppl. 2).

Van Haveren, R. A., Blank, W. J., & Bentley, K. W. (1999). *Lafeneline: Promoting sexual health through college radio.* Manuscript submitted for publication. (Available from Rick Van Haveren, Counseling Center, Georgia State University, Atlanta, GA 30303)

Vessey, J. T., & Howard, K. I. (1993). Who seeks psychotherapy? *Psychotherapy, 30,* 546–553.

Wechsler, H., Dowdall, G. W., Maenner, G., Gledhill-Hoyt, J., & Lee, H. (1998). Changes in binge drinking and related problems among American college students between 1993 and 1997: Results of the Harvard School of Public Health College Alcohol Study. *College Health, 47,* 57–67.

Wechsler, H., & Isaac, N. (1991). Alcohol and the college freshman: Binge drinking and associated problems. A report to the AAA Foundation for Traffic Safety. Boston: Harvard School of Public Health, Youth Alcohol-Drug Program.

Wendt, K. F., & Johnston, P. G. (1987). "60 seconds to think about": Radio announcements for college counseling centers. *Journal of College Student Personnel, 28,* 91–92.

Werner, M. J., & Greene, J. W. (1992). Problem drinking among college freshmen. *Journal of Adolescent Health Care, 13*(6), 487–492.

Wiggins, J. A., & Wiggins, B. B. (1987). Drinking at a southern university: Its description and correlates. *Journal of Studies in Alcohol, 48*(4), 319–324.

Wilcox, D. W., & Forrest, L. (1992). The problems of men and counseling: Gender bias or gender truth? *Journal of Mental Health Counseling, 14*(3), 291–304.

Wisch, A. F., Mahalik, R., Jr., Hayes, J. A., & Nutt, E. D. (1995). The impact of gender role conflict and counseling technique on psychological help-seeking in men. *Sex Roles, 33*(1–2), 77–89.

CHAPTER SEVEN

Psychotherapy with Men in Prison

Terry A. Kupers

The prison population in the United States quadrupled between 1980 and 2000. Although the percentage of female prisoners is increasing rapidly, more than 90 percent of prisoners are men. Most people who go to prison are poor, at least 40 percent are functionally illiterate, and people of color are vastly overrepresented among prisoners: approximately 50 percent are African American, another 15 to 20 percent are Latino, and 1 percent are Native American (a disproportionately high percentage relative to the percentage of Native Americans in the general population). The imprisonment binge has devastating effects on low-income and inner-city communities. For example, more than one-third of African American men between the ages of eighteen and twenty-nine are under the control of the criminal justice system, behind bars or on probation or parole (Mauer & Hurling, 1995). Consider the effects on children who have fathers in prison and the effects on their communities. And this society is not kind to ex-felons. It is almost impossible for them to find work; in a time when the "lock-'em-up" rhetoric prevails, laws are passed to preclude their receiving financial support to attend school. With so many states denying ex-felons the vote, over a million African American men are disenfranchised for life.

Terrible things go on inside men's prisons. For example, the kind of massive crowding one finds inside is known to increase the incidence of violence, psychiatric breakdown, suicide, and medical illness (Thornberry & Call, 1983). Gymnasiums are converted into impromptu dormitories housing over a hundred prisoners. The lights stay on all night, there is constant noise, and, not surprisingly, fights are frequent. Meaningful rehabilitation has been dismantled because law-and-order buffs have stigmatized it as "coddling," and consequently idleness is the rule. Rape is always a threat, and men learn to act tough if only to avoid harm. The male code prohibits stepping in to halt victimization and rape, as well as any display of a man's vulnerability and pain.

Is it any wonder that as many as 16 to 25 percent of prisoners and ex-prisoners suffer from significant mental disorders? Some entered prison with a history of psychiatric breakdown and hospitalization. An unprecedented number of individuals with serious mental illnesses are incarcerated today because of several intersecting trends, including deinstitutionalization, repeated budget cuts for public mental health programs in the community, the criminalization of homelessness, and courts being much less willing than they once were to consider a defendant's psychiatric disorder as a mitigating factor. Other prisoners who were emotionally stable before incarceration develop significant mental disorders while serving time. The crowding, idleness (due to the dismantling of many rehabilitation and education programs), brutality, threat of rape, and widespread use of solitary confinement in punitive segregation and supermaximum security units all add to the stress that ordinarily accompanies incarceration. The result is a large proportion of prisoners who need mental health care.

PRISON EXAGGERATES TOXIC MASCULINITY

Jim Messerschmidt (1993) claims men use crime as a resource for constructing masculinity. The assumption is that manhood is an accomplishment and not a given. Whether by pulling a heist, joyriding in a stolen car, doing a drive-by shooting to prove one is enough of a "man's man" to be in the gang, or participating in a college fraternity gang rape, young men use crime to prove their manhood and initiate others.

Toxic Masculinity in Prison

Not all of the qualities and traits we associate with masculinity are problematic. Toxic masculinity, on the other hand, is the constellation of traits in men that serve to foster domination, the devaluation of women, homophobia, and wanton violence. Toxic masculinity plays a part in accomplishing manhood, such as in the form of exaggerated bravado and male posturing, rape, and domestic violence. Of course, class and race figure prominently; although young men of all classes and races commit crimes to prove their masculinity, it is disproportionately low-income men of color who are arrested, convicted, and sentenced to long prison terms (Miller, 1996).

I do not want to give the wrong impression; 75 percent of people entering prison today have not been convicted of violent crimes. There are some very heinous criminals behind bars, but the majority of prisoners have been convicted of relatively minor crimes, usually drug related, and will be released after several years. But they are forced to dwell in brutal correctional facilities in which toughness is the key to survival, so even if they were not especially aggressive and misogynist when they entered prison, they must become versed in hypermasculine posturing and violence merely to stay alive and protect their honor. Of course, the training does not help them prepare for postrelease adjustment as caring, loving men.

Unfortunately, toxic masculinity is unrestrained and proliferates wildly in prison. The prison code is an exaggeration of the unspoken male code on the outside. The schoolyard fight in which the bully stands over the vanquished while the other boys join him in jeering the "sissy" is replayed daily on prison yards where nobody steps in to halt the fight and men are beaten, raped, and even killed. And in this world of extremity and violence, men's need to keep their cards close to their chests and refuse to disclose their needs and pains often prevents them from seeking the kind of mental health care that might help them do their time and come out of prison emotionally prepared to lead productive, noncriminal lives.

At the same time, it is quite dangerous in prison to expose one's vulnerabilities, and thus men's tendency not to express their feelings and inner experiences can serve them well to stay out of certain kinds of trouble. For example, other prisoners pick on men known to be "weak in the head," and the psychiatric notes in a man's "jacket" (file) can cause a parole board to postpone release indefinitely based on the assumption that his mental illness would make him a threat to the community.

Plight of Prisoners with Serious Mental Illness

The plight of prisoners with serious mental illness is a frightening example. The stigmatization of weakness creates a real hell for these prisoners. Other prisoners call the prisoner with a serious mental illness a "ding" or a "bug" and victimize him. He is certain to be teased and likely to be beaten and raped. When I tour a prison in the middle of the day I find a large number of prisoners in their bunks with the lights out. Many prisoners with serious mental illness elect to remain in their cells all day to avoid victimization in the dayroom and on the yard. Of course, they become depressed and their prognoses worsen, but as one man told me, "At least that way I'll survive and get out of here alive." Another group of prisoners with serious mental illness cannot control their temper, get into fights, and are sent to "the hole." Today that is likely to mean spending years in solitary confinement in a supermaximum or maxi-maxi security unit. I have toured such units in five states, and I always discover that between a quarter and a half of the residents of these high-tech isolation units have severe psychosis. Prisoners with serious mental illness are selectively confined in punitive segregation units, and they are especially prone to the psychosis-inducing effect of the extreme isolation and idleness (Grassian & Friedman, 1986).

Another tragic example is the plight of the man who has been raped or forced to become the sex slave or "galboy" of a tougher prisoner. Often he develops posttraumatic stress disorder, but the prison code and the unkindness of security staff prevent him from seeking the appropriate mental health treatment. In many prisons, if he complains to staff members that he has been raped, they will demand that he tell them the name of the perpetrator before they can offer any help. He is in a bind. If he names the rapist, he will be considered a snitch and likely killed. If he does not, he will be denied a move to a safer unit and will not be given any treatment. In many prisons there is even a rule that a mental health clinician who hears that a prisoner-client has been raped must report the incident to security staff. In addition, because mental health resources in prisons are very scarce relative to the large number of prisoners in need, most prisons concentrate their resources on prisoners actively suffering from serious mental illness such as schizophrenia and provide little or no treatment for posttraumatic stress disorder. These and other equally outrageous realities preclude the survivor of rape from attaining safety and proper treatment while he is incarcerated.

The mental health clinician attempting to offer a male prisoner or ex-prisoner psychotherapy must be well versed in the relevant gender issues, the obvious racial and class biases and tensions, the "prison code," and the stark reality and brutality of life in prison.

THERAPEUTIC ISSUES

Men who go to prison are deeply wounded, and the prison experience is generally traumatic. With a growing proportion of individuals with serious mental illness going to prison today, and many more suffering emotional deterioration inside, the challenges facing correctional mental health clinicians are great (Kupers, 2000). The potential for facilitating healing and growth are enormous as well. There are some expectable hazards and some predictable barriers to quality mental health treatment, but by identifying them and being realistic in taking them on, clinicians can accomplish much.

Independence and Collaboration

The first thing mental health clinicians must establish is a certain degree of independence from security staff—not total independence, however; clinicians rely on security staff for their safety and much of the management of their clients' everyday lives. But when mental health staff members bow to every directive from security staff, the prisoners with mental illness lose out. For instance, security staff might demand access to information a clinician considers confidential such as the identity of a prisoner that a client claims raped him. Or security staff may respond to a disturbance by moving the prisoners involved to punitive segregation, even if the clinician believes the prisoner-client's involvement in the disturbance (for example, a fight) was directly related to his mental illness (for example, a command hallucination ordering him to strike out). Or a clinician might believe that housing a certain prisoner in a punitive solitary confinement unit is causing him to regress and hallucinate, whereas security staff members say they are certain the prisoner is merely manipulating and needs to be punished harshly for the sake of institutional security.

Close collaboration is needed, and there is a security component to every treatment or management plan. But clinicians often need to advocate for their clients—for instance, by demanding a move to a nonsolitary housing situation as they work to restore a prisoner who is psychotic to stability. Clinicians need an independent mind, but too often after they have worked in a prison for any length of time they begin to think like a correctional officer and suspect every prisoner of manipulating and feigning illness. When independent-minded clinicians disagree with the security officers' management plan for a prisoner, there needs to be a higher authority to which the mental health staff can appeal (for example, an ombudsman set up for this purpose or an assistant warden who is an expert on both security and mental health).

Finding Time and Space

Next, mental health clinicians need sufficient time and space to accomplish quality clinical work. It is not sufficient for psychiatrists to make rounds on a punitive segregation unit where all the prisoners are locked in their cells and ask each man taking psychotropic medications or deemed a suicide risk how he is doing today. The prisoners will not say much if they believe prisoners in adjacent cells and security staff standing in the "freeway" can overhear them; they do not want to develop a reputation as a weakling or a "mental case." A quiet, confidential office is a minimal requirement. But often security staff members say they do not have time to usher each prisoner out of his cell and into an office. Mental health clinicians have to stand firm and demand a bare minimum of confidentiality and safety for their prisoner-clients. Likewise, when clinicians are required to "speed up" and see too many prisoners in a limited time period, they need to advocate for the prisoners' receiving adequate time in treatment.

Prison mental health staff outside designated psychiatric inpatient units are often required to spend all their time doing something other than talking to their prisoner-clients. For instance, psychiatrists are usually in short supply relative to the number of prisoners with serious mental illness, so they spend most of their time seeing prisoners briefly and prescribing medications or admitting prisoners to the inpatient unit. Psychologists in many institutions tell me that they spend so much of their time writing reports for the courts, classification panels, and parole board that they have too little time to conduct treatments. They know that many prisoners need substance abuse treatment and group therapy focused on domestic violence, fathering, anger management, and surviving trauma, but they do not have the time to conduct such groups and they have even less time for individual treatment sessions. Under these circumstances, burnout develops rapidly and they begin to care less about their prisoner-clients' suffering.

Men in prison are hungry for a sympathetic person to pay some attention and help them with their problems. They might need to make contact with a loved one, such as a partner or child who has not come to visit. Too often prisons discourage contact with outsiders and prohibit mental health staff from calling prisoners' families. This is a foolish policy. Clinicians' time would be well spent making contact with prisoner-clients' families in appropriate cases, conducting family therapy, and even making home visits. After all, prisoners who maintain healthy connections with loved ones throughout their prison terms are more likely to leave behind a life of crime after they are released.

The Horror of Prison Rape

Prison rape can lead to posttraumatic stress disorder in the victim. Posttraumatic stress disorder is not included on the list of major mental illnesses such as schizophrenia and bipolor disorder, and it is grossly underdiagnosed and undertreated in correctional settings. Symptoms of posttraumatic stress disorder include flashbacks, nightmares, panic attacks, and severe constriction in emotional range and daily activities. Depression and suicide are frequently part of the clinical picture. Treatment for posttraumatic stress disorder involves establishing safety (for example, making certain that the perpetrator and his friends do not have access to the victim and that the staff will not betray the victim's confidence) and providing an opportunity to talk about the trauma in individual or group therapy (Herman, 1992). Medications are sometimes helpful as an adjunct to the verbal processing of traumas, but they are not an adequate treatment when they are prescribed as an alternative to talking therapy.

The male prisoner faces overwhelming obstacles to talking through the trauma of prison rape. First, as previously noted, he must decide whether he is going to identify the perpetrator and face the likelihood of deadly retaliation. If the victim seeks help, the treating psychiatrist is very likely to disbelieve the patient's report of the rape and symptoms of posttraumatic stress disorder and accuse the prisoner of manipulating to gain attention. If the psychiatrist believes the victim, he or she may prescribe tranquilizing or antidepressant medications without any talking therapy because of insufficient mental health treatment resources. Even if group therapy is provided, the rape victim is faced with the shame of admitting he was raped and the prohibition against exposing his vulnerabilities and pains in front of other men. Is it any wonder so many rape victims never report the incident, never seek treatment (or are denied adequate treatment when they do tell staff about their plight), and then become depressed and eventually commit suicide?

Great Gains Are Possible

In spite of all these obstacles, practicing psychotherapy with prisoners can be very rewarding. Prisoners are the first to admit that they have made mistakes or they were young and foolish when they committed their crimes. But a therapist's attention to their plight can lead to a very meaningful therapeutic relationship, and great gains are possible. In therapy, clinicians need to cover the entire panorama of gender relations and show these men that they see how domination lies at the core of their problems: racism, the growing gap between the rich and the poor, and the class inequities in the criminal justice system, in higher education, and in the workforce. In other words, the suffering these men experience is not entirely due to their personal failings. But the ways they have reacted to inequity and injustice in the past have led to huge problems, much suffering on the part of their loved ones and communities, and terms in prison. Clinicians must have sympathy for the children these men once were, who were beaten, who were perhaps raped, or who may have witnessed their fathers get drunk and beat their mothers; clinicians must understand the real-world hazards, including poverty and racism, that played such an important role in these men winding up behind bars.

As we have discovered in men's groups in the community, some men who abuse women do not know how to express their feelings and needs any other way. Many but not all can be taught other ways and helped to empathize with the women in their lives. Men who abuse substances can be helped to look at the part early abuse at the hands of their parents has played in their developing a drug habit and an exaggeratedly tough persona. Even once-violent prisoners can be helped to understand the deep-seated pain and sadness beneath their quick, angry reactions. The degree of honesty among these men quickly belies for discerning clinicians the stereotype of the unfeeling, incorrigible, antisocial prisoner.

And mental health work inside prisons provides an opportunity to see the way oft-traumatized men cover their more deep-seated sensitivity and capacity for caring relationships with layers of toughness and feigned hyperindependence. They had to exaggerate these and other male foibles to survive a childhood of abuse and trauma, life on the streets, and adult captivity in a brutal prison world. Shame is a core element of their psychological makeup and needs to be considered in treatment (Gilligan, 1996). Clinicians have to watch out for signs of manipulation—and there are plenty of manipulators among prisoners—

but usually prisoners are seeking to make contact with an authentic human being who will treat them with respect. And if clinicians do so, the therapeutic experience can be extremely rewarding. In treatment, it is possible to take apart the aspects of toxic masculinity that have led to deep trouble.

One additional point: Many clinicians who work on the outside, especially if they work in the public mental health system or make sincere efforts to diversify their private practices, will see men who have served terms in prison. All that I have said about life in prison forms the backdrop to ex-prisoners' current challenges fitting in, forming loving relationships, and becoming productive citizens. When clinicians are able to empathize with the predicament ex-felons face, there is room to form a profound and trusting therapeutic relationship. Therapists must be honest, because prison has enhanced the ex-felons' capacity to detect insincerity. For example, a parolee might ask whether the therapist is going to report him to his parole officer if he misses an appointment, says the wrong thing, or submits a urine sample that tests positive for drugs. The clinician must realize that even though he or she is trying to avoid acting as an agent of the police, he or she will report missed sessions or turn over the chart if the parole officer has a right to see it. Sometimes the clinician has to admit that in certain situations he or she would "snitch" on the client. By carefully outlining those potential situations, the ex-felon will at least know where he stands and to what degree he can trust the therapist. And that is a beginning.

MEN'S LIVES IN PRISON

There is a tendency to generalize about prisoners, such as calling them sociopaths. But each prisoner is unique, and there are as many personal histories as there are convicts. The clinician's difficult task is to get beyond stereotypes and find the unique individual in the correctional setting. In this section I tell two of the very many stories I have heard.

Leroy, the Recalcitrant Protester

Leroy (not his real name), a young African American man in punitive segregation, refuses to return his food tray after lunch one day because, according to him, "This food stinks!" The corrections officer comes over to his cell and tells him he has to return the tray right now or the officers will come in and get it. The young man backs up a few paces, raises his fists in a boxing pose, and says, "Like hell you're going to come in here and beat me up. You're gonna have a fight on your hands!" The officer leaves, but a few minutes later he returns with a "cell extraction team" in padded uniforms, helmets with visors, and an ample supply of mace. Leroy attempts to fight them off, but they subdue him roughly and drag him out of his cell and into another cell that has a plastic (lexan) door over the regular door. The new cell is stuffy and hot, and the lexan also shuts out more sounds than an ordinary segregation cell.

After being confined in the lexan-covered cell and ignored by the staff for a few weeks, Leroy begins to hear voices commanding him to kill the guard who disrespected him. He also begins to shout obscenities most of the daytime hours and long into the night. Prisoners in neighboring cells complain that the noise is keeping them awake. A corrections officer comes to Leroy's cell and gruffly tells him to "Shut up or else!" Who is to say which prisoner is of sounder mind in this situation, the one who permits himself to be subjected to endless indignities or the one who chooses a moment to make a stand even in the face of overwhelming force? But clearly the prisoner who is hearing voices and suffering from delusions in his solitary cell is not very capable of controlling his rage. And this kind of dyscontrol is why so many severely disturbed prisoners wind up in punitive segregation and why so many are the objects of brutal cell extractions. In any case, Leroy screams incoherently at the corrections officer.

In many very similar situations, the prisoner's obscenities will trigger another cell extraction. In this case, the officer quietly returned to his post and phoned the mental health department to ask if someone could come to the unit and examine Leroy. Twenty-four hours later a psychiatrist visited the supermaximum security unit where Leroy was housed, diagnosed psychosis, and ordered administration of Haldol by injection. In this prison, it is a rule violation for a prisoner to refuse to take prescribed psychotropic medications. Leroy refused, loudly. Because he was already in "the hole within the hole" (the few cells with lexan covers are reserved for the most troublesome prisoners), it would seem there was little else the staff could do to make Leroy comply with the medication regimen. But the psychiatrist thought of something. He had the officers enter Leroy's cell in force again, but this time they threw him onto his bunk, handcuffed his extremities to the corners, and threw shackles around his waist and neck. The psychiatrist told him he would be kept in five-point restraints until he agreed to take the medication.

Discussion. It is difficult but possible to halt the cycle of violence that is an everyday occurrence in prison. A prisoner is locked in his cell, an officer says something the prisoner considers disrespectful, the prisoner acts out and perhaps insults the officer, the officer resorts to overwhelming force and subdues the recalcitrant prisoner or merely ignores him and leaves him to rot in his cell, the prisoner gets angrier and more recalcitrant, and if he is prone to psychiatric breakdown he rapidly decompensates. At this point, a mental health practitioner is called, only to discover an angry, resistant prisoner-client who refuses to cooperate with the treatment. There is much to say about this situation. Of course, the case scenario is an example of gross clinical mismanagement and cruel insensitivity on the part of both security and mental health staff. The staff members are in a difficult bind. There certainly are dangerous convicts inside prisons, although they constitute a small minority. And maintaining security is definitely a priority. But sometimes fear of truly dangerous prisoners spreads beyond its appropriate bounds and the staff members act with excessive force. There are many dedicated and caring staff members and administrators in prisons. It would be entirely inappropriate and unfair to blame all prison staff for the abuses perpetrated by relatively few. But there is also a high rate of burnout among security and mental health staff, and there are some very cruel staff. And, sadly, this scenario is all too representative of what happens in super-maximum security housing units.

Hans Toch (1997) offers a clear and effective clinical strategy for "disturbed disruptive" prisoners. His approach requires the security staff and mental health staff to work together to consider the context of the prisoner's psychiatric deterioration and behavior problems, to design an individual management plan, and to collaborate in its execution. I will merely mention a couple of key issues that were handled very badly in the case example. Medications alone are not an adequate intervention in a case such as Leroy's. Obviously the conditions of confinement are causing or exacerbating the psychiatric breakdown, so if the prisoner is to receive effective and humane treatment he must first be removed from the setting. Forcing a prisoner to take medications by brutalizing him and ignoring the proper legal safeguards is absolutely countertherapeutic and actually constitutes torture according to international human rights standards (Human Rights Watch, 1997).

Instead of mistreating Leroy, the clinical and security staff needed to collaborate to help Leroy calm down and motivate him to cooperate with treatment. Medications alone, without providing a change of setting and some competent talking therapy, will not improve the situation and might make it much worse. Better, the psychiatrist or another mental health clinician, after perceiving the extremity of the situation, might have asked the officer if the lexan cover could be removed from Leroy's door so he would be better able to breathe. If the officer responded, "Not until he stops yelling, spitting, and throwing excrement," the clinician could turn to Leroy and mention that removal of the lexan is contingent on these changes in Leroy's behavior. At this point the prisoner has little reason to trust the clinician, and the issue of trust becomes the central theme of the intervention. If Leroy is not willing to comply and have the lexan removed, the clinician might say, "Of course there's no reason for you to trust me at this point. I will leave now, but I will return each day to talk to you, and we'll see if we can't work out a plan together to improve your situation." Then the clinician can return each day and negotiate honestly with the prisoner: "If you agree to stop yelling and spitting, we can have the officers remove the lexan," "If you agree to take the medication the psychiatrist prescribed, you'll be able to calm down and maybe we can work on a way to get you out of here," and so forth. In other words, the clinician's concern, honesty, realistic negotiating, and sensitivity to the prisoner's plight foster the kind of trust and motivation needed to defuse the tense situation in the solitary confinement unit and then to initiate a reasonable treatment plan.

Jim, the Sad Batterer

Jim, white and thirty-seven, was convicted of repeatedly beating his wife. He was addicted to methamphetamine, or "crank," and the beatings always occurred after he shot up with crank and guzzled large quantities of beer. His wife had tried several times to leave him and take their two young children to a battered women's shelter, but each time she ended up choosing to return home. One night he became very violent, and she was frightened he would hurt the children so she called the police; they and the district attorney decided Jim had beaten her once too many times and prosecuted him. While in jail awaiting trial, he developed a deep, dark depression and tried to kill himself by hanging. He was found before he did any damage and placed naked in a safety cell with padded walls. After conviction he arrived at prison with a history of depression and suicide, and as a result he was referred to a psychiatrist.

The psychiatrist informed Jim that depression is often a part of detoxification from amphetamines, especially when detoxification is done "cold turkey" in a jail cell, and prescribed antidepressants. He also recommended an anger management group and substance abuse treatment. The psychiatrist, who was not a regular employee of the prison, traveled to the prison each week for a half-day medication clinic, and there was no psychiatric coverage between his visits. He assumed the anger management and substance abuse groups were available because they were included in a printout he had been handed when he arrived to conduct his first clinic. But in fact there was a long waiting list for both groups, and each lasted only twelve weeks. When Jim's name came up on the waiting list, he was so tired of waiting to be in the group that he refused to take part. His depression worsened in spite of the antidepressants, and once again he tried to hang himself.

Jim was kept in a strip cell until the psychiatrist returned. The psychiatrist asked him what had happened to the plan for him to join the groups. Jim explained that the groups were crowded, the wait was too long, and he would only be permitted to attend twelve sessions. Jim said he really did not think that would help him much, and meanwhile he had heard that his wife had taken up with another man. It was after hearing that news that he had tried to hang himself. The psychiatrist realized that antidepressants alone would not really help Jim because he needed to do some intensive therapeutic work to overcome his addiction and his proclivity toward domestic violence. Without that work, Jim would either kill himself in prison or serve his time and return to the community, where he would likely once again use drugs and commit domestic violence.

Discussion. I wish I had a happy ending to report. In fact, Jim never received the treatment he needed and was eventually released from prison, with no further follow-up. But there are many men like Jim in our prisons. We know that time spent in prison does not help people end their drug habits, whereas community substance abuse programs, even though they do not succeed in every case, report 60 to 80 percent success rates three years after completion of counseling. Although 75 percent of prisoners suffer from substance abuse, only 17 percent receive treatment in prison. In fact, in California, 15 to 20 percent of the prisoners are in prison because they violated parole, usually because of a urine sample that tested positive for drugs. Imprisonment does not seem a rational and effective approach to the massive drug problem plaguing the United States today. In 1998 the voters of Arizona approved a statewide initiative instituting community drug counseling as an alternative to incarceration for nonviolent offenders, and the outcome studies so far show that the community programs are far superior to incarceration in helping people stay clean.

Similarly, we know that community programs aimed at ending men's violence, including therapy groups for batterers, are often effective even though they are not successful in halting domestic violence in every case. In fact, the studies that show prison rehabilitation works are careful to point out that the prisoner must be motivated to some extent and must be placed in a program that addresses his needs (Palmer, 1991). In other words, some prisoners will not benefit, and the staff should not waste too much of their time trying to rehabilitate them. But in a significant proportion of cases there is great benefit. In contrast, placing batterers in prison, where they must toughen themselves and fight for their lives to defend their manhood, does not lead to a reduction in violence toward women after the men are eventually released. Corrections departments resist permitting experts on men's violence from the community to enter the prisons and train the counseling and mental health staff in running groups. This attitude is unfortunate, because group counseling could be an extremely valuable tool for diminishing men's violence toward women, especially while the men are captive.

RECOMMENDATIONS AND CONCLUSION

Changes are needed in the entire criminal justice system. Nonviolent offenders, especially those whose only crime is minor and drug related, should be diverted to noncorrectional settings where they can receive help for their problems, which often involve substance abuse and chronic unemployment. A much larger proportion of mentally ill offenders need to be diverted to noncorrectional treatment settings. We need to reinstate meaningful education and rehabilitation programs inside prisons. We need to ameliorate the racism that permeates the criminal justice system. We need to reverse the trend in recent decades to lengthen sentences and make punishment harsher. We need to put an end to the use of supermaximum control units and other forms of cruel and inhuman captivity. We need to focus much attention and many more resources on youth to keep them out of the corrections system. And we need to find strenuous means to help men who have broken the law to reform themselves, return to the community, and lead productive lives. Only in the process of achieving all of these aims will it become possible to establish quality mental health services within correctional institutions (Kupers, 1999b).

Gender is another very important issue that unfortunately rarely is addressed in discussions about treating male prisoners. We need to attend to men's issues at the same time as we reform our criminal justice system and provide adequate mental health treatment programs. I have mentioned some of the many ways men's mental disorders are intensified by male proclivities in prison. For example, their hypermasculine posturing and bravado cause many male prisoners, especially those who already have or are prone to develop serious mental disorders, to break rules and be sent to psychosis-inducing solitary confinement, where the harsh conditions worsen their mental health. Or the vulnerability of prisoners with mental disorders leads to their being raped and then having no opportunity to process the trauma in a trust-inspiring situation.

These unfortunate scenarios are made all the more tragic by the male tendency to trust nobody, to keep silent about private pains and vulnerabilities, and then to act out aggressively to keep from talking about inner turmoil. Of course, these tendencies are omnipresent among men in the outside world, but in prison they are greatly magnified by the male code. Complicating the picture is the very real danger of being perceived as weak or of trusting someone and being betrayed. Even many men who are aware they have a serious emotional disorder refuse to admit it and seek help because they fear they will be perceived as weak and will be victimized by staff members or other prisoners.

Still, to the extent it is possible to provide psychotherapy in the prison setting, a great deal of healing can occur. From well-documented efforts in the community we have learned a great deal about preventing rape, ending men's violence, helping people end their drug and alcohol dependence, and treating trauma survivors (Herman, 1992; Kivel, 1992; Warters, 1991). Community agencies around the country work with men to halt or prevent violence. These groups come together to share experiences and techniques in what has become known as the ending men's violence movement. The lessons can be applied inside the prisons by dedicated clinicians.

We should attend to men's issues while struggling to improve conditions and treat mental illness within the prisons. For example, many men are conflicted about their role as fathers, and many others would like to learn to relate better to women so that they will be successful in building intimate relationships after they are released. Men's groups can be formed, with or without facilitation by psychotherapists, in which men share their experiences as fathers, husbands, and partners and in the process develop a kind of intimacy with other men that will likely make them less prone to engage in violent altercations and rule breaking within the correctional facility. In this context, some of the men might feel safe enough with each other to begin talking about past traumas and current emotional turmoil.

A big stumbling block in the effort to work with men's issues while providing treatment is that the same kind of tough, cruel law-and-order thinking that makes it very difficult to fund rehabilitation programs and adequate mental health services behind bars makes it even more unimaginable to change men's attitudes and behaviors. In fact, there is a parallel process: The uncaring tough-on-crime, no-coddling-of-prisoners attitude that permeates political discussions today (and serves to block the reestablishment of humane prisons and programs) reflects the same kind of toxic masculine sensibility that we see in exaggerated form in the prisoners who are condemned to suffer under the harsh conditions and cruelty that result. But psychotherapists working inside with prisoners who are motivated to change can quietly accomplish quite a lot. Meanwhile, the political, profeminist men's movement, which was founded on the premise that men can and must be changed, should join the struggle to reverse the extreme cruelty and abuse that are so rampant in U.S. prisons today (Kupers, 1999a).

References

Gilligan, J. (1996). *Violence: Our deadly epidemic and its causes.* New York: Grosset/Putnam.

Grassian, S., & Friedman, N. (1986). Effects of sensory deprivation in psychiatric seclusion and solitary confinement. *International Journal of Law and Psychiatry, 8,* 49–65.

Herman, J. (1992). Trauma and recovery: The aftermath of violence—from domestic abuse to political terror. New York: Basic Books.

Human Rights Watch. (1997). Cold storage: Super-maximum security confinement in Indiana. New York: Author.

Kivel, P. (1992). Men's work: How to stop the violence that tears our lives apart. Center City, MN: Hazelden.

Kupers, T. (1999a, July 8–11). *Men in prison.* Keynote address at the Twenty-Fourth National Conference on Men and Masculinity, Pasadena, CA.

Kupers, T. (1999b). Prison madness: The mental health crisis behind bars and what we must do about it. San Francisco: Jossey-Bass.

Kupers, T. (2000). Mental health in men's prison. In D. Sabo, T. Kupers, & W. London (Eds.), *Confronting prison masculinities: The gendered politics of punishment.* Philadelphia: Temple University Press.

Mauer, M., & Hurling, T. (1995). *Young black Americans and the criminal justice system: Five years later.* Washington, DC: Sentencing Project.

Messerschmidt, J. (1993). Masculinities and crime: Critique and reconceptualization of theory. Lanham, MD: Rowman & Littlefield.

Miller, J. (1996). Search and destroy: African-American males in the criminal justice system. Cambridge: Cambridge University Press.

Palmer, T. (1991). The effectiveness of intervention: Recent trends and current issues. *Crime and Delinquency, 37*(3), 330–346.

Thornberry, C., & Call, J. (1983). Constitutional challenges to prison overcrowding: The scientific evidence of harmful effects. *Hastings Law Journal, 35,* 313–353.

Toch, H. (1997). *Corrections: A humanistic approach.* Guilderland, NY: Harrow & Heston.

Warters, W. (1991). The social construction of domestic violence and the implications of "treatment" for men who batter. *Men's Studies Review, 8*(2), 7–16.

CHAPTER EIGHT

Issues of Males with Physical Disabilities in Rehabilitation Settings

Irmo D. Marini

The impact of a sudden traumatic disability to any individual often has profound and lasting implications in relation to his or her socialization, employment outlook, and basic independent functioning. Research findings pertaining to the psychosocial adjustment of persons who sustain a paralyzing trauma such as spinal cord injury, myocardial infarction, or stroke generally describe stages of adjustment (Livneh, 1991b; Shontz, 1975) or an ongoing recurrent model of adaptation (Kendall & Buys, 1998). Although statistically these specific disabilities are sustained more often by males (for example, 80 percent of all spinal cord injuries affect men), there is scant focus on the particular disability-related issues of what males endure. Before exploring the psychosocial adjustment issues for males with severe physical disabilities and subsequent therapeutic treatment strategies, I would like to share my own experience sustaining a disability.

A PERSONAL ACCOUNT OF DISABILITY

On February 10, 1981, while playing in a varsity hockey game for Lakehead University in Thunder Bay, Ontario, Canada, I was propelled headfirst into the end boards, immediately rendering me with C5 tetraplegia at age twenty-three, paralyzed from the chest down. My entire life drastically changed within the blink of an eye. During the ensuing three weeks, I lay in traction without the ability to feed myself, move my head, or tend to my own hygiene needs. I was then flown one thousand miles from home to Toronto, Ontario, with the comforting support of my girlfriend and younger sister at my side. While in Toronto, I underwent surgery to fuse and stabilize the vertebrae in my neck. The operation went well; however, my lung collapsed the following evening. I went into cardiac arrest and after my resuscitation was placed on a respirator, where I remained for the next thirty days. During this time, I was fed through a tube, could not speak, had a halo vest screwed into my skull to immobilize my head and neck, and lost forty-five pounds of muscle I had worked hard to develop from body building since age twelve. After three months of being confined to a bed, I sat up for the first time and was wheeled in front of a mirror. I was devastated by my rapid loss of muscle mass after eleven years of body building. It had all been erased in ninety days. Up until this point, I had denied the severity and permanency of my injury despite my physician's prognosis that I would not be able to walk again. The reality of my situation left me despondent and depressed. The multitude of questions that had been racing through my head were more pronounced now than ever. Would I be able to have sex and father a child? Would I be able to work or was I to collect disability for the rest of my life? How would others relate to me? How often would I be sick and rehospitalized? Would I have to live in a nursing home? Who would take care of me? How could I replace my interest and love of playing sports? What was I going to do now that I was no longer able to do anything?

On December 6, 1981, after ten months of acute hospitalization and rehabilitation, I returned home with my girlfriend Darlene. The oddity of returning home in a wheelchair and seeing people who had last seen me standing or going to local places where I used to play hockey or golf left me with a surreal feeling. Being out in the community in a wheelchair and seeing firsthand just how inaccessible and segregating certain places were was frustrating and disheartening and a reminder that I was now disabled. Some friends and acquaintances who once enjoyed my company now appeared visibly uncomfortable in my presence. Strangers sometimes pitied me or offered me assistance when I did not ask for it. A year or more after the injury, some people still responded to me as though I were depressed . . . or should be. I suppose they rationalized that if this type of thing had happened to them, they would surely be depressed and perhaps suicidal. However, because I seemed to be OK and was going back to school, well, then, I was admired for being so strong and courageous. I began to resent the fact that society expected me to act a certain way with this disability (for example, helpless and dependent), and I began to think about how I was going to bring back some manhood and dignity to my life.

Now, nineteen years after the injury and having counseled numerous persons with severe physical disabilities, I am better able to understand some of the issues I went through and better able to appreciate some of the same issues my male clients face with their disabilities. Many of my initial fears and worries, however, have passed. Since earning my master's degree in clinical psychology in 1985, I have always been employed and subsequently earned a Ph.D. in rehabilitation in 1992. Today, I am a professor and coordinate a graduate program in rehabilitation counseling. My once girlfriend Darlene has been my wife since 1982, and we feel closer than most couples we know because of the experience we both endured. Although I have been physically capable of having sex since my injury, Darlene and I elected not to have children because of ejaculatory problems. I also have never been rehospitalized or become seriously ill since my injury, and I retain the same personality and attitude toward living that I once had. Overall, to some degree, one's disability is only as severe as one makes it.

The purpose of this chapter is to explore the unique experience of males who sustain a sudden traumatic physical disability, with a focus on the multitude of issues they may present during the acute rehabilitation phase. To fully appreciate the possible origins of these issues, I address several relevant dynamics. From a sociological perspective, I discuss societal views of masculinity and what it means to be male in Western society. Relatedly, I examine empirical findings regarding societal views and attitudes toward persons with disabilities. This examination is followed by a discussion of the impact of disability on male masculinity. I next review psychological adjustment to traumatic physical disability, with primary attention given to stage versus recurrent models of adjustment. Finally, I discuss some of the unique concerns and reactions males present in rehabilitation settings and recommend therapeutic and counseling points of discussion for male patients.

SOCIETAL VIEWS OF MASCULINITY

The concept of masculinity and masculine traits is well documented elsewhere and is only briefly addressed here (Bem, 1974, 1993; Brannon, 1976; Gerschick & Miller, 1995, 1997; Herek, 1986; Sprecher & Sedikides, 1993; Tepper, 1997; Zilbergeld, 1992). Zilbergeld (1992) claims that by age seven, most lessons about male socialization have been learned. He and earlier researchers have defined masculinity and masculine behavior as reflecting a cluster of male competency traits including strong, self-reliant, successful, having sexual interest and prowess, active, independent, tough, not prone to tears, aggressive, dominant, stoic, persistent, self-confident, athletic, assertive, and unexpressive of emotions (Bem, 1974; Herek, 1986; Spence, Helmreich, & Stapp, 1974).

The origin of gender-polarized traits is conditioned or programmed from various societal influences as projected by culture, the media, family influences, and religion. The North American culture embraces the "body beautiful" concept that focuses on youth, health, physical or personal appearance, athletic prowess, and wholeness (Roessler & Rubin, 1982; Wright, 1983; Zilbergeld,

1992). Television and movies portray successful persons as having many of the successful traits described.

Several empirical studies lend support to the notion of masculinity traits. Sprecher and Sedikides (1993) found that men express less emotion than women in close relationships, which the authors attribute to male social role expectations of self-control, toughness, and autonomy. These authors concluded that men have problems asking for support and responding to such questions as "How do you feel?" Relatedly, Belle (1987) found that, compared with women, men tend to provide and receive less social support and are less likely to seek social support. Other researchers have noted that many males do not seek social support because doing so signifies weakness and dependence or they find self-disclosure to be inversely related to trait masculinity (Butler, Giordano, & Neren, 1985; Winstead, Derlega, & Wong, 1984). As I describe in more detail later in this chapter, when a male incurs a severely disabling condition, his identity becomes conflicted because of the virtual loss of all of his perceived masculine traits.

SOCIETAL ATTITUDES TOWARD DISABILITY

Having reviewed the masculine traits typically used to describe the "real" man in Western society, I turn now to a brief review of traditional societal views toward persons with disabilities. There are a plethora of empirical and theoretical studies relating to the investigation of attitudes toward persons with disabilities (Anthony, 1972; Belgrave, 1984; Belgrave & Mills, 1981; Comer & Piliavin, 1975; Donaldson, 1980; English, 1971; Evans, 1976; Fichten, Robillard, Tagalakis, & Amsel, 1991; Marini, 1992; Yuker, 1988). Chubon (1982), however, in a critical review of the literature regarding attitudes toward disablement, found that only 60 of 102 studies reviewed were empirical in nature. The remaining studies were conceptual, with little or no empirical basis.

In the 1991 Lou Harris poll of one thousand able-bodied Americans concerning their attitudes toward persons with disabilities, results indicated that persons with disabilities are generally thought of as objects of pity or admiration and perceived to be fundamentally different from nondisabled persons (Harris, 1991). Lyons (1991) adds that our society perceives persons with disabilities as helpless, incapable, and inferior. Gething (1991) notes how societal attitudes can affect how people react toward a perceived minority. These perceptions can subsequently affect the quality of life, opportunities, and extent to which members of the stigmatized group can reach their potential.

Numerous studies have explored whether the sentiment Western society has toward persons with disabilities is positive, negative, or simply ambivalent (English, 1971; Evans, 1976; Havranek, 1991; Makas, 1988; Marini, 1992; Wright, 1960; Yuker, 1988). The answers to such questions are, however, much too complex for any one researcher to make global generalizations from. In his extensive literature review on attitudes toward disability, Yuker (1988) noted that of the studies pertaining to contact and disability, 51 percent showed a positive attitude change, 31 percent were inconclusive, and 10 percent reported a more negative attitude resulting from contact.

The literature indicates that many nondisabled persons become anxious or tense because they do not know what to say or how to behave around someone with a disability (Albrecht, Walker, & Levy, 1982; Belgrave & Mills, 1981; Evans, 1976; Marinelli & Kelz, 1973; Yuker, 1988). Albrecht et al. (1982) found that 83 percent of their nondisabled sample reported that ambiguity or uncertainty in not knowing how to behave was the major reason for social avoidance of persons with disabilities. The Harris (1991) poll confirms this sentiment; nondisabled Americans report feeling awkward around persons with disabilities. However, the same poll also suggests that previous positive familiarity with a person with a disability creates more favorable attitudes.

Another factor related to contact pertains to what Donaldson (1980) refers to as "equal status" of the person with a disability. Specifically, the likelihood of a positive attitude change toward disability increases when the person with a disability possesses a similar education, socioeconomic status, and vocational status and is roughly the same age as the nondisabled person.

Livneh (1991a) classified the origins of negative attitudes toward disability into thirteen categories: (1) psychodynamic mechanisms, (2) childhood influences, (3) aesthetic aversion, (4) minority group comparability, (5) sociocultural conditioning, (6) punishment for sin, (7) disability as a reminder of death, (8) prejudice-inviting behaviors of persons with disability, (9) threats to body image integrity, (10) anxiety-provoking unstructured situations, (11) disability-related factors associated with negative perceptions (for example, functional or organic causality, level of severity, and visibility), (12) demographic factors (for example, sex, age, socioeconomic status, and educational attainment), and (13) personality variables associated with attitudes. Each origin is empirically or theoretically supported in the literature. Although it is beyond the scope of this chapter to fully address all the origins of negative attitudes, I address two.

Dembo, Leviton, and Wright (1975) describe "psychodynamic mechanisms" as pertaining to societal beliefs that if a person does not feel badly about the disability, he or she must be in denial. This expectation of having to mourn the loss poses a problem for males, who typically attempt to hide their emotions (Bem, 1993). A related mechanism, the spread phenomenon, refers to society's belief that a disability affecting one aspect of an individual (that is, paralysis) spreads and affects all other aspects such as mental abilities and emotional stability. This belief, of course, becomes problematic for males who want to return to work and are perceived by employers as being incapable both mentally and physically of performing the job.

The concept of "anxiety-provoking situations" refers to the body of literature examining the anxiety nondisabled persons feel when interacting with someone with a disability (Albrecht et al., 1982; Cloerkes, 1981; Kleck, 1968; Marinelli & Kelz, 1973). Findings suggest that in novel encounters with visibly disabled persons, nondisabled persons fear saying something that may upset the person with a disability (for example, telling a wheelchair user you enjoy jogging, then realizing he or she cannot walk and therefore may become upset). Marini (1992) noted that nondisabled persons cognitively weigh the pros and cons of a possible interaction with someone who is disabled and decide the anticipatory anxiety and discomfort over having to guard what one should or should not say ultimately leads to avoidance.

Such findings begin to describe the potential fears, insecurities, and related difficulties some males with disabilities may feel in their attempts to attract a partner. It does not take a trained observer to notice when one is being ignored or avoided. Men with disabilities will begin to question their sexual prowess and may lose self-esteem if others continually avoid them at social gatherings. Marini (1992) and others note that it therefore becomes critical for the individual with a disability to be able to develop the social skills and strategies to be able to quickly place others at ease and convey an "I'm-OK-with-my-disability" type of attitude (Evans, 1976).

Overall, societal views of disability are somewhat similar to attitudes reserved for other minority groups. Specific to disability, however, are popular sentiments of either pity or admiration and perceptions of those with disabilities as being sick, incapable, and needing to be cared for. When surveyed, those without disabilities claim to feel awkward and anxious around persons with disabilities. These factors begin to set the stage for the identity crisis males experience after sustaining a severe physical disability.

DISABILITY IMPACT ON MASCULINITY

The assault of a physical disability on a man's sense of masculinity compromises virtually all of the traits typified by society for the male gender. Two sets of social dynamics men struggle with are, on the one hand, dealing with pressures of being masculine, while, on the other hand, trying to disprove society's perception of them as passive, dependent, pitiful, sick, and incapable (Gerschick & Miller, 1995, 1997).

From her interviews of men with chronic disabilities, Charmaz (1995) found that some males attempt to preserve aspects of there predisability selves by maintaining qualities or attributes that previously defined their self-concept. As they come to adapt to their disability, males "preserve self" by limiting the impact of the disability in their daily lives and develop strategies to minimize the limiting aspects of the disability.

Charmaz (1995) found that other males with disabilities attempt to "recapture" all aspects of their past selves by ignoring their limitations. When these men realize it is not possible to ignore their disabilities, they become despondent and depressed. Wright (1983) defines this approach as "as-if" behavior, whereby an individual denies his or her limitations by acting as if he or she does not have a disability.

Finally, Charmaz found that still other males with disabilities attempt to preserve their public predisability identity and conceal their private disability identity. These males strive to preserve the same strong public persona as they had in the past but privately at home maximize the sick, dependent role. It is important for these men to maintain their masculine image outwardly to the public. This type of male is illustrated in Hugh Gallagher's (1994) book, *FDR's Splendid Deception*. Gallagher describes President Roosevelt, who was born with polio, as having totally denied his disability, never speaking to anyone including his wife and mother about his disability. Roosevelt was adamant about never being filmed or photographed in public with his leg braces on or while sitting in his wheelchair. He feared he would be perceived as a weak and incapable leader if the public ever learned of his secret.

Gerschick and Miller (1995) conducted ten in-depth interviews using an analytic induction approach with men who sustained either paraplegia or tetraplegia (Katz, 1988). They noted three patterns of coping that interviewees with disabilities used in dealing with the dominant masculinity standards. The first pattern, reformulation, characterized males who redefined idealized masculine traits to conform to their new abilities. Males who needed a personal attendant to assist in performing activities of daily living (for example, grooming and dressing) still viewed themselves as independent because they controlled the actions of the personal attendant. They also defined the term *self-reliant* as meaning earning capacity and the ability to work and support oneself.

The second pattern of coping, defined as reliance, characterized those males who relied heavily on the masculine ideals of strength, independence, and sexual prowess. These males were deeply bothered by the fact that they could not live up to their ideals. Some attempted to function independently even when they needed assistance and refused to ask for help. Others became involved in risk-taking behavior or played wheelchair sports to remain competitive, and still others viewed wheelchair sports as not being the "real" thing and therefore did not participate.

The third pattern of coping Gerschick and Miller (1995, 1997) described was rejection of the masculine ideals. This group of men with disabilities rejected the traditional notion of what made the "real" man. They tended to create an alternative masculine identity, identifying themselves as "persons," and believed that mental ability was superior to physical strength. In all cases, those in this group attempted to come to terms with their disability in different ways.

There are essentially two views as to how individuals adjust or adapt to traumatic disability. The first is the stage model of adjustment, in which an individual progresses through a series of stages over time, and the second is the recurrent adjustment model, which asserts that individuals gradually become less distressed over time with adjustment being ongoing, experiencing periodic times of sorrow or despair.

STAGE MODEL OF ADJUSTMENT

In any stage model of adaptation to loss, there are certain consistently reported observations of which to be aware. First, adjustment to a traumatic disability is a dynamic and not a static process (Kahana, Fairchild, & Kahana, 1982). An individual may experience a regression in stages, progress through one stage only to revert back again later, or skip a stage altogether. Second, there is no predetermined time limit for any one stage or stages, and not all persons go through all stages. Third, some persons may never reach what might be considered an end stage and essentially become "stuck" at an earlier phase. Fourth, each defined stage carries with it certain behavioral, emotional, and cognitive correlates indicative of that stage. Finally, involvement in various stages is usually temporary and transitional in nature (Livneh, 1991b). After reviewing more then forty different stage of adjustment models, Livneh (1991b) synthesized five distinct stages, which I briefly outline in the following sections.

Initial Impact

In relation to the time the traumatic injury occurs, the period of initial impact generally involves immense anxiety and shock immediately following the bodily insult and may last for hours, days, or even weeks. During this period, the injured person (if alert) and his or her family often psychologically deal with the catastrophe using an "emotion-focused" coping response (Lazarus & Folkman, 1984). Emotion-focused coping allows affected individuals to deal with the incapacitating anxiety and stress by maintaining hope and keeping up morale through prayer. During such periods, the shock persons experience often impairs the ability to concentrate, problem solve, or make rational decisions. Interestingly, this idea is in contrast to findings by Stone and Neale (1984), who suggest that males tend to use problem-solving coping strategies more often than do women.

Defense Mobilization

Bargaining and denial are the two major components of the next stage, defense mobilization (Livneh, 1991b). Once the injured loved one is off the critical list, the situation may become awkward when the family and injured person begin to hope and pray for full recovery. Bargaining is perhaps a focal spiritual time period when the injured person and his or her family offer some trade-off to a higher power for complete recovery. Throughout this process, there often remains a strong wall of denial in the person injured, but the family may slowly begin to realize and reluctantly accept the imminent situation. Denial continues from the initial impact stage and occurs concomitantly with bargaining, except now the focus of denial involves healing the disability and complete recovery. It is not denying so much the injury itself but rather the permanency of its disabling effect.

Initial Realization

Mourning of the loss, possible reactive depression, and internalized anger over one's situation primarily mark the stage of initial realization. At this stage the injured person begins to fully realize the implications of his or her injury. Livneh (1991b) describes mourning (grief) as being short-lived, with a focus on the loss of a body part and past lifestyle. The reactive depression, when it occurs, tends to be longer in duration, with a focus on the consequences of the disability. Although it is generally believed that everyone mourns loss in some way, there are conflicting study findings as to whether depression is always involved (Trieschmann, 1988). Nevertheless, a traumatic, severe disability often leaves the injured person with thoughts of hopelessness and helplessness, feelings of despair and sadness, and a desire to initially avoid social contact. Also sometimes evident at this stage is internalized anger (Livneh, 1991b), marked by feelings of self-blame and guilt over what has happened. The individual searches and often finds reasons (no matter how insignificant) as to why God has justifiably punished him or her (Hohmann, 1975). Suicidal ideation and verbalizations are also common at this stage.

Retaliation

During the retaliation stage, the injured person turns his or her anger and frustration outward, sometimes lashing out at significant others and medical staff. He or she begins to displace blame for the injury away from the self and may direct fault to medical personnel perceived as incompetent, persons related to the accident itself, or God, with overt behavioral outbursts. A less overt sign of rebellion is not cooperating with the prescribed treatment regimen for rehabilitation. The patient may demand special privileges, test hospital rules, or manipulate others.

Reintegration

Livneh (1991b) subdivides this final stage into three successive substages. The first is that of acknowledgment, in which the injured person is able to realize the final implications of his or her situation. The perceived impact on social, vocational, and familial roles is met with some trepidation. Acceptance is described as the second of three substages. It is an affective assimilation of the disability and the development of a new emotional self-concept. At this stage, the individual feels that it is essentially OK to be disabled despite the inherent societally imposed attitude barriers of having a disability. Final adjustment represents the last stage. This stage is characterized by a person who feels positive, confident, and content about his or her capabilities (Shontz, 1975). The client knows his or her limitations but focuses on remaining or new strengths.

RECURRENT ADJUSTMENT MODEL

The other model of adjustment is referred to as the recurrent adjustment model of disability. B. H. Davis (1987) and others have argued that although stage models of adjustment describe the linear progression of adjusting, they do not account for the ongoing, recurrent nature of adjustment over time. The recurrent adjustment model accounts for the ongoing, reemerging periods of sorrow or despair persons with traumatic disabilities experience (Kendall & Buys, 1998). It is based on Beck and Weishaar's (1989) cognitive theory concept of cognitive schemata development. Cognitive schemata are our beliefs and assumptions of self, others, and how our environment works.

After an injury, an individual attempts to continue working from his or her preinjury schemata. Wright (1983) refers to this approach as the "as-if" behavior noted earlier. When these older schemata no longer work, the individual may experience anxiety, helplessness, hopelessness, and despair. As time goes on, the individual begins to gradually develop new schemata to function in the environment with the disability. Modification of new schemata is guided by three themes: (1) the search for meaning in this new life with a disability; (2) the need for mastery and control over the disability, environment, and one's future; and (3) the effort to protect and enhance the disability. Development of new schemata can be positive ("I can do this") or negative ("I'm a failure"), and individuals often fluctuate in their adjustment over time, analogous to a pendulum that gradually slows to center (Kendall & Buys, 1998).

MALE ISSUES IN REHABILITATION SETTINGS

Regardless of which adjustment theory one subscribes to, it is clear that persons who sustain a severe physical disability must deal with bodily function changes and with immediate and drastic changes to their past lifestyles. When a physical disability is sustained, both genders are immediately thrust into minority group status. As Gerschick and Miller (1997) indicate, men with disabilities are marginalized and stigmatized in American society. The connotations of disability in Western society are in stark contrast with societal views as to what defines a "real" man in America.

The majority of issues men experience when faced with a disabling injury most often relate either directly or indirectly to losses of their masculine identity traits. Males are unfortunately placed in a paradoxical situation when injury occurs. As Zilbergeld (1992) explains, even though men with traumatic disabilities have numerous fears and concerns, they often feel the need to conceal them and not express their despair because of the perception that revealing emotions would further diminish their manhood. Some males continue to project a stoic, tough, no-sissy-stuff, no-crying demeanor while inwardly attempting to deal with numerous concerns and fears on their own. In these situations, therapists have to initiate common topics of concern such as sexuality, employability issues, finances, feelings of helplessness and dependence, and patients' inability to express fear and frustration.

Life-Cycle Development Issues

The issues males present in an acute rehabilitation setting vary depending on their age. Although there is some overlap of concerns regardless of the age at which the injury is sustained, different stages of life bring somewhat different priorities of concern for the involved male. Teenage males who sustain a physical disability, for example, have several primary concerns. During a period when they are beginning sexual experimentation, preparing for college or work, and contemplating moving out on their own to test their independence, the impact of a severe disability temporarily or permanently compromises all these desires.

Simmons and Rosenberg (1975) found that adolescents are more concerned about changes to their physical appearance than they are about changes to any other aspect of themselves. Older adolescents are typically concerned with developing intimate relationships, dating, having sex, and bonding with their peer group (S. E. Davis, Anderson, Linkowski, Berger, & Feinstein, 1991). Several researchers have found that adolescents with disabilities expressed great concern about their social relationships, were fearful of rejection, and expressed loneliness and a sense of isolation (Blum, 1983; Minde, 1978). Because adolescence is also a time when males participate in sports and go out often, adolescent males with a physical disability are often forgotten or unable to participate in these activities, thus creating the sense of isolation noted earlier. Adolescent males may also encounter difficulties in developing vocational maturity (Brolin, 1980). Not knowing one's present abilities and not being sure of one's future ability to earn a living are additional areas of concern, especially with societal pressures for males to be breadwinners. The inability to make a living affects other issues such as ability to attract a mate, quality of life, and where and how one will live.

For males sustaining a disability in early adulthood or midlife, major concerns include career constraints, sexuality, and family role (Power, Hershenson, & Schlossberg, 1991). Depending on the severity of the disability, husbands may face reversal of traditional gender roles, in which they are no longer the independent, strong, breadwinning head of the household but rather a dependent, unemployed, insecure, and anxious person who requires personal assistance to complete simple everyday tasks. Anxiety and fear over how one will support one's family are primary concerns, as are deep-seated fears of abandonment by the spouse.

Sexuality Issues

Tepper (1997) disclosed his experience as a twenty-year-old male with tetraplegia. Although his major concerns focused on his sexual capabilities and ability to father a child, he found that the medical staff would not acknowledge his sex concerns. Indeed, research indicates that many medical professionals feel uncomfortable in discussing sex with patients. Gill (1988) discovered that although 79 percent of the rehabilitation staff in a Boston hospital stated that sexual adjustment was important to patients' recovery, only 9 percent reported feeling comfortable discussing these issues with patients. Of this sample, 51 percent reported they would discuss the topic only if the patient initiated the conversation.

Zilbergeld (1992) cited the many myths Western society has regarding male sex performance and sexuality. Sentiments such as "a real man isn't into the sissy stuff like feelings and communicating" (p. 44), "all touching is sexual and should lead to sex" (p. 45), "a man is always interested in and always ready for sex" (p. 47), "a real man performs in sex" (p. 48), "good sex requires orgasm" (p. 55), and "good sex is spontaneous with no planning and no talking" (p. 59) all perpetuate the myth. Males who attempt to conform to such pressures ultimately will have many questions regarding their sexuality.

Tepper (1997) states that treatment for males with physical disabilities should include medical staff–initiated questions and education regarding the physiological changes in sex function with a spinal cord injury. It should also include dispelling sexual myths and education on positioning, establishing sexual relationships, dating issues, and fathering. Milligan and Neufeldt (1998) found that the major concern for males with spinal cord injuries related to their capacity to succeed in present or future intimate relationships, sexual performance concerns, sexual identity, and others' perceptions of them as asexual. Overall, sexuality is a primary issue for males of all ages who have sustained physical disabilities.

Dealing with Humility and Helplessness

As a practitioner and someone with a severe physical disability, I have experienced and observed other males also struggle with the frustration of having to relearn basic activities we typically learn at age four such as relearning how to dress, eat, brush, write, and deal with the loss of bowel and bladder functions. As previously noted, because males are socialized not to express their feelings and because they must already depend on medical staff and family for physical assistance, many men perceive that it would be even more embarrassing and burdensome to then admit to having psychological problems. To suddenly and forcibly relinquish being independent, autonomous, self-reliant, dominant, and in control becomes overwhelming for many males, but that they are overwhelmed often remains their best-kept secret. It is a humbling experience that virtually all humans ultimately will grieve and may or may not become clinically depressed over (Trieschmann, 1988). Grief is related to loss of body function as well as loss of previous lifestyle and may last several weeks or months.

With a sense of helplessness may come an almost intolerable boredom due to the sudden and abrupt loss of a previously active lifestyle. A typical day in therapy rotates between physical therapy (muscle strengthening) and occupational therapy (relearning basic activities). If weekend home visits or recreational outings are nonexistent during treatment, an individual may begin to slip into depression.

RECOMMENDATIONS FOR THERAPISTS

The issues men face after sustaining a debilitating, permanent physical injury challenge the very essence of their male identity and often create an identity crisis. Because gender role expectations for males include not expressing emotions, many men continue to convey an outwardly stoic front of toughness while inwardly struggling with numerous unresolved issues. In Western society, "real" men are perceived as tough, independent, stoic, athletic, self-reliant, self-confident, strong, and in control. Conversely, persons with disabilities are viewed as passive, pitiful, incapable, dependent, and needing to be cared for. An obvious contradiction and paradox exists for males who become disabled.

The primary issue for males with disabilities in rehabilitation settings is sexuality and reproductive in nature and includes perceived loss of sexual prowess, sexual performance fears, concerns about the ability to father a child, fears about the ability to attract a mate, and loss of ability for spontaneous sex. A second major issue pertains to loss of control of bodily functions and to the surrounding medical environment because patients have to comply with hospital rules and are passive recipients of services. A third issue males may struggle with relates to finances and future employability. Concerns revolve around the ability to financially support family, job alternatives and marketability, perceived employer discrimination, and perceived social status as a poor, unemployed person with a disability. Such issues contradict the male identity of self-reliance, success, and independence. A final major issue relates to the immense frustration of having to relearn basic human functions we generally acquire by age four. Having been previously strong and independent, many males may struggle with childlike feelings of dependency and perceive having to ask for assistance to complete the simplest of tasks as embarrassing and shameful. I discuss specific counseling strategies to deal with these issues in the following sections.

Cognitive Reframing of Societal Views of Disability

The first recommendation is that therapists have a thorough understanding of Western societal views of masculinity and disability. This knowledge base provides for a solid framework and foundation from which to work. Many clients harbor some unresolved issues relating to the contradiction between masculinity and disability. As noted in the recurrent model of adjustment, many males initially strive to hold on to their preinjury schemata as if they do not have a disability (Kendall & Buys, 1998; Wright, 1983). As injured individuals continue to realize that these old schemata no longer work, they may experience anxiety and helplessness. Therapists should assist clients to reframe old schemata and build new schemata to function in the environment with the disability. Kendall and Buys (1998) recommend modifying or reframing positive new schemata around three themes: (1) the search for meaning in this new life with a disability; (2) the need for mastery and control over the disability, the environment, and one's future; and (3) the effort to protect and enhance the disability. Developing a can-do attitude while offering practical suggestions to make positive changes relative to these three themes becomes important (Kendall & Buys, 1998). For example, in working with the need to master or control one's environment, discussions centering on gaining independence in the home, in the community, or at work may include purchasing adaptive driving equipment, employing personal care attendants, furthering one's education to enhance employment marketability, and taking an assertiveness-training course.

Another aspect to cognitive reframing relates to Albert Ellis's (1973) rational emotive therapy and challenging clients' irrational beliefs that their future is predetermined. Clients who are not depressed but rather despondent and feeling hopeless or helpless about their situation could be questioned about what they believe their future holds. Those who feel their life is over should be tactfully challenged about what proof they have regarding their assertion. Therapists should be prepared beforehand, however, to back up their own arguments that an individual's life is not over. For example, persons with paraplegia who believe they will never work, marry, or have children should be shown examples of persons with paraplegia who have accomplished these activities.

The appropriate use of humor in certain instances can also be quite effective in assisting clients to view their situation from a different perspective. Again, therapists can be challenged by clients who are not clinically depressed but who make self-deprecating statements such as "Who will want me like this?" The cognitive technique of paradoxical intent described by Frankl (1967) can be effective when clients unwittingly feed their negative self-talk about their being unattractive to a potential mate. If a therapist's best attempts to convince a client that he is still attractive fail, the therapist may consider paradoxical intent. With this technique, for example, the therapist may finally agree with the client and attest as to just how ugly the client really is. The therapist might then proceed further and ask the client to exaggerate his "ugliness" by hunching over, moaning, and acting like a monster. At some point, the client will begin to see that he is really not as unattractive as the therapist claims he is and perhaps begin to view his situation from a more positive or lighter perspective. The therapist could then proceed to discuss concrete ways the client could improve his self-image (for example, by dress, hygiene, and social skills).

Initiating Talking Points with Clients

A second suggestion relates to the idea that therapists will likely have to initiate discussions regarding the issues noted earlier. For resistant clients who continue to assert that everything is fine, therapists must differentiate denial from masking what one really feels. Livneh's (1991b) five-stage adjustment theory holds that denial is common during the defense mobilization stage. If, however, clients know the implications of their situations but still claim everything is OK, therapists should begin to initiate talking points with the clients. Therapists should openly address the notion of clients not wanting to burden others with their problems so as to grant clients permission to do so. Because they know many of the most commonly cited concerns for males with severe disabilities, therapists can touch on each concern and gauge their clients' responses to various topics such as sex, abandonment, health, career, financial, and other issues. If clients see that therapists already know and empathize with the fear and anxiety they are feeling over these issues, clients may begin to open up and discuss their worries and perhaps experience their first catharsis.

In empowering clients to finally talk about their fears, therapists are better able to assist clients in problem-solving approaches geared toward alleviating uncertainties and developing strategies to concretely do something about their fears. Clients who cannot return to a former physical labor job and are concerned about how they will support their family can be assisted in exploring advanced education or specialized training for sedentary jobs that pay well. Relatedly, concerns about sexuality might be addressed by exploring the myths and misconceptions of male performance and methods for enhancing performance (for example, medications and implants).

Addressing Inappropriate Coping Mechanism Issues

The third recommendation pertains to addressing inappropriate ways of dealing with stress such as alcohol or substance abuse, avoidance, and reckless behavior. Statistics regarding persons with physical disabilities indicate that as many as 68 percent of persons who sustain traumatic injuries have been under the influence of substances. In many cases, substance abuse continues after the injury, not only because of preinjury use but also to mask the pain experienced from the disability (Heinemann, 1993). In extreme cases of addiction, referral to a substance abuse program is warranted. Ironically, drinking tolerance may be considered as macho or masculine behavior for some males and thus perceived as a way to hold on to some of their masculinity.

Avoidance and isolating oneself from others may be another type of inappropriate response observed in clients. Again, being embarrassed or ashamed can lead clients into avoiding significant others who could help bring meaning back to their lives. Therapists can help clients explore and challenge their concerns regarding the differences between a person's physical appearance and who he or she is as an individual. If therapists question their clients as to what traits they like about others, clients become aware that significant others are loved for who they are, not what they look like.

Another area to observe and discuss is a client's mental status, especially pertaining to suicidal ideation. The rate of suicide in males with spinal cord injury is about twice as high as that in the general population (Geisler, Jousse, Wynne-Jones, & Breithaupt, 1983). Death from unintentional injury and suicide are the leading causes of death for persons with spinal injury six months after injury (Brown, 1998). As such, reckless behavior or suicidal ideation is another area that therapists need to explore during acute care rehabilitation. Regarding Livneh's (1991b) five stages of adjustment, suicidal ideation may be common during the retaliation stage because of feelings of despair and frustration with one's perceived situation. It is beyond the scope of this chapter to provide detailed recommendations regarding therapeutic treatment of suicidal ideation, but consulting with treating physicians for appropriate medication prescriptions and having knowledge of clinical depression and crisis intervention become essential.

Understanding Disability-Specific Physiology

A fourth suggestion is for therapists to become thoroughly familiar with the physiological changes of specific disability populations with which they are working. Aside from reading about the limitations, therapists can talk to treating therapists and physicians about individuals' functional limitations. From this information, therapists are able to educate clients about sexual myths and functioning as well as health and wellness practices regarding taking care of oneself (for example, managing stress, nutrition, drug or alcohol use, exercise, and so forth). Knowledge of psychoneuroimmunology or behavioral medicine and relevant practice of healthy habits can help clients in minimizing the frequency of rehospitalization. For persons with tetraplegia, for example, weight gain can severely compromise independence and increase the potential for pressure sores, which are not only costly but can be deadly. Long hospitalizations can also affect job status and quality of life.

Introducing Clients to Role Models with Disabilities

Finally, despite nondisabled therapists' best efforts, nothing compares with recruiting successfully adjusted persons with disabilities for clients to interact with and from whom they can see firsthand that a quality life can still be pursued and enjoyed after a disabling injury. Role models can be introduced individually or as part of group counseling, which is particularly effective. Therapists should be cautious, however, to always first ask clients if they would like to meet and talk to someone who has lived with the disability. Most newly injured persons have a certain period (usually right after injury) during which their denial of the long-term prognosis is so great that they will resent and be unwilling to meet another person with a disability. Therapists should be prepared to broach the topic occasionally until clients are finally ready to meet the individual. In addition, it is important, of course, to locate good role models who are married, working, or otherwise have positively moved on with their lives.

Today, persons with severe physical disabilities are living longer and healthier lives thanks to advances in medicine, assistive technology, empowering legislation (for example, the Americans with Disabilities Act), and pharmacological developments. As such, the quality of life for this population continues to improve, with exciting new advances on the way. Sperm extraction and fathering a child for males with spinal cord injury, for example, had a less than 15 percent success rate fifteen years ago. With today's medical advances, the success rate now stands at over 90 percent in this regard. Physical barriers in the community and with transportation continue to be eliminated, opening the once closed doors of engaging in activities such as attending a movie or sporting event, going to restaurants, or taking a train ride. Riding the wave of the growing numbers of aging baby boomers who want alternative options to living in nursing homes, many states now allow persons with severe disabilities to live independently in their homes with the aid of personal attendants. These are all exciting changes that not only enhance the quality of life for persons with disabilities but also improve their overall mental health. Once the task of working with males with disabilities was getting them to accept their plight of living in an unfair world that functioned mainly for able-bodied people. Psychotherapists today must still be able to address the many issues described here but can now assure clients that many barriers of the past no longer exist. Indeed, perhaps the greatest remaining barriers are the sometimes negative attitudes not only of others but also of those with disabilities themselves.

References

Albrecht, G. L., Walker, V. G., & Levy, J. A. (1982). Social distance from the stigmatized. *Social Science Medical, 16,* 1319–1327.

Anthony, W. A. (1972). Societal rehabilitation: Changing society's attitudes toward the physically and mentally disabled. *Rehabilitation Psychology, 19*(3), 193–203.

Beck, A. T., & Weishaar, M. (1989). Cognitive therapy. In A. Freeman, K. M. Simon, L. E. Beutler, & H. Arkowitz (Eds.), *Comprehensive handbook of cognitive therapy* (pp. 21–36). New York: Plenum.

Belgrave, F. Z. (1984). The effectiveness of strategies for increasing social interaction with a physically disabled person. *Journal of Applied Social Psychology, 14*(2), 147–161.

Belgrave, F. Z., & Mills, J. (1981). Effects upon desire for social interaction with a physically disabled person after mentioning the disability in different contexts. *Journal of Applied Social Psychology, 11,* 44–57.

Belle, D. (1987). Gender differences in the social moderators of stress. In R. C. Barnett, L. Biener, & G. K. Baruch (Eds.), *Gender and stress* (pp. 257–277). New York: Free Press.

Bem, S. L. (1974). The measurement of psychological androgyny. *Journal of Consulting and Clinical Psychology, 42*(2), 155–162.

Bem, S. L. (1993). The lenses of gender: Transforming the debate on sexual inequality. New Haven, CT: Yale University Press.

Blum, R. W. (1983). The adolescent with spina bifida. *Clinical Pediatrics, 22,* 331–335.

Brannon, R. (1976). The male sex role: Our culture's blueprint of manhood, and what it's done for us lately. In D. David & R. Brannon (Eds.), *The forty-nine percent majority* (pp. 1–45). Reading, MA: Addison-Wesley.

Brolin, D. E. (1980). *Vocational preparation of persons with handicaps* (2nd ed.). Columbus, OH: Merrill.

Brown, W. J. (1998). Current psychopharmacologic issues in the management of major depression and generalized anxiety disorder in chronic spinal cord injury. *SCI: Psychosocial Process, 11*(3), 37–45.

Butler, T., Giordano, S., & Neren, S. (1985). Gender and sex-role attributes as predictors of utilization of natural support systems during personal stress events. *Sex Roles, 13,* 515–524.

Charmaz, K. (1995). Identity dilemmas of chronically ill men. In D. Sabo & D. Gordon (Eds.), *Men's health and illness: Gender, power, and the body* (pp. 266–291). Thousand Oaks, CA: Sage.

Chubon, R. A. (1982, Winter). An analysis of research dealing with the attitudes of professionals toward disability. *Journal of Rehabilitation, 48*(1), 25–30.

Cloerkes, G. (1981). Are prejudices against disabled persons determined by personality characteristics? *International Journal of Rehabilitation Research, 41*(1), 35–46.

Comer, R. C., & Piliavin, J. A. (1975). As others see us: Attitudes of physically handicapped and normals toward own and other groups. *Rehabilitation Literature, 36*(7), 206–221.

Davis, B. H. (1987, June). Disability and grief. *Journal of Contemporary Social Work,* pp. 352–357.

Davis, S. E., Anderson, C., Linkowski, D. C., Berger, K., & Feinstein, C. F. (1991). Development tasks and transitions of adolescents with chronic illness and disabilities. In R. P. Marinelli & A. E. Dell Orto (Eds.), *The psychological and social impact of disability* (3rd ed., pp. 70–80). New York: Springer.

Dembo, T., Leviton, G., & Wright, B. (1975). Adjustment to misfortune: A problem of social psychological rehabilitation. *Rehabilitation Psychology, 22,* 1–10.

Donaldson, J. (1980, April). Changing attitudes toward handicapped persons: A review and analysis of research. *Exceptional Children, 46,* 504–514.

Ellis, A. (1973). Humanistic psychotherapy: The rational-emotive approach. New York: Julian Press.

English, R. W. (1971). Correlates of stigma toward physically disabled persons. In R. P. Marinelli & A. E. Dell Orto (Eds.), *The psychological and social impact of physical disability* (3rd ed., pp. 162–182). New York: Springer.

Evans, J. H. (1976). Changing attitudes toward disabled persons: An experimental study. *Rehabilitation Counseling Bulletin, 19,* 572–579.

Fichten, C. S., Robillard, K., Tagalakis, V., & Amsel, R. (1991). Causal interaction between college students with various disabilities and their nondisabled peers: The internal dialogue. *Rehabilitation Psychology, 36,* 3–20.

Frankl, V. E. (1967). Paradoxical intention: A logotherapeutic technique. In V. E. Frankl (Ed.), *Psychotherapy and existentialism.* New York: Washington Square Press.

Gallagher, H. G. (1994). *FDR's splendid deception.* Arlington, VA: Vandamere.

Geisler, W. O., Jousse, A. T., Wynne-Jones, M., & Breithaupt, D. (1983). Survival in traumatic spinal cord injury. *Paraplegia, 21*(6), 364–373.

Gerschick, T. J., & Miller, A. S. (1995). Coming to terms: Masculinity and physical disability. In D. Sabo & D. Gordon (Eds.), *Men's health and illness: Gender, power, and the body* (pp. 183–204). Thousand Oaks, CA: Sage.

Gerschick, T. J., & Miller, A. S. (1997). Gender identities at the crossroads of masculinity and physical disability. In M. Gergen & S. Davis (Eds.), *Toward a new psychology of gender* (pp. 455–475). New York: Routledge.

Gething, L. (1991). Generality vs. specificity of attitudes towards people with disabilities. *British Journal of Medical Psychology, 64,* 55–64.

Gill, K. M. (1988). *Staff needs: Assessment data.* Unpublished manuscript.

Harris, L. (1991). *Public attitudes towards people with disabilities.* New York: Louis Harris & Associates.

Havranek, J. E. (1991). The social and individual costs of negative attitudes toward persons with physical disabilities. *Journal of Applied Rehabilitation Counseling, 22*(1), 15–21.

Heinemann, A. W. (1993). An introduction to substance abuse and physical disability. In A. W. Heinemann (Ed.), *Substance abuse and physical disability* (pp. 3–10). Binghamton, NY: Haworth Press.

Herek, G. M. (1986). On heterosexual masculinity. *American Behavioral Scientist, 29*(5), 563–577.

Hohmann, G. W. (1975). Psychological aspects of treatment and rehabilitation of the spinal cord injured person. *Clinical Orthopedics, 112,* 81–88.

Kahana, E., Fairchild, T., & Kahana, B. (1982). Adaptation. In D. J. Mangen & W. A. Peterson (Eds.), *Research instruments in clinical gerontology: Vol. 1. Clinical and social psychology* (pp. 145–193). Minneapolis: University of Minnesota Press.

Katz, J. (1988). A theory of qualitative methodology: The social system of analytic fieldwork. In R. Emerson (Ed.), *Contemporary field research: A collection of readings* (pp. 127–148).

Kendall, E., & Buys, N. (1998, Summer). An integrated model of psychosocial adjustment following acquired disability. *Journal of Rehabilitation, 64*(3), 16–20.

Kleck, R. (1968). Physical stigma and nonverbal cues emitted in face-to-face interaction. *Human Relations, 21,* 19–28.

Lazarus, R. S., & Folkman, S. (1984). Stress, appraisal, and coping. In R. L. Atkinson, R. C. Atkinson, E. E. Smith, & D. J. Bem (Eds.), *Introduction to psychology.* New York: Harcourt Brace Jovanovich.

Livneh, H. (1991a). On the origins of negative attitudes toward people with disabilities. In R. P. Marinelli & A. E. Dell Orto (Eds.), *The psychological and social impact of disability* (3rd ed., pp. 181–196). New York: Springer.

Livneh, H. (1991b). A unified approach to existing models of adaptation to disability: A model of adaptation. In R. P. Marinelli & A. E. Dell Orto (Eds.), *The psychological and social impact of disability* (3rd ed., pp. 111–138). New York: Springer.

Lyons, M. (1991). Enabling or disabling? Students' attitudes toward persons with disabilities. *American Journal of Occupational Therapy, 45*(4), 311–316.

Makas, E. (1988). Positive attitudes toward disabled people: Disabled and nondisabled persons' perspectives. *Journal of Social Issues, 44*(1), 49–61.

Marinelli, R. P., & Kelz, J. W. (1973). Anxiety and attitudes toward visibly disabled persons. *Rehabilitation Counseling Bulletin, 16*(4), 198–205.

Marini, I. (1992). The use of humor in counseling as a social skill for disabled clients. *Journal of Applied Rehabilitation Counseling, 23*(3), 30–36.

Milligan, M. S., & Neufeldt, A. H. (1998). Postinjury marriage to men with spinal cord injury: Women's perspectives on making a commitment. *Sexuality and Disability, 16*(2), 117–132.

Minde, K. K. (1978). Coping styles of 34 adolescents with cerebral palsy. *American Journal of Psychiatry, 135,* 1344–1349.

Power, P. W., Hershenson, D. B., & Schlossberg, N. K. (1991). Midlife transition and disability. In R. P. Marinelli & A. E. Dell Orto (Eds.), *The psychological and social impact of disability* (3rd ed., pp. 81–104). New York: Springer.

Roessler, R., & Rubin, S. E. (1982). *Case management and rehabilitation counseling.* Austin, TX: PRO-ED.

Shontz, F. C. (1975). The psychological aspects of physical illness and disability. New York: Macmillan.

Simmons, R., & Rosenberg, M. (1975). Sex, sex roles, and self-image. *Journal of Youth and Adolescence, 4*, 229–258.

Spence, J. T., Helmreich, R. L., & Stapp, J. (1974). The personal attributes questionnaire: A measure of sex-role stereotypes and masculinity-femininity. *JSAS Catalog of Selected Documents in Psychology, 4*, 127.

Sprecher, S., & Sedikides, C. (1993). Gender differences in perceptions of emotionality: The case of close, heterosexual relationships. *Sex Roles, 28*(9–10), 511–530.

Stone, A. A., & Neale, J. M. (1984). New measure of daily coping: Development and preliminary results. *Journal of Personality and Social Psychology, 46*(4), 892–906.

Tepper, M. S. (1997). Living with a disability: A man's perspective. In M. Sipski & C. Alexander (Eds.), *Sexual function in people with disability and chronic illness* (pp. 131–146). Gaithersburg, MD: Aspen.

Trieschmann, R. (1988). *Spinal cord injuries.* New York: Demos.

Winstead, B. A., Derlega, V. J., & Wong, P.T.P. (1984). Effect of sex-role orientation on behavioral self-disclosure. *Journal of Research in Personality, 18*, 541–553.

Wright, B. A. (1960). *Physical disability: A psychological approach.* New York: Harper & Row.

Wright, B. A. (1983). *Physical disability: A psychosocial approach* (2nd ed.). New York: Harper & Row.

Yuker, H. E. (1988). *Attitudes toward persons with disabilities.* New York: Springer.

Zilbergeld, B. (1992). *The new male sexuality.* New York: Bantam Books.

CHAPTER NINE

Counseling and Psychotherapy for Male Military Veterans

Gary Brooks

W hen one speaks of health care services to U.S. military veterans, one is primarily speaking of services delivered through the Department of Veterans Affairs (VA). This federally administered organization is the largest health care provider in the world and employs more counselors and therapists than any other organization.

Historically, the VA has paid little overt attention to the gender of its treatment population. In the 1990s, however, the VA experienced a dramatic rise in the number of female veterans, causing gender to emerge as an important topic of interest. According to Weiss (1995), projections call for women to make up 11 percent of the veteran population by 2040. In response to this trend, the VA has begun offering new programs to women and established the Women Veterans Program Office in 1994.

Ironically, it has been the appearance of a large number of female veterans that has helped the VA realize that it must pay greater attention to gender and must become more aware of the differential needs of male and female veterans. Dr. Kenneth Kizer, then the national VA medical director, stated that "excellence in customer service" requires that the VA "tailor the care environment" to the particular needs of special populations of patients (Kizer, 1996, p. 43). Because female veterans were identified as one of these special groups, gender could no longer be overlooked as a critical variable affecting the veteran population.

As is often the case, the appearance of a new group stimulates awareness of issues previously invisible. Because the VA treatment population has been predominantly male, most practitioners were able to ignore masculinity as a relevant aspect of their clients' lives. Much as fish are unaware of the existence of water, the VA has been relatively gender blind—that is, inattentive to how men's socialization into masculinity has affected their lives.

This chapter will further this process of creating greater gender awareness in the treatment of male military veterans. In particular, it will supplement the new literature on female veterans' special mental health needs and offer ideas about the corollary mental health needs of male veterans. I briefly review the general problems of male socialization and then focus on how military experience powerfully reinforces the most traditional aspects of this masculinity socialization and makes veterans especially susceptible to gender role strain. Informed by this information, I finally elaborate on the core elements of successful therapy with veteran men.

HOW MILITARY SOCIALIZATION EXACERBATES GENDER ROLE STRAIN

Although men have long enjoyed the political and economic benefits granted by a patriarchal culture, they have also carried substantial costs that have only recently received broad recognition. Pleck's "gender role strain paradigm" (1981, 1995) challenged previous ideas about masculine identity and pointed out that socially constructed gender roles create problems for women and for men. In many ways these gender roles are inconstant, impossible to fully satisfy, inherently dysfunctional in their expectations, and unforgiving when their rigid standards are violated. As has been extensively reported in other chapters of this volume, men have paid the price of masculinity in terms of damage to both physical and emotional well-being. From their decreased life expectancy to their common experiences of loneliness and personal powerlessness, many men have ultimately realized that the "privileged" status of manhood has multiple liabilities.

Long before they enter the military, young men have already been exposed to a rigorous and relatively unforgiving course of gender socialization. Pollack (1995) and Levant (1996) have been leading advocates of the position that the normative developmental course for young men is highly problematic. Pollack (1995) noted that this process is characterized by premature psychic separation from both maternal and paternal caregivers and by "traumatic abrogation of their early holding environment" (p. 44). Levant (1996) described this process as the "ordeal of emotion socialization" (p. 262).

In adolescence, the "male chorus" (Pittman, 1993) exerts further pressure on young men to conform to narrow ideas of manliness. This male chorus, composed of all a young man's comrades, rivals, buddies, bosses, male ancestors, and cultural heroes pushes the adolescent to "sacrifice more and more of his humanity for the sake of his masculinity" (p. 42).

The sacrifices, ordeals, and traumas of normative male socialization take on new and unimagined dimensions when the young man enters military basic training. The single most urgent mission of this training is to take a select group of immature young men and turn them into "warriors and fighting machines" (Egendorf, 1985, p. 23; see also Dunning, 1996; Wikler, 1980). Although this military socialization process provides many benefits in the national interest, it does so at a sizable cost to the young men who undergo it. In brief, the military has a principal mission of creating warriors who, if they survive the combat for which they are being prepared, must ultimately reenter a larger civilian culture in which warrior values are minimally adaptive. Let us turn to a closer examination of these warrior values.

Violence

Wartime military experience is inherently about violence, and soldiers become conditioned to its pervasive presence. To prepare for war a new recruit is exposed to a value system in which (1) violence is central, (2) the world is divided into allies and enemies, and (3) enemies are depersonalized as justifiable targets of violent impulses (Carlson, 1987).

Because wars are typically imbued with moral rationale, soldiers must adopt a value system in which violence becomes a highly legitimate mechanism, a means to serve moral goodness (Egendorf, 1985). At times, combat situations create the extremes of what Laufer (1985) calls "abusive violence." According to Laufer, this type of violence involves systematic or intentional killing when one's life is not threatened. Laufer found that one-third of his sample of Vietnam veterans had been exposed to abusive violence. One-tenth had participated in the episodes.

Emotional Insensitivity

Because soldiers do not have the luxury of emotional sensitivity, emotional suppression is an essential component of military life. Lifton (1973) described "psychic numbing" as endemic to Vietnam soldiers. Shatan (1978) noted that from the beginning of their basic training soldiers are taught to suppress their compassion by dehumanizing the enemy and ultimately distorting their own humanity.

> After consistently anesthetizing their empathic reactions and cutting themselves off from ordinary sensory experiences under fire, many ex-combatants find it painful and difficult to have humane feelings for other people—difficult because they are frozen in a state of "emotional anesthesia," painful because thawing

out their numbed reactions to the evil and death which enveloped them in combat is unsupportable. . . . Frequently they find inner peace only by devising a "dead space" in their psyches where memories live on, cut off from their enduring emotional impact. The price of this peace—alienation from feelings in general—creates a powerful obstacle to the formation of close relationships. (p. 49)

Dunning (1996) noted that because the Persian Gulf conflict relied so heavily on call-ups of reserve and National Guard members, the situation was unique and less conducive to this common psychological defense.

Paranoia and Distrust of Others

Based on their work with male soldiers and their families, Keith and Whitaker (1984) referred to the military as the "paranoid edge of the culture" (p. 150). Because paranoia is an intrinsic part of soldiering, the paranoid component is extremely difficult to displace. Hendin and Haas (1984) noted that because veterans tend to see civilian life as an extension of the wartime situation, "paranoid adaptation" is a common residual effect for combat veterans. They characterized this paranoid stance as incorporating "eternal vigilance in dealing with others, an expectation that any argument is a prelude to a violent fight, and a need to fight first in the face of potential aggression. . . . [T]he veteran perceives civilian life as an extension of the war" (p. 88).

In terms of combat-induced paranoia, special mention must be made of the plight of Vietnam veterans. The later years of Vietnam combat featured a counter-insurgency fighting style and an invisible enemy who fought sporadically through sniping, booby traps, and mines. Because the North Vietnamese and Vietcong frequently enlisted civilian support, U.S. soldiers commonly generalized their fear and antipathy toward all Asians and developed broad patterns of racial hatred toward all "gooks" (*gooks* being the pejorative term applied to all Asians) (Leventman & Camacho, 1980).

Additionally, the prolonged stress of the "unwinnable" war generated major disruptions among American soldiers. Hostilities and violence ("fraggings") within U.S. ranks reached epidemic proportions during the later phases of the Vietnam conflict (Moskos, 1980). Those who had been involved in the war only a short time distanced themselves from new arrivals, and "grunts" were resentful of rear-echelon support troops; senior sergeants were viewed as lifers and, as such, took on the negative characteristics relegated to the "brass" of earlier wars.

As if the numerous internal tensions were not enough to generate severe interpersonal distrust and a paranoid life stance, the Vietnam veteran returned to a painfully divided country. The well-documented antipathy that greeted the returning Vietnam veteran only worsened his deeply felt paranoia and distrust. Family, friends, the VA, the media, and the government were commonly lumped together as part of the distrusted civilian world. Eventually, many Vietnam veterans came to believe that only Vietnam veteran comrades could be trusted (Carlson, 1987).

Substance Abuse

The military has a long history of tacit (sometimes relatively overt) support for alcohol use as a coping mechanism (Stanton, 1980). In Vietnam, as in many other military environments, the serviceman's club, with inexpensive and readily available alcohol, was the primary recreational outlet. Jelinek and Williams (1982) charged that the military has encouraged the use of alcohol for stress reduction and used alcohol as a reward for successful combat operations. In Vietnam, alcohol use was supplemented heavily by reliance on marijuana (Bey & Zecchinelli, 1970). Even when discouraged from doing so by official policies, soldiers commonly have learned to use chemicals to cope with stresses and human problems.

To some extent, soldiers' use of alcohol and illicit drugs is related to the type of warfare they undergo. In high-intensity ground wars (such as the Persian Gulf conflict) there are likely to be more anxiety- and conversion-related disorders. War situations that include periods of prolonged stress (Vietnam War and World War II) are likely to produce higher rates of substance abuse (Koshes, 1996).

Problematic Relations with Women

Although recent scandals may have provoked certain changes, the military has historically been considered by many observers to be a bastion of male dominance and misogyny. Egendorf (1978) noted that "the military world denigrates women and treats sex as a commodity even more blatantly than the civilian world does" (p. 240). Numerous authors have commented on the military's suppression of sexuality as an important part of preparing young men for military combat (Egendorf, 1985; Tanay, 1982; VanDevanter, 1982).

But the problem is larger than sexual deprivation, because the sexual denial has commonly been accompanied by highly misogynistic views of women and sexuality. Hickman (1987) described these negative views in both mild and severe forms. The milder instances have included references to women as fickle and disloyal, as represented in the omnipresent references to "Jody" (Jody is the mythical civilian man who would take advantage of a soldier's absence and steal his girl and his job). The most serious instances of misogyny have been those in which women are routinely portrayed as "harlots, hussies, and whores" (Hickman, 1987, p. 195).

Prostitution not only is common around military settings but is considered by many to be deeply woven into the military lifestyle. In general, the military too rarely encourages the view of sex as part of a loving relationship and too commonly encourages the view of it as "a bodily indulgence to be paid for or ripped off to get your rocks off" (Egendorf, 1978, p. 241).

Work Compulsion

If obsession with work and career is considered a big problem for the civilian man, then it is a huge problem for the military man. For the soldier all else is considered secondary to his principal mission of fighting wars and completing the mission (Ridenour, 1984). Keith and Whitaker (1984) noted that all families within the military are indoctrinated with the ethos that loyalty to military duties is paramount. Dunning (1996) quoted the oft-heard military maxim, "if the military had wanted you to have a family, it would have issued you one" (p. 198).

IMPLICATIONS FOR CLINICAL TREATMENT OF MALE VETERANS

Before veterans can be assimilated into or reenter a civilian culture that has undergone substantial shifts in expectations of men and women, these veterans must be helped to understand the culture's conflict with the most anachronistic aspects of military culture.

To offer culturally sensitive clinical services to male veterans, we must recognize the powerful socializing forces that shape men, as well as the primary values or "dominant discourses" (Hare-Mustin, 1994) of both civilian culture and military culture.

Previously, I argued that treatment programs for Vietnam veterans would not be optimally successful until clinicians understood male gender role strain and viewed male veteran clients as men as well as veterans (Brooks, 1990). More recently I have described a gender-sensitive model of psychotherapy with traditional men (Brooks, 1998a, 1998b). For convenience, I use the acronym MASTERY to represent the core components of the model. In the remainder of this chapter, I briefly describe the components of this model and illustrate its applicability with male veterans through a case illustration.

Luis: Anguish of Combat Veterans

Luis was a thirty-eight-year-old divorced, Mexican American, unemployed brick-layer, who, as a Vietnam combat veteran, was eligible for services at the Temple (Texas) VA Hospital. Prior to admission he had been suicidal and homicidal in reaction to separation from his girlfriend Rose (age thirty-five). Rose had broken off the relationship after becoming impatient with Luis's moodiness and temper outbursts, usually directed at her and her three children from an earlier marriage.

When seen for the initial triage meeting with the psychiatry inpatient staff, Luis appeared angry and frustrated, though not overtly depressed. He clearly was upset about the breakup of his relationship with Rose, but bitterness and anger were his most prominent affects. In the initial meeting he was observed to be a neat, clean-shaven man, with impeccable grooming, dressed in blue jeans and a denim shirt. He was short and muscular, with a dark complexion, and had thick black hair. He had several military-theme tattoos on his arms, with the letters "L-O-V-E" on the knuckles of his left hand and "H-A-T-E" on the right. His general demeanor was marked by emotional intensity. Luis seemed to be a deadly serious man of powerful emotions. Although Luis was obviously bitter and hypervigilant, he was also fearful and desperate. He very much wanted help, yet was confused by the help-seeking process, defensive about self-revelation, and suspicious of the helping community.

As we collected information about Luis's history, we became even more uncomfortable with him. We learned that after a military career that had included two Vietnam combat tours, Luis had begun having major adjustment problems. Unable to cope with his memories of Vietnam combat, he had begun abusing alcohol and heroin and lived on the streets, literally fighting to survive. He eventually was arrested for a variety of criminal acts and spent several years in prison. During his incarceration, Luis was divorced by his first wife and became estranged from his two children.

After leaving prison, Luis began to "go straight." He quit drug and alcohol use and began work with his father as an apprentice bricklayer. In the early 1980s, he met Rose, a divorced mother of three. Luis saw Rose as a "good" woman, who was loving, supportive, and moral. He was interested but was troubled because she seemed to be from a higher social class. Of even greater concern to him was the realization that she was not at all like other women he had known. Rose was intelligent, educated, independent, assertive, socially competent, and politically active (as a barrio organizer of a Latino political action group).

An impassioned and conflictual relationship developed. Rose was drawn to Luis's strength, work ethic, and loyalty yet fearful of his intensity and moodiness. Luis was drawn to Rose as someone who not only excited his manly passions but also could understand him, soothe him, and exorcise his demons. Although he could never fully reveal the extent of his combat trauma, he nevertheless sensed that she knew and accepted his anguish. When he had experienced the sudden flashbacks, wrenching nightmares, and anguished guilt that are hallmarks of posttraumatic stress disorder, he had relied on Rose to provide comfort and compassion. Rose had been the only person who could get inside his macho facade and could tease and joke, allowing access to a playful side he had never recognized.

At the same time, however, Luis was becoming deeply fearful of the dependency he was developing on Rose. Never particularly comfortable with emotional intimacy, he was terrified that he might lose her. As his fears increased he became more possessive and sought to control her. Not surprisingly, Rose resented Luis's controlling behaviors. Intense conflicts ensued, with bitter fights, threats, separations, and impassioned reconciliations. Over the years, Rose had grown increasingly weary of Luis's insecurities yet could not imagine how to end the cycle. Luis was also tired of it but knew how to express his fears only through his rage. Although he had never become violent, he was deeply fearful of losing control.

Overview of Psychotherapy with Luis

Over the next several months I worked intensively with Luis. For a number of reasons I have explicated elsewhere (Brooks, 1996), I opted initially for intensive exposure to a men's therapy group. Luis immediately benefited from this environment through a greater sense of connection with other men in distress and a greater appreciation of potential benefits of seeking help. Because his Vietnam issues were so pressing, I referred Luis to an intensive posttraumatic stress disorder program. There he confronted the horrors of his Vietnam combat experiences and his significant survivor guilt. Although he realized that his Vietnam experiences had made permanent changes in his approach to life, he returned with a commitment to make the best accommodation he could. At this point he seemed far better prepared to begin working on his relationship with Rose and seek a marital relationship more in keeping with Rose's needs and changing times.

THE MASTERY MODEL: CONCEPT AND APPLICATION

In the remainder of this chapter I describe the conceptual basis of the MASTERY model and illustrate how it was effectively applied in psychotherapy with Luis (and Rose).

Monitor Personal Reactions to Men and Male Behavior Styles

Before describing my work with Luis, I first describe the conceptual basis of this initial step of my MASTERY model. I then illustrate its application with Luis.

Concept. Empathy, the capacity to understand the world from the perspective of a client, has long been accepted as a critical component of successful psychotherapy. One of the most respected principles of psychotherapy is that clients are more likely to entertain change when they feel they have been understood, appreciated, valued, or esteemed. In the case of therapy with traditional men, empathy is especially important because of the many ways that these men make themselves difficult to value or understand. Brooks and Silverstein (1995) noted that the "dark side of masculinity" includes a wide range of negative behaviors—violence, alcohol and drug abuse, sexual excess, emotional flight or withdrawal, sexism, and inadequate behavior as relationship partners—that frequently appear in populations of traditional men.

Therapists working with the victims of men's dark-side behavior are quite likely to have strong negative reactions to the perpetrators. These reactions are fully understandable and, to the extent that they alert therapists to the need to protect vulnerable parties, they are functional. However, in some extreme cases of dark-side behavior, men are likely to evoke unnecessarily strong reactions and be labeled as "wife beaters," "winos," "dead-beat dads," or "male chauvinist pigs." At other times, therapists must struggle to avoid generalizing their negative reactions to some male perpetrators onto all men—that is, to the entire male gender.

Already angry or defensive about entering the therapy situation, many of these men can be expected to be quite sensitive to therapist disapproval and may quickly exit if they sense it. Some men may adopt a supplicant and self-condemning stance, heaping blame and guilt on themselves while idealizing loved ones whom they have mistreated. Others may present as overwhelmed, confused, or emotionally anesthetized. Regardless of the type of client presentation, the therapist faces a significant challenge.

To establish therapeutic rapport the therapist must find a way to get behind aversive features of the male client's pretherapy behavior and highlight the client's positive or ennobling characteristics. In brief, the capacity to monitor personal reactivity and to value traditional men is one of the core elements of treatment.

Application. From the moment I first encountered Luis, I realized that I would need to monitor my affective reactivity to him. His strength and physical power were apparent. His muscular torso was barely hidden by his T-shirt and jeans. He exuded emotional intensity through his confrontational glare and tense posture. The atmosphere felt oppressive as he sat forward in his chair, clenching and unclenching his fists in an effort to cope with his discomfort. My discomfort was not helped by my recognition of his history. Because this man had been in Vietnam combat and had been in prison, he probably had become accustomed to dealing with his distress in some pretty scary ways. To work with him, I might eventually need to confront some things and/or set limits. Could I overcome my fear of him to do that?

But fear was not the only source of discomfort. In many ways, Luis was clearly different from me. He had grown up in an impoverished, ethnic minority environment. When he had gone to school, he had attended inferior ones, with less qualified teachers. Most of his "education" came on the streets. When I was attending college and protesting the Vietnam War, he had been a frontline "grunt" in the Vietnam jungles. When I was completing graduate training, he had been battling drugs and incarceration. When I began my cerebral and emotion-focused career as a psychologist, he had been sweating and enduring the rigors of physical labor. In many ways my life was going well and I was a "success." Luis was on the edge. By some traditional standards of masculinity, he was a "loser."

These realities created a number of additional affective reactions that I needed to monitor very closely. Would I be susceptible to subtle feelings of superiority and condescension in the face of this unsuccessful man? On the other hand, would I be subject to feeling inadequate in the company of a man who exuded intense physical masculinity and had minimal regard for "shrinks"? What about guilt and social justice? Luis was a member of a minority group and been raised in a culture that granted no advantages to Mexican Americans. Luis had served his country in Vietnam, while I had bettered myself in college and graduate school.

Obviously, my therapy with Luis would depend on my capacity to recognize and manage my affective reactivity to him. Over the past twenty years, I have worked assiduously to do exactly that—to recognize my multiple reactions to traditional men and their (our) methods of coping with distress. Although this is a continual struggle, I believe that I am far more empathic and realistic than when I first entered the VA system.

In the most general terms, I have found that to work successfully with male veterans, I must be both realistic and compassionate. I must not be awed or overly honoring of them (even if they are celebrated and decorated war heroes). When they run into trouble, I must find a way to develop noble ascriptions of them. Sometimes, a veteran's war injuries provide visible evidence of his victimization. At other times, however, a man's injuries are not apparent and I must recognize the less obvious wounds, whether they are from actual combat or from the more brutalizing aspects of masculinity socialization.

Sometimes I have found it necessary to curb my negative reactions to certain men and search for their more noble aspects—for example, their loyalty to their provider, protector, and family leadership roles. In the specific case of veterans, it becomes critical to put aside any lingering hatred of wars and respect the sacrifices and loyalty of the individual warriors.

Assume the Male Client Is Feeling Pain

The second step of the MASTERY model calls for attention to the emotional anguish implicit in traditional masculinity socialization. I first address this step at the conceptual level and then illustrate it in my work with Luis.

Concept. When one reviews the newly emerging men's studies literature, a critical realization emerges about the lives of contemporary men: Although there are many benefits of the traditional model of manhood, there are also many penalties. This, of course, is the heart of the gender role strain model described earlier in this chapter and throughout the handbook.

Although many men are leading very fulfilling lives, most men suffer in many areas. Most men are plagued with a degree of anxiety about whether they are "man enough"—that is, do they measure up to the next guy or to unrealistic public images of male heroes? Almost all men are susceptible to a range of health problems that are related to the way men are taught to treat their bodies. Many men die prematurely. Many men have satisfying sex lives, but a great many others are dissatisfied with the quantity or quality of their sexual activities or the physical appearances of their partners. Finally, many feel emotionally isolated and yearn for closer connections with others.

Application. Because he exuded anger and frustration, it was easy to see that Luis was in pain. But behind his enraged exterior lay the far deeper suffering that had triggered much of his dark-side behavior.

The breakthrough came in a particularly intense group session when Luis tearfully and haltingly told the group of his loss of a "normal boyhood." "I didn't have no childhood, man. . . . They needed me. . . . Somebody had to be the man of the family!" With anguish he related his efforts as a twelve-year-old boy to provide food for his mother and siblings after his father had abandoned them. He described both his humiliation and his pride at searching through garbage cans to ensure family survival. From that reverie, Luis moved to his painful memories of Vietnam—of his failure to save a comrade who had run across a field of fire to reach a departing chopper. Luis had reached down and caught the bloodied wrist of the panicked man but had lost his grip as the chopper ascended. Luis needed more than thirty minutes to describe his years of self-recrimination and vivid nightmares in which he would reexperience the images and screams of a man about to face death or torture.

Traditional working-class men are subject to intense emotional states that they poorly comprehend and rarely express directly and appropriately. Luis was no exception, as therapy began in earnest when Luis was able to access his considerable psychic pain.

See the Male Client's Problems in Gender Context

The third step of the MASTERY model calls for therapists to be gender sensitive, in both their case conceptualizations and their therapeutic interventions.

Concept. Culturally sensitive therapy adjusts its diagnostic formulations and intervention style to the dominant value system of clients. When it comes to therapy for traditional men, it follows that masculinity should come under the microscope. Solomon (1982) proposed that most men benefit from "gender role psychotherapy," in which gender role issues are explicitly agreed on as a major focus of therapy. Many others have argued for "gender-sensitive" or "gender-aware" therapies—that is, those that make gender an integral aspect of counseling and that view client problems within their social context (Good, Gilbert, & Sher, 1990; Philpot, 1991).

At their heart, these context-aware therapies urge men to see themselves in social context—that is, as products and sometimes victims of their upbringing in a gendered culture. This challenge to men's usual attribution system usually provides immense subjective relief. Men often benefit when they see their failures as less personal and as more the product of a severe and unforgiving socialization process. When they recognize that they have suffered because they have been loyalists to an anachronistic masculine code, they cannot help but experience a dramatic decrease in excessive self-blame. This process not only provides substantial comfort for many anguished men but also may generate enough energy for them to begin the corollary investigation of how socialization pressures have limited women.

Application. A special emphasis of all my men's groups is that of examining the members' problems through a gendered lens and elucidating the manner in which rigid role definitions contribute to situational problems. Repeatedly, I define the group as one that would examine the stresses we all shared as men.

With Luis, one therapeutic focus was that of his obsession with work performance as the only meaningful evidence of masculine worth. As a blue-collar male, he was realistic about the survival value of work, but he had additionally incorporated unrealistic aspects of the work ethic. For example, his rigid work ethos allowed for no possibility that he could be assisted by Rose's work, because that would be interpreted as further evidence of his failure as a male breadwinner. His capacity for providing Rose with practical help and emotional support was negated as unworthy of a man. Ironically, one of Luis's traditional ideas about male-female relationships—women are drawn to the highest-performing men—was a basic source of his insecurity with Rose.

Over the course of the therapy group, Luis was able to grasp what had formerly been in the background—his strong ideas about proper male conduct. Although that new awareness alone did not produce answers to his situational problems, it did provide a measure of subjective comfort. What he had formerly seen as a complete personal failure he could now see, in part, as a product of a changing culture, with its revolutionary ideas about what is suitable for women and men.

Transmit Empathy and Understanding

The fourth step of the MASTERY model calls for the therapist to communicate to the male client that his struggles and pain are recognized.

Concept. If hidden emotional pain is the shameful secret of traditional men, then it is especially critical that therapists establish therapeutic connection by recognizing and validating men's psychic pain. When they are not translating their vulnerable emotions into rage, men typically experience any psychic pain as humiliating weakness. Psychic pain can be so terrifying that men will go to great lengths to hide from it. Rage and frustration, because they are "manly" emotions, are the primary affective states men allow themselves. McLean (1996) stated that "the process of turning boys into men has, historically, been one of systematic abuse, both physical and emotional, designed to teach boys not to show most emotions, except in certain ritually prescribed situations, and if possible, not to feel them" (p. 21).

For growth to occur, men's pain cannot remain hidden or misunderstood. For that pain to come into the open, an environment of empathy and acceptance must be established. Before significant therapeutic change can take place, therapists must understand the dimensions of men's psychic pain and they must convince men that it is safe to encounter it. Often, a man will not feel safe unless he realizes that he is not alone, that other men also hide similar emotional burdens. As a result therapy must be conducted in a fashion that maximizes the possibility of men becoming more self-disclosing. In my experience, this self-disclosure is most likely to occur in the relative safety of a men's group, although it can certainly occur with a skillful therapist in other therapy formats.

Previously I have noted that men's groups help men reveal their pain because "participative self-disclosure" allows them to feel a sense of "universality" with other men (Brooks, 1996, 1998a, 1998b). Many times I have heard a troubled man say "*these* men can understand me because they have been there, they have walked in my shoes."

This process is also helpful because it frequently instills hope in a troubled man. Group members can bear witness and offer testimony about the benefits of therapy and the potential for therapeutic growth.

Even when groups are not feasible, this critical step of transmitting compassion and understanding can be accomplished. A therapist who has worked extensively with men can reach a troubled man by describing his or her past encounters with men in similar straits. A male therapist can, to some extent, describe his own struggles and fears. A female therapist can describe her experiences with important men in her life and demonstrate her empathic connection with these struggles.

Application. Luis had lost touch with a male reference group. Although he shared the common gender role problems of most traditional men and carried around the omnipresent and invisible psychic "male chorus" (Pittman, 1990), he had become socially and emotionally isolated from other men. He fully experienced the negative aspects of the male chorus in that he was always evaluating himself negatively against other men who seemed to be problem free. At some deep level, he truly felt that he alone was experiencing the common problems and failures of contemporary men.

Once he realized he was not alone, Luis experienced a rush of relief and enthusiasm. In the words of a fellow group member, "Luis, you're just like us." The new excitement of shared struggles allowed Luis entrée into the most positive and healing aspects of the male community through loyalty, supportive interactions, and a sense of belonging. Within a brief period of time, Luis became a central figure in the group, elevating his personal morale and injecting new energy into the group milieu.

Luis had been demoralized by his seemingly vulnerable position and confused by the vagaries of the psychotherapy process. But when he started group therapy he was buoyed by the testimonials of more experienced group members. Group veterans extolled the benefits of the group environment, describing it as a psychological haven that had enabled them to regain a sense of control over their lives. These testimonials, though overblown at times, were particularly helpful in relieving Luis's fear about the shameful or "feminizing" effects of psychotherapy.

Empower Men to Change

The fifth step of the MASTERY model calls for the therapist to push the male client not to settle for subjective relief but to make more substantial life changes.

Concept. As I noted earlier, men are likely to experience considerable subjective relief and gain substantial self-respect as they recognize the universality of these struggles among men—that is, "I am not alone in this." They may realize tension reduction through their cathartic expression of intense negative feelings. But, although these accomplishments are quite important, they are not sufficient. This is the point at which my approach to men differs markedly from that of certain others. Let me elaborate.

From Robert Bly's *Iron John* (1990) and John Gray's *Men Are from Mars, Women Are from Venus* (1996) to the controversial work of sociobiologists and evolutionary psychologists, there have been many calls for greater understanding of men's behavior and more acceptance of male modes of being. These works are helpful yet in my view are highly disappointing, even counterproductive, when they espouse essentialist philosophies and call for nothing more than improved understanding of men's behavior. It is my fervent belief that therapists cannot settle for mere understanding of men; we must also have complete commitment to helping men change. The subjective relief experienced by our male clients is a critical first step, but therapy cannot stop there. Men must be challenged to initiate a major reevaluation of their gender role values and assumptions in an effort to bring themselves into greater harmony with a changing world.

Application. Luis had made immense progress though his work in the men's group. For the first time in years, he was able to function without the constant support and emotional validation he had demanded from Rose. A crisis generated a brief relapse but also a major spurt of relational growth.

Rose was due to come to the hospital to pick up Luis for a weekend pass. One day earlier, she had called with unsettling news. To her horror, she had learned that, many years before, her oldest daughter, Marie (age twenty-two), had been sexually assaulted by her stepfather (Rose's second husband). Although tormented by Marie's pain, Rose was terrified to tell Luis. "He'll go crazy," she said. "He'll either kill the bastard or fall all to pieces." I agreed to try to help Rose talk with Luis.

Our conjoint session was superficial and uneventful, because Rose stayed clear of the troubling issue. As the hour neared an end, I suggested we needed to prepare to stop. Rose became frantic: "No! We can't stop yet." Luis was shocked and perplexed.

I asked her to talk more, but she could not. I asked her to keep trying. As the silence wore on, Luis became increasingly unnerved. "What the hell is it?" he demanded.

Rose tried but still could not speak. That was it for Luis. "Well, to hell with this, let me get to hell outta here. You've met a man haven't you? Don't bother telling me. . . . I can see it. . . . Let's get a goddamn divorce!"

Rose became even more distraught when she saw that Luis was totally misreading her messages. She looked to me in near panic: "Can you help?"

I turned to Luis. "Luis, relax. You are way off the mark . Rose needs to tell you something . . . but it's very hard for her. . . . She needs your help and support."

Luis could not let it go. "Support! I'll give her support. She can pack her damn bags and hit the road. . . . Let that other dude give her support!"

I continued to try to reach him. "Luis, it's not about divorce, . . . it's about something entirely different." That calmed him. He turned to Rose and asked in a far more tender voice, "What is it?"

Eventually Rose was able to tell him. Luis was taken completely by surprise and was awkward in trying to comfort Rose. I coached him to sit beside her. He began to get it. Slowly his put his arm around Rose, who then began wailing. Luis nearly panicked and ran to get her water. He returned and began pacing the floor. I urged him to move back beside Rose. Emboldened by my encouragement, he resumed holding Rose. For several minutes he held and rocked her, and she painfully confronted her guilt and described her fears for her daughter.

Luis had been so preoccupied with losing Rose that he could imagine only one reason for Rose to be upset. Lacking any other substantive relationships or sources of emotional support, he had become obsessed with Rose's nurturance and reassurances. He had been intensely overreactive to any interruptions in her attentions and often paralyzed by fears that she might abandon him for a worthier man.

Fortunately, in the group environment Luis had felt understood and had begun to broaden his circle of emotional support. He had become more confident of his personal assets and less needy of Rose's constant comforting. At times he was able to recognize the irrational aspects of his abandonment fears. Yet in a crisis his first response had been to panic and regress to a more dependent state.

As this vignette illustrates, the compassion and empathy of gender-sensitive therapy can provide a critical step in helping a traditional man to change. But the process should not stop at that point. The subjective relief of early therapy should be used as an inspiration for men to launch fundamental changes in their lives. Men should not only recognize the distress caused by gender role strain but also be encouraged to actually challenge the narrow and limiting masculine code that has constrained them. They need to be empowered to broaden their life options beyond those of warriors and providers to become better friends, fathers, and relational partners.

Respect Resistance and Yield Some Control to the Larger System

The final step of the MASTERY model calls for therapists to be persistent yet realistic in their efforts to help men change.

Concept. There are many metaphors from which to choose: Rome wasn't built in a day. The longest journey begins with a single step. You can only eat an elephant one bite at a time. It is my belief that the first therapy contact, whether in a men's group or in gender-sensitive individual therapy, is only one step in the therapy journey of traditional men. As a systems therapist I believe that families and larger social systems are rule governed. Therefore, any attempt to change the beliefs, attitudes, and behaviors of one person will be met with a "change-back" reaction, homeostatic pressures to return to more customary patterns. For this reason, I commonly envision the initial contacts as a critical step that prepares the way for more systematic change in the form of eventual family therapy and, for some, men's movement activism. Men are shaped by their families and by the larger culture. At the same time, they themselves contribute to creating that culture. Change needs to occur at both the individual and the societal level.

Despite my belief in the ultimate convergence of psychotherapy and social action, I recognize that many men will take only small steps. Not all traditional men will take on the larger project of reforming the culture. Most will approach therapy itself in a tentative and cautious fashion. If they feel understood and the overall experience is positive, they will return. For this reason, I consider it essential that therapists develop a high degree of respect for men's reluctance to embrace change and a high level of patience for change in the larger social system.

Application. Patience and respect were especially critical in my work with Luis and Rose. Luis had seemed greatly relieved to recognize the value of confronting some aspects of the rigid male code. At the same time, however, traditional masculinity was deeply ingrained in him and he was deeply ambivalent about even minimal change. His gender role journey would be slow and episodic, requiring continual guidance and support from an understanding therapist.

Not long after Luis entered therapy, I made contact with Rose to lay the groundwork for couples therapy and family therapy. Rose had been in therapy herself and had been impatient for Luis to become more psychologically minded. The session described here provided a marvelous springboard to family therapy that continued intermittently for the next two years.

Luis did not change every aspect of his value system or his traditional masculinity. He certainly did not become a men's movement activist. In many ways,

I would have liked to have seen him change more than he did. At the same time, however, I was pleased to see that he had become far more comfortable in and had made a far better accommodation to his life circumstances. He may not have radically changed his beliefs about masculinity, but he had incorporated more flexibility and broadened his ideas about how men and women can interact.

OVERVIEW OF THERAPY WITH LUIS AND MALE VETERANS

Luis received considerable benefit from the gender-sensitive therapy he experienced in the men's group. An environment was created in which he was able to interact meaningfully with other traditional men in similar straits—a male healing group. He became less distrustful of psychotherapy and gained markedly in self-respect from the recognition that his problems were common among other men. He realized tension reduction through cathartic expression of intense painful feelings.

However, this was not enough. When he left the group he reentered a world undergoing major cultural changes. To maximize Luis's ability to cope with this world and to facilitate more flexible role functioning in his marital and family life, further work was necessary. Luis had been made comfortable in therapy because he had been understood and validated. Discovering other struggling men had increased his comfort. Ultimate progress, however, depends on the therapist's ability to challenge men to make still further changes.

In working with veterans and other traditional men, therapists are challenged to persuade them that whatever their negative feelings about the changing culture, it is their responsibility to make appropriate accommodations in themselves. The seemingly idyllic world of yesterday will not return. Although they may consider it more masculine to be the ram that keeps buttin' that dam, they can be assured that, in most cases, this only produces dented dams and dead rams.

To accomplish its mission of "excellence in customer service," the VA needs to continue the vitally important process of refining the health care services it delivers to its veteran clients, including the innovative programs for female veterans. But the VA should not stop there. With the newly emerging findings about gender as a critical mediating variable in health, special attention must be given to how the needs of women and men are similar yet different. Health care givers in the VA must avail themselves of the information being developed in the newly emerging fields of women's studies and men's studies. In these rapidly changing times, compassionate, thoughtful, and gender-aware psychotherapists offer unique hope for the many male and female veterans who seek help in the VA health care system.

Compassionate, thoughtful, and gender-aware psychotherapists offer unique hope for challenging men to reach out to each other, to interact sensitively with women, to challenge regressive institutions, and to mentor the next generation of men. These therapies offer hope for developing couple relationships characterized by feminist principles of mutual respect and empowerment. Psychotherapists must be continually alert to the destructive potential of the darkest aspects of traditional masculinity and yet hold utmost confidence in the potential of men— men who desperately want a better deal for themselves, their culture, and their loved ones. Therapists are uniquely positioned to provide leadership in the painful but ultimately exhilarating process of helping traditional men discover realistic and compassionate masculinities, helping couples develop egalitarian relationships, and helping family systems empower women and men.

References

Bey, D. R., & Zecchinelli, V. A. (1970). Marijuana as a coping device in Vietnam. (USARV Pamphlet 40). *USARV Medical Bulletin, 22,* 21–28.

Bly, R. (1990). *Iron John: A book about men.* New York: Vintage Books.

Brooks, G. R. (1990). Post-Vietnam gender role strain: A needed concept? *Professional Psychology: Research and Practice, 21,* 18–25.

Brooks, G. R. (1996). Treatment for therapy-resistant men. In M. Andronico (Ed.), *Men in groups: Realities and insights* (pp. 7–19). Washington, DC: APA Press.

Brooks, G. R. (1998a). *A new psychotherapy for traditional men.* San Francisco: Jossey-Bass.

Brooks, G. R. (1998b). Group therapy for traditional men. In W. S. Pollack & R. F. Levant (Eds.), *New psychotherapy for men* (pp. 83–96). New York: Wiley.

Brooks, G. R., & Silverstein, L. B. (1995). Understanding the dark side of masculinity: An integrative systems model. In R. F. Levant & W. S. Pollack (Eds.), *A new psychology of men* (pp. 280–333). New York: Basic Books.

Carlson, T. A. (1987). Counseling with veterans. In M. Scher, M. Stevens, G. Good, & G. Eichenfield (Eds.), *Handbook of counseling and psychotherapy with men* (pp. 343–359). Newbury Park, CA: Sage.

Dunning, C. M. (1996). From citizen to soldier: Mobilization of reservists. In R. J. Ursano & A. E. Norwood (Eds.), *Emotional aftermath of the Persian Gulf War: Veterans, families, communities, and nations* (pp. 197–225). Washington, DC: American Psychiatric Press.

Egendorf, A. (1978). Psychotherapy with Vietnam veterans: Observations and suggestions. In C. R. Figley (Ed.), *Stress disorders among Vietnam veterans* (pp. 231–253). New York: Brunner/Mazel.

Egendorf, A. (1985). *Healing from war: Trauma and transformation after Vietnam.* Boston: Houghton Mifflin.

Good, G., Gilbert, L. A., & Sher, M. (1990). Gender aware therapy: A synthesis of feminist therapy and knowledge about gender. *Journal of Counseling and Development, 68,* 376–380.

Gray, J. (1996). *Men are from Mars, women are from Venus.* New York: HarperCollins.

Hare-Mustin, R. (1994). Discourses in the married room: A postmodern analysis of therapy. *Family Process, 33,* 19–35.

Hendin, H., & Haas, A. P. (1984). *Wounds of war: Psychological aftermath of combat in Vietnam.* New York: Basic Books.

Hickman, P. (1987). But you weren't there. In T. M. Williams (Ed.), *Post-traumatic stress disorder: A handbook for clinicians* (pp. 193–208). Cincinnati, OH: Disabled American Veterans.

Jelinek, J. M., & Williams, T. (1982). Post-traumatic stress disorder and substance abuse. In T. Williams (Ed.), *Post-traumatic stress disorder* (pp. 103–118). Cincinnati, OH: Disabled American Veterans.

Keith, D. V., & Whitaker, C. A. (1984). C'est la guerre: Military families and family therapy. In F. W. Kaslow & R. I. Ridenour (Eds.), *The military family: Dynamics and treatment* (pp. 147–166). New York: Guilford Press.

Kizer, K. W. (1996). *Prescription for change.* Washington, DC: Department of Veterans Affairs.

Koshes, R. J. (1996). The care of those returned: Psychiatric illnesses of war. In R. J. Ursano & A. E. Norwood (Eds.), *Emotional aftermath of the Persian Gulf War: Veterans, families, communities, and nations* (pp. 393–414). Washington, DC: American Psychiatric Press.

Laufer, R. S. (1985). War trauma and human development: The Vietnam experience. In S. M. Sonnenberg, A. S. Blank, & J. A. Talbot (Eds.), *The trauma of war* (pp. 31–56). Washington, DC: American Psychiatric Press.

Levant, R. F. (1996). The new psychology of men. *Professional Psychology: Research and Practice, 27,* 259–265.

Leventman, S., & Camacho, P. (1980). The "gook" syndrome: The Vietnam war as racial encounter. In C. R. Figley & S. Leventman (Eds.), *Strangers at home* (pp. 5–44). New York: Praeger.

Lifton, R. (1973). *Home from the war.* New York: Simon & Schuster.

McLean, C. (1996). The politics of men's pain. In C. McLean, M. Carey, & C. White (Eds.), *Men's ways of being* (pp. 11–28). New York: Westview Press.

Moskos, C. (1980). Surviving the war in Vietnam. In C. R. Figley & S. Leventman (Eds.), *Strangers at home* (pp. 71–86). New York: Praeger.

Philpot, C. L. (1991). Gender-sensitive couples therapy. *Journal of Family Psychotherapy, 2,* 19–40.

Pittman, F. (1990). The masculine mystique. *Family Therapy Networker, 14*(3), 40–52.

Pittman, F. (1993). Man enough: Fathers, sons, and the search for masculinity. New York: Perigee.

Pleck, J. H. (1981). *The myth of masculinity.* Cambridge, MA: MIT Press.

Pleck, J. H. (1995). The gender role strain paradigm: An update. In R. F. Levant & W. S. Pollack (Eds.), *A new psychology of men* (pp. 11–32). New York: Basic Books.

Pollack, W. S. (1995). No man is an island. In R. F. Levant & W. S. Pollack (Eds.), *A new psychology of men* (pp. 33–67). New York: Basic Books.

Ridenour, R. I. (1984). The military service families and the therapist. In F. W. Kaslow & R. I. Ridenour (Eds.), *The military family: Dynamics and treatment* (pp. 1–17). New York: Guilford Press.

Shatan, C. F. (1978). Stress disorders among Vietnam veterans: The emotional content of combat continues. In C. R. Figley (Ed.), *Stress disorders among Vietnam veterans* (pp. 43–56). New York: Brunner/Mazel.

Stanton, M. D. (1980). The hooked serviceman. In C. R. Figley & S. Leventman (Eds.), *Strangers at home* (pp. 279–292). New York: Praeger.

Tanay, E. (1982). The Vietnam veteran—Victim of war. In W. E. Kelley (Ed.), *Post-traumatic stress disorder and the war veteran patient* (pp. 29–42). New York: Brunner/Mazel.

VanDevanter, L. M. (1982). The unknown warriors: Implications of the experiences of women in Vietnam. In W. E. Kelley (Ed.), *Post-traumatic stress disorder and the war veteran patient* (pp. 148–169). New York: Brunner/Mazel.

Weiss, T. W. (1995). Improvements in VA Health Services for women veterans. *Women and Health, 23*, 1–12.

Wikler, N. (1980). Hidden injuries of war. In C. R. Figley (Ed.), *Stress disorders among Vietnam veterans* (pp. 87–108). New York: Brunner/Mazel.

SECTION TWO

PROBLEMS

CHAPTER TEN

Assessing and Treating Depression in Men

Sam V. Cochran

For many years clinicians and researchers alike have assumed that about half as many men as women experience depression. This assumption has led many to conclude that men experience fewer and less severe symptoms of depression and that men do not seek help for depression. In general, scientific studies tended to confirm these assumptions (Nolen-Hoeksema, 1987). Recently, however, increasing attention has been directed to the problem of undiagnosed and untreated depression in men in both professional venues (see Cochran & Rabinowitz, 2000; Pollack, 1998) and popular venues (see Lynch & Kilmartin, 1999; Real, 1997). These authors argue for greater sensitivity on the part of psychotherapists to the insidious and often deadly effects of depression on men.

Epidemiological studies have found that in certain population samples men experience depression just as frequently as women do. In some samples, such as the elderly, rates of depression may even be greater in men than in women (Bebbington et al., 1998). Furthermore, the course of depressive disorders is remarkably similar for both men and women diagnosed with depression (Simpson, Nee, & Endicott, 1997). In addition, conditions related to depression, such as alcohol and substance abuse, have been found to be more prevalent in men than in women (Fava et al., 1996). Finally, data on suicide indicate that men of all ages and races commit suicide at rates from four to fifteen times that of women in comparable groups (Moscicki, 1997). In light of these reports, it now appears that the commonly referenced epidemiological findings asserting

229

that women experience depression at twice the rate that men do encourage oversimplified interpretations that simply do not capture the full reality of depression as it may be experienced by many men.

In this chapter I provide an overview of recent epidemiological findings on major depression and suicide as well as psychotherapy outcome studies that report results of investigations examining the treatment of depression. Attention is directed toward what these findings tell us about depression in men. In addition, I present practical guidelines for the assessment and treatment of depression in men that are linked to these empirical findings. Indeed, the outlook is improving for men who experience depression. Increasing numbers of therapists are becoming sensitized to the problem of undiagnosed and untreated depression in men. Well-tested treatments and new, innovative therapies provide relief for men who come forward and seek treatment for their depression.

SEX, GENDER, AND DEPRESSION

Depression was long considered a woman's malady. For many years, demographic data on hospital admissions and from treatment settings were interpreted to confirm that compared with men women tended to be depressed in greater numbers and tended to have more lengthy and severe episodes of depression. Because many more women than men were treated in institutions and outpatient settings this conclusion appeared warranted.

With the development of empirically based diagnostic criteria for various mental and physical conditions, rigorous epidemiological studies on the incidence and prevalence of mental disorders, including depression, could be undertaken. One of the first large-scale investigations of this kind, the Epidemiological Catchment Area study (Robins & Reiger, 1991), found that in a sample of almost twenty thousand persons drawn from five sites in the United States the incidence and prevalence of both major depression and dysthymia were greater for women than for men. In this study lifetime prevalence estimates for major depression and dysthymia for men were 2.6 and 2.2 percent, respectively, compared with 7.0 and 4.1 percent, respectively, for women. These estimates were confirmed in a later investigation, the National Comorbidity Survey (Kessler et al., 1994). In this survey, which used a stratified sample of more than eight thousand adults from the United States, the lifetime prevalence estimates for major depression and dysthymia for men were 12.7 and 4.8 percent, respectively, and the comparable rates in women were 21.3 and 8.0 percent, respectively. Differences in prevalence estimates between the two studies were attributed to the probing life review section of the interview protocol included in the National Comorbidity Survey methodology. Although the addition of this life review section to the methodology to counter the "forgetting" effect that the investigators believed might skew the results in the direction of higher rates for women, the ratio of prevalence estimates for the depressive disorders was still two to one. In both epidemiological surveys women were approximately twice as likely as men to develop a depressive condition at some point in their lifetimes.

At about the same time that these two landmark epidemiological studies appeared, several other investigations found notable divergences from the typical two-to-one female-to-male ratio of prevalence estimates of mood disorders. One of these, the Old Order Amish study reported by Egeland and Hostetter (1983), found that in a small community of Amish in Pennsylvania the rates of bipolar disorder and unipolar depression were practically identical in men and women. Another investigation that examined the rates of depression in a community of Orthodox Jews living in London found no significant differences in rates of depression between 157 men and 182 women (Loewenthal et al., 1995). An investigation of 1,747 Chinese Americans in Los Angeles reported equivalent rates of both depression and dysthymia in low-acculturation samples but found the common two-to-one female-to-male ratio in subjects with higher levels of acculturation (Takeuchi et al., 1998). Other studies that have examined populations of Atlantic Canadians (Murphy, Olivier, Monson, Sobol, & Leighton, 1988), New Zealanders (Wilhelm & Parker, 1994), and elderly persons (Girling et al., 1995) found that under certain circumstances men in these samples experience depression at rates equal to or greater than those of women.

What might be the common factor in these studies in which the men have been found to experience depression in numbers comparable to those of women? Some investigators have hypothesized that the cultural norms of these select samples are such that the men tend to suppress alcohol abuse, drug abuse, and sociopathy, thus permitting a more direct manifestation of depression. This hypothesis is plausible for the communities with strong religious and spiritual roots such as the Amish community in Pennsylvania and the Orthodox Jewish community in London.

Consistent with this hypothesis, a model of depression that has been termed the depressive spectrum disease model proposes that alcoholism and antisocial behavior disorders are a masculine expression of an underlying genetically based depressive disorder (Winokur, 1997). Hence, in populations in which these behaviors are discouraged a greater rate of depression would be expected in some of the men.

In addition to the suppressing effect that certain cultural norms might exert on atypical depressive symptoms, two of these studies used what the investigators considered more "gender-fair" criteria for defining depression within the samples (Murphy et al., 1988; Wilhelm & Parker, 1994). When alternative criteria that might be more likely to detect depression in the men were used, the rates of depression in both the men and the women in these investigations converged to nearly identical values. These findings demonstrate that our culturally derived definitions of depression, the criteria by which we designate depression in a person, have a distinct influence on who is included in the final tally.

The results from the study sampling the Chinese American community further highlight the important role that culture plays in the manifestation of depression. In this study, investigators found that the more acculturated (that is, more like Americans) the subjects were, the more likely the women were and the less likely the men were to show depression. On the other hand, the less acculturated (that is, less like Americans, more like traditional Chinese) the subjects were, the greater the likelihood of finding an even ratio of rates of depression in these men and women.

Taken together, these findings demonstrate the critical importance cultural forces (implicit and explicit behavioral norms about appropriate masculine behavior, for example) have as intervening variables in the manner in which depression is defined and manifest in the populations studied (Manson, 1995). Indeed, research on masculinity-related psychological distress has tended to confirm that gender role–related conflicts in men are correlated with high levels of distress in general (Good, Robertson, Fitzgerald, Stevens, & Bartels, 1996) and with depression in particular (Good & Wood, 1995). Reported sex differences in rates of depression are certainly influenced by gender-related (that is, cultural) variables. Clinicians can no longer ignore the implications of culturally derived gender role values in the case definition, experience, manifestation, assessment, and treatment of depression in men.

GENDER AND SYMPTOMS OF DEPRESSION

Interestingly, studies that have evaluated symptom profiles of subjects with depression have found that the actual manifestation of clinical depression is very similar in men and women (see Young, Scheftner, Fawcett, & Klerman, 1990). By and large, men with depression report the same symptoms as women with depression. For both men and women, dysphoria is reported most commonly, followed by death thoughts, changes in appetite and sleep patterns, fatigue, concentration problems, guilt, psychomotor changes, and loss of interest (Weissman, Bruce, Leaf, Florio, & Holzer, 1991). This similarity of symptom profiles appears to hold even for those subjects with chronic depression, defined as a major depression lasting at least two years without antecedent dysthymia (Kornstein et al., 1996).

In addition to studies that have detailed the symptoms of depression in men and women, studies examining the clinical progression of depression have found that women and men are very similar in terms of the course and chronicity of the disorder (see Simpson et al., 1997). The number of symptoms reported, the time elapsed between diagnosis and recovery, and the length of time between episodes all appear to be very similar in both men and women. For practical purposes the actual clinical manifestation of depression is very similar in men and women.

In contrast to the studies that have found similarities between men and women with depression, a number of investigations have reported sex-related patterns of comorbid conditions in subjects with depression. Most important, compared with women with depression, men with depression have been found to have more comorbid alcohol and other drug abuse and dependence (Fava et al., 1996; Hanna & Grant, 1997). Men with depression are also more likely than women with depression to show increased incidence of antisocial personality traits (Black, Baumgard, & Bell, 1995), masculine gender role strains (Good & Wood, 1995; Heifner, 1997), compulsive personality characteristics, and defensive or exaggerated assertions of autonomy (Frank, Carpenter, & Kupfer, 1988).

For purposes of assessment it is important for clinicians to recognize that although men show many of the same symptoms of depression that women show there are important masculine-specific patterns of behavioral and emotional expression that uniquely characterize the male experience of depression. These patterns include significant alcohol- and drug-related comorbidity, behaviors characterized as compulsive and antisocial, and increases in interpersonal conflict such as anger, withdrawal, and defensive assertions of autonomy. Sensitive assessment of depression in men must recognize the overlap between these expressions, which may appear inconsistent with a clinical picture of depression and the likely presence of depression in the men who exhibit them.

CASE EXAMPLES

Because depression is so frequently underdiagnosed in men, in this section I present some clinical examples that illustrate issues involved in assessment and treatment. These case examples demonstrate the wide variety of triggering events and clinical presentation the clinician encounters in working with men. A follow-up to the presentations given here is provided later in the chapter as a means of illustrating some of the treatment process issues that can arise in working with depression in men.

Case I. Tim scheduled an appointment for evaluation and possible psychotherapy at the urging of his spouse, to whom he had been married less than a year. He had become increasingly withdrawn from her over recent months and spent more time at work and at the golf course with friends. When his spouse questioned him about his distance and seeming lack of interest in joint activities, he often responded by becoming argumentative and would withdraw further, sometimes stomping out of the house in anger. His evaluation with a therapist revealed an intense dissatisfaction with his current employment, sadness over having given up his "last chance" to become a professional golfer, and questioning of his commitment to his marriage and relationship with his spouse. He met the criteria for a depressive episode and was offered individual psychotherapy.

Case II. Roger was required to seek psychotherapy by his employer, a city transit office. He had tested positive for drugs and alcohol at a random drug screen that was a requirement in his workplace. He reported to his initial evaluation with an uncommon openness as he revealed his history of serious alcohol abuse, lack of friendships and relationships, and long-standing symptoms of depression. He had smoked some marijuana at a bar the night before the drug screen, and residue had remained in his system. He said he was actually glad to finally have an opportunity to discuss his current unhappiness, which he said he had felt at least since high school. He met diagnostic criteria for alcohol abuse and dysthymia. He continued in individual psychotherapy with his therapist for a year beyond his required attendance.

Case III. Robert and Arlene sought couples therapy at Arlene's behest. After his retirement, Robert had shown an initial interest in working on some projects around the house. Now, one year into his retirement, he spent most of his days watching television or reading. When Arlene asked him what was wrong, he responded, "Oh, nothing." Arlene knew better. Robert simply was not his old, cheerful, outgoing self. Together they described to their therapist that Robert had eagerly anticipated his retirement. However, one of his best friends had died unexpectedly shortly after they both had retired. Robert played a significant part in the memorial ceremony and even delivered a moving eulogy. Shortly afterward, however, Robert began to feel sad and tired and lost interest in many of the activities he had enjoyed prior to his retirement. A number of these activities he and his friend had planned to enjoy together.

These three case examples illustrate the wide range of triggering events and clinical presentations of depression in men. In the first case, the transition from bachelorhood to married life triggered withdrawal, overinvolvement with work, and anger. In the second case, the overlap of alcohol and substance abuse with depression is evident. And in the third case, the impact of loss on a man is expressed through sadness and withdrawal. In both the first and third cases an intimate partner is instrumental in motivating the man to seek help for his depression.

MASCULINE-SPECIFIC ASSESSMENT OF DEPRESSION

Clinicians must balance three tasks in assessing depression in men. First, a thorough assessment of symptoms of depression based on the diagnostic criteria outlined in the *Diagnostic and Statistical Manual of Mental Disorders (DSM-IV)* (American Psychiatric Association, 1994) must be completed. Second, because there is significant gender-specific comorbidity of depression with various depression-related disorders in many men, a thorough evaluation of the potential contribution of these comorbid disorders is warranted. Finally, because important culturally derived influences shape the experience and expression of depression across many settings and communities, a careful consideration of the contribution that these influences make to the manifestation of depression in men is essential.

The *DSM-IV* outlines nine symptoms of a major depressive episode, including (1) depressed mood, (2) decreased interest or pleasure in most activities, (3) weight loss or gain, (4) insomnia or oversleeping, (5) psychomotor retardation or agitation, (6) fatigue, (7) feelings of worthlessness or guilt, (8) trouble concentrating, and (9) thoughts of death or suicide. A man must manifest at least five of these criteria over a two-week period, and at least one of these five criteria must be either depressed mood or decreased interest or pleasure in most activities. Many men presenting for evaluation or treatment report a number of these common symptoms of depression. With patient, gender-sensitive listening and gentle coaxing many men often reveal enough symptoms to warrant an outright diagnosis of major depression.

In addition to assessing for the presence of the standard diagnostic criteria for depression, a therapist must also carefully assess the masculine-specific symptoms and comorbid conditions that are related to depression in men. Symptoms commonly associated with depression in men include alcohol and substance abuse, increased interpersonal conflict, work-related concerns and difficulties, and increased impulsive, self-destructive behavior. These symptomatic manifestations of depression in men are often rooted in important cultural and community norms that must also be considered when assessing a man for depression. Exhibit 10.1 outlines important features of a masculine-specific assessment of depression. By combining traditional diagnostic criteria with culturally sensitive inquiry into other possible manifestations of depression rather than focusing only on the traditional diagnostic criteria, a clinician is much more likely to detect and diagnose depression in men.

SUICIDE RISK IN MEN WITH DEPRESSION

Suicide is now recognized as a major public health concern that warrants national attention. Because men commit suicide at high rates compared with women, death from suicide is a significant mortality risk for men with depression. Consequently, any therapist working with men must devote time to assessing the potential risk for suicide, especially when working with men with depression (Cochran & Rabinowitz, 2000).

Exhibit 10.1. Masculine-Sensitive Assessment of Depression.

1. Assessment of *DSM-IV* criteria for major depressive episode
2. Identification of important comorbid conditions
   • Alcohol abuse and dependence
   • Substance abuse and dependence
   • Related personality features (antisocial, compulsive, and narcissistic traits)
3. Masculinity-related symptom expression
   • Somatic or physical complaints
   • Increases in interpersonal conflict
   • Work-related difficulties and conflicts
   • Wounds to self-esteem (job loss or relationship loss)
4. Culturally influenced manifestations of emotional distress
   • Class and race considerations regarding emotional expressivity
   • Level of awareness and acceptance of traditional male gender roles
   • Family of origin role models and norms regarding emotional expressivity
5. Suicide and homicide risk assessment
   • Ideation, plan, means, access, and intent
   • Alcohol or drug intoxication
   • Psychotic or delusional features
   • Capacity for cooperation with clinician

Suicide rates in men have been estimated to be between approximately twenty deaths per one hundred thousand for men between fifteen and twenty-four years of age and approximately seventy deaths per one hundred thousand for men over eighty years of age (Buda & Tsuang, 1990). These suicide rates for men range from seven to fifteen times the suicide rates for women of comparable ages. Because fewer men than women seek treatment for depression and because untreated depression greatly increases the risk of suicide, men who may be depressed are at significantly increased risk for death due to suicide.

Thoughts of death and suicide are not uncommon in depression. In fact, one of the *DSM-IV* diagnostic criteria for a major depressive episode is recurrent thoughts of death or suicide or a suicide attempt or plan for committing suicide. The specificity of suicidal ideation and a detailed plan that would be carried out with accessible means are significant risk factors in suicide assessment. In addition to these commonly identified factors that elevate suicide risk, recent alcohol or drug intoxication or antisocial behaviors, recent health-related problems, and interpersonal loss coupled with access to a firearm have been associated with completed suicides in men (Fowler, Rich, & Young, 1986; Isometsa et al., 1994).

Increased age further exacerbates suicide risk in men (Osgood & Thielman, 1990). Whether due to advanced age, the gradual accrual of the impact of deaths of friends and family, or increasing physical ailments, an alarming number of elderly men commit suicide. Assessment of depression in elderly men must directly address the issue of suicide, including the availability of lethal means for completing suicide (Adamek & Kaplan, 1996).

TREATING DEPRESSION IN MEN

Even though men are often not counted in the tally of rates of depression, there is clear evidence that many men experience depression. Furthermore, when this depression is left undiagnosed and untreated, the risk of suicide in men is exacerbated. Suicide remains a major mortality risk for men of all ages and all races. In light of possible risk of suicide and the lost productivity and negative impact on communities and families that result from not treating depression in men, gender-sensitive therapists are now beginning to recognize the importance of assessing and treating depression in the men who consult them for help.

In spite of the increased visibility of clinical and research findings pertaining to depression in men, fewer men than women schedule appointments with psychotherapists. However, once men come for an initial appointment, they are just as likely as women to continue with psychotherapy (Vessey & Howard, 1993). For men who persevere with treatment, research has demonstrated the efficacy of many types of psychotherapy used to treat depression in men.

Empirical evaluations of psychotherapeutic treatments for depression have demonstrated positive results with men. The National Institute of Mental Health Treatment of Depression Collaborative Research Program (Elkin et al., 1989) assessed the efficacy of two well-known psychosocial treatments—cognitive-behavioral and interpersonal psychotherapy. These treatments were compared with a standard, proven effective pharmacological treatment (imipramine). This investigation found the psychological treatments to be as effective as the drug treatment for most patients. The gender of the subject was not a significant predictor of outcome in this investigation. Subsequent reports from this and other randomized, controlled trials that assessed either interpersonal or cognitive-behavioral therapy have found that men respond positively to both of these treatments (see Thase et al., 1994, 1997). In addition to these individual treatments, group treatments that have yielded positive results with men experiencing depression have been reported (Kelly et al., 1993). Couples therapy approaches have also been demonstrated effective when working with men with alcohol or substance abuse problems along with concurrent relationship difficulties (Fals-Stewart, Birchler, & O'Farrell, 1996).

Taken as a whole, these studies demonstrate that men benefit from the standard psychotherapies that have been subjected to empirical testing. In most outcome studies, the gender of the subject has not been a significant predictor of outcome. Men have even recovered more quickly than women in some cases (see Frank et al., 1988). Findings from these and other investigations offer good news for men with depression in that they clearly establish the effectiveness of psychotherapy in helping men recover from episodes of depression.

In addition to these empirically verified treatments, several innovative, gender-sensitive approaches for treating depression in men have been proposed. Pollack (1998) describes a psychodynamic approach to psychotherapy with men that integrates self-psychology with psychoanalytic developmental psychology. Early relational and emotional trauma, derived from child-rearing practices based on stereotypical norms about appropriate masculine behavior, creates in many men a core emotional landscape that consists of feelings of loss, depression, and sadness. By using a therapeutic stance of empathic attunement, a therapist working from this perspective helps a man gain awareness of the impact of these traumatic losses on his life and to change his patterns of behavior.

Cochran and Rabinowitz (1996) describe an approach that emphasizes the integration of early childhood experiences of relational discontinuity and loss with other experiences of loss that accrue over a man's life span that are related to gender role strains and constraints. Many men experience failure to meet society's unrealistic and unhealthy norms about masculinity as real or symbolic loss. Full realization of these loss experiences may precipitate depression in men who are vulnerable or predisposed to mood disturbances.

These conceptualizations of psychotherapy for depression in men parallel the self-in-relation model of recovery from depression in women formulated by Stiver and Miller (1997). In this model, a core therapeutic task is the differentiation of feelings of depression from those of sadness. Depression is viewed as a clinical syndrome, whereas sadness is viewed as a natural response to experiences of loss. In women, such losses are often relational. In men, losses may also be symbolic and based on the perceived failure to meet culturally defined expectations of masculinity. For both men and women, recovery from depression is in part based on the recognition of the losses that have precipitated a depressive episode. In women, recovery involves a movement away from depression and into sadness over these losses. For men, an additional step in the process may include recognition of the roles that anger, interpersonal conflict, and withdrawal play as prominent defenses against both depression and sadness.

In addition to the approaches that address specific issues clinicians encounter when working with men with depression, Good, Gilbert, and Scher (1990) outline tenets of gender-aware therapy that explicitly incorporate elements of masculine gender role strain into the conceptualization of client problems. Brooks (1998) describes innovative approaches to dealing with men for whom therapists perceive traditional psychotherapeutic venues as inappropriate. Although not specifically designed to address depression in men, these approaches introduce important gender-sensitive values into psychotherapy with men. Such values underscore the restrictive, detrimental impact that rigid adherence to

Exhibit 10.2. Psychotherapies Used to Treat Depression in Men.

1. Empirically verified treatments
   - Cognitive-behavioral therapy (Beck, Rush, Shaw, & Emery, 1979)
   - Interpersonal therapy (Klerman, Weissman, Rounsaville, & Chevron, 1984)
   - Integrative behavioral-couples therapy (Christensen, Jacobson, & Babcock, 1995)
   - Group therapy (Kelly et al., 1993)
   - Behavioral therapy (Lewinsohn & Gotlib, 1995)

2. Innovative treatments
   - Psychodynamic therapy (Pollack, 1998)
   - Loss-focused integrative therapy (Cochran & Rabinowitz, 1996)
   - Gender-aware therapy (Good et al., 1990)
   - Psychotherapy for traditional men (Brooks, 1998)

traditional masculine gender role behaviors and values can have on men. Because masculine gender role strain has been associated with increased levels of depression in samples of men, gender-sensitive approaches that openly invite men to consider the negative impact of the constraining influence of traditional gender roles on their lives are important innovations.

Both empirically verified treatments and new, innovative treatments offer proven effectiveness and enhanced potential for improving the diagnosis and treatment of depression in men. Exhibit 10.2 summarizes the available treatments that have been described and tested in the psychological and psychiatric literature. There are many and varied possibilities available for therapists who wish to increase their effectiveness in detecting and treating depression in men.

CASE EXAMPLES

In Case I, Tim revealed in an early session that he was having difficulty adjusting to his recent marriage. He had been married about ten months, and he related much of his unhappiness to his difficulty in getting "settled in" to married life. His treating therapist decided to use an interpersonal approach (Klerman, Weissman, Rounsaville, & Chevron, 1984) enhanced with gender-aware insights to treat his depression. Tim's core conflicts were cast in terms of interpersonal disputes (conflict with his spouse over priorities, time spent together, and planning of mutual activities) and role transition (mourning the loss of single adulthood status, adjustment to new married man status, and acceptance that he would not become a professional golfer). By couching Tim's depression in terms of these changes in his life, his therapist was able to help

Tim to step back and gain some perspective on his current situation. His therapist also emphasized Tim's struggle with adjusting to his shifting expectations about the meaning of manhood (for example, settle down and get serious, give up your dreams, and do not play with old buddies). Tim was able to learn to express some of his pent-up anger to his spouse more directly and to work through the frustrations he was experiencing with having to accept the limitations of his current employment situation. He met for a total of eighteen sessions and terminated treatment with a greatly improved mood and increased satisfaction with both his marriage and his new married man status.

Roger, described in Case II, was treated for approximately one year with weekly individual psychotherapy that combined the psychodynamic approach of Pollack (1998) and the loss-focused therapy of Cochran and Rabinowitz (1996). Although Roger had never sought treatment before, he quickly and eagerly took to the weekly meetings with his therapist. It was almost as if he had wanted an excuse to talk to someone about his difficult life experiences.

Roger was the older of two boys, raised in a family in which his father was a laborer who held two jobs to support the family and his mother was a homemaker. He related many instances of feeling misunderstood, rejected, and abandoned by both his mother and his father. His father was always working and never seemed to have time for him or his brother. His mother, who was a religious fundamentalist, was involved in reading the bible, attending study groups, and imposing strict, rigid rules of living on Roger and his brother based on her religious beliefs. Roger recounted feeling intensely alone, isolated, and sad during most of his grammar school and high school years. He did not have many friends and tended to keep mostly to himself. He was expected to take care of his younger brother much of the time. He felt he never related to the traditional boyhood activities in which he saw many of his peers involved.

After graduating from high school, he enlisted in the army and spent two years in active duty, one of which was spent in two tours of duty in Vietnam. He returned to the United States and enrolled in college, took a number of different courses, and finally graduated with a degree in English literature. He had intended to continue to study creative writing but needed to work to support himself and obtained employment as a subway train driver. He quickly advanced in seniority and salary and soon found his income too high to warrant jumping to another career or entering a graduate writing program. Underneath his easy-going exterior, he felt trapped, unable to pursue his dreams. He began to abuse alcohol and marijuana as an escape from his feeling of being trapped. He was frustrated that he had not been able to "make anything more" of himself even though he earned a substantial salary with excellent benefits. He had always had a dream of making something better of himself, which for him meant something better than what his father had attained as a laborer.

Roger did not believe he had done any better than his father and felt his life was becoming what his father's life had been—"work, work, work."

Over the months, a theme emerged in therapy with Roger—that he had been forced to abandon his dreams and resign himself to a marginal and "second-rate" life. He progressively uncovered many layers of feelings about himself and his life. He was angry at his situation yet did not know whom to hold accountable. He was depressed and felt helpless and hopeless about ever accomplishing anything different from what he had already accomplished. He did not like his life but was unable to formulate any concrete strategies to change it. And toward the end of his therapy, he felt sad that his life had been what it was and mourned his failure to fulfill many of his dreams. Yet in the midst of this sadness he discovered a deep, lasting, spiritually based acceptance of his life on which he based a number of plans for changing his life within the context of "what it had turned out to be."

Robert and Arlene, described in Case III, came to a total of six sessions with their couples therapist. At the beginning, Robert exhibited many symptoms of depression, including withdrawal and loss of interest in activities he had previously enjoyed, sad and depressed mood, fatigue, and loss of energy. Robert's therapist put Robert's symptoms into the context of a normal grieving process and, with Arlene's support, helped Robert to acknowledge his feelings of loss for his close friend. In addition to grieving the loss of his close friend, Robert also recognized that he needed to grieve the loss of what he had anticipated during his retirement. He was not going to be able to share activities with his old friend. Naming and openly acknowledging these losses and Robert's feelings about them moved him quickly from his depression into a deep sadness. This sadness was acknowledged as signifying the importance of this relationship to Robert, and he was supported in his efforts to "move on" as he was sure his old friend would wish for him to do. The couples sessions ended with Robert having gained a new perspective on his emotional responses to his recent losses, decreased depressive symptoms, and a new, optimistic determination to look to the future and revise his retirement plans.

In these three cases, three different approaches are used to treat the men's depression. In the first, in which Tim is involved in adjusting to marriage, interpersonal psychotherapy with a gender-aware emphasis is used. Addressing Tim's failures to live up to his culturally based expectations of himself as a man plays an important role in this treatment. In Roger's case, the impact of early childhood neglect and trauma is integrated into the treatment and combined with addressing his "failure" to live up to his dream of surpassing his father's accomplishments. Finally, Robert and Arlene represent a common presentation for depression in a man who is prompted into treatment at the suggestion of a concerned partner. The loss of his friend had triggered a depressive episode in

Robert that he did not know how to manage. Identifying and naming his emotional reactions to his friend's death released him to move on and plan his retirement in a positive and constructive fashion.

SUMMARY

Undiagnosed and untreated depression is a serious health problem for many men. Suicide rates and levels of alcohol and substance abuse in men indicate that men with depression often slip through the net of our mental health system undetected until it is too late. Gender role–related strains further compound men's depression by contributing to feelings of failure and loss as many men are unable to meet their own or society's expectations of success and achievement. By increasing awareness of the manifestations of depression and depression-related conditions in men and by emphasizing the availability of effective treatments, more men with depression may be identified and treated.

References

Adamek, M., & Kaplan, M. (1996). Firearm suicide among older men. *Psychiatric Services, 47,* 304–306.

American Psychiatric Association. (1994). *Diagnostic and statistical manual of mental disorders* (4th ed.). Washington, DC: American Psychiatric Association.

Bebbington, P., Dunn, G., Jenkins, R., Lewis, G., Brigha, T., Farrell, M., & Leltzer, H. (1998). The influence of age and sex on the prevalence of depressive conditions: Report from the National Survey of Psychiatric Morbidity. *Psychological Medicine, 28,* 9–19.

Beck, A., Rush, J., Shaw, B., & Emery, G. (1979). *Cognitive therapy of depression.* New York: Guilford Press.

Black, D., Baumgard, C., & Bell, S. (1995). A 16- to 45-year follow-up of 71 men with antisocial personality disorder. *Comprehensive Psychiatry, 36,* 130–140.

Brooks, G. (1998). *A new psychotherapy for traditional men.* San Francisco: Jossey-Bass.

Buda, M., & Tsuang, M. (1990). The epidemiology of suicide: Implications for clinical practice. In S. Blumenthal & D. Kupfer (Eds.), *Suicide over the life cycle: Risk factors, assessment, and treatment of suicidal patients* (pp. 17–38). Washington, DC: American Psychiatric Press.

Christensen, A., Jacobson, N., & Babcock, J. (1995). Integrative behavioral couples therapy. In N. Jacobson & A. Gurman (Eds.), *Clinical handbook of couples therapy* (pp. 31–64). New York: Guilford Press.

Cochran, S., & Rabinowitz, F. (1996). Men, loss, and psychotherapy. *Psychotherapy, 33,* 593–600.

Cochran, S., & Rabinowitz, F. (2000). *Men and depression: Clinical and empirical perspectives.* New York: Academic Press.

Egeland, J., & Hostetter, A. (1983). Amish Study, 1: Affective disorders among the Amish. *American Journal of Psychiatry, 140,* 56–61.

Elkin, I., Shea, M., Watkins, J., Imber, S., Sotsky, S., Collins, J., Glass, D., Pilkonis, P., Leber, W., Docherty, J., Fiester, S., & Perloff, M. (1989). National Institute of Mental Health Treatment of Depression Collaborative Research Program. General effectiveness of treatments. *Archives of General Psychiatry, 35,* 971–982.

Fals-Stewart, W., Birchler, G., & O'Farrell, T. (1996). Behavioral couples therapy for male substance-abusing patients: Effects on relationship adjustment and drug-using behavior. *Journal of Consulting and Clinical Psychology, 64,* 959–972.

Fava, M., Abraham, M., Alpert, J., Nierenberg, A., Pava, J., & Rosenbaum, J. (1996). Gender differences in Axis I comorbidity among depressed outpatients. *Journal of Affective Disorders, 38,* 129–133.

Fowler, R., Rich, C., & Young, D. (1986). San Diego Suicide Study, 2: Substance abuse in young cases. *Archives of General Psychiatry, 43,* 962–965.

Frank, E., Carpenter, L., & Kupfer, D. (1988). Sex differences in recurrent depression: Are there any that are significant? *American Journal of Psychiatry, 145,* 41–45.

Girling, D., Barkley, C., Paykel, E., Gehlhaar, E., Brayne, C., Gill, C., Mathewson, D., & Huppert, F. (1995). The prevalence of depression in a cohort of the very elderly. *Journal of Affective Disorders, 34,* 319–329.

Good, G., Gilbert, L., & Scher, M. (1990). Gender aware therapy: A synthesis of feminist therapy and knowledge about gender. *Journal of Counseling and Development, 68,* 376–380.

Good, G., Robertson, J., Fitzgerald, L., Stevens, M., & Bartels, K. (1996). The relation between masculine role conflict and psychological distress in male university counseling center clients. *Journal of Counseling and Development, 75,* 44–49.

Good, G., & Wood, P. (1995). Male gender role conflict, depression, and help-seeking: Do college men face double jeopardy? *Journal of Counseling and Development, 74,* 70–75.

Hanna, E., & Grant, B. (1997). Gender differences in DSM-IV alcohol use disorders and major depression as distributed in the general population: Clinical implications. *Comprehensive Psychiatry, 38,* 202–212.

Heifner, C. (1997). The male experience of depression. *Perspectives in Psychiatric Care, 33,* 10–18.

Isometsa, E., Henriksson, M., Aro, H., Heikkinen, M., Kuoppasalmi, K., & Lonnquist, J. (1994). Suicide in major depression. *American Journal of Psychiatry, 151,* 530–536.

Kelly, J., Murphy, D., Bahr, R., Kalichman, S., Morgan, M., Stevenson, Y., Koob, J., Brasfield, T., & Bernstein, B. (1993). Outcome of cognitive-behavioral and support group based therapy for depressed, HIV-infected persons. *American Journal of Psychiatry, 150,* 1679–1686.

Kessler, R., McGonagle, K., Zhao, S., Nelson, C., Hughes, M., Eshelman, S., Wittchen, H., & Kendler, K. (1994). Lifetime and 12-month prevalence of DSM-III-R psychiatric disorders in the United States: Results from the National Comorbidity Survey. *Archives of General Psychiatry, 51,* 8–19.

Klerman, G., Weissman, M., Rounsaville, B., & Chevron, E. (1984). *Interpersonal psychotherapy of depression.* New York: Basic Books.

Kornstein, S., Schatzberg, A., Yonkers, K., Thase, M., Keitner, G., Ryan, C., & Schlager, D. (1996). Gender differences in presentation of chronic major depression. *Psychopharmacology Bulletin, 31,* 711–718.

Lewinsohn, P., & Gotlib, I. (1995). Behavioral theory and treatment of depression. In E. Becker & W. Leber (Eds.), *Handbook of depression* (pp. 352–375). New York: Guilford Press.

Loewenthal, K, Goldblatt, V., Gorton, T., Lubitsch, G., Bickness, H., Fellowes, D., & Sowden, A. (1995). Gender and depression in Anglo-Jewry. *Psychological Medicine, 25,* 1051–1063.

Lynch, J., & Kilmartin, C. (1999). *The pain behind the mask: Overcoming masculine depression.* Binghamton, NY: Haworth Press.

Manson, S. (1995). Culture and major depression; Current challenges in the diagnosis of mood disorders. *Psychiatric Clinics of North America, 18,* 487–501.

Moscicki, E. (1997). Identification of suicide risk factors using epidemiological studies. *Psychiatric Clinics of North America, 20,* 499–517.

Murphy, J., Olivier, D., Monson, R., Sobol, A., & Leighton, A. (1988). Incidence of depression and anxiety: The Stirling County Study. *American Journal of Public Health, 78,* 534–540.

Nolen-Hoeksema, S. (1987). Sex differences in unipolar depression: Evidence and theory. *Psychological Bulletin, 101,* 259–282.

Osgood, N., & Thielman, S. (1990). Geriatric suicidal behavior: Assessment and treatment. In S. Blumenthal & D. Kupfer (Eds.), *Suicide over the life cycle: Risk factors, assessment, and treatment of suicidal patients* (pp. 341–379). Washington, DC: American Psychiatric Press.

Pollack, W. (1998). Mourning, melancholia, and masculinity: Recognizing and treating depression in men. In W. Pollack & R. Levant (Eds.), *New psychotherapy for men* (pp. 147–166). New York: Wiley.

Real, T. (1997). I don't want to talk about it: Overcoming the secret legacy of male depression. New York: Simon & Schuster.

Robins, L., & Reiger, D. (1991). *Psychiatric disorders in America.* New York: Free Press.

Simpson, H., Nee, J., & Endicott, J. (1997). First-episode major depression: Few sex-differences in course. *Archives of General Psychiatry, 54,* 633–639.

Stiver, I., & Miller, J. B. (1997). From depression to sadness in women's psychotherapy. In J. Jordan (Ed.), *Women's growth in diversity* (pp. 217–238). New York: Guilford Press.

Takeuchi, D., Chung, R., Lin, K., Shen, H., Kurasake, K., Chun, C., & Sue, S. (1998). Lifetime and twelve-month prevalence rates of major depressive episodes and dysthymia among Chinese Americans in Los Angeles. *American Journal of Psychiatry, 155,* 1407–1414.

Thase, M., Greenhouse, J., Frank, E., Reynolds, C., Pilkonis, P., Hurley, K., Grochocinski, V., & Kupfer, D. (1997). Treatment of chronic depression with psychotherapy or psychotherapy-pharmacotherapy combinations. *Archives of General Psychiatry, 34,* 1009–1015.

Thase, M., Reynolds, C., Frank, E., Simons, A., McGeary, R., Fasiczka, A., Garamoni, G., Jennings, R., & Kupfer, D. (1994). Do depressed men and women respond similarly to cognitive behavior therapy? *American Journal of Psychiatry, 151,* 500–505.

Vessey, J., & Howard, K. (1993). Who seeks psychotherapy? *Psychotherapy, 30,* 546–553.

Weissman, M., Bruce, M., Leaf, P., Florio, L., & Holzer, C. (1991). Affective disorders. In L. Robins & D. Reiger (Eds.), *Psychiatric disorders in America* (pp. 53–80). New York: Free Press.

Wilhelm, K., & Parker, G. (1994). Sex differences in lifetime depression rates: Fact or artefact? *Psychological Medicine, 24,* 97–111.

Winokur, G. (1997). All roads lead to depression: Clinically homogeneous, etiologically heterogeneous. *Journal of Affective Disorders, 45,* 97–108.

Young, M., Scheftner, W., Fawcett, J., & Klerman, G. (1990). Gender differences in the clinical features of unipolar major depressive disorder. *Journal of Nervous and Mental Disease, 178,* 200–203.

CHAPTER ELEVEN

Treating Substance Abuse in Men

Carl Isenhart

W hen I was first asked to write this chapter for this handbook, I was struck with a sense of irony about writing a chapter about men's issues in substance abuse treatment. Because most of the substance abuse literature in general and the treatment outcome literature in particular involves male subjects, it would be reasonable to ask why this chapter is needed.

But there are some very good reasons. First, men have more significant alcohol abuse and alcohol-related problems, become intoxicated at an earlier age, and experience more alcohol-related legal and other social problems than do women (Dawson, 1996; Fillmore et al., 1997).

Second, there are gender differences in substance abuse treatment outcomes. Some reviews have found mixed or contradictory results (Moos, Finney, & Cronkite, 1990; Toneatto, Sobell, & Sobell, 1992), but Beckman (1993) suggested that women may have a slightly better outcome than men. Project MATCH (Project MATCH Research Group, 1997) results indicated that of the patients in an aftercare group men had fewer days of abstinence than did women and that being male, along with other variables, predicted more alcohol consumption during drinking days. Moos et al. (1990) noted that being male, along with having more psychiatric symptoms, was associated with increased alcohol use as length of time increased during the follow-up period.

Third, men either do not seek medical or psychological services or do so later than they should (Helgeson, 1995). This masculine reluctance to seek health care in general implies that men will be reluctant to seek substance abuse services in particular.

Consequently, there are some good reasons to address male gender issues in substance abuse treatment. Because the research has focused mostly on alcohol use rather than other drug use, alcohol abuse and its treatment are the focal points of this chapter. However, before going any further, I offer three caveats.

First, to describe what a male role is implies what a female role is not and vice versa. Obviously it is not as simple as that. Both sexes have a mix of gender expectations. There may be clusters of gender role expectations, some attributable more to men and others attributable more to women but nonetheless attributable to some extent to both sexes. Therefore, it is simplistic to think in terms of either-or; a more realistic way to think about this topic is to what extent expectations apply to both sexes and within each individual.

Some of the literature cited in this chapter (for example, Kaplan & Marks, 1995) references levels of femininity and masculinity in both women and men. Within the sexes, many men (depending on age, social status, education, and region) display some features that would traditionally be described as feminine, and many women display some features that would traditionally be described as masculine. Therefore, in this chapter I discuss issues related to masculinity with the assumption that they apply in greater proportion to men. However, clearly some of these issues do not apply to some men and may apply to some women.

The second caveat is that nothing in this chapter is intended to reduce the responsibility of men's decision to use substances and to be accountable for the resulting consequences. Men may be under pressure to comply with masculine role expectations, but everyone is under pressure to fulfill and live up to many other role expectations: father, mother, spouse, and so forth. It is up to everyone to fulfill his or her roles in ways that are beneficial to the person, his or her immediate social network, and society in general.

The third caveat is that substance abuse treatment services have been helpful to many people, and I review some relevant literature in this chapter. Consequently, it is not my intent in this chapter to dismiss those accomplishments but rather to show that there is room for improvement; toward that aim, this chapter may provide some guidance.

I describe common expectations of the traditional male role and how many of these expectations encourage alcohol use. These expectations encourage alcohol use because (1) alcohol use is associated with the traditional masculine role and (2) men use alcohol to better fit into the traditional masculine role and to better manage the stress associated with living up to the traditional masculine role. Williams and Ricciardelli (1999) referred to these styles as confirmatory and compensatory drinking, respectively. The review of the masculine role expectations is also important because such expectations may lead to conflicts with treatment and recovery expectations. Such conflicts may interfere with men's participation in alcohol abuse treatment services.

I review research describing the impact of male role expectations on health care use, both medical and psychological, to provide a context in which to understand men's health care–seeking behavior, including services for alcohol abuse. Given this background, I describe the stages of change model and motivational interviewing as strategies to address men's issues in treatment. Also, because traditional treatment may be contradictory to the traditional male role, I explore the treatment outcomes research to demonstrate that a number of treatment options are available to staff and patients. Such options provide therapists and clients flexibility in developing treatment goals and strategies. The implication is that services can be tailored to meet the patient's needs rather than wasting time trying to force a patient to adopt a particular philosophy that is inconsistent with his masculine identity.

TRADITIONAL MASCULINE GENDER ROLE EXPECTATIONS

The traditional masculine role expectations provide a backdrop against which to better understand men's substance use and behavior in treatment. As mentioned earlier in this handbook, David and Brannon (1976) identified four male role expectations: "No Sissy Stuff," "The Big Wheel," "The Sturdy Oak," and "Give 'Em Hell."

If men perceive these expectations as mandates for behavior, then stress will result when men perceive their behavior as inconsistent with or falling short of these expectations. Two concepts have been used to address the relationship between the masculine role and stress associated with that role. It should be noted that stress as referred to in this discussion relates to stress associated with fulfilling masculine role expectations and not to using alcohol to cope with stress in general. Cooper, Frone, Russell, and Peirce (1997) reported that stress or coping style could not account for gender differences in alcohol abuse.

The first concept is masculine gender role stress (Eisler & Skidmore, 1987). A man experiences masculine gender role stress in two circumstances: when he feels unable to live up to the expectations of the traditional male role or when he perceives himself as being expected to behave in ways that are inconsistent with the traditional male role. The authors identified five classes of stressful situations that constitute masculine gender role stress: (1) inadequate physical performance, (2) having to express emotions, (3) subordinating to women, (4) inferior intellectual performance, and (5) overall performance failure.

The second concept is gender role conflict and strain (O'Neil, 1982; O'Neil, Good, & Holmes, 1995; Pleck, 1995), which may result from the conflict resulting from attempting to comply with the "masculine mystique." O'Neil (1982) described the masculine mystique as a set of rigid expectations and attitudes about masculinity that prescribes the rejection of any thoughts, feelings, attitudes, or behaviors that others may see as feminine. Specifically, men traditionally have aversions to anything feminine, strive to be masculine, inhibit emotional expression, and keep emotional and physical distance from other men. The conflict and strain set up six patterns of conflict: (1) restricted emotionality; (2) homophobia; (3) behavioral demonstrations of power, control, and competition; (4) limited expression of sexual and affectionate behaviors; (5) overemphasis on achievement and success; and (6) avoidance of seeking health care.

Use of Alcohol to Meet Gender Role Expectations

Williams and Ricciardelli (1999) described compensatory drinking as individuals using alcohol to "heighten their sense of masculinity or femininity" (p. 324). In this section I review how traditional masculine role expectations promote alcohol use as a way for a man to better fit in to the masculine role and also as a way to manage the stress associated with not fitting into the role. Williams and Ricciardelli found that, for both men and women, high scores on alcohol use were associated with high scores on "negative masculinity" (for example, "being bossy") and low scores on "positive femininity" (for example, "loves children").

Blazina and Watkins (1996) reported a significant relationship between success, power, and competition and college men's admission of increased alcohol use. McCreary, Newcomb, and Sadava (1999) maintained that the more men held traditional attitudes, the more alcohol they consumed. They found that high masculine gender role stress and alcohol use were associated with alcohol problems; however, high masculine gender role stress was not associated with alcohol consumption.

In a study by Isenhart (1993), men dependent on alcohol participating in a substance abuse treatment program with high scores on selected masculine gender role stress scales had high scores on the Enhancement scale of the Alcohol Use Inventory—Revised (AUI-R) (Horn, Wanberg, & Foster, 1990). This finding would suggest that high masculine gender role stress scores were associated with using alcohol to improve social, emotional, cognitive, and interpersonal functioning. Patients with high masculine gender role stress also experienced more alcohol-related disruptions and more concern about their alcohol use than men with low masculine gender role stress scores.

Finally, McClelland, Davis, Kalin, and Wanner (1972) found that when their male subjects consumed small or moderate amounts of alcohol, the subjects reported increased fantasies of "socialized" or "altruistic" control over others. Such control is represented by acts of teaching or helping others. However, when the subjects consumed larger amounts of alcohol, the fantasies changed to "personalized" or "self-aggrandizing" control over others. This kind of control is represented by acts that are sexual or aggressive in character. McClelland and coworkers' research supports the line of reasoning in the previous paragraphs that men use alcohol to augment their ability to fulfill gender role expectations associated with power, dominance, and control.

Alcohol and "Manliness"

Alcohol use can be a major part of what defines a man socially. This idea is important because, given this relationship between alcohol and masculinity, when a man is asked (or told) to give up alcohol, he may feel like he is also giving up part of his masculine identity. Williams and Ricciardelli (1999) described confirmatory drinking as alcohol use that reinforces gender stereotypes. In this section, I review literature that shows that alcohol use has been inextricably integrated into the masculine role for many years. Pursch (1976) provided one description about the relationship between men and alcohol use:

> the hard drinking, two-fisted, pioneering frontiersman; the hard-charging tiger of an aviator who can drink all night and fly all day; the ruggedness of the guy who can hold his liquor like a man; and the notion that you can't trust a man who won't drink (p. 1656)

Lemle and Mishkind (1989) outlined how alcohol has been symbolic of being male and how alcohol use has been associated with personality features that are consistent with male role expectations: questioning authority, challenging convention, and being uninhibited. Lemle and Mishkind (1989) nicely summarized their argument: "Alcohol is the only drug which is part of the male sex role, the only mood altering drug which society overtly promotes as manly" (p. 217).

One major way in which society promotes the connection between the male role and alcohol use is through the media. Postman, Nystrom, Strate, and Weingartner (1987) concluded that beer was associated with traditionally masculine pursuits and leisure activities that required strength, endurance, and risk. Beer was presented as a source of group cohesiveness, identity, and membership, and it was a symbol for acceptance, friendship, and affection.

Also, beer was shown as a way to enhance the romantic relationships between men and women via lowered inhibitions and the creation of an amorous mood. Wallack, Breed, and Cruz (1987) found that 74 percent of beverages consumed during a sample of prime-time shows were alcoholic and that the frequency of consumption by men was twice that by women. The impact of these ads is significant. For example, Grube and Wallack (1994) reported that in a sample of fifth- and sixth-grade children, recognition of televised beer commercials was associated with positive drinking attitudes and heightened intentions to use alcohol as an adult.

ISSUES OF MEN'S UTILIZATION OF HEALTH CARE

The preceding sections suggest that the traditional masculine role has clear expectations for behavior, that alcohol use can be used to comply with those expectations, and that alcohol in itself is a part of the masculine identity. In this section I review how these expectations influence men's health care utilization. Helgeson (1995) reported that men are less likely than women to follow standard health procedures, consult physicians, and report symptoms. Kaplan and Marks (1995) found that men with high measures of femininity displayed higher levels of health concern than men with low femininity scores.

Field, Kockey, and Small (1997) reported that men avoid help-seeking behavior because it is traditionally feminine, and men are expected to be self-reliant and to minimize illness. However, these authors cautioned that such explanations are made out of context of other variables, such as age and social class. Waldron (1995) reported other cautions; she acknowledged that women seek medical care more often then men but for conditions that do not typically result in death. For example, women wait just as long or longer than men to seek services for many types of cancer and for heart disease.

Men's reluctance to seek services goes beyond medical interventions and includes seeking psychological services as well. Helgeson (1995) reported that redivorced men, when compared with redivorced women, reported twice as much depression but sought treatment for the depression less frequently. She also noted that men with depression are viewed more negatively than women with depression. Good, Dell, and Mintz (1989) reported similar findings. They found that traditional male role attitudes were associated with negative attitudes about obtaining psychological services and noted that

> The need to dispel the popular yet restrictive image of men as the "strong and silent type" appears warranted. Indeed, for men who hold traditional attitudes toward the male role, a reframing of the stigma of seeking counseling appears necessary. (Good et al., 1989, p. 300)

Helgeson (1995) attributed these findings to a gender role that dissuades men from admitting to problems and concerns and from seeking health care services. This kind of behavior is seen as inconsistent with being strong, invulnerable, and self-reliant. Eisler (1990) stressed that some men may see obtaining help as feminine, and consequently obtaining help may threaten their sense of independence. He added that the expectation of disclosing vulnerabilities and giving over power and control to others could also be stressful. He concluded: "the role we require male clients to perform in traditional counseling runs counter to the coping techniques that men have learned as essential in maintaining their sense of values as men" (p. 57).

Researchers have examined men's behavior specifically in substance abuse treatment. Beckman (1993) reported that women are more likely to be aware of their alcohol abuse problem, whereas men are more likely to experience conflicts, particularly with those in authority positions, that result in them being involuntarily referred to substance abuse treatment. Blazina and Watkins (1996) postulated a curvilinear relationship between alcohol use and masculinity: although masculinity is associated with increased alcohol consumption, after the point when the man loses control over his alcohol use (that is, manifests lower levels of success, power, and competition) perceived masculinity may be reduced. Lemle and Mishkind (1989) made a similar point: a man's ability to "hold his liquor" is consistent with the male role and not being able to do so (that is, experiencing signs of dependency and alcohol-related problems) is inconsistent with the male role. Therefore, the admission of alcohol-related problems, let alone seeking help, is patently inconsistent with the traditional masculine role.

One reason to consider substance abuse treatment options (and why this issue is reviewed later in this chapter) is that some of the expectations associated with the traditional, Alcoholics Anonymous–based treatment philosophy may be inconsistent with traditional masculine roles. Beckman (1993) reported that one reason Women for Sobriety was established was because Alcoholics Anonymous was perceived as not meeting women's needs. The same may be true for men. Because of masculine role expectations, men may find it difficult to admit to powerlessness and turn over power and control, disclose weaknesses and "character defects," and unconditionally accept a set of tenets (particularly if they are inconsistent with decades of socialization).

Moos et al. (1990) reported a significant positive correlation between men's alcohol consumption at follow-up and the level of staff control within the substance abuse treatment programs. They interpreted this relationship between staff control and outcome to be consistent with the male gender expectation of maintaining power and control. They suggested that poorer outcome may be the result of a treatment environment that is perceived as being too controlled and that promotes a feeling of powerlessness on the part of the participants. In their study, women also reacted negatively to perceptions of increased staff control in the form of more depression and less social activity. Finally, DiClemente (1993) noted that Alcoholics Anonymous–based services may not be appropriate for particularly ambivalent patients in general because of the prominence of turning over power and control to a higher power, the declaration of oneself as being an alcoholic, and the emphasis on abstinence as the only goal.

APPROACHES TO ADDRESSING MEN'S ISSUES
IN SUBSTANCE ABUSE TREATMENT

I have reviewed some of the variables that influence men's use of alcohol and health care services in this chapter: the masculine role is closely affiliated with heavy alcohol use to fit in and to manage the stress associated with not living up to these expectations, seeking help is inconsistent with the traditional male role, and men do not routinely seek out health care in general (and they show very low adherence rates to any recommended or prescribed interventions). In addition, many substance abuse services and interventions require men to behave in ways that are inconsistent with the traditional male role and that are counter to decades of socialization. With this background, I review intervention services that may be more appropriate for the treatment of men with substance abuse problems.

Ambivalence

One of the greatest challenges of working with those with substance abuse problems or any clients considering change is the reluctance and ambivalence they exhibit about making changes. The typical response by treatment staff is to attribute that ambivalence to denial, and clients are expected display less denial and become motivated for change as treatment progresses. Thus, motivation has been traditionally perceived as a dichotomy: a patient is either motivated or is not motivated.

However, this traditional attitude misses the fact that ambivalent behavior is consistent with the traditional masculine role of maintaining power and control and questioning convention and authority. Staff members' attribution of ambivalence to denial also ignores any interventions they can make to decrease this resistance, and, just as important, it minimizes the role staff members may have in increasing resistance. The net result is that men become frustrated and at best marginally participate or at worst leave treatment; these actions only reinforce staff members' beliefs about denial, which results in less effective treatment.

Readiness for Change

Studies have demonstrated inconsistencies and contradictions with this model of motivation and have supported new perspectives (Miller, 1985, 1995, 1998; Miller & Rollnick, 1991); these new perspectives have led to innovations for working with clients with substance abuse problems. For example, studies of "self-changers" (people who have changed behavior without professional intervention) have shown that ambivalence or doubt about making changes is normal and natural in the change process (Cohen et al., 1989; Orford, 1985).

Previous research by McConnaughy, Prochaska, and Velicer (1983) and McConnaughy, DiClemente, Prochaska, and Velicer (1989) identified stages of change through which patients proceed during psychotherapy: (1) precontemplation, (2) contemplation, (3) determination, (4) action, and (5) maintenance.

In *precontemplation,* the individual perceives that there is no problem and consequently sees no reason to change. A person at the *contemplation* level begins to consider the possibility that there may be a problem and begins to experience some ambivalent feelings about the possibility of change. In *determination,* the individual acknowledges the presence of a problem and makes a decision to initiate changes to address that problem in the future. The individual takes steps to implement change to address the problem behavior while in the *action* level. And a person in *maintenance* strives to establish conditions to maintain their changes.

These concepts have been applied to substance abuse and have demonstrated that people experience varying levels of motivation to change their addictive behavior (Prochaska, DiClemente, & Norcross, 1992); that is, like most change, addressing one's addictive behavior involves progressing and regressing through a range of readiness-for-change levels. Although these concepts are discussed as stages, more accurately they represent points along a continuum where one point imperceptibly merges with the next point.

Also, this view means not only that there is overlap and no clear demarcation between stages but also that clients may experience features associated with different stages simultaneously. For example, even while a client is taking action, he or she may continue to have feelings of ambivalence, which are associated with contemplation. Consequently, instead of referring to stages of change, many clinicians refer to this process as readiness for change. The term implies that change is not dichotomous and that people do not simply go from not being motivated to being motivated to change; change involves a complex and dynamic continuum that is greatly influenced by the environmental conditions in which change is being considered.

For men, one source of this ambivalence can be the perceived contradictions between treatment expectations and social role expectations regarding alcohol use. The implications of these concepts is that men are at different levels of readiness for change regarding their alcohol use. For a number of reasons that I have already addressed (for example, using alcohol to be more manly or reluctance to seek help because it is counter to traditional men's socialization), some men may be unwilling to consider change, others may be considering but not yet ready to take action, and still others may be ready to take action.

Prochaska et al. (1992) provided strategies for working with clients at different levels of motivation. These strategies work well when integrated with motivational interviewing, which I discuss in the next section. When working with a man who is precontemplative, one goal would be to increase his consciousness about his alcohol use. One strategy might be to examine the relationship between alcohol use and the man's feelings of masculinity, sense of independence and control, and how alcohol may help him manage feelings and feel dominant and confident in social situations. This process can lead to the man's increased awareness that he may be using alcohol as an artificial support and how this use of alcohol has led or can lead to problems.

Once a man is aware of his alcohol use and the potential problems, he may become contemplative—that is, ambivalent—about his alcohol use. The strategy now is to have the man generate the positive and negative past consequences and future expectations associated with both maintaining and changing his current alcohol use pattern. Acknowledgment on the part of the therapist regarding alcohol's benefits and the downside of making changes communicates acceptance and respect for the client's perspective. This acknowledgment and respect increase the likelihood that the patient will begin discussing the negative consequences of alcohol use and be willing to admit to problems and concerns. The goal is to have the client generate his own list of problems rather than have the therapist outline them for him. This approach allows the man to maintain a sense of control and not feel subordinate to the therapist.

A client within the determination range of the continuum has decided that he has a problem but has not yet initiated behavior changes. The goal would be for him to begin considering action steps to change his alcohol use. This consideration can be facilitated by discussing how seeking such services may be inconsistent with masculinity: it may feel "unmanly" to sit in a group and discuss problems, going to others for help may feel like giving up control and is inconsistent with being strong and independent, and such activities may not allow the man to engage in achievement- or success-oriented activities (for example, work at a job or take advantage of possible career opportunities). Once these distortions are identified and verbalized, the client can be encouraged to dispute them: it is OK for men to discuss problems, control can be maintained in treatment by allowing the male to state the direction and timing of services, and engagement in such services may actually facilitate achievement and success by addressing any alcohol-related career problems.

A man within the action and maintenance ranges is ready to engage in new behaviors to change his alcohol use and to maintain those changes and prevent relapse, respectively. This is where the strategies typically associated with substance abuse treatment (for example, brief interventions and mutual-help groups) are instituted. However, even these interventions need to be initiated within a therapeutic relationship and environment that addresses the masculinity issues that have been mentioned so far. For example, not requiring the man to refer to himself as an alcoholic may facilitate his admission to having "problems" with his alcohol use and consequently make him more willing to seek services.

Overall, rather than attempting to engage all patients in action-oriented strategies (because by doing so the therapist establishes the context to intensify resistance), the therapist needs to listen and understand the patient's perspective about his problems and goals, negotiate a plan for realistic change, and solicit from the patient strategies to achieve those goals. This does not mean that the therapist has to agree with these goals or strategies; I discuss constructive ways for the therapist to express his or her concerns about the patient's plans later in this chapter.

Motivational Interviewing

This process of working with clients is embodied in motivational interviewing. Miller (1985, 1995, 1998) has reported that patients' ambivalence is not a personality trait but rather a dynamic interaction between patients and their environment (including the relationship with the therapist). Also, it has been found that the type of intervention and counselor style influences whether the ambivalence (and consequently motivation) increases or decreases (Luborsky, McLellan, Woody, O'Brien, & Auerbach, 1985; Miller, Benefield, & Tonigan, 1993). Consequently, motivation can be increased (or decreased) through the therapeutic relationship, and one aspect of that relationship involves addressing clients' masculinity issues.

Miller and Rollnick (1991; Rollnick and Morgan, 1995) have developed the concept of motivational interviewing as a client-centered style that establishes an atmosphere in which the client can openly discuss his mixed feelings about change, verbalize the benefits and costs of changing and staying the same, and review possible strategies to initiate and maintain any change. Motivational interviewing is a directive approach that encourages the client to decide whether change will occur, to what degree, according to what time frame, and by what means. Although motivational interviewing has strategies and techniques, more than anything it is a therapeutic attitude or philosophy about engaging the client and establishing a therapeutic relationship.

The motivational interviewing approach is conducive to working within the context of masculine role expectations. For example, this approach encourages a man to discuss his concerns about not appearing to be masculine and his reservations about taking advice or discussing vulnerabilities. Specifically, the client retains control by directing the treatment focus, goals, and expectations. This approach supports the client's self-reliance and independence, and it allows the client to make his own decisions. The traditional power gradient is minimized, and the client is not likely to be seen as being in a "one-down" position. The client is truly allowed to maintain responsibility for the direction of his treatment. This strategy supports and encourages a questioning and critical attitude when assessing what is best for the client. The client is encouraged to do what he thinks is in his best interest rather than doing what is traditional.

Miller and Rollnick (1991) discussed five principles of motivational interviewing: (1) express empathy, (2) develop discrepancies, (3) avoid argumentation, (4) roll with the resistance, and (5) support self-efficacy.

A definition of these principles and an example of a therapeutic response follow. *Express empathy* by maintaining and demonstrating an acceptance of (though not necessarily an agreement with) the patient's perspective of the problem: "I understand that you have been getting a lot of messages for a lot of years to use alcohol; it must be tough to consider not drinking." *Develop discrepancies* by generating cognitive dissonance between where the patient currently is and where he aspires to be: "It is difficult to open up and talk about problems, but your being here tells me that you do want some help." *Avoid argumentation* and the use of confrontational dialogue in which the client will feel the need to defend himself: "You're right, there are other ways to look at this." *Roll with the resistance* instead of confronting it directly by using other strategies such as reframing (reflecting the client's statements with an added different perspective) the client's resistance to invite or volunteer a new perspective: "Yes, it is frustrating to be out of control and to have your family telling you what to do, but it sounds like they really care about you." And *support self-efficacy* and build up the individual by recognizing and highlighting past accomplishments and strivings to achieve current goals (no matter how small): "It must have been difficult for you to decide to come in and ask about our services."

Motivational interviewing uses a number of processes to engage these principles. Five opening strategies are used to initiate contact with clients (Miller & Rollnick, 1991): (1) ask open-ended questions: "How does alcohol help you feel more manly?"; (2) listen reflectively: "It sounds like you are giving up control and giving in to others if you stop drinking"; (3) affirm the client: "It takes real strength to admit to having those kinds of problems"; (4) summarize: "You're getting tired of being told what to do, you don't like being treated like a patient, and you'd just like to get all this over with"; and (5) elicit self-motivational statements: "You seem to question how things are typically done in this program; how has this helped you in the past to make changes?" Although these sound like basic interviewing strategies (and they are), they are scarce even in well-trained and seasoned staff.

Motivational interviewing also involves increasing a therapist's awareness of "counseling traps"; these traps may be particularly detrimental when working with men with high masculine expectations. Examples of counseling traps include premature focus and the expert trap. Premature focus occurs when the therapist focuses on an apparent problem before the client is ready to do so; it frequently results in increased resistance. The expert trap involves the therapist having all the answers and giving little encouragement or support for the client to generate alternatives for himself. Both of these traps take away control from the client, place him in a subordinate position, and inhibit a questioning attitude, all of which run counter to masculine role expectations. Although motivational interviewing readings are included in the reference list, this approach is best learned by participation in an experiential training session with a qualified motivational interviewing trainer. Additional information, including how to contact a trainer, can be found on the motivational interviewing Web site (www.motivationalinterview.org).

TREATMENT OPTIONS

It is critical for therapists to be aware of the treatment options available to clients experiencing substance-related disorders. This awareness is particularly important in relationship to the traditional male role, which expects the man to question standard procedures, consider alternatives, and make independent decisions. The studies discussed in this overview include men and women, although more men than women are represented in such studies. The idea that there are alternatives to traditional (that is, Alcoholics Anonymous–based substance abuse programs) was supported by the results of Project MATCH. That study compared the impact of Alcoholics Anonymous–based, cognitive-behavioral, and motivational enhancement interventions on those who abuse alcohol. The results suggested that all three interventions were equally effective and that no particular client characteristic was a better match for one intervention over the other.

Miller, Andrews, Wilbourne, and Bennett (1998) critically evaluated the alcohol treatment outcomes literature. They identified a number of different interventions that had empirical support for reducing alcohol consumption and alcohol-related problems. These interventions included brief interventions and motivational enhancement, coping and social skills training, and the community reinforcement approach. Therefore, rather then engage a client in a debate over a particular program or treatment philosophy, particularly a man who has been encouraged to maintain and demonstrate power and control and who is reluctant to seek services anyway, the therapist can help the client to explore service alternatives and encourage him to identify which strategies to try, how they will be implemented, and for what goals.

Miller et al. (1998) stressed, however, that whatever the treatment service, clients' success depends on the relationship they have with their therapists: "Clients show better short-term and long-term drinking outcomes when treated by therapists who display high levels of client-centered counseling skills" (p. 213). Client-centered counseling is the foundation of motivational interviewing and a main theme of this chapter; therapists who are aware of men's issues in treatment, who meet patients where they are at motivationally, and who incorporate the kinds of philosophies and strategies espoused by motivational interviewing (for example, reflective listening) develop strong therapeutic relationships with the clients with whom they work.

CONCLUSION

Alcohol abuse and dependence are complex disorders, and it would be naive to suggest that the use of the concepts and strategies discussed in this chapter can make these problems any less complex. However, increased awareness of these issues can enhance the quality of the therapeutic relationship, which consistently has been shown to affect treatment outcome. A therapist who communicates an awareness that alcohol is a part of the masculine identity and that alcohol is used to comply with those identity expectations builds the foundation for a strong therapeutic relationship. Also, this relationship is further enhanced if the therapist is sensitive to how seeking alcohol abuse treatment can be inconsistent with male role expectations and may require engaging in behavior that is inconsistent with the male role; this sensitivity can help a male client accept treatment and minimize any reservations or resentments associated with seeking services. Services that match the client's level of motivation will help engage him and avoid overwhelming him. Motivational interviewing strategies will allow the client to identify and prioritize problems, generate strategies, and formulate the timetable to address the problems. The therapist is in a position and has the ability to create an atmosphere that allows for the development of a truly collaborative and client-centered therapeutic relationship that considers a variety of empirically supported treatment opportunities to facilitate behavior change.

References

Beckman, L. J. (1993). Alcoholics Anonymous and gender issues. In B. S. McCrady & W. R. Miller (Eds.), *Research on Alcoholics Anonymous* (pp. 233–248). New Brunswick, NJ: Alcohol Research Documentation.

Blazina, C., & Watkins, E. (1996). Masculine gender role conflict: Effects on college men's psychological well-being, chemical substance usage, and attitudes toward help-seeking. *Journal of Counseling Psychology, 43,* 461–465.

Cohen, S., Lichtenstein, E., Prochaska, J. O., Rossi, J. S., Gritz, E. R., Carr, C. R., Orleans, C. T., Schoenbach, V. J., Biener, L., Abrams, D., DiClemente, C. C., Curry, S., Marlatt, G. A., Cummings, K. M., Emont, S. L., Giovino, G., & Ossip-Klein, D. (1989). Debunking myths about self-quitting: Evidence from 10 prospective studies of persons quitting smoking by themselves. *American Psychologist, 44,* 1355–1365.

Cooper, M. L., Frone, M. R., Russell, M., & Peirce, R. S. (1997). Gender, stress, coping, and alcohol use. In R. W. Wilsnack & S. C. Wilsnack (Eds.), *Gender and alcohol* (pp. 199–224). New Brunswick, NJ: Alcohol Research Documentation.

David, D. S., & Brannon, R. (1976). *The forty-nine percent majority: The male sex role.* Reading, MA: Addison-Wesley.

Dawson, D. (1996). Gender differences in the risk of alcohol dependence: United States, 1992. *Addiction, 91,* 1831–1842.

DiClemente, C. C. (1993). Alcoholics Anonymous and the structure of change. In B. S. McCrady & W. R. Miller (Eds.), *Research on Alcoholics Anonymous* (pp. 79–97). New Brunswick, NJ: Alcohol Research Documentation.

Eisler, R. M. (1990). Gender role issues in the treatment of men. *Behavior Therapist, 13,* 57–60.

Eisler, R. M., & Skidmore, J. R. (1987). Masculine gender role stress: Scale development and component factors in the appraisal of stressful situations. *Behavior Modification, 11,* 123–136.

Field, D., Kockey, J., & Small, N. (1997). Making sense of differences: Death, gender, and ethnicity in modern Britain. In D. Field, J. Kockey, & N. Small (Eds.), *Death, gender, and ethnicity* (pp. 1–28). New York: Routledge.

Fillmore, K. M., Golding, J. M., Leino, E. V., Motoyoshi, M., Shoemacker, C., Terry, H., Ager, C. R., & Ferrer, H. P. (1997). Patterns and trends in women's and men's drinking. In R. W. Wilsnack & S. C. Wilsnack (Eds.), *Gender and alcohol* (pp. 21–48). New Brunswick, NJ: Alcohol Research Documentation.

Good, G. E., Dell, D. M., & Mintz, L. B. (1989). Male role and gender role conflict: Relations to help seeking in men. *Journal of Counseling Psychology, 36,* 295–300.

Grube, J. W., & Wallack, L. (1994). Television beer advertising and drinking knowledge, beliefs, and intentions among schoolchildren. *American Journal of Public Health, 84,* 254–259.

Helgeson, V. S. (1995). Masculinity, men's roles, and coronary heart disease. In D. Sabo & D. F. Gordon (Eds.), *Men's health and illness: Gender, power, and the body* (pp. 68–104). Thousand Oaks, CA: Sage.

Horn, J. L., Wanberg, K. W., & Foster, F. M. (1990). *Guide to the alcohol use inventory.* Minneapolis, MN: National Computer Systems.

Isenhart, C. E. (1993). Masculine gender role stress in an inpatient sample of alcohol abusers. *Psychology of Addictive Behaviors, 7,* 177–184.

Kaplan, M. S., & Marks, G. (1995). Appraisal of health risks: The roles of masculinity, femininity, and sex. *Sociology of Health and Illness, 17,* 206–220.

Lemle, R., & Mishkind, M. E. (1989). Alcohol and masculinity. *Journal of Substance Abuse Treatment, 6,* 213–222.

Luborsky, L., McLellan, A. T., Woody, G. E., O'Brien, C. P., & Auerbach, A. H. (1985). Therapist success and its determinants. *Archives of General Psychiatry, 42,* 602–611.

McClelland, D. C., Davis, W. N., Kalin, R., & Wanner, E. (1972). *The drinking man: A theory of human motivation.* New York: Free Press.

McConnaughy, E. A., DiClemente, C. C., Prochaska, J. O., & Velicer, W. F. (1989). Stages of change in psychotherapy: A follow-up report. *Psychotherapy, 26,* 494–503.

McConnaughy, E. A., Prochaska, J. O., & Velicer, W. F. (1983). Stages of change in psychotherapy: Measurement and samples profiles. *Psychotherapy: Theory, Research, and Practice, 20,* 368–375.

McCreary, D. R., Newcomb, M. D., & Sadava, S. W. (1999). The male role, alcohol use, and alcohol problems: A structural modeling examination in adult women and men. *Journal of Counseling Psychology, 46,* 109–124.

Miller, W. R. (1985). Motivation for treatment: A review with special emphasis on alcoholism. *Psychological Bulletin, 98,* 84–107.

Miller, W. R. (1995). Increasing motivation for change. In R. K. Hester & W. R. Miller (Eds.), *Handbook of alcoholism treatment approaches: Effective alternatives* (2nd ed., pp. 89–104). Boston: Allyn & Bacon.

Miller, W. R. (1998). Enhancing motivation for change. In W. R. Miller & N. Heather (Eds.), *Treating addictive behaviors* (2nd ed.). New York: Plenum.

Miller, W. R., Andrews, N. R., Wilbourne, P., & Bennett, M. E. (1998). A wealth of alternatives: Effective treatments for alcohol problems. In W. R. Miller & N. Heather (Eds.), *Treating addictive behaviors* (2nd ed., pp. 203–216). New York: Plenum.

Miller, W. R., Benefield, R. G., & Tonigan, J. S. (1993). Enhancing motivation for change in problem drinking: A controlled comparison of two therapist styles. *Journal of Consulting and Clinical Psychology, 61,* 455–461.

Miller, W. R., & Rollnick, S. (1991). *Motivational interviewing.* New York: Guilford Press.

Moos, R. H., Finney, J. W., & Cronkite, R. C. (1990). *Alcoholism treatment: Context, process, and outcome.* New York: Oxford University Press.

O'Neil, J. M. (1982). Gender-role conflict and strain in men's lives: Implications for psychiatrists, psychologists, and other human-service providers. In K. Solomon & N. B. Levy (Eds.), *Men in transition: Theory and therapy* (pp. 5–44). New York: Plenum.

O'Neil, J. M., Good, G. E., & Holmes, S. (1995). Fifteen years of theory and research on men's gender role conflict: New paradigms for empirical research. In R. F. Levant & W. S. Pollack (Eds.), *A new psychology of men* (pp. 164–206). New York: Basic Books.

Orford, J. (1985). *Excessive appetites: A psychological view of addictions.* New York: Wiley.

Pleck, J. H. (1995). The gender role strain paradigm: An update. In R. F. Levant & W. S. Pollack (Eds.), *A new psychology of men* (pp. 11–32). New York: Basic Books.

Postman, N., Nystrom, C., Strate, L., & Weingartner, C. (1987). *Myths, men, and beer: An analysis of beer commercials on broadcast television, 1987.* Falls Church, VA: Foundation for Traffic Safety.

Prochaska, J. O., DiClemente, C. C., & Norcross, J. C. (1992). In search of how people change: Applications to addictive behaviors. *American Psychologist, 47,* 1102–1114.

Project MATCH Research Group. (1997). Matching alcoholism treatments to client heterogeneity: Project MATCH posttreatment drinking outcomes. *Journal of Studies on Alcohol, 58,* 7–29.

Pursch, J. A. (1976). From Quonset hut to naval hospital: The story of an alcoholism rehabilitation service. *Journal of Studies on Alcohol, 37,* 1655–1666.

Rollnick, S., & Morgan, M. (1995). Motivational interviewing: Increasing readiness for change. In A. M. Washton (Ed.), *Psychotherapy and substance abuse: A practitioner's handbook* (pp. 179–191). New York: Guilford Press.

Toneatto, A., Sobell, L. C., & Sobell, M. B. (1992). Gender issues in the treatment of abusers of alcohol, nicotine, and other drugs. *Journal of Substance Abuse, 4,* 209–218.

Waldron, I. (1995). Contributions of changing gender differences in behavior and social roles to changing gender differences in mortality. In D. Sabo & D. F. Gordon (Eds.), *Men's health and illness: Gender, power, and the body* (pp. 22–45). Thousand Oaks, CA: Sage.

Wallack, L., Breed, W., & Cruz, J. (1987). Alcohol on prime-time television. *Journal of Studies on Alcohol, 48,* 33–38.

Williams, R. J., & Ricciardelli, L. A. (1999). Gender congruence in confirmatory and compensatory drinking. *Journal of Psychology, 133,* 323–331.

CHAPTER TWELVE

Male Survivors of Trauma

David Lisak

I t is a measure of change that this revised edition, *A New Handbook of Counseling and Psychotherapy for Men,* includes a chapter on male survivors of trauma. When the first edition of this book was published, in 1987, no such chapter was included. The inclusion of this chapter is not the result of a sudden increase in the prevalence of trauma among men. Men—as boys, adolescents, and adults—have been experiencing trauma for as long as there have been humans on this planet. Rather, the change represented by inclusion of this chapter is one of collective consciousness.

In the years since the publication of the first edition of this book, what was a fledgling new field of men's studies has grown into a dynamic and rapidly expanding discipline. Psychology's corner of it is now represented in the American Psychological Association by the Society for the Psychological Study of Men and Masculinity (Division 51). Three scholarly journals publish the growing body of work associated with this new discipline. The discipline of men's studies serves both as a vanguard for changing consciousness and as a reflection of broad-based cultural changes that are beginning to occur.

Included among these changes is a new and still fledgling awareness that men can indeed experience trauma and its long-term effects in unique ways that are determined by men's unique patterns of gender socialization. The emergence of this awareness has been slow because it challenges many of the core assumptions about men that were not questioned until very recently.

Chief among those assumptions was perhaps the most basic of them: that men are synonymous with masculinity, that masculinity is somehow an intrinsic property of maleness. When we free ourselves of this assumption, we become capable of seeing masculinity as a kind of ideology, a set of powerfully held beliefs. Masculinity is a unique ideology in that it is exalted to the status of a gender identity: men are forced to internalize the ideology until they experience it as an intrinsic part of their being—indeed, often the very core of their personal identities. Because the essential features of masculine ideology are toughness, fearlessness, and the denial of vulnerability, it is not surprising that men and the culture that surrounds them have been slow to acknowledge that men can indeed be victimized and that like all victims they suffer.

Our culture's blindness to the suffering of male survivors of trauma can be understood as the result of clashing schemata. The schema of men as essentially synonymous with masculinity is still well entrenched. It is therefore very difficult for people to hold in consciousness the clashing view of men as tough and invulnerable on the one hand and hurt and suffering on the other. How can a man be both at the same time?

An example of this clash of schemata can be seen in some of the best writing from the field of trauma studies. In Judith Herman's excellent book *Trauma and Recovery* (1992) she uses the feminine pronoun to refer to generic victims and the masculine pronoun to refer to generic perpetrators. This usage is interesting because many of the victims discussed in the book, including war veterans and holocaust survivors, are men. The schema that men are perpetrators and women are victims was even more baldly revealed in a recent published study of victimization among navy recruits (Merrill et al., 1998). The abstract, quoted in part, speaks for itself:

> U.S. Navy recruits (n = 3,776) were surveyed for premilitary histories of adult sexual assault. They completed a survey designed to estimate rates for experiences as victims (women) and perpetrators (men) of attempted and completed rape since the age of 14.

The assumption—quite explicit in this case—is plainly that the only thing relevant about men and sexual assault is whether and how often they have perpetrated it. The possibility that they may have been victims of it never seemed to have entered the researchers' minds.

Many individual men have also experienced the clash of these schemata, although more directly and more painfully. More than once male survivors of sexual assault have told me that they were turned away by rape crisis centers. The worst example is a male victim who was told that the crisis center did not have the staff to treat perpetrators. Again, it never entered the staff member's mind that the caller was not a perpetrator but rather a victim of sexual violence.

Fortunately, the changing cultural consciousness about men and masculinity has created a new openness to studying and understanding male survivors of trauma. This development is important for three reasons. First, the evidence now makes it clear that vast numbers of men have suffered traumatic experiences. Second, although men's response to trauma is in part simply a generic human response, it is also in part shaped by their gender socialization, by their internalization of masculine ideology. Thus, the treatment of male trauma survivors must incorporate an understanding of the interaction between trauma and masculinity. Finally, the evidence also makes clear that male survivors of trauma are not only a risk to themselves, in the form of self-destructive behaviors, but also to those around them. Male survivors of trauma are more likely than women to externalize their pain, resulting in the perpetration of interpersonal violence and the tragic continuation of the cycle of pain.

COMMON FORMS OF MALE VICTIMIZATION

Men can experience trauma in an infinite number of ways. However, clinicians are likely to encounter particular forms of traumatic experience, including those described in the following sections.

Childhood Physical Abuse

Estimates of the lifetime prevalence of childhood physical abuse among men, mainly derived from self-reports of college student samples, range from 10 to 20 percent (Briere, 1992; Graziano & Namaste, 1990). Wolfner and Gelles (1993) reported rates of "minor violence" of 65 percent and "severe violence" of 12.6 percent based on responses to the Conflict Tactics Scale (Straus, 1979). Estimates of the incidence of physical abuse of children range from 3.5 to 5.7 cases per 1,000 when based on documented cases to 110 cases per 1,000 when based on surveys of households (Kolko, 1992).

From a clinical perspective, underreporting of childhood physical abuse by men is a chronic problem. Men pervasively downplay the severity of the abuse they experienced and tend to describe it the context of nonabusive discipline. Nevertheless, physical abuse is associated with a wide array of potentially long-term problems, including developmental delays, neurological impairment, disturbances in attachment, impaired self-esteem, decrements in cognitive functioning and school achievement, school discipline problems, difficulties in childhood peer relations, and a greater tendency toward physical aggression and externalizing behaviors, alcoholism, and substance abuse (Crittenden, 1998; Dembo et al., 1987; Dodge, Bates, & Pettit, 1990; Kaufman & Cicchetti, 1989; Kolko, 1992; Lisak & Luster, 1994; Salzinger, Feldman, Hammer, & Rosario, 1991; Schaefer, Sobieraj, & Hollyfield, 1988).

Childhood Sexual Abuse

Once considered a rarity, sexual abuse of males is now beginning to receive the attention it has always deserved. It has been difficult to pin down the prevalence of sexual abuse—that is, the percentage of adult men who experienced sexual abuse at some point during their childhood—but increased research over the past decade has provided some solid estimates. Holmes and Slap (1998) reviewed 166 studies in which the prevalence estimates ranged from 4 to 76 percent. These estimates vary because of differences in sampling and survey techniques, but there has been a narrowing in the range of estimates. Perhaps the best indicators are studies of nonclinical samples in which standardized survey techniques and roughly equivalent abuse definitions have been used. Among these studies, the range of estimates narrows to the neighborhood of 15 to 20 percent (see Finkelhor, Hotaling, Lewis, & Smith, 1990; Fromuth & Burkhart, 1989; Lisak, Hopper, & Song, 1996).

Childhood sexual abuse is associated with an array of long-term negative consequences, although here too there is a great range in the diversity and severity of the impact. In male samples, a history of childhood sexual abuse has been associated with disrupted intimate relationships (Dimock, 1988; Hunter, 1990; Lew, 1988; Lisak, 1994; Lisak & Luster, 1994), substance abuse (Krug, 1989; Lisak & Luster, 1994; Rogers & Terry, 1984), sexual problems (Lisak, 1994; Rogers & Terry, 1984), and an array of psychiatric symptoms (Briere, Evans, Runtz, & Wall, 1988; Fromuth & Burkhart, 1989), including suicidal impulses and attempts (Darves-Bornoz, Choquet, Ledoux, Gasquet, & Manfredi, 1998; Garnefski & Arends, 1998; Lisak, 1994). Gartner (1999) and Mendel (1995) provide summaries and analyses of this literature.

Witnessing Parental Violence

It is extremely difficult to obtain reliable data on the number of children who have witnessed violence between their parents, let alone a breakdown of those numbers according to the sex of the child. Studies of the prevalence of domestic violence rarely query about the presence of children or whether children witnessed the acts described. Further, it has been shown that parents' accounts of their children's exposure are not reliable (O'Brien, John, Margolin, & Erel, 1994). Nevertheless, it is estimated that between 3.3 and 10 million American children each year are witnesses to acts of violence between their parents (Margolin, 1998). The effects of exposure to domestic violence are potentially diverse and long lasting for children and may include depression, impaired social competence and empathic abilities, and aggression. Retrospectively, witnessing violence has been associated with an increased risk among men of committing dating violence and marital violence (Margolin, 1998).

Witnessing Community Violence

For many children, violence is a pervasive feature of the landscape outside their homes. Growing up in such environments is a chronic stressor, is a threat to safety, and can have important long-term effects. Several studies in the 1990s have documented the prevalence of exposure to community violence among particular at-risk groups. For example, Bell and Jenkins (1993) reported that approximately 30 percent of African American children between seven and fifteen years of age who live in Chicago had witnessed either a shooting or a stabbing. Among slightly older children, the proportions increased to more than a third, and 23 percent had by then witnessed a killing. Although there is variability in the reported effects of such exposure, it is generally associated with increased distress, depression, symptoms of posttraumatic stress disorder, and acting-out behavior (Horn & Trickett, 1998).

Combat

Until quite recently, war was the exclusive province of men. It still is a predominantly male endeavor. At the end of the twentieth century, America could look back on two world wars, two protracted regional wars (in Korea and Vietnam), and countless other more contained or brief military engagements. There are currently about 25 million veterans, about 80 percent of whom served during a period of active hostility or war. Of these, a significant number, from senior citizens to young adults still launching their lives, have experienced combat. Many of these men—hundreds of thousands—have symptoms of trauma related to those experiences.

It is probably safe to say that without the Vietnam War there would be no official diagnosis of posttraumatic stress disorder. There certainly would be a much smaller body of literature on the cognitive, emotional, medical, and neurobiological consequences of trauma, because the study of Vietnam veterans has produced the single largest body of research of any type of trauma. As Herman (1992) noted, the antiwar movement provided veterans with the political muscle they needed to force society to acknowledge the psychological impact of combat and ultimately to change the very institutions of society. The suffering of Vietnam veterans has been well documented and has inspired scores of books and movies. The trauma of the Vietnam veteran has become part of America's national consciousness.

Nozmsv talk.

This focus has provided a much-needed corrective. The traditional view of the heroic warrior served society's purposes by laying the groundwork for the next generation of young men who would be needed to fight the next war and by salving the consciences of those who stay behind, those who vote to send those young men off to war. But war has always been hell, and it has always scarred its participants. The Vietnam War may have finally exposed the nation to the toll that war exacts from those who survive it, but it was not unique in exacting that toll. Eric Dean, in his book *Shook over Hell* (1999), uncovered evidence of the psychological toll of the American Civil War on its veterans. Similarly, the Korean War, World War I, and World War II caused untold suffering among their veterans, many of whom suffered in isolation because society provided no language, no diagnosis, and no opening for them to speak about the legacy of their experiences.

A colleague of mine treated a World War II veteran for more than two years, the final two years of this man's life. He had survived Normandy, the Battle of the Bulge, the liberation of two concentration camps, and an unimaginable sequence of daily horrors. The seventy-year-old man had never been diagnosed with posttraumatic stress disorder, even though he had suffered a variety of psychiatric symptoms for decades. It was his wife who finally revealed the true scope of his posttraumatic symptoms when she described the decades of nightmares and flashbacks that both of them had endured. For the final two years of his life, this World War II veteran recounted horror after horror, all long stored in his memory and never before revealed. To the end he told his therapist that he would spare her the worst of it, and he did.

Many hundreds of thousands of war veterans suffer in isolation and silence, some because they cannot or will not speak and others because they have never been asked to.

Assault

It is (hopefully) standard practice now when conducting a psychological assessment to inquire about traumatic childhood experiences. If the client is a woman, inquiring about possible sexual assaults would be equally advisable. It ought to be similar standard practice to inquire of men whether they have been victims of assault or other forms of violence.

According to statistics compiled by the Bureau of Justice Statistics, a branch of the U.S. Department of Justice, men outnumber women as victims of violent crime in the United States (*National Crime Victimization Survey,* 1994). In 1994, the most recent year for which a breakdown by sex is available, more than six million American males experienced some form of violent assault, as follows:

Homicide	17,448
Rape/sexual assault	32,900
Robbery	857,300
Aggravated assault	1,658,700
Simple assault	4,012,500

These are the numbers for a single year. Clearly, the odds are excellent that a male client experienced a violent victimization at some point during his lifetime.

Masculinization

I am not simply trying to make a political point by including masculinization in the list of common traumas experienced by men. Nor am I asserting that all men experience their gender socialization as traumatic. However, many men have had profoundly negative and traumatic experiences in the course of their socialization into masculinity, experiences that have branded them and that shape and distort their personalities in much the way that other forms of trauma do. Very often, the most traumatizing masculinization experiences are those that come at the hands of peers—vicious taunting, humiliation, rejection, and degradation. Such experiences become etched in the memories of their victims in much the way that other traumas do, so it behooves therapists to conduct sensitive assessments, both to unearth information and to help their clients understand the enduring impact of these experiences on their behavior.

INTERACTION OF TRAUMA AND MASCULINE SOCIALIZATION

Masculine ideology was in all likelihood constructed over thousands of generations to capitalize on a couple of relatively minor differences between human males and females. Human males tend to have a larger muscle mass and to be more predisposed to aggressive action. A culture that takes these characteristics and dramatically amplifies them would garner an advantage in any conflict with competing human groups or simply in the struggle to survive in harsh environments. By creating an ideology of masculinity and through various traumatic socialization practices forcing males to internalize that ideology, a culture would produce an entire class of humans who struggle mightily to reject within themselves any semblance of vulnerability, any sign or feeling of fear, and who certainly never manifest externally any sign of those dreaded internal experiences. Such a class of humans would be extraordinarily useful as fighters or as scavengers of prey, because they would do very dangerous things despite their fear—that is, they will have been trained to disregard the biologically ingrained fear signals that tell them to run and would instead move forward into the maw of the beast.

The primary function of the ideology of masculinity has always been to confront particular aspects of human biology and quell them—to train individuals to disregard their biological signals to run in fear or to cry in grief and pain. And so one can easily see what this ideology is likely to do to the human male who is unfortunate enough not only to be subjected to such a socialization but also to suffer some other form of victimization, such as childhood physical or sexual abuse. The experience of victimization produces intense biological states of fear, grief, and distress, the very states that masculine ideology was designed to expunge. So the man who experiences abuse is subjected to an apparently irresolvable conflict between his biology and the ideology of masculinity he has internalized.

What do men who are caught in this vicious vise do? Most simply suffer, squeezed by two opposing and converging forces—masculine ideology and the emotional legacy of victimization. Men who have experienced abuse are for the most part destined to feel internally branded by the experience, not intrinsically by the fear and grief it evoked but rather by the inevitable conclusion they must come to that because they most definitely have and continue to experience intense states of fear and vulnerability they can never truly possess what masculinity ideology offers—the identity of being men. To be men under the dictates of this ideology, they cannot experience the vulnerability that is forever the legacy of their victimization.

Branded internally as nonmale, they feel insecure and inferior, and they bring these handicaps with them into many of their life endeavors, relational and occupational. They may spend many decades being productive, raising children, and supporting their community and all the while internally feel themselves to be frauds who at any moment will be discovered as such and exposed as nonmen in a world of true men.

For victimized men who spend long decades in this vise, squeezed between the psychobiological legacy of trauma and masculinity, the only escape is through breaking one of the two jaws of the vise. Which one? Well, there is no choice. They cannot break their biology or erase the psychological legacy of trauma. So their only choice is to break the jaw of masculinity. They must recognize and confront their internalization of that ideology, reconnect with their human biological heritage, and with the heat and energy of that confrontation force open the jaws of the vise sufficiently to make their escape.

Unfortunately, there is another method of escape from the vise, but it is only an apparent escape, not a real one, and the consequences are tragic for men and often for those around them. Some victimized males, squeezed between their biological heritage and masculinity, attempt to renounce biology. They attempt to deny the fear and powerlessness and vulnerability that are essential, biological parts of them, because through such a renunciation they can clutch at the "I am a man" identity offered to them by the ideology of masculinity. It is a classic deal with the devil. In exchange for the cherished object—the masculine identity—victimized males give up so much of what makes them human that they are left profoundly distorted. Emotionally and empathically crippled, they are unable to relate meaningfully to other humans.

And as in all stories about dealing with the devil, the cherished object too turns out to be tainted. The masculine identity garnered through such a deal is a brittle shell founded on illusion. The devil may promise that fear and vulnerability will disappear, but it is not a promise that can be kept. Those vulnerabilities, intrinsic human qualities that they are, will forever haunt their hosts, as biology is wont to do, and so the hosts will forever strain to hold them at bay.

Men who attempt to bury their victimization in this way are likely to react harshly, even violently, when they are confronted externally by the ghosts of their own vulnerability. So when they see vulnerability in their children they will lunge at it in fear and hatred, because it evokes the ghosts of their own. Because their culture bombards them with messages that women as a group are vulnerable and weak, they will hate them, too, and they may attack the vulnerability they see in women.

IMPLICATIONS FOR TREATMENT

Male survivors of trauma are best conceptualized as suffering from dual and interacting traumas. They have been socialized, often traumatically, into an ideology of masculinity that in many cases has severely limited the resources with which they live their lives. In addition, they have suffered a traumatic experience that while leaving its own legacy also tends to massively complicate the legacy of their masculine socialization. The implication of this conceptualization is that the treatment of male survivors of trauma should in most cases proceed on two fronts: (1) confronting the trauma and its legacies and (2) confronting masculinization and its legacies.

Although this conceptualization may seem abstract, it has very concrete implications. Consider some of the likely interactions between men's gender internalizations and the basic work of trauma-focused therapy. No matter which therapeutic school the therapist is anchored in, treatment of trauma includes, typically as its primary component, the active emotional processing of traumatic memories. Trauma therapists routinely work in creative ways to help their clients feel sufficiently safe to approach traumatic memories, to expose themselves to them, and to integrate their cognitive and emotional components. For many male trauma survivors, these basic avenues for healing are partially or wholly blocked by the proscriptive dictates of masculine ideology. To render themselves open and vulnerable to such extreme emotional states, to such states of pain and vulnerability, is to flagrantly violate the norms of masculinity. Any therapist who embarks on such a treatment strategy with a male trauma survivor had better be cognizant of this added impediment to treatment.

At the core of most traumatic experiences are overwhelming states of fear, helplessness, and vulnerability. These are extremely difficult states for anyone to deal with, but they carry an added message and burden for male trauma victims. Most men carry around some degree of scarring resulting from their masculinization experiences. Virtually all men feel to some degree that they do not measure up to the standards of masculine ideology; this "failure" is a certainty because the standards literally defy men's basic humanity. Therefore all men carry with them underlying insecurities about their identity as men, insecurities that almost certainly will be enormously exacerbated by any attempt to approach the emotional legacy of victimization experiences.

Consequently trauma therapy with male victims must incorporate an active effort to treat the legacies of masculine socialization. Those legacies stand like a giant roadblock on the path toward healing from trauma; without actively confronting the legacies, the roadblock will remain.

Treating gender internalizations is essentially the same process as treating any other type of internalization that a therapist perceives to be destructive to clients. For example, clients who were psychologically abused as children would very likely retain many internalized messages from that abuse. They would likely feel themselves to be inferior, bad, spoiled, selfish—whatever the particular words and messages their emotionally abusive parents conveyed to them. A therapist would need to confront those internalizations by identifying them when they crop up, giving them labels, and helping clients trace them back to their source. And the therapist would take an active rather than neutral stance. It is hard to imagine a therapist saying, in effect, "Maybe your parents were right, maybe they were wrong." Rather, few therapists would hesitate to actively challenge such negative internalizations and label them as internalized distortions.

A similar stance is required when confronting the negative, distorting internalizations that result from masculine socialization. The therapist must be prepared to challenge the ideology of masculinity, including its rigid prescriptions and proscriptions and its distorting norms and dictates. Consider the following simple example: When a male trauma client finally approaches the threshold of tears and automatically pulls himself back from "the brink," the therapist must actively identify the full meaning, the consequences, and the roots of that choice. Often, it is helpful to incorporate large measures of psychoeducation in the process, teaching the client the biology of emotions and the role of emotions in human evolution and adaptation. Such lessons in human evolution and biology carry both explicit and implicit messages. Explicitly, they familiarize the client with his emotional systems and help demystify them. Implicitly, they begin to erode his identity as a man and supplant it with an identity as a human.

CONFRONTING THE SCARS OF ABUSE

Paul was a successful investment banker with a six-figure income, an expensive car, a high-priced home in the suburbs, and a work week that typically spanned dawn until dusk six days per week. He was also married and the father of three young children. The superficial indicators of success in his life—his career, financial well-being, and family—actually belied deep undercurrents of fear, insecurity, and profound feelings of inferiority. Virtually no one in Paul's life was aware of those undercurrents, although he was and always had been conscious of them. He simply kept them under tight wraps and compensated for them with a zealous devotion to his work.

Paul's adaptation is not unusual among male survivors of childhood abuse. Although he was profoundly scarred by sexual abuse perpetrated by an uncle throughout his early childhood, Paul sealed away the overt signs of his pain and buried his fears and insecurities to survive the gauntlet of masculine socialization. He emerged from it with at least a superficial hold on the masculine identity he viewed as absolutely crucial to his existence. He was by no means hypermasculine. His gender persona was designed not to flaunt his masculinity but rather to display just enough of it to ward off the critical gaze of other men. It was not that other men saw through him or gave him any reason to doubt himself. Rather, Paul's own feelings of inferiority were so vivid and pervasive that he was constantly vigilant about how other men perceived him, always fearing that they judged him to be less than a man. No matter how successfully he managed his career, no matter how much money he earned, Paul—in the classic manner of male survivors of sexual abuse—felt himself to be branded internally by the abuse, a man who was less than a man.

There was of course a great cost to Paul's adaptation to his trauma and gender socialization, and it was this cost that ultimately forced him to seek treatment. The great seal he placed over his childhood pain—the wall he built to contain all those overwhelming emotions—also walled him off from his capacity to connect emotionally to his wife and children. Thus, with the birth of each child Paul drifted further and further into a one-sided existence, a drift that was virtually preordained by the constraints instilled in him by his abuse history and his experiences of abuse. His disconnection was so great that his wife's threat of separation if he did not seek treatment hit him like a blow from a phantom punch. He had not had a clue that she was that much in despair.

This scenario is not unusual for the initiation of treatment of a male client, and, not surprisingly, Paul was skeptical, guarded, and evasive. He professed genuine bafflement at his wife's desperation about the state of their relationship. Such initial sessions with male clients present therapists with a difficult choice. Do you hold back, shy away from confrontation, and try to establish a degree of trust in an effort to delay what often feels like the man's inevitable judgment that psychotherapy is meaningless? Or do you use the opposite strategy: move in quickly and show the skeptic that things can really happen in the space of one hour?

There can be no rigid rule about such choices, but I almost always choose the latter strategy. I try to quell my fears about scaring the male client away by telling myself that he is already halfway out the door anyway. It is my job to pull him in, not to simply avoid a mistake that hastens his departure.

r Paul's opening remarks I made a deliberately provocative comment. I
n that he was certainly not the first man to sit in that chair without a
)ut why his life was about to crash and burn around him and that if he
uinely interested in figuring out what had happened to him and per-
.iding the disaster I was there to try to help him. I also told him that it
did not seem as though we had much time and that he had better make a decision quickly. Paul was predictably taken aback by my remarks and was genuinely frightened by them. So I apologized for scaring him, but I did not back
off. By the end of the hour we had established a relationship; it was not warm
and fuzzy, but it was a relationship built around a job we had to do.

Paul did not disclose his history of sexual abuse to me until the third session.
It was by then painfully clear that he was holding back something and becoming unbearably uncomfortable with the strain. Partway through the session I
interrupted him and simply asked him to tell me what was scaring him. It was
all the prompt he needed.

With the secret out, our work began to take shape. Within a few sessions,
we invited Paul's wife to join us so that he could tell her about the abuse and
begin to talk about the fears he had been masking for so many years. From then
on, couples work became an integral part of the treatment.

I also began giving Paul homework, in the form of readings. He began with
Victims No Longer (Lew, 1988), a book for male sexual abuse victims. As I
began to actively challenge his internalized masculine ideology, he became curious about the language I was using, terms such as *masculinization* and *gender
conformity*. So he started reading men's studies texts and was soon immersed
in a new universe of ideas that served to validate the changes that he was facing within himself. To help offset the erosion of his former masculinized identity, I gave him LeDoux's book *The Emotional Brain* (LeDoux, 1996). The new
discoveries about the neurobiology of emotions, the information about the long
evolutionary development of the human repertoire of emotions, and the links
between humans and other animal species all served to underscore his more
essential identity as a human being, an identity rooted in his biology and one
that could eventually supplant the rigid masculinity that he had for so long
clung to.

Of course this description does not convey the hard slugging of such treatment—the moments of despair and the impulses to retreat to familiar ground,
the ill-timed interpretations and the inevitable misunderstandings. Nevertheless,
Paul persevered. He began to meet and experience the emotional legacy of his
abuse, simultaneously stretching and eventually breaking the bonds of masculine ideology. His newfound emotional life was a stormy one, and he found himself at times overcome by strange tides of rage, at other times awash in
unexpected tears. Had these been the only consequences of his new emotional
openness he might well have retreated. But there was an enormous benefit that

soon made itself felt: Paul discovered his love for his wife and children, and his emotional connection to them was reciprocated. He soon found himself chafing at the demands of his job, regretting the time spent away from his family. As Paul altered his fundamental adaptation to life as a man who had been abused, he found that the life he had built no longer matched his altered self, and he began looking for ways to make further changes.

There are hopeful signs that men are beginning to challenge masculine ideology, to alter their views of themselves and thereby to alter the way society views them collectively, as a gender. One of the immediate consequences of this change is an increase in the number of men who are seeking treatment, and among these men are many who have experienced psychological trauma. The psychological community must prepare itself to meet these men; mental health professionals must be well informed and capable of providing the treatment these men need and deserve.

However, these emerging changes are part of a much broader cultural change that has immense social and political implications. Further, recent history suggests that for such fundamental—and personal—changes to be successful, individual men need the support and validation of a movement. Heroic individuals can sometimes overcome the tidal forces of culture independently and provide the rest of us with an example and an inspiration. But for such changes to reach the many, we need more than heroism. We need a movement that can provide its own tidal force, one that can create the new language forms and the new ideas that serve to liberate the many millions of men who are increasingly ready to abandon the maladaptive tenets of masculine ideology.

References

Bell, C. C., & Jenkins, E. J. (1993). Community violence and children on Chicago's Southside. In D. Reiss, J. E. Richters, M. Radke-Yarrow, & D. Scharff (Eds.), *Children and violence* (pp. 46–54). New York: Guilford Press.

Briere, J. (1992). *Child abuse trauma.* Newbury Park, CA: Sage.

Briere, J., Evans, D., Runtz, M., & Wall, T. (1988). Symptomatology in men who were molested as children: A comparison study. *American Journal of Orthopsychiatry, 58*(3), 457–461.

Crittenden, P. M. (1998). Dangerous behavior and dangerous contexts: A 35-year perspective on research on the developmental effects of child physical abuse. In P. K. Trickett & C. J. Schellenbach (Eds.), *Violence against children in the family and the community* (pp. 11–38). Washington, DC: American Psychological Association.

Darves-Bornoz, J. M., Choquet, M., Ledoux, S., Gasquet, I., & Manfredi, R. (1998). Gender differences in symptoms of adolescents reporting sexual assault. *Social Psychiatry and Psychiatric Epidemiology, 33,* 111–117.

Dean, E. T. (1999). *Shook over hell.* Cambridge, MA: Harvard University Press.

Dembo, R., Dertke, M., La Voie, L., Borders, S., Washburn, M., & Schmeidler, J. (1987). Physical abuse, sexual victimization, and illicit drug use: A structural analysis among high risk adolescents. *Journal of Adolescence, 10,* 13–33.

Dimock, P. T. (1988). Adult males sexually abused as children: Characteristics and implications for treatment. *Journal of Interpersonal Violence, 3*(2), 203–221.

Dodge, K. A., Bates, J. E., & Pettit, G. S. (1990). Mechanisms in the cycle of violence. *Science, 250,* 1678–1683.

Finkelhor, D., Hotaling, G., Lewis, I. A., & Smith, C. (1990). Sexual abuse in a national survey of adult men and women: Prevalence, characteristics, and risk factors. *Child Abuse and Neglect, 14,* 19–28.

Fromuth, M. E., & Burkhart, B. R. (1989). Long-term psychological correlates of childhood sexual abuse in two samples of college men. *Child Abuse and Neglect, 13,* 533–542.

Garnefski, N., & Arends, E. (1998). Sexual abuse and adolescent maladjustment: Differences between male and female victims. *Journal of Adolescence, 21,* 99–107.

Gartner, R. B. (1999). *Betrayed as boys.* New York: Guilford.

Graziano, A. M., & Namaste, K. A. (1990). Parental use of physical force in child discipline: A survey of 679 college students. *Journal of Interpersonal Violence, 5,* 449–463.

Herman, J. L. (1992). *Trauma and recovery.* New York: Basic Books.

Holmes, W., & Slap, G. (1998). Sexual abuse of boys: Definition, prevalence, correlates, sequelae, and management. *Journal of the American Medical Association, 280,* 1855–1862.

Horn, J. L., & Trickett, P. K. (1998). Community violence and child development: A review of research. In P. K. Trickett & C. J. Schellenbach (Eds.), *Violence against children in the family and the community* (pp. 103–138). Washington, DC: American Psychological Association.

Hunter, M. (1990). *Abused boys.* Lexington, KY: Lexington Books.

Kaufman, J., & Cicchetti, D. (1989). Effects of maltreatment on school-age children's socioemotional development: Assessments in a day-camp setting. *Developmental Psychology, 25,* 516–524.

Kolko, D. J. (1992). Characteristics of child victims of physical violence. *Journal of Interpersonal Violence, 7,* 244–276.

Krug, R. S. (1989). Adult male report of childhood sexual abuse by mothers: Case descriptions, motivations, and long-term consequences. *Child Abuse and Neglect, 13,* 111–119.

LeDoux, J. (1996). *The emotional brain.* New York: Simon & Schuster.

Lew, M. (1988). *Victims no longer.* New York: Nevraumont.

Lisak, D. (1994). The psychological consequences of childhood abuse: Content analysis of interviews with male survivors. *Journal of Traumatic Stress, 7,* 525–548.

Lisak, D., Hopper, J., & Song, P. (1996). Factors in the cycle of violence: Gender rigidity and emotional constriction. *Journal of Traumatic Stress, 7,* 507–523.

Lisak, D., & Luster, L. (1994). Educational, occupational, and relationship histories of men who were sexually and/or physically abused as children. *Journal of Traumatic Stress, 7,* 507–523.

Margolin, G. (1998). Effects of domestic violence on children. In P. K. Trickett & C. J. Schellenbach (Eds.), *Violence against children in the family and the community* (pp. 57–101). Washington, DC: American Psychological Association.

Mendel, M. P. (1995). *The male survivor.* Thousand Oaks, CA: Sage.

Merrill, L. L., Hervig, L. K., Newell, C. E., Gold, S. R., Milner, J. S., Rosswork, S. G., Koss, M. P., & Thornton, S. R. (1998). Prevalence of premilitary adult sexual victimization and aggression in a navy recruit sample. *Military Medicine, 163,* 209–212.

National Crime Victimization Survey. (1994). Washington, DC: U.S. Department of Justice, Bureau of Justice Statistics.

O'Brien, M., John, R. S., Margolin, G., & Erel, O. (1994). Reliability and diagnostic efficacy of parents' reports regarding children's exposure to marital aggression. *Violence and Victims, 9,* 45–62.

Rogers, C. M., & Terry, R. (1984). Clinical intervention with boy victims of sexual abuse. In I. R. Suart & J. G. Greer (Eds.), *Victims of sexual aggression: Treatment of children, women, and men* (pp. 91–104). New York: Van Nostrand Reinhold.

Salzinger, S., Feldman, R. S., Hammer, M., & Rosario, M. (1991). Risk for physical child abuse and the personal consequences for its victims. *Criminal Justice and Behavior, 18,* 64–81.

Schaefer, M. R., Sobieraj, K., & Hollyfield, R. L. (1988). Prevalence of childhood physical abuse in adult male veteran alcoholics. *Child Abuse and Neglect, 12,* 141–149.

Straus, M. A. (1979). Measuring intrafamily conflict and violence: The Conflict Tactics (CT) Scales. *Journal of Marriage and the Family, 41,* 75–88.

Wolfner, G. D., & Gelles, R. J. (1993). A profile of violence toward children: A national study. *Child Abuse and Neglect, 17,* 197–212.

CHAPTER THIRTEEN

Homicide, Violence, and Male Aggression

David Lisak

In the twelve months preceding the writing of this chapter, millions of American women and children were subjected to acts of violence. Simultaneously, untold thousands of American men were raped in prison and hundreds of thousands more were murdered or physically assaulted. Repeatedly, the national consciousness has been rocked by an unrelenting series of mass killings: by "disturbed youths" at schools in Colorado and Georgia and by "angry white men" in Illinois, California, and Texas.

The vast majority of this violence and mayhem is being perpetrated by males, and males are most often the casualties of this violence (Gilligan, 1996). As the United States reels from its impact and meaning, citizens question the roots of violence in American culture, about the source of our national obsession with guns, and about the problems besetting our children. Most rare among the questions raised in the wake of this violence is perhaps the simplest and most obvious one: *Why men?*

Men and violence, as well as men and guns, have been inextricably intertwined in our national myths. If a culture depicts something essential about itself in its legends of its origins, then America's legends are revealing. The stories we tell about our origins, the images of heroism we choose to represent ourselves, are replete with the mixture of men and guns: the stalwart men at Lexington, flintlocks cradled in their arms, facing the redcoats across the green; the courageous pioneer, ax in one hand and rifle in the other, braving the dangers of the wilderness; Daniel Boone, out of ammunition, swinging his rifle in his final moments at the Alamo; the jaunty cowboy, fists ever ready, six-shooter strapped to his hip. The images represent almost inseparable connections among men, violence, and the instruments of violence.

Historically, American men used violence to secure the country's independence and to colonize the continent and wrest it from its original peoples. Historically, it was the British, the Mexicans, and the native peoples of this continent who bore the cost of this violence, while America the nation benefited. However, it may be argued that increasingly America the nation is bearing the cost. Therefore, if for no other reason than self-interest, it behooves us to seek an understanding of the origins of male violence.

ORIGINS OF MALE VIOLENCE

There are many perspectives from which to explore what sometimes seem to be almost inseparable connections among men, violence, and the instruments of violence.

From Predator to Prey

As Barbara Ehrenreich (1997) has reminded us, we humans have only very recently altered our basic position in that most fundamental of natural hierarchies, the predator and the prey. During the vast aeons of our evolution, we humans were the prey. We lived in abject terror of nature's predators, the true meat eaters. Our brain and nervous system adapted to this station in life. We developed a very healthy capacity to experience fear, to anticipate danger, and to respond to the slightest sign of this danger. Such a pervasive need for vigilance must have evoked considerable reality-based anxiety. And that anxiety no doubt fueled our quest to alter our abilities, to change our original role within nature's food-acquisition balance, and ultimately to alter our very position in the hierarchy of predator and prey.

Our closest cousins are the chimpanzees, with whom we share approximately 98 percent of our genetic material. In evolutionary terms, we diverged from the chimps very, very recently. Chimpanzees are opportunistic feeders. Their main diet consists of the vegetable matter they can fairly easily procure from the trees around them. Termites provide an important source of protein and occasionally so do baby baboons, bush babies, or other small mammals they can catch in one of their group hunts (Heltne & Marquardt, 1989). At night, these food gatherers and occasional hunters climb thirty to forty feet up into the trees, build nests of bunched leaves and branches, and sleep away the night out of reach of the predators who stalk the ground beneath them.

At some point after our divergence from the chimpanzees, our humanlike ancestors began walking upright with increasing ease (Tattersall, 1999). We traded in the anatomy specialized for tree climbing in favor of one specialized for walking and running upright. Armed with this new anatomy—which included the ability to see over tall grass and to walk with our hands free to hold on to objects such as stones and sticks—we began to compete for food in the protein- and danger-rich open grasslands. Almost certainly, our initial (for aeons) strategy was that of a scavenger. Because anatomically and physiologically we remained—essentially—members of the prey class of species, we could not go head to head with the lions, leopards, and cheetahs. However, we could go after the kills those animals produced. If a pack of scrawny hyenas can intimidate a pride of lions away from a recent kill, then so may have a pack of stone-throwing and stick-waving early humans. The prize: a veritable supermarket of protein. The cost: imagine the fear of challenging a group of lions at a recent kill, armed with a four-foot stick or a stone.

No matter how any of us might weigh the relative costs and benefits of our divergence from the chimpanzees—our move from the trees to the ground—evolution has spoken. We humans have evolved into what our planet has never before experienced—a superpredator. Humans are the only species that preys on virtually all other species. In fact, it would be hard to argue with the notion that we are preying on the planet itself, systematically consuming the very substances of which the planet is constructed.

What a heady experience this must be for an animal that spent—in the time scale of evolution—the vast majority of its existence cowering in terror, suffering endlessly the nightmare, both real and constantly imagined, of the predator's savage teeth and claws. Those aeons of terror are not some distant, ancestral memory, etched in pale drawings on dimly lit cave walls. They are etched in our bodies. As the new research on the biology of trauma is revealing, they live on in our neurons, in the very structure of our brains (LeDoux, 1996). The terror can be and still is evoked within us constantly. If we were more honest with ourselves, the animals we would choose to adorn our national symbols would be the zebra, the antelope, and perhaps the chimpanzee, because no matter how many eagles we print on our stamps and dollar bills and missiles and war planes we cannot alter our heritage. We are not eagles. We are not lions. We may soon succeed in destroying all of the lions, leopards, wolves, and bears that terrorized us for so many generations; we may soon succeed in devouring our entire planet. Yet this course of action will only tragically underscore our still frantic need to reassure ourselves that when we lie down at night we will not be awakened by the hot breath of the predator.

It is a never-ending battle we wage to deny, even to expunge from within ourselves, the evidence of our evolutionary heritage: our great reservoir of fear and the vulnerability of which it so eloquently speaks. Because the fear and vulnerability are ineradicable, because they are entrenched in our very biology, to choose to deny them is to choose a never-ending struggle. It is no wonder that both human cultures and individuals are so often virtually surrounded by symbols that serve to bolster and support this endless struggle. Many of our cars are named after predators, as are many of our sports teams. We tend to choose predators as our national symbols. We yearn to identify with them because in so doing we imagine we can leave behind that always-nagging vulnerability.

Human Vulnerability and Human Violence

I have spent considerable time interviewing prisoners on death row units around the United States. In compiling life histories of these men, I have interviewed not only the men themselves but also their family members and former teachers, neighbors, and friends, and I have reviewed enormous volumes of medical, psychiatric, school, social service, and court records. Through these efforts, it is often possible to reconstruct the sequence of tragedies that stretches backward and forward, from past generations into the lives of the prisoners and then forward into the lives of the prisoners' victims.

It is not a pleasant task, but it is an informative one. And one of the secrets revealed again and again in these efforts is that, with very few exceptions, hidden behind the tattooed shell of the cold, murdering predator resides that same, cowering, terror-stricken human. Not a predator at all, just another terrorized human, arms raised over bowed head to fend off the blows, body curled up in the fetal position to protect the vulnerable abdomen. I have always found it bizarrely reassuring that behind the pervasive American myth of the cold-blooded killer we actually find the same terribly vulnerable humanity that is both more real and ultimately more familiar than the myth.

This vulnerability is not simply a possibility, not a potential human frailty, but rather a core characteristic of our species and therefore of each and every one of us. Female and male. This vulnerability can separate us and cast us into warring roles or provide us with a commonality that can bridge our differences.

This vulnerability is not synonymous with fear. It is much more than that. It is a state of being. Vulnerability is surely shot through with fear, but it is also our helplessness and powerlessness in the face of so much in life that has the potential to overwhelm us. Perhaps its prototype truly is that moment when we come face to face with the predator, when instinctively we measure our frailty against those rippling muscles, those enormous canines, and those razor claws, and we know in our deepest being that we are powerless to prevent what is now inevitable.

But of course so many other scenes can and do evoke this state of vulnerability. As many theorists have pointed out eloquently, it is a state that fairly characterizes human infancy. And in various ways it follows us throughout our lives. The beast is always out there, ready to pounce, be it a lion, the sound of a hundred thousand marching boots, or a doctor's voice saying *cancer.*

Each of us must come to terms with this fundamental vulnerability. We are not given the choice of whether we wish to; come to some terms with it we will. We may choose to deny our vulnerability; we may choose to plaster our walls and cars and perhaps our very bodies with the images of predators and in so doing identify with the beast that in reality terrorizes us. We may even go beyond the image and actually act the predator. As one college student rapist once told me: "All of us in the fraternity would be on the lookout for good-looking girls, especially freshmen, the real young ones. They were the easiest, it's like they were easy prey."

By preying on others, we of course ward off the nagging doubts about our power, the persistent inner fear that the beast can and will turn on us. By turning someone else into our prey, we force them to hold for us all of our terror of that horrible state of helplessness and vulnerability. But it is a terribly fragile plot that the predator weaves, because it can foster only the illusion of invulnerability. It is so fragile, its reassurance so ephemeral, that the predator must constantly find new victims to be his prey, to hold his fear. It is not surprising therefore that so many predators hurt, rape, and kill over and over.

Why is it that so many of these predators are men? Why is it that our prisons, that death row, is such a bastion of masculinity? Certainly biology has its role. But if men were so inexorably more violent and so inexorably more afraid of vulnerability than women, then why would almost every human culture expend so much time and energy to ensure that biological men come to embody the characteristics we know as masculinity (Gilmore, 1990)?

Cultural Utility of Masculinity

To the extent that masculinity has evolved, survived, and thrived as a creation of cultures, it must have yielded an important adaptive advantage for those cultures. An examination of the core features of masculine ideology reveals some important clues about what those advantages might have been.

We are all quite familiar with core masculine ideology: the prescription to be tough, independent, and fearless, to shake off pain, and to betray no vulnerability. Cultures typically do not simply put out this ideology and allow males to take it or leave it. Typically, masculine ideology is given the exalted status of a *gender identity*—that is, the culture dictates that all humans born of the male sex shall adopt masculine ideology and internalize it as part of their identity.

The result of this process is a radical transformation of a human being. Toughness, independence, and the capacity to suppress fear and pain—all human capacities—are available to males and females alike. But they represent only a portion of human capacities. Humans are also intrinsically capable of experiencing the vulnerable spectrum of emotions, those empathic capacities that produce our potential for nurturing and tenderness. When people feel their own fear they can recognize and resonate with the fear in fellow humans. When they feel their own vulnerability they can sympathize with the vulnerability in others.

When a culture grants masculine ideology the status of gender identity it sets in motion a radical transformation of those males who follow the path. Their very humanity is truncated. In the service of accentuating one end of the spectrum of human capacities, the other end is necessarily expunged. This is a radical event, one that has many potentially negative consequences for both the individual male and his society. What good could possibly offset these negative consequences?

To find an answer to that question, start with the assumption that there must indeed have been some substantial gain, because otherwise the cultural evolution of masculinity would not logically have run this particular course.

Next, try the following thought experiment: You are on a Civil War battlefield. You are shoulder to shoulder with thousands of other men, each clutching a rifle. You hear the officer's order and at once you start advancing with your unit across an open field. Two hundred yards ahead you can see the glint of rifles and bayonets, your enemy, waiting to send thousands of screeching balls of lead directly into you. Every human cell in your body is screaming for you to run; these cells reach back through time to your ancestors in the savanna who fled from the signals of death and so lived to produce the generations that ultimately produced you. Yet now you are not fleeing the signals of death but rather marching directly into its maw. With every step you take, the inevitability of your death comes closer, and yet you march forward.

Masculine ideology has long been intertwined with war and warriors, with hunting and killing, and with overcoming the fear of being killed. It would not be a great leap to imagine that cultures that exalted such an ideology and that created a whole class (gender) of humans who were uniquely prepared to overcome their intrinsic fear of being killed—a gender that was uniquely shaped to deny its links to other prey species and to instead identify itself as belonging to the predator species—would create a significant adaptive advantage for themselves. They would create an advantage in the struggle to survive in harsh environments, an advantage in any competition for protein with other animal species, and an advantage in any competition with other human groups.

To return to the thought experiment: Imagine the two armies facing each other across that field, each army consisting of men facing the apparent certainty of death, men struggling to defy their instinctual impulses to flee. Now, imagine that one army represents a culture such as we have been describing, in which masculine ideology is exalted to the status of gender identity. This army now is composed of men whose very identity is linked to this masculine ideology. For these men, to flee is to relinquish that core identity that they have internalized. That they do not flee tells us that they view the loss of that identity as—quite literally—a fate worse than death. Now imagine that the opposing army represents a culture in which masculine ideology has never been exalted to such an extent. This army is composed of men whose identity is more fully human, men who have never forcibly expunged from themselves their link to human vulnerability, men whose instincts to flee from near-certain death are still largely intact.

Which army would you bet on?

The army of highly masculinized males may well have the advantage. The culture they represent accrues some benefits as a consequence of its strategy of masculinization. Yet there are also costs associated with this strategy. Such highly masculinized males, being much-truncated human beings, can be liabilities to society when they are not either at war or engaged in some other similar activity. Because they have expunged their capacities for nurturing and tenderness and have little capacity for empathy, they are not very useful as caregivers and parents and they may well be prone to antisocial behaviors, including violence toward other members of the culture.

The balance between the benefits and the costs of any particular adaptive advantage is not a static thing. As the environment changes, the balance between costs and benefits shifts. For example, in a physically harsh environment in which competition for resources is strong, a culture may accrue more benefits than it suffers costs by instilling an extreme masculine identity in its males. However, if changes in the environment make competition less productive and cooperation more productive, then this culture may suddenly find that the costs of masculine ideology outweigh its benefits.

If we permit speculation on a grand scale for a moment, is it possible that the twentieth century brought human cultures—collectively—to just such a threshold point? Human history has been characterized by intra- and inter-species competition, precisely the conditions that tend to favor cultures with rigid codes of masculinization. Yet development of the technologies of mass destruction rather suddenly altered the balance of benefits and costs associated with warrior masculinity. If the outcome of competition is death for all, then there is suddenly nothing to be gained by outmasculinizing the enemy. Rather suddenly, the needs for cooperation, for trust, for negotiating, for empathy, and for understanding the other become far more critical to survival. The human capacities that underlie these abilities are by and large very different from those that underlie traditional masculinity. Thus, suddenly—in the time frame of human cultural evolution—cultures are faced with a radically altered balance of benefits and costs associated with the masculinization of their males. Suddenly, the costs to societies seem to be far outweighing the benefits. Suddenly, questions are raised about "angry white men" and "troubled [male] youths." Suddenly, the image of the man with a gun—an image that for so long represented heroism in the service of the collective—has become an image of collective terror and anguish.

CAN MASCULINITY AND VIOLENCE BE UNLINKED?

Yes.

The answer is that easy because masculinity is a creation of culture. While human males may be biologically predisposed toward aggression and dominance behavior (Wrangham & Peterson, 1996), human societies have built a multithousand-year layer of culture that channels and amplifies those predispositions. As the evidence mounts that traditional forms of masculine socialization have become maladaptive, the press to alter those forms will intensify. It seems already to be happening. The spate of excellent books about the socialization of boys (for example, Garbarino, 1999; Pollack, 1999) and the widespread media interest in the topic are indications that American culture is beginning to grapple with this problem. However, there is always a great lag between the recognition and identification of a problem and the fixing of it. Therefore, in the meantime, what is psychology's role in dealing with the problem of male violence?

IMPLICATIONS FOR TREATMENT

The scale of the violence referred to in the opening paragraph of this chapter invites some skepticism about whether the problem of male violence is one that falls within the domain of counseling and psychotherapy. At such a scale, do we not need to consider the client to be society itself or the cultures that comprise it? What meaning can there be in treating an individual when there are millions to be treated?

Collective Responsibility

Fortunately, treating individuals and treating the society of which they are a part are not mutually exclusive. In fact, it may be argued that they are related. I would argue that treating a violent male is a political act, a statement to the larger society that this man and the men whom he represents are not simply monstrous perpetrators of hideous crimes but rather are human beings who have been subjected to particular life experiences and patterns of socialization that have had very predictable and unfortunate consequences. Whether a particular individual is ultimately treatable is far less the issue than that the group he represents be regarded as treatable and the group members' damaging behaviors be regarded as preventable. Sometimes the real value of treatment is not in the percentage of "successful" cases but simply in the reminder to society that these delinquents, batterers, rapists, and murderers are still human beings, human beings whose damaging behavior could have been prevented.

Such a reminder carries with it a message about responsibility: It is our collective responsibility to take the actions necessary to stop male violence, and this responsibility goes far beyond building more prisons and execution chambers.

Masculinization and Violence

Male violence is also masculine violence and stems directly from the masculinization of male children and adolescents. Masculinization is a cultural endeavor, and altering it will also be a cultural endeavor. Consequently, this is not a problem that can be effectively treated by the conventional means of psychotherapy. For one, we intervene after the violence has been committed and new traumatized victims have been created. For another, the very forces that shape the violent man make him extremely unlikely to seek treatment. So if he does come in, it is usually by coercion, which makes for a very poor prognosis. Finally, it should be noted that treatment for certain types of violence, most notably sexual violence, is a highly specialized field and should never be attempted outside the context of specifically designed programs or by anyone other than specially trained clinicians.

Treating Underlying Trauma

Certain therapeutic targets should be addressed in the treatment of violent men because they are frequently common characteristics. Men who perpetrate violence were very often themselves victimized and traumatized (Lisak, Hopper, & Song, 1996; Widom, 1989). It is therefore imperative to treat this underlying trauma. Traumatized, violent men typically suffer from a pronounced deficit in empathy (Miller & Eisenberg, 1988). This empathic disconnection must be treated directly (Lisak, 1998). However, it is often if not typically the case that the first stop on the road to empathic reconnection is empathy for the self—that is, violent men must learn to feel sympathy for their own pain before they can feel sympathy for the pain of others. Further, such self-empathy must often be preceded by their experiencing the empathy of therapists. This chain of empathy learning often boils down to an enormous countertransference problem for therapists who treat violent men. It is a significant challenge: Can therapists connect to the humanity buried in the person who sits before them, a person who has committed violent and abusive acts toward others? This is not a minor challenge, because it often hits therapists at the fault lines of their training and their worldview.

The study of psychological trauma has had a torturous history in the field of mental health: discovered, politically attacked, suppressed, only to be rediscovered. The study of trauma has been birthed and nurtured largely through the passionate vision and work of victim advocates, whose work is often informed by a clear political perspective. These women and men have brought the healing salve of recognition and legitimacy to forgotten and neglected groups of traumatized individuals. And simultaneously they have brought out the pain and suffering of these individuals and confronted the larger society with the reality of the pain and suffering. The larger society of course has not always wanted to receive the news. Advocates for the traumatized are always just a breath away from suffering the same fate as the traumatized.

Faced with this omnipresent wall of denial, advocates for the traumatized have little else to shield themselves with other than passion and commitment. We know that we see what others either cannot or refuse to see. We know that in the face of society's need to deny, our role as advocates becomes ever more critical.

Beyond Polarized Realities

In this embattled context, it is not surprising that we sometimes see with too much clarity. So we come to see reality through a polarizing filter, a reality neatly divided into good and evil, into victims and perpetrators. Such a polarized reality is often a needed barricade against the onslaught of denial and delegitimization to which we are subjected, but it is nevertheless an illusory reality.

As an embattled field we have dealt gingerly—or not at all—with such dissonant realities as mothers who abuse their children and soldiers who commit atrocities. Both to support our own besieged vision of reality and to present a united front against the onslaught of societal denial, we have constructed a world in which much of the haze that characterizes human life has been erased by our polarizing filters. We have made use of somewhat arbitrary distinctions to define the boundaries within our world.

Perhaps the greatest single arbitrary distinction that we have fostered and depended on is the distinction between victim and perpetrator. It is a distinction embedded in the language we use and the terms and pronouns we apply to people. It is a distinction that divides and subdivides the institutions that govern professional training and that conduct the research that informs our field. The field of trauma includes professionals who treat and study victims and professionals who treat and study perpetrators, but they are rarely found in the same room and few professionals treat both victims and perpetrators.

This arbitrary distinction between victim and perpetrator is irrevocably erased when a therapist honestly and openly confronts the humanity of the violent man he or she is there to treat. In this confrontation, the therapist is placed squarely in an uncomfortable terrain in which good and evil and victim and perpetrator coexist within the same individual and sometimes even at the same moment in time.

Participating in this process challenges one to tolerate ambiguity and to move forward without the distinctions that make the world at least apparently clear. It is an emotionally and intellectually draining challenge. But it is one that also has its rewards. Paradoxically, by standing firmly on this uncomfortable ground, truths about the capacity of human beings to change, truths that can be a genuine source of optimism about the future of our species, can be revealed.

THERAPY ON DEATH ROW

Prisoners on U.S. death row units live in what can hardly be denied are a unique set of conditions. They live with the constant knowledge that their society has judged them unfit for life. This knowledge is their ever-present companion for the many years they spend on death row as they wait out, usually as passive and helpless bystanders, the arcane legal procedures that connect two critical points in time: the date of their sentence and the date of their execution. They live with a knowledge that is almost unimaginable to most of us: the knowledge of the exact day of their death. For most, it is a repeated process. Their execution date appears on their calendar, it is removed by a stay, and a new one soon appears to take its place.

Daily life on death row is different from the image many of us have of the violent environment of maximum-security prisons. Typically, it is considerably calmer, if only because on most units death row prisoners spend most of their time secluded in their individual cells. This seclusion provides endless hours in which to think, to remember, to regret, and to suffer.

Early Roots

From the perspective of psychological science, Roger was born into a maze of risk factors and into a virtual vacuum of protective factors. His parents both had substance abuse problems and had led unstable, unhappy, and violent lives. His siblings were all considerably older than he, and so by the time Roger was five years old they were largely out of the house, certainly out of his life. Roger came into the world as an afterthought, and that was certainly the theme of his childhood.

He suffered severe nutritional, emotional, and medical neglect. Formal meals were a rarity, and Roger often was left to scrounge for food on his own. He ate his parents' leftover pizza, learned to love white bread coated with mayonnaise, and even developed a taste for cat food, at times his surest source of dietary protein. Many nights he went to bed hungry, often locked in his room while his parents partied with their friends. Being locked away was perhaps the most accurate metaphor for Roger's emotional development. He was warehoused, because neither of his parents were capable of providing him with the nurturing that every growing child needs and both were preoccupied by their own miseries and the drugs they used to anesthetize them. Not surprisingly, Roger was often sick as a child. Because of the lack of even rudimentary medical care, several of his childhood illnesses left him with permanent medical problems that plagued his adult life.

Compounding Factors

Given this atmosphere of neglect and deprivation, it is not surprising that Roger's cognitive development lagged far behind that of his peers. In school he was quickly labeled as learning disabled. In fact, his deficits were so pronounced that he was twice evaluated specifically to determine whether he met the formal criteria for mental retardation. He did not, but the numbers placed him at the borderline level. The expectations for his potential were scaled down accordingly.

Roger's peers quickly tagged him with an array of derogatory nicknames. His mental slowness, physical clumsiness, and interpersonal awkwardness all ensured that he would be the prime target of derision in every one of his classes. He vainly tried to gain some measure of acceptance by being a clown, but his efforts only consolidated his role as an outcast and earned him the reputation as a behavior problem among his teachers. From the early grades, his school records are filled with notations reflecting his teachers' utter disapproval of him and their despair over his potential.

Victimization

Neglected by his family and rejected by his peers, Roger became a prime target for neighborhood pedophiles. A maintenance worker at his school noticed the outcast boy when Roger was in second grade and soon began to "groom" him. Because Roger's parents never noticed what time Roger returned from school, he was free to roam at will after school hours. Soon he was spending afternoon hours with the maintenance worker, who showered him with sweets and attention. To Roger, even reflecting on it four decades later, this seemed a fair bargain for the oral sex that he was soon obliged to provide the maintenance worker in return for his affections.

Two other perpetrators sexually abused Roger over the course of his childhood, but it was not until he was an early adolescent that he was again targeted for chronic abuse. By the time he was thirteen, Roger had managed to insinuate himself into a small group of teenage outcasts who roamed their neighborhood looking for empty bottles and getting into minor mischief. This little band of rejected kids was soon picked out by a pedophile who lived alone in the neighborhood. He offered them small change for doing chores around his house, fed them snacks, and soon enticed them with the promise of watching "dirty movies." He began molesting the boys as they watched the movies and eventually singled out Roger as his prime target. Soon Roger was being offered special viewings alone. By this time, Roger knew what the quid pro quo would be, and once again he viewed it as a fair deal. He became the pedophile's sexual toy.

Hypermasculinity

The pedophile also inducted Roger into a new doctrine of masculinity. Despite turning the boy into his sexual object, the pedophile indoctrinated Roger in an ideology of hypermasculinity, which had as its prime tenet the degradation of women. So Roger watched violent pornography in which women were humiliated and debased, internalized a view of himself as the dominator of these women, and all the while was himself being used and debased by the pedophile.

By the age of sixteen Roger was effectively a dropout. He worked at several jobs under the watchful eye of relatives but was always regarded as more a burden than a help. Looking for a way out of his misery, as soon as he was old enough, he went to his local army recruiting office. The army held out the promise of a home to Roger—and an overt validation of the masculine identity he held on to with such tenacity. Fate was on his side; despite his absolute inability to meet the army's rudimentary entrance standards, he managed to enlist because the standards were lowered to meet recruitment targets. It was the height of the Vietnam War, and Roger had finally found a place where he was wanted.

From Soldier to Civilian

The army found a place and use for Roger, and he reciprocated with absolute loyalty. He volunteered for dangerous jobs with such a reckless enthusiasm that his fellow soldiers regarded him as a fool rather than a hero. During the months he served in Vietnam, Roger was never physically injured. However, he witnessed scenes of barbarity that were to have a lasting impact on him. He saw tortured and mutilated bodies, he witnessed rapes, and he ingested an atmosphere of unrestrained impulses. He also discovered drugs.

When his term of enlistment expired Roger immediately sought to reenlist. He fully intended to make the army a career. The army saw it otherwise, however, and rejected his request. The rejection was a staggering blow to Roger's fragile identity and self-esteem. For the first time in his life, friends and family members started to see an angry Roger, a now full-grown man prone to sullen moods and angry outbursts. He had no job and spent his days cruising in his beat-up car, drinking beer, and using pornography.

From Victim to Perpetrator

When Roger started to kill and mutilate women, he did so with a guileless depravity that seemed an almost precise amalgam of the neglect, abuse, and violence that he had absorbed over the course of his tragic life. His murderous acts were fueled by his anger, but they were also the products of the distorted and aggressive masculine ideology that he had internalized, an ideology that was Roger's distorted distillation of the pedophile's indoctrination, the army's training, and Vietnam's lessons.

For almost his entire life, Roger lived the life of the vulnerable one, the prey. He was subject to his parents' abuses and profound neglect, he was tormented by his peers, and he was the sexual toy of pedophiles. The army gave him his first taste of the other side of the coin. It armed him and trained him to kill. It showed him what killing meant. It gave Roger his first taste of self-esteem but simultaneously gave him a taste of what it is like to be the predator. For a period of months, immersed in the unreality of Vietnam, Roger played the role. Predictably, he found it far preferable to the abject rejection and victimization that had until then characterized his life. It is not surprising perhaps that once he tasted the role of predator, given his lifelong history of serving as prey to other predators, Roger was at grave risk for finding some way to restore the feeling he had tasted so briefly in Vietnam. Tragically, with his limited cognitive and emotional resources, Roger could only find his way back to that feeling in the most concrete way imaginable, re-creating the barbarity he had witnessed when he had been a "true" predator.

Roger's story may serve as a cautionary tale for us. Masculine ideology did not by itself cause him to commit murder. But masculine ideology played a central role in the long chain of causation. And his story may be representative of the dangers that we face as a society when we seek to use masculine ideology to serve our purposes. When it is used to transform a human being into a predator, it is not always possible to control who will become the prey.

References

Ehrenreich, B. (1997). *Blood rites.* New York: Henry Holt.

Garbarino, J. (1999). *Lost boys.* New York: Free Press.

Gilligan, J. (1996). *Violence.* New York: Putnam.

Gilmore, D. D. (1990). *Manhood in the making.* New Haven, CT: Yale University Press.

Heltne, P. G., & Marquardt, L. A. (1989). *Understanding chimpanzees.* Cambridge, MA: Harvard University Press.

LeDoux, J. (1996). *The emotional brain.* New York: Simon & Schuster.

Lisak, D. (1998). Men and violence: Treating the violent male patient. In W. S. Pollack & R. F. Levant (Eds.), *New psychotherapy for men: Case studies* (pp. 214–236). New York: Wiley.

Lisak, D., Hopper, J., & Song, P. (1996). Factors in the cycle of violence: Gender rigidity and emotional constriction. *Journal of Traumatic Stress, 7,* 507–523.

Miller, P. A., & Eisenberg, N. (1988). The relation of empathy to aggressive and externalizing/antisocial behavior. *Psychological Bulletin, 103,* 324–344.

Pollack, W. S. (1999). *Real boys: Rescuing our sons from the myths of boyhood.* New York: Owl Books.

Tattersall, I. (1999). *Becoming human: Evolution and human uniqueness.* New York: Harcourt Brace.

Widom, C. S. (1989). Does violence beget violence? A critical examination of the literature. *Psychological Bulletin, 106,* 3–28.

Wrangham, R., & Peterson, D. (1996). *Demonic males.* Boston: Houghton Mifflin.

CHAPTER FOURTEEN

Confusion of Sex and Violence

*Counseling Process and Programming
Considerations for College Men*

Mark A. Stevens

Mike, a twenty-one-year-old junior, did not consciously plan to scare, humiliate, and sexually violate his date. He wanted to have a good time and possibly start a relationship with this woman. So what turned this level-headed, bright young man into a criminal? Was it the alcohol? Was it poor communication skills? Was it pressure from his peers? Was it MTV? Was it the *Playboy* magazine his older brother introduced to him at age twelve? Was it the lack of mentoring about male sexuality and intimacy? Is there something in particular about Mike's developmental history that would explain such behavior? How different is Mike from the average Joe next door? How different is Mike from the man spending his life in jail for raping a stranger at gunpoint?

I address these questions and more with the intention of providing guidelines for counseling and facilitating workshops for college men that focus on issues of sexual violence. Sexual violence continues to be an important issue on college campuses (Koss, Gidycz, & Wisniewski, 1987). As the campus culture has become more educated about and sensitive to the issues of sexual violence, the number of reported rapes and rapelike behaviors (Stevens, 1993) has increased. According to directors of student conduct offices and women's resource centers, the number of reported rapes and other sexual violating behavior complaints against college men has increased more than 50 percent during the past ten years (S. Rhoten, personal communication, October, 1992, and E. Davenport, personal communication, September 1999). Subsequently, universities face new issues and dilemmas, including the practice of the university providing educational and prevention services to men accused or convicted of sexual violence. The chapter is divided into two sections. In the first section I provide an overview of therapeutic issues and considerations related to counseling college men who are accused or convicted of sexual violence and subsequently self-referred or mandated to undergo counseling at the university counseling center. In the second section I provide an overview of sexual violence–prevention (rape-prevention) programs for college men.

COUNSELING PROCESS

It is important to review several contextual issues to better understand the counseling process with college men accused or convicted of sexual violence. More specifically, I address terminology, rape statistics, reason for counseling, substance abuse, and influence of masculine socialization.

Terminology

The first contextual issue is that of terminology. *Rape* is a legal term that denotes a crime. Often colleges and universities use the terms *rape, sexual assault,* and *sexual imposition* interchangeably, and the wording in their student conduct codes may not coincide with the legal definition of rape in their city or state codes. Consequently, the (alleged) perpetrator, no matter what he is being charged with, believes the community views him as a rapist. He rejects this label because he has a stereotypic view of a rapist as a "sleazy, deranged" male who sneaks through women's bedroom windows at night (Burt, 1991).

Although the term *rape* may be helpful in a court of law or in university conduct hearings, a more elaborate definition is needed to understand the goals and process of counseling. Legal definitions must be expanded to include moral, psychological, and sociopolitical perspectives on sexual violence. These definitions would include the following concepts:

1. Sexual violence stems from the individual's confusion of sexuality and violence and has nothing to do with mutual intimacy or pleasure.

2. Sexual violence is an act of power and control.

3. Sexual violence is degrading and humiliating to the victim.

4. Sexual violence has negative consequences for men and women.

This definition is inclusive of behaviors and attitudes such as physically forced intercourse, sexual harassment, and unwanted sexual attention (for example, staring and cat calls). Although it may not be specific enough for a court of law, the definition can help counselors and clients better understand the nature of sexual violation (Scher & Stevens, 1987). In this chapter I use the term *sexual violence* as an inclusive working definition.

Rape Statistics

The second contextual issue is that of understanding statistics about reported acts of sexual violence. Because the number of complaints by college women against college men has increased over the past five years (Berkowitz, 1992) one might wonder whether college men have become more sexually violent. The most likely explanation for the increase in reporting is public attention, expanded definitions of sexual violence, and friendlier, more accessible judiciary reporting and review procedures on college campuses (Koss & Dinero, 1989).

Reason for Counseling

Therapists need to understand the background reasons for referral to counseling. College men who are accused or convicted of sexual violence come into counseling primarily because they are referred by a university conduct panel. Students may be required to see a therapist at the university counseling center to remain or reenter the university. Sometimes a specific number of sessions is mandated, although typically the length of treatment is left open to the counselor's discretion. A significant number of college men who are self-referred seek counseling after a sexual violation charge has been or is threatened to be filed against them. College men who self-refer without external pressure because they are concerned about their sexual violating behavior (past or present) are rare.

Mandatory counseling for college students convicted of violating student conduct codes is an important and controversial issue that university administrators and counseling centers have struggled with over the years. Although I am not a strong advocate for mandatory counseling, researchers have found that many students who come for a required one-time-only counseling interview continue treatment. They may continue treatment as a result of being educated about confidentiality and assured that the university will only know they came in for the one required session. A variety of sexual violating behaviors may prompt a university conduct panel to refer a student for counseling, assuming the panel has that power. Typically students are referred because they (allegedly) engaged in behaviors or attitudes such as inappropriate touching, taking advantage of an intoxicated person, silently participating in gang sexual violence, and other behaviors that are degrading to women and reinforce men's confusion of sexuality and violence (O'Sullivan, 1991; see also Koss & Dinero, 1989; Malamuth, 1986; Martin & Hummer, 1989). Violations that involve weapons, excessive physical force, and sexual intercourse call for expulsion, and therefore the student is usually not referred to counseling.

Substance Abuse

An alarming percentage of the sexual violating behaviors in which college men engage occur while the men are under the influence of alcohol (Richardson & Hammock, 1991). Although alcohol intoxication by no means excuses their behavior, it expands treatment considerations to include assessment and lessening of alcohol abuse or dependency.

Influence of Masculine Socialization

The final contextual issue involves an understanding of the relationship between traditional male sexuality socialization and sexual violence (Boeringer, 1996; Rapaport & Burkhart, 1984). Generally speaking, the male socialization process emphasizes sexual relations as a conquest and a way to build self-esteem and gain peer acceptance (O'Neil, 1981) rather than the process of developing intimacy and emotional connection (Fracher & Kimmel, 1987). The media, pornography, and "locker room lies" teach and reinforce this type of self-expression, so male sexuality becomes objectified and performance and conquest driven (Messner & Stevens, forthcoming) Potential sex partners become objectified as numbers, body parts, and notches on the belt, for example. As they objectify potential sexual partners, men become less empathetic; as empathy decreases and self-centeredness increases, men become more likely to commit acts of sexual violation. Initially men are often confused about why their behavior is considered offensive. Because myths of male sexuality are so ingrained in their way of thinking, some men believe they are "doing what guys are supposed to do" (Connell, 1995; Muehlenhard & Linton, 1987).

Counselors need to understand their personal beliefs and have a professional understanding of the influence of male sex role socialization, male sexuality training, and consequent propensity toward sexual violence. Such understanding does not excuse violent behavior; rather, it increases empathy for perpetrators and provides guidelines for treatment interventions.

TREATMENT GUIDELINES AND CONSIDERATIONS

I now provide a developmental perspective as an overview of the counseling process with college men accused or convicted of sexual violence and then briefly present two case examples with discussion of relevant clinical issues and outcomes.

I. First treatment phase
   A. Build relationship
   B. Clarify confidentiality

C. Clarify the student's expectations

D. Clarify the counselor's role

E. Clarify the university conduct panel demands

The steps in the first phase of treatment are essential for helping to establish the boundaries of the therapeutic relationship, as determined by answers to the following questions: (1) Is the student mandated to come into counseling and, if so, for how many sessions? and (2) What type of documentation does the university conduct panel need or want? For example, the student may assume that the counselor will report back to the conduct panel his or her opinions about whether the sexual violence occurred. When treating students mandated to counseling it is important for counselors to clarify with students what the counselors are willing to submit in written or oral reports to the conduct panel. During the first phase of treatment the counselor can also communicate his or her role to the student. For example, it is important for the counselor to let the student know that he or she is there to support the student through the judiciary process while also hoping to serve as a catalyst for the student's personal growth during the crisis.

II. Second treatment phase

A. Build relationship

B. Hear the student's story

C. Do not take sides

D. Acknowledge and encourage feelings, whatever they may be associated with

E. Assess relevant history

The second phase sets the tone for counseling and will influence the degree of personal sharing and risk taking by the student. Most students feel a deep sense of embarrassment, shame, and confusion in this situation; they anticipate that they will not be understood and will have a "critical finger" pointed at them. Students may feel victimized and unjustly treated by the system. They may feel impending doom, such as the loss of respect from others and punishment from school officials (for example, expulsion, suspension, or eviction from housing). Although they may show some remorse, clients are typically self-absorbed in shame, confusion, and fear. By carefully listening to their stories and acknowledging their feelings without taking sides counselors earn credibility that will come in handy during the next phase of treatment.

III. Third treatment phase

A. Continue relationship building and support

B. Challenge student to take more responsibility in relation to his sexual violating behaviors and attitudes

C. Look more closely at the impact of alcohol on the student's life

D. Introduce the student to men's issues, in particular male sex role socialization and male sexuality

The third phase is intended to help the student move out of the victim-victimizer role, as accomplished through increasing the student's willingness and ability to empathize with the feelings and thoughts of the individual who was the target of his behaviors or attitudes.

Through learning about male socialization issues, a student can better understand the roots of his sexual violating behaviors or attitudes, which may lower his internal voice that says he is a "bad boy." In other words, the student increases his own capacity for "self-empathy." His fear of the critical finger may indicate a projection of his internal voice. Assignments to read articles or books on men's issues may help facilitate this process.

A thorough assessment of the client's alcohol and other drug use and attitudes is crucial. Students should be educated about the myths and facts of alcohol use and sexual violence (Richardson & Hammock, 1991). Many students want to excuse their behaviors if they are intoxicated but at the same time place blame on the woman if she has been drinking. This double standard also contributes to the perception that women who get drunk are "easy."

Most clients are unaware of the laws related to consent and intoxication. In many states if a person is alcohol impaired he or she cannot give consent for sex and thus the partner can be convicted of sexual violation (rape) if he has sex in these circumstances. The assessment of alcohol dependence and abuse is critical to the treatment process, and interventions to reduce drinking may take precedence over other concerns.

IV. Closing phase of treatment
  A. Continue relationship building and support
  B. Refer to rape education and prevention program; discuss assigned readings
  C. Discuss how the crisis has been integrated into a learning opportunity
  D. Discuss where to go from here

During the fourth phase of treatment the student attempts to make peace. The edge of criticism toward the system, victim, and self is reduced. He is ready to move on and does so by finding some answers about himself and understanding larger psychosocial issues.

Referral to rape-prevention programs helps reinforce some of the concepts discussed in counseling. More importantly, it gives the student an opportunity to make public his struggles and learning, which often is a relief and reduces shame. He is no longer a man in hiding and knows that he can talk about the event as a learner rather than as a victim. As with most therapy termination, it is important to review the process of treatment including leftover feelings and identified new learning.

Rick's Story

Rick is a twenty-one-year-old junior from a large Midwestern university; he is a member of a fraternity but does not live in the fraternity house. He was referred to counseling by a university conduct panel for sexual misconduct and alcohol abuse. No charges were filed against him through the district attorney's office. Rick indicated that while at a fraternity party he had met a young woman who was "partially" drunk. They both continued to drink and went upstairs and had sexual intercourse. According to Rick the young woman gave full consent and there was no indication that she did not want to have intercourse with him. A short time later a friend of his came into the room and Rick left and went down to the party. Later that evening the young woman came down the stairs and said with considerable emotion that Rick's friend had raped her.

Counseling Process and Outcome. Rick was obviously anxious about coming to counseling. The first phase of treatment revealed that he assumed the counselor had control of his future: the counselor would decide whether he could stay in school. Clarification of the counselor's role was needed. The counselor explained to Rick the concept of confidentiality and agreed that the university conduct panel would only be sent a note that Rick came into counseling; Rick double-checked with the conduct panel to see if that was enough. But Rick was confused and angry about the university conduct hearing decision that suspended him for one semester. He did not understand why he was punished. He disclosed that he was sexually active and had had similar experiences without any complaints. He was not sure what had happened between his friend and the woman, but he was positive that he did not rape the woman.

After the initial tension subsided, Rick became quite enthusiastic about individual counseling. He felt relieved that he could openly talk about his feelings and confusion. He had been "hiding" from others out of shame, and the hiding was very uncomfortable.

Rick contracted to meet for five sessions, read *Men on Rape* (Beneke, 1982), and attended a rape-prevention workshop. He appeared to find relief in discussing personal issues to which he had not paid much conscious attention: alcohol use, sexuality and intimacy, and definitions of legal and moral consent.

Rick saw himself as an above-average "party person." He was accepted and felt proud of his reputation of being a guy who could easily "get" women. He had not had much conscious thought or feeling as to what it meant to have so many casual sexual experiences without real intimacy. He revealed that being sexually active helped him with the illusion that he was a likeable guy, but underneath he felt unsure of his ability to be liked in a long-term relationship. He was envious of his fraternity brothers who were in long-term relationships.

Rick was unaware of the laws regarding consent while intoxicated. When asked if the woman would have had intercourse with him if she had not been drinking, Rick seemed quite affected. He had never asked himself that question before. The question produced a moral dilemma, which was important for Rick, as was another moral issue: whether Rick had encouraged his friend to have intercourse with the woman. If so, could he be held morally accountable for the sexual violation? Rick's actions showed little empathy for the woman. She was somebody who was "easy" and a stimulus for "male bonding." Although Rick never admitted saying directly to his friend that he should try to have intercourse with the woman, he did reveal that he was not concerned about her well-being and thought she would have intercourse with his friend under Rick's definition of consent. Clearly part of Rick's lack of empathy was connected to his self-centeredness; it was compounded by his alcohol abuse.

His alcohol use was not a major issue in our counseling process, but Rick was required to attend Alcoholics Anonymous meetings. It appeared that Rick saw alcohol as a problem only because "it" reduced his judgment abilities. Although his day-to-day life was not affected by alcohol use, he clearly had the potential for developing severe alcohol problems but was not motivated to explore that potential.

Rick appeared to benefit from the counseling contract. He shared his story openly with others in the workshop. By that time, he had participated in four sessions and was clear about his role in the sexual violation. He appeared to have increased empathy toward women in terms of viewing them as important in their own right and not just as sexual objects for his self-esteem. He realized that it is important to gain sexual consent and to be sexual with someone who is not drinking. Others in the workshop responded to Rick quite positively and reinforced his self-disclosure by sharing their own stories.

The counseling termination phase was short. Rick was appreciative of having a place to share his story and not feel negatively judged. He recounted what he had learned and was thankful that his bitterness toward the system had been significantly reduced.

Kent's Story

Kent is a twenty-year-old junior who was on the sailing team. He came into counseling on his own after being accused of sexual assault by a female team member. Kent does not remember the event because he was intoxicated, but he strongly denies that he would ever try to hurt another person. Kent was a good friend of the woman and had volunteered to walk her home after a party. Both individuals had been drinking. According to the female student, Kent tried to kiss her and touch her breasts without her consent. She tried to run away, but he wrestled her to the ground. When she did get away, she ran into her on-campus residence and Kent broke a window trying to get to her. The woman called security and filed a report. A few days later Kent called and made an appointment to see a counselor.

Counseling Process and Outcome. Kent was quite distraught when he came into counseling. He was fearful of losing his academic scholarship and his friends. Kent worried that his parents would find out and disown him. He had never been in "trouble" before and characterized himself as a "goody-two-shoes." His immediate concern was whether to hire a lawyer.

The first phase of treatment was to clarify confidentiality and his expectation of the terms of counseling and of the counselor. Kent stated that he wanted to talk to someone who was "anonymous." He was having difficulty concentrating on school and was experiencing loss of appetite and sleep. He was not suicidal but did show clinical signs of acute depression. He was crying throughout most of the initial sessions and was focused on how the charges against him were going to ruin his life.

Kent participated in fifteen sessions. Early phases of treatment concentrated on crisis intervention and stabilization. A clinical history revealed that Kent grew up in a strict, close-knit second-generation Slavic family. He feared his father's temper and became the obedient child. He was afraid of being sexual and described himself as shy and awkward with women; he had never been in a long-term relationship, and he was a virgin. Kent said he drank on social occasions but never before college. He said that recently he had begun drinking larger amounts of alcohol at social gatherings.

Our sessions wove together several foci: (1) coping with and understanding the alleged sexual violation, (2) the father-son relationship, and (3) social discomfort with women. Because Kent had been intoxicated, his memory of the event was limited. He said he would have no trouble feeling remorse for what he allegedly had done, but he thought he was not capable of such actions. He believed that, because the woman was drunk, she had distorted the events. Around the fourth session, Kent realized that the counselor had some doubts about the certainty of his account. This session was an important transition in the counseling process. Kent was fearful of not being trusted (akin to his fear of his father) by the counselor. But he became willing to confront his counselor, and that appeared to help lift the acute depression and empower him out of the victim role that perpetrators often experience.

Kent appeared to benefit from counseling. By the time the university conduct hearing took place, he was able to articulate his confusion and remorse even though he did not remember what had occurred. He made a commitment to work further on himself, specifically in the area of relationships with women and with his father. He accepted and followed through on a referral for outside counseling. He decided to stop drinking, motivated by his fear of losing control and having to go through another ordeal.

SEXUAL VIOLENCE–PREVENTION PROGRAMS

Historically, sexual violence–prevention (rape-prevention) programs on college campuses (and in the community) were developed by women and for women and included self-defense, safety, and awareness workshops, with the primary goals of protection and education (Cummings, 1992). Not until the early 1980s was programming on college campuses directed toward the perpetrators of sexual violence, college men (Koss et al., 1987). In 1983, the Ohio State University Rape Education Prevention Project created a men's curriculum task group that developed prevention workshops for college men (Stevens & Gebhart, 1984). Currently, many colleges have sexual violence–prevention programs for men, including mixed-gender and male-only workshops. In this section I highlight the goals, strategies, and facilitation issues associated with sexual violence–prevention workshops for college men.

Male students look forward to the workshops much like the general population anticipates spending an evening at traffic school. They resent having to attend, anticipate a critical finger being pointed in their direction, and often enter the room with an air of unfriendliness and bravado. On the other hand, I have noticed underneath this veneer of aloofness a detectable curiosity. Engaging the audience is an essential component of the rape-prevention learning process. Understanding participants' resistance while expanding their curiosity helps increase the engagement process. Working with male-only groups is often quite challenging. Facilitators need to be prepared for a unique type of intimidation that may take the form of loud side conversations, off-the-wall questions followed by loud laughter from other participants, insider jokes, and uncomfortable silences accompanied by nonexpressive staring. Although there are plenty of unique challenges to offering rape-prevention programs to all-male groups, I have found a variety of facilitation tools and approaches that are useful in creating a safe learning environment that reduces resistance and increases positive engagement. These tools and approaches include the following:

• *Self-disclose.* Keeping in mind appropriate selectivity and timing, facilitators can share their own personal experiences, which in turn will help set the expectation for risk taking and lessen the us-versus-them mentality.

• *Reward honesty.* Participants will be more verbal if they feel respected and heard. When they feel rewarded for taking the risk to share their thoughts and feelings, even if they happen to be "politically incorrect," they become engaged in the workshop and do not shut down.

• *Get their attention.* Facilitators can provide statistics or ask provoking rhetorical questions to get students' attention, such as "How many of you would like to know with 99 percent certainty that you will never be accused or convicted of date or acquaintance rape?" Almost all the participants raise their hands. With the full attention of the students, the facilitators let the students know that simple principles and practices of gaining full consent will be discussed later on in the workshop.

• *Be firm, yet at times roll with the chaos.* Male groups can be quite loud, and participants may feed off of one another and create a chaotic learning environment. The participants need to know that facilitators have a bottom line and will expect participants to treat facilitators with the respect they show their coaches or other authority figures. On the other hand, it is important for facilitators to allow room for this chaos to exist and perhaps join in at appropriate times.

• *Respectfully challenge.* Participants will present opinions and beliefs that need to be challenged. Doing so is part of the educational process. It is essential for facilitators to find ways to challenge the participants in a manner that will lead to continued dialogue. One such way is to become curious rather than critical as to how participants developed certain opinions or beliefs.

WORKSHOP AGENDA

I have designed and used a variety of tools and exercises to promote increased empathy, understanding of full consent, and courage to break the codes of silence.

Increasing Empathy

Empathy is the ability to take into consideration and respond accordingly to the feelings of another person. Empathy allows one to measure the impact and consequences that a certain behavior will have on another human being. Men who engage in sexual violating behaviors have been shown to have limited empathy skills (Stevens, 1993). Increasing empathy skills is understandably a key component of rape prevention. Most men never give much thought to the fact that women are often consumed by fear of rape. Additionally, most men are unaware that woman feel neither flattered nor safe when whistled at, stared up and down, or propositioned. In fact, many men are socialized to view these behaviors as essential to the mating ritual. Furthermore, men are systematically taught to hide, avoid, and deny their own feelings of pain, hurt, and embarrassment. When boys are told not to cry, they are also being denied the opportunity to learn how to empathize and feel for the other. I have designed and used a variety of tools and exercises to help motivate men to improve their empathy skills.

Imagining Twenty-Four Hours Without Rape. The men are asked to imagine what their lives would be like if they knew there was no such thing as rape (Stevens, 1987). Facilitators then ask the men to imagine how women would feel and act differently if they knew there was no such thing as rape.

Being Bullied. The facilitators ask the men to remember an experience when they were threatened or picked on by someone who was larger, was stronger, or had more perceived power than them. The men are asked to describe how they felt during and after the attack.

Relating Rape to a Sister or Girlfriend. The participants are encouraged to discuss the variety of ways they try to "pick up" or "hit on" women. Facilitators then ask participants to imagine other guys using the same behaviors toward their sisters or girlfriends. Feelings and reactions are discussed, along with the awareness that the women they are "hitting on" also have a brother or boyfriend (perhaps sitting in the room).

Gaining Full Consent

Rape or sexual assault cannot happen if there is full and mutual consent. How to gain full consent is both a complicated concept and a difficult task. I attempt to teach the concept of the "consent table," whereby certain variables need to be out on this table before one can really know if there is full consent. These variables include permission, sobriety, truthful intentions, and any other information that would influence one's decision to become sexual. What men are asked to do to gain full consent is antithetical to the male experience and brings up strong fears of rejection and embarrassment. Men are taught to believe that they must figure out when a women is ready to be sexual; they believe that asking permission or clarifying the ambiguity of the situation is unromantic and may lead to rejection. Facilitators can offer for discussion and clarification a metaphor and scenarios to enhance the participants' understanding of full consent.

Traffic-Light Metaphor. Consent for sex is discussed in the context of how participants respond to a red, green, or yellow traffic light. They share a clarity of response to the red or green light. Yet approaching a yellow light is confusing and they typically speed up rather than slow down. Discussion follows about how sexual interactions are often confusing and there are a myriad of yellow lights that need to be understood and clarified before full consent can be obtained. Participants are encouraged to identify and brainstorm ways that one can respond to yellow-light situations that are respectful and ensure that sex is consensual.

Is This Full Consent? The following scenarios are used to help the audience more fully understand the concept and behaviors associated with full consent.

Scenario one. You are exclusively dating someone who likes you considerably more than you like her. In fact, you are thinking about dating others and have no intention of marrying this person. You have been sexual with each other, without having intercourse. Your girlfriend has told you on numerous occasions that she is a virgin and having sexual intercourse is something very sacred and special. On a special anniversary night, one thing leads to another, and you decide to have sexual intercourse. She finds out a few days later that you are thinking about dating others and have in fact asked someone else out. How does she feel? Was there full consent? Was she raped?

Scenario two. You meet someone at a party; both of you are sober and you decide to become sexually involved. You go back to her apartment and have an enjoyable evening of foreplay, oral sex, and eventually intercourse. Three days later you are sharing some of the highlights of the evening with your friend, when he tells you that the person you had sex with has tested positive for the human immunodeficiency virus (HIV). How do you feel? Was there full consent? Were you raped?

The discussion of these two scenarios brings to light the fact that one must put everything on the consent table to gain full consent. In the first scenario, the man kept secret his intentions to date others. In the second scenario, the woman kept secret her HIV status. The true litmus test for achieving full consent is to ask the following question: Would we be involved in this sexual behavior if all the information was out on the table? Although it is doubtful that either of the individuals in the scenarios could be legally convicted of rape, their partners may certainly feel they have been betrayed, degraded, and raped.

Speaking Out

I have found that many men are disgusted about the ways they see other men objectify and degrade women. Yet when confronted with this reality, they often say nothing or give a courtesy sign of approval. I believe that the root of this silence is that men are afraid of other men. Almost all male groups are reluctant to break the silence in fear of being humiliated, ostracized, or beaten up. One way I confront this issue in the workshops is to explore the concept of positive male bonding. For instance, the participants are asked what is likely to happen at a party if two or three of their friends take a very drunk woman into a room to have sex with her when she is clearly not in a condition to give full consent. Is it not part of the loyalty to their friends and to themselves to bravely step in and stop something like this from happening? In the workshops, I discuss openly why it is so difficult to break this code of silence. As a result of these discussions, it is hoped that a gentle shift may occur in terms of reducing the culture of silence.

IMPLICATIONS AND FUTURE DIRECTIONS

Sexual violence has become a larger public issue in recent years. The attention and subsequent dialogues created in reaction to the Tyson, Kennedy, and

Thomas-Hill trials have been significant if not profound. Now more than ever men are thinking they will be held accountable for their sexual violating behaviors, and this is a gigantic step forward. The grassroots efforts of feminist communities in the 1960s and 1970s, along with the college campus date and acquaintance rape research and the media splash of the 1980s are paying off.

Finding ways to help educate and empower men to change their attitudes and behaviors that promote or perpetuate our "rape culture" (Brownmiller, 1977) is essential. In many ways most of the work with men has only just begun. We must hold men accountable for their behaviors by being both firm and affirming. Promoting change must incorporate compassion and understanding of male socialization along with sensitivity to the destructiveness and power differential of male sexism.

Campus communities must find creative ways to reach college men and provide all-male forums of "alternative locker rooms" that promote dialogue. These alternative locker rooms can help break down the isolation created by homophobia, competition, and hypermasculinity training (Harris & Gertner, 1992; Stevens, 1992). Continuing programs are needed to encourage dialogue between women and men in which directness and honesty are valued more than political correctness. Berkowitz (1992) has proposed a model that helps clarify the complex intra- and interpersonal interactions of men and women that promote sexual violence.

In this chapter I have provided ideas and guidelines for helping college men better understand and become more able to change their sexual violating attitudes and behaviors. Research is needed to more clearly understand the effectiveness of interventions directed toward promoting such changes (Heppner, Neville, Smith, Kivlighan, & Gershuny, 1999). In other words, we need to determine how to evaluate whether sexual violence prevention programs are working. Attitudinal changes that are theoretically linked to sexual violating behaviors can be measured over time, but how do we know such attitudinal changes translate into behavioral changes? Measuring such changes is a difficult endeavor and should include not only self-reports but also observations from others.

References

Beneke, T. (1982). *Men on rape*. New York: St. Martin's Press.

Berkowitz, A. (1992). College men as perpetrators of acquaintance rape and sexual assault: A review of recent research. *Journal of American College Health, 40*, 175–181.

Boeringer, S. (1996). Influences of fraternity membership, athletics, and male living arrangements on sexual aggression. *Violence Against Women, 2*, 134–147.

Brownmiller, S. (1977). *Against our will*. New York: Simon & Schuster.

Burt, M. (1991). Rape myths and acquaintance rape. In A. Parrot & L. Bechofer (Eds.), *Acquaintance rape: The hidden crime* (pp. 26–40). New York: Wiley.

Connell, R. W. (1995). *Masculinities.* Berkeley: University of California Press.

Cummings, N. (1992). Self-defense training for college women. *Journal of American College Health, 40,* 183–188.

Fracher, J., & Kimmel, M. (1987). Hard issues and soft spot: Counseling men about sexuality. In M. Scher, M. Stevens, G. Good, & G. Eichenfield (Eds.), *Handbook of counseling and psychotherapy with men* (pp. 83–96). Newbury Park, CA: Sage.

Harris, J., & Gertner, D. (1992). *Exploring masculinity: Experiential exercises to help students explore men's issues.* Fort Collins: Colorado State University, Residential Life.

Heppner, M., Neville, N., Smith, K., Kivlighan, D., & Gershuny, B. (1999). Examining immediate and long-term efficacy of rape prevention programming with racially diverse college men. *Journal of Counseling Psychology, 46,* 16–26.

Koss, M., & Dinero, T. (1989). Predictors of sexual aggression among a national sample of male college students. In R. Prentky & V. Quinsley (Eds.), *Human sexual aggression: Current perspectives. Annals of the New York Academy of Science, 528,* 133–146.

Koss, M., Gidycz, C., & Wisniewski, N. (1987). The scope of rape: Incidence and prevalence of sexual aggression and victimization in a national sample of higher education students. *Journal of Counseling and Clinical Psychology, 55,* 162–170.

Malamuth, N. (1986). Predictors of naturalistic sexual aggression. *Journal of Personality and Social Psychology, 50,* 953–962.

Martin, P., & Hummer, R. (1989). Fraternities and rape on campus. *Gender and Society, 3,* 457–473.

Messner, M., & Stevens, M. (forthcoming). Scoring without consent: Confronting male athletes' violence against women. In M. Gatz, S. Rokeach, & M. Messner (Eds.), *A sporting chance: Youth and sport in urban settings.* Albany: SUNY Press.

Muehlenhard, C., & Linton, C. (1987). Date rape and sexual aggression in dating situations: Incidence and risk factors. *Journal of Counseling Psychology, 34,* 186–196.

O'Neil, J. (1981). Male sex role conflicts, sexism, and masculinity: Psychological implications for men, women, and the counseling psychologist. *Counseling Psychologist, 9,* 61–80.

O'Sullivan, C. (1991). Acquaintance gang rape on campus. In A. Parrot & L. Bechhofer (Eds.), *Acquaintance rape: The hidden crime.* New York: Wiley.

Rapaport, K., & Burkhart, B. (1984). Personality and attitudinal characteristics of sexually coercive college males. *Journal of Abnormal Psychology, 93,* 216–221.

Richardson, D., & Hammock, G. (1991). Alcohol and acquaintance rape. In A. Parrot & L. Bechhofer (Eds.), *Acquaintance rape: The hidden crime* (pp. 83–95). New York: Wiley.

Scher, M., & Stevens, M. (1987). Men and violence. *Journal of College Development, 65,* 351–356.

Stevens, M. (1987). 24 hours without a rape. In *C.A.R.E. manual.* Los Angeles: University of Southern California, Office of Women's Advocacy.

Stevens, M. (1992, August). *Introducing college men to men's issues.* Symposium presentation at the 100th annual convention of the American Psychological Association, Washington, DC.

Stevens, M. (1993). College men and sexual violation: Counseling process and programming considerations. In L. Whitaker & J. Pollard (Eds.), *Campus violence: Kinds, causes, and cures* (pp. 239–258). Binghamton, NY: Haworth Press.

Stevens, M., & Gebhart, R. (1984). *Rape education for men curriculum guide.* Columbus: Ohio State University, Rape Education and Prevention Program.

CHAPTER FIFTEEN

Male Gender Role Issues in the Treatment of Sexual Dysfunction

Cathryn G. Pridal

Sexual functioning is an integral part of the male concept of self. In Western culture, part of being male is being sexually active, and male socialization stresses both sexual conquests and virility. As a result, male sexual dysfunction is often experienced as a major threat to core esteem rather than as just another problem to be solved. Men who experience sexual dysfunction may become withdrawn from their partners or may even become depressed as they attempt to cope with this failure to live up to the expectations of male sexual socialization. Because men often attempt to cope with negative feelings by becoming defensive and aggressive, their intimate relationships also may be affected by an increased level of hostility. The partners of men who are experiencing sexual dysfunction often report that these men are unwilling to discuss the problem and may become angry, even blaming their partners for the dysfunction. This reaction exacerbates the problem and leads partners to emotionally and physically withdraw from the relationship.

Occasionally partners are contributing to the dysfunction. For example, a man with erectile difficulties whose partner refuses to touch his penis may not be receiving the physical stimulation he needs to get an erection. Similarly, a man whose partner wants to have an orgasm only during intercourse will typically feel more pressure to have an erection than one whose partner is comfortable enjoying orgasms from other types of sexual activity as well.

More commonly, the sexual partners are frustrated and would gladly engage in sexual activities other than intercourse, but the men refuse to even discuss the situation. Generally, these men are quite reluctant to consider therapy and have problems discussing their sexual functioning when there (Good & Wood, 1995). In fact, many men prefer a medical diagnosis and medical solution to their dysfunction. Before the advent of Viagra, urologists reported that their patients with erectile problems would not accept a referral for sex therapy but would be willing to have penile prosthesis implant surgery (that is, these men preferred having their penises cut open and implants inserted to create more rigid penises—a painful process and one that risks infection and the like) (Stewart & Gerson, 1976). Male socialization led them to prefer a physical solution because it implied a disease process was the cause of the dysfunction. In this way men with sexual dysfunctions did not feel responsible for the dysfunction or that they had failed to live up to the male script. Sex therapy was unappealing to these men because it implied that they themselves were at fault. Men who do present for sex therapy, then, are dealing with many issues in addition to the sexual dysfunction. These individual issues often include a feeling of failure, or lack of competence; shame; a desire to measure up to some implicit external standard; a reluctance to trust another individual with personal details; and a global aversion to asking for help. Additionally, couples issues such as lack of emotional intimacy, pent-up resentment, and blaming each other for the problem commonly are also present.

The symptoms of each sexual dysfunction interact with male gender issues to create unique problems for the therapist and client. In each case, the gender role expectations interfere with entering therapy and with the therapy process, but the interference varies for the different dysfunctions. For example, men with low sexual desire are coping with violating different gender "rules" than men with premature ejaculation, erectile dysfunction, or orgasmic disorders. Thus, the therapist must carefully assess each situation to determine which social expectations are interacting with which symptoms to maintain or exacerbate the dysfunction.

INTERACTION BETWEEN THE MASCULINE SEX ROLE AND SEXUAL DYSFUNCTION

Much has been written about the male sexual script (see, for example, Brooks, 1995; Gross, 1978; Levant & Brooks, 1997; Michael, Gagnon, Lauman, & Kolata, 1994; Zilbergeld, 1999). Based on a review of the literature, J. A. Doyle (1989) identified five themes of masculinity that pervade the male role. Although only one of these themes is directly associated with male sexual functioning, all five are related to expectations of how men will behave sexually and with regard to entering and participating in therapy. One theme, *do not be female,* implies that men should not be gentle, receptive, or passive because those are elements of the feminine role. A man who appears to be sensitive or vulnerable is likely to be ridiculed as a wimp or sissy. This prohibition carries over into sexual functioning such that men are often awkward with the tenderness and gentle touching that many women enjoy. They also find themselves reluctant to receive pleasure without performing (earning it) in some way and thus put pressure on themselves to always take an active role in sexual encounters.

A second theme, *be successful,* also has implications for sexual functioning. In the sexual realm, "success" places performance pressure on men and includes a number of elements. One element of success relates to physical functioning. A successful man can achieve an impressive erection on demand. This erection can then be fully maintained until the man decides that he wishes to enjoy the release of orgasm. Another element of successful sexual functioning relates to interaction with the partner. It is no longer enough that the man reach orgasm; first he must give pleasure to his partner and bring her to multiple orgasms. Therefore, he must not ejaculate too quickly or need extra stimulation from his partner. To be a skilled, successful lover he must be able to function autonomously while delivering overwhelming pleasure to his partner.

A third theme, *be aggressive,* implies that a man should initiate sex and persist in this request even in the face of resistance by the partner. Fortunately, public awareness of date rape has reduced the pressure on men to sexually force themselves on unwilling partners, but this element of the male role still exists and leads to confusion for many individuals. Because Western culture condones male aggression in many arenas, male sexual "aggression" may not be limited to initiating sexual activity. This element of masculinity also interacts with the conservative social proscription against female sexuality, setting up an impossible situation for both partners. Because women are not supposed to be openly sexual, being "swept away" by desire is a way to act on sexual impulses while still adhering to the female role. Who, then, is to do the "sweeping"? The man, of course. Herein lies the problem. Many of today's men are sensitive to the issue of date rape, yet they also know the social expectations regarding female sexual behavior. Men must then negotiate a tricky path between being too aggressive and not being persuasive enough to satisfy both their own gender expectations and those of their partner. Clearly social mores for both genders need to change to ultimately solve this problem. In other words men need to be able to be open about their sexual needs while respecting their partners' desires, and women also need to feel comfortable expressing their sexuality and being assertive about their desires at any particular time.

The fourth theme of masculinity Doyle described is *be sexual.* This theme means that to be masculine sex must be a central part of the definition of self. Men are expected to be interested in sex all the time. Having sex is supposed to be the number-one priority, and men should be ready to have sex anywhere, anytime. If sex is a possibility, no "real man" should do anything other than strip off his clothes and jump into bed. Additionally, men are supposed to have multiple partners. The stereotype of the experienced man leading the virgin woman to heights of passion is still operative in today's society. Men are supposed to reluctantly accept monogamy after marriage but should have lots of partners before marriage. Men who have affairs after marriage are subject to less social sanction than women who have affairs. The implication of this theme is that men are sex machines, able and eager to perform at any and all times with as many different partners as possible.

Doyle's fifth theme, *be self-reliant,* not only relates to sexual interactions but also has implications for therapy. Before sex, men should not need physical stimulation to get aroused. The mere thought of having sex should be enough to produce an erection. During sex, men should enjoy anything their partners do and should not need to ask for specific types of stimulation or certain activities to maintain an erection or to reach orgasm. Also, they should intuitively know what their partners need. They should not have to ask about intensity or type of stimulation; they should be able to cause great pleasure and multiple orgasms simply because they are male and know how to do it. If there is a problem, men should solve it themselves. They should not talk to their partners about any difficulty and should certainly not bring a "stranger" (therapist) into the situation. Asking for help is weak and dependent and violates the rules of this theme.

SEXUAL MYTHS THAT RESTRICT MEN'S SEXUAL FUNCTIONING

In addition to these general themes regarding masculinity, social expectations also relate specifically to male sexual functioning. Zilbergeld (1999) suggests that ten sexual myths relate to male sexual functioning. Most men do not subscribe to all of the myths Zilbergeld described, but most believe some of them. One challenge for therapists is to identify which myth or myths are contributing to the sexual dysfunction. Considerable probing is often required to uncover beliefs in these areas. Many men are vaguely aware that these beliefs are irrational, but they secretly (and often without full awareness) have these expectations for themselves anyway. In therapy, it is often effective to use Zilbergeld's list of myths as a framework to focus therapeutic questioning. This format encourages discussion of the major areas of the male sexual script and can awaken the male client to the unrealistic standards he holds for himself.

Myth one: We are liberated folks who are very comfortable with sex. In reality, most people are not comfortable with sex at all. We are reluctant to endorse sex education in our schools, and most parents are awkward and uncomfortable with discussing sex with their children. As a result, young people learn about sex from their peers, and much of what they learn is inaccurate and even harmful. What they do not learn also can be harmful; for example, one young man had permanent damage to his penis during a heavy petting session with his girlfriend. He was wearing tight jeans, and his penis became erect but was held in a bent-down position by the jeans while he was lying on his back. His girlfriend straddled him and was rubbing and bumping her pubic area against his penis. As they became more aroused their activity became more vigorous until a loud pop and intense pain signified damage to the one of the corporal bodies in his penis. This medical problem could have been avoided with the provision of adequate, basic, accurate information about male sexual arousal mechanisms in the penis.

Myth two: A real man is not into sissy stuff like feelings and communicating. This myth relates to the *be self-reliant* theme. Both require men to be stoic and to avoid talking about their feelings. As a result, many men use sex to communicate and as an attempt to get emotionally close to their partners. The idea of talking about their feelings, hopes, dreams, and desires is frightening to many men. Instead, they blindly engage in sex, hoping to connect and feel fulfilled in the relationship. However, because this connection is physically based, it is shallow, imprecise, tenuous, and ultimately unsatisfying. This resultant dissatisfaction frequently leads to attempts for real intimacy with other partners using the same misdirected strategy. Additionally, a lack of communication before and during sex can be very problematic. Because there are many sexually transmitted diseases, some discussion of past sexual behavior is prudent prior to engaging in sexual contact. Also, a conversation about contraception and preventing the transmission of disease should occur before sex. Dissatisfaction with the sexual encounter itself can be prevented or handled by talking about preferred activities and level of stimulation throughout the sexual contact. In all of these situations, the prohibition against men discussing feelings interferes with optimal and safe sexual functioning.

Myth three: All touching is sexual or should lead to sex. This myth leads to a number of problems and miscommunications in relationships and also creates specific difficulties for men with low desire. If men believe that touching leads to sex, then they will avoid touching their partners at all so that they can avoid facing their lack of desire for sex. However, a lack of physical affection can be damaging to even the strongest relationship and can completely destroy it over time. For men with erectile difficulties, this myth can be part of the anxiety spiral associated with the erectile dysfunction. In this case, the men perceive affection from their partners as pressure to achieve erection. They then are upset if an erection does not immediately result, criticize themselves as failures, and are even less likely to have erections in the future. Relationship problems can also occur with erectile dysfunction. Men with erectile difficulties often pull away and reject their partners' affectionate gestures, leaving their partners confused and hurt.

Myth four: A man is always interested in and always ready for sex. This myth is clearly related to the theme of *be sexual.* Both themes support the expectation that men are sex machines. Machines do not get tired or distracted. Machines are always able to function, regardless of the situation. Human males, on the other hand, do get tired. They also on occasion drink too much alcohol. Human males also find themselves distracted by thoughts of job pressures, family issues, and personal problems. Human males are not attracted to every potential sexual partner and may even want an emotional connection before engaging in sexual relations. This myth does not allow for any of these human elements, and men may feel they are less than fully masculine if they do not have sex whenever the opportunity is presented. Ironically, this myth can actually cause sexual dysfunction. For example, Bill had difficulty getting an erection because he was tired and distracted from a demanding day at work. He then began to worry that he would not get an erection the next time he tried to have sex. This worrying detracted from his arousal during his next sexual encounter, and he again failed to achieve an erection. Unfortunately, once this pattern has begun, it is difficult to break out of the anxiety spiral, in part because of the very myth that started the process. Men with sexual dysfunctions have an additional problem related to this myth. Because the dysfunction interferes with their ability to behave according to this myth, they perceive themselves as continual failures in the masculine arena. As a result, they are often reluctant to admit having a dysfunction, much less seek therapy for it.

Myth five: A real man performs in sex. Sex is seen as an opportunity to prove masculinity by performing well (Zilbergeld, 1999). The standards for performance are not clearly laid out; men have to infer what is expected by observing descriptions of sexual activity in magazines, books, movies, and videos. One problem with this method relates back to cultural discomfort with sex. Men who read and watch graphic material are suspected of being perverts. Therefore, information must be obtained in minute bits and pieces and strung together from often unrealistic depictions of sexual behavior. These inferences often lead to expectations about sexual performance that are impossible to fulfill. For example, few movies show foreplay that includes direct touching of the penis (too graphic for an R rating) or that is as lengthy as most people enjoy (it would lose viewers' attention). However, as men age they need more direct penile stimulation to achieve a full erection. This normal part of the aging process is definitely not included in this performance-oriented myth and is not widely known in U.S. culture.

This myth also compounds the problem for men with sexual dysfunction. By definition, sexual dysfunction means that men cannot perform sex the way that they are "supposed" to. This myth then adds a layer of pressure to an already difficult situation and may interfere with therapeutic progress by causing men to expect rapid change if they work diligently enough. In other words, men with premature ejaculation or erectile difficulties perform the therapy in much the same way they attempt to perform sex. They expect that if they work hard enough, they will quickly overcome "the problem." This performance approach to therapy produces yet another impediment to men connecting with their own feelings and desires instead of aiding therapeutic progress. This myth amplifies the self-deprecation of not being adequately masculine for men with low desire. Instead of leading them to work more diligently to solve the problem, it may lead them to avoid the topic entirely (or anything vaguely associated with it) because they know they do not measure up.

Myth six: Sex is centered on a hard penis and what is done with it. For men with erectile difficulties, this myth is devastating. They are clearly inadequate if they think that sex requires a hard penis and they do not have one. As a result, many men with erection problems avoid any type of sexual activity. Unfortunately, this myth is not only believed by men but also by many women. For example, one couple presented for therapy at the wife's request, to deal with her husband's lack of erection. When a variety of sexual activities other than intercourse were recommended, she responded, "If he can't give me the real thing, I don't want him getting me all hot and bothered." Obviously, a shared belief in this myth was interfering with sexual enjoyment for both partners.

Myth seven: If your penis is not up to snuff, we have a pill that will take care of everything. This myth stems from the idea that real men do not have sex problems, but if they do there is a medical solution for the problem. If one follows the social prescription for good sex, then obviously no problems should result. This notion ignores contradictions among myths, aging changes, medication effects, and the results of disease processes. Gender socialization is full of contradictions, and not just in the area of sexual functioning. Our ageist society does not consider sex appropriate for people over age forty-five or for persons who are ill. Even the medical profession supports this idea. For example, many physicians do not talk with their patients about the potential effects of prostate surgery on erection and ejaculation (L. Schover, personal communication, 1991). The implication is that the individual is lucky to be alive so he should not be concerned about sexual functioning. In reality, this omission by physicians is often the result of their own discomfort with the topic of sex (see myth one), but their patients get the message that they are no longer expected to be sexually functional.

This myth suggests that psychotherapy is not needed to cope with sexual dysfunctions and thus creates an impediment to both entering and fully participating in therapy. If real men do not have sex problems and it is important to be a "real man," then admitting a dysfunction means admitting one is not a real man. If an individual man has spent much of his life struggling to meet the social expectations for masculinity, this sort of admission strikes at the very heart of his identity. If he acknowledges a sexual dysfunction, then he has to face up to all of the other ways in which he falls short of the male ideal. He decides it is much better to ignore the problem or blame it on something or someone else. Alternatively, if the man admits to having a problem, he will look for a medical solution to the difficulty (for example, just "pop a pill"). He will resist entering therapy, and once in therapy (perhaps initiated by his partner) such a man will frequently be defensive and uncooperative. Despite being off-putting, the therapist must sense the man's distress and realize that these behaviors are self-protective rather than purposefully aimed at thwarting therapy. Of course, because these defenses are designed to enable men to avoid thinking about their feelings ("real men don't cry" and so forth), they will interfere with the progress of therapy unless these gender role expectations are also addressed.

Myth eight: Sex equals intercourse. This myth is an extension of myth six in that sex requires not only a rigid penis but also intercourse and orgasm. Interestingly, about one-third of women report not having orgasms during intercourse (Hite, 1976). However, men persist in thinking that they must be able to engage in intercourse for their sexual performance to be adequate. Men with either erectile dysfunction or premature ejaculation do not measure up by this standard. Men who have erectile difficulties do not have the required equipment (a rigid penis) to allow intercourse to occur, and men with premature ejaculation do not last long enough for the intercourse to "count." In both cases, the pressure to have intercourse to have sex means that performance anxiety is likely to interfere with enjoyment of sexual activity. This expectation also interferes with the therapy process because men who subscribe to this myth expect sustained intercourse to be the goal of therapy. Sustained intercourse is a reasonable goal for men with premature ejaculation but only after they have completed a series of steps that does not include intercourse at all. For men whose erection problems are due to physical complications, returning to having intercourse with the erections that they had when they were eighteen is not a reasonable therapy goal.

Myth nine: Men should be able to make the earth move for their partners or at the very least knock their socks off. Because women are not supposed to be openly sexual, one measure of male sexual prowess is men's ability to bring their partners to powerful orgasms. "Real men" will instinctively know all the right things to do to achieve this goal. This myth ignores the fact that many women do not have multiple orgasms or even one orgasm during intercourse. If men believe in this myth, they will try to delay their orgasms to extend intercourse, expecting that their partners will ultimately have orgasms because of their "magic penises." Other kinds of sexual activity may be permitted with this myth, because the goal is for the great lovers' partners to experience amazing pleasure.

Myth ten: Good sex is spontaneous, with no planning and no talking. Wild, passionate sex requires spontaneous abandon to desire rather than thoughtful consideration of a comfortable time and place and an awareness of health and birth control protection, according to this myth. Sexual performance requires constant readiness by the penis but does not allow for preparations such as discussing the idea with the potential sex partner. Both persons simply get turned on and want sex, seemingly on the spur of the moment. Carrying a condom implies that one has been planning to have sex, which is seen as insulting or sleazy, depending on the gender of the person carrying the condom. If a man brings a condom along, his date may be insulted that he thinks she is "easy" rather than flattered by his hopeful concern for both their well-being. If a woman carries a condom, she is viewed as promiscuous rather than as prudently comfortable with her own sexuality.

A study by Levant et al. (1992) suggests that for some men some of these myths are less compelling than they were in the past. This study asked undergraduate men at a large, northeastern university whether they agreed or disagreed with a series of statements. Several of these statements related to Zilbergeld's (1999) myths. Interestingly, the undergraduate men disagreed with statements that were similar to myths three, four, and ten: *For men, touching is simply the first step toward sex; A man should always be ready for sex;* and *For a man, sex should be a spontaneous, rather than preplanned, activity.* However, they endorsed a statement similar to myths five and nine—*It is important for a man to be good in bed*—and disagreed with a statement that contradicts myth six—*A man does not need to have an erection in order to enjoy sex.* In other words, these young men believed that an erection was important to the enjoyment of sexual activity.

Although the results of this study are encouraging, they should be viewed with caution. The participants in the study were not representative of the male population as a whole. Additionally, the study did not explore the actual beliefs of these men but only measured their responses to a paper-and-pencil questionnaire. With some probing, therapists often discover their clients initially give the "correct" response but actually hold far different standards for themselves. Finally, the participants in the study still endorsed some of the most damaging myths (regarding sexual dysfunction)—it is important for a man to be good in bed, and a man needs an erection to enjoy sex.

IMPLICATIONS FOR SEX THERAPY WITH MALE CLIENTS

The masculine role has implications for many aspects of sex therapy with men. It especially affects the assessment and psychoeducation aspects of therapy.

Assessment

Detailed assessment of clients' presenting complaints and their underlying beliefs is important for successful sex therapy (LoPiccolo, 1999). A cursory discussion of symptoms can result in treatment directed at the wrong sexual activity. Omitting exploration of the myths and stereotypic beliefs held can result in resistance to change and even dropping out of therapy. Clinicians approaching a sexual assessment interview may be anxious about raising this topic. Sex is usually a highly emotional, private subject, and clinicians may find themselves feeling uncomfortable in response to clients' embarrassment, hesitancy, and reticence in discussing sexual behavior.

As an introduction to the assessment of sexual dysfunction and the myths and beliefs a client holds, the therapist should acknowledge that sex is a sensitive and difficult area to discuss. The therapist should go on to state that the intent is to make the process as easy for the client as possible and to request that the client tell the therapist if there is anything the therapist could do to make the client more comfortable. The therapist might also mention that he or she is experienced in this area and reassure the client that he will not shock or embarrass the therapist by anything he describes. In many cases, a male client with sexual dysfunction presents for therapy at his partner's insistence, and so the partner's reticence about this topic should be addressed as well.

Given the messages about masculine gender roles, male clients with sexual dysfunctions usually do not enter therapy as their initial reaction to the problem. As mentioned, many present for therapy because their wives insist that the couple enter therapy. This insistence can even take the form of threats of divorce, and of course the fear of divorce can cause additional anxiety that will hinder therapeutic progress. Other men enter therapy despite the concerns of their partners, who may have their own issues about sex such as a reluctance to discuss sex with a stranger or relief that the sexual aspect of their relationship has ceased. For example, some women who were raised in conservative families of origin have "done their duty" while their husbands were sexually functioning but are relieved when erectile dysfunction results in a cessation of sexual intercourse. Clearly, entering therapy with an unwilling or uncooperative partner also hinders progress in treating the sexual dysfunction.

Other clients enter therapy on the referral of a physician, often a urologist. These men have sought medical treatment for their problem, and the physician believes psychological issues are involved. For example, most erectile dysfunction "cases involve major psychologic etiology (regardless of degree of organic impairment present)" (LoPiccolo, 1999, p. 188), and a responsible physician will make a referral for psychotherapy. Unfortunately, in today's managed care climate, the referral may not be made until after some significant degree of failure to "cure" the problem using medical treatments has occurred. In erectile dysfunction cases, for example, a prescription for Viagra may be written, and then if patients are still dissatisfied, the physician will refer them for psychotherapy.

Another important aspect of assessment is clients' objectives for therapy. Most of the time, male clients enter sex therapy with a very clear goal to "make it work right." This goal is frequently tied to myths about sexual functioning and therefore is often unrealistic. For example, working "right" may be defined as "hard as steel and goes all night" for men with erection problems (Zilbergeld, 1999). If the therapist accepts clients' unrealistic goals or goals based on the male sexual script, therapy is unlikely to succeed. Sometimes the most important part of sex therapy is educating clients about the way sex actually works. This education should include both the physiology and psychology of sexual functioning. Couples need to know the physical mechanisms involved in obtaining an erection and ejaculating and understand the limitations imposed by these mechanisms. Information about how aging affects these mechanisms and about the effects of medication (see Crenshaw & Goldberg, 1996) and disease (see Kresin, 1993; Wise, 1987) is also helpful. In addition, therapy should involve education about the psychological aspects of sexual functioning and the ways that stress, depression, anger, fear, and the like can affect sexual desire and performance. During the course of this education, the therapist can begin to counteract some of the myths and male sexual script beliefs held by the clients. After education about "normal" functioning based on physical and psychological knowledge, therapists and clients can set realistic goals for therapy.

Psychoeducation

The education phase of therapy can serve a function in addition to counteracting sex role stereotypes and setting realistic goals. This phase can also lower clients' resistance to change in therapy by removing some of the clients' investment in following the male sexual script. Additional techniques to deal with resistance may be needed, however. According to LoPiccolo (1999) client "resistance" can be caused by the therapist's conceptual error in failing to adequately assess all the factors involved in the dysfunction. If clients "resist," the therapist must more deeply assess the meaning of the dysfunction for male clients or for couples. If he or she knows the male sex role script and the expectations that result, the therapist can explore the adaptive value of the dysfunction for clients. Once this value has been identified, the therapist and clients can determine other ways to meet those needs. If the "needs" appear to be the result of believing one or more of the male sex role myths, the therapist can challenge these beliefs. Bibliotherapy can help challenge these beliefs, and the therapist can suggest that the client read *The New Male Sexuality* (Zilbergeld, 1999) and *Men and Sex: New Psychological Perspectives* (Levant & Brooks, 1997). Sex therapy is often threatening to male clients, so the importance of acknowledging clients' need to maintain dignity and self-respect cannot be overstated. Resistance to thera-peutic techniques can be avoided if the therapist proceeds cautiously and con-tinually assesses clients' levels of comfort and the functional value of the dysfunctions. This value may change as therapy progresses, so the assessment must be ongoing throughout therapy.

TREATING SPECIFIC SEXUAL DYSFUNCTIONS

As mentioned previously, gender role expectations interfere with both entering therapy and the process of therapy. Additionally, each dysfunction involves spe-cial issues that interact with the role expectations to produce unique challenges for therapists in developing treatment strategies and objectives.

Low Desire

In theory, the definition of low desire can be debated. However, in practice low desire is a misnomer—it is actually no desire for most clients. These men say, "If my wife didn't mention it, I don't know when I'd think about having sex" or "I realize my wife is upset and when I try to think about the cause, I realize that I've forgotten again and it has been two months since we made love." Men with low desire are challenging in therapy because this disorder involves behav-ing in a manner that is inconsistent with the Western cultural sexual script for men. This inconsistency may be the reason that there is a paucity of objective, empirical research in this area (Meggers & LoPiccolo, forthcoming). Case stud-ies and theories of etiology suggest that family-of-origin issues and issues in the current relationship are often involved in low desire (LoPiccolo & Friedman, 1985; Zilbergeld & Ellison, 1980). Some men have experienced erotic feelings in their family of origin and learned to turn off their feelings to avoid arousal in that situation. This avoidance of sexual thoughts and contact continues even after the individuals have left home. Others have witnessed a highly conflicted relationship between their parents and want to avoid such a situation in their own lives. As a result, they avoid intimacy, believing that distance is protection against conflict. Some men have been influenced by an extremely conservative upbringing in which sex was a taboo topic and physical affection was exceed-ingly rare. They learned to squelch their natural desire for affection in childhood and extended that repression to sexual feelings in adolescence and adulthood.

Current relationship issues also can play a role in low desire. Some men no longer love their partners, and so lack of desire is indicative of lack of love. Some are even having affairs outside the marriage and have high desire for these partners and appear to have low desire for their mate. Clearly, these issues must be explored instead of rushing to treat the low desire. Additional relationship issues may include power discrepancies, unresolved conflicts, and lack of connection to the partner. Any relationship issues must be identified and treated before therapy for the low desire can be successful. In some cases, resolving the relationship issues with couples therapy ameliorates the low desire. In others, once the relationship is back on track, sexual desire issues can become the focus of therapy and treatment can progress in this area.

Treatment of low desire itself should include focusing on feelings and cognitions about sex as well as on specific sexual behaviors (Pridal & LoPiccolo, 2000). In the first stage of therapy for low desire, *affectual awareness*, clients explore negative emotions that are associated with sexuality and sexual behaviors. Often, these emotions were learned in clients' families of origin. Negative emotions about being sexual can also arise from bad experiences in past relationships or from current relationship issues. Therefore, this stage of therapy can be conducted concurrently with the exploration of family-of-origin and relationship issues noted earlier. Perhaps because negative emotions about sexuality are in direct contradiction to the male sex role, it is often difficult for men to identify these emotions. Many male clients describe an indifference to sex—"I can take it or leave it, no big deal"—instead of acknowledging that they are afraid of sexual intimacy. In addition to fear, other negative emotions that men are likely to find blocking their sexual desire are revulsion, anger, and disgust. Skilled exploration is needed to reveal these emotions. Men are supposed to want sex, and therefore negative emotions associated with sex are not acceptable to individuals who are living by the male sex role script. If the therapist bluntly assumes negative emotions, clients are likely to protest and resist becoming aware of any negative emotions associated with sex. Instead, the therapist must guide clients to awareness of these emotions through nonthreatening questions about past and current experiences with sex. Sometimes imagery can be a useful technique. Clients are asked to recall their most recent sexual encounters as vividly as possible. If that is not possible, then clients are asked to imagine a potential partner initiating sex as vividly as possible. With the images in mind, clients are asked to describe their feelings. (Preparatory work on identifying and describing feelings may be needed for some male clients who enter therapy completely disconnected from their emotions—again following the male role.)

In the second stage, *insight and understanding*, the therapist attempts to help clients understand the causes of their problems. He or she explains that low drive involves multiple causality, in that there is usually a set of "initiating" causes and a set of "maintaining" causes. In addition to thinking of initiating and maintaining causes, it is also useful to conceptualize causation as individual, couple systemic, or medically based. After exploring past experiences as possible individual initiating causes, the therapist asks couples about other common individual factors, such as depression, aging concerns, masked sexual deviations, gender identity issues, fear of having children, life stress issues, fear of loss of control over sexual urges, unresolved childhood sexual abuse, fear of failure secondary to sexual dysfunction, and unresolved grief following the loss of a previous mate.

Similarly, couple systemic causes also should be explored in this stage of therapy. Common couple systemic causes of low sexual desire include inability to resolve marital conflict, lack of physical attraction to the partner, poor sexual skills in the partner, inability to fuse feelings of love with feelings of sexual desire (Freud's princess-prostitute syndrome), fear of closeness, vulnerability and trust concerns, personal space concerns, and differences in emotional expressiveness.

Stage three, *cognitive and systemic therapy,* follows established procedures used in other types of therapy. The individual issues can be conceptualized in a model similar to cognitive therapy for depression. For example, the therapist may ask clients to develop lists of the negative thoughts and beliefs that are mediating their negative emotions about sex and thus blocking their sexual drive. Then, they develop a matching list of coping statements that counter each of those negative items with a positive self-statement. Additionally, systemic therapy for the relationship problems that are suppressing sexual drive occurs during this stage. In cases in which the problem of low drive in one partner results from a clear power imbalance in the relationship, for example, the therapist is actually more able to help the couple than if there was not coexisting low drive and the couple was experiencing marital distress only. In such cases, the person with the power is often rather unmotivated to change. If sexually frustrated, however, this person may be willing to reconsider the structure of the relationship.

Finally, in stage four, *behavioral interventions,* the therapist explores with clients methods to increase affectionate behavior and undertakes initiation and refusal training. Couples are helped to identify and then begin to engage in a wide range of simple affectionate behaviors that they agree will not be ways to initiate any sexual activity. These activities are ones they both can enjoy, knowing that they are not to lead to greater sexual exchange. Most clients with low sex drive enjoy these sorts of affectionate behaviors and are happy to be affectionate with their spouses without worry that these behaviors will be misinterpreted as an invitation to have sex. After partners are consistently being more affectionate with each other, the focus of therapy then turns to the initiation of sexual activity. Most of these partners have a limited understanding of each other's feelings about requests for sex, and misunderstandings often occur. Role playing is used to learn about each partner's preferences and feelings. It first focuses on current interactions between the partners and then switches to preferred ways of initiating and refusing sex. Initially, any refusal sounds unacceptable to the partner with higher sex drive, because of the history of deprivation, so that partner is asked to assume that he or she is making love more often. Under these conditions, the therapist approaches the question of what would be an acceptable refusal. For most couples, a detailed, specific discussion of the reason one is "not in the mood" is unnecessary, but reassurance about loving the partner and having sexual feelings for the partner, statements about when lovemaking can be expected, and suggestions for what would lead to being "in the mood" typically make a refusal easier to accept.

Another major component of this stage of therapy is a set of procedures labeled drive induction. Sexual drive is somewhat different from other biological drives in that a clear set of bodily sensations is not associated with it. Rather, our sexual drive depends on external cues and stimuli. Yet even a more basic biological drive such as hunger sometimes requires stimulation by an external source before we become aware of our internal state of need. We are sometimes not aware that we are hungry until we smell or see delicious food (or look at a clock). The external cues are even more important with sex drive, and persons with low sexual desire are masters at avoiding awareness of sexually relevant cues. Drive induction, then, encourages clients with low sex drive to be more aware of the external cues that are continually presented in the environment. This awareness may take the form of a diary of sexual stimuli, note cards containing sexual fantasies, consciousness of advertisements that are arousing, and so forth. If there is any actual sexual dysfunction in terms of arousal or orgasm, the dysfunction would be dealt with at this point in therapy, after the preceding stages have been completed. Even for clients without a specific dysfunction, the therapist should routinely inquire about enjoyment experienced in lovemaking activities and consider trying to help couples to improve the quality of their lovemaking sessions as an aid to increasing sexual desire. After all, one cannot expect people to have much interest or desire for an unrewarding experience.

This four-phase treatment of low desire is quite successful, especially if the therapist can identify clients' maladaptive beliefs in the male script and alter them to more realistic notions about male sexual functioning (LoPiccolo & Friedman, 1988).

Erectile Dysfunction

Differential diagnosis has been the focus of most of the recent research on erectile dysfunction (Meggers & LoPiccolo, forthcoming). Differential diagnosis involves the determination of the mix of physiological and psychological problems that combine to cause erectile difficulties in a particular client. The typical physiological problems that contribute to erectile dysfunction are neurological diseases, hormonal abnormalities, and failure of blood flow to the penis. These physiological problems are involved in a considerable percentage of cases of erectile failure, with or without corresponding psychological origins (Tanagho, Lue, & McClure, 1988). It seems that part of the reason for this current research focus is the availability of medications such as sildenafil (Viagra) to treat "organic" erectile dysfunction. It may seem logical to simply refer all patients with erectile difficulty to a medical doctor without further therapeutic contact. However, although evaluation for organic impairment is an important part of the assessment aspect of therapy for erectile problems, the presence of such impairment does not automatically negate the need for psychotherapy (Meggers & LoPiccolo, forthcoming). Often, men with some organic impairment can still function well with the appropriate relationship conditions and adequate stimulation. A referral to a qualified urologist to determine the level and nature of physiological impairment can be followed with therapy to work on the psychological issues that are impeding the remaining erectile capacity.

The advent of sildenafil as a medical treatment for erectile dysfunction may make men with this problem even more likely to avoid entering therapy, opting instead for a visit to a medical doctor. However, this strategy is not recommended for a number of reasons. Given that taking sildenafil is not risk free—headaches, flushing, and dyspepsia are potential side effects, as is the risk of myocardial infarction for men with cardiac problems (Rosenberg, 1999)—men whose erection difficulties are not due to physical causes should not expose themselves to this drug. It may be difficult to determine the precise level, if any, of organic impairment; for example, in comparison studies 16 to 20 percent of men given a placebo reported improved erections and successful intercourse (Pallas, 2000). Additionally, sildenafil may not restore erections if the relationship is troubled to the extent that the partner is not perceived as sexually stimulating; even if erections are restored, relationship issues are not addressed by "popping a pill" and may be exacerbated by an abrupt return to sexual functioning (Rosenberg, 1999). Sildenafil is best viewed as an adjunct to psychotherapy and as such can be very useful. For example, Pallas (2000) found that 6 percent of clients benefited simply from having a prescription for sildenafil in that it reduced their performance anxiety and allowed their erectile capacity to function at its peak. Another 38 percent used sildenafil regularly to accomplish intercourse that was satisfying to both partners. Unfortunately, 20 percent developed psychological, sexual, or relationship problems after attempting to use sildenafil without psychotherapy. In some cases intercourse was still occurring, despite the new sexual problem (3 percent), but in general these new problems resulted in a lack of intercourse and dissatisfaction in the relationship. In light of these findings, psychotherapy is warranted for the majority of patients with erectile dysfunction.

LoPiccolo (1992) has identified some good prognostic indicators for therapeutic outcome in patients with erectile dysfunction. He suggests that if clear behavioral deficits or maladaptive thinking patterns can be identified, the prognosis is much better than when such problems are not clearly associated with the erectile difficulties. These positive prognostic indicators relate to elements in a couple's sexual relationship that can be identified as less than effective and that can be changed by providing information and support for rejection of the sexual script for either partner. Briefly, these positive prognostic indicators are as follows:

1. Lack of adequate sexual stimulation
2. Partner's sexual gratification currently depends on the mate obtaining an erection
3. Lack of knowledge about age-related changes in sexual functioning
4. Cognitive distortions regarding the male sex role stereotype, leading to unrealistic demands on the man for sexual performance
5. Individual dynamic, relationship system, unresolved family-of-origin, or operant reinforcement issues that make it functionally adaptive for the erectile failure to continue to occur; although long-term therapy in such cases is often indicated, the prognosis is good if such functional issues can be identified

Likewise, negative prognostic indicators, according to LoPiccolo (1992), are as follows:

1. An unwillingness on either the client's or the partner's part to reconsider male sex role demands, the role of the partner in providing adequate stimulation for the client, or the means of stimulation by which the partner reaches orgasm
2. Presence of a sexual deviation
3. Extreme religiosity, with religious beliefs about sex interfering with sexual performance
4. Severe clinical depression

In the past, therapy for erectile dysfunction began with sensate focus exercises to reduce performance anxiety and eliminate the self-evaluative spectator role (Masters & Johnson, 1970). However, since the 1970s, there has been much coverage of modern sex therapy techniques in books, magazines, newspaper columns, and television talk shows. As a result, most clients entering therapy are aware of the supposed effects of sensate focus—to reduce anxiety and therefore produce an erection. These clients now suffer from meta-anxiety about why eliminating performance anxiety does not lead to erection, and thus sensate focus is no longer effective as a therapeutic technique. Another problem with relying on sensate focus to "cure" erection problems is the one-third to two-thirds of men who have some degree of organic impairment of their erectile capability. These men may require direct and intense genital stimulation for erection regardless of the absence of performance anxiety and degree of pleasure experienced in sensate focus (LoPiccolo, 1992).

Instead of routinely beginning with sensate focus, it is recommended that therapy begin with a detailed analysis of the couple's actual sexual behavior. If the couple has not tried manual and oral stimulation of each other because of sex role expectations, inhibitions, or lack of knowledge, these behaviors should be discussed as options for sexual fulfillment. Discussion of these options may require support for both partners to reexamine their sexual values and expectations of each other because sex role stereotypes can be very powerful for both partners.

If the couple can accept manual and oral stimulation of the genitals as a route to sexual satisfaction, performance anxiety will be reduced for the client with erectile difficulties. Knowing that he can give pleasure to his partner in ways other than intercourse allows the male client to feel competent as a lover and therefore removes the pressure to have an erection to satisfy his partner. Likewise, direct manual and oral stimulation of the penis is important because of normal aging processes and the likelihood of some level of organic impairment. If couples understand that the erection response slows as men age, their expectations are more realistic and performance pressure again is reduced. Thus, manual and oral stimulation of the penis for a longer period is needed for an older man to have an erection. Explicit films and books can be used for couples who have not included such activities in their sexual repertoire.

Sometimes the partners of men with erection problems make demanding or derogatory statements about the men's sexual abilities. It is important for the therapist to recognize the origins of these statements. It is quite common for partners to interpret erectile difficulties as indicative of the state of the relationship. Some typical thoughts are that the mate no longer finds his partner attractive, does not love his partner, is having an affair, and so forth. As a result of these fears, the partner may make critical and demanding statements to the mate with erection problems. The therapist must gently explore these issues in the treatment of erectile dysfunction, so that the partner's inner anxieties, despair, and even depression do not inadvertently sabotage treatment.

One variety of erectile dysfunction is very difficult to treat: global, lifelong erectile failure. This diagnosis applies to a man who has never been able to achieve an erection, in any way, in his entire life (Schover, Friedman, Weiler, Heiman, & LoPiccolo, 1982). Because neither sensate focus nor expanding the sexual repertoire of such a client is usually successful, LoPiccolo (1992) suggests the therapeutic use of nocturnal penile tumescence after ruling out physiological causes of erectile failure. However, before attempting this procedure the therapist must carefully assess the role that lack of erection has played in the individual's life and the couple's relationship. After dealing with any adaptive value of lack of erection, then the couple can proceed to use naturally occurring nighttime erections. In this procedure, the man goes to bed and falls asleep while his partner remains in another room. After one to two hours have passed, the partner begins checking on him approximately every fifteen minutes. At some point the partner will observe that he has an erection while he sleeps. When this happens the partner is to begin gently caressing his penis. He will then gradually awaken to an erection during sexual activity—a new experience for him. This "milestone experience" can lead to remarkable treatment progress in previously unsuccessful cases and is recommended as a last resort technique (LoPiccolo, 1992).

Premature Ejaculation

As in the case of low desire, there are no objective criteria for premature ejaculation (Meggers & LoPiccolo, forthcoming). As such, this sexual dysfunction depends on the subjective rating of satisfaction by both partners. In this situation, it is easier to define what is not premature ejaculation: if both partners agree that their lovemaking is not negatively affected by efforts to delay ejaculation, then there is no dysfunction. Duration of intercourse is not a good measure of the presence of premature ejaculation because a man may manage five minutes of intercourse, but only by engaging in extreme mental and physical manipulations. For example, he cannot engage in foreplay because any touching of his genitals or those of his partner leads to such high arousal that he ejaculates. During intercourse he does not touch his partner for the same reason, and he thinks distracting thoughts (about taxes, job worries, and so forth) to avoid arousal to ejaculation. This situation is not pleasurable for either partner and so would qualify for a diagnosis of premature ejaculation regardless of the duration of intercourse. Additionally, the myth that men should be able to make the earth move for their partners (Zilbergeld, 1999) may result in a man wishing to prolong intercourse beyond what his partner actually desires in an effort to be a great lover. In this case, the partner may be very satisfied with the quality of lovemaking and the duration of intercourse, but the male client may feel inadequate. This situation would not warrant a diagnosis of premature ejaculation, and attempting to treat it as such would not be successful. Once again, the importance of a thorough assessment is clear. The motivations of both partners and their sexual behaviors and thoughts must be explored to determine if the couple would benefit from therapy for premature ejaculation.

The cause of premature ejaculation is also unclear at this time. Evolutionary psychologists have suggested that perhaps it is a remnant of an earlier time when it was to the couple's advantage to quickly finish intercourse and thus is built into the human organism (Hong, 1984). Other theorists have suggested that a man with premature ejaculation is unaware of his own level of arousal (Kaplan, 1974). Yet another theory suggests that premature ejaculation is caused by a low frequency of sexual activity (Kinsey, Pomeroy, & Martin, 1948). None of these theories is empirically supported, so the client who is searching for a "cause" will be dissatisfied.

However, despite the lack of empirical evidence for etiology and a clear definition of the symptom picture, premature ejaculation responds well to treatment. The standard treatment for premature ejaculation is the pause procedure

(Semans, 1956) or pause and squeeze procedure (Masters & Johnson, 1970). Because masturbation is usually less arousing than partner stimulation or intercourse, it is suggested that the treatment procedure begin during the male client's individual masturbation. He masturbates until a high level of arousal is reached, then pauses to allow the arousal to subside somewhat, and then resumes masturbating. This process is repeated several times, until the client is able to masturbate for five to six minutes before pausing. Treatment then includes manual stimulation by the partner, with pauses as in the masturbation procedure, until again five to six minutes of stimulation can occur before a pause. The final step is stimulation by intercourse—beginning in the least arousing position, with pauses as needed to reduce arousal, progressing to more arousing positions and activities.

The male sexual script can interfere with therapy for premature ejaculation if the client focuses on achieving immediate results. Although this procedure has been reported to be successful for 90 to 98 percent of clients (Kilman & Auerbach, 1979) men who put pressure on themselves to succeed may have difficulty. For most men, anxiety inhibits arousal, but for some the physical sensations associated with anxiety are incorporated into sexual arousal and ejaculation happens even more rapidly. In other cases, the emphasis on achievement interferes with awareness of pleasurable sensations. In these cases, the treatment aspect that involves self-monitoring of arousal and changing stimuli to slightly reduce arousal is impeded by the focus on correct performance of the procedure. In both of these situations, letting go of the male achievement mode and relaxing are critical to a successful therapy outcome.

Male Orgasmic Disorder

Male orgasmic disorder is rare, and the etiology is unclear (Meggers & LoPiccolo, forthcoming). However, there is little empirical evidence that psychological factors cause the disorder. Instead, this dysfunction appears to have several physical causes: multiple sclerosis (Kedia, 1983), damage to the hypothalamus (Kosteljanetz et al., 1981), medication side effects (Ban & Freyhan, 1980), and other neurological impairments.

For patients with clear organic impairment, some treatment success has resulted from the use of drugs that activate the sympathetic nervous system (Murphy & Lipshultz, 1988). In addition, education about the male ejaculatory reflex can make couples more comfortable with increasing stimulation of the scrotal, perineal, and anal areas. Stimulation in these areas can trigger the reflex arc and result in ejaculation.

Therapists can use some of the standard sexual therapy strategies to treat male orgasm dysfunction for patients with no obvious physical factors. Attempting to eliminate performance anxiety and ensuring adequate physical stimulation, including of the previously mentioned areas, is the preferred approach. If the male client is viewing sex as a performance (myth five), then ejaculation is seen as the culmination of the performance. Requiring male orgasm to complete the performance can result in a level of anxiety such that ejaculation is inhibited. Performance anxiety can also result when pregnancy is the desired outcome. If a couple is trying to become pregnant, the emphasis on ejaculation is even greater. This level of anxiety may be enough to cause orgasm dysfunction, but another possible cause also exists in this situation. The husband may not feel ready to parent but knows his wife really wants to conceive. He is not able to directly communicate his concerns, and so they are translated into anxiety that inhibits ejaculation. In this case, the man's concerns should be directly addressed in therapy and shared with his wife. The couple can then discuss the decision to try to become pregnant and remove the pressure for ejaculation to please the wife.

Finally, the treatment program developed for female anorgasmia may be appropriate for some men who buy into the myths about male sexual performance. This program involves examining values about sexuality and learning to focus on pleasure during sexual activity (Heiman & LoPiccolo, 1988). Men can use this program to learn about their beliefs and values and how they may be interfering with reaching orgasm. They can then move on to learning about the kind of stimulation most likely to lead to ejaculation and then share that knowledge with their partners. Men who believe that they should automatically reach orgasm during every sexual activity are prime candidates for this approach.

THERAPIST TRANSPARENCY

Given the social inhibitions regarding the discussion of sexual behavior, the therapist should be extremely cautious regarding self-disclosure in the therapy session. Male therapists who try to use themselves as role models by revealing aspects of their own feelings about sex may find they have engendered competitive feelings or a sense of hopelessness in their clients. Male therapists who try to use themselves as coping models may have clients who think, "Why should I listen to this guy? He can't do it right either."

Female therapists face additional pitfalls when working with male clients who have sexual dysfunctions. If they reveal aspects of their own sex lives, they may trigger voyeuristic feelings in their male clients. Male clients may tend to sexualize their therapeutic relationship with a female therapist anyway, so it is best to avoid sharing information that will augment that tendency.

To provide a safe environment in which to foster progress in therapy, it is best to clearly maintain appropriate therapeutic boundaries when working with male clients with sexual dysfunctions. Providing a safe environment does not mean eliminating warmth or a supportive demeanor but rather maintaining clear professionalism when conducting sex therapy. As mentioned previously, discussing sex and sexual dysfunctions is difficult for most people raised in a Western culture. Providing a safe environment in this case, then, means providing an environment in which the client is free from distracting thoughts about the therapist as a sexual individual.

FRANK: ISSUES AND TREATMENT

Frank presented for therapy when he was thirty-six years old. He had recently taken a new job as director of a health care provision group and was also recently separated from his wife of fifteen years. He stated that he had experienced erectile difficulty since he was an adolescent, specifically since his first experience with attempting intercourse. While recounting his relationship history, Frank displayed no insight into the factors that might have been related to his erection problems. He mentioned that his first intercourse experience was initiated by an older woman (she was twenty-two, he was seventeen), and he knew she was sexually experienced because several of his friends had reported sexual experiences with her. He felt that he was supposed to want to have sex with her, because "that's what teenage boys dream of, isn't it? Sex with an older, experienced partner?" He expected an immediate erection when she invited him to have intercourse and was ashamed when it did not happen. She made some comment about his penis "hiding" and assured him that she would "bring it out so they both could enjoy it." He then watched in horror as she tugged on his penis but was unable to produce an erection. Finally, he closed his eyes and imagined kissing one of the models in *Playboy* and was able to achieve a semi-rigid penis. He "faked" an orgasm from oral stimulation and fled.

After this experience, Frank decided that he was somehow defective as a man and avoided sexual situations for several years. While a junior in college, he met a waitress who seemed to be attracted to him and impressed by his impending college degree. He decided that he should marry her, because he knew she would agree, based on her anticipation of his earning potential, and maybe she would not mind that he was defective in the sexual performance arena. This marriage lasted for about eight months, during which his wife routinely belittled him because of his erection difficulties. Frank was confused by her criticisms because he liked engaging in oral sex and thought she enjoyed having orgasms that way too. They were divorced, and a few months later Frank met the woman who was to become his second wife.

This relationship began in the college library; she did not attend the same college he did but was in the college library researching material for a paper. Frank was doing a similar assignment and they encountered each other several times in different areas of the stacks, and he finally asked her to have coffee after they finished. They quickly became close friends, and Frank felt comfortable enough to reveal his terrible secret—his impotence. She responded in a supportive manner, and Frank decided to ask her to marry him. They were married right after they graduated from college and both obtained employment in the health care field. They had two children within the first four years of their marriage, and, although Frank continued to have occasional erectile problems, they were generally happy together. When they had been married for seven years they had a third child, who was severely disabled. Frank's wife believed that as a good mother she needed to care for this child herself instead of placing him in an institution. She quit her job (which placed a financial strain on the family) and devoted herself to caring for their disabled son. As the years went on, this situation placed an increasing strain on their marriage; for example, they rarely went out together because of the difficulty in finding a sitter and the expense. Instead, they each joined organizations and attended meetings separately about once a week. During this time their sexual relationship suffered, they rarely had the time and energy to have intercourse, and Frank felt he should produce an erection on demand on the few occasions they attempted sexual relations.

After about eight years of this lifestyle, Frank's wife met an independently wealthy widower through one of the volunteer organizations to which she belonged. He convinced her that she should focus on her needs for a change, and, after some deliberation, she decided to leave Frank and their children. One of the reasons she gave for ending the marriage was her dissatisfaction with his sexual performance—she was tired of having to work so hard for him to get an erection and wanted a "real man" in her life. (This explanation helped the woman neatly avoid having to face the issue of her own unrealistic expectations for "good mother" behavior and the resulting stress and exhaustion.) Frank was devastated by her pronouncement and accepted her conceptualization of their relationship as one huge failure on his part.

When Frank entered therapy they had been separated for six months and their divorce was pending. His disabled son had been placed in an institution, and his other two children resided with him. He did not have a sexual partner, so the initial focus of therapy was on unpacking the male sexual script he was carrying. He clearly subscribed to the majority of the myths identified by Zilbergeld (1999), despite his exposure to contradicting information in the human sexuality class he had taken in college. The first few months of therapy involved exploration of his learning history regarding these myths and the resultant unrealistic expectations he held. Family-of-origin issues had laid the groundwork, and his sexual experiences had reinforced these expectations and resultant critical self-evaluation. Cognitive strategies were used to allow Frank to confront and reject the destructive beliefs that were interfering with his sexual functioning. Relaxation training coupled with cognitive therapy enabled him to learn to reduce his anxiety level at work and when dealing with his children. When Frank felt that he was no longer under the control of his previously held sexual beliefs he was encouraged to "take a break" from therapy until he found a sexual partner. He was instructed to decide at that time if he felt he (or they) needed additional therapy to deal with the actuality of having sexual relations.

Frank returned to therapy about a year later, when he had met a woman whom he really cared about. He found that all of his old thoughts regarding the need for him to perform sex to be acceptable resurfaced when faced with the potential for having sexual intercourse. A few sessions were devoted to confronting these beliefs, and then role playing was used to help Frank tell his potential partner about his experiences with erection difficulties. When he told her about his erection problems, she was supportive and suggested that they attend a few therapy sessions together. In these sessions she revealed that, although she enjoyed intercourse, her "best" orgasms occurred during oral sex. Frank visibly brightened at this statement and indicated that he felt much less pressure to produce an erection if he knew they could enjoy sexual activities without having intercourse.

Frank attended one final session of therapy to describe a fulfilling sexual and emotional relationship with this woman, whom he now intended to marry. He mentioned that he felt he had been damaged by the beliefs he had held for so long but now was able to see how irrational they were and believed he would be able to avoid thinking that way in the future.

This case illustrates the importance of carefully assessing the irrational beliefs held by male sex therapy clients. Even individuals who are well educated and introspective may still endorse one or more of the myths about male sexual functioning identified by Zilbergeld (1999). Believing these myths interferes with male sexual functioning and also with men seeking psychotherapy. Instead, many opt for the "quick fix" they see being offered by some of the recent medical advances, such as sildenafil. Unfortunately, men are not sex machines, and dealing with the physiology without the psychology is typically doomed to failure. It seems very likely that advances in medical treatments will continue, and these new technologies and medications will have an important place in the treatment of male sexual dysfunction. However, without the addition of social changes to the male gender role script the medical advances will not be effective in eradicating male sexual dysfunction. Until Western culture changes the messages conveyed to boys and men, psychotherapy to address these issues will still be a necessary component of a successful treatment approach.

References

Ban, T., & Freyhan, F. (1980). *Drug treatment of sexual dysfunction.* New York: Karger.

Brooks, G. R. (1995). *The centerfold syndrome: How men can overcome objectification and achieve intimacy with women.* San Francisco: Jossey-Bass.

Crenshaw, T., & Goldberg, J. (1996). *Sexual pharmacology: Drugs that affect sexual function.* New York: Norton.

Doyle, J. (1989). *The male experience* (2nd ed.). Dubuque, IA: W. C. Brown.

Good, G. E., & Wood, P. K. (1995). Male gender role conflict, depression, and help seeking: Do college men face double jeopardy? *Journal of Counseling and Development, 74,* 70–75.

Gross, A. (1978). The male role and heterosexual behavior. *Journal of Social Issues, 34,* 87–107.

Heiman, J., & LoPiccolo, J. (1988). *Becoming orgasmic: A sexual growth program for women* (2nd ed.). New York: Simon & Schuster.

Hite, S. (1976). *The Hite report.* New York: Macmillan.

Hong, L. (1984). Survival of the fastest. *Journal of Sex Research, 20,* 109–122.

Kaplan, H. (1974). *The new sex therapy.* New York: Brunner/Mazel.

Kedia, K. (1983). Ejaculation and emission: Normal physiology, dysfunction, and therapy. In R. Krane, M. Siroky, & I. Goldstein (Eds.), *Male sexual dysfunction* (pp. 37–54). Boston: Little, Brown.

Kilman, P., & Auerbach, R. (1979). Treatments of premature ejaculation and psychogenic impotence: A critical review of the literature. *Archives of Sexual Behavior, 8,* 81–100.

Kinsey, A., Pomeroy, W., & Martin, C. (1948). *Sexual behavior in the human male.* Philadelphia: Saunders.

Kosteljanetz, M., Jensen, T. S., Norgar, B., Lunde, I., Jensen, P. B., & Johnson, S. G. (1981). Sexual and hypothalamic dysfunction in the post concussion syndrome. *Acta Neurologica Scandinavia, 63,* 169–180.

Kresin, D. (1993). Medical aspects of inhibited sexual desire disorder. In W. O'Donnohue & J. Geer (Eds.), *Handbook of sexual dysfunctions: Assessment and treatment* (pp. 15–52). Boston: Allyn & Bacon.

Levant, R., & Brooks, G. (Eds.). (1997). *Men and sex: New psychological perspectives.* New York: Wiley.

Levant, R., Hirsch, L., Celentano, E., Cozza, T., Hill, S., MacEachern, M., Marty, N., & Schnedeker, J. (1992). The male role: An investigation of norms and stereotypes. *Journal of Mental Health Counseling, 14*(3), 325–337.

LoPiccolo, J. (1992). Post-modern sex therapy for erectile failure. In R. Rosen & S. Leiblum (Eds.), *Erectile failure: Assessment and treatment* (pp. 171–197). New York: Guilford Press.

LoPiccolo, J. (1999). Psychological assessment of erectile dysfunction. In C. Carson, R. Kirby, & I. Goldstein (Eds.), *Textbook of male erectile dysfunction* (pp. 183–194). Oxford, U.K.: Isis Medical Media.

LoPiccolo, J., & Friedman, J. (1985). Sex therapy: An integrative model. In S. Lynn & J. Garske (Eds.), *Contemporary psychotherapies: Models and methods* (pp. 459–493). Columbus, OH: Merrill.

Masters, W., & Johnson, V. (1970). *Human sexual inadequacy.* Boston: Little, Brown.

Meggers, H., & LoPiccolo, J. (forthcoming). Male sexual dysfunction. In W. Craighead & C. Nemeroff (Eds.), *Encyclopedia of psychology and neuroscience* (3rd ed.). New York: Wiley.

Michael, R. T., Gagnon, J. H., Lauman, E. O., & Kolata, G. (1994). *Sex in America: A definitive survey.* Boston: Little, Brown.

Murphy, J., & Lipshultz, L. (1988). Infertility in the paraplegic male. In T. Tanagho, F. Lue, & R. McClure (Eds.), *Contemporary management of impotence and infertility* (pp. 279–284). Baltimore: Williams & Wilkins.

Pallas, J. (2000). A study using Viagra. *Journal of Sex and Marital Therapy, 26,* 41–50.

Pridal, C., & LoPiccolo, J. (2000). Treatment of low desire. In S. Leiblum & R. Rosen (Eds.), *Principles and practice of sex therapy* (3rd ed., pp. 57–81). New York: Guilford Press.

Rosenberg, K. (1999). Sildenafil. *Journal of Sex and Marital Therapy, 25,* 271–279.

Schover, L., Friedman, J., Weiler, S., Heiman, J., & LoPiccolo, J. (1982). A multi-axial diagnostic system for sexual dysfunctions: An alternative to DSM III. *Archives of General Psychiatry, 39,* 614–619.

Semans, J. (1956). Premature ejaculation: A new approach. *Southern Medical Journal, 49,* 353–357.

Stewart, T., & Gerson, S. (1976). Penile prosthesis: Psychological factors. *Urology, 7,* 400–402.

Tanagho, T., Lue, F., & McClure, R. (Eds.). (1988). *Contemporary management of impotence and infertility.* Baltimore: Williams & Wilkins.

Wise, T. (1987). Sexual problems in cancer patients and their management. *Psychiatric Medicine, 5,* 329–342.

Zilbergeld, B. (1999). *The new male sexuality* (Rev. ed.). New York: Bantam Books.

Zilbergeld, B., & Ellison, C. (1980). Desire discrepancies and arousal problems in sex therapy. In S. Leiblum & L. Pervin (Eds.), *Principles and practice of sex therapy* (pp. 29–64). New York: Guilford Press.

CHAPTER SIXTEEN

Men and Divorce

Caren C. Cooper

Bill (age sixty-eight) entered therapy for the first time, after his wife announced she had filed for divorce after forty-five years of marriage. Bill was confused and outraged by his wife's decision. His wife insisted that she had given him several warnings, but Bill adamantly denied that he had been given any information that she was so unhappy with their relationship. Bill hoped that the therapist could give him some quick advice to help him save his marriage.

Michael (age forty-two) began therapy for the first time, after he and his partner ended a committed relationship of fourteen years. The last three years of the relationship had been very conflictual. Michael reported working seventy to seventy-five hours per week for the last six months of the relationship and having three to five drinks to help him relax after work and get to sleep. One evening, Michael's partner announced that he was leaving Michael that very night. Michael reported becoming very angry. Unable to verbalize anything other than "I can't believe you're doing this to me," he stormed out of the house. When he returned several hours later, he found that his partner had indeed left.

Bob (age forty-eight) entered therapy for the third time, after his second wife announced she wanted to end their marriage of five years. Bob's wife suspected that he was having an extramarital affair; however, when confronted, Bob vehemently denied that he was involved with anyone else and expressed anger at his wife's mistrust of him. At a later point, Bob's wife found out via a friend that Bob had been seeing another woman for the past year. She then filed for divorce. Bob reported to the therapist that his wife was "just too demanding" and "didn't understand his needs."

John (age twenty-six) entered therapy for the second time, after his girlfriend of five years told him she thought the relationship was over. They cohabited for the last three years of their relationship. Over the course of the last year, there were many heated arguments. John told the therapist that he knew the relationship was in trouble but that his girlfriend "was his whole world, his best friend and confidant." In fact, John's social network was made up of only his girlfriend. John expressed hope that his girlfriend would be impressed that he was beginning therapy and that she might give the relationship another chance.

These scenarios are becoming increasingly common for mental health professionals. Although women still comprise the larger percentage of persons entering therapy prior to, during, and after a divorce, more men than ever are seeking mental health services. Also, as the preceding scenarios highlight, the age range of male clients seeking services is widening. Furthermore, therapists are seeing a broader range of relationship scenarios (for example, a male client who was married thirty years; a male client who was in a long-term committed relationship, heterosexual or gay).

Statistically speaking, comparison data are available only for married, heterosexual relationships. Over the course of the past four decades, the divorce rate among this group has dramatically increased in the United States. The 1960s and 1970s witnessed the most significant increases. In 1950, there were 385,000 divorces in the United States. By the mid-1970s, there were over 1 million divorces. In 1996, there were more than 1.1 million divorces (Crooks & Baur, 1999). These recent statistics indicate a leveling off of the divorce rate, which is attributed largely to the choice of more couples to cohabit (Crooks & Baur, 1999). However, in spite of this leveling off, there is an increase in divorces occurring in middle and later adulthood (Berk, 1998).

Because of the significant increase in divorce rates since the 1960s, mental health professionals have sought greater understanding of the process of separation and divorce (Myers, 1999; Vaughan, 1990). However, an area that has been insufficiently explored in light of the new psychology of men is how men differ from women with respect to the ending of a relationship and the adjustment period that follows. As Levant (1997) noted, researchers and therapists alike are just beginning the process of examining the traditional male gender role and "reconstructing" masculinity. The challenge for mental health professionals is to work with this evolving, reconstructed conceptualization of masculinity and develop therapy that effectively addresses the needs of male clients.

Another issue that has received insufficient attention is the experience of gay male clients going through relationship endings (Myers, 1999). The majority of the self-help literature addresses these matters from a heterosexual point of view and does not adequately address issues salient for gay men. In this chapter, I include in the discussion important aspects of divorce for gay men. The term *divorce* is used inclusively to refer to the ending of a committed relationship, regardless of the sexual orientation of the men involved.

PSYCHOLOGICAL PROCESSES OF DIVORCE

Before exploring issues that may be specific to men going through divorce, it is important to examine what is known about the psychological processes of separation and divorce in general. Although there are many important aspects to the divorce process such as financial and legal issues, the subsequent discussion focuses on the psychological challenges during the divorce process.

A person going through the divorce process is confronted with a significant amount of cognitive and emotional work, as well as interpersonal challenges. Vaughan (1990) examined the issue of how people end relationships, or "uncouple," and delineated a multilevel redefinition of self. Initially, the partners are confronted with the intrapersonal challenge of disentangling their identities and redefining themselves. The disentangling of identities occurs at a concrete level (for example, separating belongings) and at a psychological level (for example, thinking of oneself as single). Then persons who are divorcing have to deal with the interpersonal or public aspect of their separation. Vaughan contends that a divorce is complete when each partner and his or her social network perceive each partner as independent of the other. Particularly helpful in Vaughan's conceptualization is her emphasis of the intrapersonal, or cognitive-emotional, aspects of divorce and the interpersonal aspects.

Cognitive-Emotional Aspects of Divorce

Most people approach a committed relationship with the hope that it will be fulfilling and that it will last. Divorce means dealing with the loss of that hope. In addition to dealing with the loss of one's partner, a person is forced to confront other losses such as loss of a lifestyle, loss of familiarity, and possible loss of a social network. Women are more likely to experience a reduced standard of living, whereas men are more likely to experience loss of regular contact with their children (Berk, 1998).

Dealing with these losses and others has led several mental health professionals to conceptualize divorce as the death of a relationship, with a grieving process that follows (Berk, 1998; Fisher & Alberti, 1999; Jacobson & Jacobson, 1987; Myers, 1999; Napolitane, 1997; Rice & Rice, 1999). Over the course of the last thirty years, several authors have proposed various stage and phase models of grieving (see, for example, Kübler-Ross, 1969; Parkes, 1970). Mental health professionals who write on the topics of grieving or divorce usually refer to one or more stage or phase models. However, regardless of the particular stage or phase model of grieving, Rice and Rice (1999) noted four key elements that are common to most models of grieving: a period of denial, a period of anger or protest, a period of mourning, and a period of detachment and readjustment. In addition, Rice and Rice noticed that most models make reference to three distinct time periods: a pre-divorce period, a transition period, and a recovery period.

Because of the increased recognition that each individual grieves differently, there has been much debate as to the accuracy and utility of stage or phase models. As an alternative, Worden (1991) elected to describe grieving as a process of four psychological tasks: (1) accepting the reality of the loss, (2) experiencing the emotional pain of grief, (3) adjusting to a context in which the ex-partner is no longer a part, and (4) detaching from the ex-partner and becoming psychologically available for new relationships.

In moving through the divorce process and struggling with the requisite psychological tasks, a person may experience a broad range of negative emotions (Berk, 1998; Fisher & Alberti, 1999; Myers, 1999; Worden, 1991). Often, people experience an initial period of shock or emotional numbness followed by a period of disorganization. This initial experience is usually followed by a mixture of other emotions such as anger, shame, guilt, anxiety, loneliness, helplessness, and sadness. These emotions tend to ebb and flow, with one or two emotions predominating. They may vary in intensity and may surface at seemingly random points in time. At some future point, a person begins to experience a sense of relief and acceptance of the relationship loss. For most people, this point does not come for at least several months to a year.

In addition to the emotional aspects, a person going through divorce may also experience certain cognitive difficulties (Fisher & Alberti, 1999; Myers, 1999; Worden, 1991). Initially, there may be disbelief that the relationship is ending. This disbelief can range from intermittent periods of "I can't believe this is happening" to massive denial. Many clients report substantial confusion and difficulty concentrating. Clients, especially male clients, may become hyper-intellectual or hyperrational. There is usually a significant amount of obsessive thinking as clients come to grips with the reality of their relationship situation. Clients are often invested in thinking and rethinking their decision, their behavior, their partner's behavior, and the related outcomes.

Aside from the many negative reactions to divorce, there may also be some positive aspects. Several authors have emphasized the potential for personal growth in the aftermath of a relationship ending (Fisher & Alberti, 1999; Myers, 1999; Napolitane, 1997; Rice & Rice, 1999; Vaughan, 1990; Weiss, 1975). As previously noted, Vaughan (1990) focused on the multilevel process of redefining oneself. Rice and Rice (1999) highlighted the tendency for therapy to become overly focused on the negative aspects of the divorce process and minimize the potential for personal transformation. These authors propose a developmental framework that views divorce similarly to other significant developmental transitions in one's life (for example, leaving home). Although these developmental transitions involve significant stress, they offer an opportunity to get acquainted or reacquainted with oneself and provide the opportunity to reassess one's life and set new goals.

Interpersonal Aspects of Divorce

There are two central interpersonal issues in divorce. The first issue has to do with the client dealing with others' reactions to his divorce. The second issue has to do with the importance of social support while going through the divorce process. With regard to the former, most authors address the challenges of dealing with one's social support system in the aftermath of divorce (Myers, 1999; Vaughan, 1990; Weiss, 1975).

In the wake of a divorce, responses from people in the client's social network can be quite varied. For example, a client may experience all or almost all his social support system to be helpful and affirming. In the most problematic situations, however, he may perceive the majority of his social support system as rejecting. Friends, relatives, and coworkers have their own views of the situation and may verbalize these views directly or indirectly. Regardless, most clients find this interpersonal aspect of the divorce process to be quite stressful and upsetting.

As a divorce unfolds, clients often feel pressured to "defend their honor" and to manage public perception. If a client feels abandoned and rejected by some or most of his social network, he may withdraw from social contact and grieve in isolation. It is vitally important for people going through a divorce to receive social support. The importance of social support is clearly reflected in the literature about determinants of adaptive reactions to divorce and the healing process (Crooks & Baur, 1999; Markides & Cooper, 1989; Napolitane, 1997; Pierce, Sarason, & Sarason, 1996; Rice & Rice, 1999). Although the effects of divorce cannot be neutralized, social support can provide an important "emotional net" and reality check for a person adjusting to divorce.

ISSUES FOR MEN

Researchers in the area of men's issues have emphasized the need for a reconstruction of masculinity (A. R. Fischer & Good, 1998; Levant, 1995; Levant & Kopecky, 1996). In particular, these researchers have examined gender role socialization and the resulting "code of masculinity" (Levant, 1997). They have explored the male traits and values that are prescribed by the traditional male gender role and evaluated the degree to which they should be retained in the reconstructed conceptualization of masculinity.

With respect to ending a committed relationship, some traditionally male traits and values may assist a man as he works his way through the divorce process. For example, helpful traits and values include the ability to take risks, the tendency to remain calm when confronted with difficult situations, and persistence in solving difficult problems (see Levant, 1995, 1997; Levant & Kopecky, 1996). Conversely, other male traits and values may serve as barriers to or impede the healing process. When faced with the ending of a relationship, problematic male traits and values include alexithymia, overuse of anger, and hyperindependence (see A. R. Fischer & Good, 1997; Levant, 1995, 1997; Levant & Kopecky, 1996; Myers, 1999; Pasick, 1990).

Ending a Committed Relationship

For most, making the decision to end a relationship and then actually ending the relationship are complex and emotionally intense steps. Persons electing to take these steps are confronted with significant losses and the attendant grief. In the United States, however, the "code of masculinity" suggests that boys should limit their emotional experience and expression, if not ignore it altogether. Boys are admonished to "not cry" and "keep a stiff upper lip" when confronted with loss. Men may view dealing with loss as "something one should do quickly and privately, without prolonged or intense displays of emotion" (Pasick et al., 1990, p. 162). Thus, a male client going through a divorce may find himself caught in a double bind. He is working his way through a major life stressor and grief issues but is "supposed" to not experience his emotions. On the other hand, if he acknowledges or expresses his emotions, he has "failed" the code of masculinity.

Levant (1997) has observed that traditional male socialization teaches boys to restrict their emotional experience; thus a significant proportion of men do not have adequate access to their emotions. These men suffer from alexithymia, or the inability to recognize or express emotion. Levant (1997) believes that alexithymia is so common among men that it can be considered normative.

If a male client is alexithymic, he will be unable to cope effectively with the major loss experience of divorce. Furthermore, if this problem is not addressed, he will carry unresolved issues, or "baggage," into his next relationship. Sadly, men's difficulty in connecting to emotional experience has cumulative effects and initiates an escalating spiral of emotional distress. That is, alexithymia produces relationship strain that sometimes results in divorce. The same alexithymia precludes men from effectively coping with divorce. This poor coping, in turn, makes future relationships even more problematic.

To further complicate matters, as a result of cultural sanctions against male emotional experience and expression, men learn to depend on women for emotional support and expression. Brooks and Gilbert (1995) noted the tendency for many men to view marriage as a provider of emotional security and as a method for dealing with emotional deficits. Pleck (1980) claimed that men experience their emotions via women and learn to depend on women to express emotions for them. Doyle (1995) noted the tendency for the wife to serve as a "socioemotional bridge." That is, the wife serves as a spokesperson in charge of conveying the husband's feelings to others. Because of this dependency on women for emotional support and expression, men who are facing divorce may experience significant fear of losing that relationship and trepidation about coping on their own.

Another factor complicating the divorce process is the importance men place on the institution of marriage. Marriage provides critical validation and support for men. Brooks and Gilbert (1995) highlight a paradox for men with regard to marriage. On the one hand, male socialization and popular lore view marriage as a relationship that should be avoided or put off for as long as possible. On the other hand, however, a significant body of research has shown that men fare better when married and that marriage is actually very good for men's emotional and physical well-being. In fact, in comparison with women, men report being more satisfied with marriage (see Whitehurst, 1977), are less likely to seek divorce (see Pettit & Bloom, 1984), remarry more quickly and more often after divorce (see Nordstrom, 1986), and die sooner after being widowed (see Nordstrom, 1986). Thus for men divorce means the loss of an arrangement that offers psychological sustenance.

Transition Period

When a person is confronted with the ending of a committed relationship, he or she may feel in transition, or "in limbo," for a significant period of time. As discussed previously, social support is important when dealing with any life stressor. However, when dealing with divorce, social support is especially critical.

In the U.S. culture, however, the traditional code of masculinity suggests that to be a man, one must be self-sufficient (Feldman, 1990; Gordon & Meth, 1990). In fact, the implied message is that in times of personal crisis, a man should need others even less in times of personal crisis. In spite of this injunction of self-sufficiency, the literature reveals that the true situation is quite different and indicates that a man going through divorce is in a highly perilous situation.

Frequently, men's social networks are quite limited. In fact, Brooks and Gilbert (1995) noted that many heterosexual men rely solely on their wives for intimate friendship. Other than this relationship, men often have few social contacts beyond those arranged and managed by their wives. This reliance on women for intimate friendship is reflected in research such as that conducted by D. S. Fischer and S. L. Phillips (1982), who found that after marriage men's friendship networks become smaller, whereas women's friendship networks remain the same or increase.

Given traditional men's dependence on their female partners as their primary sources of support, men's networks of male friends and nonsexual intimate friendships are often sparse. And, in light of male socialization, there is little cultural permission to develop this type of social support. Furthermore, while in the midst of the divorce process, men often channel their distress into their work. The resulting increase in work hours leaves little time for developing new friendships, reestablishing old ones, or deepening existing friendships. In addition, men may not know how to go about describing their experience to a friend or may not want to risk having an intimate discussion with a friend. Such discussions are especially unlikely with male friends, because a man may fear being perceived as weak or out of control.

Therefore, with regard to social support, it is readily apparent that the male client going through the divorce process is once again placed in a double bind. Social support is crucial to the healing process. However, if a man reaches out for social support, he may believe he is weak or likely to be perceived by others as weak. On the other hand, if he does not reach out, he will suffer in isolation. This inability to experience the caring and support of others jeopardizes both his psychological and his physical well-being.

CLINICAL INTERVENTION

The preceding discussion makes clear the central nature of grief work and social support to the healing process for male clients who are ending committed relationships. Furthermore, with regard to grief work and social support, it is important for therapists to be cognizant of the double binds in which men may find themselves. In the paragraphs that follow, gender issues are highlighted with respect to assessment and treatment of male clients going through the divorce process.

Assessment

As with all therapy, the initial assessment period is crucial for effective treatment of men undergoing divorce. Although there are many areas to cover during this initial part of therapy, the information that follows addresses the issues that are specifically relevant to male clients going through this divorce process.

Several authors have noted the tendency for male clients to avoid therapy and ultimately seek it only when subjected to external pressures (Brooks, 1998; Myers, 1999; Pasick et al., 1990; Scher, 1990). Therefore, it is often helpful to note who made the appointment or who referred the client. For example, it is not unusual for a well-intentioned friend or relative to make the initial phone contact. If this is the case, the therapist already has some important information about the client's view of therapy. Also, it can be helpful to note the source for referral. For example, was he referred by an employee assistance program?

Work supervisor? Physician? Clergy? As the following case illustrates, this information can alert the therapist to possible problems.

Tom, age thirty-four, was referred to his employee assistance program for an evaluation. He was then referred for therapy by his employee assistance program, whose personnel arranged the intake appointment. Tom and his wife had decided to divorce after ten years of marriage and were in the process of discussing custody arrangements for their two children. During a two-week period, Tom's work supervisor had called him into his office on three occasions after Tom "exploded" at coworkers. When his supervisor inquired about his angry outbursts, Tom replied, "I don't think I sounded angry. I'm not angry about anything or at anybody."

Assessing for anxiety and depression. Before moving into gender issue questions, it is very important for the therapist to assess for anxiety and depressive symptoms. When clients are in the midst of grieving, they have anxiety and depressive symptoms. The key issue here is to explore the breadth and intensity of symptoms. If clients are moderately to markedly anxious or depressed, their capacity for emotional experience and expression and their motivation to seek out social support are significantly impaired.

One of the most common errors new therapists make is to underdiagnose the distress of a newly divorced male client (Myers, 1999). Because of early male socialization and the cultural expectation that men should be self-reliant, the male client is likely to work very hard to avoid appearing "weak," dependent, or vulnerable. Therefore, the therapist must be particularly careful about accepting a divorcing man's facade of well-being.

It is critical that therapists understand the difference between appropriate grief and depression. Although it is sometimes very difficult to differentiate the two, especially when a divorcing male client is working hard to appear in control, the distinction is vital. Worden (1991) noted that a loss of self-esteem is usually present with depression and not with grief. However, depending on the circumstances of a divorce, a client may indeed experience a loss of self-esteem. For example, if a male client believes he has "failed" at marriage, he may believe that he is less of a man. This self-perception and the attendant shame often result in a significant loss of self-esteem.

Assessing for substance abuse. In addition to assessing for anxiety and depressive symptoms, it is also important for therapists to inquire about substance use and possible abuse in male clients undergoing divorce. Myers (1999) emphasized the "inextricable link" between the code of masculinity and substance abuse and addiction. For men in the United States and many other countries, substance use and abuse are viewed as acceptable methods for dealing with upsetting emotions. If a client is abusing alcohol or other substances, then sobriety must be the first order of therapeutic business.

Assessing for role strain. For many men, scheduling a therapy appointment and attending the initial intake session require a great deal of courage (or a profound sense of desperation). Making an appointment for therapy is "asking for help," which runs counter to the traditional code of masculinity that promotes hyperindependence and self-sufficiency. Therefore, in the initial assessment session, it can be helpful to assess the man's discomfort from having violated the male code of self-sufficiency. This information may provide clinical data regarding the client's location on the continuum of traditional masculinity. It will also offer a gauge of the client's capacity for insight into his emotional experience and help the therapist to pace future questions, especially emotion-focused questions.

John, age fifty-one, had divorced his second wife after eleven years of marriage. When he called to make an appointment, he spoke very quickly and succinctly. It was obvious he wanted to make the phone contact very brief. During the intake session, John was noticeably anxious. His hands were clasped very tightly, his face became more flushed as the session progressed, and he was perspiring on his forehead by midsession. When asked if coming to his appointment was a hard step to take, he let out a huge breath of air and said, "This is the most embarrassing thing I think I have ever done."

Having elicited important information about this man's sense of humiliation, the therapist was in a position to further explore the client's concerns and to provide gender-sensitive reassurances. The therapist could reassure the client that his admissions were confidential and would not generate public embarrassment. Equally important, however, the therapist could assure the male client that he was not alone; that is, problems of this type are relatively common among contemporary men.

Upon further exploration, the therapist gathered some important information that helped reveal the male client's beliefs about masculinity and acceptable male behavior. The therapist learned that this man had grown up in a small, rural community with a very stoic father. The client was concerned that his father would somehow find out that he was "so weak he had to see a shrink."

In spite of the public perception gains made by the American Psychological Association and other mental health professional groups, many men still view therapy as a "shameful forum for the weak." Commonly, they expect therapy to be an emotionally focused process that is either uncomfortable or awkward for them (Brooks, 1998; Pasick et al., 1990). It is important to check out a male client's preconceived notions about therapy. As discussed next, if a male client has these views of therapy, the therapist will be in a difficult situation when grief work is at the center of the therapy process.

Assessing loss history. As previously discussed, dealing with divorce means dealing with loss. It is important for a therapist to obtain a "loss history" for a male client going through the divorce process and assess how much loss he has experienced in his life. Furthermore, it is equally important to assess how he has previously dealt with loss. Frequently, themes of loss and coping patterns will emerge.

Steve, age thirty-three, had been in a committed relationship for nine years. One night he came home from work and discovered that his partner had left him; there was no note, but all of his partner's belongings were gone. He had experienced one other long-term relationship, of three years, that was terminated quickly one afternoon by his partner. Steve's mother died in an accident when he was ten years old.

In exploring these three significant losses, it became clear that all three losses occurred suddenly and Steve had no control over or input into these events. In terms of coping, Steve reported that his father sternly instructed him to "toughen up" when he was crying one week after his mother's death. A well-intentioned friend gave him the same "instructions" when his first long-term relationship ended. Steve received strong messages from his father and peers to adhere to "the code" even when faced with major life events.

Assessing the stage of grief. With respect to the divorce process and coping with current losses, it is important to assess where the male client is in the grieving process. For example, has he accepted the reality of the divorce or is he "stuck" in denial? Myers (1999) cautions therapists to be on the lookout for male clients who have put their grief "on hold." He suggests that therapists watch for clients who get into new relationships too quickly and become overly preoccupied with those new relationships. Myers also cautions therapists to watch for clients who submerge themselves in work or deny that their relationships have ended.

Charles (age thirty) was referred for therapy by his physician. For five years, Charles had lived with his girlfriend. One Friday evening, he arrived home from work and his girlfriend announced she wanted to end the relationship and would be moving out that night. Charles did not say much and, after sitting on the couch quietly for a few minutes, grabbed his car keys and returned to the office. He slept at the office that night and worked at the office the entire weekend. Over the course of the next month, he reported working no less than ninety hours per week, ostensibly because he had several projects due.

In addition to assessing where the male client is in the grieving process, it is important to assess how he is coping with his emotional experience. For example, is he dealing with his emotions in a positive manner such as meeting a friend for coffee and talking about his frustrations with the divorce process? Or is he dealing with his emotions in a destructive manner? For example, several authors have noted the tendency for men who are upset to overuse anger (Long, 1987; Myers, 1999; Pasick et al., 1990). Long (1987) described the "emotional funnel system," whereby men are prone to channel most of their painful emotions into anger. Because most men view anger as a "masculine" emotion and therefore an acceptable emotion to express, it is not surprising that men going through divorce commonly overuse anger to mask hurt and other emotions that make them feel vulnerable.

James (age forty-seven) had been married for twenty-seven years. He decided he wanted to go hunting for the weekend, as he often did. When he informed his wife of his plans, she became upset and explained that "she just couldn't take it anymore." This was a common sequence of events in this relationship, and James was very aware of his wife's dissatisfaction with their marriage. However, each time she expressed her discontent, he was fearful that she was going to leave him. Instead of verbalizing his fear and having a constructive conversation, he would become enraged and hit the wall or throw something across the room. His wife would then become silent. The destructive manner in which James dealt with his anger prevented important conversations from taking place.

As a therapist explores a male client's loss history, where he is in the grieving process, and how he is dealing with his emotional experience, the therapist is able to gather information regarding how much access he has to his emotional experience. Does he recognize that he is hurting? Can he put language to his emotional experience? As Levant (1997) explained, if a client has only a vague sense something is wrong and is unable to articulate much content, the therapist can be relatively certain that alexithymia is present.

Assessing the social support network. Finally, it is important to assess the extent of the male client's social support network. The therapist needs to get an idea of the breadth and depth of the client's social system. If a male client states that he has several close friends, the therapist should probe what the client means by "close."

Dan (age fifty-two) divorced after twenty-five years of marriage. When asked about his social support network, he stated that he had several close friends and that he had good relationships with both his parents and his two older brothers. However, in gathering more information about Dan's "significant others," the therapist learned that "several close friends" meant there were four other people who worked in his section at work and that he only spoke occasionally to two of them. None of them were aware he was going through a divorce.

Psychotherapy

Mental health professionals inevitably accompany many clients as they confront different forms of loss. Regardless of theoretical orientation, most therapists agree that helping clients discuss various cognitive and emotional aspects of the loss experience is central to the healing process. In general, however, male clients tend to be more comfortable talking about the cognitive aspects than the emotional aspects. Therefore, for a male going through the divorce process, one of the primary goals of therapy is to address and work through the emotional aspects of the grieving process.

Challenge of emotion work. When working with male clients, emotion work often proves to be a significant challenge for therapists. Walking a therapeutic tightrope of sorts, therapists have to balance the need to do emotional work with the need to not make the male client feel so uncomfortable that he abandons the therapy process. To a male client who adheres to a traditional masculinity code, doing the emotional work of grieving may feel like the therapist is asking the client to be "unmanly" and to defy his masculine heritage. If the therapist pushes too hard in this direction, he or she risks being perceived as insensitive to the male experience and therefore dismissed as unlikely to be helpful.

Most therapists have been trained to emphasize emotional expressiveness. During sessions, therapists routinely ask clients emotion-focused questions such as "How do you feel?" or "How did that make you feel?" With male clients, it is helpful to not overuse the words *feel* and *feelings*. Although it is an important therapeutic goal to help the client articulate his feelings and work through these feelings, timing is of the utmost importance. Early in the therapeutic process, it can be helpful to ask male clients about their reactions rather than using the word *feeling*. Most times, male clients offer a mixture of behavioral and physiological details that imply emotional responses.

For example, a male client stated, "and my heart was pumping like crazy and I was making a fist with my hand!" This client did not say, "I was really angry when . . ." but provided behavioral and physiological information that confirmed his emotional experience.

In the preceding example, many therapists would go ahead and ask, "What were you feeling at that moment?" There are two problems with this approach. The first problem is that therapists are not recognizing that the male client has already stated how he felt using other modes of communication. Too often, therapists focus too much on exact identification and verbalization of emotion and are not open to "hearing" other types of emotional expression. The second problem is that asking about feelings too early in the therapy experience may make the client uncomfortable and lead to the client abandoning therapy.

For example, during an intake, a practicum student asked a newly divorced client, "And how did that make you feel?" The male client, obviously agitated by the question, responded, "I knew you were going to ask me about my feelings. . . . This is not going to work!" It is crucial for therapists to be open to other ways of communicating feelings while supporting and promoting increased emotional understanding and expression in male clients.

Psychoeducational work. If clients are not able to recognize and differentiate their emotions or give language to their emotional experiences, the therapist needs to provide psychoeducation in this area. Given most male clients' preference for and comfort with cognitive work, providing clients with information about emotions can lay a foundation for future therapeutic work that is more directly focused on emotions. Levant (1997) recommends providing historical information regarding socialization processes and gender roles. He also recommends providing clients with research findings that support the idea that emotions are just as natural for men as they are for women. Psychoeducation regarding factors such as socialization processes can provide clients with the "cultural" permission to do emotion-focused work. It also conveys a message that the therapist is affirming of male emotional experience. Furthermore, it can have a calming effect on clients because it gives them a conceptual framework for understanding their experiences. Without first getting the cognitive framework, few male clients going through the divorce process are willing to move directly into the emotional aspects of grief work.

In addition to psychoeducation regarding gender role socialization and related issues, it may be useful to provide information about emotions themselves. For example, Levant (1997) teaches male clients about the physiology of emotions. He also includes exercises that will help male clients develop a "vocabulary for emotions." Because of socialization processes and sanctions against emotional experiences, male clients are often inarticulate about emotions or present with an impoverished emotional vocabulary. Therefore, it can be quite frustrating and shaming for male clients to be asked frequently about their emotional experiences when they may not have language to give expression to their experiences.

Increasing emotional competence. As clients gain understanding about emotions themselves and how male socialization silences healthy emotional experience and expression, it is important to begin the process of helping clients identify their own emotional experiences. To provide language for clients' experiences, as with initial sessions, the therapist needs to be open to several modes of communication. For example, in the previous example of the male client stating, "and my heart was pumping like crazy and I was making a fist with my hand!" the therapist at this point might interpret the man's physical experience of his emotions and assist him in labeling them. The therapist might say something like, "It sounds like you were feeling upset and angry. Is that accurate?"

In addition to assisting clients in identifying their own experiences, it is also important for clients to develop skills in recognizing others' emotional states. It is not uncommon for male clients to report being caught off guard by their partners' decision to leave the relationship. Given men's difficulty in connecting with their own emotional experiences, it is not surprising that they are not adept at reading others' emotional states. During the divorce process, clients usually have to communicate with their ex-partners regarding various issues (for example, dividing up the household, child care issues, or taxes). These scenarios often provide useful practice opportunities. For example, if a male client stops by his ex-partner's house to inquire about something, the client can be encouraged to study the reactions of his ex-partner throughout the conversation and see if he can recognize the different emotional states exhibited by his ex-partner.

Increasing social support. In addition to doing the cognitive and emotional work of grieving, it is crucial for male clients to have social support. It is especially vital that male clients understand the difference between expanding their networks of friends and prematurely entering a new intimate relationship to substitute for the lost relationship. As noted previously, traditional heterosexual men are far too dependent on marriage as their primary form of social support and need special encouragement to expand their networks of male friendships and nonsexual intimate relationships.

As with grief work, it can be helpful to provide psychoeducation regarding socialization processes, the conventional sanctions against men asking for support, and the multiple barriers to male friendships. After offering this psychoeducation, it is important for the therapist to take the time to discuss possible avenues and strategies for obtaining social support. The therapist should be pragmatic and set attainable goals; he or she can help male clients to think of non-work-related possibilities and to think in terms of underdeveloped areas for personal growth. Among the many possibilities is participating in a men's support group.

Special issues for gay clients. A therapist needs to be sensitive to certain issues of social support if the male client is gay. He or she needs to inquire as to whether the client is "out" and if so with whom (for example, family, friends, or coworkers). If a significant proportion of the client's social network is not aware he is gay or that he has been in a committed relationship, it may be difficult for the client to access adequate social support during the divorce process. It is also important for the therapist to be aware of the size of the local gay community and whether the client is active within that community. If a client lives in a small- to medium-sized community, the gay community may be small and close-knit, making relationship endings particularly difficult if a male client's partner lives in the same community.

Additionally, if persons in the client's social network are aware that the client is gay, find out if they have been supportive and affirming of his lifestyle and relationship, as well as how they are reacting to the ending of his relationship.

Jim ended a twelve-year committed relationship. In the midst of his dealing with all the aspects of divorce, a female heterosexual coworker whom Jim described as a close friend said, "You people are so lucky; you don't have to deal with all the legal crap!" To say the least, Jim felt his experience minimized at many levels. Subsequent comments by a couple of other coworkers implied that because it was a gay male relationship, the breakup should not hurt as much.

It is not uncommon for members of the client's social support system to make comments that inadvertently minimize the importance and impact of a gay divorce. It is important for the therapist to process such incidents with the client, to hear and validate the emotional elements of the incident, and to acknowledge the reality that some will not understand that the client's experience of a divorce is no different from that of a heterosexual person.

Concluding remarks. As a final note, it important for the therapist to offer hope and to offer it frequently. Divorce, although painful, is a time-limited experience and can offer several personal growth opportunities for male clients. Given that gender socialization is such a powerful force and begins early in childhood, sometimes it takes a powerful life event such as divorce to force an internal psychological reassessment.

Some have argued that clients can only connect with others insofar as they are able to connect with themselves. As a result of male socialization, men disconnect from themselves in some important ways that result in a compromised capacity for intra- and interpersonal understanding and connection. Divorce may serve as a catalyst for the male client to develop insight into his internal experience and to develop skills that promote a healthier relationship with oneself. In turn, he may then be able to experience understanding of and connection with others that was previously not possible.

References

Berk, L. E. (1998). *Development through the lifespan.* Boston: Allyn & Bacon.

Brooks, G. (1998). *A new psychotherapy for traditional men.* San Francisco: Jossey-Bass.

Brooks, G., & Gilbert, L. A. (1995). Men in families: Old constraints, new possibilities. In R. F. Levant & W. S. Pollack (Eds.), *A new psychology of men* (pp. 253–279). New York: Basic Books.

Crooks, R., & Baur, K. (1999). *Our sexuality* (7th ed.). New York: Brooks/Cole.

Doyle, J. A. (1995). *The male experience* (3rd ed.). Dubuque, IA: W. C. Brown.

Feldman, L. B. (1990). Fathers and fathering. In R. L. Meth & R. S. Pasick (Eds.), *Men in therapy: The challenge of change* (pp. 88–107). New York: Guilford Press.

Fischer, A. R., & Good, G. (1997). Men and psychotherapy: An investigation of alexithymia, intimacy, and masculine gender roles. *Psychotherapy, 34,* 160–170.

Fischer, A. R., & Good, G. (1998). New directions for the study of gender role attitudes: A cluster analytic investigation of masculinity ideologies. *Psychology of Women Quarterly, 22*(3), 371–384.

Fischer, D. S., & Phillips, S. L. (1982). Who is alone? Social characteristics of people with small networks. In L. A. Peplau & D. Perlman (Eds.), *Loneliness: A sourcebook of current theory, research, and therapy.* New York: Wiley-Interscience.

Fisher, B., & Alberti, R. (1999). *Rebuilding: When your relationship ends* (3rd ed.). New York: Impact.

Gordon, B., & Meth, R. L. (1990). Men as husbands. In R. L. Meth & R. S. Pasick (Eds.), *Men in therapy: The challenge of change* (pp. 54–87). New York: Guilford Press.

Jacobson, G. F., & Jacobson, D. S. (1987). Impact of marital dissolution on adults and children: The significance of loss and continuity. In J. Bloom-Feshbach & S. Bloom-Feshbach (Eds.), *The psychology of separation and loss* (pp. 316–344). San Francisco: Jossey-Bass.

Kübler-Ross, E. (1969). *On death and dying.* New York: Macmillan.

Levant, R. F. (1995). Toward the reconstruction of masculinity. In R. F. Levant & W. S. Pollack (Eds.), *A new psychology of men* (pp. 229–251). New York: Basic Books.

Levant, R. F. (1997). *Men and emotions: A psychoeducational approach.* New York: Newbridge.

Levant, R. F., & Kopecky, G. (1996). *Masculinity reconstructed.* New York: Plume.

Long, D. (1987). Working with men who batter. In M. Scher, M. Stevens, G. Good, & G. A. Eichenfield (Eds.), *Handbook of counseling and psychotherapy with men* (pp. 305–320). Newbury Park, CA: Sage.

Markides, K. S., & Cooper, C. L. (1989). Aging, stress, social support, and health: An overview. In K. S. Markides & C. L. Cooper (Eds.), *Aging, stress, and health* (pp. 1–10). New York: Wiley.

Myers, M. F. (1999). *Men and divorce.* New York: Guilford Press.

Napolitane, C. (1997). *Living and loving after divorce.* New York: Signet.

Nordstrom, B. (1986). Why men get married: More and less traditional men compared. In R. A. Lewis & R. E. Salt (Eds.), *Men in families* (pp. 31–53). Newbury Park, CA: Sage.

Parkes, C. M. (1970). The first year of bereavement: A longitudinal study of the reaction of London widows to the death of their husbands. *Psychiatry, 4,* 444–467.

Pasick, R. S. (1990). Friendship between men. In R. L. Meth & R. S. Pasick (Eds.), *Men in therapy: The challenge of change* (pp. 108–127). New York: Guilford Press.

Pasick, R. S., Gordon, S., & Meth, R. L. (1990). Helping men understand themselves. In R. L. Meth & R. S. Pasick (Eds.), *Men in therapy: The challenge of change* (pp. 152–180). New York: Guilford Press.

Pettit, E. J., & Bloom, B. L. (1984). Whose decision was it? The effects of initiator status on adjustment to marital disruption. *Journal of Marriage and the Family, 32,* 54–67.

Pierce, G. R., Sarason, B. R., & Sarason, I. G. (Eds.). (1996). *Handbook of social support and the family.* New York: Plenum.

Pleck, J. H. (1980). Men's power with women, other men, and society: A men's movement analysis. In E. Pleck & J. H. Pleck (Eds.), *The American man* (pp. 417–433). Englewood Cliffs, NJ: Prentice Hall.

Rice, J. K., & Rice, D. G. (1999). *Living through divorce: A developmental approach to divorce therapy.* New York: Guilford Press.

Scher, M. (1990). Effect of gender-role incongruities on men's experience as clients in psychotherapy. *Psychotherapy, 27,* 322–326.

Vaughan, D. (1990). *Uncoupling: turning points in intimate relationships.* New York: Vintage Books/Random House.

Weiss, R. S. (1975). *Marital separation.* New York: Basic Books.

Whitehurst, C. (1977). *Women in America: The oppressed majority.* Santa Monica, CA: Goodyear.

Worden, J. W. (1991). *Grief counseling and grief therapy: A handbook for the mental health practitioner* (2nd ed.). New York: Springer.

SECTION THREE

NORMATIVE ISSUES
OF THE MALE LIFE CYCLE

CHAPTER SEVENTEEN

The Crises of Boyhood

Ronald F. Levant

Boys today are in crisis even though many appear to be doing just fine on the surface. Over the past decade we have become aware of how difficult it is to grow up female in U.S. society and of the major crisis many girls experience in adolescence, manifested in a dramatic loss of self-confidence and self-esteem. We are less aware of the problems for boys. In fact, we have a cultural blindness to the problems of boys, in part because of our assumption that males should be self-sufficient and in part because boys are required to keep their problems to themselves. However, recent work in the new psychology of boys and men indicates that boys suffer from not one but two crises: the first at the point of entrance into school (between the ages of five and seven) and the second in adolescence.

The first crisis is actually several years in the making and is fundamentally the result of how we socialize our sons' emotions. Because of widespread beliefs in U.S. society about how boys and men ought to behave (what I call the "code of masculinity"), we tend to get swept up in a process of shaping and channeling boys' expression of emotions so that, although boys start out life more emotional than girls, they wind up much less so. By the time a boy enters school he has learned to hide and feel ashamed of two important sets of emotions: those that express vulnerability in one way or another (fear, sadness, loneliness, hurt, shame, and disappointment) and those that express neediness, caring, or connection to others. As a result boys become deeply alienated from themselves and from those closest to them, from whom they feel they must hide their shameful sense of vulnerability and neediness (Levant & Kopecky, 1995; Levant & Pollack, 1995). Thus boys enter school with a fragile personality, which—interacting with the stress of the school situation—manifests itself in an array of problems. Hence, the problems that boys manifest at the start of school are but the tip of the iceberg of deeper-lying difficulties that will not only profoundly influence boys' subsequent development but will also give boys' adolescent crisis its unique character.

THE FIRST CRISIS: SCHOOL DAZE

Quite apart from these underlying problems, boys are vulnerable at the point of entry into school because of the state of their maturation. They are less able than girls to adapt to the school environment; they are slower to learn to read and write, have greater needs for large-muscle activity, and have much less ability to sit quietly and listen to the teacher. The school environment simply has not been planned to accommodate boys' needs. Schools that are doing away with recess may exacerbate this problem for boys.

Boys' Symptoms

Boys also have more symptomatic behavior than girls. At the onset of the school experience boys begin to express more symptoms than girls—in learning, behavior, and emotions. Boys are twice as likely as girls to be diagnosed with learning disabilities. Although girls are diagnosed with dyslexia (a specific learning disability that affects the ability to read) nearly as frequently as are boys, they are more likely to overcome it so that after intervention girls' rates drop to 25 percent that of boys. In terms of behavior, compared with girls, boys are five times more likely to have conduct problems, three times more likely to be enrolled in special education classes, and six times more likely to be diagnosed with attention-deficit/hyperactivity disorder. Of the one million children taking Ritalin for attention-deficit/hyperactivity disorder, 75 percent are boys. In terms of emotions, although girls are eight times more likely to attempt suicide, boys are four times more likely to complete it (Bushweller, 1994; Kiselica & Horne, 1999; Pollack, 1998).

Why do boys have so many problems at the point of entry into school? Partly because of differing rates of maturation of physical and cognitive abilities of boys and girls, such that girls are simply more ready for school than boys, a problem that could be remedied by redesigning the primary grades to take into account boys' needs. But the difference in maturation rates only explains part of the problem. There is a deeper level that is harder to see, hidden as it is by our assumptions about how boys ought to behave. This deeper level concerns the way our sons' emotions and behavior are molded. Just as we discourage our daughters from being too aggressive and (when they are older) too sexual because of our beliefs about how girls ought to behave, we discourage our sons from expressing a whole set of needs and emotions that we consider inappropriate for boys: dependency, vulnerability, and even caring and affection. The net effect of this discouragement is that we inadvertently compound our sons' slower maturation, creating emotional difficulties and vulnerability to symptom formation.

"Snips and Snails and Puppy Dog Tails": Our Beliefs About Boys

I have been studying our beliefs about how boys and men ought to behave for the past decade and have found that the major beliefs in our society are that males must (1) be independent and self-reliant, (2) not express their emotions (particularly those that show vulnerability or their attachment to another person), (3) be tough and aggressive, (4) seek high social status, (5) always be ready for sex, (6) avoid all things "feminine" lest there be any confusion about their masculinity, and (7) reject homosexuality. Together these beliefs make up the code of masculinity—which is quite a demanding set of behaviors, at once stoic and heroic (Levant et al., 1992).

To put these beliefs in context, the code of masculinity fits best with harsh social conditions, such as those that occurred in the United States from the period of industrialization through World War I, the Great Depression, and World War II. In such conditions certain male traits such as toughness, self-reliance, and lack of awareness of emotions are likely to be more adaptive.

Although the code is waning, it still holds sway and in fact profoundly affects how we raise our sons. It is interesting that the code is more strongly endorsed by males than by females and shows differential endorsement in different ethnocultural subgroups in U.S. society (Levant & Fischer, 1998; Levant & Majors, 1997; Levant, Majors, & Kelley, 1998; Levant, Wu, & Fischer, 1996). Nonetheless, we all get caught up in the code, whether we explicitly endorse it ourselves, carry it as a set of unexamined assumptions, or have it forced on us by others (for example, our spouses, other children acting on their parents' views, teachers, coaches, or the culture at large). The net result is that it has a profound influence on the shaping of our boys' emotional lives.

Boys' Emotional Shaping: Birth to Six Years

In this section, we discuss the emotion socialization of boys, showing that, although boys start out more emotionally expressive than girls, they wind up much less so due to their socialization by parents and peers. This emotion socialization process is aimed at curbing boys' expression and ultimately their awareness of both their caring and connection emotions (such as affection, fondness, etc.) and their vulnerable emotions (like fear, sadness, etc.). However, as we shall see, anger and aggression are permitted and even encouraged.

Boys' emotional beginnings. One interesting biological difference between the sexes is that boys seem to be more emotional than girls at birth and remain so until at least one year of age. A review of twelve studies (eleven of which were of neonates, studied just hours after birth) found that boys cry more often and more intensely, but they also coo, gurgle, and smile more often, and they fluctuate more rapidly between emotional states than do girls (Haviland & Malatesta, 1981). Another study found that infant boys were judged to be more emotionally expressive than were infant girls, even when the judges were misinformed about the infants' actual sex, thus controlling for the effects of gender role stereotyping on the part of judges (Cunningham & Shapiro, 1984, cited in Brody & Hall, 1993). Finally, boys remain more emotional than girls at least until six months of age; compared with girls, they exhibit "more joy and anger, more positive vocalizations, fussiness, and crying, and more gestural signals directed toward the mother" (Weinberg, 1992, p. vii).

Crossover in emotional expression. Despite this initial advantage in emotional expressivity, boys learn to tune out, suppress, and channel their emotions, whereas the emotional development of girls encourages their expressivity. These effects become evident with respect to verbal expression by two years of age and with respect to facial expression by six years of age. One study found that two-year-old girls refer to feeling states more frequently than do two-year-old boys (Dunn, Bretherton, & Munn, 1987). Another assessed the ability of mothers of four- to six-year-old boys and girls to accurately identify their children's emotional responses to a series of slides by observing their children's facial expressions on a television monitor. The older the boy, the less expressive his face, and the harder it was for his mother to tell what he was feeling. This researcher found no such correlation among the girls: their mothers were able to identify their emotions no matter what their age. The author concluded that between the ages of four and six years, "boys apparently inhibit and mask their overt response to emotion to an increasing extent, while girls continue to respond relatively freely" (Buck, 1977, p. 234).

Socialization and how it works. What would account for this "crossover in emotional expression" such that boys start out more emotional than girls and wind up much less so? The socialization influences of mother, father, and peer group combine to result in the suppression and channeling of male needs and emotions and the encouragement of female emotionality. These influences are wrought through (1) selective reinforcement, modeling, and direct teaching of desired behavior; (2) the different kinds of experiences that boys and girls have with parents and peers; and (3) punishment for breaking the code of masculinity. These matters were treated in greater detail in another publication (Levant & Kopecky, 1995); hence I simply present a brief overview here.

In infancy, mothers work hard to manage their more excitable and emotional male infants. They smile more when their sons are calm, thus reinforcing calm, inexpressive behavior when they play with their sons. In fact, mothers may go to special lengths to ensure that their sons are contented. Mothers also control their own emotional expressivity to avoid "upsetting their sons' more fragile emotional equilibria" (Haviland & Malatesta, 1981, p. 202). In contrast, mothers expose their infant daughters to a wider range of emotions than they do their sons (Malatesta, Culver, Tesman, & Shephard, 1989).

In the toddler years, fathers take an active interest in their children. This interest becomes apparent in the thirteenth month of life, and from that point on fathers tend to interact with their toddler sons and daughters along gender-stereotyped lines (Lamb, 1977; Lamb, Owen, & Chase-Lansdale, 1979). Fathers interact more with infant sons than they do with infant daughters (Lamb, 1977). With older children, fathers engage in more verbal roughhousing with sons and tend to speak more about emotions with daughters (Greif, Alvarez, & Ulman, 1981; Schell & Gleason, 1989). Fathers also express more disapproval to sons who violate the code of masculinity by engaging in doll play or expressing emotions such as neediness, vulnerability, and even attachment (Langlois & Downs, 1980). Many adult men whom I have counseled recall experiences in which their fathers made them feel deeply ashamed of themselves for expressing vulnerable emotions such as sadness or fear or attachment emotions such as caring, warmth, or affection.

Both parents participate in the development of language for emotions, differentiated along the lines of gender. Parents discourage their sons from learning to express vulnerable emotions; although they encourage their daughters to learn to express their vulnerable and attachment emotions, they discourage their daughters' expression of anger and aggression. It should be noted that females' language superiority also plays a role in their greater ability to express emotions verbally (Brody & Hall, 1993). One investigative team found that mothers used more emotion words when speaking with daughters than with sons (Dunn et al., 1987). Another found that mothers spoke more about sadness with daughters than with sons and only spoke about anger with sons. With daughters, mothers discussed the experience of emotions, whereas with sons they discussed the causes and consequences of emotions, which would serve to help sons learn to control their emotions (Fivush, 1989). A third study had parents "read" stories to their children using wordless books and videotaped and transcribed their conversations. Mothers talked about anger twice as frequently with sons as with daughters (Greif et al., 1981). Finally, another team of researchers found that school-age sons expected their parents to react negatively to the expression of sadness, whereas school-age daughters expected their mothers to react more positively to the expression of sadness than they would to the expression of anger (Fuchs & Thelen, 1988).

Sex-segregated peer groups complete the job. Young girls typically play with one or two other girls, and their play consists of maintaining the relationship (by minimizing conflict and hostility and maximizing agreement and coopera-tion) and telling each other secrets, thus providing experiences that foster their learning skills of empathy, emotional self-awareness, and emotional expressiv-ity. In contrast, young boys typically play in larger groups in structured games—experiences in which they learn skills such as how to play by the rules, teamwork, stoicism, toughness, and competition (Lever, 1976; Maccoby, 1990; Paley, 1984). One study found that boys experience direct competition in their play half of the time, whereas girls experience it very infrequently (less than 1 percent of the time) (Crombie & Desjardins, 1993, cited in Brody, 1996). Boy culture is also notoriously cruel to boys who violate male role norms, such as expressing vulnerable emotions, showing affection, or being unwilling to fight (Krugman, 1995).

Hardening of boys' hearts. Many adult men recall that their first experiences with limitations on expressing caring emotions actually occurred in the context of their relationships with their fathers, for, in the typical postwar family, hugs and kisses between father and son came to an end by the time the boy was ready to enter school. In addition to whatever messages boys hear at home, they also get the message from their peers that it is not socially acceptable to be affectionate with their mothers (lest they be a "mama's boy"), girls (for fear of being teased by friends), or boys (where anything but a cool, buddy-type rela-tionship with another boy can give rise to the dreaded accusation of homosex-uality). Childhood experiences of this type set up powerful barriers to the overt expression of attachment and caring emotions, which thus get suppressed (Levant & Kopecky, 1995).

Overdevelopment of aggression. Through a similar process boys become ashamed of expressing vulnerable emotions such as fear, sadness, loneliness, or hurt, so that they lose touch with their ability to express these emotions as well. On the other hand boys are allowed to feel and become aware of emotions in the anger and rage part of the spectrum, as prescribed in the toughness dimension of the male code. As a result males express anger more aggressively than do females (Brody & Hall, 1993; Campbell, 1993; Eagly & Steffen, 1986; Frodi, Macaulay, & Thome, 1977). The aggressive expression of anger is in fact one of the very few ways boys are encouraged to express emotion; as a conse-quence, the outlawed vulnerable emotions, such as hurt, disappointment, fear, and shame, get funneled into the anger channel. This rechanneling of emotions has been called "the male emotional funnel system," the final common path-way for all those shameful vulnerable emotions that are too unmanly to express directly (Long, 1987). Some boys learn to actively transform these vulnerable emotions into anger, rage, and aggression, as when a boy is pushed down on the playground and knows that it is expected that he come back up with a fist-ful of gravel rather than a face full of tears. This facility to transform vulnera-ble emotions into aggression is learned in boy culture and accounts for the fact that many adult men get angry when their feelings are hurt. It may also have played a role in the school killings by adolescent boys in Jonesboro, Arkansas, Pearl, Mississippi, and Paducah, Kentucky.

The Net Result

These socialization experiences not only prevent boys from being able to express a wide band of the spectrum of human emotions but also make them feel very ashamed of themselves for even having these emotions. Because aggression is encouraged, it becomes boys' only outlet and as a result overdevelops.

This socialization creates a tremendous burden for boys, who come to feel that parts of themselves are unacceptable and even shameful and that they dare not let others see these parts of themselves. Hence boyhood socialization puts boys at odds with parts of themselves and cuts them off from other people, thus creating low self-esteem and a self-imposed isolation. Although this isolation is socially sanctioned, it is also destructive because boys have many needs and feel many vulnerable and caring emotions. As a consequence boys must live a lie and learn to deaden themselves to it.

When you combine these results of socialization with boys' biologically based preference for large-muscle motor activity and later development of read-ing and writing skills, is it any wonder that our boys are having so many prob-lems when they enter school? However, as already noted, the problems that boys manifest at the start of school are but the tip of the iceberg of deeper-lying difficulties that will not only profoundly influence the boys' subsequent devel-opment but also give boys' adolescent crisis its unique character.

THE SECOND CRISIS: TEEN YEARS

Whereas girls experience their major crisis in early adolescence, boys actually have two crises: the school crisis discussed previously and the crisis of adolescence. Boys' adolescent crisis revolves around issues that all children share, such as inde-pendence versus dependence, identity, self-confidence, and sexuality. However, it has a particular character because of boys' early training to hide and feel ashamed of their caring and vulnerable emotions, their resultant feelings of being at odds with parts of themselves and unable to go to others for emotional support, their often problematic relationships with their fathers, and the influence of boy culture and the culture at large. These unique effects are seen in such problematic areas as sexuality, alcohol and drug use, risky behavior, and finding a direction in life.

Problematic Sexuality

The way we have traditionally raised our sons to be strong, competitive, and emotionally stoic fosters a problematic sexuality. In adolescence, when interest in sexuality dawns thanks to the combined effects of hormones and culture, boys' caring and connection emotions and their more vulnerable counterparts are nowhere to be found because of boys' earlier emotional training. Hence the basis for letting oneself be vulnerable, for exchanging emotional intimacy, and for the integration of emotional with physical intimacy is simply not there.

Rather, prevailing images in our society of females as sex objects encourage boys to view girls as vehicles for the release of their sexual urges. Acting on messages from their peers and the culture at large, adolescent boys also develop the need to prove their manhood by "scoring" with girls. As a result sexuality for boys becomes nonrelational and self-centered, in contrast to girls' greater emphasis on relational intimacy (Brooks, 1995; Levant & Brooks, 1997). In support of these differing views of sexuality by gender, recent research has found that only half as many males as females reported that affection for their partner was the reason for having sexual intercourse for the first time (Michael, Gagnon, Laumann, & Kolata, 1994).

Some research that I and colleagues have recently conducted on the major concerns of adolescent boys today is relevant to this discussion (Levant, Brooks, & Pitta, 2000). The question teachers (confederates in the study) posed to the boys was, "If you had the chance to have a private and confidential conversation with an expert with a great deal of knowledge and understanding about the concerns of adolescent boys today, what would you want to ask him or her? Please write down six questions about anything at all that is on your mind." Well over 90 percent of the responses concerned sex. Hence sexuality for teenage boys seems to be a looming, every-minute type of obsession.

Why does sex loom so large for boys? For basically the same reasons that anger, rage, and aggression serve as proxies for boys' more vulnerable emotions such as hurt, disappointment, sadness, shame, and loneliness: namely, that boys have been trained to so thoroughly suppress the expression of caring, attachment, neediness, and dependency that these emotions can only emerge in a very disguised, certainly unacknowledged, form hidden in the sexual experience. Like being angry when you are hurt, being lustful when you are needy is the only acceptable way a teenage boy trained under the code of masculinity can behave: powerful, dominant, aggressive, and self-sufficient and in no way vulnerable or needy. Teenage boys are rarely able to articulate this subterranean expression of caring emotions in their overt sexuality, but adult men have acknowledged to me how truly close and intimate they can feel with their wives during the act of sex.

With regard to the specific research results, boys had a lot of questions about sex. Some of these questions concerned anatomical aspects of genitalia, mechanical aspects of intercourse, sexually transmitted diseases, birth control, pregnancy, impotence, premature ejaculation, virginity, homosexuality and what causes it, how to know if you are gay, masturbation, oral sex, the experience of sex (many questions), and girls and how they think about, desire, and experience sex. This long list of questions highlights boys' isolation and underscores how difficult it is for them to talk to adults (parents and teachers) about things that matter a lot to them.

Influence of Popular Culture

For aeons parents have had to battle the influence of popular culture in their attempts to raise their children. Recently, malignant elements that foster misogyny and debasement of sex, as seen in the lyrics of contemporary rap music and MTV shows, have entered into the culture. One result is predatory sex, such as in the infamous "spur posse" (a gang of well-to-do boys who competed by victimizing girls), the "whirlpool" phenomenon (in which a group of boys surround a girl in a public swimming pool, swim around her to create a diversion, and then pull off her swimsuit or worse), "wilding" (in which a group of boys went on a rampage in Central Park, New York, assaulting women), and the like. In addition, the Internet offers too easily accessible XXX-rated pornography and provides pedophiles with a powerful means by which to lure children. These dangers are very real, and parents struggle to know what to do about them.

Alcohol and Drugs

The need to keep the communication channels open becomes even more important in relation to alcohol and drugs. Many teenage boys are involved with drugs of various sorts. Surveys conducted by the National Institute of Drug Abuse indicate that more than 60 percent of high school students have smoked cigarettes at least once, 90 percent have drunk alcohol at least once, and 44 percent have smoked marijuana at least once (Witters, Venturelli, & Hanson, 1992).

Peer pressure plays a large role in substance use. But drugs and alcohol have a particular appeal to teenage boys because they can have the effect of temporarily deadening boys' sensitivity to their emotional turmoil—the struggle between their needs and emotions (if these are not yet fully suppressed) and their beliefs about how boys are supposed to behave. In addition some drugs can temporarily assuage adolescents' bitter feelings of low self-esteem and embarrassment and shame about natural parts of themselves that violate the masculine code.

Because of boys' isolation from self and others and their need to appear self-sufficient, parents may miss the opportunity to discuss these matters at a time when it might make a difference. Many boys who use drugs have reported that there were periods of confusion and ambivalence, when having a way to talk to an empathic and concerned adult might have made a difference in their choice to use drugs.

Lack of Adult Supervision

Drugs, sex, and other problematic teen behaviors are aided and abetted by the lack of adult supervision that is widespread in U.S. society. Many changes in the family and neighborhood have taken place in the space of a generation. When the baby boom generation grew up, only a handful of mothers were in the workforce while children were small, and there were always adults around in the neighborhood after school. Children appear to have been more adequately supervised then. Now 75 percent of mothers are in the workforce, and the typical middle-class neighborhood is bereft of adults from 2 to 6 P.M. on school days. We became aware of this problem in the 1980s and termed the children "latchkey" or "self-care," as if giving them a label somehow dealt with the problem. However, we did not deal with the problem, and it has gotten much worse. For example, violent crime committed by juveniles soars during the 2 to 6 P.M. time slot. And of course, this is prime time for nonrelational sex. In the 1950s there were many obstacles to teen sex, which usually took place in the back seat of a car. Today it happens in the comfort of the child's home—usually the boy's. Once again this is a very difficult problem. Parents need guidance on what they can do to ensure that their children are adequately supervised during this highly vulnerable time.

Finding a Direction in Life

As has been noted, boys often have a problematic relationship with their fathers, which profoundly affects their ability to find a sense of direction in life and to visualize themselves as adult men. The father's role tends to vary a great deal today, from highly involved coparent to traditional breadwinner in two-parent homes, from custodial parent to visitation father to disengaged noncustodial parent in divorced families, and the role of stepfather in remarried families. However, three themes tend to recur with a high degree of consistency.

The first theme is that fathers tend to be the transmitters and chief enforcers of the code of masculinity. As noted, men tend to endorse the code to a much higher degree than do women. Furthermore, fathers believe that it is their job to "make men" out of their sons and as a consequence tend to deliver the shaming message that "big boys don't cry" or that males do not express affection to each other.

The second theme is that fathers tend to remain somewhat emotionally distant from the family, either by staying on the periphery or by focusing on the instrumental rather than the interpersonal and emotional aspects of family life.

The third theme is that fathers, like the men Henry David Thoreau described, "lead lives of quiet desperation." Themselves the servants of the code of masculinity, fathers tend to be breadwinners, or at least think of themselves that way, even when their wives earn half or more of the family income. They often approach their work as joyless duty, something that must be done to "put bread on the table and a roof over their heads."

IMPLICATIONS FOR COUNSELORS AND THERAPISTS

The dominant myths that males should be tough and stoic made more sense when social conditions were harsh, such as in the United States from the period of industrialization through World War I, the Great Depression, and World War II. However, in today's world emotional intelligence and the ability to balance one's own perspective with that of others—to be relational instead of nonrelational—is vitally important. Hence we need to debunk the myths and construct new, more flexible images of manhood. The women's movement succeeded in expanding women's adult roles, so that a woman can be both an aggressive marketer and a loving mother. We have yet to do the equivalent for men. We seem to fear that men will lose their essential manhood if they are not tough enough.

Counselors and psychologists are in a unique position to help boys, their parents, and their teachers respond to these crises. However, to do so requires developing a gender-aware perspective on boys and their emotional development, such as has been offered in this chapter and elsewhere (Pollack, 1998), and applying this perspective to the boys in counseling, their parents, and their teachers.

With regard to counseling boys, it is important to not take a boy's apparent self-sufficiency and emotional disengagement at face value. The counselor should also work at developing a relationship that will allow the boy to feel a strong and trusting bond, a sense of safety, and a secure knowledge that he will not be made to feel ashamed of himself, so that he can begin to explore his feelings of vulnerability and shame. Some adolescent boys have already been so thoroughly socialized that they are unable to experience and express their emotions. These boys could be considered mildly alexithymic and might benefit from my psychoeducational program designed to enhance males' emotional self-awareness (see Chapter Twenty-one).

As a family psychologist, I generally prefer to see the child in the family context. In addressing the problems of boys, parents are in great need of guidance for how to raise their sons in what many parents perceive as a sea of trouble. They need help on a range of matters such as (1) how to help their sons succeed in school (for example, addressing complaints or concerns voiced by teachers about their sons' performance or behavior, including blunt statements that the boy has "attention-deficit/hyperactivity disorder and needs an evaluation," which a teacher made to a family I counseled); (2) how to deal with the cruelty of boy culture (including how to handle bullies); (3) how to deal with peer pressure and the influence of other parents who may have different standards (for example, one couple I counseled was fairly strict and needed help in dealing with their son's complaints that "all the other boys get to do X"); (4) how to deal with the influence of the culture at large (including television, popular music, film, and of course the Internet); (5) how to find adult supervision during the vulnerable after-school period; and (6) for older children, how to deal with sex, alcohol, and drugs.

Finally, counseling professionals could have a significant influence on these problems (above and beyond the help they provide in the consulting room) by offering talks, workshops, and in-service training programs to groups of parents and teachers designed to raise their level of awareness of the influence of the code of masculinity and how it affects our boys.

References

Brody, L. (1996). Gender, emotional expression, and parent-child boundaries. In R. Kavanaugh, B. Zimmerberg-Glick, & S. Fein (Eds.), *Emotion: Interdisciplinary perspectives* (pp. 139–170). Hillsdale, NJ: Erlbaum.

Brody, L., & Hall, J. (1993). Gender and emotion. In M. Lewis & J. M. Haviland (Eds.), *Handbook of emotions* (pp. 435–460). New York: Guilford Press.

Brooks, G. R. (1995). *The centerfold syndrome.* San Francisco: Jossey-Bass.

Buck, R. (1977). Non-verbal communication of affect in preschool children: Relationships with personality and skin conductance. *Journal of Personality and Social Psychology, 35*(4), 225–236.

Bushweller, K. (1994). Turning our backs on boys. *American School Board Journal, 181,* 20–25.

Campbell, A. (1993). *Men, women, and aggression.* New York: Basic Books.

Dunn, J., Bretherton, I., & Munn, P. (1987). Conversations about feeling states between mothers and their children. *Developmental Psychology, 23,* 132–139.

Eagly, A. H., & Steffen, V. J. (1986). Gender and aggressive behavior: A meta-analytic review of the social psychological literature. *Psychological Bulletin, 100*(3), 309–330

Fivush, R. (1989). Exploring sex differences in the emotional content of mother child conversations about the past. *Sex Roles, 20,* 675–691.

Frodi, A., Macaulay, J., & Thome, P. R. (1977). Are women always less aggressive than men? A review of the experimental literature. *Psychological Bulletin, 84*(4), 634–660.

Fuchs, D., & Thelen, M. (1988). Children's expected interpersonal consequences of communicating their affective state and reported likelihood of expression. *Child Development, 59,* 1314–1322.

Greif, E. B., Alvarez, M., & Ulman, K. (1981, April). *Recognizing emotions in other people: Sex differences in socialization.* Paper presented at the meeting of the Society for Research in Child Development, Boston.

Haviland, J. J., & Malatesta, C. Z. (1981). The development of sex differences in non-verbal signals: Fallacies, facts, and fantasies. In C. Mayo & N. M. Henly (Eds.), *Gender and non-verbal behavior* (pp. 183–208). New York: Springer.

Kiselica, M. S., & Horne, A. M. (1999). Preface: For the sake of our nation's sons. In A. M. Horne & M. S. Kiselica (Eds.), *Handbook of counseling boys and adolescent males* (pp. xv–xx). Thousand Oaks, CA: Sage.

Krugman, S. (1995). Male development and the transformation of shame. In R. F. Levant & W. S. Pollack (Eds.), *A new psychology of men.* New York: Basic Books.

Lamb, M. E. (1977). The development of parental preferences in the first two years of life. *Sex Roles, 3,* 475–497.

Lamb, M. E., Owen, M. J., & Chase-Lansdale, L. (1979). The father daughter relationship: Past, present, and future. In C. B. Knopp & M. Kirkpatrick (Eds.), *Becoming female* (pp. 89–112). New York: Plenum.

Langlois, J. H., & Downs, A. C. (1980). Mother, fathers, and peers as socialization agents of sex-typed play behaviors in young children. *Child Development, 51,* 1217–1247.

Levant, R. F., & Brooks, G. R. (Eds.). (1997). *Men and sex: New psychological perspectives.* New York: Wiley.

Levant, R. F., Brooks, G. R., & Pitta, P. (2000). [The concerns of adolescent boys.] Unpublished raw data.

Levant, R. F., & Fischer, J. (1998). The Male Role Norms Inventory. In C. M. Davis, W. H. Yarber, R. Bauserman, G. Schreer, & S. L. Davis (Eds.), *Sexuality-related measures: A compendium* (2nd ed., pp. 469–472). Newbury Park, CA: Sage.

Levant, R. F., Hirsch, L., Celentano, E., Cozza, T., Hill, S., MacEachern, M., Marty, N., & Schnedeker, J. (1992). The male role: An investigation of norms and stereotypes. *Journal of Mental Health Counseling, 14,* 325–337.

Levant, R. F., & Kopecky, G. (1995). *Masculinity reconstructed.* New York: Dutton.

Levant, R. F., & Majors, R. G. (1997). An investigation into variations in the construction of the male gender role among young African American and European American women and men. *Journal of Gender, Culture, and Health, 2,* 33–43.

Levant, R. F., Majors, R. G., & Kelley, M. L. (1998). Masculinity ideology among young African American and European American women and men in different regions of the United States. *Cultural Diversity and Mental Health, 4,* 227–236.

Levant, R. F., & Pollack, W. S. (Eds.). (1995). *A new psychology of men.* New York: Basic Books.

Levant, R. F., Wu, R., & Fischer, J. (1996). Masculinity ideology: A comparison between U.S. and Chinese young men and women. *Journal of Gender, Culture, and Health, 1,* 207–220.

Lever, J. (1976). Sex differences in the games children play. *Social Work, 23*(4), 78–87.

Long, D. (1987). Working with men who batter. In M. Scher, M. Stevens, G. Good, & G. A. Eichenfield (Eds.), *Handbook of counseling and psychotherapy with men* (pp. 305–320). Newbury Park, CA: Sage.

Maccoby, E. E. (1990). Gender and relationships: A developmental account. *American Psychologist, 45,* 513–520.

Malatesta, C. Z., Culver, C., Tesman, J., & Shephard, B. (1989). The development of emotion expression during the first two years of life. *Monographs of the Society for Research in Child Development, 50* (1–2, Serial No. 219).

Michael, R. T., Gagnon, J. H., Laumann, E. O., & Kolata, G. (1994). *Sex in America: A definitive survey.* Boston: Little, Brown.

Paley, V. G. (1984). *Boys and girls: Superheroes in the doll corner.* Chicago: University of Chicago Press.

Pollack, W. S. (1998). *Real boys: Rescuing our sons from the myths of boyhood.* New York: Random House.

Schell, A., & Gleason, J. B. (1989, December). *Gender differences in the acquisition of the vocabulary of emotion.* Paper presented at the annual meeting of the American Association of Applied Linguistics, Washington, DC.

Weinberg, M. K. (1992). *Sex differences in 6-month-old infants' affect and behavior: Impact on maternal caregiving.* Unpublished doctoral dissertation, University of Massachusetts, Amherst, MA.

Witters, W., Venturelli, P., & Hanson, G. (1992). *Drugs and society.* Boston: Jones & Bartlett.

CHAPTER EIGHTEEN

Addressing the Implications of Male Socialization for Career Counseling

Mary J. Heppner
P. Paul Heppner

A curious irony exists in the literature on the career development of men. In some ways, most of the history of the field has been male centered. Frank Parsons, who is widely regarded as the father of career development, began this field in the early part of the twentieth century by emphasizing the importance of "matching men and jobs." Throughout the century, researchers and theorists have continued to emphasize men in their longitudinal research and in their development of vocational assessment measures, career theories, and normative work patterns. As Leona Tyler (1977) argued, "much of what we know about the stages through which an individual passes as he [sic] prepares to find his [sic] place in the world of work might appropriately be labeled 'The Vocational Development of Middle Class Males' " (p. 40). Given that history, it is rather amazing how little is actually known about the influence of male gender role socialization in various facets of career development for contemporary American men.

The irony is that much of the foundational work in the area of career development was conducted at a time when men were viewed as homogeneous. The men studied were, as Tyler noted, typically white and middle class. Their career development patterns were studied at a time when most men followed what today would be labeled a traditionally masculine gender role pattern. During this time researchers and practitioners gave little attention to differences among men, particularly in terms of gender role socialization. No one thought much about the gender socialization context of a man's chosen career path or about the psychological or physical consequences created by living the career pattern of the traditional male. Even in the early twenty-first century, we find that men's career development has not been extensively studied within a gendered perspective.

The purpose of this chapter is twofold. First, we highlight ten critical issues that we perceive emerging from both the new psychology of men literature (Levant, 1996) and our own experience in counseling men; it is particularly important for counselors to understand these issues in counseling male clients about career choices. Second, using a model of the career counseling process (Gysbers, Heppner, & Johnston, 1998), we illustrate how these themes often emerge in actual career counseling sessions. Throughout this final section, we provide numerous case examples from the lives of men that portray the lived experiences of men as they struggle with career issues.

Before we proceed we offer two caveats: First, it is important to underscore that providing career counseling for men is similar in many respects to providing career counseling in general; however, special gender dynamics often arise that can either facilitate or hinder the career counseling process. Gender issues do not always affect the career counseling process, but we conceptualize these gender dynamics as an additional set of variables (among many) that can affect the career counseling process (see Heppner & Gonzales, 1987). Second, because there are virtually no empirical data on gender-related career counseling with men, the information and suggestions provided in this chapter are based largely on our own experience and observations from the professional literature. Thus, until empirical data emerge, it is important to realize that it is unclear to what extent these observations are generalizable. We know from our experience that men differ greatly in how they respond to the various suggestions we make. For example, although reinforcing a man's strength for coming into counseling may feel validating to one man, it may seem condescending to another. Thus, the suggestions and observations that follow are not meant to be a foolproof recipe but rather a list of possible potent ingredients that the individual counselor will need to sensitively apply given the uniqueness of each individual man's experience.

TEN CRITICAL ISSUES IN CAREER COUNSELING WITH MEN

In examining the literature and thinking about our own counseling experiences when working with men, a host of issues could be addressed. Here we highlight ten that we consider to be the most important for counselors to understand to work effectively with men in career counseling.

Relationship Between Men's Life Goals and Their Male Socialization

Perhaps the most overarching issue is the importance of placing gender awareness at the core of career counseling with men. At each step of the career counseling process, it is important to understand how a man's early and current gender role socialization may have influenced the man in the past and may continue to affect his life choices. For example, some men might be unaware of the impact of early messages they received about what it is to be a boy (for example, strong, resilient, unexpressive emotionally, and aggressive) on choices they are now making about careers. Other men might be unaware of the pressure they experience from working multiple jobs to obtain a certain lifestyle for their family. Thus, the counselor might discuss how early attitudes about sex-appropriate and sex-inappropriate occupations were formed (Gettys & Cann, 1981). Often by the time boys or men seek career counseling, the socialization process affects all parts of the process, including whether they seek career services at all, how they interact with the counselor, how open or closed they are in discussing their problems, what career fields they may be considering, and their willingness to engage with the process that career counseling entails.

In short, it is helpful to continually seek to understand the many facets of a male client's life goals in terms of his prior socialization as a male; such a perspective often is helpful in understanding the psychological dynamics (that is, cognitions, affect, and behaviors) related to the man's motivation and career choices and development. Moreover, gender role constructs may well affect the type of psychological problems that exist, their associated symptoms, and how people respond to problems (Cook, 1990; Eisler & Blalock, 1991). For example, research indicates that strong adherence to particular standards and expectations within a man's gender role ideology may have both negative physical and negative psychological effects (Pleck, 1995). In addition, research has indicated that men use different ways of coping with stress than women use during some stressful career transitions (Heppner, Cook, Strozier, & Heppner, 1991). Thus, understanding the career issue within the broader gender socialization context gives the counselor a much more complete picture of the male client's process.

Critical Role of Work in Most Men's Lives

Men often define who they are in the world through work. As Skovholt (1990) poignantly expressed, "Painting a picture of men's lives often results in a work-dominated landscape" (p. 39). For example, Keen (1991) described the first job as a rite of passage into manhood. At this point work often begins to influence a man's identity, either directly or indirectly, to the point that work and self become inseparable for many men. To be a man is to be successful in one's career, to achieve, to make money, and to be able to afford possessions that also become symbols of a man's worth (David & Brannon, 1976). "Whether the job is loved, hated, intrinsically satisfying, or boring, is much less relevant than the expectation that a man will work. A long term non-working male adult violates this strong male principle and is usually shunned or rejected" (Skovholt, 1990, p. 42). It is not surprising, given the importance of the role of work for many men, that there is often an imbalance between the amount of time a man devotes to work and the amount of time he devotes to leisure activities and even personal relationships and family life (O'Neil, 1981). O'Neil and his colleagues have found that conflict between work and family relations is a major source of gender role conflict in men (see O'Neil, Good, & Holmes, 1995). Thus, it is important for the counselor to understand how central the role of work is to many men and that it often means a great deal more than earning a living; it is really about earning a self. It is thus important to understand the role of work in a male client's life, how work affects other aspects of his life, and how career-related decisions affect the man's physical and psychological well-being.

Variations Among Men: Individual Differences That May Influence Men's Career Development

It is critical that career counselors not continue to subscribe to the homogeneity myth that all men are alike. Men in need of career services are a diverse group and differ in all sorts of individual areas, including racial and ethnic minority status, age and developmental stage in the career planning process, sexual orientation, and physical stature and appearance, all of which contribute to how they view themselves as men and the career paths they may want to pursue. Moreover, men differ on a multitude of personality variables such as self-esteem, need for control, locus of control, and problem-solving style and have acquired a unique set of values. Thus, it is critically important that career counselors be sensitive, aware, and skillful in working with a diverse range of male clients and not be biased in their assumptions and myths about men in general.

Recent career texts have devoted considerable attention to the unique needs of various groups (Gysbers et al., 1998; Leong, 1995). Today's career counselors need to continue to review current research on specific groups and ways of meeting their career planning needs most effectively. This knowledge can include such varied competencies as understanding how racial and ethnic identity development may influence the career development process (Helms, 1990; Helms & Piper, 1994) and becoming knowledgeable of the guidelines of the Americans with Disabilities Act of 1990 and the amendments of 1992 and how these guidelines influence the career options of clients with disabilities. As is probably evident, this knowledge base is large; highly skilled professionals are needed to serve the unique career development needs of an increasingly varied clientele (and in this case a varied clientele of men). Thus, it is important for counselors not only to be knowledgeable about male gender role socialization and its many intragroup variations but also to continually check the accuracy of assumptions and conclusions we draw about a particular client, preferably in dialogue with the client.

Assessment of Male Gender Role Attributes and Traditional Career Assessments

Assessment is an important, ongoing process in career counseling and can consist of both formal and informal assessment methods (see Gysbers et al., 1998).

Moreover, a number of formal assessment measures are designed to specifically assess aspects of the male gender role. These assessments can be used along with traditional career interest assessments (such as the Strong Interest Inventory [Harmon, Hansen, Borgen, & Hammer, 1994] and the Self-Directed Search [Holland, 1985]) to provide a more complete picture of the issues facing contemporary men. It may also be useful for counselors to take the assessments to evaluate their own gender role socialization, which may affect the efficacy of their work with clients (see Heppner & Gonzales, 1987).

Thompson and Pleck (1995) reviewed the available instruments on men and masculinity-related constructs. Four of the most used and researched instruments are (1) the Gender Role Conflict Scale (O'Neil, Helms, Gable, David, & Wrightsman, 1986), (2) the Masculine Gender Role Stress Scale (Eisler & Skidmore, 1987), (3) the Male Roles Scale (Brannon & Juni, 1984; Fischer, Tokar, Good, & Snell, 1998; Thompson & Pleck, 1986), and (4) the Gender Role Journey measure (O'Neil, Egan, Owens, & McBride, 1993). As assessment tools, these four instruments provide a context in which and a language with which to discuss the complex issues of gender and career planning. Counselors can use them with male clients to introduce gender role constructs and incorporate these constructs as integral parts of the career counseling process. Used in concert with more traditional career planning measures, gender-informed formal assessments can help male clients understand their career development process. In addition, informal assessment of clients' cognitions, affect, and behaviors is equally important to understand the messages particular clients have received or incorporated into their worldviews about being men, particularly related to the world of work. Thus, useful information about male clients can be obtained through formal assessment or by asking clients throughout the counseling process about their beliefs, thoughts, feelings, and actions related to male gender role socialization.

Integration of Psychological Adjustment with Issues of Career Choice or Adjustment

An unfortunate dichotomy of separating career adjustment from issues of psychological adjustment has existed in the field of career development for years (see Hackett, 1993). This dichotomy has led to some serious problems for clients in that most if not all career concerns are intertwined with psychological issues. Research indicates that most adult clients seeking career services also have psychological adjustment issues (such as depression or anxiety) (Multon, Heppner, Gysbers, Zook, & Ellis, 1998). Because work tends to be such a vital part of men's lives, chances are very good that when men seek counseling for psychological problems, their problems relate to their work life or their psychological distress affects their work life. Thus, it is critical that career counselors use a holistic approach to working with men and see career as just one part, albeit a very important part, of a broader picture of how male clients are functioning.

This holistic approach would also include examining the role of relationships with family and friends, exercise, and leisure activities. Again, the integration of psychological adjustment with career issues emphasizes the need for a broad, thorough, and careful assessment.

Strengths That Male Socialization Often Develops

Oftentimes only the negative aspects of the male role are discussed. For example, men in general have been described as tending to be emotionally restrictive (see O'Neil, 1981), unaware of their own feelings or the feelings of others (see Heppner & Gonzales, 1987), and often requiring control and dominance (Farrell, 1975). Although considerable evidence suggests that male gender role socialization and subsequent gender role conflict are linked to a host of problems for many contemporary men (see Cournoyer & Mahalik, 1995; Good et al., 1995; O'Neil, Good, & Holmes, 1995; Sharpe & Heppner, 1991), focus on only these potentially negative aspects of the male role may leave men feeling stripped of any redeeming characteristics. It is vitally important that counselors recognize and affirm strengths related to male gender role socialization. For example, male socialization is typically linked to a myriad of skills such as the ability to persist in difficult situations until problems are resolved; the ability to strategize, think logically, take risks, and stay calm in the face of danger; willingness to sacrifice personal needs to provide for others; willingness to withstand hardship to protect others; and ability to express love through action, or doing things for others (Levant, 1996). It is helpful for counselors to not only emphasize and bring into clients' awareness these and other skills related to problem solving in particular but also to draw on these skills in developing career paths with clients. In short, affirming these and the other strengths that many men possess can be very helpful in the career counseling process and instrumental in achieving the desired career planning outcomes.

Men and the Difficult Art of Help Seeking

The constellation of self-reliance, emotional restrictiveness, and the need for control defines the traditional male gender role (David & Brannon, 1976). To be able to take care of oneself, to not need others, and to be independent are all well-socialized characteristics for many men. Thus, to seek counseling services goes against the very core of many contemporary men (Good & May, 1987; Good, Dell, & Mintz, 1989). It is not surprising that compared with women, men underuse all forms of social services, including career counseling services (Gysbers et al., 1998). It is often very difficult for men to admit not only to others but even to themselves that they need assistance to solve a problem. As Scher (1979) noted, "his pride will be suffering" (p. 253). Thus, counselors should consider the cost to the self-esteem of men who have to admit they cannot deal with their lives and must enlist the aid of others to resolve their problems (Heilbrun, 1961). It is also important for counselors to recognize that when men actually seek counseling, they are likely to be experiencing a fair amount of distress in some aspect of their lives. Often it is useful for counselors to acknowledge the strength it takes to come to counseling and that the male clients have taken an important first step in improving their life situation. Moreover, some men who seek psychological assistance find it difficult to complete counseling and thus end counseling prematurely. Thus, we have found it helpful to occasionally process with clients how they are experiencing counseling and if they are progressing in the intended manner.

Men, Relationships, and the Formation of the Working Alliance

The importance of building a strong working alliance with clients to achieve successful outcome has been well documented in the literature (Beutler, Machado, & Nuefeldt, 1994; Meara & Patton, 1994). Meara and Patton described the alliance as the part of counseling that can be characterized as mutuality, collaboration, and cooperation of two individuals working together toward common goals through a mutual bond. Research has also indicated that this alliance needs to be formed early in the counseling relationship and that in most counseling the alliance is either firmly in place (or not) by the third session (Eaton, Abeles, & Gutfreund, 1988). Building a strong working alliance with male clients can pose some challenges. Much has been written about the traditional male socialization process with regard to interpersonal relationships (see Goldberg, 1976; Lewis, 1978), but surprisingly little has been written about how best to establish a strong working alliance with different types of men. Because of the traditional male socialization process, building a relationship with male clients may sometimes be difficult. For example, if the counselor is male, the male client may feel vulnerable, competitive, or uncomfortable with this unfamiliar intimacy with another man (see Heppner & Gonzales, 1987). If the counselor is a woman, the client may feel more or less comfortable, defensive, or resistant, depending on his past relationships with women (see Carlson, 1987).

It is important that the client perceive that the counselor understands and accepts his situation. Appreciating the pride of the man and empathizing with his discomfort and inadequacy may be important for the formation of a working alliance. Self-disclosure of relevant and appropriate information from the counselor's own life may help model the appropriate expression of emotion and assist in building the bond. As the counselor begins building the working alliance he or she can also reinforce client strengths; such reinforcement may be especially important because the client may feel he has few strengths left if he has reached the point of coming for help.

Intricate Dance Between Taking Action and Focusing on the Process

The process of career counseling with many men involves a delicate balance between the push to take action and the pull to focus on issues of self-awareness. In general, men tend to be problem focused and are typically inclined to take action to solve their problems (see Scher, 1979). However, many men are less interested or comfortable with a discussion of how their feelings or socialization may have influenced their career development (see Heppner & Gonzales, 1987). Some men use a variety of techniques to avoid dealing with their feelings about themselves as men. For example, one man said quite directly, "I don't care about this touchy-feely stuff; I am here to find a new job." Others simply intellectualize the issue away. Sometimes men are simply unaware of their feelings, whereas other times fear and anxiety drive this avoidance. Thus, the counselor needs to achieve a balance between problem solving and taking action, on the one hand, and identifying important psychological issues related to the process that some men would rather not talk about, on the other hand. During the dance between process and action, the counselor needs to monitor whether the male client has sufficient self-knowledge and occupational knowledge to make these critical life choices.

The Changing Job Market and Skills Requirements

The contrast between the workplace of the current generation and the workplace of previous generations is vast. In essence, the changes that are currently taking place raise questions about the very basic assumptions of what it is to be a worker and what it is to have a career. Specifically for men, the personal characteristics so important to the last generation such as competitiveness, ability to rise within a hierarchical structure, longevity, and stability are not necessarily the most valued traits in today's workforce. In many of today's companies, individual accomplishment is no longer highly valued because workers function primarily as part of a larger group brought together to work as a team on specific projects (Feller & Waltz, 1995). This team structure requires far different skills than those needed in the traditional, more individualistic structure. For example, interpersonal skills become paramount in these kinds of organizations; one must be able to work with diverse people (including both men and women and people of diverse races and social backgrounds), have excellent verbal skills, and be able to disagree or express conflict in appropriate ways. For some men, this new marketplace requires skills they have not developed. They are being asked to be interdependent with their team, to cooperate for the good of the team, to express their thoughts and feelings by using interpersonal skills, and to collaborate on resolving problems. This changing work environment can create new stresses for some men. For the counselor, it may be especially important to address these differences and to help the client find ways of enhancing his skills to better meet the changing needs of today's marketplace.

INTEGRATING ISSUES OF MALE GENDER ROLE SOCIALIZATION INTO THE CAREER COUNSELING PROCESS

It is often difficult to take an intellectual understanding of a topic such as male gender role socialization and apply it to your own work with career clients. Thus, we provide a model of the career counseling process developed by Gysbers and his colleagues (1998) and then discuss examples of integrating the issues relevant to the gendered context for men into this structure. The Gysbers et al. (1998) model proposed a number of activities within the career counseling process, which for clarity are identified chronologically as phases and subphases. Although Gysbers et al. presented these phases in a linear fashion, they emphasized the nonlinear nature of the career counseling process and the need to return to various phases and subphases as counseling progresses.

The first phase is client goal or problem identification, clarification, and specification, which includes the subphases of (1) opening and forming the working alliance, (2) gathering client information, and (3) understanding and hypothesizing about client behavior. The second phase is client goal or problem resolution, which includes (1) taking action, (2) developing goals and plans of action, and (3) evaluating results and closing the relationship. We describe these phases and subphases in the following sections, along with particular aspects of the male gender role that might be important in each phase. Although we selected issues that often occur in a particular phase of career counseling, any of the ten issues previously described can be important throughout the counseling process.

First Phase of Treatment

The first major phase of the career counseling process is one of defining and building the relationship, gathering and evaluating client information, and using this information to understand and hypothesize about client behavior.

Opening. The opening phase of career counseling has as its central goals (1) identifying the client's goals or problems and the internal thoughts and feelings that might be involved, (2) beginning to form the working alliance, and (3) defining and clarifying the client-counselor relationship and responsibilities.

Given that most men tend to avoid career counseling, some men may feel threatened in some way if they seek assistance. Thus, as the initial counseling session begins, it is often useful to affirm the man's strength in seeking counseling. A subtle reassurance concerning the wisdom and courage he is exhibiting, such as the following statement, may be helpful to some men:

> Many men stay in jobs they hate for their whole working lives. Other men, like you, are clear that they want something better for themselves and their families. I am glad that you have taken an important first step by coming here today.

In addition, the working alliance begins to form in this first session. As we have indicated, building a strong alliance with men requires sensitivity to what will build and conversely what will diminish this alliance. For example, although self-disclosure by the counselor is often seen as a positive way of emphasizing communality with the client, such strategies can backfire, as a client of ours recently stated:

> Yes, I was in counseling once before, but the guy I worked with kept telling me how his parents had never let him cry and how he is less able to express himself than he would like. . . . I thought the guy was a flake and maybe needed more help than I did.

Our suggestion is to take the lead from the client. For example, if the man tends to be task oriented, then the counselor can communicate that he or she is willing to work with him on the tasks and goals that are most important to him at this time in his life. In this way, the counselor can communicate caring in a way that some men are better able to receive.

Another example of communicating understanding of a male client might relate to the close link between work and self. Although a career change, job layoff, or firing can begin to seem a normative and routine experience for many career counselors, it is often critical for the counselor to communicate understanding about the importance of these events to the individual man. It can be helpful to build a working alliance by communicating that the counselor really understands how hard it can be to lose a job, for example.

Another important part of building the working alliance in this early phase is identifying and acknowledging that each man has developed strengths that will be helpful to him at this time. For example, as the counselor learns more about his or her client's career history, the counselor may search for skills such as the client's ability to persist in difficult situations, to work on problems until they are resolved, or to think logically (see Levant, 1996). For purposes of career counseling, the skills associated with male gender role socialization can be strengths for the career planning process. Recognizing and affirming them can also help to build the working alliance, as a recent client emphasized in a closing session:

> I don't know, when I came in here, I was at an all-time low. I kind of felt like a dinosaur. . . . Like who I was, and the way I was raised wasn't good enough. My wife kept telling me I needed to communicate with her and tell her I loved her more and express my feelings. While I definitely know I do need to work on being more open, you helped me see that I do communicate love, only in a dif-

ferent way than she does, and that I do have strengths, I just need to—what did you call it?—"expand my repertoire."

As the relationship grows with the individual, the counselor might start helping the client examine his goals through a gender filter (for example, "Which of your goals are motivated from your upbringing as a man?" or "Which of your difficulties are the result of environmental pressures and a need to prove some aspect of the traditional male role?") The counselor might also note to what extent the client tends to express emotions freely and honestly, even if they include feelings of vulnerability or fear. Does the client appear to be setting authentic goals based on a full knowledge of relevant information? If relevant, the counselor can openly discuss these questions with the client. With some clients, the counselor may need to approach the questions later and less directly. It may also be important to make explicit that the goal of such exploration is to help the client make more life-affirming choices about his work life.

Greg's situation is a good example. Greg was in his late forties when he came in for counseling, had held a variety of jobs in business, and had worked his way up to a very comfortable and high-status position. But he reported being unhappy in his work. The counselor noted that even though all of Greg's formal jobs had been within conservative financial firms, Greg's Daydreams list on Holland's Self-Directed Search indicated he had dreamed of being a social worker, a Peace Corps volunteer, and a minister at earlier times in his life. However, it seemed difficult for him to talk about the inconsistency between his dream jobs and his real jobs, and so the counselor provided the following type of rationale:

> Greg, it seems like you are telling me that you have a position that pays well and has a great deal of status in your firm and yet you feel unhappy. I see that you had earlier dreams of becoming a social worker, Peace Corps volunteer, or minister. It seems important to explore how it was that you left that socially oriented path and followed the business path you did. By understanding more about some original dreams, we may be better able to help you decide what path might be most beneficial for you right now.

This initial phase is also a time for clarifying the counselor-client relationship and responsibilities. Counselors whose philosophy includes working together in a collaborative manner with the client need to clarify this orientation from the start. Some men view the counselor as an "answer dispenser." Their expectations are to go in and get fixed, not to work in a collaborative relationship that emphasizes self-awareness. Also the counselor and client may need to discuss the role of the environment in shaping the individual. In essence, the client has a right to be informed in his choice of a career counselor. The counselor's philosophical base is important information in making that choice.

Gathering client information. The clarification and information-gathering subphase of the career counseling process has as its central goal learning more about the client. Any of the assessments discussed earlier in this chapter can be used to supplement any other standardized or nonstandardized career-related assessment measures. The Gender Role Conflict Scale, Masculine Gender Role Stress Scale, Male Role Norms Scale, and Gender Role Journey are all effective assessment measures to gather information about experiences that may affect the client's career planning process. If a counselor uses one of these measures with a client, it is important to discuss the rationale for doing so. The counselor might say something like the following:

> I think it would be helpful for you to take a series of instruments to help us both get a better picture of where you are in your life right now. A couple of these will be instruments that assess your career interests and values. Another one relates to how you view yourself as a man and how that may be influencing your career planning.

Assessment instruments such as those mentioned can also be used in creative ways, perhaps as a stimulus for journal writing. For example, the counselor might ask the male client to take one of the gender role instruments and then write in a journal to help explore the various themes further. For example, the following was a portion of a client's journal entry after taking the Male Role Norms Scale:

> When I was growing up, I was always critical of my dad for being so materialistic. He was never with us, because he was always out there trying to earn a buck. Now that I have my own family, I am struck with how much like him I have become. Partly I understand more the pressures he was facing, but partly I also want to achieve a better balance in my own work and family life.

Combining both traditional career measures such as Holland's Self-Directed Search and gender role measures such as the Gender Role Journey measure by O'Neil and his colleagues can provide a comprehensive assessment of what would be most helpful to the client. For example, Don had what would be considered a very low, flat profile on the Self-Directed Search, with only high scores in the Realistic area (indicating that the client was expressing interests in working independently, primarily with his hands, on very tangible kinds of products). Don's scores on the Gender Role Journey measure indicated that he was at the gender role stage characterized by gender role ambivalence, confusion, anger, and fear. By talking through the antecedents of his ambivalent feelings, it became clear that he wanted to be more open to different occupations but felt confused about whether he could be involved in more interpersonally oriented occupations and still feel like a man.

Understanding and hypothesizing about client behavior. The specification subphase of the career counseling process has as its central goal understanding clients more fully and hypothesizing about their unique dynamics and the psychological and environmental reasons behind their actions. Thus, in this phase it may be appropriate to examine how a male client's psychological adjustment may be influencing his career adjustment. It may also be an appropriate place to discuss how the environmental changes in today's labor force might have changed which characteristics are valued in some workplaces and how these changes may be affecting the individual. Thus, in this phase the counselor is trying to probe deeper and understand more about how the client is making meaning out of himself and his occupational world.

During this phase the counselor may assess the psychological adjustment of the client, either formally or informally, and determine how psychological adjustment may be influencing career adjustment. For example, James came into career counseling at the urging of his wife. He had lost his job when his company downsized and had been unable to find work for the past six months. As he talked, the counselor noted his flat affect and slow speech. She began hypothesizing that James was depressed, perhaps clinically. It was clear that he had been unable to conduct an active and successful job search, due in large part to his depression. When he went for interviews, he presented himself as a low-energy person with little zest for the position. Thus, in this case both formal and informal assessments provided useful information to the counselor and client and altered the course of counseling.

In this phase it may also be appropriate to assess how environmental change such as the changing culture of the workplace may be influencing an individual client. The following scenario occurred after the counselor noted that the client was having difficulty interpersonally in the workplace:

COUNSELOR: You said you feel uncomfortable at work, like you don't fit in. Can you say more about that?

CLIENT: I don't know. . . . It just seems like I used to know the rules. I came up with an idea, I brought it to my boss, and if he liked it I ran with it. . . . Now everything goes through my team. I have to sell my idea to eight other people, some of whom I don't get along with at all. I don't know, I was always able to talk to my boss—and we would see eye to eye most of the time—but some of those people on my team, particularly the two ladies, . . . we just don't seem to be on the same wavelength.

This type of interchange helps the counselor understand more about the interpersonal dynamics of the client and what strategies might be effective in helping him.

In this phase the counselor may hypothesize about and understand how unique aspects of the man such as his race, ethnicity, sexual orientation, or physical stature may be influencing his career choices. This process can take many forms; for example, it may be a time to talk with a gay client about how his sexual orientation may be influencing his career planning process. It might also be important that the client understand the phenomenon of internalized homophobia and recognize whether he has internalized society's heterosexist messages and beliefs. It may be a time to talk to an African American client about his own black racial identity and how this identity may be influencing his career choice or adjustment. For example, he may be at the immersion-emersion status, which is characterized by high racial saliency and idealization of black standards and denigration of white standards (Helms, 1990). If so, his racial identity as an African American may be influencing many facets of his career, including where he feels comfortable working and with whom he wants to work. Thus, these individual difference variables may be important influences on the career planning process and ones that need in-depth exploration at this phase.

Second Phase of Treatment

The second major phase of the career counseling process is one of action taking. In this phase counseling moves from gathering and evaluating information to actually taking steps to act on this information. Getting to this phase means that the counselor and client have examined all the major aspects of the client's situation and the client is in a position to make an authentic life decision based on as complete a set of information about himself and the world of work as possible.

Taking action. Taking action is sometimes an easier phase of the counseling process than earlier ones for many men because it typically is consistent with their gender role training. Nonetheless, it is important to be sure men have the necessary self-knowledge and occupational knowledge to make career decisions before proceeding with the action phase. Consider the following example of a midcareer man, Bill, who came to a career planning center and began speaking rapidly, in an authoritative tone:

> Well, you could say I am in a bit of a mess. I just lost my job—was fired for what my idiot boss described as "insubordination"—and then my wife decides "we have grown too far apart" and moves out, all in the course of one week. I need to get a job and fast. I heard you people could help people find a job. Where can I begin looking?

Even from this short introduction, it is easy to determine there are many issues here and most likely a great deal of pain. Underneath the assertive exterior, the man is probably very scared, hurt, and angry, and yet his main goal is action—to get a job quickly. This man's situation is a good example of when being able to do the dance between taking action and staying with the process becomes important. Thus, even though this man's life is difficult, it is important to help him slow down a bit and live with the ambiguity inherent within the career transition to increase the probability of making good choices.

Developing career goals and plans of action. Individualized career plans are particularly important when the counselor is helping a male client incorporate parts of his gender role ideology into the career planning process. It can be very helpful to a client to carefully examine each step of the plan of action in terms of how he is likely to handle the particular action steps given his gender role upbringing. For example, if a counselor is helping a man who may likely come off as arrogant when interviewing with women, building the client's awareness about the consequences of various interpersonal styles might be helpful. If one is helping a gay man apply for positions in an employment setting that may not be open to gay men, discussing each choice point he has in the job application and interview process is often important (Hedgepeth, 1979/1980). In essence, many times it is useful to role-play and strengthen various skills or thoroughly discuss choice points to increase the probability of the client's action plan being successful and producing long-term satisfaction.

Evaluating results and closing the relationship. The closing sessions are a time to examine whether goals have been met and what the process was like for the counselor and the client. When examining the closure sessions through a gender filter, several issues are often important.

The counselor and client can reflect on the journey the career counseling process has taken. For some men this may have been the first time that they identified the need for help and sought counseling. It is sometimes very important for the counselor to reflect on and again reinforce the courage of that act. It may be helpful to the client to see the experience of asking for help as a sign of strength rather than a sign of weakness.

It is also sometimes helpful to reflect on the entire counseling process to examine whether new things can be learned from the process. For example, is there anything to be learned from how the working alliance developed? Or if there were tears in the working alliance, is there anything to be learned from how they were mended? How are both the counselor and client feeling about termination of the counseling? In short, it can be helpful to talk about how the counseling relationship developed, how communication became more honest, and other important events that might be transferable to other situations or relationships in the man's life.

The counselor may want to encourage the client to return for additional sessions or just to update the counselor on the client's progress. It is often especially important for men to know that the support system that was provided during counseling will remain if they meet with difficulties after counseling has closed.

Although the field of career counseling has focused since its inception at the turn of the twentieth century primarily on understanding men, much more information is needed about being effective in career counseling with contemporary men in the twenty-first century. In this chapter we have highlighted some aspects of the male gender role socialization process that seem to affect the career counseling process with men. Helping clients understand how their male gender role socialization might affect their life path is an important but complex goal for counselors. We hope that future researchers will investigate this important issue and provide the next generation with much-needed data to inform the career counseling process with contemporary men.

References

Beutler, L. E., Machado, P. P., & Nuefeldt, S. A. (1994). Therapist variables. In A. E. Bergin & S. L. Garfield (Eds.), *Handbook of psychotherapy and behavior change* (pp. 229–269). New York: Wiley.

Brannon, R., & Juni, S. (1984). A scale for measuring attitudes toward masculinity. *JSAS Catalog of Selected Documents in Psychology, 14,* 6 (MS No. 2012).

Carlson, N. L. (1987). Woman therapist: Male client. In M. Scher, M. Stevens, G. Good, & G. A. Eichenfield (Eds.), *Handbook of counseling and psychotherapy with men* (pp. 39–50). Newbury Park, CA: Sage.

Cook, E. P. (1990). Gender and psychological distress. *Journal of Counseling and Development, 68,* 371–375.

Cournoyer, R. J., & Mahalik, J. R. (1995). Cross-sectional study of gender role conflict examining college-aged and middle-aged men. *Journal of Counseling Psychology, 42,* 11–19.

David, D. S., & Brannon, R. (1976). *The forty-nine percent majority: The male sex role.* Reading, MA: Addison-Wesley.

Eaton, T. T., Abeles, N., & Gutfreund, M. J. (1988). Therapeutic alliance and outcome: Impact of treatment length and pretreatment symptomatology. *Psychotherapy, 25,* 536–542.

Eisler, R. M., & Blalock, J. A. (1991). Masculine gender role stress: Implications for the assessment of men. *Clinical Psychology Review, 11,* 45–60.

Eisler, R. M., & Skidmore, J. R. (1987). Masculine gender role stress: Scale development and component factors in the appraisal of stressful situations. *Behavior Modification, 11,* 123–136.

Farrell, W. T. (1975). *The liberated man.* New York: Random House.

Feller, R., & Walz, G. R. (1995). *Optimizing life transitions in turbulent times: Exploring work, learning, and careers.* Greensboro, NC: ERIC Clearinghouse on Counseling and Student Services.

Fischer, A. R., Tokar, D. M., Good, G. E., & Snell, A. F. (1998). More on the structure of male role norms: Exploratory and multiple sample confirmatory analyses. *Psychology of Women Quarterly, 22,* 135–155.

Gettys, L. D., & Cann, A. (1981). Children's perceptions of occupational sex stereotypes. *Sex Roles, 7,* 301–308.

Goldberg, H. (1976). The hazards of being male: Surviving the myth of masculine privilege. New York: Nash.

Good, G. E., Dell, D. M., & Mintz, L. B. (1989). Male roles and gender role conflict: Relationships to help seeking in men. *Journal of Counseling Psychology, 3,* 295–300.

Good, G. E., & May, R. (1987). Developmental issues, environmental influences, and the nature of therapy with college men. In M. Scher, M. Stevens, G. Good, & G. A. Eichenfield (Eds.), *Handbook of counseling and psychotherapy with men* (pp. 150–164). Newbury Park, CA: Sage.

Good, G. E., Robertson, J. M., O'Neil, J. M., Fitzgerald, L. F., Stevens, M., Debord, K. A., Bartels, K. M., & Braverman, D. G. (1995). Male gender role conflict: Psychometric issues and relation to psychological distress. *Journal of Counseling Psychology, 42,* 3–10.

Gysbers, N. C., Heppner, M. J., & Johnston, J. A. (1998). *Career counseling: Process, issues, and techniques.* Boston: Allyn & Bacon.

Hackett, G. (1993). Career counseling and psychotherapy: False dichotomies and recommended remedies. *Journal of Career Assessment, 1,* 105–117.

Hedgepeth, J. M. (1979/1980). Employment discrimination law and the rights of gay persons. *Journal of Homosexuality, 5*(12), 67–78.

Heilbrun, A. B. (1961). Male and female personality correlates of early termination in counseling. *Journal of Counseling Psychology, 8,* 31–36.

Helms, J. E. (1990). *Black and white racial identity: Theory, research, and practice.* New York: Greenwood Press.

Helms, J. E., & Piper, R. E. (1994). Implications of racial identity theory for vocational psychology. *Journal of Vocational Behavior, 44,* 124–136.

Heppner, P. P., Cook, S. W., Strozier, A. L., & Heppner, M. J. (1991). An investigation of coping styles and gender differences with farmers in career transition. *Journal of Counseling Psychology, 38,* 167–174.

Heppner, P. P., & Gonzales, D. S. (1987). Men counseling men. In M. Scher, M. Stevens, G. Good, & G. A. Eichenfield (Eds.), *Handbook of counseling and psychotherapy with men* (pp. 30–38). Newbury Park, CA: Sage.

Keen, S. (1991). *Fire in the belly: On being a man.* New York: Bantam Books.

Leong, F.T.L. (1995). *Career development and vocational behavior of racial and ethnic minorities.* Mahwah, NJ: Erlbaum.

Levant, R. F. (1996). Masculinity reconstructed. *Independent Practitioner, 16,* 1. American Psychological Association, Division 42, Bulletin of the Division of Independent Practice.

Lewis, R. A. (1978). Emotional intimacy among men. *Journal of Social Issues, 34,* 108–121.

Meara, N. M., & Patton, M. J. (1994). Contributions of the working alliance in the practice of career counseling. *Career Development Quarterly, 43,* 161–177.

Multon, K. D., Heppner, M. J., Gysbers, N. C., Zook, C. E., & Ellis, C. (1998). Relationship of personal adjustment outcomes to process in career counseling. In D. Luzzo (Chair), *Career counseling process and outcome research.* Symposium conducted at the annual meeting of the American Psychological Association, San Francisco.

O'Neil, J. M. (1981). Male sex-role conflicts, sexism, and masculinity: Psychological implications for men, women, and the counseling psychologist. *Counseling Psychologist, 9,* 61–81.

O'Neil, J. M., Egan, J., Owens, S. V., & McBride V. (1993). The gender role journey measure: Scale development and psychometric evaluation. *Sex Roles, 28,* 167–185.

O'Neil, J. M., Good, G. E., & Holmes, S. (1995). Fifteen years of theory and research on men's gender role conflict: New paradigms for empirical research. In R. F. Levant & W. S. Pollack (Eds.), *The new psychology of men* (pp. 164–206). New York: Basic Books.

O'Neil, J. M., Helms, B. J., Gable, R. K., David, L., & Wrightsman, L. S. (1986). Gender Role Conflict Scale: College men's fears of femininity. *Sex Roles, 14,* 335–350.

Pleck, J. H. (1995). The gender role strain paradigm: An update. In R. F. Levant & W. S. Pollack (Eds.), *The new psychology of men* (pp. 11–32). New York: Basic Books.

Scher, M. (1979). On counseling men. *Personnel and Guidance Journal, 58,* 252–253.

Sharpe, M. J., & Heppner, P. P. (1991). Gender role, gender-role conflict, and psychological well-being in men. *Journal of Counseling Psychology, 38,* 323–330.

Skovholt, T. M. (1990). Career themes in counseling and psychotherapy with men. In D. Moore & F. Leafgren (Eds.), *Men in conflict* (pp. 39–53). Alexandria, VA: American Association for Counseling and Development.

Thompson, E. H., & Pleck, J. H. (1986). The structure of male role norms. *American Behavioral Scientist, 29,* 531–543.

Thompson, E. H., & Pleck, J. H. (1995). Masculinity ideology: A review of research instrumentation on men and masculinity. In R. F. Levant & W. S. Pollack (Eds.), *A new psychology of men* (pp. 129–163). New York: Basic Books.

Tyler, L. E. (1977). *Individuality.* San Francisco: Jossey-Bass.

CHAPTER NINETEEN

Contemporary Marriage

Challenges for Clients and Therapists

Lucia Albino Gilbert
Sarah J. Walker

I n this chapter we deal with specific ways therapists can assist male clients who are struggling with the normative issues of intimacy, mutuality, and role sharing in contemporary marriages. Unlike in earlier times, relationship commitment and stability today are closely tied to views of personal happiness, relational satisfaction, work-family convergence, and egalitarian values. Yet vestiges of tradition, embedded in assumptions about what it means to be a man or a woman, inadvertently enter into marriage and undermine its stability and quality.

Contemporary marriage has a great deal to do with gender—with changing views of what is possible and desirable for men and women today. Gender is not simply biological sex. A person is not born with gender. Rather, one learns how to become a man or a woman (Clatterbaugh, 1990; deBeauvoir, 1970). Learning one's gender is a highly complex sociopsychological process that varies across cultures and historical periods. The period since the 1960s in particular has witnessed large changes in societal values and expectations associated with one's biological sex. Indeed there is considerable debate today about what behaviors and roles are to be associated with men and women and whether earlier distinctions between the sexes have any real meaning or validity. These debates are about constructions of

The material in this chapter is adapted from other published works by the authors, including Gilbert (1993, 1999), Gilbert and Scher (1999), Gilbert and Walker (1999), and Walker (1998).

gender—about how a society defines and enforces what it means to be a man or a woman via formal and informal practices within the society and culture.

In this chapter we first discuss barriers to effective therapeutic work. We then present some facts and figures on modern marriages and consider three areas of particular therapeutic importance.

CONSIDERING OUR OWN ATTITUDES TOWARD GENDER AND MARRIAGE

According to Hare-Mustin (1994, p. 22), "The therapy room is like a room lined with mirrors. It reflects back only what is voiced within it." Because major changes have occurred with regard to gender and marriage, therapists must first consider their own attitudes, values, and behaviors with women and men. Therapists act as the carriers and enforcers of values in their work with clients. They can reinforce gender stereotypes and patriarchal values that in turn limit the considerations and exploration of nontraditional perspectives in counseling and psychotherapy. If both the client and the counselor hold a certain set of beliefs about what it means to be a man or a woman, these are the only beliefs voiced in therapy.

Exhibit 19.1 summarizes and provides examples of three interconnected factors that reinforce traditional societal views and stereotypes about gender in therapeutic settings and thus work against effective therapeutic interventions with men in contemporary marriages. These factors are (1) using essentialist, "opposite sex" beliefs to guide work with clients; (2) conceptualizing clients' concerns stereotypically; and (3) isolating or separating the concerns of clients from the context in which they occur, including the context of the counseling relationship.

Recognizing Opposite Sex Beliefs

For decades theorists and researchers have assumed that the sexes were opposite and thus possessed totally different and opposite attributes and abilities. Men, for example, were thought to be independent and rational, and women were thought to be dependent and irrational. The causes of these differences were assumed to be innate and thus essential to being male and female. Numerous studies conducted since the mid-1970s indicate that these assumptions are incorrect. Women and men are not opposite; they possess similar abilities and personal characteristics (Gilbert & Scher, 1999). It is crucial for therapists to familiarize themselves with this large and important body of literature so that they can better assist clients to comprehend that the sexes are not opposite and that marital partners are not opposite in their abilities and goals.

Exhibit 19.1. Factors Contributing to Ineffective Therapy.

- Using essentialist, "opposite sex" beliefs to guide work with male clients
  Example: Viewing men as competent in instrumental areas and incompetent in relationships
  Example: Viewing men as independent and women as needing men

- Conceptualizing clients' concerns stereotypically
  Example: Conceptualizing a man's unhappiness as his spouse's responsibility
  Example: Considering a male client's engaging in sex with multiple partners as possibly problematic only if safe sex practices are not used
  Example: Assessing a man's level of functioning on the basis of his success at his occupational work

- Isolating or separating the concerns of clients from the context in which they occur
  Example: Conceptualizing a man who takes paternity leave as bringing on his own problems at work
  Example: Viewing a professionally competent man choosing nondemanding employment as compensating for or acting out of unresolved issues from childhood

Source: Adapted from Gilbert, 1999, p. 124.

This understanding is particularly important for men who enter marriages based on principles of mutuality and partnership.

Challenging Stereotypes

In addition, assumptions that the sexes were opposite traditionally defined standards for men's (and women's) healthy behavior and good psychological functioning. Indeed, assessing clients' levels of functioning on the basis of how well they fit conventional gender roles is still normative for many therapists (Gilbert & Scher, 1999). Especially detrimental to men, personally and interpersonally, are myths and conventional discourses about what it means to be a man (Ker Conway, 1994). These discourses include viewing men as independent and self-contained, oriented toward occupational success, and entitled to both women's nurturance and their bodies (Levant & Brooks, 1997; Levant & Pollack, 1995).

Remembering Context

It is particularly crucial for therapists to grasp the third factor, isolating or separating the concerns of male clients from the context in which they occur. All behavior occurs in a context, but one's tendency is to attribute the cause of behavior almost entirely to something about that individual actor, as if there was no context associated with the behavior. A man's hesitation to take paternity leave, for example, has a context—the context of his work situation, his marital relationship, his own history and values, and so forth. These three factors are further considered in the later section "Issues for Men in Contemporary Marriage."

Interviews with couples conducted by Blain (1994) provide some excellent illustrations of how these factors inadvertently emerge in marriage and cause difficulties for partners. In explaining their own behavior and the behavior of their spouses, partners in her study relied on supposedly essential characteristics on which women and men differ (notion of the sexes as opposite) and ignored the sociopolitical context of women's and men's lives. One common explanatory theme partners used was "individual choice," which assumes that all tasks in marriage are chosen freely by partners. Such an explanation of course ignores the larger social context of power relations in marriage. A second theme partners used to explain who does what in their marriage was "differential abilities." Women were presumed more competent at caretaking and men more competent in pursuits outside the home. Such an explanation by partners does not take into account that the abilities of women and men are more similar than they are different. A third theme to explain how family tasks were divided was "women naturally nurture." This theme reflects the view that it is necessary for mothers but not fathers to nurture children. There is no evidence that men are not suited for infant and child care.

Recognizing and challenging traditional stereotypes relate not only to how clients present themselves but also to what therapists view as important areas for intervention. As the examples provided from Blain's interviews with couples illustrate, therapists first need to be able to see the implicit opposite sex themes and how they operate to perpetuate patterns that are problematic. They then need to mirror them back to clients in ways that challenge their validity, not further reinforce them. Clients put trust in their therapists to assist them to develop broader conceptions of themselves as human beings and to establish the support systems to buttress these broader conceptions. Thus, it is crucial for therapists to personally reflect on their work with clients and to consider whether and how they can effectively work to empower clients to go beyond conventional gendered views of themselves.

CONTEMPORARY MARRIAGE: KEY CHANGES FROM THE PAST

Marriage today represents dramatic changes in conceptions of love, enduring relationships, and social structures. Foremost among these transformations are changes associated with assumptions of male superiority, male authority over women, and the good provider role (Bernard, 1981). Traditionally men were to use their talent, ambition, and drive to move along occupational paths and be successful providers. Societal arrangements and custom reinforced this view and largely ignored the emotional and physical health costs and enormous role strain many men experienced (Pleck, 1981).

Women, in turn, provided the love, nurturance, and caretaking needed to sustain men's goals. When men were able to execute their defined roles, society rewarded them well. Unfortunately, society largely ignored women's contributions to male success and women's capacity for independent achievement. For men, the rewards went for achievement. For women, rewards were dispensed for attention to men and families. Women were seen through men; their status and economic well-being were derived from the men in their lives. Contrary to the wisdom of our chapter's epigraph, the pillars of the temple did not stand apart.

The situation today is quite different. Male-female relationships and roles have changed irreversibly since the 1970s. Employment is now widely recognized as an appropriate, normative, healthy, and intrinsically rewarding aspect of women's and men's adult lives. Women have increased access to education, good job opportunities, laws to protect them from discriminatory practices, and a status and meaning separate from their affiliations with men. Similarly, connections with family—feeling loved and loving and providing interpersonal care and nurturance within the family—are also widely recognized as appropriate, normative, healthy, and intrinsically rewarding aspects of women's and men's adult lives. Indeed, less than 3 percent of American families today fall into the category of breadwinner father and stay-at-home mother. About 63.1 percent of married women with children under six years old are in the labor force, and approximately 71 percent of married women with children under the age of eighteen are employed (U.S. Bureau of Labor Statistics, 1999).

Among dual-earner families and across various ethnic groups, both spouses are employed full-time in three-fourths of families ("National Report on Work and Family," 1998). Dual-earner couples comprised 60 percent of all marriages in 1996 and 45 percent of the labor force. Thus, almost half of the workforce is married to an employed spouse. The majority of spouses surveyed by Catalyst (1997) classified their occupational work of equal importance and wanted to balance work and family. There is also evidence that employed women and men report similar levels of success and kinds of work-family trade-offs (Milkie & Peltol, 1999) and similar benefits with regard to health and well-being (Barnett & Rivers, 1996).

Despite the fundamental and dramatic changes reflected in these facts and figures, it is not easy to establish the contemporary marital relationship many men and women envision in courtship. There are formidable pressures to conform to gender roles that seem polarized, arbitrary, and contrived. Depictions of women and men in dual-career families, for example, often exaggerate stereotypic cross-gender characteristics. A cover of a popular newsmagazine depicted a harried husband and father standing over a messy stove with a toddler pulling at his apron and an infant in one arm. The accompanying cover story on dual-career families intimated that men were being made into women. Women, in turn, were shown wearing masculine-looking suits, carrying briefcases, and being asked about "the little husband." The reality is quite different. Nonetheless, it is difficult to allow women and men to engage in roles traditionally assigned to the other sex and not see them as somehow "becoming" that sex. Men who devote themselves to child rearing may find their masculinity questioned. Women who aspire to high-powered careers run the risk of being viewed as denying their femininity. The compulsion to keep certain characteristics and behaviors as female and thus as belonging only to women and others as male and as belonging only to men, the opposite sex thinking described in the previous section, attests to the continuing power of conscious and unconscious gender processes in society.

ISSUES FOR MEN IN CONTEMPORARY MARRIAGE

In this final section we describe three areas associated with gender stereotypes and discourses that pose challenges for men (and women) interested in contemporary marriage. We provide a case example with each area described.

Sexuality and Intimacy

Heterosexual intimacy is negotiated within the context of traditional assumptions about what is "normal" and appropriate sexual behavior for men and women. Discourses about sexuality draw on social constructions of gender and are reflected and sustained in language and cultural practices (Gavey, 1989; Hare-Mustin, 1994). Discourses about male sexuality can impede newer and more adaptive ideas about how to be a man.

Hollway (1984) identified the "male sexual drive" discourse as a principle discourse in the production of meanings concerning contemporary sexuality. This discourse has its origin in sociobiological views of men's role to pursue and procreate and hence in the primacy and importance of the male sexual drive. Themes associated with the male sexual drive discourse are well documented (Brooks, 1995; Walker, 1998) and include "relationships and sexual consequences are a woman's responsibility, not a man's," "male sexuality is all about performance," and "men want sex and are always ready to have it."

As relationships move to commitment and marriage in adulthood, acceptance of the male sexual drive discourse continues to have wide-ranging implications. Although sexuality is only one part of a committed relationship, several studies support the view that sexual problems interact with relationship problems (Sprecher & McKinney, 1993; Stock, 1985). In addition, public surveys indicate that sexual satisfaction is widely considered essential to relationship success (Tiefer, 1995). Negotiating the details of a sexual relationship—who initiates intimacy, frequency of intercourse, length of foreplay, and the communication of desires and preferences—takes place in a gendered context. Here, the male sexual drive discourse may create problems because it calls for men to be in charge and to perform in particular ways and for women to defer to men's sexual desires.

"Performance," or the frequency of sexual intercourse, is often viewed as a measure of the quality of a sexual relationship. A performance-oriented approach, however, neglects the subtle impact of male sexual entitlement and duties that are associated with this dominant discourse. Performance ignores the psychosocial aspects of sexual expression and discounts the multidimensional nature of sexuality and its expression (Pinney, Gerrard, & Denney, 1987). Thus, one needs to be careful in using frequency of sex as a proxy for marital and sexual satisfaction. Doing so limits work with clients because it obscures discussion of their lived experiences.

Viagra effect. Current practices regarding Viagra help illustrate how successful treatment is framed by views of performance. Indeed Viagra provides somewhat of a "natural experiment" of how we talk about and think about male sexuality (Brooks, 2000; Walker, 1998). What we hear about Viagra is its ability to restore an erection. We hear nothing about how taking this drug relates to emotional or relational dynamics—for example, how Viagra changes the terms of sexual negotiation in relationships, particularly for couples who do not talk about impotence or who became content with alternative means of sexual expression before Viagra.

In a culture in which great sex is defined by male erection and female penetration, dysfunction can be considered "cured" by taking a pill to ensure erections. But for therapists the case of Viagra instead provides an opportunity to reopen discussion and dialogue of what constitutes sexual dysfunction and where it is located—in the penis, in the biology, or reciprocally in the relationship. At least one approach is for therapists to explore how they define good sex—is it through performative measures such as number of sex acts or number of orgasms per week? Or is sexuality considered multidimensional and qualitative? Therapists need to work with male clients in ways that delve deeply into the emotions, attitudes, assumptions, and power dynamics of sexual behavior to better illuminate alternative possibilities, choices, and ways of relating (Brooks, 2000; Muehlenhard & Cook, 1988; Tiefer, 1995).

Case of Roland. Roland, a stylishly dressed, handsome man, complains of bouts of anger and depression and describes a series of recent crises with his spouse, who is doing well in her occupational work; they have been married for four years. His story relates a good deal of sexual activity prior to marriage and a history of inconsistent performance in school and in work. He describes himself as experiencing a growing uneasiness about the marital relationship and about his inability to feel successful in the marriage. He is finding himself increasingly attracted to other women and has on occasion acted on this attraction.

Several gender-related issues pertain to this case. Male socialization emphasizes concealing emotions, especially when one is in pain; being successful at work; and looking to sex as a way to feel good about oneself. Working with Roland therapeutically will necessitate discussions about sexuality and its expression, but these issues may be best addressed later in therapy after there has been time for trust to develop. It is likely more important to address early in therapy Roland's feelings of inadequacy and loneliness. In this situation suggesting couples counseling also appears premature. Suggestions to bring the spouse into therapy would run the risk of conceptualizing Roland's unhappiness as his spouse's responsibility and prematurely focusing the therapy on the relationship (see Exhibit 19.1).

Roland appears to have difficulty in establishing close personal relations. He may, for example, withhold himself from relations to provide an illusion of an independent, strong man, but doing so keeps him emotionally remote, disconnected, and lonely. In addition, Roland may be looking for validation of himself as a man through his sexual relations with women. His sense of alienation and failure may leave him feeling needy and dependent on women for strength, on the one hand, but angry that he feels so dependent on women, on the other. Alternatively, his inconsistent work performance may leave Roland feeling financially at risk. His depression may come out of the anger and frustration associated with his sense of failure as a man.

Working empathically with Roland to understand his intrapersonal and interpersonal dynamics (including male socialization issues) would set the stage for later considerations of sexuality within his relationship and other issues related to the marriage. At this later point it might be useful to discuss couples work.

Multiple Role Involvement and the Politics of Housework

Recent data on the division of family labor in dual-earner families indicate that although some husbands do far less than their fair share, others are in an equitable arrangement (Barnett & Rivers, 1996; Pleck, 1996). Overall, men's participation in family work has continued to increase since 1970, more so in the area of parenting than in the area of household work. At the same time, there is a good deal of variation among dual-earner families and how they manage work and family roles. On average, men in dual-earner families do 34 percent of the housework and larger percentages of the parenting, with a sizable number close to 50-50 in both areas (see Crouter & Manke, 1997; Gilbert, 1993; Milkie &

Peltol, 1999). Approximately one-third of dual-career families achieve a role-sharing marriage (Gilbert, 1993).

Although the traditional emblems of masculinity still abound in the culture at large, many men today question the adequacy of traditional male norms and seek expanded definitions of self-worth and self-confidence (Good & Mintz, 1993; Levant & Pollack, 1995). Men's greater involvement in relationships, caring, and parenting is likely the hallmark of the 1990s (Levine & Pittinsky, 1997). Heterosexual men today appear less defined by the traditional "good provider role" long associated with male privilege and power (Bernard, 1981) and as a group are much more involved in household work and parenting (Silverstein, 1996) than men were in the past. Research surveys show that nearly one-third of working fathers have refused a new job, a promotion, or a transfer that threatened to reduce their family time (Malcolm, 1991). In a 1996 poll of men in their thirties and forties working at Levi Strauss & Co., 84 percent equated "success" with being a good father (cited in Levine & Pittinsky, 1997). (See Chapter Twenty for a more in-depth discussion of fathering.)

Nonetheless some men seem confused about their roles, with some trying to redefine masculinity and still others trying to ignore the obvious changes in women's lives. Findings from a study (Weiss, 1991) of upper-middle-class heterosexual white men who "do well at work" provide a good illustration. Although most of their spouses were employed, the seventy men in the survey showed little interest in their wives' lives or with how they managed to juggle work and family. Their concern was with their own success.

The focus on how well one is doing by traditional standards of male success can keep men from seeing the reality of women's lives and from supporting changes that would benefit both partners. Rather than pitching in to cook dinner or clean up, they may wait to be asked. They may view their time as too important to devote to "women's work." One male client who lived with a female partner took her out to dinner whenever she complained that he was not doing his fair share of the meal preparation. He saw this response as "fair"; she saw it "as his not getting it" and eventually left the relationship.

Politics of housework. For some time now, partners have struggled with what has come to be known as the politics of housework. This situation causes a good deal of conflict for families and has produced a huge body of literature ranging from studies on coping to studies on work-family policies (see Blain, 1994). Generally speaking, relationships do better when partners hold similar attitudes about women's and men's roles (see Huston & Geis, 1993) and when they discuss their visions of occupational, household, and parenting roles prior to marriage (Gilbert, 1985). When both partners hold egalitarian views, couples are more likely to share the responsibilities of the household and parenting and report greater marital happiness (Sanchez & Kane, 1996; Thompson & Walker, 1989).

Partners' satisfaction with participation in work and family roles of course depends on many other factors. Generally conflict and day-to-day stress associated with parenting and careers are lowest under the following conditions:

- Employers of both partners have benefit policies that are family responsive
- Both partners actively participate in parenting
- Partners feel comfortable sharing the parenting with child care personnel
- Partners view each other's involvement in home roles as fair
- Partners are satisfied with the child care they are using
- Partners are happy in their occupational work
- Partners employ understanding strategies in coping with stress

Historically, women have expressed much more dissatisfaction than men have with how tradition has defined their lives, and they have done more to change their situation. Recently, however, increasing numbers of men have begun seeking self-definitions that allow love, relationships, and work to be at the center of their lives.

Case of Patrick. Patrick, married for nearly ten years, has two preschool-age children and works for a high-tech firm in a large city. Patrick enters therapy with a presenting problem of "feeling down, fatigued, and unmotivated." The client has been in the same job for the past ten years and is disappointed by the absence of any significant promotions. The therapist begins by asking the client the reasons for the lack of promotions. Patrick attributes it to working only forty hours a week and not going into the office on weekends. He avoids working overtime to make time for family recreation and chores. In addition, Patrick admits to being less assertive and less well organized than coworkers (adapted from Rencher, Schillaci, & Goss, 1995).

Patrick mentioned avoiding working overtime to make time for family activities and responsibilities. In counseling him, a therapist may question whether he has made the right choices and question his marriage and the possibility that his spouse is too dominant and demanding. Successful therapy may be viewed as helping Patrick be more successful at work and more assertive at home.

By doing so, however, therapist would be interacting with the client in ways that preserve societal views of men's roles and responsibilities and perhaps the therapist's own deeply held views of a "healthy" man. Patrick may leave the first therapy session feeling that the solution to his problem is to change his priorities at home and work longer hours so that he can be more successful and thus happier, behaviors that would preserve the traditional societal view of what men do. Conveying to Patrick that "if he didn't have to take care of the darn children and spend time with his family, he would be happier and healthier" in the therapist's eyes might also undermine the client's successful attempt to engage in nontraditional behaviors, leave him with feelings of shame about his needs to nurture and connect with his children, and further add to his presenting feelings of depression.

Patrick may need assistance in recognizing and effectively confronting sexist attitudes at work and among friends and family members. He may feel alienated from other men or feel he cannot let coworkers know about the time he devotes to his family. He too may be engaging in gendered processes such as avoiding interactions with male coworkers and friends or using stereotypic models of male aggression and assertiveness in assessing his own assertiveness. Validation of his experiences would be important, as would understanding his and his spouse's vision for their relationship and the personal, family, and societal sources of support for this vision.

Mutuality of Spousal Support and Affirmation

The importance of mutual spousal support and affirmation to successful marriages cannot be overemphasized. Jessie Bernard (1974) noted some time ago that spousal support and sensitivity play a key role in dual-career families. Spousal support involves not only valuing and affirming a partner's abilities and goals but also providing emotional support, listening empathically, and nurturing. It requires putting aside one's own immediate needs and doing for another. Men have typically depended on women for support and affirmation (Pleck, 1981), just as they have expected themselves to be primary providers (Bernard, 1981). In modern marriages, men's ability (and freedom) to give women the emotional support and encouragement women traditionally give to men is especially crucial to spouses' marital happiness.

How one views dependence and the need for support influences models for effectively providing support. Early therapeutic practices assumed dependency was a personal variable (characteristic of women) and not a dynamic interpersonal variable characteristic of an ongoing relationship. Thus, dependence was a characteristic on which wives and husbands differed—women were considered essentially dependent and stayed that way, and men were considered nondependent—regardless of the behaviors in which they engaged. Contemporary marriage requires dependence to be reframed as an interpersonal process involving both giving and receiving and mutual empowerment and strength. It is an interpersonal process that serves as a vehicle for the development of mutuality between partners. To be able to rely on others and have them able to rely on you is enhancing and empowering to partners and to the relationship.

Communication is particularly important in achieving mutuality between partners, especially in asking for and receiving support. The language of interactions, especially language that challenges implicit notions of the sexes as opposite, provides important information to therapists about how partners communicate concern, support, and liking in their efforts to maintain a loving relationship. A woman who tells her spouse that she wants him to be listen to and hear her rather than solve her problems would be working toward relationship mutuality; so too would be a man who tells his female partner that he just needs to be held. In describing examples of how they provided mutual support, one husband in a past study about work and parenting said, "After our daughter was born I kept reassuring her about the quality of her work (they were in the same profession) and she kept reassuring me that I was a competent and loving father" (Gilbert, 1985, p. 70).

Case of Rick and Darlene. Rick, a thirty-six-year-old carpenter, enters counseling. Darlene, his thirty-one-year-old wife, is a product manager with a major food corporation in a small city in the South. They have recently found out that she is pregnant, something they both very much want. Darlene assumed she would take the maternity leave offered by her company and then return to work after that three-month period. Rick believes that she should stay home with the child full-time and that if the mother is not the primary person in the baby's life, especially during the first year, the baby will have psychological problems. He also believes Darlene would be missing out on an important aspect of womanhood. He is very anxious and upset over their past arguments in this regard and is also concerned with how this situation is affecting their sexual intimacy. Darlene has tried to accommodate his fears by suggesting that she use the flextime options her company offers and he change his work schedule for that year to do child rearing (which he can do because he works independently). He feels that she is being unreasonable and that she is asking too much of him. Although he feels strongly about his opinions, Rick questions whether he is going to be sorry in the long run. He is worried about what this situation is going to do to their relationship (adapted from Gilbert & Scher, 1999).

This case illustrates characteristic issues in contemporary marriages. Exhibit 19.2 summarizes relevant factors to consider in working with this client. Initial issues to consider in working with Rick pertain to possible challenges to his feelings of authority in the marriage and feelings of incompetence regarding his ability to care for his child. For example, Rick may feel Darlene is not being sufficiently sensitive to disruptions to his work. He is self-employed and works by word-of-mouth referrals; as a white man reared to evaluate himself through his provider role he may feel more threatened than reassured when she reminds him that her position offers greater financial stability and a higher income than his, in addition to providing their health care coverage.

It may be particularly important to explore the relationship factor of partner support and how the partners express intimacy. Neither partner may feel supported at the moment, and instead both may feel that the other is trying to push him or her into a decision both are reluctant to make. By focusing on how

Exhibit 19.2. Factors Associated with Gender That Influence Men in Modern Marriages.

- Equity and power (for example, how decisions are made; what seems fair; and how partners come to agreements about household work, parenting, money, and how to deal with sexism and racism in their own lives and in the lives of their children)
- Partner support (for example, how support is expressed and given)
- Dominant discourses that prevail in the culture (for example, "men want sex and are always ready to have it" and "men are entitled to women's care")
- Views of women and men as opposite and possessing nonoverlapping attributes and abilities (for example, women as natural nurturers and men as superior to women)
- Structure of work (for example, flexibility of work hours, presence of sex or race discrimination, and provision of health care benefits, including coverage of partners)
- Employer's views (for example, kinds of family policy provided and general attitude about men who involve themselves in family life)
- Child care availability and quality
- Support systems (for example, family, friends, colleagues, church, and community)

Darlene and Rick typically support each other and by exploring how each would like to be supported in this area, new options are likely to emerge. Thus, although Rick may have the more flexible position, depending on her work situation, Darlene may be able to arrange more flexible hours so that parenting can be shared more equally between them. These kinds of discussions would lay the groundwork for Rick's discussing any anxieties and fears he may have about being a caregiver and assuming responsibilities for taking care of an infant.

The therapist's job in this situation likely centers on helping Rick and perhaps the couple explore their basic beliefs and increase their awareness of the values they are currently using to make decisions. However, given the value-laden aspects of the situation regarding women's and men's traditional roles, the therapist may need to first explore his or her own values in the areas of work and family and decide whether he or she can ethically work with Rick or with the couple.

Numerous variables influence men and relationships, but none are likely as profound as the stereotypes and discourses tied to views of women and men as opposite sexes. Therapists who understand and embrace contemporary views of women and men as similar in their rights and roles and as entering egalitarian relationships will do well in assisting male clients who struggle with the normative issues of intimacy, mutuality, and role sharing in marriage.

References

Barnett, R. C., & Rivers, C. (1996). *She works/he works: How two-income families are happier, healthier, and better off.* New York: HarperCollins.

Bernard, J. (1974). *The future of motherhood.* New York: Dial.

Bernard, J. (1981). The good provider role: Its rise and fall. *American Psychologist, 36,* 1–12.

Blain, J. (1994). Discourses of agency and domestic labor: Family discourse and gendered practice in dual-career families. *Journal of Family Issues, 15,* 515–549.

Brooks, G. R. (1995). *The centerfold syndrome.* San Francisco: Jossey-Bass.

Brooks, G. R. (forthcoming). Challenging dominant discourses of male (hetero)sexuality: The clinical implications of new voices about male sexuality. In P. Kleinplatz (Ed.), *New directions in sex therapy.* New York: Brunner/Mazel.

Catalyst. (1997). Work and family. (Available from 250 Park Ave. South, New York, NY 10003)

Clatterbaugh, K. (1990). *Contemporary perspectives on masculinity: Men, women, and politics in modern society.* Boulder, CO: Westview Press.

Crouter, A. C., & Manke, B. (1997). Development of a typology of dual-earner families: A window into the difference between and within families in relationships, roles, and activities. *Journal of Family Psychology, 11,* 62–75.

deBeauvoir, S. (1970). *The second sex.* New York: Bantam Books.

Gavey, N. (1989). Feminist poststructuralism and discourse analysis. *Psychology of Women Quarterly, 13,* 459–475.

Gilbert, L. A. (1985). *Men in dual-career families: Current realities and future prospects.* Hillsdale, NJ: Erlbaum.

Gilbert, L. A. (1993). *Two careers/one family: The promise of gender equality.* Beverly Hills, CA: Sage.

Gilbert, L. A. (1999). Reproducing gender in counseling and psychotherapy: Understanding the problem and changing the practice. *Journal of Applied and Preventive Psychology, 8,* 119–128.

Gilbert, L. A., & Scher, M. (1999). *Gender and sex in counseling and psychotherapy.* Boston: Allyn & Bacon.

Gilbert, L. A., & Walker, S. J. (1999). Dominant discourse in heterosexual relationships: Inhibitors or facilitators of interpersonal commitment and relationship stability? In J. M. Adams (Ed.), *Handbook of interpersonal commitment* (pp. 393–406). New York: Plenum.

Good, G. E., & Mintz, L. B. (1993). Toward healthy conceptions of masculinity: Clarifying the issues. *Journal of Mental Health Counseling, 15,* 403–413.

Hare-Mustin, R. T. (1994). Discourses in the mirrored room: A postmodern analysis of therapy. *Family Process, 33,* 19–35.

Hollway, W. (1984). Gender differences and the production of subjectivity. In J. Henriques, W. Hollway, C. Urwin, C. Venn, & V. Walkerdine (Eds.), *Changing the subject* (pp. 227–263). London: Methuen.

Huston, T. L., & Geis, G. (1993). In what ways do gender-related attitudes and beliefs affect marriage? *Journal of Social Issues, 49*(3), 87–106.

Ker Conway, J. (1994). *True north: A memoir.* New York: Random House.

Levant, R. F., & Brooks, G. R. (1997). *Men and sex: New psychological perspectives.* New York: Wiley.

Levant, R. F., & Pollack, W. S. (1995). *A new psychology of men.* New York: Basic Books.

Levine, J. A., & Pittinsky, T. L. (1997). *Working fathers: New strategies for balancing work and family.* San Diego: Harcourt Brace.

Malcolm, A. H. (1991, June 16). A day of celebration for a more active kind of dad. The *New York Times*, p. 14.

Milkie, M. A., & Peltol, P. (1999). Playing all the roles: Gender and the work-family balancing act. *Journal of Marriage and the Family, 61,* 467–490.

Muehlenhard, C. L., & Cook, S. W. (1988). Men's self-reports of unwanted sexual activity. *The Journal of Sex Research, 24,* 58–72.

National Report on Work and Family. (1998). *National study on the changing work-force, 11*(8), 81–83.

Pinney, E. M., Gerrard, M., & Denney, N. W. (1987). The Pinney Sexual Satisfaction Inventory. *Journal of Sex Research, 23,* 233–251.

Pleck, J. H. (1981). Men's power with women, other men, and society: A men's move-ment analysis. In R. A. Lewis (Ed.), *Men in difficult times: Masculinity today and tomorrow* (pp. 234–244). New York: Prentice Hall.

Pleck, J. H. (1996, June). *Paternal involvement: Levels, sources, and consequences.* Paper presented at the Co-Parenting Roundtable of the Fathers and Families Roundtable, New York, NY.

Rencher, L. L., Schillaci, J., & Goss, S. (1995, August). *Gender as interpersonally cre-ated in the therapeutic relationship: Client considerations.* Paper presented at the meeting of the American Psychological Association, Washington, DC.

Sanchez, L., & Kane, E. W. (1996). Women's and men's constructions of perceptions of housework fairness. *Journal of Family Issues, 17,* 385–387.

Silverstein, L. B. (1996). Fathering is a feminist issue. *Psychology of Women Quarterly, 20,* 3–37.

Sprecher, S., & McKinney, K. (1993). *Sexuality.* Newbury Park, CA: Sage.

Stock, W. (1985). The influence of gender on power dynamics in relationships. In D. C. Goldberg (Ed.), *Contemporary marriage: Special issues in couples therapy* (pp. 62–99). Homewood, IL: Dorsey Press.

Thompson, L., & Walker, A. J. (1989). Women and men in marriage, work, and parenthood. *Journal of Marriage and the Family, 51,* 845–872.

Tiefer, L. (1995). *Sex is not a natural act and other essays.* Boulder, CO: Westview Press.

U.S. Bureau of Labor Statistics. (1999). *Labor force statistics derived from the current population survey.* Washington, DC: Author.

Walker, S. J. (1998, August). *Nonrelational sexuality versus sexual integrity: Contrasting discourses for contemporary men.* Paper presented at the meeting of the American Psychological Association, San Francisco.

Weiss, R. S. (1991). *Staying the course: The emotional and social lives of men who do well at work.* New York: Free Press.

CHAPTER TWENTY

Therapeutic Interventions with Fathers

Jerrold Lee Shapiro

Although many of the early chapters of this handbook stress the importance of outreach and nontraditional therapy settings appropriate for men, my personal experience is somewhat different. For the past thirty years my clients in private practice have been predominantly men and couples. In general, the therapy has been long-term and theoretically existential and insight oriented. It has been an interesting contrast to my work as a professor in graduate counseling training programs in which fully 75 percent of all my students have been women. The practice is unusual in its gender balance but not totally unique. Men seek therapeutic help on a regular basis, but because of the imperatives of gender role strain (Pleck, 1995), they do so primarily when they are experiencing major stress in their lives. Generally, stress occurs during major transitions. In this chapter, I focus on the transformations that accompany fatherhood.

GENERAL PRINCIPLES IN WORK WITH MALE CLIENTS

Fathers are men. Therefore, before turning to the special issues of working with fathers, it is helpful to look at some general principles in working with men. Therapeutic interventions with fathers are somewhat unique and time sensitive, but the most salient issues involve making psychotherapy more user-friendly for men in general.

The typical male client has been socialized to believe in the primacy of success, power, competence, self-reliance, and emotional control (see Brooks, 1998; Harris, 1995; Levant & Pollack, 1995; Pollack & Levant, 1998). Such beliefs and the attendant defenses (often cited as examples of gender role strain for men) are anathema to traditional therapy.

This discrepancy between the masculine patient and the "sensitive" demand characteristics of therapy has been the object of interest in the popular media. In both the Billy Crystal–Robert DeNiro vehicle *Analyze This* and HBO's spectacularly successful series *The Sopranos,* the juxtaposition of the powerful gangster suffering from anxiety with the difficulties of the therapist creating a relevant environment for treatment underscores this crucial discrepancy. At times, each seems like a fish out of water. Yet at other times the therapy, both in these dramas and in real life, really works.

The creation of a working, masculine therapeutic environment behooves sensitivity and adjustment to implications of male gender role strain (Mahalik, 1999; Pleck, 1995). With awareness of those special cultural pressures, therapists must work within their clients' personal frameworks to promote understanding and behavior change. Thus, for example, when a client presents with alexithymia (Levant, 1998), both the therapist and the client are aware that there is a greater need for the client to identify and express his feelings more directly and clearly. Yet prodding him to focus more on feelings is tantamount to asking the client to use the absent skills that are the supposed successful end point of therapy as a means to get to that point. This approach is both nonempathic and frustrating for the therapist and the client. It stands as another example that the client's needs, desires, and styles of behavior are undesirable. For most men, such treatment, which purportedly is designed to promote behavior change, has a paradoxical effect.

Although we begin the training of all therapists with the dictum "always begin where the client is, not where we think he should be," we somehow often fail to speak the same language as our male clients. Successful psychotherapy with any client requires a deep, compassionate involvement with the language and metaphors of his or her life. Both dynamic and systems-oriented theoretical perspectives train psychotherapists to be particularly sensitive to the relational aspects of communication, something Tannen (1990) identifies with stereotypical female conversation. Many therapists hear clearly the relational aspect of communication. Yet when they bridge such issues with male clients, the therapy may become too confrontational, threatening, or incomprehensible.

In working with men, therapists must be carefully attuned to their indirect communication. Whereas women in therapy may be more aware of the changing relationship between therapist and client, men are more likely to be attuned to the words and their meaning, constantly looking for the bottom line. To avoid the risk of rejection, men often focus primarily on what they must do to be right.

For men, language is used primarily to pass information and identify or establish a hierarchy (Haley, 1963). Emotional language for men is likely to be expressed indirectly in story or metaphor. Because men typically connect intellectually or physically as a means to connect emotionally, they are more likely than women to talk about common topics and shared experiences. Among topics that are often rich in metaphor for men are work, technology, cars, tools, and sports.

I saw Ben for a year while he was facing a conflict between his competitive desire to be a "player" in the fast-paced Silicon Valley arena and the desire to be close to his wife and children. Ben did not have the "obsessed" personality of the seventy-five-hour-work-week set. Yet comparisons to suddenly wealthy former classmates, other workers, and neighbors left him feeling diminished.

Two metaphors worked particularly well to help him set a better balance for his own life. One was the high-tech metaphor that we called "Which Steve?" The reference was to two founders of Apple Computer—Steve Wozniak, who took his fortune and became a teacher and philanthropist, and Steve Jobs, who started other companies and is now working harder than ever as CEO of Apple. Ben had a much greater affinity for the "Woz" position. By thinking about it externally as styles of others, he could explore his own life with less defensiveness or threat.

Ice hockey provided the second metaphor that defined Ben's therapeutic change. A native Canadian, Ben was an avid hockey fan and former player. A simple question about his favorite players indicated that all were goalies. As a player himself, he always played defense or goal. Talking about hockey served to establish that Ben was a security-first person. Once he acknowledged that he was a defender rather than an offensive player by personality and history, we could delve into the work-home balance conflict, respecting his need to be conservative. He was then able to find ways of accepting the relatively lower advancement at work in return for protecting his "true goal" by staying home more with his family.

Patrick was another client who illustrates the use of metaphors. He had a lengthy history of poor relationships with women and refused to discuss problems that had to do with his "sainted Irish mother." This woman had severe emotional problems and deserted Patrick and his two younger sisters when he was fourteen. Although he had rage about rejections by women, he was a master of creating situations in which women would abandon him as an adult. He adamantly refused to relate it at all to his childhood, dismissing any such theorizing as "psycho-crap."

Patrick left his prior therapist when she began to prepare him for a hiatus in therapy instigated by her own pregnancy. During the first session with me, he insisted that "all shrinks care about is money and blaming mothers for their problems." He made it clear that speculation about the relationship between the abandonment by his second wife (and children) and that of his mother was not to be a point of discussion.

Patrick was a computer science engineer who took great pride in his work. The metaphor that finally broke the logjam and allowed him to explore the impact of his history on current relationships was a multisession meandering exploration about his work. As he complained about the hardware group at work that made his life miserable, I asked him whether he would characterize his personal problem as a "software" or "hardware" problem. He responded, "hardware of course; after all I'm a software engineer." This response led me to suggest that he was being limited by defects on his "internal motherboard." He laughed at the obvious connection and jokingly accused me of trying to get into "shrink talk" with my attempt at "technological buzzword compliance."

Despite his articulate protest, the metaphor of his psyche-as-computer gave him sufficient distance to explore his long-standing terror of future abandonment. He responded by writing a new "personal software program." In his "default" program he avoided the larger fear of loss by anticipating a woman's rejection and then unconsciously behaved to create a self-fulfilling prophecy that guaranteed the abandonment he was so focused on avoiding. In the revised program he found a way to face his fear of rejection directly without guaranteeing a negative result in advance.

Although he stuck to his principle of never complaining about his mother, he was able to identify a personal basic deficit and override it in his future behavior with women. Patrick was able to tolerate and use the intervention because it came in a language in which he was comfortable and an expert and it was nonconfrontational. Because it was delivered in an indirect and metaphorical manner, Patrick could experience it almost as if it were from within and thus it generated far less resistance. The specifics of the intervention were less important than its respectful delivery, which validated Patrick's personal process.

Several observers have opined that for men the four deadliest words in the English language are "We have to talk!" If a man experiences emotional communication and confrontation primarily as criticism and rejection, it is unlikely that he will find such communication successful in therapy. Typically, men report that when they had to talk to mom, it meant punishment for wrongdoing. When a man does wrong, he expects to suffer the consequences—typically rejection. By using metaphor and "masculine" language, a therapist can address sensitive issues such as abandonment and loss in a way that the male client can approach instead of defend.

HOW THERAPY MAY BE INHOSPITABLE TO FATHERS

As a father, each man experiences inevitable vulnerabilities, challenges, and fears. At such times, the pathways to a man's heart, soul, and psyche become more open, but only to those who prove themselves sensitive to male needs and language. Even with the best of intentions, therapists may fail to properly serve men for reasons that are intrinsic to the common practice of psychotherapy.

Gaps in Knowledge of Men and Pathology

In some significant ways, psychotherapists do not know men and their lives as well as we know women. From a gender-centric position, it is possible to argue that our century-old profession falls into two major periods. For the first two-thirds of the century, predominantly male therapists studied predominantly female clients and found them to be pathological by reference to inferred male standards of being. The final third of the twentieth century was marked by studies of women that were then used to find pathology in men by reference to the female standard. This result certainly was not the hope or promise of prominent feminists and civil rights activists. Truly understanding male needs in therapy requires the study of men and male ways.

Not Recognizing Therapy as Unmasculine

It is easy to view the roles, tasks, and ambience of psychotherapy as promoting more traditional feminine than masculine traits. Core conditions for therapists are warmth, openness, and focus on and expression of feelings, intimacy, and congruence. These traits fit much better with notions of Mom than with those of Dad. Indeed, as Gottman (1994), Pollack (1995), and Shay and Maltas (1998) have indicated, these traits are apparently incongruent with self-sufficiency, detachment, and other male roles that follow the protect-and-provide prime directive. All therapists are trained in interview methods that focus on rapport building, relationship, sensitivity to feelings, and so forth. If the therapy room has the look and feel of a late-nineteenth-century drawing room appropriate for the content of romance novels, where is a traditional man even to find a place to sit?

Gaps in Knowledge About Fatherhood

Since the mid-1980s, authors such as Greenberg (1985) and Shapiro (1987) have underscored the need for a greater understanding of the "forgotten parent" (Diamond, 1995a). Until recently, information on fatherhood has been minimal and offered from a maternal-centric position. Issues common and normal for men undergoing the transition to fatherhood (see Michaels & Goldberg, 1988) have not been well explored or understood in the therapeutic community.

HELPING MEN WITH THE TRANSITION TO FATHERHOOD

Fatherhood is a crucial marker in men's lives (see Shapiro, Diamond, & Greenberg, 1995), and the transition to fatherhood is the psychological prototype for all fatherhood-related issues. It is a state that demands a man's attention to his inner life, often for the first time. When a man becomes a father, he is faced with many issues for which he is a complete rookie. During his partner's pregnancy, a man may well reflect on his personal mortality, the legacy he carries from his own childhood, and a new sense of adult responsibility. In addition, he faces a new level of vulnerability, a greater potential for rejection and loss, and pressures to behave in ways that are less characteristically masculine.

Many expectant fathers begin to reassess the fathering that they received as children and simultaneously relive psychologically feelings they experienced as boys. They may also begin a deeper reflection on their inner selves (see Osherson, 1987). Because most men are not fully conscious of the extent of these internal shifts, it is the therapists' job to help tease them out and help the male client focus on and find meaning in the changes.

Over the course of a pregnancy, expectant fathers experience fears, anxieties, concerns, and new sensitivities to relationships, children, and the world as a whole. Shapiro (1987) documented four basic areas of concern for expectant fathers. These concerns match well with the issues facing men, as described by Diamond (1992), Keen (1991), and Osherson (1992). Clinical practice with large numbers of fathers and a second series of studies of fatherhood over the lifetime (Shapiro, 1993) indicate that certain issues are predominant in the thinking of men throughout their adult lives. These issues are manifested as concerns about performance, security, relationships, and existential issues.

Performance Concerns

Ehrensaft (1994) indicates that modern American culture treasures men for "doing" but not for "being." In a less academic but certainly still powerful way, Farrell (1986) makes the observation, "Hey, look at the size of the wallet on that guy." The message to boys is that every encounter is a potential competition—either we win or lose; "to the victors belong the spoils" (Marcy, 1832). In war, those who lose, perish. In less mortal pursuits, those who lose become less attractive and feel rejection and abandonment. Expectant fathers have two primary performance concerns that counselors and therapists should be aware of: performance in financial and emotional realms and performance in the delivery room.

Performance in financial and emotional realms. In modern Western cultures, the prime yardstick of the protect-and-provide male standard is fiscal success. Nowhere is the socioeconomic programming so hardwired as in the intense pressure fathers feel to provide financial support for their families.

One twenty-two-year-old father of three days managed to capture in a sentence the sudden inevitable rush of economic responsibility: "One day I was going along happy-go-lucky. The next day I was the sole support of three people."

The new child demands financial, physical, and emotional adjustments in the relationship. For most couples, the first pregnancy brings with it, at least temporarily, a change from two incomes for two people to one income for three. Tradition and social expectations and the inequity in male and female salaries typically mean that the father bears the brunt of the enhanced financial burden. It is common during a pregnancy for a father to moonlight or switch jobs. Of course, such endeavors take him away from his pregnant partner and direct connection to the child growing in her womb.

These feelings of enhanced responsibility and the attendant disconnection from family that results from longer hours at work seem to exist in men regardless of their financial wherewithal. Men with sufficient resources or high-paying jobs report similar anxiety to those with far more realistic financial worries. It is important for therapists to focus on both a man's fear of failure to carry out this prime directive and the fiscal realities. When these are discrepant, the former bears primary inspection in therapy.

Judd, a thirty-six-year-old first-time father, had a director-level job in a high-tech firm. He had a six-figure income at the time. When he came to therapy, he worried aloud about his wife's decision to quit her teaching job several months before the baby was due. Over time, he acknowledged that he had "run the numbers many times and they always came up OK." Nonetheless, he kept worrying about being disabled, a stock market downturn, or being laid off by his company. He was losing sleep and ruminating through the day. On reflection in therapy he was able to discern that he was terrified of failure to provide for his wife and new baby not because of fiscal considerations but because with the added responsibility he felt he worried most that he would be "a failure." When queried about the implications of being a failure, he surprised himself by blurting out, "then my wife would find someone better."

Performance in the delivery room. In North America, fully 85 percent of all men expect to be present at the births of their children (Shapiro, 1995). Although many men describe some ambivalence, most want to share the birth experience with their partners. Unfortunately, desire to be a part of the pregnancy and birth does not reduce anticipatory discomfort regarding an abundance of blood and other bodily fluids. An expectant father anticipating his first birth participation wonders about his ability to "keep it together" and truly help his wife instead of fainting or "losing his cookies" during the delivery. The importance of this concern is revealed in recent fathers' accounts of the births of their children. Immediately after describing the births as "wonderful" and commenting on the courage of their wives, they described with pride how well they personally came through the pregnancy with the contents of their digestive tracts intact (Shapiro, 1995).

The reassurance that very few men actually have such trouble does not diminish the concern. In addition, what passes for humor by physicians and the popular media contributes to men's fears of experiencing the birth of their children from a prone position under the table on a delivery room floor.

From a therapy perspective, these concerns need to be taken very seriously and normalized. Indeed, one therapist indicated that she always asks specifically about what the expectant father anticipates during the labor and delivery. It is also advisable for men to discuss these fears with peers, especially those who have recently become fathers. It is essential to understand that for many men, failure to perform well is tantamount to being rejected.

Security Concerns

Closely related to performance concerns are security issues. If one accepts the contention that boys' development leads normatively to fears of abandonment and rejection (see Pleck, 1995; Pollack, 1998), then one recognizes that an expectant father's anticipation of loss of control can only exacerbate such situations. For most men, feeling a sense of control over a situation is reassuring even if the actual influence is illusory. A man with a plan is usually less anxious than one who feels subject to the whims of fate. During a pregnancy and birth, men are truly not in control. In addition to the obvious lack of influence over physical processes, three factors common to expectancy diminish feelings of being in control: difficulties in dealing with the obstetrics and gynecology establishment, insecurity about paternity, and fears about the health and safety of spouse and infant.

Difficulties in dealing with the obstetrics and gynecology establishment. The branch of medicine that deals with female reproductive anatomy remains mysterious and alien to many men. Expectant fathers often experience feelings of dehumanization, infantilization, and embarrassment during their initial contacts with obstetrics and gynecology staff. Several men who accompanied their wives to prenatal pelvic exams reported rejection from the same obstetrical staff who had previously praised their involvement. Their questions were frequently silenced with looks that implied "only a fool would not know that" (Shapiro, 1987).

During a pregnancy, men often develop a disquieting sense that they are simultaneously encouraged to be involved and told that many parts of them are undesirable. This *cultural double bind* (Shapiro, 1987) requires men to be aware of and expressive about their feelings but to censor expression of any "negative" feelings such as fear, anger, sadness, or the like. The conflict often promotes withdrawal.

Although many men first experience this cultural double bind during their wives' pregnancies, it is not limited to the experience of expectant fatherhood. Indeed, most fathers report that they consistently must deal with a request for the more emotional side of their experience and simultaneously are told that such expression is potentially harmful to wife and children.

Dave, a self-described "computer nerd," was the father of three young children. He reported that his wife sent him into therapy "to learn to communicate." As a client, he was able to express his thoughts quite well, albeit with painstaking care. When asked about his feelings, he had more difficulty but soon was able to label and discuss his emotional experiences with the same care. After approximately six sessions, he came in and reported that his wife had encouraged him to quit therapy because his "emotional outbursts were scaring the children." In the specific incident to which she referred, Dave informed her that he was going to take the three children with him on an excursion. When she disagreed, he said that he wanted to do it anyway. At that point she told him that he was being intimidating. Dave and his wife were subsequently able to resolve this and similar issues, but for a period of three months he reported that he was caught between what she requested and what she wanted. Until they worked it through, the only "acceptable" feelings were agreement and acquiescence.

To be successful, the therapist must acknowledge the reality of the double bind and explore in an understanding way an expectant father's feelings of rejection. The therapist must first help the expectant father discover and discuss the whole array of his feelings and thoughts. Then it is important to examine the advisability of discussing these concerns with his pregnant partner. Under most circumstances, this sharing of the multiplicity of feelings with a pregnant woman and with other expectant or recent fathers is well received.

Insecurity about paternity. A client once said to me, "I jokingly told my wife, if that kid has blond hair and blue eyes, I'm gone." What is surprising about this "joke" is that more than 50 percent of the men surveyed by Shapiro (1987) acknowledged a fleeting thought that they were not the biological father of the child. This discomfort, often reinforced by unintentionally cruel jokes referencing the physical appearance of the mailman or other service providers, was based less on any real concern that the wife had been unfaithful than on a general feeling of inadequacy to be part of anything so monumental as the creation of life.

The general feeling of inadequacy to create life also manifests itself for men (and women) in psychological denial of the pregnancy—a phenomenon that may last for men until after the birth—and in a repetitive concern that the hospital staff has mixed up the babies in the nursery.

Therapists must approach this concern with great sensitivity. Normalizing the father's experience and exploring his core feelings of inadequacy are the natural focal point of therapy. Only in the rare circumstances in which there is good reason to question the paternity and this issue is paramount to the expectant father is a factual exploration potentially advisable. An expectant father's insecurity about being sufficiently powerful to sire a child allows therapeutic exploration of fears of general adequacy, a sense of heightened (potentially excessive) responsibility, and a subsequent fear of being discarded and abandoned. These explorations often lead to therapeutic examination of the relationship with the client's own father, a sense of abandonment as a child, and a fear of future unknowns.

Fears about the health and safety of spouse and infant. Among the most powerful ways an expectant father can feel out of control is in his worry that something terrible might happen to his partner or baby. This very common fear usually arises during the second trimester. Often based on dreams of such a loss, refreshed family memories, or tragic stories, this fear may also be rooted in personal fears of abandonment or of being replaced. Because his pregnant spouse is normally turning inward toward the infant and away from him at a time when he is feeling particularly insecure and emotionally open, it is easy for his unconscious mind to transform her temporary emotional distance into a premonition of permanent loss.

The related fear that something will be wrong with the child often thrusts itself into the consciousness of both expectant parents. It is a rare parent who does not worry about birth defects or neglects to count fingers and toes on the newborn.

For most men, reassurance and planning for likely problems may be the best way to focus the therapy. Therapists may do well to encourage the expectant father to talk to his pregnant partner about these particular fears. In fact, a few couples sessions either within the purview of his therapy (with the pregnant woman invited in as a consultant) or in separate couples therapy can often be an excellent stage for this conversation. In my experience as a therapist working with couples without serious pathology, the vast majority of pregnant women experience their husbands' fears about health and safety as reassuring. To her overprotective husband's surprise, one woman spontaneously hugged him during a session, saying, "I am so happy you are worried about the same things I am. I feel so much closer to you." Although her husband did not understand her reaction, he liked it and responded by slowly sharing more of his feelings.

Relationship Fears

There is considerable documentation that most men have primary fears of abandonment (Bly, 1989; Pollack, 1995; Shapiro, 1997). These fears are particularly exacerbated during pregnancy because of a real loss of their wives' attention at a time when men are feeling more vulnerable and less in control. It is common and important for pregnant women to turn inward and begin bonding with the life growing inside. At such times, husbands may feel neglected. It is not surprising that expectant fathers fear the loss of their most important relationship. Many have survived periods of great turmoil in their marriages. Expectant fathers of today may well have experienced firsthand the pain of their parents' divorce or the loss of their own prior relationships. As children and young men, most have experienced a feeling of abandonment by a mother or other women.

If a man's own father, committed to the "earning a living," division-of-labor standard, was somewhere in the background (away at work or in the garage), the primary bond in the home was between mother and child. Can he not then expect that as a father, he will also be pushed aside, relegated to the role of provider?

Several types of intervention may be crucial in addressing the fear of being replaced. One involves normalizing the experience of a wife's inward bonding. The therapist may encourage the expectant father to indicate to his spouse need for her to make space available for him in the parental triad (Greenberg, 1997). Diamond (1995b), in discussing the watchful role of fathers, indicates the value of therapeutic reification that the father is clearly approaching the mother-baby bond as an outsider. Indeed, the father's role is to support the individuation aspects of his child's development while the mother focuses more naturally on the supportive role. As such, the father's feelings of being on the outside are both real and functional.

Another class of interventions becomes salient when the new father has little knowledge of fathering from his own history. Explorations of a man's relationship with his own father are often the core of therapy for fatherhood issues. A man's examination of his father's life is often revealing and significant (Osherson, 1987; Shapiro, 1993). Therapy may well turn on issues of "destiny," a sense of inadequacy and meaninglessness, feelings of improper preparation, and low self-esteem. A reconsideration of one's own father as a real person with strengths and flaws and the development of an understanding, potentially an acceptance, of the choices he made are valuable in a man's decisions to make similar or different choices in his own life as a father and man. Often therapists encourage men to contact their fathers and reconnect in new ways to learn about their fathers' lives.

At forty-four, Jack was in therapy for almost two years to work through his divorce and loss of contact with his children from his first marriage. When his second wife became pregnant with their first child, he was plagued with a sense of potential loss of another child and a feeling that he had not been much of an involved father to his two daughters from the first marriage.

In discussing where he learned to be a father, Jack described his own father as a stern, taciturn farmer who "believed in action not words." He spoke with a mixture of pride, anger, and concern that at age eighty his father was still running the Indiana farm on which Jack was born and raised. Each time he tried to discuss what he wanted to learn from his father, he cried. After several weeks of planning and encouragement from the therapist and his wife, Jack took a trip to Indiana to have a "big talk" with his father. His plan was to talk while he was helping his father on the farm. They spent two labor-intensive days repairing a fence, during which Jack began to ask his father to reminisce about the days when Jack and his brother were young. The older man was quite able to remember and describe the events and his own reactions.

When Jack returned to California, he claimed, "It was the best time I ever had with my dad." Quickly focusing on the new term to describe his father, Jack's eyes moistened and he stated, "I guess it's the first time I realized how much he loves me."

As therapy progressed, Jack resolved to let his daughters and the new baby know clearly how he felt about them "and not wait for them to have to seek me out in some senior residence."

Existential Fears

Expectant fatherhood prompts men to examine their mortality. As one man put it, when his wife was pregnant, "I became aware that I no longer had any right to die. I stopped taking such huge risks. I found myself driving slower, avoiding rougher areas of town, actually listened to a life insurance salesman."

Of all the changes, fears, and novel experiences a wife's pregnancy brings to men, none is so subtle and yet so dramatic as a new consciousness of the biological life cycle. In reflecting on their intimate involvement with the beginnings of life, many men describe feeling closer to their own deaths. They also describe an increased sense of connection to their own fathers.

Because death is anathema in a youth- and action-centered culture, most men are surprised by their sudden feelings about the fragility of human existence and particularly with their own mortality. Until a man is a father, he remains identified as a member of the younger generation. His living parents or grandparents act as a psychological buffer against death, because he expects to outlive them. When he becomes a father, there is now a new, younger generation, one he cannot expect to outlive. This concern over life and death epitomizes all fears portending loss, helplessness, inadequacy, or limitations. As the ultimate limitation, mortality colors the experience of expectant fathers.

Most clients are not able to discuss easily these mortality fears. It is valuable for the therapist to gently introduce the issues of fears of mortality and loss into the therapeutic dialogue. Discussions of mortality precipitate more in-depth examinations of limitations and fears of the unknown that are part and parcel of becoming a father to an infant.

The issue of intense vulnerability emerges during the pregnancy and continues throughout a father's life. Frequently, in therapy, the pathway to a man's feelings about mortality revolve around his concerns for his children's safety and well-being. Many fathers can better discuss their own frailties and fears, as well as hopes and dreams, when a therapist begins by focusing on their feelings about their children.

THERAPY ISSUES WITH LATER-STAGE FATHERS

Pregnancy and birth initiate major transformations for men, but fathers' fears and challenges grow as do their children. Unaddressed and unchecked, these fears produce enough anxiety to prevent a dad from full participation in his family. As Pasick (1992) and Pleck (1995) have described, when men experience a discrepancy between what they feel and what they think is expected of them, they often react with withdrawal and feelings of low self-esteem.

Early Fatherhood

From a therapeutic perspective, each of the fears described previously as normative for expectant fathers and early fathers must be anticipated, explored, and addressed by the therapist. For example, the therapist must address unconscious performance anxieties if the patient does not initiate such a conversation.

Chuck came into therapy late in the first trimester of his wife's pregnancy. He reportedly made the appointment at the urging of his wife, who thought that he was depressed and had an anger problem. In the initial session, he reported that soon after becoming pregnant, Mary "celebrated" by quitting her job. With the help of her mother and two friends, she began preparing the home for the new arrival. Reactively and automatically, Chuck began increasing his hours of overtime and found a second job. He said that he was unhappy and that Mary was very angry with him for "working all the time."

Because his increase in work was "automatic," he was apologetic about her reaction and wondered aloud if he should wait until she was asleep before beginning his second (home-based) job. Once the therapist began to ask about the performance concerns and fear of failure, Chuck became aware of how he was "always wrong" in his wife's eyes and how she and her mother were spending more money than he could make. He confessed to thinking he "should just leave." When his need to perform was explored in therapy, he became aware of his feelings of anger and helplessness.

With this insight and supported by the therapist, Chuck was able to discuss his concerns with Mary. He was surprised both by the depth of his feelings about being a provider and at how responsive she was when he described these feelings to her. When she told him it was more important to her that he be available to her, they were able to negotiate both a reduction in her baby-related spending and a renewal of her salary-producing work into the third trimester.

The solution is not always that obvious. Soon after the birth of their second child, Alan found himself increasing his time at work with Karen, a female partner. Although there was no physical involvement, he saw her as his confidant and best friend. Angry and jealous comments from his wife only propelled him more toward Karen. When he came into therapy, he was working more than seventy hours per week and was angry at his wife for showing no understanding of the pressures he had as the sole wage earner. He described his frustration that his wife was so unlike his caring coworker.

By viewing Alan's reaction as a subconscious replacement fear, the therapist focused attention on what Alan was not receiving at home. When Alan stated, "She has the baby and is fine with that," the therapist responded, "So at home you feel like a fifth wheel." Alan replied vehemently, "No! I'm not like a fifth wheel, I'm like the engine with two hundred thousand miles and I'm breaking down."

Continuing with the car metaphor, the therapist explored with Alan what it was like to be running on fumes and feeling like there was no time to even stop for fuel or maintenance. Alan replied, "It's like at home I get to do all the work and she gets to be with the baby." When the therapist suggested that the client was feeling so rejected he might be preparing for the worst by starting a new relationship as an exit strategy, the patient immediately began discussing how he lost his father when his mother "stopped giving him sex." The topic then turned to his feeling of being out of control, rejected, and "like it's my destiny to lose my family again."

While Alan continued with his own personal work revolving around his fears of rejection, he eagerly accepted the therapist's referral for couples therapy with his wife. Soon thereafter, he began insisting on more time alone with the baby and with his wife.

Later Fatherhood

The transition to fatherhood is a precursor to subsequent transitions throughout a man's life as a father. Being a parent is not a time-limited job. As many have opined, parenthood continues far beyond launching the children from home in their late teens or early twenties. The amount of hands-on time may diminish, but the feelings of responsibility and caring and the potential for guilt seem to persist well into our children's adulthood. Behaviorally, the major shift is from manager to consultant. Whatever the shift, fatherhood remains emotionally powerful and complex.

Each developmental stage of childhood brings new challenges for fathers. Not only are the specific developmental challenges different, but at each stage of a child's development, fathers tend to relive emotionally their own development at that stage. Being present at a back-to-school night or on the sidelines at a soccer game, for example, brings out some interesting regressive behaviors in many parents.

In a study of almost two thousand fathers and couples, Shapiro (1993) noted four overriding concerns for fathers. Each is notable for its therapeutic implications. Among the concerns expressed by the men in this sample were (1) becoming a "Mr. Mom," (2) losing male friends, (3) avoiding conflict with women, and (4) needing to overcome a disconnection from their own fathers.

Becoming a "Mr. Mom." It is understandable that for the past several decades, parenting has been equated with mothering. Most men were primarily parented by women, and the model of parenting most common in the 1930s through the 1970s was the father at work away from the home and the mother at home with the children. Yet mothers and fathers normatively approach parenting differently. Shapiro and Bernadett-Shapiro (1998) have argued that, stereotypically, mothers parent from the inside out, and fathers parent from the outside in. Fathers typically approach their children with a greater focus on the outside world and rules, whereas mothers tend to focus on the momentary feelings of their children. A combination of approaches is quite beneficial to the children. Men tend to discipline, communicate, touch, and play with their children differently than do women. However, because it is assumed that a mother's style is the "correct" way, men are often criticized for parenting in a way that is natural for them. Indeed, the model that the media and many child care experts hold up as ideal fathering (and subsequently ridicule) is the "Mr. Mom" standard.

Many men enter therapy feeling inadequate as fathers because they do not measure up to that standard. They describe feeling like second-class parents and have a tendency to respond by withdrawing, thereby accelerating and solidifying those feelings. Therapists need to acknowledge and challenge the social pressure to be a substitute mother. They need to support the father's way of relating to the children and help him educate the mother about his parenting style. In addition, the father will need support to face his own fears of engaging in behaviors that are novel and with unknown contingencies of reinforcement.

Although there may be a power struggle at home for a while, the establishment of equality in parenting minimizes the mother as supervisor–father as underling ambience. A father who experiences his equality as a parent will doubtlessly increase the quantity and quality of father-child time. Several studies have indicated the salience of such time for children's healthy development (see Bernadett-Shapiro, Ehrensaft, & Shapiro, 1996; Secunda, 1992).

One of the reasons that men are pressured in the "Mr. Mom" direction is that they lack the experience and resources to defend their masculine styles of contributions to their children's development. In their own lives, many men have few solid male models of parenting. Indeed, most men do not remember much nurturance from their fathers and consequently feel insecure about their ability to nurture their own children. To make matters worse, the popular media offer few positive examples of male behavior and tend toward unhelpful extremes. Thus a man can feel inadequate by an inability to live up to a father-knows-best style or diminished by being lumped into the caricature of a dolt like Homer Simpson.

Losing male friends. With little to support their natural inclinations toward fathering, a man would normally turn to male friends for examples. However, there is a phenomenon in modern culture that discourages men from getting together. It is a combination of priorities for their time and a fear of what men will do when influenced by their male friends. When a man becomes a father he is often expected to eschew his former friends and focus his energy on the family. This loss may be compounded because most men have a harder time making new friends as they age. This difficulty is due in part to competition, in part to lack of opportunity, and in part to a deficit in intimate social skills.

The dominant implication of reduced contact with male friends is a loss of touch with male ways of "being in the world." A father without peers who provide access to the knowledge he desires naturally turns to others he loves. However, because his partner is a mother, she is better equipped to teach him about being a mother than about being a father. Regardless of both parents' positive intentions, when a man tries to parent as his female partner recommends, he experiences a feeling of being inadequate by a female standard.

Avoiding conflict. Many men avoid any confrontation with their wives for fear of rejection. Indeed, the fear of rejection or abandonment, which is based in childhood experiences (see Cath, Gurwitt, & Ross, 1982), often causes men to withdraw into work, television, the garage, or "projects." Paradoxically, the rejection they fear is actually augmented by these actions.

During the developmental stages in which separation and individuation are dominant, conflict is commonly associated with limit setting and punishment. Because mothers, female teachers, and other women are often the dominant parental figures in a young boy's life, he may well associate conflict and rejection from women. Common social failures throughout the adolescent years reinforce these fears of abandonment. Many men in therapy have an automatic "yes, dear" approach to relationships with significant women in their lives. Therapists need to encourage and support fathers to stand up more for what they want. Initially, this assertiveness will produce some confusion and anxiety related to anticipatory conflict. Once such men begin to focus on personal desires and express their feelings, they offer their partners the opportunity to collaborate and deepen their intimacy.

Overcoming disconnection from father. Since the Industrial Revolution, when men left the home to pursue work at distant locations, boys and girls have had to grow up with little day-to-day male influence. When a man becomes a father, his model is often that of an absent person (Rotundo, 1993). For boys in particular the lack of an adult male influence during crucial years can have a powerful impact, especially as it affects gender role learning (Pollack, 1998).

Most men are well served if they can be helped to rediscover who their father was—for example, as a child, a young man, a new parent. Indeed, knowing the pressures, motivations, successes, and failures of one's own father decreases the likelihood of unconsciously replicating or deliberately reversing one's fathering in a new generation. A man can create a new destiny by choosing what he wants to replicate and what he wants to change.

The example of Jack, cited earlier, who turned a visit with his aging father on the Indiana farm into a resolve to be closer to his daughters is particularly germane here. Shapiro (1993) provides a series of methods for reconnecting with an adult father, even if he is unavailable physically.

EXISTENTIAL THERAPY WITH FATHERS

Because of its emphasis on here-and-now choices, existential therapy is particularly well suited to men in transition. During major life transformations, there is a consistent tension between the fear of change (the unknown) and the security of maintaining the status quo. To meet the challenges of fatherhood, a man must face his fears of the unknown, especially his personal limits and mortality. If instead he chooses the security of continuing to behave as he always has, he must endure the guilt and stagnation of the mental or behavioral status quo. Existential therapists believe that individuals must face their fears of the unknown to grow. Facing fears of the unknown does not demand counterphobic behaviors. Rather, healthy adaptations require that a client examine the payoff and price of change and make an informed decision.

Bob was referred to therapy by his minister, who told him that he was quite depressed. His appearance at the first session supported that impression. Bob reported that he was extremely distraught about his twenty-two-year-old daughter's choice of a boyfriend. He described her as emerging from a difficult breakup with a fiancé. He admitted that he initially had trouble with the fiancé because of a racial difference, but "as I got to know him as a person, I began to love him as a son." Bob was still mourning the loss of the engagement when his daughter brought home her current romantic interest.

Bob reported that he was intensely affected by the events in his only daughter's life. He attributed this deep involvement to their three years alone after his first wife died. He also described a hands-off pattern they had evolved when it came to her romantic interests. In examining the payoff for this lack of involvement, he spontaneously muttered, "Well, if I make it a choice between him and me, she'll leave me." In addition, he admitted that he was particularly embarrassed about his feelings toward the new boyfriend because of a deep personal prejudice. Alcohol sensitive all of his life, Bob was uncomfortable with this man's penchant for beer.

Bob was the sixth child of an immigrant family with a history of alcoholism. As the only moderate drinker and professional among his siblings, he was proud of his emergence from the six-pack-after-a-hard-day's-labor lifestyle of his family of origin. He was extremely threatened by the image of his daughter returning to that kind of hard life.

Bob's daughter was planning to visit without her boyfriend for Thanksgiving when Bob and the therapist discussed his dilemma. Bob was afraid that if he said nothing, she would view it as his acquiescence and ultimately he would end up as "father-in-law to my own personal demon." By contrast, if he told her how he felt, he worried that she would see how prejudiced he was and would reject him for the new romantic interest.

In this "launching" transition, Bob was feeling stuck. When Bob and the therapist explored Bob's fears, the discussion immediately reverted to the loss of his first wife and mother. He cried when he spoke about both of their deaths and immediately responded that he could not stand to lose his daughter. The payoff for continued silence was that he got to avoid facing the fear of abandonment. The downside was that he was depressed and felt like a failure as a father.

Therapy revolved around supporting him, acknowledging the dilemma, exploring the payoff and cost of his "safety," and helping him find a way to face the risk realistically. Several times Bob and the therapist role-played "the big conversation," with Bob playing his daughter and the therapist taking Bob's role. In addition, therapy included intense work with Bob's fear that he would be abandoned by another important woman in his life; the work involved mourning the loss of his mother when he was twenty-two (his daughter's current age).

Bob discussed the matter with his daughter, who acknowledged her own pain about the broken engagement and her need for a "transition" relationship rather than a serious one. She also laughed fondly about her dad's sensitivity to "drunks in the family," a sensitivity she shared. At his suggestion, she entered individual therapy to examine her reasons for her current choice and her part in ending the prior relationship.

From an existential perspective, Bob had to confront his fears of abandonment and explore whether it was worth the depression and stagnation to avoid that fear. This launching-stage transition is typical of similar conflicts that may emerge during any stages of fatherhood.

The goals of therapy with fathers are many and varied. Successful fathering requires confidence, a strong sense of self, and comfort in parental interactions with children. It requires the ability to have an equal say in parental decision making, an appreciable quantity of time with children, modeling of male compassion and strength, and courage to face the inevitable vulnerabilities that accompany fatherhood. Therapy with men dealing with such issues offers a unique opportunity to foster psychological growth. Yet therapy with men who are dealing with issues of fatherhood often seems equivalent to dealing with progressive levels of insecurity.

Several factors magnify this sense of insecurity. Cultural pressures on men to protect and provide are exacerbated during pregnancy and extend throughout their lives as fathers. In addition, despite a significant increase in literature about fathering since the 1980s, positive models and knowledge of appropriate fathering still lag and are unavailable to many. The popular media continue to identify men in general and fathers in particular as appropriate objects of derisive humor. In addition, male bonding and friendships tend to recede over time, and connections between fathers are far less common than is desirable.

In addition to the cultural pressures, there are many significant intrapsychic barriers to effective fathering. Because of the basic fear of abandonment that many men carry from childhood, they are loath to risk rejection, especially by women who are significant in their lives. When their fathering is questioned or criticized, men commonly try to comply by stuffing down feelings of anger or withdraw to avoid the aversive situations. Both of these defensive adaptations are likely to have long-term negative consequences.

The therapist's task is manifold. In working with fathers, therapists are most effective when they attend to the core fear of abandonment. To avoid exacerbating the fear and driving the clients from therapy, approaching the fear of abandonment is best done indirectly, metaphorically, and sensitively. Often the latch that opens the doors of that exploration is a consideration of the dynamic tension between a man's fear of the unknown and guilt about maintaining the status quo. Exploring the cost of opting for the status quo allows many fathers to begin to explore their anxieties when faced with matters that are out of their control and fears that they will be abandoned for failure.

On a pragmatic level, a therapist can encourage a man to pursue male relationships, support his appropriate disagreements with his wife's emotional certainty, and help him examine his relationship with his father. When a man becomes a father he often lets a number of nurturing aspects of his life slide in favor of the new responsibilities. Frequently, his world contracts to the point that he is distant from friends, has given up playful pastimes or hobbies, and experiences an erosion of personal time. Despite the new opportunities for pleasure afforded by a family, he may find his life out of balance.

In the words of one thirty-one-year-old father of two, "There's two pots in our house—hers and ours." What he was missing was the personal side of his life. It is the therapist's job to help him remember what he has historically found nurturing and to prod him to recapture some of that feeling. This process can then allow him to be more present with his family. Encouragement for his getting together with male friends, talking to his father, exploring how other men resolve this dilemma, and setting personal limits with his partner may be particularly important therapeutically.

Because any such changes will tap men's resistance, based in a fear of rejection or abandonment, different clients may need to begin at opposite ends of the dilemma. Thus, some fathers will look for the pragmatic behavior change as a means of gaining relief and as a method of probing deeper psychologically.

Other fathers may prefer intrapsychic insight as a precursor to behavioral change. Still others may need to work from both ends toward the middle. Although it is essential that the therapist help clients make both adjustments, the cue for access points and appropriate metaphors must be from within individual male clients.

References

Bernadett-Shapiro, S. T., Ehrensaft, D., & Shapiro, J. L. (1996). Father participation in childcare and the development of empathy in sons: An empirical study. *Family Therapy, 23*(3), 77–93

Bly, R. (1989). *A gathering of men: An interview with Bill Moyers* [Videocassette]. New York: Mystic Fire Video.

Brooks, G. R. (1998). *A new psychotherapy for traditional men.* San Francisco: Jossey-Bass.

Cath, S. H., Gurwitt, A. R., & Ross, J. M. (1982). *Father and child: Developmental and clinical perspectives.* Boston: Little, Brown.

Diamond, M. J. (1992). Creativity needs in becoming a father. *Journal of Men's Studies, 1,* 41–45.

Diamond, M. J. (1995a). Becoming a father: A psychoanalytic perspective on the forgotten parent. In J. L. Shapiro, M. J. Diamond, & M. Greenberg (Eds.), *Becoming a father: Contemporary social, developmental, and clinical perspectives* (pp. 268–285). New York: Springer.

Diamond, M. J. (1995b). The emergence of the father as the watchful protector of the mother-infant dyad. In J. L. Shapiro, M. J. Diamond, & M. Greenberg (Eds.), *Becoming a father: Contemporary social, developmental, and clinical perspectives* (pp. 243–254). New York: Springer.

Ehrensaft, D. (1994). Bringing in fathers: The reconstruction of mothering. In J. L. Shapiro, M. J. Diamond, & M. Greenberg (Eds.), *Becoming a father: Contemporary social, developmental, and clinical perspectives* (pp. 43–59). New York: Springer.

Farrell, W. (1986). *Why men are the way they are.* New York: McGraw-Hill.

Gottman, J. (1994). *Why marriages succeed or fail.* New York: Fireside.

Greenberg, M. (1985). *The birth of a father.* New York: Continuum.

Greenberg, M. (1997, June). *Becoming a father.* Paper presented at the annual meeting of the American Psychiatric Association, San Diego, CA.

Haley, J. (1963). *Strategies of psychotherapy.* New York: Grune & Stratton.

Harris, L. M. (1995). *Messages men hear: Constructing masculinities.* Bristol, PA: Taylor & Francis.

Keen, S. (1991). *Fire in the belly.* New York: Bantam Books.

Levant, R. F. (1998). Desperately seeking language: Understanding, assessing, and treating normative male alexithymia. In W. S. Pollack & R. F. Levant (Eds.), *New psychotherapy for men* (pp. 35–56). New York: Wiley.

Levant, R. F., & Pollack, W. S. (1995). *The new psychology of men.* New York: Basic Books.

Mahalik, J. R. (1999). Incorporating a gender role strain perspective in assessing and treating men's cognitive distortions. *Professional Psychology: Research and Practice, 30*(4), 333–340.

Marcy, W. L. (1832, January). Speech in the U.S. Senate. In Bartlett, J. (1980). *Bartlett's familiar quotations* (rev. 15th ed., p. 455). Boston: Little, Brown.

Michaels, G. Y., & Goldberg, W. A. (1988). *The transition to parenthood: Current theory and research.* Cambridge, U.K.: Cambridge University Press.

Osherson, S. (1987). *Finding our fathers: The unfinished business of manhood.* New York: Fawcett.

Osherson, S. (1992). *Wrestling with love.* New York: Fawcett.

Pasick, R. S. (1992). *Awakening from the deep sleep: A powerful guide for courageous men.* San Francisco: Hardon.

Pleck, J. H. (1995). The gender role strain paradigm: An update. In R. F. Levant & W. S. Pollack (Eds.), *The new psychology of men* (pp. 1–32). New York: Basic Books

Pollack, W. S. (1995). A delicate balance: Fatherhood and psychological transformation—a psychoanalytic perspective. In J. L. Shapiro, M. J. Diamond, & M. Greenberg (Eds.), *Becoming a father: Contemporary social, developmental, and clinical perspectives* (pp. 316–331). New York: Springer.

Pollack, W. S. (1998). *Real boys.* New York: Random House.

Pollack, W. S., & Levant, R. F. (1998). *New psychotherapy for men.* New York: Wiley.

Rotundo, A. E. (1993). *American manhood.* New York: Basic Books.

Secunda, V. (1992). *Women and their fathers.* New York: Delacorte.

Shapiro, J. L. (1987). *When men are pregnant: Needs and concerns of expectant fathers.* San Luis Obispo, CA: Impact.

Shapiro, J. L. (1993). *The measure of a man: Becoming the father you wish your father had been.* New York: Delacorte.

Shapiro, J. L. (1995). When men are pregnant. In J. L. Shapiro, M. J. Diamond, & M. Greenberg (Eds.), *Becoming a father: Contemporary social, developmental, and clinical perspectives* (pp. 118–134). New York: Springer.

Shapiro, J. L. (1997 June). *Becoming a father.* Paper presented at the annual meeting of the American Psychiatric Association, San Diego, CA.

Shapiro, J. L., & Bernadett-Shapiro, S. T. (1998). No, I want daddy: Stages of parent preference. *Bay Area Parent, 15*(3), 29–32.

Shapiro, J. L., Diamond, M. J., & Greenberg, M. (1995). *Becoming a father: Contemporary social, developmental, and clinical perspectives.* New York: Springer.

Shay, J. J., & Maltas, C. P. (1998). Reluctant men in couple therapy: Corralling the Marlboro man. In W. S. Pollack & R. F. Levant (Eds.), *New psychotherapy for men* (pp. 97–126). New York: Wiley.

Tannen, D. (1990). *You just don't understand: Men and women in conversation.* New York: Morrow.

CHAPTER TWENTY-ONE

Desperately Seeking Language

Understanding, Assessing, and Treating Normative Male Alexithymia

Ronald F. Levant

NORMATIVE MALE ALEXITHYMIA

In this chapter I focus on a fairly specific aspect of psychotherapy for men, but one that has general significance—namely, the understanding, assessment, and treatment of normative male alexithymia.

Alexithymia literally means the inability to put emotions into words. The term is composed of a series of Greek roots: *a-* (meaning without), *lexus* (meaning words), and *thymos* (meaning emotions)—without words for emotions. Sifneos (1967) and Krystal (1982) originally described this condition to characterize the severe emotional constriction that they encountered in their (primarily male) patients with psychosomatic disorders, drug dependence, and posttraumatic stress disorder (see also Sifneos, 1988). They were dealing with cases of severe alexithymia, which is at the far end of the continuum of this disorder. Through my work on this topic in the Boston University Fatherhood Project (Levant & Kelly, 1989) and in my subsequent research and clinical practice (Levant & Kopecky, 1995), I have found that alexithymia also occurs in garden-variety or mild-to-moderate forms; these forms are very common and widespread among men. I have come to term this condition *normative male alexithymia.*

Simply put, as a result of the male role socialization ordeal, boys grow up to be men who are genuinely unaware of their emotions and sometimes even their bodily sensations, as is illustrated in the following clinical vignette:

> George, age fifty-three, a self-made multimillionaire, collapsed one day in his office. He was rushed to the emergency room, where a complete examination revealed no medical illness. He was simply out of touch with the cues that his body was sending him—in this case exhaustion from taking a red-eye back from the West Coast and running a sales meeting after two hours of sleep. His hobby was competing in car races, and he complained in the first interview that he had a better idea of what was going on with his car, as he put it through its paces, than he did with himself. He wanted a set of "dials and gauges" that would allow him to know what was going on inside him.

When men are required to give an account of their emotions and are unable to identify them directly, they tend to rely on their cognition to logically deduce what they should feel under the circumstances. As is illustrated in the following anecdote, they cannot do what is so easy and almost automatic for most women—to simply sense inward, feel the feeling, and let the verbal description come to mind.

> I once asked a father: "What were your feelings, Don, when your son stood you up for the father-son hockey game?" Don's response: "He shouldn't have done it!" "No, Don," I said, "I didn't ask you what you thought he should have done. I asked you what you felt." Don's response: "Oh. Let me think. I guess I felt, I think I felt, I must have felt . . . upset."
>
> In contrast, ask a woman what she felt when her daughter stood her up for an afternoon of shopping at the mall and listen as she peels off layer after layer of her feelings: "At first I was angry. Then I got worried, because I didn't know what had happened to her. Then I was really disappointed, because I was really looking forward to spending this time with her before she left for college."

This widespread inability among men to identify emotions and put them into words has enormous consequences. It blocks men who have it from using the most effective means known for dealing with life's stresses and traumas—namely, identifying, thinking about, and discussing one's emotional responses to a stressor or trauma with a friend, family member, or therapist. Consequently it predisposes such men to deal with stress in ways that make certain forms of pathology such as substance abuse, violent behavior, sexual compulsions, stress-related illnesses, and early death more likely. It also makes it less likely that such men will be able to benefit from psychotherapy as traditionally practiced.

I hasten to point out that by viewing men's traditional inability to put emotions into words as a mild form of alexithymia I do not mean to characterize maleness as pathological. Rather, I hope to engage the reader in a consideration of the idea that this aspect of traditional masculinity does not serve men well in today's world and is therefore dysfunctional, although it served a purpose in earlier eras (Grunebaum, 1996). I also hope to point out that normative alexithymia, like the more severe forms, is a result of trauma—in this case the trauma of the male role socialization process, a trauma that is so normative that we do not think of it as trauma at all (see also Betcher & Pollack, 1993; Pollack, 1995, 1998a, 1998b).

MALE ROLE SOCIALIZATION PROCESS

To fully understand how male socialization harms men, one must understand the shift that has recently taken place in the conceptualization of gender roles. This shift is represented best by a fundamentally new variant of gender ideology—the gender role strain paradigm.

Gender Role Strain Paradigm

The gender role strain paradigm (Pleck, 1981, 1995) is the best developed representative of the social constructionist perspective on gender in the new psychology of men. In contrast to the older gender role identity paradigm, the strain paradigm does not assume that masculinity and femininity are the same thing as, nor are they essential to, being male or female, respectively, but rather sees these definitions of gender as historically relative and socially constructed. Further, the strain paradigm proposes that, to the extent that parents, teachers, and peers subscribe to a particular gender role ideology extant in a society or historical era, children will be socialized accordingly. Prior to the late 1960s in the United States, what have been termed *traditional gender role ideologies* prevailed (Thompson & Pleck, 1995). Hence, male children brought up in the postwar era were reared to conform to traditional norms of masculinity, of which Levant et al. (1992) identified seven: (1) avoidance of all things feminine, (2) restrictive emotionality, (3) toughness and aggression, (4) self-reliance, (5) achievement and status, (6) nonrelational attitudes toward sexuality, and (7) fear and hatred of homosexuals.

To put these norms in context, traditional masculinity ideology fits best with harsh social conditions, such as those that occurred in the United States from the period of industrialization through World War I, the Great Depression, and World War II (Gilmore, 1990; Rotundo, 1990). In such conditions certain male traits such as toughness, self-reliance, and lack of awareness of emotions are likely to be more adaptive.

The strain paradigm also proposes that gender roles do not fit individual personalities particularly well, resulting in gender role strain. Of the several types of gender role strain that have been described, the most relevant in this context is trauma-strain, the notion that the processes required to develop this role are traumatic (Pleck, 1995). The concept of trauma strain has been applied to certain groups of men whose experiences with gender role strain are thought to be particularly harsh, such as professional athletes (Messner, 1992), war veterans (Brooks, 1990), survivors of child abuse (Lisak, 1995), men of color (Lazur & Majors, 1995), and gay and bisexual men (Harrison, 1995). But above and beyond the recognition that certain classes of men may experience trauma strain, a perspective on the male role socialization process that views socialization under traditional masculinity ideology as *inherently* traumatic has emerged (Levant, 1996). The traumatic aspects are seen most clearly in the emotion socialization process, through which boys' natural emotional expressivity is suppressed and channeled.

Emotion Socialization Ordeal for Boys

Because of what seem to be biologically based differences, boys start out life more emotionally expressive than girls do. Haviland and Malatesta (1981), reviewing data from twelve studies (eleven of which were of neonates), concluded that male infants are more emotionally reactive and expressive than their female counterparts—that they startle more easily, become excited more quickly, have a lower tolerance for tension and frustration, become distressed more quickly, cry sooner and more often, and fluctuate more rapidly between emotional states. Furthermore, Cunningham and Shapiro (1984, cited in Brody & Hall, 1993) found that infant boys were judged to be more emotionally expressive than were infant girls, even when the judges were misinformed about the infants' actual sex, thus controlling for the effects of gender role stereotyping on the part of judges. Finally, boys remain more emotional than girls at least until six months of age. Weinberg (1992, p. vii) found that six-month-old boys exhibited "significantly more joy and anger, more positive vocalizations, fussiness, and crying, [and] more gestural signals directed towards the mother . . . than girls."

Despite this initial advantage in emotional expressivity, males learn to tune out, suppress, and channel their emotions, whereas the emotion socialization of females encourages their expressivity. These effects become evident with respect to verbal expression by two years of age and with respect to facial expression by six years of age. Dunn, Bretherton, and Munn (1987) found that two-year-old girls refer to feeling states more frequently than do two-year-old boys. Buck (1977) assessed the ability of mothers of four- to-six-year-old boys and girls to accurately identify their children's emotional responses to a series of slides by observing their children's facial expressions on a television monitor. The older the boy, the less expressive his face, and the harder it was for his mother to tell what he was feeling. Buck found no such correlation among the girls: their mothers were able to identify their emotions no matter what their age. Buck (1977) concluded that between the ages of four and six years, "boys apparently inhibit and mask their overt response to emotion to an increasing extent, while girls continue to respond relatively freely" (p. 234). (See also Allen & Haccoun, 1976; Balswick & Avertt, 1977; Brody & Hall, 1993; Stapley & Haviland, 1989.)

What socialization processes would account for this "crossover in emotional expression" (Haviland & Malatesta, 1981, p. 202), such that boys start out more emotional than girls and wind up much less so? Levant and Kopecky (1995) proposed that the socialization influences of mother, father, and peer group combine to result in the suppression and channeling of male emotionality and the encouragement of female emotionality. The mechanisms of emotion socialization include selective reinforcement, direct teaching, differential life experiences, and punishment.

1. Mothers work harder to manage their more excitable and emotional male infants: They "employ more contingent responding (and particularly contingent smiling) in playing with their sons. Mothers may go to special lengths to ensure that their sons are contented" (Haviland & Malatesta, 1981, p. 202). Mothers also control their own expressivity to "preclude upsetting their [sons'] more fragile emotional equilibria" (Haviland & Malatesta, 1981, p. 202). In contrast, mothers expose their infant daughters to a wider range of emotions than they do their sons (Malatesta, Culver, Tesman, & Shephard, 1989).

2. Fathers take an active interest in their children after the thirteenth month of life (Lamb, 1977) and from that point on socialize their toddler sons and daughters along gender-stereotyped lines (Lamb, Owen, & Chase-Lansdale, 1979; Siegal, 1987). Fathers interact more with infant sons than they do with infant daughters (Lamb, 1977). With older children, fathers engage in more verbal roughhousing with sons and tend to speak more about emotions with daughters (Greif, Alvarez, & Ulman, 1981; Schell & Gleason, 1989). Fathers also express more disapproval to sons who engage in gender-inappropriate play (Langlois & Downs, 1980). Many adult men whom I have counseled recall experiences in which their fathers made them feel deeply ashamed of expressing either vulnerable (such as sadness and fear) or caring or connection emotions (such as warmth and affection).

3. Both parents participate in the gender-differentiated development of language for emotions. Parents discourage their sons from learning to express vulnerable emotions; although they encourage their daughters to learn to express their vulnerable and caring or connection emotions, they discourage their daughters' expression of anger and aggression. It should be noted that females' language superiority also plays a role in their greater ability to express emotions verbally (Brody & Hall, 1993). Dunn, Bretherton, and Munn (1987) found that mothers used more emotion words when speaking with daughters than with sons. Fivush (1989) found that mothers spoke more about sadness with daughters than with sons and only spoke about anger with sons. With daughters,

mothers discussed the experience of the emotion, whereas with sons they discussed the "causes and consequences of emotions," which would serve to help sons learn to control their emotions. Greif, Alvarez, and Ulman (1981) had parents "read" stories to their children using wordless books and videotaped and transcribed their conversations. Mothers talked about anger twice as frequently with sons as with daughters. Finally, Fuchs and Thelen (1988) found that school-age sons expected their parents to react negatively to the expression of sadness, whereas school-age daughters expected their mothers to react more positively to the expression of sadness than they would to the expression of anger.

4. Sex-segregated peer groups complete the job. Young girls typically play with one or two other girls, and their play consists of maintaining the relationship (by minimizing conflict and hostility and maximizing agreement and cooperation) and telling each other secrets, thus fostering their learning skills of empathy, emotional self-awareness, and emotional expressivity. In contrast, young boys typically play in larger groups in structured games, in which they learn skills such as how to play by the rules, teamwork, stoicism, toughness, and competition (Lever, 1976; Maccoby, 1990; Paley, 1984). One study found that boys experience direct competition in their play half of the time, whereas girls experience it very infrequently (less than 1 percent of the time) (Crombie & DesJardins, 1993, cited in Brody, 1996). Boy culture is also notoriously cruel to boys who violate male role norms, such as expressing vulnerable emotions, showing affection, or being unwilling to fight (Krugman, 1995).

The suppression and channeling of male emotionality by mothers, fathers, and peer groups has four major consequences: the development of "action empathy," normative alexithymia, the overdevelopment of anger, and the channeling of caring emotions into sexuality.

Action Empathy

Empathy can be defined in cognitive-developmental terms as "interpersonal understanding" (Selman, 1980), which puts the emphasis on the ability to "decenter" from one's own frame of reference and take another person's perspective. In this view, many men develop a form of empathy that I call "action empathy," which can be defined as the ability to see things from another person's point of view and predict what they will or should do (Brody & Hall, 1993; Eisenberg & Lennon, 1983; Hall, 1978; Levant & Kopecky, 1995). Action empathy is in contrast to emotional empathy, which involves taking another person's perspective and knowing how that person feels. Action empathy also differs from emotional empathy in terms of its aim: emotional empathy is usually employed to help another person and is thus prosocial, whereas action empathy is usually (though not always) employed in the service of the self. Action empathy is usually learned in the gymnasiums and on the playing fields from gym teachers and sports coaches who put a premium on learning an opponent's general approach, strengths, weaknesses, and body language to be able to figure out how he might react in a given situation.

Normative Alexithymia

Normative alexithymia is a predictable result of the male gender role socialization process. Specifically, it is a result of boys being socialized to restrict the expression of their vulnerable and caring or connection emotions and to be emotionally stoic. This socialization process includes both the creation of skills deficits (by not teaching boys emotional skills or allowing them to have experiences that would facilitate their learning these skills) and trauma (including prohibitions against boys' natural emotional expressivity and punishment, often in the form of making the boy feel deeply ashamed of himself for violating these prohibitions).

Emotions consist of three components (Taylor, 1994): (1) the neurophysiological substrate, which includes both autonomic and endocrinological components (for example, in the fight-flight response the sympathetic nervous system is activated and the adrenal glands release epinephrine); (2) the motor or behavioral response, which involves the activation of the skeletomuscular system in facial expression, tone of voice, and body language or in direct action, such as a physical attack or an embrace; and (3) the cognitive or affective component, which includes the subjective awareness of the emotion and the ability to put it into words. Men with normative alexithymia typically lack the third component, and some also lack the second.

Some men report that their wives know what they are feeling when they themselves do not. In these cases the men may lack the third component of the emotion but have the second component, from which their wives can read their emotions in their facial expression and tone of voice.

Men who are having an emotion that they cannot bring into awareness often experience it in one of two ways:

1. As a bodily sensation, which may be the result of the neuroendocrinological or the skeletomuscular components of the emotion, examples of which are tightness in the throat, constriction in the chest, clenching of the gut, antsy feeling in the legs, constriction in the face, difficulty in concentrating, and gritting of the teeth. This particular way of experiencing emotions as bodily sensations has been described by Buck (1984) as "internalizing," which he defines as physiological arousal coupled with facial inexpressiveness, and by Gottman and Levenson (1988) as the way that men in conflicted marriages experience marital conflict.

2. As a response to external pressure (that is, feeling "stressed out," "overloaded," "zapped," or having the need to "just veg out").

Overdevelopment of Anger and Aggression

An important corollary of normative alexithymia is the overdevelopment of anger and aggression. Boys are allowed to feel and become aware of emotions in the anger and rage part of the spectrum, as prescribed in the toughness dimension also known as the "Give 'em Hell" injunction of the male code (David & Brannon, 1976). As a result men express anger more aggressively (as a motor or behavioral response) than do women (Brody & Hall, 1993; Campbell, 1993; Eagly & Steffen, 1986; Frodi, Macaulay, & Thome, 1977). The aggressive expression of anger is in fact one of the very few ways boys are encouraged to express emotion, and as a consequence the outlawed vulnerable emotions of hurt, disappointment, fear, and shame get funneled into the anger channel. Long (1987) refers to this rechanneling of emotions as "the male emotional funnel system," the final common pathway for all those shameful vulnerable emotions that are too unmanly to express directly (see also Keltikangas-Jarvinen, 1982).

In truth, though, for some men the process is more active. For these men the vulnerable emotions are actively transformed into anger, a process learned on the playing fields, as when a boy is pushed down on the ground and he knows that his job is to come back up with a fistful of gravel rather than a face full of tears.

In addition, because of the general lack of sensitivity to emotional states that characterizes alexithymia, many men do not recognize anger in its mild forms, such as irritation or annoyance, but only detect it when they are very angry. Consequently, angry outbursts often come too readily in men. Such men are victims of what Levant and Kelly (1989) call the "rubber band syndrome."

Suppression and Channeling of Tender Feelings into Sexuality

Boys experience sharp limitations on the expression of caring or connection emotions. This message often comes from the father, as is illustrated in the following anecdote:

> The father drove into the driveway, and his children bounded out to greet him. He first hugged and kissed one little daughter and then hugged and kissed the second daughter. His four-year-old son stood waiting to be hugged and kissed. The father said: "No, Timmy, men don't hug and kiss." Slowly, Timmy got reorganized and offered a stiff manly little hand for a handshake.

Boys also get the message from their peers that it is not socially acceptable for boys to express affection either to girls (a peer might taunt, sing-song fashion: "Johnny loves Susie") or to boys (lest they be called "faggots"). Socialization experiences of this type, often accompanied by enormous feelings of shame, set up powerful barriers to the overt expression of caring or connection emotions. Later, in adolescence, the pent-up caring or connection emotions get channeled into sexuality. Fueled by the hormonal changes that accompany puberty and fused with the adolescent boy's need to prove himself, this expression often takes the form of nonrelational sexuality or unconnected lust (Brooks, 1995; Hudson & Jacot, 1991; Levant & Kopecky, 1995).

Zilbergeld (1992) describes how teenage boys learn about sex. An absence of realistic, compassionate portrayals of sexuality combined with ubiquitous fantasy images of the woman as sex object fosters the development of unconnected lust:

> The message is clear: For men sex doesn't have to be connected to anything except lust, and it doesn't matter much toward whom it's directed. . . . The female in his fantasies is simply a tool to gain release. And then to do it again, and again, and again. Next time it will probably be with a different female. And he certainly doesn't have to like the girl to have sex with her. . . . Sex is a thing unto itself for adolescent boys, cut off from the rest of their life and centered on their desire for physical release and the need to prove themselves. (pp. 34–35)

Hence, the male role socialization ordeal, through the combined influences of mothers, fathers, and peer groups, suppresses and channels natural male emotionality to such an extent that boys grow up to be men who develop an action-oriented variant of empathy, who cannot readily sense their feelings and put them into words, and who tend to channel or transform their vulnerable feelings into anger and their caring feelings into sexuality.

I began working with men to help them identify and process their emotions in a preventive program that I ran in the 1980s, the Boston University Fatherhood Project (Levant & Kelly, 1989). Since then I have experimented with the treatment of men with normative alexithymia individually and in groups. My approach integrates cognitive-behavioral, psychoeducational, skills-training, and family systems components. The program that I have developed is an active, problem-solving approach that relies on the use of homework assignments. I have found that many men find such an approach congenial, because it is congruent with aspects of the male code. In addition, men who are demoralized for one reason or another may find that it restores their sense of agency by giving them something that they can do to improve their situation.

Helping men overcome normative alexithymia is useful at the beginning stages of therapy for many men, because it enables them to develop the skills of emotional self-awareness and emotional expressivity that will empower them to wrestle with the deeper issues. Such was the case with Raymond.

A NUMB EXPECTANT FATHER

Raymond, a forty-one-year-old successful software designer currently racing to bring a new, "preemptive" telecommunications product to market, called for an appointment because he "felt nothing" about the fact that he and his wife of twenty years were expecting their first child. He and his wife had met in high school and had postponed having a child because Raymond's work required many moves over the years. Raymond was a hard-driving man who met or exceeded most of the requirements of the male code. The firstborn son of a rural family, responsibility was his middle name. He took care of various members of his family of origin and his extended family.

Apart from the fact that his wife was pregnant and he thought he "should" feel something about that, Raymond did not find it particularly odd that he "felt nothing." He usually felt nothing. The last time he had cried was when his dog was hit by a car. That was ten years ago.

Assessment: Session One

During the first interview, in addition to taking a standard history, I also assess the male client's ability to become aware of his emotions and put them into words. Here is the format I typically follow:

1. To what extent is the patient aware of discrete emotions, as contrasted with either the neuroendocrinological and skeletomuscular components of emotions (that is, tension in the forehead or tightness in the gut) or signs of stress (that is, feeling "overloaded" or "zapped")? Some specific questions include the following: Do you have feelings that you cannot quite identify? Is it easy for you to find the right words for your feelings? Are you often confused by what emotion you are feeling? Do you find yourself puzzled by sensations in your body? (Questions were borrowed or adapted from the Twenty-Item Toronto Alexithymia Scale [TAS-20], Bagby, Taylor, & Parker, 1994.)

2. What emotions does the patient become aware of? Is he aware of his emotions in the vulnerable part of the spectrum—that is, emotions that make us feel vulnerable such as worry, fear, anxiety, sadness, hurt, dejection, disappointment, rejection, or abandonment? ("When you are upset do you know if you are sad, frightened, or angry?" Question was adapted from the TAS-20, Bagby, Taylor, & Parker, 1994.) If he is not aware of his vulnerable emotions, are these emotions transformed into anger and expressed as anger, rage, or violence?

3. Is the patient aware of his emotions in the caring or connection part of the spectrum such as caring, concern, warmth, affection, appreciation, love, neediness or dependency, closeness, or attachment? Is he limited in his ability to express caring or connection emotions? Does he express them primarily through the channel of sexuality?

4. Is the patient aware of his emotions in the anger part of the spectrum? Does he become aware of an emotion such as anger only when it is very intense?

5. At what intensities does the patient experience his emotions? Some specific questions include the following: Would "cool, calm, and collected" describe you? When you are angry is it easy for you to still be rational and not overreact?

Does your heart race at the anticipation of an exciting event? Do sad movies deeply touch you? When you do something wrong, do you have strong feelings of shame and guilt? (Questions were borrowed or adapted from the Affective Intensity Measure [AIM], Larsen & Diener, 1987.)

Raymond was not aware of discrete emotions but instead experienced them as signs of stress. He did not tend to transform vulnerable emotions into anger and in fact was not often aware of his anger. He felt most connected to his wife during sex.

Alexithymia Treatment: Sessions Two Through Four

The program for the treatment of alexithymia that I have developed has five steps.

Step one: psychoeducation about normative alexithymia. For the patient to be able to make sense of his experience and use the treatment techniques, he needs to know his limitations in his ability to name and express his emotions and how these limitations came about. An important part of this step is helping the patient develop his ability to tolerate certain emotions (such as fear or sadness) that he may regard as unmanly and therefore shameful (Krugman, 1995). I tailor this step to the individual patient, drawing on the material in the first two sections of this chapter (see also Krystal, 1979).

Step two: develop a vocabulary for emotions. Because men tend not to be aware of emotions, they usually do not have a very good vocabulary of words for emotions. This limited vocabulary also follows from the literature (reviewed earlier) on the development of language for emotions. The next step, then, is to help the man develop a vocabulary for the full spectrum of emotions, particularly the vulnerable and caring or connection emotions. I asked Raymond to record as many words for feelings as he could several times during the week.

Step three: learn to read the emotions of others. The third step involves learning to apply emotional words to feeling states. Because it is often less threatening to do this step with other people than with oneself and because men can readily build on their action empathy skills to learn emotional empathy, I recommend focusing on other people at this stage. I taught Raymond to read facial gestures, tone of voice, and other types of body language in other people. I encouraged him to learn to identify the emotions of other people in conversations, while observing other people, or while watching movies. I instructed him to ask himself questions during this process such as "What is he feeling?" and "What does this feel like from her perspective?"

Step four: keep an emotional response log. The next step involves teaching the application of emotional words to a man's own experiences. To do this, I asked Raymond to keep an emotional response log, noting when he experienced a feeling that he could identify or a bodily sensation or sign of stress that he became aware of and what circumstances led up to it. The instructions for keeping an emotional response log are as follows:

- Record the bodily sensation or sign of stress (or feelings, if you notice them) that you become aware of and when you first started to experience them

- Describe the social or relational context within which the emotion was aroused: Who was doing what to whom? How did that affect you?

- Go through your emotional vocabulary list and pick out the words that seem to best describe the emotion that you were experiencing

Raymond was pretty good at recording the emotions or sensations and the context within which they occurred. But, as with many other men, the third task required discussion in the session to develop the connections between his emotional experiences and language.

Step five: practice. The fifth and final step involves practice. Emotional self-awareness is a skill, and like any other skill it requires practice to become an automatic part of one's functioning. In the Fatherhood Project (and the fatherhood course that I currently teach), we use role playing, videotaped for immediate feedback, to practice the skill. Fathers are taught to tune in to their feelings through watching and discussing immediate playbacks of role playing in which feelings were engendered. By pointing out the nonverbal cues and asking such questions as "What were your feelings, Tom, when you grimaced in that last segment?" fathers learn how to access the ongoing flow of emotions within. The video playback is often so effective that we have come to refer to it as the "mirror to a man's soul."

Although working on these matters in a group context with video feedback is obviously advantageous, one can also practice this skill without such arrangements. By systematically keeping an emotional response log and discussing the results in therapy, one can gradually build up the ability to recognize feelings as they occur and put them into words.

Some colleagues were surprised that men can learn this skill fairly easily. But it really should not be a surprise, because what we are teaching men is a skill that young girls learn as matter of course and that they might have learned themselves had they not been shunted onto the male emotion socialization track. And when men learn this skill, they feel very empowered. One man said that it was as though he had been living in a black-and-white television set that had suddenly gone to color.

During sessions two through four Raymond worked on increasing his capacity to recognize his emotions by using the five-step program with an emphasis on the emotional response log. Raymond was a quick study, and although he did not feel vulnerable emotions very intensely and he certainly could not yet let his feelings pour out, he was able to discern quite subtle differences in his emotional states by the fourth session.

Fatherhood Issues: Sessions Two Through Five

Raymond said at the outset that he thought that a lot of his problems had to do with his father. His father was eleven years older than his mother, was thirty-eight when Raymond was born, and had died thirteen years before Raymond came to therapy. Raymond believed that his father had a great and adventurous life as an air force officer during World War II—a life that he had had to leave behind when he married and started a family and one that he seemed to miss greatly throughout Raymond's childhood. Because of the age difference and his father's detachment, Raymond never felt that he knew his father. And yet he admired him greatly and yearned to know him. For example, Raymond's lifelong hobby was participating in Scottish rites and learning about his Scottish ancestry, an activity in which he had earlier hoped he could involve his father. The first time I saw Raymond display emotions openly was in an unguarded moment when he spoke of how he had always wanted to see his dad in a kilt, carrying a set of pipes.

Raymond's father was a hard-driving publisher of a local newspaper who, even when he was home for an evening or weekend instead of traveling or working late, was usually closeted in his den with paperwork or tied up in meetings with community leaders who were always paying late-evening calls. He had had a heart attack three years before he died and had to drastically curtail his activities. At that time Raymond was in the service, stationed in the northwestern part of the United States and did not have time for a visit home. In fact he did not visit at all during the last three years of his father's life.

During the fifth session Raymond's tone had shifted from detachment to curiosity. As we explored it, he found he had many questions about his father. Using this curiosity, we constructed a therapeutic ritual during the fifth session, in which Raymond would spend thirty minutes in the evening, two evenings a week, writing down the questions that he had for his father on three- by five-inch note cards. Using his newly developed emotional self-awareness, he also described the emotions that accompanied the questions and represented them with colors, using felt-tipped pens with different colors to represent different emotions and indicating the intensity of the emotion by the amount of color. I also asked him to try to locate some family photos from when he was a child.

Sadness Emerges: Session Six

Raymond came in with a thick sheaf of photos and an equally thick folder of questions. The questions he came up with were as follows: Did his father not feel anything toward him and was that why he was so distant? Is there a "family curse" of nonfeeling fathers? Was the family (Raymond, mother, and younger identical twin sisters) a burden on his father? And did his father resent the family for this burden? Was that why he was so detached? Raymond said that he could have written more, except that he ran out of cards. But that didn't matter, he realized, because if he took all of his questions and rolled them into one, what he came up with was that he did not "know a damn thing about [his] father."

The photos provided an epiphany of sorts. He could find no pictures of him and his dad together. At first he thought his mother had kept them, but he called her to ask if she could send him a couple and she did not have any either. He shook his head and laughed a hard-edged laugh: "It fits, see?"

"What does?"

"The photos, the questions." His face was flushed now. "Of course I don't know anything about my dad. He was never there! He was always too busy with more important things, except spending time with his own son. And later, after his heart attack, when he did have time it was like, 'Fuck you, I can be busy too.' And then—" his voice cracked. He gazed out the window, tears welling in his eyes, lifted a hand to his face, and began to cry. He did not cry long, but long enough to feel a sense of relief (as well as some of the predictable embarrassment).

Visit to His Aunt: Session Seven

Raymond had an opportunity between the sixth and seventh sessions (three weeks apart) to get some of his questions answered. He had a business trip that took him to the city where his aunt lived.

After settling in for our first session after his return, Raymond reached inside his jacket pocket, pulled out what looked like an old snapshot, placed it gently on the table in front of him, and stared at it for a moment before starting to speak. He had seen his Aunt Millie and had dinner at her house.

They had been sitting around the table enjoying an after-dinner coffee when Raymond casually mentioned that he had been thinking about his dad lately, realizing he had never really known him all that well.

His aunt's eyes lit up. Then she got up, left the room, and came back with photo albums and boxes of old letters. He wanted to know about his dad, her beloved older brother? "It was almost like she'd been waiting for me to ask." They spent the rest of the night sifting through his aunt's trove of memorabilia and talking. "She talked. I listened." He shook his head. "All this stuff—all this stuff I never knew."

Raymond had known his father's own father had died when Raymond's father was six years old and he and his aunt had been raised by a stepfather. Raymond had not known the stepfather had been a drinker who beat his wife and stepchildren until, at age twelve, his father had put a stop to the beatings by shoving the man against a wall and threatening to kill him if he laid a hand on them again. Raymond had known that this stepfather had died when his dad was fifteen. He had not known that his dad had quit school then to get a job to help support the family and that he had finished high school and put himself through college by working days and taking classes at night. He had known that his dad had always managed money wisely. He had not known that, when his parents married, his dad had put the money his in-laws had given him toward a down payment on a house into college savings bonds for his future children instead. He had known his dad as an aloof, unavailable, taciturn man who never showed emotion. He had not known that his dad actually had shed tears once—the first time he held his newborn son in his arms.

And the snapshot? A present from Raymond's aunt—of his father at age two. He picked it up and held it cupped in one hand. "I'd never seen a picture of him as a baby before." Smiling, he passed it to me. "It's uncanny, really. Even my wife says so. If I didn't know better, I'd think it was me."

Visit to the Grave: Session Eight

The denouement to the therapy occurred when Raymond visited his mother and his father's grave. He described the experience as "raw emotion." His grief poured out of him as he stood alone at his father's headstone, reading though his color-coded cards filled with unanswered questions.

Fear Emerges and Turns to Excitement: Sessions Nine and Ten

Having broken through the walls that protected him from his grief, Raymond began to experience some strong feelings about his expectant fatherhood, specifically fear, worry, and anxiety. He began to worry about whether the baby was going to be all right, given his wife's age (also forty-one). He also investigated some obscure genetic diseases that run in families of Scottish descent. I encouraged him to address his worries directly by attending one of his wife's visits to her obstetrician. He did so and was reassured about the baby's health and also heard the baby's heartbeat. His fear then turned to joy and excitement. We terminated therapy after the tenth visit, one month before the baby was due. I got a postcard two months later:

> Ron, the baby was 2 weeks late. But he's a big guy, 8 lbs. 13 oz. And he definitely looks Scottish!
>
> *Raymond*

In this chapter I considered the problem of normative male alexithymia. After a brief introduction to the gender role strain paradigm, I examined in depth the male emotion socialization process and revealed how, guided by traditional masculinity ideology, mothers, fathers, and peer groups conspire to channel and suppress natural male emotional expressivity to such an extent that males come to be normatively alexithymic. I further pointed out the traumatic nature of that process, not only in its resultant deformation of men's ability to experience and express the full range of their emotions but also in the process in which fathers and peer groups in particular dole out shame-based forms of punishment for violations of the male code. I presented a method to assess the degree to which male patients have normative male alexithymia, along with a five-step psychoeducational program that is useful at the beginning stages of treatment.

I also presented the case of Raymond—an expectant father whose chief complaint was that he felt nothing about his future baby. Raymond was assessed to be normatively alexithymic and treated with the psychoeducational program. As is typical with many of the men I treat, an action-oriented approach to therapy, in which the patient is asked to do something to get better, was well received, and Raymond willingly did the assigned homework. As a result of psychoeducational treatment, long-buried issues about his own father started to surface by the fifth session. Using his emerging curiosity, a therapeutic ritual was constructed in which Raymond was asked to identify the questions he had about his father. In addition he was asked both to identify his emotional responses to the questions verbally and to color code them, using felt-tipped pens. I used this latter suggestion, which draws on right-brain processes, to bypass any defensive equivocation that might have come into play. Finally, I used family photo reconnaissance to stimulate memories and perhaps additional questions. The combined effect of these interventions was to bring the patient face-to-face with his bitterness about his father's psychological absence, which initiated a long-delayed grieving process.

Fortuitously, Raymond had an opportunity to visit his aunt (his father's younger sister) at a time when he was receptive to learning more about his father and was treated to a wealth of information about the man his father was. This experience helped him begin to see his father as a whole man, far from perfect but doing the best he could with what he had—and doing quite well at that. But it was not until he visited his father's grave that Raymond was able to fully grieve the father he never knew, until now.

After doing a brief but significant piece of grief work, Raymond found that his feelings about becoming a father had come unblocked. The first set of feelings he had were on the anxious end of the spectrum. A visit to his wife's doctor addressed his worries and allowed him to hear his baby's heartbeat. At that point his anxiety turned to excitement, and the therapy ended.

Is this therapy useful for all types of male patients? I certainly do not have enough experience to answer that question, but I can say that it seems to work best with male patients with normative alexithymia who are motivated to comply with treatment—that is, are willing and motivated to follow a directive, homework-based form of therapy. It seems to be less useful to patients who tend to defy treatment, for whom resistance is a much larger matter.

References

Allen, J. G., & Haccoun, D. M. (1976). Sex differences in emotionality: A multidimensional approach. *Human Relations, 29*(8), 711–720.

Bagby, R. M., Taylor, G. J., & Parker, J.D.A. (1994). The Twenty-Item Toronto Alexithymia Scale, II: Convergent, discriminant, and concurrent validity. *Journal of Psychosomatic Research, 38,* 33–40.

Balswick, J., & Avertt, C. P. (1977). Differences in expressiveness: Gender, interpersonal orientation, and perceived parental expressiveness as contributing factors. *Journal of Marriage and the Family, 39,* 121–127.

Betcher, W., & Pollack, W. S. (1993). *In a time of fallen heroes: The recreation of masculinity.* New York: Atheneum.

Brody, L. (1996). Gender, emotional expression, and parent-child boundaries. In R. Kavanaugh, B. Zimmerberg-Glick, & S. Fein (Eds.), *Emotion: Interdisciplinary perspectives* (pp. 139–170). Hillsdale, NJ: Erlbaum.

Brody, L., & Hall, J. (1993). Gender and emotion. In M. Lewis & J. M. Haviland (Eds.), *Handbook of emotions* (pp. 435–460). New York: Guilford Press.

Brooks, G. R. (1990). Post-Vietnam gender role strain: A needed concept? *Professional Psychology: Research and Practice, 21*(1), 18–25.

Brooks, G. R. (1995). *The centerfold syndrome.* San Francisco: Jossey-Bass.

Buck, R. (1977). Non-verbal communication of affect in preschool children: Relationships with personality and skin conductance. *Journal of Personality and Social Psychology, 35*(4), 225–236.

Buck, R. (1984). *The communication of emotion.* New York: Guilford Press.

Campbell, A. (1993). *Men, women, and aggression.* New York: Basic Books.

David, D., & Brannon, R. (Eds.). (1976). *The forty-nine percent majority: The male sex role.* Reading, MA: Addison-Wesley.

Dunn, J., Bretherton, I., & Munn, P. (1987). Conversations about feeling states between mothers and their children. *Developmental Psychology, 23,* 132–139.

Eagly, A. H., & Steffen, V. J. (1986). Gender and aggressive behavior: A meta-analytic review of the social psychological literature. *Psychological Bulletin, 100*(3), 309–330

Eisenberg, N., & Lennon, R. (1983). Sex differences in empathy and related capacities. *Psychological Bulletin, 94*(1), 100–131.

Fivush, R. (1989). Exploring sex differences in the emotional content of mother child conversations about the past. *Sex Roles, 20,* 675–691.

Frodi, A., Macaulay, J., & Thome, P. R. (1977). Are women always less aggressive than men? A review of the experimental literature. *Psychological Bulletin, 84*(4), 634–660.

Fuchs, D., & Thelen, M. (1988). Children's expected interpersonal consequences of communicating their affective state and reported likelihood of expression. *Child Development, 59,* 1314–1322.

Gilmore, D. (1990). *Manhood in the making: Cultural concepts of masculinity.* New Haven, CT: Yale University Press.

Gottman, J., & Levenson, R. (1988). The social psychophysiology of marriage. In P. Noller & M. A. Fitzpatrick (Eds.), *Perspectives on marital interaction* (pp. 182–200). Clevedon, U.K.: Multilingual Matters.

Greif, E. B., Alvarez, M., & Ulman, K. (1981, April). *Recognizing emotions in other people: Sex differences in socialization.* Paper presented at the meeting of the Society for Research in Child Development, Boston.

Grunebaum, H. (1996, May). Discussant in symposium, *Treating the reluctant male,* presented at the annual meeting of the American Orthopsychiatric Association, Boston.

Hall, J. A. (1978). Gender effects in decoding nonverbal cues. *Psychological Bulletin, 85*(40), 845–857.

Harrison, J. (1995). Roles, identities, and sexual orientation: Homosexuality, heterosexuality, and bisexuality. In R. F. Levant & W. S. Pollack (Eds.), *A new psychology of men* (pp. 359–382). New York: Basic Books.

Haviland, J. J., & Malatesta, C. Z. (1981). The development of sex differences in nonverbal signals: Fallacies, facts, and fantasies. In C. Mayo & N. M. Henly (Eds.), *Gender and non-verbal behavior* (pp. 183–208). New York: Springer-Verlag.

Hudson, L., & Jacot, B. (1991). *The way men think: Intellect, intimacy, and the erotic imagination.* New Haven, CT: Yale University Press.

Keltikangas-Jarvinen, L. (1982). Alexithymia in violent offenders. *Journal of Personality Assessment, 46,* 462–467.

Krugman, S. (1995). Male development and the transformation of shame. In R. F. Levant & W. S. Pollack (Eds.), *A new psychology of men* (pp. 91–126). New York: Basic Books.

Krystal, H. (1979). Alexithymia and psychotherapy. *American Journal of Psychotherapy, 33,* 17–30.

Krystal, H. (1982). Alexithymia and the effectiveness of psychoanalytic treatment. *International Journal of Psychoanalytic Psychotherapy, 9,* 353–378.

Lamb, M. E. (1977). The development of parental preferences in the first two years of life. *Sex Roles, 3,* 475–497.

Lamb, M. E., Owen, M. J., & Chase-Lansdale, L. (1979). The father daughter relationship: Past, present, and future. In C. B. Knopp & M. Kirkpatrick (Eds.), *Becoming female* (pp. 89–112). New York: Plenum.

Langlois, J. H., & Downs, A. C. (1980). Mother, fathers, and peers as socialization agents of sex-typed play behaviors in young children. *Child Development, 51,* 1217–1247.

Larsen, R. J., & Diener, E. (1987). Affect intensity as an individual difference characteristic: A review. *Journal of Research in Personality, 21,* 1–39.

Lazur, R. F., & Majors, R. (1995). Men of color: Ethnocultural variations of male gender role strain. In R. F. Levant & W. S. Pollack (Eds.), *A new psychology of men* (pp. 337–358). New York: Basic Books.

Levant, R. F. (1996). The new psychology of men. *Professional Psychology: Research and Practice, 27,* 259–265.

Levant, R. F., Hirsch, L., Celentano, E., Cozza, T., Hill, S., MacEachern, M., Marty, N., & Schnedeker, J. (1992). The male role: An investigation of norms and stereotypes. *Journal of Mental Health Counseling, 14*(3), 325–337.

Levant, R. F., & Kelly, J. (1989). *Between father and child.* New York: Viking.

Levant, R. F., & Kopecky, G. (1995). *Masculinity reconstructed.* New York: Dutton.

Lever, J. (1976). Sex differences in the games children play. *Social Work, 23*(4), 78–87.

Lisak, D. (1995, August). *Integrating gender analysis in psychotherapy with male survivors of abuse.* Paper presented at the annual meeting of the American Psychological Association, New York.

Long, D. (1987). Working with men who batter. In M. Scher, M. Stevens, G. Good, & G. A. Eichenfield (Eds.), *Handbook of counseling and psychotherapy with men* (pp. 305–320). Newbury Park, CA: Sage.

Maccoby, E. E. (1990). Gender and relationships: A developmental account. *American Psychologist, 45,* 513–520.

Malatesta, C. Z., Culver, C., Tesman, J., & Shephard, B. (1989). The development of emotion expression during the first two years of life. *Monographs of the Society for Research in Child Development, 50*(1–2, Serial No. 219).

Messner, M. A. (1992). *Power at play: Sports and the problem of masculinity.* Boston: Beacon Press.

Paley, V. G. (1984). *Boys and girls: Superheroes in the doll corner.* Chicago: University of Chicago Press.

Pleck, J. H. (1981). *The myth of masculinity.* Cambridge, MA: MIT Press.

Pleck, J. H. (1995). The gender role strain paradigm: An update. In R. F. Levant & W. S. Pollack (Eds.), *A new psychology of men* (pp. 11–32). New York: Basic Books.

Pollack, W. S. (1995). No man is an island: Toward a new psychoanalytic psychology of men. In R. F. Levant & W. S. Pollack (Eds.), *A new psychology of men* (pp. 33–67). New York: Basic Books.

Pollack, W. S. (1998a). Mourning, melancholia, and masculinity: Recognizing and treating depression in men. In W. S. Pollack & R. F. Levant (Eds.), *New psychotherapy for men: Case studies* (pp. 147–166). New York: Wiley.

Pollack, W. S. (1998b). The trauma of Oedipus: Toward a new psychoanalytic psychotherapy for men. In W. S. Pollack & R. F. Levant (Eds.), *New psychotherapy for men: Case studies* (pp. 13–34). New York: Wiley.

Rotundo, E. A. (1990). *American manhood: Transformations in masculinity from the Revolution to the modern era.* New York: Basic Books.

Schell, A., & Gleason, J. B. (1989, December). *Gender differences in the acquisition of the vocabulary of emotion.* Paper presented at the annual meeting of the American Association of Applied Linguistics, Washington, DC.

Selman, R. L. (1980). *The growth of interpersonal understanding: Developmental and clinical analyses.* New York: Academic Press.

Siegal, M. (1987). Are sons and daughters treated more differently by fathers than by mothers? *Developmental Review, 7,* 183–209.

Sifneos, P. E. (1967). Clinical observations on some patients suffering from a variety of psychosomatic diseases. In *Proceedings of the Seventh European Conference on Psychosomatic Research.* Basel, Switzerland: Kargel.

Sifneos, P. E. (1988). Alexithymia and its relationship to hemispheric specialization, affect, and creativity. *Psychiatric Clinics of North America, 11,* 287–292.

Stapley, J. C., & Haviland, J. M. (1989). Beyond depression: Gender differences in normal adolescents' emotional experiences. *Sex Roles, 20*(5–6), 295–308.

Taylor, G. J. (1994). The alexithymia construct: Conceptualization, validation, and relationship with basic dimensions of personality. *New Trends in Experimental and Clinical Psychiatry, 10,* 61–74.

Thompson, E. H., & Pleck, J. H. (1995). Masculinity ideology: A review of research instrumentation on men and masculinities. In R. F. Levant & W. S. Pollack (Eds.), *A new psychology of men* (pp. 129–163). New York: Basic Books.

Weinberg, M. K. (1992). Sex differences in 6-month-old infants' affect and behavior: Impact on maternal caregiving. Unpublished doctoral dissertation, University of Massachusetts, Amherst, MA.

Zilbergeld, B. (1992). *The new male sexuality.* New York: Bantam Books.

CHAPTER TWENTY-TWO

Psychotherapy with Men Navigating Midlife Terrain

Sam V. Cochran

For many years social and behavioral scientists considered middle age the "latency" period of adulthood, paralleling the latency of childhood in which little active development was thought to be occurring. Psychoanalytic theorists viewed childhood as formative, and the years after puberty received scant attention from most scientific and psychological writers in the first half of the twentieth century. Two notable exceptions were Carl Jung and Erik Erikson. Unlike Freud, who believed that psychological structures and functions were fixed by childhood experiences, Jung believed that psychological changes occurred throughout life and that important transformations occurred in particular at midlife (see Jung, 1969). Erikson (1956) outlined the tasks of ego and identity development from childhood through adulthood. His model of development contributed important understandings to issues that are activated in midlife and beyond.

Psychological inquiry focused on sex differences related to midlife has occurred more recently. Since 1980, several groundbreaking investigations that charted the developmental and psychological challenges that men experience in adulthood have been reported (see Farrell & Rosenberg, 1981; Levinson, Darrow, Klein, Levinson, & McKee, 1978; Vaillant, 1977). Several issues that characterize men's experiences at midlife have emerged from these studies. Men navigating midlife terrain struggle with issues of commitment to family and work, personal and psychological integrity, real and symbolic loss, and mortality.

In this chapter I review current psychological perspectives on midlife or middle age in men and integrate these perspectives with a new psychology of men. Attention is paid to several important empirical investigations of men that have tended to shape our psychological understanding of the challenges men face at midlife. In addition to these empirical reports, a number of clinical reports have further documented the various issues that men navigating midlife terrain encounter. A perspective that integrates these empirical and clinical viewpoints yields an empathic and depth-oriented understanding of men and provides groundwork for suggestions for psychotherapy with men as they navigate this midlife terrain.

DEFINING MIDLIFE IN MEN'S LIVES

Definitions of midlife or middle age tend to be inconsistent and highly variable. This variability most likely reflects the difficulty scholars, scientists, and clinicians have had in clearly outlining the parameters of middle age for both men and women. Several perspectives can be used to define the boundaries of midlife or middle age. Biological perspectives rely on actuarial estimates of expected life span as well as predictable timetables for natural biological processes associated with aging to play out over the life span. Role transition perspectives emphasize expected changes in typical social and occupational roles as individuals grow older and progress through roles of worker, parent, and family and community member. Life stage perspectives seek to chart the various developmental stages from childhood through young adulthood, middle adulthood, and old adulthood and to describe the developmental challenges encountered as an individual passes through each stage.

Biological Perspectives

The average life expectancy for a man born in 1950 is 65.6 years. For a man born in 1960 the life expectancy increases one year to 66.6 years. Medical advances and changes in personal life style have extended the life expectancy for many men since that time. In 1996, a white man who was forty years old could expect to live for seventy-six years, whereas a forty-year-old African American man could expect to live for sixty-seven years. Based on these average life expectancies, middle age for most American men would be somewhere between thirty-three and thirty-eight years of age (National Center for Health Statistics, 1998).

Physiological change occurs rapidly at birth, in adolescence, and in old age. Although physiological changes continue in middle age, for most people this time is characterized by relative stability, in contrast to the rapid changes of other periods of life. Perhaps the most significant naturally occurring physiological process of middle age is menopause in women. Some investigators have suggested that men may experience a similar sex hormone–based process. Age-associated testosterone decline in men has been noted as a contributing factor to many problems in men that appear to be associated with advancing age (Sternbach, 1998). Manifestations of this normal decline in male hormone levels may include depression, anxiety, irritability, insomnia, weaknesses, decreased libido, impotence, poor memory, reduced muscle and bone mass, and reduced sexual body hair. Such changes would be expected to garner a reaction in most men as they enter middle age, especially if they have based aspects of their identity on traditional definitions of masculinity that emphasize physical and sexual prowess, strength, and vigor.

Social Role Perspectives

Analysis of social roles has also proved to be a useful approach to studying midlife. Moen and Wethington (1999) emphasize how men's and women's roles shift as the requirements of certain social roles change and evolve over time. For men, for example, the requirements of the social role of provider may shift as economic requirements of supporting a family evolve. In addition, men at midlife may experience family roles in a much different manner than women at midlife.

Huyck (1999) summarizes the differential impact of gender roles on the experience of middle age in women and men. Family relationships, work relationships, and community relationships are the most important domains in which men's and women's roles are defined throughout adulthood. In comparison to women, men's midlife role transitions have been found to be more closely connected to shifts in work, career, and men's perceived role as the family provider (see Levinson et al., 1978). In addition to these shifts, other investigators have found an increased sense of commitment to family relationships (see Farrell & Rosenberg, 1981) and work and community relationships (see Weiss, 1990) and an increased valuing of the parental role in men (see Guttman, 1987).

Life Stage Perspectives

Another perspective that has proved useful in studying changes over the life cycle is a perspective that views these changes as occurring at distinct stages. Erikson (1956) was one of the first developmental theorists to define the tasks of adult (male) development, including negotiating intimacy in young adulthood and, later, generativity and integrity. Neugarten (1968) detailed personality changes that paralleled chronological age in adults and located distinct shifts in perspective in the fifth decade of life that resulted in greater reflection and introspection.

Results of Levinson and colleagues' (1978) investigation confirmed that men passed through definable stages, or "eras," of life. Levinson and his colleagues were able to identify distinct transitions from young adulthood, during which the early aspects of a life structure (occupation and family) are put in place, into middle adulthood, during which the elements of this life structure are reviewed and revised. In addition to this finding with American men, Guttman (1976) confirmed the existence of a midlife transition period or "crisis" in five different cultural groups that included men from urban American, American Indian, Middle Eastern Druze, and lowland and highland Mayan samples.

Although these and other studies have yielded important findings that have helped to define the midlife terrain for men, developmental stage approaches have also been controversial. Feminist researchers have challenged developmental stage models for their reliance on exclusively male samples from which conclusions are drawn (see Gilligan, 1982). Nonetheless, in terms of studying a specific segment of the population, these findings provide convenient markers or signposts that designate the challenges and tasks many men encounter at various points across the life cycle.

Are there unique, masculine-specific challenges that arise in midlife? I examine two perspectives that have illuminated many important midlife issues for men. Empirical studies that have used longitudinal and cross-sectional methodologies have defined the issues men encounter in midlife (see Ciernia, 1985; Cournoyer & Mahalik, 1995; Farrell & Rosenberg, 1981; Levinson et al., 1978; Vaillant, 1977). In addition to these empirical findings, clinical case reports have also contributed to an understanding of the midlife challenges that at times become so severe as to overwhelm coping resources and bring men to therapy (see Braverman & Paris, 1993; Cochran & Rabinowitz, 1996; Kernberg, 1985; Rabinowitz, 1998). In general, these findings converge to point to the importance of four separate but interrelated issues as important for men at midlife: work, health, family relationships, and death awareness.

MEN AT MIDLIFE: EMPIRICAL FINDINGS

In this section I explore the empirical findings about men at midlife. In particular, I describe research investigating the seasons of a man's life, men's adaptation to life, men and midlife, and staying the course.

The Seasons of a Man's Life

Levinson et al. (1978) studied forty men from diverse backgrounds representing four different occupational groups: hourly workers, executives, academic scientists, and novelists. These men were between the ages of thirty-five and forty-five and were studied using a qualitative-quantitative methodology. Levinson and his colleagues' specific purpose in this investigation was to examine the middle years and to explore what was considered to be an important life transition that the investigators hypothesized occurred in men around age forty. Results of this study identified a distinct process of transition from that segment of the life span that was characterized as the early adult era into the middle adult era. They called this entry into middle age the "midlife transition" to imply that it is a transition between early adulthood and the settling-down phase that characterized middle age.

The tasks of middle age include revising "the dream" and resolving the four polarities of life. Revision of the dream entails measuring actual occupational achievement against childhood dreams and fantasies that provided a sense of identity and purpose for a young boy. Often, midlife conflict can occur in relation to discrepancies between the persistent force of the dream of boyhood and the reality of occupational accomplishment in adulthood. For some men, too great a discrepancy may result in despair and frustration at midlife and beyond. These sentiments may give rise to a "midlife crisis" in some men.

Resolution of the four polarities of life involves reconciliation of conflicts related to age (old versus young), purpose or direction (destructiveness versus creativity), identity (masculinity versus femininity), and intimacy (attachment versus separateness). Interestingly, a number of men in the four cross-sectional samples experienced a period of tumult or struggle around the midlife transition. This period of tumult was revealed in questions concerning the life plan or life accomplishments and feelings of anger and recriminations against the self and significant others. Faced with the challenges of resolving life polarities, the men in this study found that they must either choose a new path or modify the old one. For some men, this challenge was met with relatively little upheaval; for others, it amounted to a midlife crisis that resulted in considerable disruption in family and work relationships.

Adaptation to Life

Vaillant (1977) reported the results of a longitudinal study of 268 men who were chosen as exemplars of health and promise as college students. These men, like those in the Levinson et al. (1978) report, were studied using a quantitative-qualitative methodology over a span of thirty years. The purpose of the study was to explore how individuals adapt to the challenges that life presents over a period of time. One of the main findings of this study was that maturity of psychological defenses was the strongest predictor of an individual's capacity to manage life challenges. The use of immature defenses (such as projection, acting out, and denial) tended to ensure marginal adjustment over the life span regardless of age. Use of mature defense mechanisms (such as sublimation, altruism, and humor) tended to be associated with better adjustment over the life span. In regard to men's use of immature defense mechanisms, Mahalik, Cournoyer, Cherry, and Napolitano (1998) identified the associations between immature coping mechanisms and masculine-specific gender role strain. They found that men who experienced greater strain related to issues of power and competition, expression of emotions, and expression of affection to other men tended to also use immature psychological defense mechanisms. The persistent use of such defense mechanisms would be expected to increase the likelihood of unsuccessful coping with various developmental crises over the life span.

Men at Midlife

Farrell and Rosenberg (1981) studied a total of 433 men in two age groups, a younger group of men between twenty-five and thirty years of age and an older group of men between thirty-eight and forty-eight years of age. The purpose of their investigation was to examine men's responses to midlife challenges and to verify differences in responses that might be related to the age differences of the two groups. For both age groups Farrell and Rosenberg identified four general types of response styles: the antihero or dissenter, the transcendent-generative, the pseudodeveloped man, and the punitive-disenchanted-authoritarian type. In Farrell and Rosenberg's study, the men of both age groups evidenced dramatic variation in how they responded to middle age stresses. In general, this investigation found that men tended to avoid the stresses and pressures of middle age.

Staying the Course

As the subtitle of the book indicates, Weiss (1990) and his colleagues studied the emotional and social lives of eighty men who were considered to be successful at work. Although the study was not designed to investigate midlife, the subjects in this study were between thirty-five and fifty-five years—ages generally considered to encompass the midlife years. This study used a cross-sectional or contemporaneous design, permitting in-depth analysis of the men's lives at a given point in time.

Not surprisingly, one of the main findings of this particular study is that work plays a significant role as the foundation of successful men's lives. For the men in this sample, a successful career established a place within the community and was the basis of respect, self-worth, and identity. Success in the community enabled these men to function happily and effectively at home as spouses and parents.

Paradoxically, for most of the men in this study family relationships and commitments were always viewed as more important than work. There was a synergistic effect between these two domains: success and pride derived from each tended to facilitate success in the other. Success at work enabled the men to feel positive about themselves as providers, parents, and spouses. Success at home as providers, spouses, and fathers tended to provide additional value and meaning to the sacrifice and effort endured at work.

Consistent with the findings of these studies, Cournoyer and Mahalik (1995) found that compared with college-aged men, middle-aged men experienced less masculine-specific gender role conflict in issues of power, success, and competition but experienced greater conflict in issues related to balancing work and family. This finding confirms that for middle-aged men, issues of commitment to family and work are highly salient and can be a significant source of stress. In contrast to this finding, Stillson, O'Neil, and Owen (1991) failed to discover differences in levels of gender role conflict among three different age groups of men. However, it is possible that their sample did not contain a wide enough age spread for the hypothesized conflicts to emerge because they used men between the ages of twenty-two and thirty-nine compared with a range of thirty-six to forty-five years of age in Cournoyer and Mahalik's sample.

MEN AT MIDLIFE: CLINICAL FINDINGS

Clinical work with men at midlife has uncovered the meaning men attribute to the life changes they may be experiencing that have brought them to seek the assistance of a psychotherapist. Cochran and Rabinowitz (1996) underscore the importance of attending to issues of loss in the lives of men at all points in the life span. Men often experience the realities of middle age as losses—losses of physical strength, deaths of family members and friends, loss of children as they leave home, and loss of relationship for those men who experience separation and divorce. Cultural prohibitions against the experience of sadness, loss, and grief in men make the open acknowledgement of these experiences difficult. Braverman and Paris (1993) view midlife challenges as a reflection of a narcissistic vulnerability in some men that is secondary to childhood neglect. Their perspective views the midlife crisis in men as a reactivation of an unresolved depressive response that occurred because of inadequate childhood emotional supplies. Both Cochran and Rabinowitz (1996) and Braverman and Paris (1993) suggest an open engagement with the emotional content of this depressive response to loss that middle age is prone to activate in many men.

Another consistent theme in these and other reports based on clinical work with men at midlife is the increasing awareness of mortality that results in a confrontation with death anxiety. Yalom (1980), Jacques (1965), Cochran and Rabinowitz (1996), Erikson (1956), Kernberg (1985), and Braverman and Paris (1993) all emphasize the importance of facing this reactivation of the "depressive position" associated with increased awareness of personal mortality. With the prospect of a finite life span, deaths of parents and children, and the limitations of creativity, men at midlife are presented with both a challenge and an opportunity as they come to terms with the meaning of death in their lives.

A major challenge for men at midlife is to embrace this death awareness and anxiety and the ensuing depression fully, to experience the grief and loss that attends this awareness, and to bear the painful affect states that are activated in this process. Men who are willing to persevere with their own emotional work on this issue have an opportunity to reconcile the ultimate polarities of life. These men may genuinely achieve a sense of resolution and serenity in the face of the prospect of death and may finally be ready to fully recommit to the remaining years of life with a renewed sense of perspective, appreciation, and wisdom.

Both empirical inquiry and clinical inquiry have contributed to an increased understanding of the issues and emotional challenges that men face at midlife. As they navigate midlife terrain men experience shifts in roles, reevaluations of commitments, and the challenge of facing inevitable losses and working through death awareness. For many men midlife challenges reawaken earlier conflict-laden aspects of development. However, with the added perspective of maturity and life experience, many men are also able to positively navigate this terrain and enter older adulthood with an enhanced sense of perspective on their lives.

CLINICAL PRESENTATION OF MIDLIFE ISSUES

From the empirical and clinical reports it is clear that men vary widely in their experiences of midlife. Clinical presentation may yield direct evidence of midlife issues. However, it is more likely that a man in midlife will present with a number of various and seemingly unrelated issues from which the psychotherapist, through careful listening, may discover the theme of midlife challenge. The following case presentation illustrates the manner in which midlife issues may be activated and presented in a man seeking psychotherapy.

Bill consulted a therapist for help "coping with stress." Bill was a successful forty-two-year-old education professional. He was married and had two children, a daughter age twelve and a son age nine. His spouse worked as a nurse in the local hospital. Bill and his spouse had moved several states away from their hometown area for Bill's career at the time of their oldest child's birth. Since then, Bill had advanced in his career and was now a popular and successful superintendent of the local school district.

At the time Bill scheduled his appointment he had been having a number of physical problems that concerned him. He was finding he experienced a noticeable shortness of breath as he played his usual pickup basketball game over the lunch hour with his friends. He had various pains in his chest and had been having an increasing number of headaches throughout the day at work. He had consulted his family physician, who found no physical problems. His physician suggested that stress might be at the bottom of Bill's physical problems and recommended a consultation appointment with a therapist.

As Bill and his therapist explored the various aspects of Bill's life that were stressful, Bill disclosed that his mother had died about ten months ago. He told his therapist that his mother's death was unexpected and was quite a shock for him. She was sixty-five years old and had died quite suddenly from a cerebral hemorrhage. Bill remembered the phone call when his father told him of his mother's death. "I knew something was wrong, and when he said Mom had passed away I felt this awful, sinking feeling in my stomach. I just knew then that my life would never be the same. It was terrible."

Sensing the obvious emotional intensity of this event, Bill's therapist invited Bill to talk more about his mother. "She was always there for me, was one of my biggest supporters. She gave me totally unconditional love. I feel like a part of me is gone now."

"I'm so sorry," Bill's therapist responded. "This sounds like a profound loss. How have you coped with it since then?"

"I've been pretty busy, I guess. The service and the wake were very emotional, but I felt like I really was able to let go and get all my emotions out." Bill paused. "I don't know. Do you think that has something to do with how I'm doing now?"

As Bill and his therapist explored his reactions to his mother's death and how he had coped with it several themes emerged. Bill's general emotional state had been mainly sad, and he attributed it to his mother's death. But as he and his therapist talked, his sadness extended to a number of other areas of his life, too. He had feelings of sadness and loss over his decline in physical strength and well-being over the past few years. "I'm just not my old self," Bill lamented to his therapist as he discussed the limitations he perceived in his physical endurance and strength.

He felt sad as he worked to reestablish a closer relationship with his father, who now relied on him more and more for emotional support. Bill found himself thinking about his father's death as their visits increased in frequency. He felt sad at times when he found himself contemplating his own death and how he would miss his spouse and his children.

In addition to Bill's sad mood, he reported feeling bored and at times frustrated with his work. He felt he was "solving the same old problems over and over" yet could not just quit and move somewhere else for the sake of a new challenge. "I have devoted a lot of my life to this community. My kids are well established. We know a lot of people. It wouldn't be fair to them. And I know, too, the grass is rarely greener."

Over a period of six months of weekly therapy sessions, Bill and his therapist explored what began as grief work over his mother's death but quickly branched out to encompass a number of areas of his life. Bill noticed how several of the issues he discussed were related to an increasing awareness of his own mortality. The impact of his mother's death was the most obvious of these issues. But his reflections on his father's advancing age and increasing reliance on Bill as a caregiver and support system brought Bill in touch with questions about how his father would probably need more attention and support as he got older. And then, finally, Bill's increasing awareness of his own aging process, played out on the basketball court at lunchtime with his buddies, brought him face-to-face with his own mortality. As Bill and his therapist explored the interrelations of all these issues, Bill gradually developed an increased sense of acceptance of his mother's death, the aging of his father, and ultimately his own aging process.

At forty-two years of age, Bill was beyond the statistical definition of midlife. If Bill were to live out his expected life span he would in fact be past middle age by at least five years. Bill's initial visit to his therapist was based on a referral from his physician. Physical concerns and symptoms had initially set the wheels in motion for Bill to seek help. It is not uncommon for middle-aged men to notice the effects of advancing age, as was apparent in Bill's concerns over shortness of breath and decreased physical endurance.

Bill's stress and his attention to his declining physical health signified for him a transition to a different stage in his life. At several points in his sessions with his therapist he engaged in comparisons that highlighted that he believed his physical strength and conditioning had changed from when he was a younger man. His workouts with his buddies on the basketball court served as daily reminders of the vulnerability of his body to the aging process. These changes also heightened his awareness of his own mortality and the evolution of his own place in the life cycle.

In Bill's situation, the death of his mother dramatically altered his role as his mother's son. The role of dutiful, responsible son who worked hard for his mother's love and approval was now challenged because his mother was dead. The comforts and support he had internalized were still in him, but the real person who had provided those vital supplies was no longer living. This shift for Bill catapulted him into examining the nature of his role not only as his mother's son but also as his father's son and as a father himself. As noted, he experienced a sense of sadness and loss as he examined these shifts in the roles he had played for such a long time. Bill's therapist expressed interest and empathy for this emotional aspect of Bill's situation and focused on Bill's feelings of grief and loss.

IS MIDLIFE A CRISIS?

The term *midlife crisis* has been applied to both men and women. But for men there exists an unfortunate stereotype popularized through media portrayals. This particular narrative involves a middle-aged man who suddenly and inexplicably plunges into a despairing crisis, leaves his spouse and children, quits his job, buys a sporty red convertible, and races off into the sunset accompanied by a voluptuous younger woman. Of course, such depictions are nothing more than negative stereotypes of men behaving badly when faced with this so-called midlife crisis. In general, research has failed to confirm the existence of such a crisis for men.

Although they worked with a highly select sample, Vaillant (1977) and his colleagues did not find compelling evidence for a midlife crisis in the men they studied. Vaillant speculated that the middle years are not without challenge but reports that the notion of a midlife crisis is simply a creation of the popular press and was rarely observed in the men in his sample. Similarly, after reviewing several longitudinal and cross-sectional studies Nydegger (1976) found little evidence for a midlife crisis in middle-aged men. Her conclusion was that the years between age forty and age fifty are characterized more by stability than by upheaval. Farrell and Rosenberg (1981) also did not find any evidence of a crisis response in the men they studied. Instead, they found that a common response style was to avoid or deny the issues of midlife. Weiss (1990), in his study of successful middle-aged men, found an occasional instance of a man who engaged in an extramarital affair or a man who became frustrated and discouraged at his place of work. These reports are consistent with Vaillant's (1977) conclusion that "divorce, job disenchantment, and depression occur with roughly equal frequency throughout the adult life cycle" (p. 223).

In summarizing their perspective on middle age, Reid and Willis (1999) conclude that the notion of a midlife crisis that has been popular since the 1970s or 1980s has been overdramatized. They, too, find midlife characterized by a period of reevaluation, reflection, introspection, and prioritization. Some men respond to this challenge with vigor and perspective, whereas others are demoralized and dejected by it. Optimally, an emerging sense of perspective and reflection is a by-product of successful navigation of these years.

In recognizing the limitations of conclusions drawn from group-derived data, Rosenberg, Rosenberg, and Farrell (1999) suggest a shift to a personal narrative conceptualization of midlife crisis. The personal narrative perspective is based on the application of narrative psychology to the experience of midlife. Narrative psychology proposes that individuals construct narratives, or stories, of their lives that give meaning and coherence to their lived experience. For Rosenberg et al. (1999), a narrative perspective can give meaning to what may be experienced as a chaotic, tumultuous midlife crisis. The midlife crisis construct can be invoked to account for dramatic shifts in an individual's life narrative that may occur at various points in the life span. This shift is particularly notable in the fourth and fifth decades of life, as narratives of stability and achievement may be revised to include an element of tragedy, romance, or decline.

In contrast to these findings that question the validity of the midlife crisis construct, Ciernia (1985) reported results of a study that found that a large percentage of men (70 percent of his sample) did in fact experience a midlife crisis. This study questioned 227 businessmen about their experiences of midlife crisis and the extent that death awareness played a part in this crisis. In general, the older subjects reported they had experienced a midlife crisis and that a concern over their mortality had been a central aspect of this crisis.

In spite of this single study that lends some support to the validity of this construct, empirical findings do not support the notion that most men experience a crisis as they navigate midlife terrain. The construct may be helpful for some men as they adjust to changes in their lives and are faced with the challenge of revising their life narrative (see Rosenberg et al., 1999). Some men, such as those in Vaillant's (1977) study, most likely experience crisis as a result of immature coping strategies. However, generalizations about men's midlife crises are not warranted from the existing data.

CLINICAL PERSPECTIVES ON WORKING WITH MEN AT MIDLIFE

Three themes emerge from the clinical and empirical literature regarding midlife developments that are relevant for clinical work with men navigating the midlife terrain. First, there is a heightened awareness of evolving roles and relationships at work, in the community, and with intimate others including family of origin and family of choice. Second, there is an emerging awareness of individual mortality and a confrontation with the reality of death. This awareness occurs not only through the individual growth, maturation, and change that reinforce the decline of physical health but also through the death and disability of close friends and family members. Finally, the opportunity that midlife reflection affords for revision of aspects of a man's identity can be both liberating and daunting. If midlife is indeed a crisis for some men, then the Chinese character for crisis as both danger and opportunity is an appropriate representation for this stage of life.

Shifts in Male Roles at Midlife

A number of studies have pointed to the importance of shifts in roles that occur at midlife. For men, these shifts occur mainly in the context of family relationships and work relationships. Changes in family relationships can be triggered through separation and divorce, deaths of parents, and shifting roles of other family members such as spouse, partner, or children. Old assumptions and expectations concerning self and others must be reexamined as men face increasing demands for equality from women and as children leave home and strike out on their own. Divided allegiances may require reconciliation as conflicts between work and family relationships emerge (see Cournoyer & Mahalik, 1995). In addition, changes in health status of parents and ultimately parental death significantly affect how a man views himself and his relationships with family members (see Kernberg, 1985). Renewed commitments to family are commonly reported outcomes of having navigated the midlife terrain (see Farrell & Rosenberg, 1981; Guttman, 1987; Levinson et al., 1978).

Shifts in work roles, responsibilities, and interests occur as men advance in their careers. Sometimes new challenges emerge that require a revision of the original motive or impetus for pursuit of a particular career path. Career stagnation or career failure can also serve as a jarring precipitant for reexamination of the meaning of a man's job and the intrinsic value it continues to hold for him and his identity. Revision of "the dream" (Levinson et al., 1978) affords men an opportunity to examine the childhood fantasy of integrity and purpose that is established through a meaningful work role. This examination, when measured against actual occupational accomplishments, results in either a shift in occupational direction or a recommitment to an already established occupation.

Social roles, which were often seen as relatively simple and straightforward in the early adulthood years, are now viewed as more complicated and tinged with considerable ambivalence. This ambivalence is often unsettling for men who have been socialized to be decisive and in control. Such ambivalence is frequently experienced as a loss and may trigger a depressive episode that might lead to a visit to a therapist (see Cochran & Rabinowitz, 1996). Increasing commitments to other roles (such as career and family) frequently trigger a reexamination of priorities and an assessment of the ultimate value of the various roles in a man's life.

Managing Death Anxiety in Middle Age

Jacques (1965) constructs a model of midlife crisis around the impact of confrontation with death and mortality. For him, midlife begins around age thirty-five and is initially characterized by an increasing awareness of the reality of death. Yalom (1980) points out the subtle ways that individuals experience (and deny) the existence of death as an integral issue in their lives. This realization is particularly heightened in middle age as awareness of individual physical decline and the death of parents and peers begin to occur with increased frequency. Cochran and Rabinowitz (1996) also highlight the significance of death awareness for men and recommend the use of an existential approach to psychotherapy with men that focuses on the meaning of actual and symbolic losses at various points over the life span.

Kernberg (1980) views the confrontation with loss and death as one of the main developmental tasks of middle age. Through this confrontation, triggered by decline in health and the deaths of parents and peers, it is possible to work through both the real and anticipated losses while maintaining a sense of hope and generativity. The existence of adequate inner resources (sufficient internalized self and object representations) is a key element in a man's capacity to manage the mourning that is required in navigating midlife terrain.

Through their clinical experience with successful middle-aged men Braverman and Paris (1993) discovered a common theme of struggle with a depressive position in middle age that was thought to be secondary to the parental neglect the men experienced and that left them with a deficit in the self. The therapeutic tasks for these men often revolved around assisting the men to develop a healthy sense of generativity as a substitute for the wish for acquiring the supplies that were not provided in childhood. Awareness of these deficits and a shift from reparation to generativity often were accompanied by an increased awareness of personal mortality.

Overall, increased awareness of the reality of death can lead to an increased appreciation of a man's individual contribution to children, family, community, and profession. For men, a shift of values often occurs in midlife. This shift is reflected in increased time spent with those with whom a man feels close attachments, a desire to value work and achievement in greater perspective, and an increased interest in passing on gifts to the succeeding generation. Guttman (1987) emphasizes the importance of this shift in middle age, because men from a number of cultures were found to exhibit an increased valuing of the parental role.

Existential Psychotherapy: Facing Midlife Challenges

The changes characteristic of midlife activate issues that resonate deeply in many men. Changes in relationships at work and in the family, increased awareness of mortality, reconciliation of dreams with actual accomplishments, and renewed commitments in various domains of life are all highlighted as men navigate the midlife terrain. Levinson et al. (1978) identified the importance of the four polarities of life that are activated in midlife: age, purpose and direction, identity, and intimacy. An existential approach to psychotherapy (see Cochran & Rabinowitz, 1996; Yalom, 1980) directly addresses these concerns. Loss and death (age), isolation and connection (intimacy), meaning and values (identity), commitment (purpose and direction), and responsibility are core themes in the existential approach to psychotherapy. The existential approach reaches directly into these core elements of the midlife terrain and offers empathic understanding and perspective on these universal human challenges.

Existential psychotherapy focuses directly on the emotional dimension and the meaning of these core issues. As normative changes unfold over the course of a man's life, he is faced with both the emotional content of these changes and their meaning. For example, the death of a parent triggers strong emotional reactions as well as a reflection on the reality of death for everyone. The experience of reaching a career plateau forces an examination of both emotional reactions to this common occurrence and a rededication to a chosen career or a shift to another career pathway.

One inclusive theme that characterizes these and other elements of midlife challenges is the theme of examining and affirming or revising elements of a man's identity. Choices of work, family, values, leisure, and friends all accrue over the life span to constitute elements of a man's identity. As he examines and weighs the value of these elements as a result of midlife changes, a man has the opportunity to affirm a clearer sense of his own identity, meaning, and purpose in life. Existential approaches to psychotherapy directly address the personal meaning of these many facets of individual identity and invite revision as warranted.

Deficits in self and identity, failure of psychological defenses to contain anxieties associated with change and increased awareness of mortality, and lack of enduring relationships to family, friends, and community may combine to yield a sense of despair and depression for some men at midlife. In contrast, most men successfully navigate midlife terrain and emerge with renewed appreciation for the fullness of the life cycle and sensitivity to their own and others' place within it. For these men, there is a deep sense of satisfaction and resolution of the conflicts that may have been activated by midlife changes. Such resolutions set the stage for entry into the subsequent life stages.

EXAMINING LIFE AT MIDDLE AGE

A common element of clinical reports of men who are facing midlife is the challenge of examining the meaning of choices and commitments and how they contribute to a sense of fulfillment or failure in a man's life. Often, a crisis precipitates such an examination and sometimes leads to a sense of despair and depression. The following case example illustrates how a crisis can often be a point of departure for examining a number of aspects of a man's life.

Barry was a forty-five-year-old man who was referred by his work supervisor for anger management therapy. Barry had been reprimanded on two occasions for slamming doors and kicking a hole in the wall of the warehouse building where he was employed. One more outburst would jeopardize his job. He readily accepted a referral from his supervisor for counseling. At his initial session he and his therapist discussed what these angry outbursts meant for him.

"It's like a frustration. It just builds up and then I explode," Barry said as he attempted to explain what had happened.

"Hmmm. Like a frustration. I'm not sure I follow what you mean here, Barry," his therapist responded.

"You know, it's like a frustration. Something doesn't go the way I want it to go. Or I do something that I look back on and realize is a mistake or is stupid."

"You get angry if you make a mistake or look stupid?"

"Yeah."

"I don't follow the connection there. Why does doing something that is what you think is a mistake or that looks stupid make you angry?" his therapist continued.

"I guess these situations make me realize that I've done some stupid things, or that I'm not really very confident or happy with myself. So I get mad, and BAM I just lash out," Barry replied.

"Not very confident or happy with yourself. That sounds like an important connection here. What do you mean by that?"

"I've been working this same old job for over twenty years now. I've had some administrative duties and a chance at a promotion but I guess I couldn't handle those. They never worked out. Then I look back at my divorce. I never really have felt very confident of myself since then. I blame myself for that. It's just a lot of things that have gone wrong over the last twenty or so years, and they have all built up, and sometimes it just gets to be too much and I get frustrated and angry and I lash out."

In Barry's next session, he and his therapist discussed his feelings of dissatisfaction with his life and what he could do to improve his sense of self-worth and happiness. Barry looked back over the past twenty years of his life and reflected, "I have done a lot of things that I'm not happy with. The divorce really threw me. I started drinking a lot after that. And I got into some trouble."

"Got into some trouble? Like what?"

"Well, I got arrested for drunk driving. And I got into some fights with some guys when I was drinking. Just stupid stuff."

Barry's therapist picked up on the replay of the word *stupid*. "You keep referring to yourself and to the things you have done as 'stupid.' What's that about?"

"I guess I've never felt like I've accomplished much. And here I am, forty-five years old, working at the same old job and not taking advantage of any advancements that come my way. I just go to work and come home and plop down on the couch. I don't do anything for myself. I'm divorced. I don't really have much contact with my daughter anymore. She's eighteen now and that's when my custody payments end. So I don't know if we will ever see each other again. Doesn't that sound like stupid to you?"

Barry paused. His therapist sat in silence with him, then probed, "Barry, what's it like to be talking about yourself in this way?"

"It's sad. Like my life hasn't really amounted to much. Like it may never really amount to much. This is what gets me frustrated and why I lash out with anger."

"You feel sad. It sure sounds like you've had to contend with a lot of disappointments with yourself."

"Yeah."

In subsequent sessions Barry and his therapist explored Barry's deep sense of sadness and despair at the state of this life. They discussed how his anger outbursts appeared to be a wake-up call for Barry to begin to make some decisions about how he was conducting his life.

Barry introduced the term *midlife crisis* to describe his experiences at work and to convey his sense of frustration and disappointment in himself. He conscientiously attended his therapy sessions, and over time he began to activate aspects of himself that had been dormant for many years. He rediscovered his interest in music and began to attend local meetings of a folk music club. He began to view his employment as providing him material comforts and the opportunity to engage in some self-improvement activities. He returned to exercise as he had done during his years in the service and prior to his divorce. He lost some of his "excess baggage," his term for the forty pounds he had gained over the past ten or so years and that he attributed to just sitting in front of the television in his spare time.

Barry's case contains several themes that are identified in clinical writings on working with men at midlife. His relationships at work were deteriorating, and he was faced with a threat of loss of employment. Although he had been divorced for several years, he still struggled with what the divorce meant for him and held to the notion that he had failed in his marriage and family. Barry struggled with feeling isolated and disconnected from these important relationships both at work and with his own ex-spouse and daughter. He expressed considerable discomfort and shame as he recounted how he felt responsible for these disconnections. He felt "stuck" as he considered what he might do to repair these relationships. These concerns all represented an increased sensitivity to his isolation and his fears that his own "stupidity" and "badness" were to blame for this situation.

He was also concerned with his state of health. As a younger man he had been an athlete in high school and had been in good shape in military service. He had gained considerable weight after his divorce and perceived himself as a "couch potato" who spent his free time sitting in front of his television "wasting away." He expressed feelings of loss and sadness as he recounted his previous state of well-being and how that contrasted with how he now felt about himself physically.

His general mood state was depressive, although his therapist focused on this depression as a natural reaction to the losses he had accumulated in adulthood and the fact that as he looked back on his life he concluded that he had failed at most things he had tried. His sense of despair over his perceived failures at work was found to be directly related to his increasing awareness of his advancing age and the limited time he felt he had left to make changes if he was going to do so. As Barry and his therapist discussed his options, Barry's awareness of a limited, finite number of years left in his work life and his life in total left him feeling depressed. He disclosed that he frequently spent time contemplating whether "life was even worth it." In the depths of his despair he said that because he had failed so badly at his work and at his marriage and because there was no time left to really make any meaningful changes, perhaps death was not such a bad option after all. At other times, he found meaning in working, attending antique shows, and playing the piano.

Barry's situation represents how a man who faces midlife challenges can plunge into despair and depression. The accumulation of losses and perceived failures may finally break through the defenses and produce a deep sense of failure, shame, and sadness that can be paralyzing and can inhibit working through the conflicts that produce these feelings. In Barry's case, he found a therapist who was sensitive to his pain and grief but who was also willing to offer him a positive, supportive, empathic relationship. The therapist helped Barry to recognize and repair his damaged sense of self and to pick up the pieces and move on with his life. Barry made significant progress in his efforts to relieve some of his sense of failure by examining the meaning of some of his perceived failures. He decreased some of his feelings of depression by facing the reality of the losses he had accrued over his life and by constructing realistic and positive plans for engaging in meaningful activities. By learning to accept himself and his "failures" more fully, he became less angry with himself for having failed and found himself less prone to angry outbursts at work or in social settings.

Midlife can present significant challenges as well as opportunities for men. Research has confirmed that men experience common themes as they navigate midlife terrain, including shifts in social, familial, and occupational roles and relationships, increases in awareness of mortality and death anxiety, and increases in opportunities to reconcile unresolved conflicts that may have been repressed at earlier ages. Most men face these challenge and move through the midlife terrain with little difficulty. However, a few men may experience the midlife terrain as particularly rocky and may experience this time of life as a crisis.

There is little empirical evidence to support the universality of the midlife crisis. Stability and perseverance are characteristic of midlife for most men. However, some men do plunge into despair and depression as they face losses that become evident in middle age. Combined with increased anxiety about what to make of the little time that is left in life, these losses can indeed create a crisis situation.

Psychotherapy that focuses on the core constituents of midlife terrain can assist men in working through the complex feelings associated with their own mortality, deaths of family and friends, and shifts in roles at work and in their families. An existential approach to these concerns may prove beneficial for most men because this approach directly addresses these concerns in the context of death anxiety, isolation, meaning and values, responsibility, and commitment.

References

Braverman, S., & Paris, J. (1993). The male mid-life crisis in the grown-up resilient child. *Psychotherapy, 30,* 651–657.

Ciernia, J. (1985). Death concern and businessmen's mid-life crisis. *Psychological Reports, 56,* 83–87.

Cochran, S., & Rabinowitz, F. (1996). Men, loss, and psychotherapy. *Psychotherapy, 33,* 593–600.

Cournoyer, R., & Mahalik, J. (1995). Cross-sectional study of gender role conflict examining college-aged and middle-aged men. *Journal of Counseling Psychology, 42,* 11–19.

Erikson, E. (1956). The problem of ego identity. *Journal of the American Psychoanalytic Association, 4,* 56–121.

Farrell, M., & Rosenberg, S. (1981). *Men at midlife.* Boston: Auburn House.

Gilligan, C. (1982). *In a different voice.* Cambridge, MA: Harvard University Press.

Guttman, D. (1976). Individual adaptation in the middle years: Developmental issues in the masculine mid-life crisis. *Journal of Geriatric Psychiatry, 9,* 41–59.

Guttman, D. (1987). Reclaimed powers: Toward a new psychology of men and women in later life. New York: Basic Books.

Huyck, M. (1999). Gender roles and gender identity in mid-life. In S. Willis & J. Reid (Eds.), *Life in the middle: Psychological and social development in middle age* (pp. 209–232). New York: Academic Press.

Jacques, E. (1965). Death and the mid-life crisis. *International Journal of Psychoanalysis, 46,* 502–514.

Jung, C. G. (1969). *The structure and dynamics of the psyche. The Collected Works of C. G. Jung* (Vol. 8). (R. F. C. Hull, Trans.). Princeton, NJ: Princeton University Press.

Kernberg, O. (1985). *Internal world and external reality.* New York: Aronson.

Levinson, D., Darrow, C., Klein, E., Levinson, M., & McKee, B. (1978). *The seasons of a man's life.* New York: Knopf.

Mahalik, J., Cournoyer, W., Cherry, M., & Napolitano, J. (1998). Men's gender role conflict and use of psychological defenses. *Journal of Counseling Psychology, 45,* 247–255.

Moen, P., & Wethington, E. (1999). Midlife development in a life course context. In S. Willis & J. Reid (Eds.), *Life in the middle: Psychological and social development in middle age* (pp. 3–24). New York: Academic Press.

National Center for Health Statistics, Centers for Disease Control. (1998). *National Vital Statistics Report, 47*(13).

Neugarten, B. (1968). Adult personality: Toward a psychology of the life cycle. In B. L. Neugarten (Ed.), *Middle age and aging* (pp. 137–147). Chicago: University of Chicago Press.

Nydegger, C. (1976). Middle age: Some early returns—a commentary. *International Journal of Aging and Human Development, 7,* 137–141.

Rabinowitz, F. (1998). Psychotherapy with depressed middle-aged men: A grief based model. *Bulletin of the Society for the Psychological Study of Men and Masculinity, 3*(3), 16–17.

Reid, J., & Willis, S. (1999). Middle age: New thoughts, new directions. In S. Willis & J. Reid (Eds.), *Life in the middle: Psychological and social development in middle age* (pp. 275–280). New York: Academic Press.

Rosenberg, S., Rosenberg, H., & Farrell, M. (1999). The midlife crisis revisited. In S. Willis & J. Reid (Eds.), *Life in the middle: Psychological and social development in middle age* (pp. 47–73). New York: Academic Press.

Sternbach, H. (1998). Age-associated testosterone decline in men: Clinical issues for psychiatry. *American Journal of Psychiatry, 155,* 1310–1318.

Stillson, R., O'Neil, J., & Owen, S. (1991). Predictors of adult men's gender-role conflict: Race, class, unemployment, age, instrumentality-expressiveness, and personal strain. *Journal of Counseling Psychology, 38,* 458–464.

Vaillant, G. (1977). *Adaptation to life.* Boston: Little, Brown.

Weiss, R. (1990). *Staying the course: The emotional and social lives of men who do well at work.* New York: Free Press.

Yalom, I. (1980). *Existential Psychotherapy.* New York: Basic Books.

CHAPTER TWENTY-THREE

Psychotherapy with the Young Older Man

Jack Sternbach

How we define age is undergoing radical transformation. Our life span is extended because of enhanced public health, medical advances, diet, and fitness. We now have a far healthier, more active, and more functional population of aging people than ever before. Men at an age once considered old are more like yesterday's middle-aged person than yesterday's older person.

In this chapter I focus on how to best meet the mental health needs of these active, functional "young aged" (American Association of Retired Persons, 1999) men in their late fifties, sixties, seventies, eighties, and beyond. Many of these men are still in the workforce. If not, they often work part-time, are active as volunteers, and are prime consumers of educational and recreational resources.

The consciousness of aging occurs when "the equilibrium of losses and gains becomes upset in favor of an accumulation of losses with which older persons have to cope" (Orr, 1986, p. 317). Having spent their earlier years striving in the workplace and providing and caring for their families, men in this age range are often preparing for or are in retirement (some have lost their jobs), aware of

I thank Jean Hay, my wife and colleague, for her acumen and editing skill in bringing this chapter into a readable form; and the men in my monthly writing group: Dennis Balcolm, John Hubbell, Richard Jacobs, and Larry Rosenberg. Their trenchant feedback and comradely warmth has sustained and encouraged me in my writing. I also thank Charles Dietrick for his magic use of the Internet in discovering and locating Erikson's later works on aging.

diminishing energy levels, caring for ill parents, or mourning the loss of family members and friends. They are often at the same time experiencing continued vitality and somewhat greater objective freedom in terms of time, pressure, and gender role expectations.

In addition to the general principles of gender-aware therapy (Good, Gilbert, & Scher, 1990), work with functional older men requires a range of specific attitudes, knowledge, and therapeutic approaches that respond differentially and specifically to the particularities of this age group. I have made use of a number of resources, in particular Erikson's works (1950, 1982, 1986), Levinson, Darrow, Klein, Levinson, and McKee's timeless book, *The Seasons of a Man's Life* (1978), and Vaillant's empirical work with the aged, *The Wisdom of the Ego* (1993).

BASIC PRINCIPLES AND ESSENTIAL HELPING ATTITUDES

To work successfully with the young older man, the therapist would do well to observe certain basic principles and consider some essential helping attitudes, as described in the following sections.

Assume the Capacity for Growth

In my work, I always assume that, unless contraindicated by organic impairment, my clients have an innate biological and psychological capacity for growth. Recent research challenges traditional assumptions that equate aging with a disabling decline in mental capacity. The current state of knowledge (Aarts & Op den Velde, 1998) is that older persons, despite declines in physical and psychological vigor, have more than adequate neurophysiological capacity for processing and integrating information and task demands. One can also correctly assume that men have dormant capacities for nontraditional male roles and behaviors. One study (Hirsch & Newman, 1995) found that older men who took on caregiving roles for ill wives were quick to adapt and were competent in assuming unfamiliar and often unpleasant tasks, regardless of any socioeconomic or educational differences. What was striking was the equanimity and acceptance of these very traditional men toward this new stress and responsibility.

Recognize Enduring Sexual Interest

Sexual interest and activity do not cease at any particular age. Both older men and younger men vary considerably in their interest and capacity for sex. A Consumers Union Report (Brecher, 1984) indicated that an overwhelming number of older men and women who responded, including those in their ninth decade, enjoy a satisfying sexual life.

New knowledge of male sexuality tells us, for example, that erectile dysfunction is not a normative condition, inevitable with aging, but rather a pathological condition stemming from illness, injury, prostate surgery, or lowered cardiovascular capacity due to nicotine, other substances, or lack of physical activity. This knowledge shifts our attention from an earlier overemphasis in our field on psychological or relational factors to one that also emphasizes physical self-care.

The range of sexual activity among my young older male clients is quite striking. Martin, a retired chief executive officer who worried after becoming a widower whether he could "get it up," now enjoys a new relationship of freedom and closeness where "sex is not that big a deal." Paul, age sixty-six, an austere Yankee, circumspect and prudent in all things, is willing to work on a difficult new relationship because, among other things, "the sex is so fantastic." A sidebar is that Martin was until recently a lifelong smoker and heavy drinker. Paul was not.

Promote the Capacity for Deeper Human Connection

The deforming rituals of male socialization work against close connections throughout men's lives. As men become older, however, a new sense of subjective time and often freedom from the breadwinner demands may open men to new connections. I see it in my hometown as older men become involved in both impersonal ways (by fund-raising for the historical society) and more intimate capacities (by volunteering at the hospice). It is primarily through human connection that we can successfully do the meaning making that can expand our spirit, offer us the opportunity to make amends, and restore integrity that may well have been bruised.

A wonderful example is the book and movie *The Prince of Tides*. In a striking scene in the movie the protagonist's father, who was a brutal and abusive parent, relates to his grandchildren with a tenderness and love with which he never blessed his son.

CRITICAL KNOWLEDGE BASE

It is vital to expand one's knowledge base so as to have a sufficient cognitive understanding of what an older man has experienced and is encountering biologically, culturally, and historically.

Biology of the Older Man

Late middle age is the time of life when a man usually receives a number of reminders that his body is changing. Even with overall good health, physical aches and pains such as lower back problems or arthritis, dental issues, and a decline in vision and aural keenness often occur. Adult diabetes and blood pressure problems may surface. Many traditional men face these changes with embedded patterns of denial and disregard of both preventive and palliative health care. Harrison's (1978) landmark warning that "the male sex role may be dangerous to your health" is especially pertinent.

On the other hand, traditional men often overrely on mainstream medicine and are highly skeptical of alternative remediation. Charles, a busy attorney in his late fifties, has chronic back pain. Although he is willing to take regular cortisone shots, he will not do back stretches, see a chiropractor, or get a massage.

Regular medical exams and care for chronic conditions are critical. The American Heart Association and American Cancer Society guidelines for healthy lifestyles and regular checkups and screenings for pathological conditions are widely publicized. The therapist needs to act as an informed consultant and motivator of good health care. Particular concern for prostate health is vital. Prostate cancer is for men—as breast cancer is for women—a leading (and often treatable) cause of early death.

When men during these years experience a major health problem such as a heart attack or a stroke it is critical to pay close attention to whether they are doing the recommended follow-up exercise and diet changes. Too often men open themselves to receive care initially but then very quickly put their ongoing health care needs aside. It is as if any decline in the image of invulnerability can lead a man to a sense of total despair or, on the other hand, unwarranted optimism that no more care is required.

Anxiety about sexual interest or performance during these years is also common. Yet men have many ways of defending, deflecting, and denying this issue, whether through humor, irony, or silent withdrawal. Arnie, a blue-collar man in his late fifties, told me one day that his wife had asked him to talk about sexuality because he had stopped having sex with her. It took the most gentle and detailed questioning for Arnie to reveal that he did not think his erection was hard enough. He took a deep breath and said: "It looks like it is over for me, huh?" As it turned out, it was not.

For every Arnie who voices this fear, there are many who simply stay silent and stop exploring their sexuality. The biological decline in testosterone does not mean a man's sex life need be finished. Information, medication, a broader range of sexual practices, and other interventions are now available.

It is the task of the therapist to be well informed, to be a resource for male clients, and to be unafraid to talk specifically in a very detailed way about health concerns. It also helps if the therapist presents a vitality and sense of well-being that reflect his or her informed and self-respecting level of lifestyle choices and self-care.

Cultural Diversity

To work effectively with older men the therapist must understand the many faces of cultural diversity (race, ethnicity, sexual orientation, social class, and others). But this understanding must be broadened. It can be correctly assumed that the older the man, the more likely it is that he carries self-ascriptions, beliefs, and attitudes specific to the particularity of his cultural background, in ways much more pronounced than the homogenized consumer culture of today, which tends to obscure and minimize such cultural differences in behalf of marketing strategies. Of course, at the same time, some cultural differences are spotlighted and exaggerated in behalf of social control (for example, the denigration of blue-collar culture).

Diversity for the young aged has two aspects. On the one hand older men came of age when racism, sexism, and other forms of oppression were scarcely recognized as such and were even less commonly challenged. White women were generally confined to the home and were economically dependent. Gays and lesbians were both invisible and subject to legal penalties. Blacks were segregated in a separate America. Anti-Semitism was rampant among all classes. Some older men have trouble "coming up to speed"—that is, discarding old, invidious distinctions and projections. One of the tasks of the therapist is to engage with men who are struggling to make sense of these changes.

Older men also grew up in a time of localism, provincial attitudes, and minimal exposure to cross-cultural differences. The cultures of place, region, and formal religious affiliation loomed much larger than they do today.

Generational Marker Events

Therapists must be aware of critical generational marker events. Knowledge of these critical experiences shared by an age cohort is of particular pertinence when the therapist is younger (a probable scenario) than the older man. Empathy is necessary but hardly sufficient to convey to an older man that his life experience is known and understood. He may with encouragement tell his story but will be considerably more confident in the therapist's ability and more forthcoming if the therapist demonstrates that he or she has taken the time to learn at least a little of the events common to his age cohort. I describe some of those events in the following paragraphs.

The worldwide flu epidemic of 1918. This medical horror killed forty million people (more than World War I) and often struck the young, vigorous, and healthy. I have worked with a number of men in their late seventies and eighties who never knew their fathers, who died in that epidemic. The randomness, meaninglessness, and lifetime sense of loss was embedded in them.

The Great Depression of the 1930s. This economic catastrophe deeply affected many men, creating a pervading mistrust of fate, conservatism about money and risk, a certain holding-on attitude, and a profound remembrance of how terribly grinding unrelenting poverty can be. Therapists need to know that the so-called safety nets of unemployment compensation, Social Security, and the like were legislated only after years of suffering. Men of that generation paid cash, took pride in paying off their debts, and kept their cards close to their vests.

The Depression brought about considerable class consciousness and passionate beliefs about social justice. The modern trade union movement was born during this period, and the Marxist vision was attractive to millions.

World War II. Now that the film *Private Ryan* has expanded our consciousness, we know a little bit more of that last great "just war"—when good was arrayed against evil. Moral reasoning did not mitigate the horror and terror, but there was some redemption for those who fought (and survived). The daughter of one veteran tells me how his silence about the war isolates him from the family. He has become mute in so many other ways as well.

Tom, a World War II veteran, recently revisited the people in Belgium, who greeted him as affectionately today as they did fifty years ago when he helped liberate them. Tom's comment to me: "If I ever had any doubt [and he must have had to give it voice] about the rightness of what I did back then, visiting those people laid it to rest." Tom reminds us of how each man, even though he is part of the epic narrative, must do his own unique meaning making.

The Korean War. This almost forgotten war, misnamed as a "conflict" or "police action" due to peculiar historical circumstances, was fought under the most adverse conditions of freezing cold. The suffering was incalculable. The fact that there has never been a memorial and this war continues to have a low profile occasions much bitterness and sense of abandonment among its veterans, most of them now in their seventies.

Forced migrations and multigenerational trauma. In the twentieth century many people became refugees and émigrés. Many Holocaust survivors are just now beginning to be able to speak out. As our appreciation of diversity expands, we are attuned to the losses of Central and South American refugees and to those of Southeast Asia and Africa. Here again it is not just the experience of death camps or exile but also the epic stories of suffering, disconnection, and rootlessness embedded in the family systems over several generations that need to be explored. The concept of multigenerational trauma is applicable to many ethnic groups. For instance, Frank McCourt's *Angela's Ashes* (1996) reminds us of the Irish oppression and diaspora.

For a full therapeutic alliance is to be forged, the therapist requires intelligent knowledge of and active inquiry into the sense of marginalization, displacement, and tribal suffering. I have yet to work with an older man from an immigrant ethnic group who is not marked by that experience, even several generations removed.

Vietnam War, antiwar movement, and sociocultural change. No man, even several decades later, in my experience, has remained untouched by the Vietnam War and its effects. On the one hand there are the combat veterans, victims and perpetrators often in the same moment. Then there are the resisters or simply the men who escaped the draft; many of these men experience guilt about those who suffered or died. This war tore apart the United States, not unlike the Civil War. It created huge internal and external fault lines in individuals, families, and institutions.

And lest we forget: the civil rights movement, the women's movement, gay liberation, and "sex, drugs, and rock and roll." Some men may have strong feelings of antipathy and judgment, whereas others may have strong feelings of identification and a sense of personal freedom and aliveness. Many men, now in their mid to late fifties, fought either in or against the Vietnam War, participated in leftist politics, took drugs, came out, sat in, felt new challenges from sisters and wives. Therapists need to work with each individual to discover how these experiences have been integrated or disowned. Inquiries about contemporary "recreational" use of marijuana are definitely in order.

The AIDS epidemic. Most now have knowledge of an AIDS victim. Therapists must consider how much this disease has affected older gay men who have been deprived of friends and mentors, just at a time in life when social supports are so important. One older gay man specifically joined a heterosexual group; he could not bear any longer being in gay men's groups with so many members who were ill or dying.

OLDER MEN'S NEED FOR THERAPY

The entrance of the young older man into therapy has two derivations: a precipitating event of a situational nature, often accompanied by the surfacing of a long-term endogenous process.

Situational Events

Common situational events that might lead to therapy are those involving loss, change, or dislocation. These events include job loss or retirement, financial concerns, loss of community and old friendship networks, illness or death of spouse, acute or debilitating chronic physical conditions, and relationship problems.

Sometimes the dislocating factor is a consequence of a positive change. Most men, regardless of social class, welcome retirement. However, there are real social class differences related to retirement. Blue-collar and lower-level service people are usually all too ready to leave jobs that either held little intrinsic value or involved grinding physical demands on the body. Higher-status men in more rewarding positions may experience tinges of regret about loss of control and command.

More to the point, there is often a profound alteration in the previously complementary but unequal marital relationship. The wife, previously willing to keep her own needs under wraps, now emerges as an independent actor. Men who were reared in times when women kept their own needs under lock and key frequently resist grappling with the emergence of their women partners. Some men feel profoundly abandoned or victimized when their entitlement is challenged.

Long-Term Endogenous Processes

The endogenous processes contain the common theme that I refer to as growth too long deferred. Deferred growth frequently presents as depression, anxiety, and somatic complaints. Marital difficulties are common. It is as if the dam has sprung a leak and earlier developmental tasks, trauma, or unresolved losses not adequately attended to emerge into troubling consciousness.

The absence of distraction and satisfaction in a regular work routine can bring realizations and anxieties to the fore that were previously contained. Just aging itself, with its accompanying diminution of physical energy and sense of fragility, can be the trigger. Jim, age sixty-two, a highly placed systems manager, burst into tears in the group after an angioplasty. He told the group how difficult it was for him to keep on doing the dirty work of firing people.

Chronic undiagnosed depression. Men in this age group often endure chronic depression that is sometimes masked by substance abuse. Real (1997) explored this phenomenon in an instructive and touching manner. He identified the terrible price so many men have paid as they have stifled their emotional life to conform to gender prescriptions.

Restimulated trauma and unresolved grief. Van den Kolk, McFarlane, and Weisaeth (1998) include in their book on trauma a chapter on the emergence of trauma among the aged. The authors hypothesize that the normative developmental tasks of that life stage may in and of themselves restimulate past trauma, often in random and unexpected ways.

Frederick was a vital, energetic, highly successful professor of humanities, justly known for his openness to students, his capacity to mentor them, and his scholarship. He had always busied himself during his summer vacations with travel and research until he took a full year's sabbatical in our small community. All of a sudden, he was by himself, tucked away in the woods, without the daily positive feedback that had been his daily fare. He went into a deep depression that required medication and came to see me to work on unresolved grief at earlier deaths and losses in his family of origin.

Reentry after a midlife moratorium. I have worked with a considerable number of men who have reengaged with life after taking time out to rebuild shattered lives. Many are in substance abuse recovery. Some were wounded by bitter divorces. Many have operated for decades as "rogue males," unattached and marginalized. Some have been grossly inappropriate and neglectful as fathers and husbands. Their own immaturity and adherence to traditional masculine values, as well as the distortions of alcoholism (for some), have left them at a much earlier stage of development than would be expected for their age. Therapy is seen as opening the possibilities for reconnection to the community, capacity to be in a new relationship, or making amends and receiving the hurt and pain of adult children.

Some older men are simply overwhelmed by all the changes around them. They may retreat behind a wall of opinionated argumentation (the stereotype of the "grumpy old man"). Such men enter therapy only after family members have issued an or-else ultimatum.

Accompanying and underlying all of the mentioned issues is the reality of the aging process, with its universal and inevitable outcome: death. This realization can evoke late-life concerns for spiritual wholeness. Most of these men are now the elders of their generation, aware of a diminishing time line and a last chance to "make things right."

IMPLICATIONS FOR PSYCHOTHERAPY WITH OLDER MEN

Based on the previously presented material, I offer in the following sections a number of suggestions for therapeutic approaches with older men.

Conduct Thorough Initial Screenings

Because of the complex interactions of biological and psychological variables in older men, it is especially important that therapists screen carefully for a number of complicating conditions.

Substance abuse. In his multiple interviews with several cohorts of older people, Vaillant (1993) made an impressive discovery about the intersection of substance abuse and health. Ongoing depression and untreated substance abuse (primarily alcoholism) are unfailing predictors of an unsatisfactory aging process. We are fortunate today to have a variety of remedial interventions available for both these conditions.

For alcoholism there are inpatient facilities, twelve-step groups, and a growing body of self-help literature. Many older men came of age when heavy and regular alcohol intake was a normative, culturally sanctioned activity. (Reviewing some old Hitchcock classics reveals that none of the characters seem able to utter a line of dialogue without cigarettes in their mouths and drinks in their hands.) They may be unaware of the possible connection between alcohol and their presenting problems such as chronic depression and despair, relational conflict, and loneliness. Problem identification and acknowledgment may take time.

It is particularly gratifying when an older man achieves sobriety. The results can be quite heartening for family members who have either kept vigil or become estranged through decades of alcohol-induced distance and misbehavior. Delwin became sober at age sixty-four and was available, in his wife's words, for the relationship "she had waited forty years for." His action had a cascading effect on the family system; one of his sons, in the grip of a cocaine habit, requested help only after his dad became sober.

Chronic depression. Only recently has chronic depression begun to be recognized as a normative experience for American men (Real, 1997). Although depression can be treated through a number of approaches, the merits of short-term psychopharmacological interventions are clear. I have found that older men often need this kind of buffering to avoid becoming overwhelmed by feelings they have never learned to tolerate. Short-term medication can help these men turn the corner and become accessible for talk therapy. Men of this generation often resist taking medication and seeing a "shrink."

Medication problems. In my experience, older men's medications are often poorly prescribed. This problem may take two forms: prescription at subtherapeutic levels or at levels so high as to precipitate dangerous or noxious side effects. It is important for therapists to become well informed and to work with psychiatrists who are both sensitive to psychotherapeutic factors and up-to-date on psychopharmacology and the interaction with medications for other problems.

Physical health. As noted earlier, it is important for the therapist to function as a knowledgeable mentor of the physical health and well-being of older male clients. This role is particularly important because the optimism and hope of aging men become increasingly connected with their biology and physical status. Health screenings, healthy lifestyle, and informed use of alternative therapies are effective in maintaining bodily function. At the same time, the therapist can help clients avoid reactivity (the first few memory lapses call up the specter of Alzheimer's disease these days) and place their health concerns in context.

Social relationships and supports. Whatever a man's age, social and emotional isolation is correlated with a low level of both physical and emotional well-being. It is heartrending to hear from an older man, often successful at work, well regarded in the community, and with at least the formalism of family contact, that there is no one he can speak to "from the heart." For many of these men there is nothing as salutary as exposure to the sustained support of a men's group.

When Delwin returned from the treatment center the first thing he did was give me a bear hug. He then went on to tell of the burden that was lifted by his participation in a small treatment group in which, for the first time in his life, he could touch and trust other men.

Cultural identity. To fully understand an older man it is imperative that the therapist be knowledgeable about his background, including the generational marker events discussed. Many men in this age group wear their identity as a badge, one that has to be noticed and appreciated. Paul, discussed earlier, was very intent on telling me how important it was that I appreciate him as a real

"Yankee," with all that implied about probity, high ethical standards, and suspicion of change, including psychotherapy. Labeling this identity as simply resistance would have alienated him and foreclosed our work.

Validate a Man's Accumulated Wisdom and Ego Strength

One of the keys to a good therapeutic relationship is calling forth the wholeness, the strengths, the proved capacities of a man who has lived parts of his life with great skill. Therapy requires regression, something scary for anyone at any age but particularly problematic for older men. I make it a point to explicitly speak to the capacity for self-care, judgment, and informed understanding that can make this process more productive and palatable to older men.

Help Mourn Losses and Celebrate Acceptance

Sometimes men's losses seem overwhelming. Rick, a physically fit outdoors type, was struck down with a major stroke in his midsixties. He pulls himself up the two stairs to my office, saying "meet the cripple." He can no longer drive or read. Sometimes all we can do is sit with and join in the mourning, which is what I did.

For the most part, however, the losses are less catastrophic. They occur as a series of small, progressive, narcissistic injuries that open a man to his vulnerability and fragility. As men move through their fifties and sixties, in the prime of their lives, they experience an unhappy paradox. Although they have "arrived" and now wield the power they longed for, they are simultaneously becoming aware of their declining physical capacities and the temporary nature of their new status. For these men it is hard enough to feel the loss of physical and sexual vigor. It is even more difficult when their economic security and their sense of social value are undermined. (Think, if you will, of the layoffs of managers in all sectors of economic life.) It is the task of the therapist to sit with a man without denying the reality of loss or downplaying the grief involved. I concur with Bly, who stated that "grief is the door to a man's soul" (as cited in Bliss, 1986, p. 18).

Despite these many losses, many men are still finding their way. In my senior men's group, Harry shares a story about how he and his wife find that cuddling and emotional closeness are every bit as satisfying as their formerly more active genital sex was. Massey has made it clear at work that leaving early for the group is a priority and that taking care of himself is important. Bart, a seventy-three-year-old retired developer keeps telling us that relational growth is "not worth the trouble—to hell with it!" yet he stays in the group and continues to work hard.

Challenge Denial, Avoidance, and Entitlement

Based on an empirical study of several hundred men, Farrell and Rosenberg (1981) coined the term *indirect generativity* to describe an impersonal, non-intimate mode of community service. Delwin, a member of the board of directors of a prestigious organization, was representative of this type of involvement. However, when he joined the men's growth group he was able bring forth his natural capacities for caring and intimacy.

Hemp, a newly retired investment banker, self-described as the "prince" of the family, encountered rough going in his retirement. Now that he no longer controlled the purse strings, he no longer called the shots. His wife was no longer compliant, including with regard to sexual access. The men's group gently supported his right to a satisfying sex life. At the same time, however, the men also made it clear that Hemp had to forego his entitlement and learn how to engage and struggle to get his needs met, both in the group and in the marriage.

Men's groups can be extremely effective in dealing with denial and avoidance. Thad was a rough and ready guy, with "street smarts." He could not see how his sarcasm and tough-guy persona had so alienated his wife that she was seeking a divorce. He had trusted me enough to join my men's group, but that did not seem to be enough. I tried to reach him, but his defenses only gave way when he connected with Patrick, a group member from a similar ethnic, blue-collar, alcohol-driven family system. Thad was busy telling us how he just did not "get this business about verbal abuse." Patrick listened for a while and then listed the specific ways in which he, Patrick, had been verbally abusive. Patrick concluded that neither he nor Thad had intended to be verbally abusive but both had inappropriately applied their street smarts to an intimate connection that required more empathy and gentleness. When Patrick finished speaking, Thad poignantly admitted, "I guess I've been rough in tender places."

Sometimes a sense of humor helps. Bill, age sixty-four, came up the hard way. His working-class background had prompted him to launch a rabid, right-wing rant that included racist, sexist, and homophobic elements. His new wife could not tolerate this behavior. In one of his first sessions he began one of his tirades. After ten minutes or so I said: "Bill, you've come to the right place, I'm a knee-jerk, left-wing radical and I like nothing more than being paid to argue politics." There was a pause and Bill broke up. After a bit he said that maybe he had a problem with coming on too strong and pushing people away. I agreed, and thereafter we did some good therapeutic work.

Receive the Stories

Older men have a special need to tell their stories. "We make up stories to place our present between past and future, to complete what is missing, to steady that which is in flux and order the chaotic" (Ezrahi, 1997, p. 267).

A therapist can be especially helpful to a man in the later stages of his life. The man needs to let someone know that he came from somewhere, that he had triumphs and tragedies, and that there is a meaning and a substance to his life. However, before he can tell a therapist about his private self, he needs to tell where he was brought up, how life was in that long-ago time, how he made his way in the world, how he formed a self from the raw material he was granted. Often these stories are a source of pride. They are the material from which meaning has been forged. If a therapist listens well, the older man will find his personal voice and will permit the therapist to help him.

Accommodate Older Men's Style

It is important to make several accommodations to the stylistic preferences of older men.

Validate the use of reminiscence. Therapists should encourage and value the older man's use of reminiscence as a joining and connecting act on his part. Empathy is a critical issue, because many older men have already lived through what most therapists can only imagine. Therapists might be helped by considering an older man's sometimes rambling discourse as his attempt to seek a union with the therapist. This behavior can be seen as the man's empathy for the therapist's life stage. Although the man may be judgmental or off target, he may nevertheless be seeking to connect with the therapist.

Learn to decode and respond to indirect requests for help. Men of the era of the Great Depression and men of the World War II generation grew up with strictures against direct statements of need and desire. Effective therapy with these men is helped by the ability to decode indirect speech. Many of these men have been models of correct, upright stoicism all their adult lives. For them, a direct request is not only a sign of vulnerability but also an expression of selfishness and bad manners.

Brooks, my eighty-two-year-old friend, came into the house and said, "Jack, don't get old!" (I reassured him I was working on it, but without much success.) It turned out he could no longer raise the mainsail on his boat without help. I picked up on it and offered to come out with him and do the lifting while he captained the boat. He smiled shyly and said, "If you don't mind."

Recognize and confront difficulties with dependency and subjectivity. Brooks is a retired attorney and considers himself to be a BASP (black Anglo-Saxon Protestant). He is a man of rectitude, containment, and propriety. He wants closeness and companionship but is leery of intrusiveness or neediness. We did manage to talk about his loss of strength and agility, but it was not easy. My response was that of a friend. If we were in a therapy context I might have explored further what he really needed and could not quite bring himself to ask for directly.

Support and affirm a man's right to claim his subjectivity. Older men such as Brooks have been taught that a focus on self is selfish and that openness to others makes one too vulnerable. Such lessons in self-denial are often accompanied by a playing out of legitimate unmet dependency needs in inappropriate and self-destructive ways. Older men need considerable connection and support to risk behaviors that will introduce vulnerability and openness into a life organized around containment and caution.

Initiate Family-of-Origin Work

Hemp could not really begin to grasp what was required until he allowed himself to recall and feel the pain of his boyhood in a family in which emotional distance was the norm. Like all older men I have worked with, Hemp was carrying significant pain about his relationship with his father. The exploration inherent in family-of-origin work is often the path into deeper work for older men who may be otherwise resistant to the language and assumptions of therapy.

The "father wound" is part of the normative male experience (Osherson, 1986). Until recently, the cultural message to "grin and bear it" has been the only context for male development. To help men, however, it is important to pinpoint the specific traumas they have endured.

Delwin could never understand why his father, a college All-American football player, never taught him sports. Hemp needed to acknowledge and grieve the total absence of any emotional closeness with his father. He had replicated his father's life including, to his anguish, emotional distance from his own children. Paul had to do some hard work to wrest one of the painful realities about his "war hero" father—that is, that his father was a chronic alcoholic who irresponsibly delegated Paul to assume a caretaker role at age fourteen. "Paul," his mother would say, "make sure you wait up for Dad and see that he gets in to the house safely when he comes home."

Despite the wealth of attention men's studies literature gives to the father wounds of men, I have found the situation complicated. In my experience, exploration of the "mother wound" is, with many men, even more unsettling than work with the father wound. Almost always it seems to uncover preverbal and primal emotions that are highly troubling and shaming for many men.

Acknowledge That Men Are Both Wounded and Wounding

In working with older men, therapists often have to seek out hidden caches of guilt and shame, where clients have hidden their moral lapses and wounding behaviors. Therapists cannot be afraid to hold clients' "feet to the fire" on behalf of their growth. This approach must always be used carefully, with continual awareness of how men's behavior fits within the pressures and expectations of their gendered situation. When therapists must confront men's behavior, it should be done in the context of gender-sensitive therapy (Brooks, 1998).

In the Arthurian legend, Lancelot, Arthur's closest and dearest companion, explained why he could not go on the quest for the grail with these simple words: "I am far too soiled by life." An older man knows only too well how many compromises, ethical lapses, and wounding behaviors he has to acknowledge. The grail may be beyond reach, but there is always meaning to be made, and redemption, forgiveness, and grace may be possible. And integrity is always within reach.

Sometimes the shame-based issues are far less substantive, though they are still problematic. In many cases the shame is the result of no-fault events. For instance, Tom, from an elite family, was ashamed that he had never learned to water-ski like his brothers. Of course, he was only eight years old and his siblings were all teenagers at the time. For such men and such events discussion and education about gender role oppression can be a real benefit that enables them to let go of such unnecessary suffering.

Consider a Men's Group

Over the past decade, many therapists have identified the all-male group as the treatment of choice for many men (Andronico, 1996; Brooks, 1998; Sternbach, 1992). In so many ways a group can be the ideal place for men to overcome shame, isolation, and denial, to receive validation, to learn how to struggle, and to develop interpersonal intimacy. Therapists may need to obtain referrals to groups for particular clients or start groups themselves.

Attend to Countertransference and Therapist Reactivity to Older Men

As Levinson et al. (1978) have said so eloquently, "The recognition of vulnerability in myself becomes a source of wisdom, empathy, and compassion for others. I can truly understand the suffering of others only if I can identify with them through an awareness of my own weakness and destructiveness" (p. 30).

So many therapists carry hurt and disappointment about their fathers, men who were often not known or were unavailable. They must be careful to neither expect too little nor, on the other hand, try to redo what they could not do with their fathers with their older male clients. Therapists must be alert to how an ageist society can undercut their ability to value an older man, including themselves as they move through the aging process. Depending on the older man's race, class, ethnicity, or sexual orientation therapists need to be alert to their own issues of dominance-submission, control, or dependency. Above all else, therapists need to develop the ability to relate empathetically—to "be with" the older male client.

Many of the issues confronting the older man involve contradictions that are, by their nature, beyond resolution. There is a richness in age to the extent that a man can both remain vital and committed to his growth and accept the inevitability of decline and loss. Work with the older man can provide the therapist with that most desirable of opportunities—the chance to see the many models of aging, some successful, others less so.

With some luck and hard work, therapists can help their older male clients, as well as themselves, to grow into wider and more generous dimensions of masculinity, as "lover, friend, mentor, healer, leader, mediator, companion, colleague, nurturer, creator, and appreciator of the human heritage" (Levinson et al., 1978, p. 221).

Eric Erikson, in his classic *Childhood and Society* (1950), said that the task of age was to resolve the polarities of integrity and despair. In this context I can do no better than to quote from a very vigorous seventy-two-year-old man who came to see me after being diagnosed with terminal cancer. He wanted to see if he could somehow make peace with forty years of a rancorous marriage. He was courageous enough to recognize how his excessively rational and aloof approach had distanced and shamed his wife. He said, "knowing what I do now, from this work with you, things are bittersweet. To realize how my logic left Anne hanging out there and provoked her even more, when she needed me so badly. I know now what I missed and I'm sorry but I'm also thankful for the knowledge."

It is sad that he waited for his death sentence before seeking the help he came to value. It is my hope that more young older men will seek therapists out when there is still time to reset the compass, even if it is only for a short time. Let therapists' work with these men be guided by the mantra "It is never too late too grow."

References

Aarts, P., & Op den Velde, W. (1998). Prior traumatization and the process of aging: Theory and clinical implications. In B. A. Van den Kolk, A. McFarlane, & L. Weisaeth (Eds.), *Traumatic stress: The effects of overwhelming experience on mind, body, and society* (pp. 359–377). New York: Guilford Press.

American Association of Retired Persons. (1999, Summer). *AARP Bulletin*, p. 8.

Andronico, M. (Ed.). *Men in groups: Insights, interventions, and psychoeducational work.* Washington, DC: American Psychological Association.

Bliss, S. (1986, Winter). Revisioning masculinity. *Nurturing News, 18.*

Brecher, E., and the Editors of Consumer Reports Books. (1984). *Love, sex, and aging.* Boston: Little, Brown.

Brooks, G. (1998). *A new psychotherapy for traditional men.* San Francisco: Jossey-Bass.

Erikson, E. (1950). *Childhood and society.* New York: Norton.

Erikson, E. (with Erikson, J.). (1982). *The life cycle completed.* New York: Norton.

Erikson, E. (with Erikson, J., & Kivnick, H. Q.). (1986). *Vital involvement in old age.* New York: Norton.

Ezrahi, Y. (1997). *Rubber bullets: Power and conscience in modern Israel.* New York: Farrar Strauss Giroux.

Farrell, M., & Rosenberg, D. (1981). *Men at midlife.* New York: Auburn.

Good, G., Gilbert, L. A., & Scher, M. (1990, March/April). Gender aware therapy: A synthesis of feminist therapy and knowledge about gender. *Journal of Counseling and Development, 68,* 376–380.

Harrison, J. (1978). Warning, the male sex role may be dangerous to your health. *Journal of Social Issues, 34,* 65–86.

Hirsch, C., & Newman, J. (1995). Microcultural and gender role influences on male care givers. *Journal of Men's Studies, 3*(4), 309–333.

Levinson, D., Darrow, C., Klein, E., Levinson, M., & McKee, B. (1978). *The seasons of a man's life.* New York: Ballantine Books.

McCourt, F. (1996). *Angela's ashes.* New York: Scribners.

Orr, A. (1986). Dealing with the death of a group member: Visually impaired elderly in the community. In A. Gitterman & L. Shulman (Eds.), *Mutual aid groups and the life cycle* (pp. 315–322). Itasca, IL: Peacock.

Osherson, S. (1986). *Finding our fathers.* New York: Fawcett Columbine.

Real, T. (1997). *I don't want to talk about it: Overcoming the secret legacy of male depression.* New York: Scribner.

Sternbach, J. (1992, Fall). A men's study approach to group treatment with all-male groups. *Men and Mental Health (Special issue). Men's Studies Review, 9*(2), 14–22.

Vaillant, G. (1993). *The wisdom of the ego.* Cambridge, MA: Harvard University Press.

Van den Kolk, B. A., McFarlane, A. C., & Weisaeth, L. (Eds.). (1998). *Traumatic stress: The effects of overwhelming experience on mind, body, and society.* New York: Guilford Press.

NAME INDEX

SUBJECT INDEX

246–250; and religious affiliations, 822–823; and sexual violence, 296–298; sports counseling, 109–111; young older men, 472–473. *See also* Substance abuse
Alcohol Use Inventory-Revised (AUI-R), 249
Alcoholics Anonymous (AA), 252, 258, 300, 823
Alexithymia, 28, 424–439, 530, 532, 624, 700; action empathy, 429–430; assessment interview, 433–434; and boys, 55; case study, 432–439; channeling of feelings into sexuality, 431–432; and cognitive therapy, 544; defined, 54; and emotion socialization ordeal, 427–429; emotional vocabulary/ feeling states, 434–435; and ending a committed relationship, 340–341; and fatherhood issues, 436; and gender role strain, 426–427; and male role socialization, 425–432; myths and realities of, 54–55; normative alexithymia, 430; overdevelopment of anger/ aggression, 431; treatment program for, 434–436
Ambivalent behavior, and substance abuse treatment, 253
American Men's Studies Association, 845
Anabolic-androgenic steroids, 100
Androgyny, 623; and spiritual health, 819
Anger, overdevelopment of, 431
Anticomplementary interactions, 133
Anxiety disorders, 30–31; and divorce, 343; performance-inhibiting of athletes, 111–112
Asian American men, 780–792; diversity of, 782; fatherhood role, 785; gender role conflicts, 784–784; identity issues, 788–790; masculinity concept, 780–781, 786–787; modified cognitive therapy, 790–791; obstacles to gender redefinition, 781–782; traditional values of, 783, 786; and the workplace, 785–786
Assault, and male victimization, 268
Athletes. *See* Sports settings, counseling in
Attention disorders, 356; and athletes, 113–114

B
Bem Sex Role Inventory (BSRI), 25
Binge drinking: and athletes, 109–110; college men, 153–154, 162
Biofeedback training, 111–112
Bisexual men, 796–811; changing sexual orientation, 801; college counseling, 150; diversity issues, 797, 811; families of, 805–806; and heterosexual men, 809–811; normative devel-

opment, 797; psychotherapy with, 796–811; social stigma and harassment of, 800–801
Black masculine identity, 745. *See also* African American men
Blueprint for manhood, 24–25, 93, 105
Body image: aging issues, 101–102; and athletes, 99–100; athletes with injuries, 109; and masculinity, 187; and steroids, 100; strength, 100; weight and size, 99–100
Boosting Alcohol Consciousness Concerning Health of University Students (BACCHUS), 110
Boston University Fatherhood Project, 424, 432, 435
"Boy code," 93
Boyhood. *See* Adolescence
Boys. *See* Adolescents and boys
Business and industry, consulting with, 126–145; applicable mental health skills, 131; case examples, 137–139, 142–144; coaching vs. counseling approach, 128; interpersonal theory, 132–134, 136–137; key practices, 139–142; leadership training, 141–142; masculine role and interpersonal theory, 134–145; ongoing consultation to executives, 140; organizational changes, 127–130; return on investments, 139–140; succession planning, 140; team building, 140–141; working with upper management, 129–130. *See also* Career counseling

C
Capitalization hypothesis, 28–29, 593
Career counseling: action vs. self-awareness focus, 376; building working relationships, 375; changing job market and skills requirements, 376; in college setting, 151–152; critical issues in, 370–376; difficulty of seeking help, 374–375; executive coaching, 126, 128–130, 142–144; and gender role socialization, 369–384; and individual differences, 372; and life goals, 370–371; male gender role attributes, 372–373; male socialization strengths, 374; psychological/career choice adjustment, 373–374; work as critical life role, 371–372
Career counseling model, 377–384; closing the relationship, 383; developing career goals and action plans, 383; evaluating results, 383; first phase of treatment, 377–382; gathering client information, 380–382; opening phase, 377–379;

Stage model of adjustment (to disability), 192–194; defense mobilization, 192–193; initial impact, 192; initial realization, 193; reintegration, 193–194; retaliation, 193

Stage-related resistance, 594–595

State-Trait Anxiety Inventory, 112

Stress, 30–31. *See also* Anxiety disorders; Masculine gender role stress

Strong Interest Inventory (career assessment), 373

Substance abuse, 31, 246–259; and boyhood, 363; college counseling, 153–155; and depression, 229, 231, 233; and disabled men, 200; and divorce, 343; gender differences in, 246; and "manliness," 250; and military socialization, 210; peer pressure, 363; and sexual violence, 296–298; sports counseling, 109–111; traditional gender role expectations, 248–249; treatment for, 246–259; utilization of health care services, 252; young older men, 472–473

Substance abuse treatment, men's issues in, 253–258; ambivalence, 253; motivational interviewing, 256–258; readiness for change, 253–256

Suicide, 29, 148; and depression, 229; and religious affiliations, 824

Suicide risk, and depression, 235–237

T

Team building, 140–141

Team identity, 97

Teamwork, as coping strategy, 78

Therapeutic process, 33–34; capitalization hypothesis, 28–29; effectiveness for mental health problems, 28–33; implication and future study, 33–34; male-friendly with school-age boys, 43–55; practice guideline for, 61–62; reexamination of professional constraints, 52–54; sexual therapy and therapist transparency, 329–330. *See also* Client-practitioner relationship; Integrative therapy; Treatment models for adult/young adult men

Total Quality Management (TQM), 131

Toxic masculinity, 171–172

Traditional male relational style, 44–45

Transference, and women therapists-men clients, 708–710

Transference issues, 597

Trauma: and assault, 268; case study example, 272–275; childhood abuse, 265–266; and combat, 267–268; community violence, 267; forced migration, 469; implications for treat-

ment, 271–272; and masculine socialization, 269–271; multigenerational trauma, 469; parental violence, 266; restimulated trauma and unresolved grief, 471; survivors of, 263–275; trauma (gender role) strain, 427; and violence, 286–287. *See also* Victimization

Trauma and Recovery (Herman), 264

Treatment models for adult/young adult men, 527–542; biological imperatives of, 532–535; case study example, 536–537, 539–541; covert abandonment depression, 537–539; empathic treatment, 535–536; and gender roles, 531–532; male-friendly approach to, 46–52; theory of treatment, 528–531

V

Veterans. *See* Military veterans

Viagra effect, 310, 323–324, 393

Victim-victimizer role, 298

Victimization, 6–7; and assault, 268; case study example, 272–275; childhood abuse, 265–266; and combat, 267–268; common forms of, 265–269; community violence, 267; death row case study, 288–291; implications for treatment, 271–272; and masculine socialization, 269–271; parental violence, 266; survivors of, 263–275

Victims No Longer (Lew), 274

Vietnam War veterans, 209, 469, 604; and trauma, 267

Violence, 30, 32, 278–291; and collective responsibility, 285–286; community violence, 267; cultural utility of masculinity, 282–284; death row case example, 288–291; evolutionary heritage of, 279–281; implications for treatment, 285–288; and male aggression, 278–291; and masculine socialization, 550, 555; men as perpetrators, 4–5; and military socialization, 208; origins of, 279–284; sexual assault by athletes, 106–107; sexual violence, 293–294; and sports, 103–106; stopping violence against women, 689–691; and vulnerability, 281–282. *See also* Sexual violence

Vulnerability, 281–282

W

Weekend retreats, for men's growth, 664–681; and fathers, 679–680; Mankind Project, 671–672; and psychotherapy, 673–674; role of leaders, 678; screening and referrals, 678679; use of rituals, 672–673; value of group setting, 675–677

THE AUTHORS

Gary R. Brooks, Ph.D., received his doctorate from the University of Texas at Austin in 1976. He currently is an associate professor at Baylor University. He is a fellow of the American Psychological Association and has been president of the American Psychological Association's Division of Family Psychology and the Society for the Psychological Study of Men and Masculinity. He has written more than thirty articles and book chapters. He has authored or coauthored four previous books—*The Centerfold Syndrome* (Jossey-Bass, 1995), *Men and Sex: New Psychological Perspectives* (Wiley, 1997), *Bridging Separate Gender Worlds* (American Psychological Association, 1997), and *A New Psychotherapy for Traditional Men* (Jossey-Bass, 1998). He received the 1996 Distinguished Practitioner Award of the American Psychological Association Division of Men and Masculinity and the 1997 Texas Distinguished Psychologist Award.

    Glenn E. Good, Ph.D., is an associate professor and director of the counseling psychology program (accredited by the American Psychological Association) in the Department of Educational and Counseling Psychology at the University of Missouri–Columbia. He earned his doctorate in counseling psychology from Ohio State University. Dr. Good has provided more than one hundred presentations at national and international conferences and authored more than fifty scholarly articles, chapters, and books. His research has documented the detrimental consequences of masculine gender roles on men's mental health and on men's degree of willingness to use psychological services. He is coeditor (with Murray Scher, Mark Stevens, and Gregg Eichenfield) of the *Handbook of*

Counseling and Psychotherapy with Men (Sage, 1987). He has served as president of the Society for the Psychological Study of Men and Masculinity (American Psychological Association Division 51), a representative to the American Psychological Association Council of Representatives, and a member and an officer of the Missouri psychology licensing board. He is the recipient of the Society for the Psychological Study of Men and Masculinity Researcher of the Year Award, the Kathryn Hopwood Award for meritorious contributions to counseling psychology, the Annuit Coeptis Award given by the American College Personnel Association, and numerous university teaching awards. Dr. Good is a fellow of both the Division of Counseling Psychology and the Society for the Psychological Study of Men and Masculinity of the American Psychological Association. He also maintains a private practice in Columbia, Missouri. His life is enriched by his wonderful wife, Laurie, and their two delightful daughters, Jennifer and Allison.

Aaron Carlstrom is currently a Ph.D. candidate in urban education with a counseling psychology specialization at the University of Wisconsin–Milwaukee. He holds a bachelor's degree in psychology from Marquette University and a master's degree in educational psychology with a community counseling specialization from the University of Wisconsin–Milwaukee. In addition to organizational consulting and men's issues, his clinical and research interests are in the areas of vocational psychology, multiculturalism, temporal perspective, spirituality, decision making, and student success and retention interventions.

Sam V. Cochran, Ph.D., is the assistant director of the University Counseling Service and an adjunct assistant professor of psychiatry at the University of Iowa in Iowa City. He received his doctorate in counseling psychology from the University of Missouri in 1983. Since then he has worked with men in therapy, written about men's issues, and researched depression in men. He is coauthor of the books *Men and Depression: Clinical and Empirical Perspectives* (Academic Press, 1999) and *Man Alive: A Primer of Men's Issues* (Brooks/Cole, 1994). He has also written several papers on assessing and treating depression in men and on psychotherapy with men.

Caren C. Cooper, Ph.D., is an independent practitioner who specializes in couples therapy. She received her doctorate in counseling psychology from the University of North Texas. She serves as chairperson for the Men and Relationships Task Force for Division 51 of the American Psychological Association. She is an adjunct faculty member at Concordia University in Austin, Texas. Her primary areas of interest include gender issues, ethical issues, and professional training and development.

Will H. Courtenay, Ph.D., L.C.S.W., received his doctorate from the University of California at Berkeley and is an adjunct professor at Sonoma State University, California. His research focuses on the influence of masculinity on the health of men and boys and gender-specific health interventions with men.

He is a regular contributor to professional journals and is currently completing a book on men's health (Temple University Press). He was recently invited to serve as guest editor for the first professional journal to devote a special issue to the subject of men's health *(Journal of American College Health)*. He provides consultation, program development assistance, continuing education, and training to colleges, public health departments, medical centers, and health professionals nationwide. He is also a psychotherapist in Berkeley and San Francisco, California.

Margaret Evanow is a Ph.D. candidate (counseling psychology) in the Department of Urban Education at the University of Wisconsin–Milwaukee. She holds a master of science degree in educational psychology (community counseling) from the University of Wisconsin–Milwaukee. In addition to gender-based issues, her clinical and research interests are in the area of interpersonal violence and familial abuse. Currently, she coordinates a school-based intervention to reduce and prevent adolescent violence in an urban setting. She also coordinates an aftercare treatment program for women recovering from alcohol and drug addictions.

Lucia Albino Gilbert, Ph.D., is vice provost, former director of the Center for Women's Studies, and professor of educational psychology at the University of Texas at Austin. Dr. Gilbert, who teaches in the department's doctoral program in counseling psychology, is a fellow of the American Psychological Association and current editorial board member of the *Journal of Family Issues, Journal of Family Psychology,* and *Journal of Counseling Psychology.* She is the author of four books and numerous articles and the recipient of awards for teaching and research excellence, including the Carolyn Wood Sherif Award recognizing her contributions to the field of the psychology of women as a scholar, teacher, and mentor. Her research focuses on understanding gender processes in dual-career families and in psychotherapeutic treatment. Recent books include *Two Careers, One Family: The Promise of Gender Equality* (Sage, 1993) and *Sex, Gender, and Counseling/Psychotherapy* (Allyn & Bacon, 1999). Dr. Gilbert holds a master's degree from Yale University and a doctoral degree from the University of Texas at Austin.

Mary J. Heppner, Ph.D., is an associate professor in the Educational and Counseling Psychology Department and an associate director of the Career Center at the University of Missouri–Columbia. She has written numerous articles, book chapters, and two books, primarily in the area of career development of adults and rape prevention interventions. Her most recent book is *Career Counseling: Process, Issues, and Techniques* (Allyn & Bacon, 1997). She won the 1999 William T. Kemper Fellowship for Excellence in Teaching and the 1999 Early Scientist Practitioner Award from Division 17 (Counseling Psychology) of the American Psychological Association.

P. Paul Heppner, Ph.D., received his doctorate in 1979 from the University of Nebraska–Lincoln and was a Fulbright Research Scholar at both the University of Göteborg (Sweden) and the University College Cork (Ireland), a visiting fellow at the University of London, and a visiting faculty member at the University of the Western Cape (South Africa). He has been an active researcher and has published more than one hundred articles and chapters; his primary areas of interest are the relationship between coping or problem solving and psychological adjustment, health psychology, supervision, and men and masculinity. He is a frequent presenter at conferences and symposiums across the United States and Canada and has been an invited speaker in Sweden, Norway, England, Taiwan, and South Africa. He has served on several national and international editorial boards and currently serves as the editor of the *Counseling Psychologist*. He has contributed to professional psychology in numerous ways, such as in various roles for Counseling Psychology (American Psychological Association Division 17), as a site visitor, and as an external reviewer of tenure and promotion. On the University of Missouri campus, he has been awarded the prestigious William T. Kemper Fellowship for Excellence in Teaching (1993) and has been very active in developing the doctoral training program, including serving as training director and most recently as one of the founders and codirectors of the Center for Multicultural Research, Training, and Consultation.

Hope I. Hills, Ph.D. (Virginia Commonwealth University, 1986), currently consults with businesses and is president of the Circle Consulting Group, Inc., in Milwaukee, Wisconsin. She teaches at both the Department of Urban Education (Counseling Psychology Program) at the University of Wisconsin–Milwaukee and the College of Business at Marquette University and maintains a small private practice. Her publications and presentations have focused on paradoxical interventions, interpersonal theory, multicultural training, and women in academia and organizational consulting. Since leaving the faculty of the University of Missouri's counseling psychology program in 1991, she has consulted with many organizations, helping leaders to recognize that ongoing leadership problems can be effectively approached through awareness of their early decisions about self and others. Because management and executive ranks remain largely male, she has developed interventions designed to break through men's reluctance to look at this more personal perspective on performance. She loves Milwaukee, where she lives with her husband, Dave, a retired Milwaukee Symphony musician whom she originally met on the Internet.

Carl Isenhart, Psy.D., L.P., is a psychologist and coordinator of the Addictive Disorders Section at the Minneapolis Veterans Affairs Medical Center. He is an assistant professor in the Department of Psychiatry and clinical assistant professor in the Department of Psychology at the University of Minnesota. He holds a Certificate of Proficiency in the Treatment of Alcohol and Other Psychoactive

Substance Use Disorders from the American Psychological Association's College of Professional Psychology, and he is a trainer in motivational interviewing. He has published journal articles, reviews, and book chapters. He is conducting research in the areas of assessment of substance use disorders, motivation and stages of change, and masculinity and male gender roles.

Mark S. Kiselica, Ph.D., N.C.C., L.P.C., is associate professor and chairperson of the Department of Counselor Education at the College of New Jersey. He has conducted fifty juried convention presentations and is the author or editor of forty juried publications, including *Multicultural Counseling with Teenage Fathers: A Practical Guide* (Sage, 1995), *Confronting Prejudice and Racism During Multicultural Training* (American Counseling Association, 1999), and *Handbook of Counseling Boys and Adolescent Males: A Practitioner's Guide* (Sage, 1999). He is a former consulting scholar to the Clinton administration's Federal Fatherhood Initiative and the immediate past president of the Society for the Psychological Study of Men and Masculinity (Division 51, American Psychological Association). Dr. Kiselica was named Counselor Educator of the Year (1996–1997) by the American Mental Health Counselors Association and was the recipient of the Publication in Counselor Education and Supervision Award for 1999.

Terry A. Kupers, M.D., M.S.P., practices psychiatry in Oakland, California, and teaches at the Wright Institute. He received his M.D. and M.S.P. degrees from the UCLA School of Medicine and trained in psychiatry at UCLA and the Tavistock Institute. His books include *Revisioning Men's Lives: Gender, Intimacy, and Power* (Guilford, 1993) and *Prison Madness: The Mental Health Crisis Behind Bars and What We Must Do About It* (Jossey-Bass, 1999). He is also coeditor of *Prison Masculinities* (Temple University Press, 2000).

Ronald F. Levant, Ed.D., earned his doctorate in clinical psychology and public practice from Harvard University in 1973. Since then he has been a clinician in solo independent practice, clinical supervisor in hospital settings, clinical and academic administrator, and academic faculty member. He has served on the faculties of Boston, Rutgers, and Harvard Universities. He is currently dean and professor, Center for Psychological Studies, Nova Southeastern University. Dr. Levant has authored, coauthored, edited, or coedited more than 150 publications, including 12 books and 80 refereed journal articles and book chapters in family and gender psychology and in advancing professional psychology. Dr. Levant has also served as president of the Massachusetts Psychological Association, president of American Psychological Association Division 43 (Family Psychology), cofounder and the first president of American Psychological Association Division 51 (Society for the Psychological Study of Men and Masculinity), two-term member and two-term chair of the American Psychological Association Committee for the Advancement of Professional

Practice, two-term member of the American Psychological Association Council of Representatives, and member at large of the American Psychological Association Board of Directors. As a member of the board of directors he chaired the task force that resolved the long-standing issue of representation of small state psychological associations and divisions on the American Psychological Association Council of Representatives through the creation of the "Wildcard Plan," which created an expanded council in January 1999. He is currently serving as recording secretary of the American Psychological Association.

David Lisak, Ph.D., is an associate professor of psychology at the University of Massachusetts–Boston, where he conducts and supervises research on the causes and consequences of violence (in particular, the long-term effects of childhood abuse in adult men) and on the relationship between early abuse and the later perpetration of interpersonal violence. He received his doctorate from Duke University in 1989. His research has been published in the *Journal of Traumatic Stress,* the *Journal of Interpersonal Violence, Psychotherapy*, and other journals. He is currently the editor of *Psychology of Men and Masculinity,* published by the American Psychological Association. In addition to his research and teaching, Dr. Lisak maintains a private practice specializing in the treatment of men, serves as an expert witness in death penalty cases in which child abuse issues are raised, and contributes to judicial education programs on issues of sexual violence.

Irmo D. Marini, Ph.D., C.R.C., is an associate professor and graduate coordinator of the master of science program in rehabilitation counseling at the University of Texas–Pan American. He received his Ph.D. in rehabilitation from Auburn University in 1992. Dr. Marini has made more than fifty international, national, and state presentations and has more than thirty publications on disability-related studies. He serves on four journal editorial boards and is a commissioner for the Commission on Rehabilitation Counselor Certification. Dr. Marini was the recipient of two research awards while at Arkansas State University and currently maintains a private practice in forensic rehabilitation consulting.

Fred B. Newton, Ph.D., is the director of University Counseling Services and a professor of counseling and educational psychology at Kansas State University. His doctorate in counseling psychology was granted by the University of Missouri–Columbia in 1972. Early in his career, Newton was a teacher and coach in the public school system and directed a community recreation program. Later, he joined the faculty of the University of Georgia (1972–1978) and was the coordinator of career counseling and an associate professor of education at Duke University (1978–1980). Newton has contributed chapters to fifteen books and written more than fifty articles for various professional journals. Internationally, he has been invited to give presentations in Europe and Asia, and his publications have been printed in Japan and Australia. A significant emphasis in his clinical work has been the development of programs and counseling approaches for athletes at the Division I level of the National Collegiate Athletic Association and the establishment of workshops and training programs in the areas of leadership, peer counseling, and organizational development.

Cathryn G. Pridal, Ph.D., received her doctorate in clinical psychology from the State University of New York at Stony Brook in 1982. She is currently on the faculty at Westminster College in Fulton, Missouri, and maintains a private practice. She has seen a variety of male clients with sexual dysfunctions in her therapy practice and has written several chapters in professional books on the treatment of sexual dysfunctions.

John M. Robertson, Ph.D., is a licensed psychologist in practice at University Counseling Services, Kansas State University. He also teaches for the Department of Psychology and is a member of the graduate faculty in the Department of Counseling and Educational Psychology. In addition, he maintains a part-time private practice for children and adults in northeast Kansas. His doctorate in counseling psychology was granted by the University of California at Santa Barbara in 1989. Clinically, Robertson has focused on the clinical needs of college men at Kansas State University. Areas of particular interest have included the special demands placed on student athletes and the experiences of college men exploring religious questions. In addition to providing individual counseling to men, he has conducted groups for men on recovering from sexual and physical abuse, managing aggression and violence, developing emotional expressiveness, and improving relationship skills. Robertson's published research has addressed a variety of issues related to masculinity: the gender biases therapists have toward male clients, emotional expressiveness in men, predictors of aggression in boys, male depression symptoms, the help-seeking preferences of college men, the experiences of voluntary male homemakers, and the measurement of psychological distress in men.

Jerrold Lee Shapiro, Ph.D., is Professor of Counseling Psychology at Santa Clara University, President of PsyJourn Corp., and a partner of Family Business Solutions. He is the author of *The Measure of a Man: Becoming the Father You Wish Your Father Had Been* (Berkeley, 1995), *When Men Are Pregnant* (Delta, 1993), and *Methods of Group Psychology and Encounter* (Peacock, 1976); the coauthor of *Trance on Trial* (Guilford, 1989; winner of the 1991 Manfred S. Guttmacher Award) and *Brief Group Treatment* (Brooks/Cole, 1997); and coeditor of *Classic Readings in Educational Psychology* (Ginn, 1986) and *Becoming a Father: Contemporary Social, Developmental, and Clinical Perspectives* (Springer, 1995; winner of the 1995 Book of the Year Award from the *American Journal of Nursing*). He has also authored more than 200 professional papers, presentations and symposia, and a poster: "A Father's Declaration."

Dr. Shapiro has appeared on well over 100 radio and television programs, including the *CBS Morning Show; The Oprah Winfrey Show; Sonya Live; CNN; People Are Talking* (San Francisco), and *Special Reports Television.* His work on fatherhood has been carried internationally in print media and cited in *TIME* magazine; the *New York Times;* the *Los Angeles Times; San Francisco Chronicle; San Jose Mercury News; Self* magazine; *Parents* magazine; *Bridal Guide,* and *Psychology Today.* In addition, he has served on the boards of directors of a software company and a health care organization and is a member of the Family Business Forum Advisory Board at Santa Clara University. He has also been a member on editorial boards of professional journals and publishing companies.

A graduate of Boston Latin School (1960), Colby College (A.B. 1964), Northwestern University (M.A. 1967), and the University of Waterloo (Ontario, Canada; Ph.D. 1970), Dr. Shapiro has maintained a private practice of psychotherapy and family therapy since 1970, is licensed in Hawaii and California, and holds a Diplomate from the American Board of Medical Psychotherapists. His clinical office is in Los Altos, California.

Nancy B. Sherrod, M.A., is currently an advanced doctoral student in the counseling psychology program (accredited by the American Psychological Association) of the Department of Educational and Counseling Psychology at the University of Missouri–Columbia. She graduated *summa cum laude* with a bachelor's degree in psychology from the University of Colorado. She conducts research in the areas of gender, sexual assault, trauma, stress, and psycho-oncology. She has coauthored ten articles, book chapters, and presentations at national conferences. She worked for two years as a coordinator of the University of Missouri Rape Education Office. Ms. Sherrod was awarded the William Gregory Fellowship and the Robert S. Daniel Teaching Fellowship. She is a student affiliate of the American Psychological Association and a member of Phi Beta Kappa.

Jack Sternbach, Ph.D., L.C.S.W., is an independent practitioner who specializes in group therapy with men in the Martha's Vineyard and Boston areas of Massachusetts. He received his master's degree in social work from the University of Pennsylvania in 1955 and his doctorate from the University of Wisconsin in 1969. Before entering private practice in 1974, he was a social work faculty member at the University of Wisconsin and the University of Pennsylvania. His descriptions of his work with men have appeared in *Social Work with Groups, Men's Studies Review, Voices,* and *Men in Groups* (American Psychological Association, 1996). His primary interest in group work for men is expressed through direct clinical service, training, and consultation.

Mark A. Stevens, Ph.D., has been a psychologist and coordinator of training at the University of Southern California Student Counseling Services since 1986. He is also an adjunct professor in the counseling psychology program at the University of Southern California. In 1983, Dr. Stevens was the first cochair of the Men's Rape Prevention Project at Ohio State University. In 1986, he founded the CARE (Creating Attitudes for Rape-Free Environments) Program at the University of Southern California. Since 1984, Dr. Stevens has presented his work at colleges across the country. He has written extensively and has participated in several video and television productions in the area of men's issues and rape prevention. Dr. Stevens received his doctorate in clinical psychology from the California School of Professional Psychology–San Diego in 1982.

Sarah J. Walker, M.A., is a doctoral candidate in counseling psychology at the University of Texas at Austin. She was awarded the Florence Geis Memorial Dissertation Fellowship for her dissertation, *The Meaning of Consent: College Women's and Men's Experiences with Nonviolent Sexual Coercion.* She is the coauthor of several articles and chapters addressing the role of dominant discourses about gender in heterosexual relationships.